CATHERINE THE GREAT

CATHERINE THE GREAT

SIMON DIXON

An *Imprint of* HarperCollins*Publishers*

To my parents

HarperCollins books may be purchased for educational, business, or sales promotional use. For information, please write: Special Markets Department, Harper-Collins Publishers, 10 East 53rd Street, New York, NY 10022.

First published in Great Britain in 2009 by Profile Books Ltd.

FIRST U.S. EDITION

Library of Congress Cataloging-in-Publication Data is available upon request.

ISBN: 978-0-06-078627-4

09 10 11 12 13 OFF/QBF 10 09 08 07 06 05 04 03 02 01

CONTENTS

Genealogies and Maps   vi

*A Note on dates, spelling, transliteration
and names*   xv

Introduction   1

Prologue   The coronation of a usurper 1762   3

Chapter 1   From Pomerania to St Petersburg
1729–1744   23

Chapter 2   Betrothal and marriage 1744–1745   41

Chapter 3   Living and loving at the Court of
Empress Elizabeth 1746–1753   65

Chapter 4   Ambition 1754–1759   91

Chapter 5   Assassination 1759–1762   108

Chapter 6   'Our Lady of St Petersburg' 1763–1766   126

Chapter 7   Philosopher on the throne 1767–1768   156

Chapter 8   Imperial ambitions 1768–1772   184

Chapter 9   Paul, Pugachëv and Potëmkin 1772–1775   215

Chapter 10   The search for emotional stability
1776–1784   241

Chapter 11   Zenith 1785–1790   270

Chapter 12   End of an era 1790–1796   293

Epilogue   The afterlife of an empress   316

Abbreviations   336

Notes   340

List of illustrations   388

List of maps   388

Further reading   390

Acknowledgements   396

Index   398

Catherine's Family Tree

Frederick IV
Duke of Holstein
d. 1702

◄----------------------------- (brothers) -----------------------------

Karl Friedrich, = Anna Petrovna (Romanov)
Duke of Holstein   1708–1728
1700–1739   daughter of Peter the Great

Christian August = Johanna Elisabeth
Prince of Anhalt-Zerbst   of Holstein-Gottorp
1690–1747   1712–1760

Karl Peter Ulrich/Peter Fëdorovich = Sophie Auguste Friderike/Catherine
Duke of Holstein, 1739–1762   Princess of Anhalt-Zerbst, 1729–1744
Grand Duke of Russia, 1742–1761   Grand Duchess of Russia, 1744–1761
Peter III, 1761–1762   Catherine II, 1762–1796
(1728–1762)   (1729–1796)

Wilhelm Christian
1730–1742

1. Natalia Alekseyevna =
1755–1776

Paul Petrovich
Grand Duke of Russia, 1754–1796
Paul I, 1796–1801
(1754–1801)

Anna Petrovna
1757–1759

2. Maria Fëdorovna =
1759–1828

Alexander
Grand Duke of Russia, 1777–1801
Alexander I, 1801–1825

Constantine
1779–1831

Alexandra
1783–1801

Yelena
1784–1803

Maria
1786–185

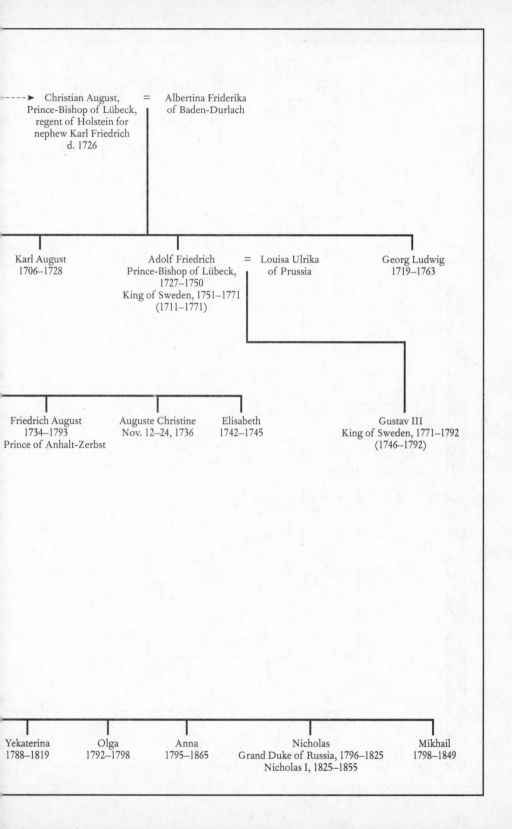

Christian August, = Albertina Friderika
Prince-Bishop of Lübeck,   of Baden-Durlach
regent of Holstein for
nephew Karl Friedrich
d. 1726

Karl August   Adolf Friedrich   = Louisa Ulrika   Georg Ludwig
1706–1728   Prince-Bishop of Lübeck,   of Prussia   1719–1763
                       1727–1750
                 King of Sweden, 1751–1771
                       (1711–1771)

Friedrich August   Auguste Christine   Elisabeth   Gustav III
1734–1793   Nov. 12–24, 1736   1742–1745   King of Sweden, 1771–1792
Prince of Anhalt-Zerbst   (1746–1792)

Yekaterina   Olga   Anna   Nicholas   Mikhail
1788–1819   1792–1798   1795–1865   Grand Duke of Russia, 1796–1825   1798–1849
                                            Nicholas I, 1825–1855

Romanov rulers of Russia from Aleksey Mikhailovich to Nicholas I

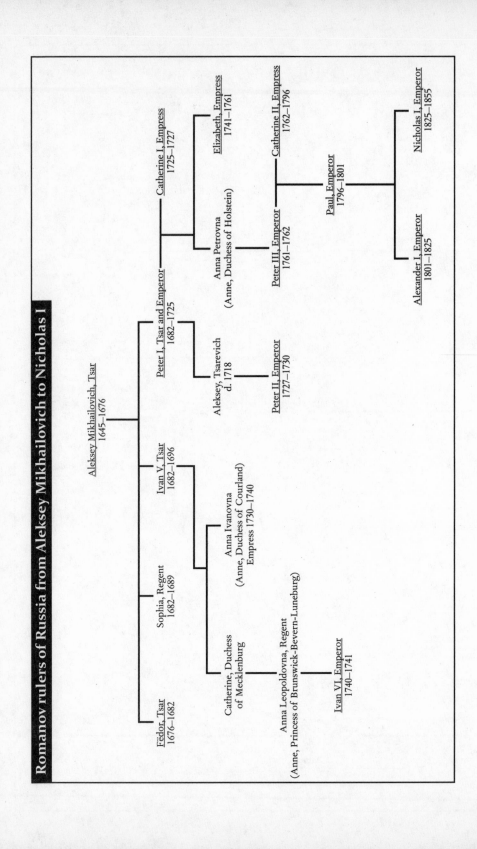

Aleksey Mikhailovich, Tsar
1645–1676

Fëdor, Tsar
1676–1682

Sophia, Regent
1682–1689

Ivan V, Tsar
1682–1696

Peter I, Tsar and Emperor
1682–1725

Catherine I, Empress
1725–1727

Anna Ivanovna
(Anne, Duchess of Courland)
Empress 1730–1740

Catherine, Duchess
of Mecklenburg

Anna Leopoldovna, Regent
(Anne, Princess of Brunswick-Bevern-Luneburg)

Ivan VI, Emperor
1740–1741

Aleksey, Tsarevich
d. 1718

Peter II, Emperor
1727–1730

Anna Petrovna
(Anne, Duchess of Holstein)

Elizabeth, Empress
1741–1761

Peter III, Emperor
1761–1762

Catherine II, Empress
1762–1796

Paul, Emperor
1796–1801

Alexander I, Emperor
1801–1825

Nicholas I, Emperor
1825–1855

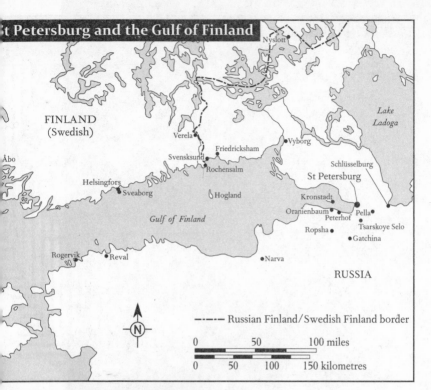

t Petersburg and the Gulf of Finland

Nyslott

FINLAND
(Swedish)

Lake
Ladoga

Verela

Vyborg

Friedricksham

Svensksund

Schlüsselburg

Rochensalm

St Petersburg

Helsingfors

Sveaborg

Hogland

Kronstadt

Oranienbaum

Pella

Peterhof

Tsarskoye Selo

Ropsha

Gatchina

Åbo

Gulf of Finland

Rogervik

Reval

Narva

RUSSIA

N

---·---·--- Russian Finland/Swedish Finland border

0   50   100 miles

0   50   100   150 kilometres

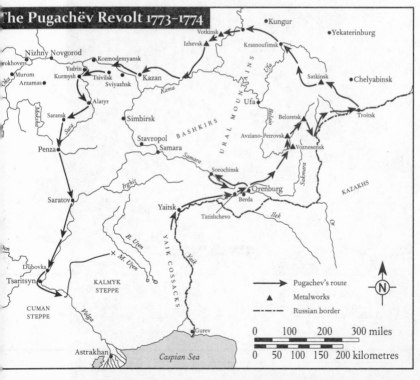

he Pugachëv Revolt 1773–1774

Kungur

Votkinsk

Yekaterinburg

Nizhny Novgorod

Izhevsk

Krasnoufimsk

Kozmodemyansk

rokhovets

Ufa

Murom

Yadrin

Kurmysh

Tsivilsk

Kazan

Satkinsk

Chelyabinsk

Arzamas

Sviyazhsk

Kama

Alatyr

Ufa

Saransk

Simbirsk

BASHKIRS

Beloretsk

Troitsk

Sura

Belaia

Stavropol

Avziano-Petrovsk

Penza

Samara

Voznesensk

Moksha

Samara

Sakmara

KAZAKHS

Irghiz

Sorochinsk

Orenburg

Saratov

Yaitsk

Berda

Tatishchevo

Ilek

Or

B. Uzen

YAIK COSSACKS

Dubovka

M. Uzen

Yaik

Tsaritsyn

KALMYK
STEPPE

Volga

CUMAN
STEPPE

on

Don

Gurev

Astrakhan

Caspian Sea

→ Pugachev's route

▲ Metalworks

---·---·--- Russian border

N

0   100   200   300 miles

0   50   100   150   200 kilometres

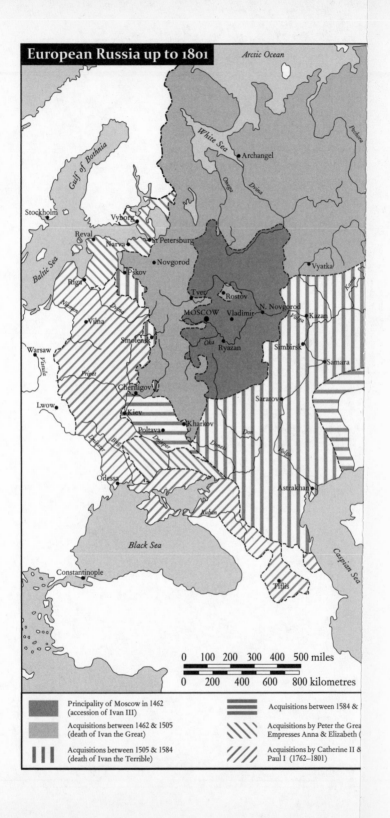

European Russia up to 1801

Arctic Ocean

White Sea

• Archangel

Gulf of Bothnia

Stockholm •

Vyborg •

Reval •
Narva •

• St Petersburg

Riga •

• Novgorod

Pskov •

Baltic Sea

Tver • • Rostov

• Vyatka

Vilna •

• MOSCOW • Vladimir

• N. Novgorod

• Kazan

Warsaw •

Smolensk •

Oka

Ryazan •

• Simbirsk

Chernigov •

Pripet

Saratov •

• Samara

Lwow •

Kiev •

Poltava •

• Kharkov

Don

Dnieper

Donets

Volga

Odessa •

Dniester

Bug

Astrakhan •

Kuban

Black Sea

Constantinople •

Caspian Sea

Tiflis •

| 0 | 100 | 200 | 300 | 400 | 500 miles |

| 0 | 200 | 400 | 600 | 800 kilometres |

Principality of Moscow in 1462
(accession of Ivan III)

Acquisitions between 1584 &

Acquisitions between 1462 & 1505
(death of Ivan the Great)

Acquisitions by Peter the Grea
Empresses Anna & Elizabeth (

Acquisitions between 1505 & 1584
(death of Ivan the Terrible)

Acquisitions by Catherine II &
Paul I (1762–1801)

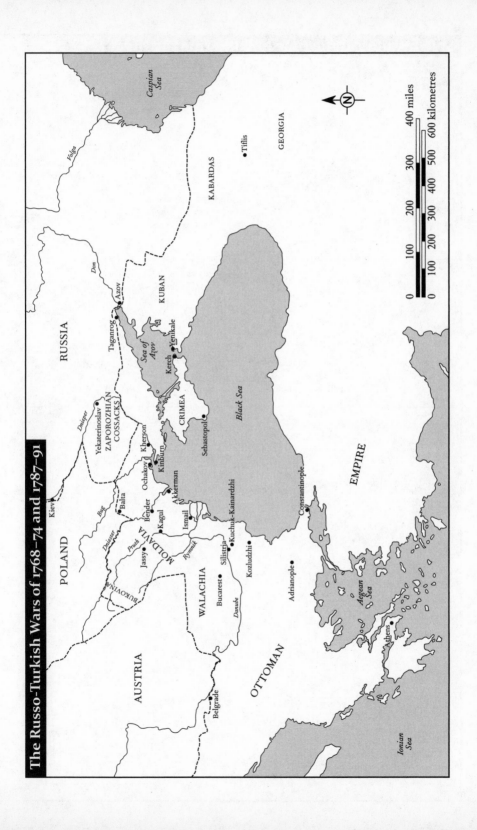

The Russo-Turkish Wars of 1768–74 and 1787–91

RUSSIA

POLAND

AUSTRIA

Volga

Don

Dnieper

Bug

Dniester

Prut

Kiev

Yekaterinoslav

ZAPOROZHIAN COSSACKS

Balta

Bender

Jassy

MOLDAVIA

BUKOVINA

Belgrade

WALACHIA

Bucarest

Silistria

Danube

Kozludzhi

Adrianople

OTTOMAN

Kagul

Ismail

Rymnik

Kuchuk-Kainardzhi

Akkerman

Ochakov

Kinburn

Kherson

Taganrog

Azov

KUBAN

Sea of Azov

Kerch

Yenikale

CRIMEA

Sebastopol

Black Sea

Constantinople

EMPIRE

Aegean Sea

Athens

Ionian Sea

KABARDAS

Tiflis

GEORGIA

Caspian Sea

N

0   100   200   300   400 miles

0   100   200   300   400   500   600 kilometres

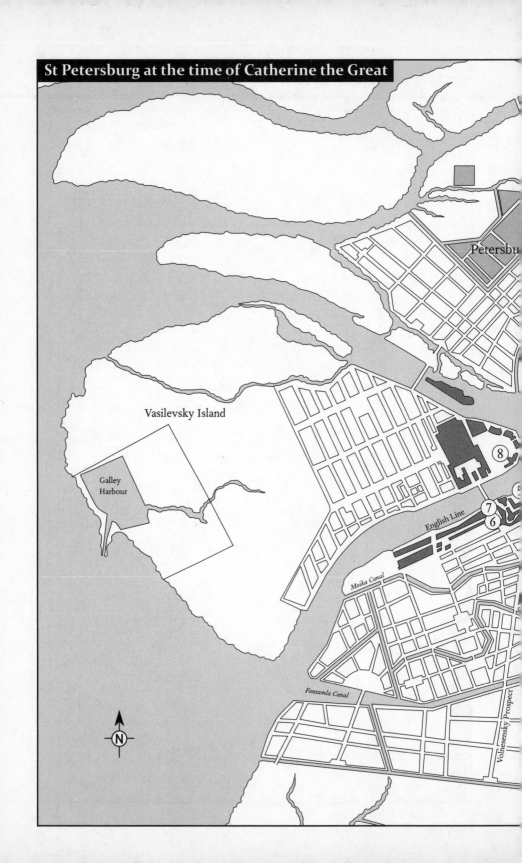

St Petersburg at the time of Catherine the Great

Vasilevsky Island

Galley
Harbour

Petersbu

English Line

Moika Canal

Fontamla Canal

Volnesensky Prospect

8

7

6

N

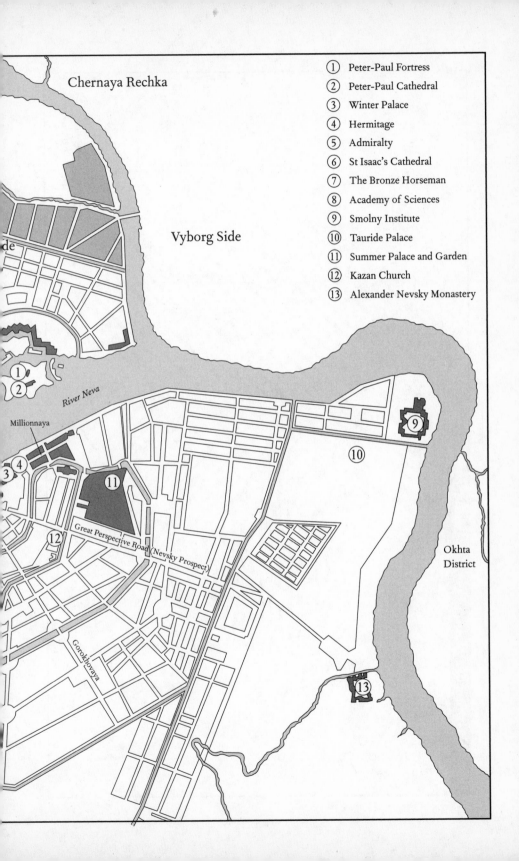

Chernaya Rechka

Vyborg Side

de

River Neva

Millionnaya

Great Perspective Road (Nevsky Prospect)

Gorokhovaya

Okhta
District

1. Peter-Paul Fortress
2. Peter-Paul Cathedral
3. Winter Palace
4. Hermitage
5. Admiralty
6. St Isaac's Cathedral
7. The Bronze Horseman
8. Academy of Sciences
9. Smolny Institute
10. Tauride Palace
11. Summer Palace and Garden
12. Kazan Church
13. Alexander Nevsky Monastery

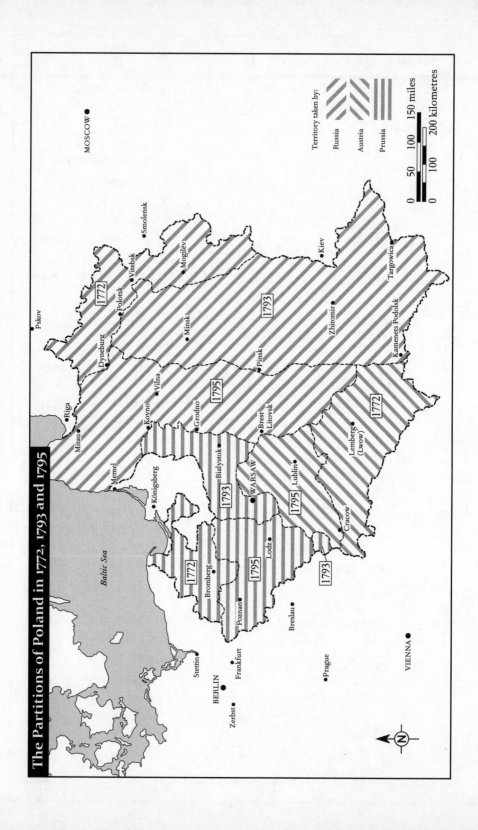

The Partitions of Poland in 1772, 1793 and 1795

Territory taken by:

Russia

Austria

Prussia

MOSCOW

Pskov

Smolensk

Vitebsk

Polotsk

Mogilëv

1772

Dyneburg

Minsk

1793

Kiev

Zhitomir

Targowica

Kamenets Podolsk

Pinsk

1795

Riga

Mirau

Vilna

Koyno

Grodno

Brest Litovsk

1772

Memel

Königsberg

Bialystok

WARSAW

Lublin

1795

Lemberg (Lwow)

1793

Baltic Sea

Stettin

Frankfurt

BERLIN

Zerbst

Bromberg

Poznan

1772

Lodz

1795

Cracow

1793

Breslau

Prague

VIENNA

N

50   100   150 miles

100   200 kilometres

A NOTE ON DATES, SPELLING, TRANSLITERATION AND NAMES

Dates: All Russian domestic dates are given according to the Old Style (Julian) calendar, which in the eighteenth century was eleven days behind the New Style (Gregorian) calendar in use in most European states by 1800. New Style dates, when given for events outside Russia, are marked NS.

Spelling and punctuation: English spelling and punctuation have generally been modernised, as has the use of capital letters, even in quotations from eighteenth-century sources.

Transliteration: There is no universally satisfactory system of transliteration for the Cyrillic alphabet. While the endnotes and the Further reading section adopt the Library of Congress system now in widespread scholarly use, a modified version is used in the text. Diacritical marks are omitted. The soft vowel 'ia' becomes 'ya': so, Yaroslavl rather than Iaroslavl; Trubetskaya rather than Trubetskaia. The soft vowel 'e' sometimes becomes 'ye': so, Tsarskoye Selo rather than Tsarskoe Selo. 'ii' and 'iy' endings on masculine proper names become 'y': so, Vyazemsky not Viazemskii. The soft vowel 'e', pronounced 'yo', is given as 'ë': so, Potëmkin rather than Potemkin or Potyomkin.

Names: Catherine's name, along with those of other ruling monarchs, is anglicised according to convention; otherwise the Russian is normally retained, e.g. Nicholas I but Nikolay Novikov. In some cases, e.g. Peter and Alexander, the anglicised version is always used. Although Russian makes extensive use of the patronymic in forms of address, most Russian names are given with Christian name and surname only: so Nikolay Novikov, rather than Nikolay Ivanovich Novikov or N. I. Novikov.

INTRODUCTION

J esus Christ, Napoleon and Richard Wagner are said to have inspired more biographies than any other figures in history. Catherine the Great cannot be far behind. Fascinated by a German princess who captured the Russian throne and corresponded with the leading minds of her age, her contemporaries started to tell her story from the moment she died on 6 November 1796. Ever since, her political achievements as ruler of the most powerful emergent empire in Europe have been set against rumours about the amorous liaisons on which she embarked in search of elusive personal fulfilment.

Over 200 years after the empress's death, when both aspects of her life still make headlines in Russia and the West, my aim has been to bridge the gap between formidable historical scholarship and the popular accounts that risk trivialising a woman whose life requires no embellishment to reveal its interest and importance. There is no need to invent her conversations: though her writings can rarely be taken at face value, they tell us much about her active mind. And there is no shortage of acute contemporary comment on her personality and reign (what posterity made of it is the subject of my final chapter). Unless otherwise acknowledged, translations from these sources are my own, though readers who want to explore for themselves now have access to a growing range of excellent English versions, listed in the Further reading section. In addition to identifying the sources of my quotations, the endnotes offer a further (if necessarily inadequate) guide to the scholarship on which I have drawn. A comprehensive list would fill a book far larger than this one.

The Russian historian and journalist Vasily Bilbasov made the same discovery at the end of the 1880s. In addition to filling a fat bibliographical volume, he took more than a thousand lively pages to cover only half of Catherine's life before the reigning tsar, Alexander III, intervened to prevent further revelations about his controversial predecessor. Since comprehensiveness is clearly an impossible goal, it is important to have a guiding purpose in choosing what to discuss and what to omit. In attempting to give a fully rounded portrait of the empress, I have taken a broadly chronological approach that helps to emphasise the very wide variety of problems with which an absolute monarch was confronted at any one time. (Corrections to generally accepted dates are largely silent, except where they significantly revise our understanding of the course of events, as, for example, in the case of the funerals of Empress Elizabeth and Alexander Lanskoy.) Above all, however, I have sought to recover a sense of place, situating Catherine in the context of the Court society in which she grew up in Germany and lived most of her long life in Russia. For all that she did to reshape the values of the Court of St Petersburg, it still preserved in the 1790s many of the features of the Baroque Courts which she had first experienced, at Stettin, Zerbst and Brunswick-Wolfenbüttel. Here the Court is understood in the multiplicity of senses familiar to her and her contemporaries: an institution alive with intrigue extending from the monarch at its heart to the servants at its outer penumbra; a network of rival aristocratic clienteles at the centre of politics in much of Europe before the French Revolution; the symbolic authority to which foreign ambassadors were accredited; an extraordinary range of palaces, both urban and surburban; and a glittering cultural icon representing the power and majesty of the ruler to her subjects, great and small. That was how Catherine experienced the Court. And no single event did more to reveal its kaleidoscopic significance than her coronation, with which my version of her story begins.

THE CORONATION OF A USURPER
1762

'Nowhere perhaps is the vicinity of a church more disagreeable than in Russia,' complained a Swedish prisoner of war in 1760, tormented by the 'perpetual dinging' from St Petersburg's Peter-Paul Cathedral.[1] Its bell tower was only a few feet from his cell. Yet had Count Johann Hård been incarcerated in the Moscow Kremlin, his ears would have been even sorer. While the Russians long continued to attribute magical powers to their bells, ringing them out to drive the devil from their parishes, their eighteenth-century rulers had co-opted the instrument as a symbol of the sacralisation of tsarist power.[2] Empress Anna could think of no better way of adding to her glory in the 1730s than by commissioning the world's largest bell. Fatally cracked by fire in May 1737, before it had been raised from its casting pit, *tsar-kolokol* – 'the tsar bell' – lay buried in the Kremlin until 1836, escaping the designs of an enterprising Moscow freemason who planned to smelt it in the 1780s and use the metal for fonts to print a new children's Bible.[3] But while Hård was languishing in the Peter-Paul Fortress, Empress Elizabeth had commissioned a rival instrument, almost as massive, measuring more than forty feet in circumference. Alongside depictions of Christ, the Virgin Mary and John the Baptist, the bell's founder Konstantin Slizov had adorned it with portraits of the imperial family. His inscription drove home the dedication:

In the year from the creation of the world 7268 and from the Incarnation of God the Word 1760, this bell has been cast in Moscow during the prosperous reign of the Most Pious and Most Autocratic Great Sovereign, Yelizaveta

Petrovna, Empress of All Russia, in the 19th year of her reign and in the time of their Imperial Highnesses, the gracious Lord, Grand Duke Peter Fëdorovich, and his consort, the gracious Lady, Grand Duchess YEKATERINA ALEKSEYEVNA, and in that of the gracious Lord [their son], Grand Duke PAVEL PETROVICH.[4]

By the time the bell was finished in 1762, the scene had radically changed. Elizabeth was dead; her successor, Peter III, overthrown and assassinated within six months of his accession. And so it was that on the morning of Sunday 22 September, Slizov's bell unexpectedly rang out for the first time to herald the coronation of Peter's widow, Yekaterina Alekseyevna, as Catherine II of Russia.

At the stroke of ten, a fanfare of trumpets and drums heralded the empress's ceremonial emergence from her private apartments in the Kremlin into the vaulted audience chamber of the Palace of Facets.[5] She can hardly have had much sleep. Thousands of lesser bells had tolled from every church in the city at three in the morning for vespers and then again at six o'clock to call worshippers to the vigil service that preceded Russian coronations. Two hours later, Slizov's 'great new bell' summoned the clergy to the Cathedral of the Dormition, emitting the 'deep hollow murmur' that a later visitor described, vibrating all over Moscow 'like the fullest and lowest tones of a vast organ, or the rolling of distant thunder'.[6] The empress herself had been fasting in preparation for the coronation communion service and before she could make her public appearance there were still some intricate personal devotions to perform. In these she was guided by her confessor, archpriest Fëdor (Dubyansky), who had grown so close to the pious Elizabeth that she conferred hereditary nobility on all his children (he himself died in possession of some 8000 serfs).[7] But ritual observance was always a duty rather than a consolation to Catherine's sceptical mind, and she was less anxious about her prayers than about the need to present a suitably majestic image to her new subjects. Comforted by the servants who had taught her the Russian proverbs in which she took a childish delight, she set about composing herself for the ceremony that was to mark the ultimate stage in the transformation of an insignificant German princess, born Sophie Auguste Friderike of Anhalt-Zerbst on 21 April 1729, into 'the most serene and all-powerful Princess and lady, Catherine the Second, Empress and Autocrat of all the Russias'.

She had plenty of time to think while she dressed for the part. Catherine had spent at least 20,000 roubles on her wardrobe, almost half as much as the initial 50,000-rouble budget for the coronation itself (the final bill was for 86,000 roubles, though such was the variety of funds that supported this extraordinary event that the total costs may never be known).[8] As a succession of startled subordinates had discovered in the brief interval since her accession on 28 June, no matter was too trivial to escape their new sovereign's attention to detail. Gone were the days of haphazard accounting under the profligate Elizabeth. Catherine, who valued precision above all else, always remembered what she had commissioned and always insisted on value for money. Her new coronation robe – a shimmering confection of silver brocade, trimmed with ermine and embossed with eagles and gold braid – had already been pored over for imperfections. Now it remained only to manoeuvre into place the bulky train that required seven gentlemen-in-waiting to carry it in her wake. The most senior was one of Russia's richest magnates, Count Peter Sheremetev, who had served the empress at her wedding banquet seventeen years earlier.[9] Only once she was satisfied that everything was secured was Catherine ready to face the world.

Outside in the Kremlin's Ivanov Square, the four Guards regiments, summoned from their barracks by a 21-gun salute at 5 a.m., were already on parade, the colourful satins of their uniforms etched sharply against the pale stone walls of the three great Kremlin churches.[10] Though these were all monuments to Muscovy's imperial pretensions in the reign of Ivan III (1462–1505), only the tsars' diminutive chapel royal, the Cathedral of the Annunciation, had been built by Russians. The Cathedral of the Archangel Michael, which preceded St Petersburg's Peter-Paul Cathedral as the royal necropolis, was the work of a Venetian architect. And it was a man from Bologna, Aristotele Fioravanti, who designed the most important church in Muscovy, the Cathedral of the Dormition, where the sixteen-year-old Ivan the Terrible had been the first to be crowned tsar in January 1547. Although the Muscovite coronation rite had been a single, stand-alone ceremony, Peter the Great had changed all that when he crowned his second wife, Catherine, in May 1724. Subsequent eighteenth-century coronations were followed by a week-long litany of receptions, balls and firework displays and preceded by a triumphal 'entry' into the city – a 'glorification of force' intended to show that the monarch's power derived as much from conquest as from consecration.[11] However, since even this entry procession culminated in a service at the Cathedral of the Dormition, which was followed by a recessional to the remaining two cathedrals,[12] Catherine's guardsmen had grown all too familiar with these hallowed buildings in the exhausting period of drills and rehearsals that had occupied them since the first detachments left St Petersburg on 4 August. They had scarcely been allowed to rest during the week of festivities and proclamations that had passed since Catherine formally entered Moscow on Friday 13 September. As their sergeants barked a final series of commands to send each platoon to its post, the soldiery probably faced the great day itself with a mixture of anticipation and relief.

More complicated emotions affected some of their officers. Among the proud subalterns marshalling the Horse Guards into position was the newly promoted Second Lieutenant Grigory Potëmkin, with whom Catherine was to fall in love in February 1774. She was probably betrothed to him in a secret ceremony sometime that summer, sharing with him not only a passionate and very public affair, but also some of the most important decisions in the second half of her reign.[13] For the moment, however, she remained committed to Grigory Orlov, a handsome hero of the Seven Years' War by whom she had given birth to an illegitimate son as recently as 11 April. While Potëmkin passed unnoticed among several young bucks who had pledged their allegiance to the new empress in return for lavish rewards, Orlov had been closely involved in the preparations for the coronation, taking a particular interest in arrangements made for the artists who had been commissioned to record the event for posterity.[14]

Catherine was no less concerned with the reactions of a more immediate public. On top of the Kremlin ramparts, a separate troop of guardsmen wheeled into place the cannon that would proclaim crucial moments of the ceremony to an expectant crowd on Red Square. From that unpaved thoroughfare at the heart of the sprawling old capital, the throng spilled over into a maze of narrow lanes. Visiting in 1780, Joseph II of Austria found Moscow 'much larger than anything I've seen. Paris, Rome, Naples, in no way approach its size'.[15] Two years earlier, the British traveller Archdeacon William Coxe declared it 'certainly the largest town in Europe, its circumference within the rampart ... being exactly 39 versts or 26 miles'.[16] Though contemporary estimates of the city's population varied widely, and it fluctuated according to the season, as many as 300,000 people could cram into the city after the summer harvest.[17] All of them, it seemed, had turned out to witness Catherine's triumphal entry nine days before the coronation.

Silken carpets, draped over the balconies of the grander houses, added a splash of semi-Asiatic colour to this most verdant of cities. Even the meanest streets through which the parade passed were strewn with festive fir-branches, carved and formed into decorative trellises.[18] Yet Moscow was by no means wholly synonymous with squalor. 'Some parts of this city have the look of a sequestered desert,' Coxe reported, 'other quarters of a populous town, some of a contemptible village, others of a great capital'.[19] Often dismissed as unplanned and unkempt by comparison with the geometrically regimented St Petersburg, the old capital could boast some impressive modern architecture of its own. The Kremlin Arsenal, begun in 1702 but completed only in 1736, was an early example of Russian classicism, the university (Russia's first, founded in 1755), one of the most recent at the time of Catherine's coronation. To these had been added four new triumphal arches, built by 3000 labourers under the supervision of architects working for Prince Nikita Trubetskoy's Coronation Commission.[20] Each arch featured two full-scale portraits of the empress by the Synodal artist Aleksey Antropov, and incorporated a mixture of classical and panegyric motifs chosen by Trubetskoy's stepson Mikhail Kheraskov, the curator of Moscow University and one of the leading Russian writers of the age.[21]

Nor was it only the foreign elements in Russian culture that were mobilised to welcome the new sovereign. Priests bowed from the porches of every church in the city as a carillon rang out on the eve of the second great feast in the Orthodox liturgical calendar, the Exaltation of the Life-Giving Cross. Spectators who could find a ticket or bribe the guards mounted galleries erected in all the city's main squares to gain a better view of their empress as she swept past in an open eight-horse carriage through streets lined with cheering subjects on her way to the Nikolsky Gate. There, at the north-eastern corner of the Kremlin, Catherine was formally greeted by Metropolitan Timofey (Shcherbatsky), while a choir of students from Moscow's Slavonic-Greek-Latin Academy, dressed in white and holding forth laurel branches, hymned God's chosen ruler before accompanying her to a service of celebration at the Cathedral of the Dormition. 'Sing solemnly, Russia,' the seminarists chanted: 'raise your voice to the heavens.'[22]

———

Catherine's entry into Moscow could hardly have presented a more impressive spectacle. Behind the scenes, however, the government worried that an unprecedented influx of migrants might destabilise an already overcrowded city. The Court and all its acolytes had decamped en masse from St Petersburg, leaving the Earl of Buckinghamshire, who arrived there as the new British ambassador on 11 September, stranded without hope of reaching Moscow in time for the coronation (he had to be satisfied with the celebrations presided over by Ivan Neplyuev, the Senator left in charge of the capital in the empress's absence).[23] Already softened by the autumn rains, the roads to the old capital were 'very bad, and the horses so much fatigued with the concourse of people who have lately travelled that way, as to make any degree of expedition impracticable'.[24] Some 395 horses were required at each posting station merely to transport the 63 carriages needed by Catherine's small entourage of 23. Since the tsarevich's suite demanded 257 horses for 27 carriages, the Postal Chancellery took more than a month to assemble the necessary animals. By one estimate, some 19,000 horses were hired to haul the remaining notables, the wheels of their carriages splashing mud over the lines of straggling rustics, beggars and petty tradesmen who flocked to the old capital in the hope of sharing in the bounty traditionally distributed by a 'merciful' new monarch. In 1903, the contrast between richly attired courtiers and ragged peasants would wreck Nicholas II's quest for national reconciliation at the canonisation of St Serafim of Sarov. Anxious to avoid any such comparison during Catherine's coronation, her officials belatedly banned the import of fabric woven in gold and silver thread on 17 September.[25]

Fears that speculators might cause unrest by artificially inflating bread prices proved unfounded. Though Moscow remained a paradise for petty criminals throughout the festivities, the mood among the crowds was jubilant from the moment that Catherine arrived in the city. On the eve of her coronation, thousands of men and women streamed towards the Kremlin, where those lucky enough to acquire tickets would be admitted the following morning to places reserved for the populace. Undeterred by forecasts of wind and rain, their less fortunate fellows clambered up onto neighbouring rooftops in the hope of catching a glimpse of their sovereign.[26]

In the event, the day dawned dry, if gloomy, and those intrepid enough to secure a vantage point did not have long to wait. The participants in the coronation had been summoned to their various assembly points across the Kremlin at the same early hour as the soldiers,[27] and at ten o'clock Prince Trubetskoy began to count out the elaborate procession that flowed slowly through the Holy Vestibule on the first floor of the Palace of Facets, out onto the ceremonial Red Staircase, and down into Cathedral Square.

Though Catherine would ultimately come to question the baroque extravagance of Elizabethan ceremonial, deeming classical self-restraint better suited to a monarch who claimed to rule in the public interest, her initial aim was simply to outdo her predecessors by staging the grandest coronation in living memory. Whereas there had been twenty sections in Empress Anna's procession in 1730 and forty-two in Elizabeth's in 1742, Catherine's boasted no fewer than fifty-one.[28] They represented a microcosm of Russia's multinational elite, constituting at once an impressive demonstration of political unity and an equally visible reminder of the various potentially conflicting interests that the empress would need to reconcile if she was to consolidate her position on the throne.

Leading off down the Red Staircase, thirty Chevaliers Gardes, three abreast, were the first to set foot onto a specially erected wooden walkway '21 English feet wide' which stretched across Cathedral Square, its railings draped with colourful silks and carpets in the manner of its prototype in 1742.[29] On reaching the Cathedral of the Dormition, the cavaliers fanned out on either side of its great south door to allow the thirty-one pages behind them to pass inside. Since there was no room for them during the coronation service, they processed straight out through the north door into the Synodal Palace to await the end of the ritual.[30] Behind them, two masters of ceremonies took up their positions near the throne of Monomakh, the tsar's place of worship just inside the cathedral, ready to guide the main body of the procession to their places.

First came representatives of Catherine's non-Russian subjects, headed by twenty-two townsmen from the Baltic lands and Russian Finland, territories conquered from Sweden by Peter the Great in the Great Northern War of 1700–21. Two Englishmen formed part of a seven-strong cohort of foreign-born merchants who had pledged their loyalty to the Russian monarchy: John Tames, a member of the linen manufacturing dynasty whose Dutch founder had been friendly with Tsar Peter, and Martin Butler, joint proprietor of a wallpaper business whose establishment of a privileged manufactory in Moscow in 1751 had provoked British rivals to protest to the Lords Commissioners for Trade.[31] Even in their finest attire, such worthies must have cut a sober figure alongside the Zaporozhian and Don Cossack officers who followed them down the Red Staircase bedecked in strident colour. Next came four delegations from Little Russia (Ukraine), and nine German knights from Livland and Estland. Only then did Russians themselves join the procession, led by members of the twelve administrative Colleges established by Peter the Great as Russia's principal institutions of central government. Seventeen groups of officials culminated in a delegation from the College of Foreign Affairs including the empress's influential secretary, Grigory Teplov. Behind them followed eight of the twenty-five members of the Senate, Russia's highest secular court and principal governing body, in the customary order of seniority, juniors first.[32]

Once some of Catherine's closest allies had assumed their places in the procession, bearing the imperial regalia, the appearance at the top of the staircase of Prince Trubetskoy was the signal for the emergence of the empress herself.[33] Beneath a silken canopy carried by nine senior officials – another mark of the sacral status of the monarch, adopted from ecclesiastical processions – could be seen the unmistakeable silhouette of the woman who was soon to become the most celebrated monarch in Europe.[34] Already statuesque at the age of thirty-three, Catherine had never been blessed with conventional good looks. Admitting that her 'features were far from being so delicately and exactly formed as to compose what might pretend to regular beauty', Buckinghamshire was too polite to single out her long, aquiline nose. At least it was compensated by 'a fine complexion, an animated and intelligent eye, a mouth agreeably turned, and a profusion of glossy chestnut hair', all of which combined to 'produce that sort of countenance which, a very few years ago, a man must have been either prejudiced or insensible to have beheld with indifference'.[35] The overall effect – a streak of masculinity running through her feminine form – would fascinate her contemporaries for the rest of her life. Catherine did nothing to dispel their puzzlement. Years of isolation at the Court of Empress Elizabeth had taught her never to reveal her innermost thoughts.

Impassive as the empress seemed as she paused at the top of the Red Staircase, she might have been forgiven a moment of private trepidation. Catherine had first processed across Cathedral Square to commemorate her engagement to Grand Duke Peter shortly after her arrival in Russia in 1744, a ceremony she recalled with distaste. Scarcely less miserable was the memory of the extraordinary occasion in 1753 when Elizabeth had chosen to celebrate the eleventh anniversary of her own coronation by re-staging the ritual in every respect bar the placing of the crown on her head.[36] For everyone except the empress, who moved into the Kremlin apartments on the eve of the ceremony, the proceedings proved tiresome in the extreme. Catherine and her husband had to travel in state from the draughty wooden palace on the Yauza River where the Court resided during its visits to Moscow, their servants trotting alongside the carriage for several miles. Neither did matters improve once the ceremony began. As Catherine later recalled:

> It was as cold and damp in that church as I had ever felt in my life. I was blue all over and freezing cold in a Court dress open at the neck. The Empress told me to put on a sable stole but I had none with me. She had her own brought to her and took one, wrapping it round her neck. I saw another in her box and

thought that she was going to give it to me to put on, but I was wrong. She sent it back. It seemed to me to be rather a clear sign of ill will.[37]

After the service, while Elizabeth dined alone in the Kremlin, Peter and Catherine returned to the suburbs in the pouring rain – and in no better a temper than Elizabeth had displayed during the ceremony itself.

More sinister than any temporary discomfort were the wider cultural values represented by the old capital. Catherine instinctively disliked almost everything Moscow stood for. To a monarch obsessed by the value of time, the city merited condemnation as 'the seat of sloth'. Its very size was an obstacle to efficiency. 'When there,' she wrote later, 'I make it a rule not to send for anyone, since one never finds out until the following day whether the person will come or not and to pay a visit oneself is to waste a whole day in the carriage.' Nobles lived in Moscow 'in idleness and luxury', tended by too many 'useless domestic servants', and 'apart from that, nowhere do people have before their eyes so many symbols of fanaticism, miraculous icons at every step, churches, priests, and convents, side by side with thieves and brigands'.[38] Since 'Moscow' signified many of the vices that Catherine would seek to extirpate from her Enlightened empire during her thirty-four years on the Russian throne, there was every reason for her to sympathise with the subjugation of the Muscovite past symbolised by her triumphal entry into the city.[39] However, since she nevertheless acknowledged the old capital as the repository of a national heritage that she was determined (and committed) to defend, her decision to be crowned there, confirmed within ten days of her accession, suggests that she was equally anxious to mobilise the Kremlin's sacred historic associations in support of her own precarious regime.

So shaky were the foundations of Catherine's authority in September 1762 that it was by no means certain that she would reach the first anniversary of her accession. She owed her power to a conspiracy shared with Grigory Orlov and a handful of fellow guards officers, who had deposed her unpopular husband, Peter III, in a bloodless coup accomplished with unexpected ease on the night of 28 June. 'We have ascended the All Russian throne to the acclamation of the whole people and, as the whole world can attest, the former Emperor has himself willingly renounced the throne in a letter written in his own hand.'[40] This was a hollow boast. Peter was assassinated soon afterwards in circumstances that still remain mysterious and his death left Catherine exposed as both usurper and assassin. Any shred of legitimacy she might possess was vested in her sickly son Paul, still to reach his eighth birthday. As a further complication, Ivan VI, deposed as an infant by Elizabeth in 1741, remained a prisoner in the Schlüssel-burg fortress, a few miles east of St Petersburg. Remarking on Russia's 'great facility to sudden and dangerous revolutions',[41] many of Europe's wisest heads predicted that Catherine's coup would be merely a prelude to another in which she herself must surely be overthrown. Barely a week after seizing the throne, she had already resolved that attack remained the best form of defence. On 7 July, the same day that she issued a risible manifesto proclaiming that her mur-dered husband had perished from an attack of his haemorrhoids, she announced her intention to stage a coronation, on an unspecified date in September, 'in the manner of our former Orthodox Monarchs, and of the pious Greeks [the Byzan-tine emperors], and of the most ancient Kings of the Israelites, who were custom-arily anointed with Holy oil'.[42]

Here, it seemed, was a classic case in which the need for a ritual celebration of the crown's legitimacy had increased as the stability of the state became less certain.[43] Yet Catherine was undoubtedly playing for high stakes in holding the coronation so soon after her coup. Some of her most influential supporters, headed by Paul's tutor, Count Nikita Panin, had expected her to rule as regent for her son, and no Russian regent had yet been crowned.[44] The precedents could scarcely have been less encouraging. Tsarevna Sophia, who governed Muscovy on behalf of the boy tsars Ivan V and Peter I from 1682 to 1689, had fatally undermined her authority by campaigning for recognition as ruler in her own right. In *The Antidote* (1770), a polemical work intended to convince sceptical Europeans of Muscovite achievements, Catherine later claimed that Sophia had 'not been given the credit she deserves': 'She conducted the affairs of the Empire for a number of years with all the sagacity that one could hope for.' But the empress can hardly have relished the prospect of ending her life under house-arrest in a convent, the fate that befell Sophia following the coup that installed Peter the Great as de facto sole ruler.[45] In principle, there was no need to hurry: nowhere in Europe was the interval between accession and coronation prescribed, and Louis XIV, given pause by noble unrest during the Fronde, had set a French record by waiting eleven years before staging his in 1654.[46] Yet the fate of Peter III warned Catherine against delay. By putting off his coronation on the grounds that the regalia were not yet ready, her husband had merely advertised the con-tempt for Orthodox tradition that contributed to his downfall. Determined to learn from his mistakes, Catherine, as a hostile French diplomat reported in early October, missed 'no opportunity to convey to her people a great idea of her pro-found piety and devotion to the Greek religion'.[47]

The vision of Peter III's strangled corpse was not the only violent image that might have flashed across the empress's mind as she descended a flight of stairs that had borne silent witness to some of the bloodiest scenes in Russian history. A reference in her memoirs to the 'famous' Red Staircase suggests that tales of the Moscow rebellion that brought Sophia to power in May 1682 might have been part of the folklore she learned from her pious lady-in-waiting, Praskovya Vladislavova ('that woman was a living archive who knew the scandalous history of every family in Russia from the time of Peter the Great and beyond').[48] It was then that the boyar Artamon Matveyev, once the leading minister to Tsar Aleksey Mikhailovich (1645–76), had allegedly been hurled from the top of the stairs onto the pikes of the mutinous musketeers. Reformed into new regiments by Peter the Great, the Guards had been guarantors of the Russian throne ever since. Conscious that resentment of her relationship with Orlov extended even to supporters of her own coup, Catherine knew as she gazed down on the serried ranks of extravagantly plumed helmets that it would take only one treacherous officer to ignite a riot. The threat was real enough: not long after the coronation, some fifteen guardsmen were arrested and tortured on suspicion of a conspiracy to dethrone her in favour of Ivan VI.[49] On the morning of 22 September, however, all remained tranquil as the crowd waited patiently in silence – a sign not of popular disapproval, as it would have been in France, but rather of awed anticipation, as the official record of the coronation was anxious to stress.[50]

———

Seeking to invent a myth of legitimacy for the new empress, Catherine's supporters set out to demonstrate the parallels between her and Elizabeth, and beyond Elizabeth to her father, Peter the Great. 'Elizabeth has risen for our sakes,' proclaimed Mikhailo Lomonosov in his 'Ode on the Accession of Catherine II': 'Catherine is the unity of both!'[51] To drive home the analogy, artists painted Catherine in poses already familiar from portraits of Elizabeth. To ensure that the new empress's coronation followed the same format as Elizabeth's twenty years earlier, Trubetskoy refreshed his memory of that event by researching the historical precedents.[52] Even as Catherine's procession made its stately progress towards the Cathedral of the Dormition, her leading supporters offered a visible representation of continuity among Russia's governing elite.

Although that elite served the tsar in a variety of military and bureaucratic organisations, their institutional hierarchies were then overlaid (as they have been ever since in Russia) by a network of informal patronage groups too flexible to be classed as factions. By marrying into the Romanov dynasty, the Saltykovs and the Naryshkins, themselves related by marriage to the Trubetskoys, had cornered an increasing number of leading offices since the reign of Peter the Great.[53] So it is no surprise to find Peter Naryshkin among the gentlemen-in-waiting carrying the empress's train and Lev Naryshkin among her closest friends. The imperial mantle was entrusted to Field Marshal Peter Saltykov, a hero of the Seven Years' War whom Catherine admired as 'a very good man, active and full of good sense'.[54] She made him Governor General of Moscow. The state sword, first used in 1742, was carried by the Master of the Horse, Peter Sumarokov, whose service in the Senate stretched back to Anna's reign in the 1730s. Admiral Ivan Talyzin, who had ridden out into Cathedral Square to shower coins over the populace at Elizabeth's coronation, now carried the state seal.[55] During Catherine's coup at the end of June, he had been responsible for turning away the deposed Peter III from the island fortress of Kronstadt. The crown itself was borne by Aleksey Razumovsky, a Ukrainian of Cossack extraction whom Elizabeth had promoted as her Grand Master of the Hunt after plucking him from the choir loft to become her lover thirty years earlier. In his case, lineage was less important than loyalty, and no one was more loyal to Catherine than Count Aleksey Petrovich Bestuzhev-Ryumin. Having initially opposed her invitation to Russia in 1744, Bestuzhev had been arrested fourteen years later as one of her most faithful supporters. Now, 'debauched, profligate, deceitful and interested to excess',[56] the old man was about to enjoy a brief Indian summer.

Waiting to greet her at the south portal of the cathedral, Archbishop Dimitry imparted a vital sense of authority to the whole proceedings. At the beginning of the nineteenth century, the story circulated that he made Catherine tremble by inquiring severely, 'Why have you come?'[57] In reality, however, there could hardly have been a more reassuring figure for the empress to meet at the start of a ritual intended to symbolise the harmony of the earthly and the celestial spheres – he had been rewarded for his support during her coup with the personal grant of 1000 serfs.[58] Surrounded by no fewer than twenty bishops, thirty-five archimandrites and a host of lesser clergy resplendent in their finest vestments, Catherine kissed the life-giving cross, believed to be studded with a fragment from Christ's crucifix, and followed Dimitry and Metropolitan Timofey past the massive, copper-plated doors into an aesthetic world that, for all her professions of loyalty to the Orthodox faith, she never fully understood.

Already installed on tiered benches erected between the cathedral's four great internal pillars was a select congregation of Court ladies, native dignitaries and foreign diplomats who had not taken part in the procession and had, as usual, been left uncertain about the arrangements until the last moment. Like the others, the French ambassador received his invitation only on 20 September, after frantic negotiations about precedence in the seating plan: 'There was nothing they could have done to persuade me to appear at the coronation as a gawping tourist.'[59] Facing the altar, in a gallery in front of the west wall, the diplomats occupied the first row with the Baltic nobility behind them, brigadiers in the third row and the Baltic merchants at the back. Female guests sat along the north wall, ranged according to rank behind Countess Anna Vorontsova, and the empress's ladies and maids of honour. Opposite them was a gallery for the foremost Russian officials. Holders of the first three ranks on the Table decreed by Peter the Great in 1722 sat at the front with lesser-ranking bureaucrats further back.[60]

At the heart of the cathedral, within full view of all three stands, twelve steps led up to a dais, six feet high, fourteen feet long and five and a half feet wide, draped in red velvet and surrounded by balustrades carved with gilded hieroglyphs. Catherine's throne had been sent from Persia for Tsar Boris Godunov at the end of the sixteenth century. To its right stood a gilded table for her regalia; to the left was a place for the young tsarevich. Above the throne, a huge velvet canopy, decorated with gold braid and fringed with lace, was suspended from the ceiling by a chain, joined to each corner by silken ropes in the shape of a pyramid. Into the lining of this canopy was sewn the imperial coat of arms, so that the empress, should she glance to the heavens during her coronation, would stare straight into the eyes of a double-headed eagle.[61]

By combining his knowledge of Renaissance engineering with rare sensitivity to Russian tradition, Fioravanti had created a building whose conventional exterior, modelled on the twelfth-century Cathedral of the Dormition in Vladimir, concealed one of the lightest and most spacious interiors in the Orthodox world. Yet it was by no means so cavernous as it was made to seem in the commemorative illustrations of Catherine's coronation by Jean-Louis de Veilly, a French artist who had had a chequered career since arriving in St Petersburg from England in 1754. (His appointment to teach at the Academy of Fine Arts was terminated 'thanks to the peculiarities of his character' and the figures he painted on the floor of the Chinese Room at Tsarskoye Selo seemed 'flushed and somehow drunken because of their slitty eyes'.[62]) De Veilly evidently used illustrations of the Bourbon coronations as one of his models. But even had the Orthodox Church permitted the use of musical instruments to accompany the liturgy, there would scarcely have been room for the 100-piece orchestra hidden behind the altar at Reims for the coronation of Louis XVI in 1775.[63] Barely a quarter of the size of Reims or Westminster Abbey, and much more intimate in atmosphere, the Dormition Cathedral had only limited space for guests. Competition for places was intensified by two eighteenth-century developments: the expansion of the noble elite and Peter the Great's insistence that both sexes should attend Court ceremonials in a church conceived by its Muscovite founders as a strictly male preserve.

Catherine's nineteen-year-old friend, Princess Dashkova, who might have expected to benefit from the new dispensations, was mortified to discover that instead they militated against her. Having travelled from St Petersburg in the empress's own carriage, Dashkova found that her membership of the Order of St Catherine, to which only thirteen candidates had been appointed during Elizabeth's twenty-year reign, counted for nothing at a ceremony where precedence depended on rank alone. As the wife of a mere colonel, the most junior officer admitted to the coronation, the princess was relegated to the back of the stand, even though her husband, as one of the two masters of ceremonies, had the honour of leading the procession of the imperial regalia from the Senate Palace, where they had been stored overnight, to the Palace of Facets.[64] The slight still rankled when Dashkova came to write her self-serving memoirs in 1804. Blaming her humiliation on the Orlovs, who distrusted her as the younger sister of Peter III's disgraced mistress, Elizabeth Vorontsova, she was forced to swallow her pride or absent herself altogether, as friends advised her to do. There was never really a choice. 'I said to myself that if they were putting on an opera I wanted to see and the only seats were in the gods, then I should, as a passionate music-lover, take my place there rather than miss the performance.'[65]

———

Catherine's coronation was a performance in three acts, of which the first was purely liturgical. As the empress processed to kiss the icons before taking her seat on the throne, the choir chanted Psalm 101 from their specially constructed stalls to the side of the holy gates: 'I will sing of mercy and judgement: unto thee, O Lord, will I sing.'[66] By the time they reached King David's final menacing verse – 'I will early destroy all the wicked of the land; that I may cut off all wicked doers from the city of the Lord' – there had been plenty of time for the congregation to contemplate the frescoes of the Last Judgement on the west wall. Though many of these masterpieces had been damaged by condensation – Catherine herself later paid for their renovation in the early 1770s[67] – their message was given added urgency in a cathedral built at a time when many Muscovites anticipated the imminent end of the world in 1492 (the year 7000 according to the Byzantine calendar numbered from the Creation).[68] Now that fears of the Apocalypse had subsided, Catherine's courtiers were less inclined to dwell on divine punishment than on the rewards to be anticipated by the righteous. Though the empress may privately have mocked superstition, the overwhelming majority of her subjects, including many of the most eminent, never abandoned their belief in the power of icons and relics to cure all manner of afflictions. As the most important church in Muscovy, the Cathedral of the Dormition housed some of Orthodoxy's most precious relics, including the head of John Chrysostom, the right hand of the apostle Andrew, one of Basil the Great's fingers, part of a leg of St John the Baptist, and the remains of many lesser, local saints.[69]

It mattered that the cathedral also contained the most famous miracle-working image in all Russia, the icon of Our Lady of Vladimir, because it had become an established literary convention to associate female Russian monarchs with the Virgin Mary. In sharp contrast to St Petersburg, Marian imagery was prominent all over Moscow, which claimed to have inherited the Virgin's traditional role as protectress of Constantinople when the 'second Rome' fell to the Turks in 1453. (The church now famous as St Basil's Cathedral at the southern end of Red Square was officially known as the Cathedral of the Protecting Veil of the Mother of God because it had been consecrated in memory of the fall of the Tatar stronghold of Kazan to Ivan the Terrible on the feast of the protective veil in 1552.) Orthodox writers who had celebrated the feast of the Nativity of the Mother of God as recently as 8 September now portrayed Catherine in the image of a virginal queen capable of restoring happiness and leading her people to paradise. But while it was convenient to associate the empress with the Virgin by virtue of her sex, her office led to analogies with Christ himself. Since the image of the sun king had been commonplace in absolute monarchies since the time of Louis XIV, there was nothing apparently extraordinary in Alexander Sumarokov's depiction of Catherine, in the ode he dedicated to her 'On the First Day of 1763', as the light to drive out all darkness (by which he meant any surviving vestige of support for Peter III). Sophisticated Russian readers, however, would have had no difficulty in recognising an additional allusion to the transfigured Christ. Vasily Petrov, the empress's 'pocket poet', later made still more explicit references to Catherine as 'the beginning and end of all things' and the 'image of the all-powerful Deity', pouring 'light from [her] lofty throne'.[70] Whilst the jewels in the empress's regalia reflected hundreds of flickering candles and glinted in the pale light filtering through windows set high in the cathedral walls, the most important illumination at her coronation was that which radiated metaphorically from Catherine herself.

Only the most accomplished of actresses could have carried off the part of a Christ-like virgin queen when all present knew her as both an adulteress and a usurper and many suspected her of regicide to boot. Yet while the Russian elite suspended its disbelief in the face of the realities of power, Catherine's theatrical talents were never in doubt. No less a rival than Louis XV acknowledged shortly before the coronation that her courage and powers of dissimulation marked her out as 'a princess capable of planning and executing great deeds'.[71] Unlike contemporaries unwisely tempted to regard coronations as so much mumbo-jumbo, Catherine was determined to take hers with all seriousness. Whereas Austria's Francis Stephen had seemed playfully to wave his regalia during the procession that followed his installation as Holy Roman Emperor in 1740 – a ceremony that his wife Maria Theresa dismissed as 'a comedy'[72] – Catherine invested even those elements of the ritual in which she could scarcely believe with the dignity expected of a rightful sovereign, beginning with a confident public declaration of her adherence to the articles of the Orthodox faith.[73]

She was at her most convincing in the investiture – the central act of the coronation, developed from the ceremony invented in the sixteenth century, on the basis of selective use of Byzantine ideas, to give religious sanction to the conquests of Ivan the Terrible. As Catherine passed Tsar Ivan's elaborately carved throne of Monomakh on her way into the cathedral, she can hardly have forgotten the promise she had made six years earlier to her confidant, the British ambassador Sir Charles Hanbury-Williams, when she recalled seeing a treaty signed by Queen Elizabeth and Ivan himself: 'That prince, tyrant though he was, was a great man; and since I shall try, as far as my natural weakness will allow me, to imitate the great men of this country, I hope one day to adorn your own archives with my name, and I shall be proud to go wrong in the steps of Peter the Great.'[74] Now she emulated the tendency of Tsar Peter and his successors to elevate the importance of the monarch in the coronation ritual at the expense of the Church.

First she invested herself with the ermine imperial mantle, decorated with the insignia of the Order of St Andrew the First Called, the highest of the Russian orders of chivalry established by Tsar Peter, ceremonially presented to her by Countess Vorontsova and her successor as the Court's senior lady-in-waiting,

Yelena Naryshkina.[75] Then Aleksey Razumovsky approached the throne bearing on a cushion the new crown designed by the Court jeweller, Gérémie Pauzié. Working on characteristically explicit instructions from Catherine herself, Pauzié had fashioned a diadem to rival any in Europe. At its centre was a cross mounted on a 389-carat ruby purchased in Peking from the Emperor Kangxi on the orders of Tsar Aleksey Mikhailovich. Further encrusted with 75 unusually large pearls, 2500 diamonds and more than 5000 other precious jewels, Catherine's crown weighed almost two kilograms and was valued at 2 million roubles at the time of the coronation.[76] Following the precedent set by Elizabeth in 1742, she lowered it onto her own brow.

As cannon fired a 101-gun salute and the bells rang out to signal the high-point of the ceremony, the newly crowned empress stood before her throne, grasping in her left hand the great golden orb and in her right a sceptre made only a fortnight earlier when a panic-stricken search for the old one ended in failure.[77] Three times the deacon chanted 'many years', and three times the congregation of notables prostrated themselves before her. As silence fell, Catherine returned both orb and sceptre to their bearers and prayed to God to preserve her 'in the hearing of all present'. While she remained standing, the congregation sank to its knees to hear Dimitry pray for her in the name of the whole people.[78] Then the archbishop – 'a prelate of great learning' who 'combined with his other qualities a moving and manly eloquence that entranced his audience'[79] – made a congratulatory speech, driving home Catherine's central theme of selflessness. Not for her the temptations of worldly power and glory, Dimitry insisted. 'Only maternal love for the fatherland, only faith in God, and ardour for piety, only compassion for the suffering and oppressed Russian children impelled You to take on this great service to God.'[80]

Only now, once the investiture was over, did the anointment take place (in France and England, it was significantly the other way around).[81] Having removed her crown, the empress processed towards the iconostasis, where the gates swung open to admit her to the holy sanctuary. There the final act of her coronation was completed as this sceptical convert from Lutheranism became the first female ruler of Russia to take her own communion bread from the platen, a sacerdotal privilege hitherto restricted to members of the Orthodox priesthood.[82]

Nothing in the coronation rite implied the existence of any contract between monarch and subjects. Neither did they expect it. Monarchy in Russia was intensely personal and Catherine intended that it should remain so. Since she was nevertheless aware that 'power without the confidence of the nation is nothing', it was a relief to emerge from the cathedral's north door to be greeted by cheering so wild that she allowed it to continue for half an hour before continuing her procession.[83] Convinced that such popular acclaim owed more to stage-management than to genuine affection, the French ambassador gleefully reported the alarm which ensued when a section of the soldiery and crowd unexpectedly hailed not Catherine, but 'Our Emperor Paul Petrovich': officers were immediately sent to silence them.[84] This, as even Breteuil admitted, was an isolated incident in an otherwise well-ordered ceremony. As her procession snaked along the wooden walkway into Ivanov Square, round the Ivan the Great bell tower and then back into Cathedral Square – first to allow the empress to pay her respects at the tombs of her Muscovite predecessors in the Cathedral of the Archangel Michael and then to kiss the relics in the Annunciation Cathedral – Catherine rewarded the attendant populace for their devotion by showering them with gold and silver coins from 120 oak barrels, each containing coins worth 5000 roubles.[85]

Naturally, the elite were not forgotten. Still in full regalia, Catherine lavished rewards on them when she returned to the Palace of Facets. Dashkova recovered some pride when she was made a lady-in-waiting; the title of count was conferred on all five Orlov brothers. For the remainder of her reign, Catherine was to remain powerfully attached to Aleksey, the scar-faced giant who had been responsible for guarding her husband at the time of his death. Vladimir became the president of the Academy of Sciences; Fëdor kept an eye on proceedings in the Senate; and Ivan was close enough to the empress to broker her eventual split with Grigory in 1772. Now, however, Grigory was appointed Adjutant General, an office that carried ceremonial duties to allow the favourite to remain at his sovereign's side. Nor were titles and promotions the only gifts on offer. Catherine's coup was by far the most expensive in eighteenth-century Russia. Between July and December 1762, she paid out 1.5 million roubles to buy support at a time when the annual state budget amounted to little more than 16 million. By the following March, she had given away 21,423 male peasants since her accession – almost three times as many as Peter III had distributed to his henchmen during his short reign.[86]

Not until three in the afternoon did Catherine finally process to a banquet that was to last long into the evening. As late as 17 September, Trubetskoy remained uncertain of the guest list because the Synod had characteristically failed to tell him how many clergy would be attending. In the end, on the model of Elizabeth's coronation, he arranged for four tables to be laid in the Palace of Facets for the churchmen and 102 senior courtiers, while 259 lesser ranking guests were accommodated in the hall above and 26 more in a neighbouring gallery. Catherine, as was customary, dined alone on a dais under a silken canopy. To her right, Countess Anna Vorontsova sat at the head of a table of Court ladies. To the left of the throne, the leading male courtiers occupied the second table; the third, placed opposite, was for the clergy; gentlemen of the third rank were served at the remaining table. Although de Veilly's illustration of the banquet depicts a far from solemn occasion, every effort had been made to ensure that it proceeded in an orderly way. Count Karl Sievers, one of four Court stewards, had instructed his chamberlains in the sternest terms to organise the liveried servants in teams for each table, to take good care of the silver, and to report drunken or disorderly lackeys to the Court administration so that none should escape a fine.[87]

The ceremonies were brought to a close with a magnificent firework representing a statue of Russia under an arched colonnade in front of a cathedral. Above the arch, two allegorical figures crowned a shield with the emblem of the new empress. The colonnade was adorned with six allegorical statues, including Faith, Hope and Plenty. In the foreground another emblem in the form of a flaming star stood on a pedestal surrounded by a railing decorated with whirling Catherine wheels.[88] Hoping to get a better view of the illuminations that transformed the Ivan the Great bell tower into a pillar of flame, the empress herself stepped out incognito onto the Red Staircase at midnight. But it was no use. Immediately spotted by the crowd, she was forced to acknowledge yet another prolonged bout of applause. Three days later, she found it 'impossible to describe' to her ambassador in Warsaw 'the delight of a numberless crowd to see me here. I cannot go out, nor even put my face to the window, without the acclamations beginning all over again.'[89] And still the public's appetite was not sated. Such was the popular fascination with the monarchy that some 122,138 people of various ranks filed past the regalia when they were put on public display between 6 and 25 October.[90]

The coronation had revealed in microcosm many of the tensions that a successful Russian tsar had to be able to resolve: between tradition and innovation; between the noble elite and the peasantry; between multinational *Rossiya* and native, ethnic *Rus*. Underlying them all lay the dilemma facing any ruler. How far should she seek to build consent? When should she resort to force? In the immediate aftermath of her coup, Catherine had passed a series of crucial tests. She had staged a coronation that fused Orthodox tradition with classical imagery in a symbolic reconciliation of mercy and conquest. More important still, she had demonstrated the personal qualities that persuaded all those who met her that success lay within her grasp. 'Affability and dignity,' Buckinghamshire reported at the end of October 1762, 'are blended in her manner, which inspires you at once with ease and respect. When the hurry, the unavoidable consequence of a revolution is over, she has every talent to make this a great and powerful country.'[91] Propagandists insisted that victory was already hers. 'Listen, universe!' urged Sumarokov during the great street pageant 'Triumphant Minerva', staged under the direction of Russia's leading actor Fëdor Volkov in Moscow in January 1763: 'Astraea is on earth, Astraea has settled in the lands of the Russians, Astraea has ascended the throne.'[92] In April, Aleksey Rzhevsky's 'Birthday Ode' returned to the same theme: 'Astraea has now descended to us, the golden age has already begun in Russia, and wisdom has come to the throne as a result of the holy will of the Almighty.'[93]

Catherine was understandably more cautious. 'I can congratulate myself on my growing popularity, but must be wary of it in spite of all the manifestations in my favour. This must not, however, prevent me from acting as though it were real ... I may be too young to become a favourite sovereign, but I must behave as though I believed myself to be one.'[94] Since arriving in Russia as the fourteen-year-old prospective fiancée for Grand Duke Peter, she had devoted many of her most private moments to preparing for the challenge.

CHAPTER ONE

FROM POMERANIA TO
ST PETERSBURG 1729–1744

In a scene far removed from the splendour of the Moscow Kremlin, Princess Sophie Auguste Friderike of Anhalt-Zerbst was born in a merchant's house in the Grosse Domstrasse, nestled in the shadow of St Mary's Church, just inside the northern city wall of Stettin (now Szczecin in Poland).[1] The house offered temporary quarters to her father, Prince Christian August, who was stationed there as a general in the service of Frederick William I of Prussia (r. 1713–40), Europe's most uncompromising soldier-king. Whereas Christian August was already thirty-nine, his wife, Princess Johanna Elisabeth of Holstein-Gottorp, was not quite seventeen when she gave birth to their first child in the early hours of the morning of 2 May 1729 (21 April according to the Julian calendar then in use in Russia, eleven days behind the Western Gregorian calendar in the eighteenth century). Never one to suffer in silence, the young mother soon made it clear to her daughter that it had been a painful, life-threatening delivery. Though her father did his best to disguise his disappointment, Sophie was left in no doubt that both parents would have preferred a boy.[2]

They were lucky that she had survived at all. Since death made little distinction between the cradles of rich and poor in the eighteenth century, twenty-nine out of every thousand infants in Europe's ruling families were stillborn, a further forty-seven were dead within a week, and 106 more failed to complete the first year of their life.[3] To the fortunate infants who passed that early milestone, smallpox offered the greatest threat. Though its impact in the eighteenth century can be estimated only approximately, the total number of European deaths per annum caused by the disease is commonly put at 400,000 and the secretary of the Royal

Society of London calculated that smallpox had killed a fourteenth of the city's population between 1680 and 1743.[4] When Catherine had herself inoculated against the greatest killer of the age in her fortieth year, she told her Prussian ally, Frederick the Great, that she had suffered 'a thousand sorrows' in her attempts to overcome her childhood fear of the disease. Every time she fell ill, however slight the infection, she imagined that it must be the dreaded pox.[5] Though no eighteenth-century royal letter was sent without careful official consideration – and this one was evidently intended to portray Catherine as an Enlightened monarch confronting the forces of unreason – the emotion it implied was sincere enough. As it transpired, her worries were unnecessary. Right from the start, Sophie showed all the signs of the hearty constitution that was to carry her through to the age of sixty-seven. A bout of pneumonia when she was seven seems to have been her only serious childhood illness. Apart from that, she chose to recall only a skin infection, generally assumed to be impetigo or some form of scrofula, whose periodic attacks forced her to cover her shaven, powdered scalp with a bonnet and to wear gloves until the scabs fell off her hands.[6]

Until Christian August inherited the family seat at Zerbst in 1743, the greater part of Sophie's childhood was spent in her bleak Baltic birthplace. Situated near the mouth of the River Oder, a hundred miles north-east of Berlin, Stettin in 1729 could boast about 11,000 inhabitants and more than 900 stone houses. Describing the town fifty years earlier, an English writer claimed that 'the greatest beauty thereof is the palace, or prince's Court, which is built with such art and magnificence, that none of the Italian Courts can equal it'.[7] By then, however, Stettin's princely glories already lay in the past. Duke Philip II of Pomerania-Stettin (r. 1606–18) had indeed been a leading artistic patron who commissioned a celebrated *Kunstschrank* – a cabinet made in Augsburg which opened to reveal hidden paintings, symbolic carvings, and precious objects that were believed to constitute an epitome of the universe.[8] But when his Greifen dynasty expired in 1637, both Stettin and the surrounding duchy of Pomerania rapidly became battle-scarred pawns on the chessboard of international politics.

Sweden, the dominant Baltic power in the seventeenth century, was the first to take control, counting Stettin and Western Pomerania among its spoils at the end of the Thirty Years' War in 1648. But while the Swedes regarded their new German possessions primarily as a means of exerting pressure on Denmark from the south, Brandenburg-Prussia, the rising power in northern Germany, never gave up hope of capturing them. Serious damage was inflicted on Stettin during a six-month siege in 1677. Two years later, France's diplomatic intervention on behalf of its Swedish satellite forced the Prussians to abandon their gains at the Treaty of Saint-Germain, so that it was not until 1713 that the Great Northern War again brought the town under their control, this time by agreement with Peter the Great's Russia, the second emergent power in the Baltic. Only in February 1720, five years after the death of Louis XIV had temporarily loosened France's stranglehold on European diplomacy, was Frederick William I finally able to purchase the town and the surrounding area for 2 million thalers under the terms of the Peace of Stockholm.[9]

It was as an officer in Prussian service that Sophie's father, the impoverished scion of a cadet branch of the princely House of Anhalt, had been obliged to make his career. By 1729, having served in the Low Countries during the War of the Spanish Succession, he had reached the rank of major general and was stationed at Stettin in command of the 8th infantry regiment. Following his promotion to command the garrison, Christian August and his family moved from the house on the Domstrasse into the nearby ducal castle, which had been denuded of its more exuberant decoration in keeping with the king's militarist ideals.[10] Having had himself crowned 'king in Prussia' in 1701 at a ceremony in Königsberg that cost roughly twice the annual revenues of the Hohenzollern administration, Frederick William I's father (Frederick, Elector of Brandenburg, 1688–1713) had gone on to establish an elaborate Baroque Court.[11] Almost every feature of it except the hunt was dismantled by his son. Whereas the Court of Berlin had spent 17,000 thalers on confectionery alone in 1707, its total annual expenditure was limited under Frederick William I to 52,000 thalers.[12] Surrounded by rubble from the town's newly strengthened fortifications, Christian August's circumstances in Stettin were even more spartan. Sophie saw little of him, though she always respected his integrity, his piety, and his knowledge of classical Rome. That was what she meant when, shortly before her fiftieth birthday, she told the Prince de Ligne that she had been 'brought up in the army with respect for republics'.[13]

In the gloomy, granite castle, the little girl and her nurses occupied three vaulted rooms on the upper floor of the wing adjoining the chapel. Every morning and evening, Sophie knelt to say her prayers in a bedroom next to the bell tower, where she remembered being disturbed by phantom noises from the organ, allegedly made by mischievous servants. As she told her principal correspondent in adult life, Baron Melchior Grimm, on discovering that he was contemplating a visit to Stettin in 1776, 'I gambolled across the whole of this wing three or four times a day to visit my mother, who lived on the other side.'[14]

Johanna Elisabeth, however, had little time for her first-born, paying more attention to her lame son, Wilhelm Christian Friedrich, who came into the world eighteen months after Sophie and was taken from it by scarlet fever at the age of thirteen. Of the three further children, only Friedrich August, born in 1734, survived to adult life: Auguste Christine Charlotte lived but twelve days in 1736; the third daughter, Elisabeth, born in 1743, not long after Wilhelm's death, was left behind when her mother took Sophie to Russia, causing both of them grief when she died in 1745.[15]

Since there could be no question of formal schooling for the female offspring of a minor German prince, Sophie's education was entrusted from the age of four to her Huguenot governess, Elisabeth (Babet) Cardel (b. 1712), the younger sister of her nurse, Magdalena. Babet taught her to spell and to read, and introduced her to a pleasure that was to remain with her for the rest of her life: listening to friends read aloud. A dancing master was employed to teach the basic courtly arts, though this was later dismissed as 'a waste of money, because really I only learned to dance much later – this is how a precocious education usually leads nowhere'. The rudiments of a more formal curriculum in French, German and the Scriptures were taught by the Pietist pastor Friedrich Wagner, a chaplain in her father's regiment.[16] This was a far more prestigious position than it sounds. The Pietist pastors chosen to become army preachers (*Feldprediger*) in Frederick William I's Prussia were a zealous elite appointed directly by the king, who relied on them to transform illiterate peasant recruits into God-fearing, disciplined soldiers. Their most prominent convert was Prince Leopold of Anhalt-Dessau, Christian August's cousin and the king's leading general.[17] Since the very notion of childhood was barely developed among princely households at the time – all Sophie's dolls and toys were removed at the age of seven on the grounds that she was 'a big girl, for whom they were no longer suitable'[18] – it probably never occurred to her father that an army preacher's methods might not suit a girl of tender age. She certainly failed to respond to them. 'I bear no grudge against Monsieur Wagner,' Catherine told Grimm in 1778, 'but I am intimately persuaded that he was a blockhead, and that Mademoiselle Cardel was an intelligent girl.'[19]

She developed the contrast in a memoir begun on her forty-second birthday in 1771. Here Wagner is portrayed as a dull pedant, keen to resort to the rod in the face of her impudent questions (she claimed to have challenged the Creation story and asked him about circumcision). Refused permission to beat his young pupil, he took his revenge by frightening her with stories of the Last Judgement and imposing an unforgiving regime of rote learning which helped to harden her mind against organised religion. Since the Word was central to Pietism – an emotional brand of religiosity which stressed the intensely personal bonds between individual believers and their God – its pastors regarded the Scriptures as the main source of religious authority and the ultimate guide to everyday behaviour. Wagner was no exception. 'I do not believe that it could be humanly possible to remember all that I had to learn by heart,' Catherine later complained, 'nor that there was any point in doing so. I have kept to this day a German Bible, in which all the verses I learned from memory are marked in red ink.'[20] By contrast, Babet Cardel appears in the empress's memoirs as 'a model of virtue and wisdom'. 'She possessed a naturally elevated soul, a cultivated mind, and an excellent heart: she was patient, gentle, gay, just, steadfast – in truth, everything one could wish to find in people who look after children.' Babet's gentle inquisitiveness generated a sympathetic response: 'I yielded to her alone; she smiled to herself and reasoned with me so gently that I could not resist her. All my life, indeed, I have preserved this inclination to yield only to reason and gentleness: I have always resisted pressure of any kind.'[21]

Artless as they may seem, such reflections form part of a carefully constructed persona which Catherine had already begun to fashion in her first brief memoir, written six years before she seized the Russian throne. Taking a detached view of her own character and conduct, she anticipated many of the features of the classic Enlightenment autobiographies by presenting herself as a rational, independent spirit – 'I was excessively lively and rather wayward in my childhood' – struggling to overcome the superstitious adults who supervised her upbringing.[22] While Sophie's parents consulted leading German doctors in their attempts to cure Wilhelm's lameness, and sent him to take the waters at Aix-la-Chapelle, Teplitz and Karlsbad, a specialist in 'dislocation' proved harder to find when it seemed that Sophie might grow up with a curvature of the spine. In the end, they resorted to the public hangman, who recommended that a local girl be summoned every morning to rub Sophie's back with her saliva and designed a primitive corset to straighten her limbs. She wore it until she was ten, growing increasingly self-conscious about her appearance. 'I don't know whether it is true that I was ugly as a child,' the mature empress mused, 'but I certainly know that people often told me so.'[23]

To compensate for lack of beauty, Sophie tried to be amusing instead. If we believe her memoirs, she also learned to be secretive. Since a degree of dissimulation was regarded as an important weapon in any successful ruler's armoury – 'Behave cleverly in public,' Catherine told Potëmkin at the height of their affair in 1774, 'and that way no one will know what we are thinking. I so enjoy being crafty!'[24] – we should not be surprised at her claim to have mastered the skill so early. But for all the careful construction in the empress's memoirs, there seems little reason to doubt that she was accustomed to keeping things to herself from an early age. Most children do, as the adult Catherine came to realise. 'One never knows what children are thinking,' she warned Grimm in 1776, a year before the birth of her first grandson, 'and children are difficult to get to know, especially when a severe education has turned them into docile listeners and they have learned from experience not to tell things to their teachers. From that, if you please, you will derive the fine maxim that one should not scold children, but put them at their ease, so that they do not hide their blunders from you.'[25]

The greatest legacy of Sophie's early education was a form of secularised Pietist work ethic that stayed with her for the rest of her life. 'I have always been able to concentrate hard,' she boasted in 1785, regularly peppering her instructions to subordinates with exhortations not to waste time. 'Waste as little time as possible,' she urged her favourite, Peter Zavadovsky: 'Time belongs not to me but to the empire.'[26] Crucial as this sense of duty was to become, the mature empress gave her childhood teachers no credit for it. On the contrary, as a celebrated patron of the Enlightenment and correspondent of Voltaire, she looked back on Stettin as an isolated provincial backwater. 'Is it my fault that I do not share the taste of my century?' she once asked Grimm, in mock defence of her alleged aesthetic shortcomings. 'I think that Mlle Cardel and M. Wagner belonged to another age.'[27]

––––––

Frustrated by the constraints of Stettin's narrow society, the vivacious Johanna Elisabeth escaped as often as she could, shuttling back and forth across the north German plain to visit better-connected relatives. At the age of three, Sophie accompanied her on the first of several trips to her maternal grandmother in Hamburg. Here, as she grew older, she would experience an exceptional degree of freedom: 'I did what I wanted and ran about from morning until night in every corner of the house.' On that first visit, however, the frightened child apparently had to be removed, screaming, from the opera house. 'This scene left such an impression on me that I remember it even now,' she wrote in 1771.[28] Another frequent destination was the family seat at Zerbst, an insignificant town fifty miles south-west of Berlin and roughly equidistant between Magdeburg and

Wittenberg, where Martin Luther had famously nailed his ninety-five theses to the door of the church in October 1517. Best of all, the ambitious Johanna Elisabeth liked Berlin, where they regularly spent part of the winter.

Zerbst and the Prussian capital, however, were primarily calling points en route to the Court of Brunswick-Wolfenbüttel in Lower Saxony, where Sophie's mother had herself been raised and where her godmother, the dowager Duchess Elisabeth Sophie Marie of Brunswick-Lüneburg, had paid her dowry and arranged her marriage to Christian August at the palace at Vechelde, six miles west of Brunswick, in 1727.[29] More at ease than her husband in the *grande monde*, Johanna Elisabeth willingly returned to spend several months of the year with her benefactress. For the growing Sophie, it proved to be a memorable experience: 'I was cajoled and made much of, small as I was. I heard it said so often that I was clever, and that I was a big girl, that I fancied it must be true. I stayed up for all the masquerade-balls and festivals and went all over the place. I chattered like a magpie and was excessively forward.'[30]

There was much for an inquisitive child to see. The Court of Brunswick had been an important centre for the arts since the time of Shakespeare's contemporary Duke Heinrich Julius, himself a notable playwright. Duke Anton Ulrich (r. 1685–1714) was an even more prolific Baroque novelist and poet, and it was during his reign that the built environment of the Court was transformed. That seasoned observer of European Court life, Baron Pöllnitz, particularly admired the duke's homage to Versailles, his new country seat (*Lustschloss*) at Salzdahlum, a stone-clad timber palace halfway between Brunswick and Wolfenbüttel: 'It has a great gallery with a collection of pictures by the chief painters which is not to be met with elsewhere.'[31] Salzdahlum's architect Hermann Korb also designed a celebrated rotunda to house the Duke August Library at Wolfenbüttel – then, as now, one of Europe's leading scholarly collections – of which no less a philosopher than Gottfried Wilhelm Leibniz was chief librarian between 1691 and 1716.[32] The interior of the residence itself, one of the largest castles in northern Germany, was reshaped by the addition of a suite of Baroque staterooms.[33] The long reign of Duke Karl I (r. 1735–80) proved to be a flourishing period for the arts during which Gotthold Lessing, the greatest literary figure of the German Enlightenment, took charge of the Duke August Library in the 1770s and the Court maintained both an Italian opera company and a French ballet.[34] As a result of such lavish expenditure, Brunswick's national debt rose from 1 million thalers in 1693 to 11 million in 1750, by which time Karl's Court had more than doubled in size to around 400 people.[35] Even so he never doubted the value of the splendour he created, and there was no sign of a decline in his dynasty's fortunes at the time of Sophie's visits.

Though the regal status achieved by their more powerful rivals in Dresden and Berlin proved beyond the reach of second-division German princes such as the dukes of Brunswick, there was no shortage of royalty to be found at their Court. Duke Karl's sisters included not only Elisabeth Christine, who in 1733 had married the future Frederick the Great of Prussia (r. 1740–86), but also Sophie's exact contemporary, Princess Juliana Maria, who corresponded with her in later life after becoming queen of Denmark. Among their brothers were Prince Ludwig of Brunswick, who became tutor to the Stadtholder of the Netherlands and Prince Ferdinand, subsequently a general in Prussian service. Sophie got to know them all. As she later recalled in a passage of her memoirs intended to show that she had by no means arrived in Russia as a naïve provincial:

> The Court of Brunswick was then a truly regal one, judging by the quantity of fine houses it occupied and their decoration, by the good order that reigned at this Court, and by the number of people of various sorts whom it maintained, and by the crowd of foreigners who visited it continually, and the grandeur and magnificence that characterised every aspect of its life. Balls, operas, concerts, hunts, promenades, banquets followed one another every day. That was what I saw for three or four months of the year, every year between the ages of seven and fourteen. The Prussian Court was by no means so well regulated, nor did it seem as splendid as that of the Duke of Brunswick.[36]

Petty German princes may have strained every sinew to emulate Versailles, but according to the French historian Adrien Fauchier-Magnan, writing shortly after the end of the Second World War, all they achieved was 'a puerile, grimacing parody, an extravagant caricature of the luxury and elegance of the *Roi Soleil*'.[37] In this way of thinking, the best that could be expected of a German ruler was harmless eccentricity. In all too many cases, however, oddity seemed to border on insanity – 'Germany teems with princes and dukes,' Count Manteufel observed in 1738, 'three-quarters of whom are not right in the head' – so that the political landscape was dotted by a profusion of self-indulgent despots, each extorting taxes from his benighted subjects to fuel his obsession with personal glory.[38]

Like all caricatures, this one incorporates a recognisable grain of truth. As Sophie was soon to discover, flagrant marital infidelity was a feature common to hothouse Court societies all over Europe. Though German Courts were no exception, there was no doubt about the identity of the monarch who had set new standards of shamelessness in his relationships with the opposite sex. When Duke Eberhard Ludwig of Württemberg scandalised his Lutheran officials in 1707 by declaring his intention to marry his paramour while his first wife was still alive, he countered their objections by pointing to the example of Louis XIV.[39] Louis had sired a string of royal bastards – so-called 'children of France' – by a succession of mistresses which ended only with his secret second marriage to Madame de Maintenon in 1683. Only then, as a recent biographer remarks, did the king undergo a 'drastic conversion to monogamy', coming to resemble 'a reformed alcoholic who will not have a bottle in the house'.[40]

Versailles was equally inspirational in matters of Court culture. The Elector of Saxony, Augustus the Strong, was so impressed by his youthful visit to the French Court in the late 1680s that the image of Louis XIV continued to fascinate him even from the grave. Aspiring to resemble his idol as precisely as possible at his son's wedding, Augustus ordered his Parisian agent in 1717 to send a costume doll to Dresden wearing an outfit 'such as the late King of France wore on great occasions like his wedding'. A drawing would not suffice, Augustus insisted: it had to be a doll.[41] Those unable to marvel at Louis XIV's palace in person avidly collected the illustrated descriptions that the Bourbon kings were eager to see published as a way of propagating French culture. Karl Eugen of Württemberg employed a full-time agent in Paris from 1748, charged solely with sending to Stuttgart all new publications relating to the Court or to palace design. Goethe expressed a widespread contemporary ambivalence about the whole enterprise:

> Duke Karl, to whom one must concede a certain grandeur of vision, worked nevertheless to gratify his momentary passions and to act out a series of ever-changing fantasies. But in that he strove for status, show, and effect, he had a particular need for artists. And even when his motives were less than noble, he could not help but further a higher cause.[42]

Fauchier-Magnan's condescension is therefore seriously distorted. Not only does he fail to see the way that most of the smaller German Courts had risen above the drunken rusticity that disfigured some of the earliest attempts to imitate Versailles, he also misses the central political purpose of representational display. Monarchs in early-modern Europe exercised power over their subjects not by keeping them under observation (as the modern state seeks to do), but by directly representing their exalted status through a series of symbolic gestures, clothing, rhetoric and rituals.[43] Everything at Versailles was designed to glorify Louis XIV, from the paintings on the ceiling to the clock that made Fame crown his statue with a laurel every time it struck the hour.[44] Princes throughout Europe exhausted their revenues to compete. Since there could be no more lavish setting in which to impress their leading subjects and dynastic rivals than a magnificent palace and Court, cultural rivalry between monarchs was intense. 'For the baroque prince,' Tim Blanning has rightly insisted, 'representational display was not self-indulgence, it was his *métier*.'[45] And as Sophie discovered when she left Stettin for the last time in 1743, it was a métier practised even by such a minor potentate as Prince Christian August of Anhalt-Zerbst.

Dwarfed by their Saxon and Prussian neighbours, the princes of the House of Anhalt were among the poorest and most insignificant in Germany. Since being divided into four tiny principalities in 1603, their lands had 'been partitioned so much that there has remained little to partition', as the mature Catherine observed from the throne of the largest territory on earth since the fall of the Roman Empire.[46] That did not mean that their Courts were culturally barren. No less a composer than Johann Sebastian Bach was appointed Court *Kapellmeister* to Prince Leopold of Anhalt-Köthen in 1717. Sandwiched between periods of even more astonishing creativity at Weimar and Leipzig, Bach's six years in Leopold's service produced the six Brandenburg Concertos and the first book of the Well-Tempered Clavier (forty-eight preludes and fugues).[47] Yet scarcely anyone beyond the area knew anything of his genius at the time. There was nothing unusual about that in the introverted confessional world of Protestant northern Germany. The only prince of Anhalt to make a wider European impact was Sophie's contemporary, Leopold III Friedrich Franz of Anhalt-Dessau, who created the first English-style landscape garden in eighteenth-century Germany at Wörlitz between 1763 and 1790, complete with islands named after Rousseau and Herder. Designed to symbolise the reconciliation of technical progress with sentimentalist philosophy, the garden boasted a model volcano whose eruptions were intended to represent the transformative power of Enlightened political reform.[48]

Although his volcano has long since gone, Franz's elegant neoclassical architecture still stands as an oasis of civilisation in the desert of decaying chemical plants that disfigure the former East Germany. The House of Anhalt-Zerbst can boast no such living legacy. Whereas the princes of Anhalt-Dessau survived to witness the formation of the Weimar Republic, Sophie's father's line came to an end even within her own lifetime at the death of her brother, Friedrich August, in 1793. Since little remains of the castle at Zerbst, it is tempting to suppose that it must have been no more distinguished than the town which surrounded it. In fact, like so many Baroque palaces in Europe, it was a quintessentially cosmopolitan creation of considerable elegance and beauty.

When its Dutch architect Cornelis Ryckwaert died in 1693, the central block planned in 1680–81 was already complete. By 1710, the addition of the west wing by the Swiss stucco-master Giovanni Simonetti provided the prince's small retinue with all the ceremonial apartments of a Baroque Court in miniature: a central reception room (*Festsaal*), with ceiling paintings on themes from the *Iliad* and the *Aeneid*; a smaller reception room whose ceiling painting glorified the investiture of the first prince of Anhalt in 1212; and a formal dining hall (*Speisesaal*). By the time that Johann Friedrich Friedel completed the east wing in the spirit of Potsdam rococo, between 1744 and 1748, Sophie had already left for Russia, but she would have worshipped in the ornate chapel at the southern end of the west wing, where Francesco Minetti worked with other artists between 1717 and 1718, inspired by motifs from the Zwinger in Dresden, and she would also have been familiar with the tower built over the castle's main entrance between 1718 and 1722 by Johann Christoph Schütze, who later took charge of construction at the Saxon Court.[49]

In such a modest palace, it was neither possible nor necessary to replicate every element of the etiquette practised at Versailles, which had never been the only available model for the smaller German Courts. Many of them – especially though not exclusively the Catholic ones – adopted the ceremonial of the imperial Court at Vienna, where the Habsburgs preserved, in the relatively unpretentious surroundings of the Hofburg, a ritual tradition adopted from Burgundy and Spain in the sixteenth century. Whereas almost everything in the life of the kings of France was a public spectacle – from the moment they rose in the morning (*lever du roi*) to the moment they retired to bed (*coucher*) – the Austrian emperors lived in comparative seclusion, appearing in public only for a limited number of formal meals.[50] We do not know which ceremonial model was adopted at Zerbst. Neither can we be sure how far the various procedural manuals potentially available to Christian August were translated into everyday practice.[51] However, the unusual fact that his private apartments were built alongside those of his wife, rather than being in separate wings or divided by the main staircase, implies a degree of domestication that serves as a reminder that the Courts of early-modern Europe were by no means monolithic. While itinerant medieval princely households had everywhere settled at a permanent dwelling place (*Residenz*) by 1700, the transformation took place in different ways and at different speeds, and even as more or less regular institutions formed around departments responsible for ceremonial, banqueting, the stables and the hunt, Courts remained complex social organisms, following their peripatetic monarchs to a range of summer and winter palaces, sometimes for whole seasons but often for only a few days at a time.[52] Even Christian August had his own country seat at Dornburg on the Elbe, not far from Zerbst, where Schütze had worked his magic so that Sophie found the castle 'not only very well situated, but embellished as much as possible, both inside and out'.[53]

By the time she moved to Zerbst, Sophie was already chafing at the restrictions of her restricted family society. She found a more attractive model on a visit to Countess Bentinck at Varel in the duchy of Oldenbourg. 'I found her charming. How else could she have seemed to me? I was fourteen; she rode, danced whenever the fancy took her to do so, sang and laughed and skipped about like a child, though she was well over thirty at the time – she was already separated from her husband.'[54] That phrase in the mature Catherine's memoirs acquires an extra frisson in the light of the fate of her own assassinated spouse. At the time, however, minds were naturally concentrated on the initial task of finding her a partner.

Though both Prince William of Saxe-Gotha and Prince Henry of Prussia (who was later to visit her twice in St Petersburg) had started to pay her attention at the age of twelve or thirteen, her most assiduous suitor as she approached marriageable age was a close relative.[55] Under the disapproving gaze of Babet Cardel, Georg Ludwig of Holstein-Gottorp, her mother's younger brother, became infatuated with Sophie when he was twenty-four and she was ten years younger. How far he awakened her adolescent sexuality remains uncertain, though the passage in her memoirs in which she refers to 'galloping astride her pillows' has often been interpreted as a veiled reference to masturbation.[56] Sophie saw no harm in his kisses – 'he was thoughtful and affectionate' – and apparently agreed to a wedding provided her parents consented. But while Johanna Elisabeth seems to have done little to stem her brother's ardour, ambition had already prompted her to cast her eyes further afield.

Even when she began to look for a more promising match, closer in age to her daughter, there was no need to look beyond the confines of her well-connected family. At Eutin in 1739, on a visit to her elder brother, Adolf Friedrich, then Prince Bishop of Lübeck, Johanna Elisabeth had introduced Sophie to her second cousin, Karl Peter Ulrich, who had inherited the dukedom of Holstein-Gottorp earlier that summer at the age of eleven. Since his late father, Duke Karl Friedrich, had been nephew to the childless Charles XII of Sweden, Peter was widely expected to inherit the Swedish throne. His late mother, Anna Petrovna, who died a few months after his birth, had been the eldest daughter of Peter the Great of Russia, and he was a far more eligible prospect than Georg Ludwig. As Court gossip began to link his name with Sophie's, Johanna Elisabeth watched his future with interest.[57]

Peter's fortunes sharply improved when Peter the Great's surviving unmarried daughter, Elizabeth, deposed the infant Ivan VI of Russia in a bloodless coup on 25 November 1741. The following February, she brought her nephew to St Petersburg, obliged him to convert to Orthodoxy, and in November formally declared him her heir in accordance with her father's law of 1722, which permitted reigning tsars to nominate their own successors. This move not only helped to secure the succession in Russia, but also forced Peter to renounce his claim to the throne of Sweden, with which Russia was at war between 1741 and 1743. At Elizabeth's insistence, the Swedish succession now passed to Sophie's uncle, Adolf Friedrich of Holstein-Gottorp, giving her scheming mother an added incentive to cultivate her relationship with the empress, who had been engaged to another of her brothers, Karl August, before he died of smallpox in May 1727.

Egged on by Frederick the Great, who promoted Sophie's father to the rank of field marshal to enhance the family's prestige, Johanna Elisabeth sent her daughter's portrait to the tsaritsa, who responded with a diamond-encrusted picture of herself. Elizabeth knew nothing of Sophie's personality. Aside from ties of sentiment to the House of Holstein-Gottorp, she was attracted mainly by the prospect of a marriage alliance with a Protestant family in Prussian service. This promised the Court of St Petersburg a foothold in northern Germany to balance the diplomatic alliance with Austria which had dominated Russian foreign policy since 1726. Against the advice of her pro-Austrian vice chancellor, Aleksey Bestuzhev-Ryumin, who would have preferred a Catholic Saxon fiancée for Grand Duke Peter, Elizabeth invited Sophie to Russia at the end of 1743.

Catherine's memoirs paint a remarkably domesticated portrait of the scene at Zerbst when the invitation arrived:

On 1 January 1744, we were all seated at the table when my father was handed a big packet of letters. After tearing open the first envelope, my father passed to my mother several letters addressed to her. I was sitting beside her and recognised the hand of the marshal of the Court of the duke of Holstein, the Grand Duke of Russia. This was a Swedish gentleman, named Brummer. My mother had written to him several times in 1739 and he had replied. My mother opened the letter and I saw the words: *'with the princess, her elder daughter'*. I knew at once what it meant – I guessed the rest and it turned out that I had guessed right. My mother had been invited by him on behalf of the Empress Elizabeth to come to Russia under the pretext of thanking Her Majesty for all the benefits she had conferred on my mother's family.[58]

Despite Catherine's claims that the decision to accept this invitation was her own, taken in the face of her Lutheran father's profound misgivings, the invitation had in reality been engineered by Johanna Elisabeth, who had already learned from Frederick the Great that the empress intended to pay 10,000 roubles for their travel expenses.[59] Faced with what amounted to an imperial summons, mother and daughter departed for St Petersburg without delay on 10 January 1744 NS.

Though Sophie's feelings as she set out for Russia can only be imagined, excitement was surely tempered by trepidation. Isabella of Parma, who married the future Joseph II of Austria twelve years later, described a predicament shared by many European princesses in the eighteenth century: 'There she is, condemned to abandon everything, her family, her country – and for whom? For an unknown person, whose character and manner of thinking she does not know.'[60] Thanks to her meeting with Peter at Eutin, that was not quite Sophie's situation. Indeed, as a German prince, born and raised in Kiel, the grand duke might have been expected to offer her a measure of familiar comfort in alien surroundings. Kiel, after all, was almost as insignificant as Zerbst in the eyes of the Russian elite, who scoffed that the whole city was no bigger than St Petersburg's Summer Garden.[61]

Neither is it necessary to suppose, as Catherine's memoirs later implied, that she faced a stark choice between obeying her future husband and overthrowing him. Though it was by no means easy for an intelligent woman to live a fulfilled life as a royal consort in the eighteenth century, it was certainly not impossible. Cultural patronage offered a natural opportunity for uncontroversial activity, eagerly grasped by most European queens. The more determined among them could also play a significant role in government, either as political hostesses or as surrogate rulers behind the scenes. We shall never know how the philosophically minded Isabella would have coped with Joseph II, because death (a constant pre-occupation in her prolific writings) snatched her from him not long after their wedding. However, Sophie's childhood friend, Juliana Maria, overcame both shyness and a stutter to become the effective ruler of Denmark in conjunction with her favourite for twelve years after the coup of 1772.[62] And although it was obviously easier for a female consort to dominate a weak king – Elizabeth Farnese, the ambitious second wife of Philip V of Spain, became notorious across Europe for her influence over her depressive husband[63] – consorts of even the most powerful monarchs could carve out a workable division of labour. Freder-ick the Great despised Court flummery and spent progressively more of his time in male company at Potsdam to avoid its offensive trappings. But since it was unthinkable for a king entirely to dispense with a Court, the gap was filled by Juliana Maria's elder sister, Queen Elisabeth Christine, whose summer palace at Schönhausen and regular reception days at Berlin provided a crucial meeting place for diplomats and foreign visitors.[64]

However uncertain she may have been about her future, Sophie was acutely conscious of how much she was leaving behind, subsequently portraying her journey to Russia in terms of sacrifice rather than opportunity. By convention, Christian August was not invited, though he accompanied his daughter to Berlin, where Frederick looked her over while instructing her mother about her conduct in St Petersburg. Though few of her contemporaries were to play such an impor-tant part in Sophie's life, she never saw the king again. She caught her last glimpse of her father at a tearful parting at Schwedt an der Oder on 17 January, the day after leaving Berlin. 'The separation was as sad as one could possibly imagine,' she remembered in 1756.[65]

After that, she faced an uncomfortable trek across the wastes of Pomerania and East Prussia, so bereft of snow that winter that the journey had to be made in carriages rather than sleighs. Peering through narrow eye-slits in the woolly hats that protected their faces, they left Stargardt (now Szczecinski) in icy condi-tions on 18 January. From there, it was a tortuous progress eastwards through Keslin, skirting Danzig, and over the Vistula to Marienwerder.[66] Although Fred-erick William I had already attempted to drain the Oder Marshes in the 1730s with the help of Dutch hydraulic engineers, the epic work of transforming the watery landscape east of the Oder still lay in the future in 1744. Over the next thirty years, it would be the king's son, Frederick the Great, and his colonists who transformed the valleys of the Elbe, the Oder, the Warthe, the Netze and the Vistula into productive agricultural land. ('Making domain lands cultivable interests me more than murdering people,' Frederick remarked in a characteristic jibe against his brutal father.)[67] At the time of Sophie's departure for Russia, the whole area remained a patchwork quilt of stagnant pools and marsh, punctuated by areas of thick, waterlogged brush – an unregulated paradise for outlaws and bandits, offensive in itself to the standardising instincts of Frederick's Enlightened administration. Like much of the rest of Europe, such a landscape was barely passable in spring and autumn, when flooding washed away the tracks that snaked across the marshes. In winter, it was a perilous wilderness. Sophie and her mother avoided the worst dangers by keeping close to the coast. 'Our journey was long, very boring, and very painful,' she later remembered of their odyssey between primitive roadside inns. 'My feet were so swollen that I had to be lifted in and out of the carriage.'[68]

During a rare day of rest at Königsberg, where another product of Pietism, the philosopher Immanuel Kant, was already a twenty-year-old student at the university, Sophie wrote to her father (in French). Mindful of the instructions he had signed at Zerbst on 3 January that no one must persuade her to renege on her religious beliefs, she adopted her most dutiful tone:

> Monseigneur,
> I have received with all imaginable respect and joy the letter in which Your Highness does me the honour of reassuring me about his health, about his remembrance of me, and his good wishes. I beg to reassure him that his exhortations and his counsel will remain eternally engraved in my heart, just as the seeds of our holy religion will be in my soul, for which I ask God to lend all the strength that I shall require to resist the temptations to which I am preparing to expose myself.[69]

Before she faced those temptations, however, there was still almost two-thirds of the journey to go. Passing north-eastwards into Courland – 'at all times a desert country', as a British diplomat had been warned by the canny purveyors of Königsberg four years earlier – she saw the 'terrible' comet first observed from Sweden and the Netherlands at the end of November 1743.[70] At its brightest in the following March, it displayed as many as twelve fanning rays in the manner of a peacock's tail. 'I have never seen a bigger one,' the mature empress declared;

'it seemed very near to the earth.'[71] She was not alone in her fascination. Though clouds obscured the comet from much of the continent until the New Year, news of it spread rapidly in the European press. 'The Comet this Evening appeared exceeding bright and distinct,' recorded an Oxford astronomer on 23 January, 'and the Diameter of its Nucleus nearly equal to that of Jupiter's; its Tail, extending above 16 Degrees from its Body, pointed towards Andromeda; and was in Length (supposing the Sun's Parallax 10") above 23 Millions of Miles; but cloudy Weather succeeding, we lost this agreeable Sight till Feb. 5th.'[72] That must have been roughly when Sophie saw it. Since comets had until recently been regarded as portents of disaster, she might have been forgiven for wondering what such an apparition beheld for her in a distant foreign land.[73] But she would mock Empress Elizabeth for holding such superstitious views in 1756, when popular scientific accounts of comets were about to appear in Russian journals.[74] And twenty-one years after her experiences on her journey to St Petersburg, Grigory Orlov, a keen amateur astronomer, would read aloud from one such treatise while Catherine amused the rest of the company by fantasising about what might happen if a comet carried them away and turned them all to glass.[75]

It was a very different Russian nobleman who met Princess Sophie just beyond Mitau (now Jelgava in Latvia) and guided her over the frozen River Dvina into the Russian empire. Johanna Elisabeth and her daughter had first encountered the thirty-three-year-old Semën Naryshkin in Hamburg on his return from London. As a youthful ambassador to the Court of St James, he had gained ample practice in the diplomatic niceties that would serve him well as a future Marshal of Elizabeth's Court. Now Master of the Hunt, no one was better equipped than this most flamboyant of courtiers to flatter Sophie's mother, who assumed he must be a prince and exposed her delusions of grandeur with a gushing travel account that placed her at the centre of events. Since it had proved impossible to heat the imperial apartments at Riga, where they gained eleven days by reverting to the Julian calendar, she and Sophie were given tastefully furnished rooms at the house of a wealthy merchant, not unlike the one in which her daughter had been born. In every other respect, theirs was a royal progress, intended to overwhelm them with a sense of Russia's imperial power and prestige as they drove through crowded streets to fanfares of trumpets and drums. 'It feels as though I am part of the entourage of Her Imperial Majesty or some great princess,' wrote the disingenuous Johanna Elisabeth: 'It never enters my head that all this is for poor me.'[76]

Until they entered Russian territory, Sophie's mother had been travelling incognito as Countess Rheinbeck, accompanied by only the most modest of suites: her chamberlain, her lady-in-waiting, four chambermaids, a valet, a handful of lackeys and a cook. Now, wrapped in the priceless sables presented to them by Naryshkin, they continued their journey under cavalry escort in long imperial sleighs drawn by ten horses. As Catherine later recalled, it was quite an art even to climb into these elaborate vehicles, in which passengers lay recumbent on bulky feather mattresses, lined with silk and covered with satin cushions.[77] Still, there was little enough to see as they traversed a snowy landscape razed by the Russians in the first decade of the century when it seemed that the invading Swedish army might triumph in the Great Northern War. Not until the 1770s did Russia's Baltic provinces recover their pre-war population levels after a campaign in which as many as 70 per cent of the population of Livland and Estland may have perished. At Dorpat (now Tartu in Estonia), which the Russians had taken from the Swedes in 1704, the signs of the bombardment were still visible.[78] Their final calling point was Narva, where 11,000 Swedish troops had humiliated Peter the Great's 40,000-strong army in November 1700, prompting far-reaching military reforms that helped to underpin tsarist imperial expansion for the remainder of the century. From there, it was a relatively short distance along the southern shores of the gulf of Finland to the Russian capital, where they arrived on the afternoon of 3 February towards the end of the carnival season.

CHAPTER TWO

BETROTHAL AND MARRIAGE
1744–1745

Though unaware of it at the time, Sophie had arrived in St Petersburg at a pivotal period in the city's short history. Its origins are shrouded in mystery. Legend has it that on 16 May 1703, Peter the Great landed with a group of military companions on Hare Island, digging two turves with a bayonet and laying them crosswise as he pronounced: 'Here a city is to be!' But since there are no records of the occasion in the Court journals, and no first-hand accounts have survived, it is not even certain where Peter was on the date in question.[1] There can be no doubt, however, of the importance of the new capital which began to emerge after the tsar's victory over the Swedes at the battle of Poltava in 1709. Whereas Turin and Madrid had grown by having a Court imposed upon them, St Petersburg was the ultimate *Residenzstadt*: a city expressly developed as the site of the imperial Court. 'Petersburg is just the Court,' the *philosophe* Denis Diderot would remark following his visit to Catherine in 1774: 'a confused mass of palaces and hovels, of *grands seigneurs* surrounded by peasants and purveyors.'[2] For the first twenty years of its existence, the city was little more than a building site. While Russian noblemen grumbled about being forced to settle in such inhospitable surroundings, visitors were astonished by the sheer speed of construction. By the early 1720s, the new capital was consuming almost 5 per cent of the Russian empire's total revenue: between 10,000 and 30,000 labourers worked there every year; thousands more were conscripted to replace those who sacrificed their lives in the effort to sink reliable foundations into the bog.[3] Struck by such awesome ambition and progress, the Hanoverian envoy duly ranked St Petersburg as 'a wonder of the world, was it only in consideration of the few years that have been employed in the raising of it'.[4]

Foreign verdicts such as this helped to generate the city's lasting reputation as a fantastic place where nothing is quite as it seems.[5] Tsar Peter and his image-makers did their best to enhance the illusion by investing the place he called his 'paradise' with layer upon layer of symbolic significance, designed to transform it at once into a New Amsterdam (a symbol of trade and prosperity), a New Rome and New Constantinople (symbols of power and kingship), and not least a New Jerusalem, a symbol of piety and devotion 'coming down out of heaven from God' and bisected by a 'river of water of life' (Revelation 21: 2; 22: 1).[6] These were probably not comparisons that entered the minds of most of St Petersburg's 70,000 inhabitants at the time of Sophie's arrival in 1744. She herself claimed fifty years later that only three of the city's streets had then been built in stone: Millionnaya (Millionnaires' Row, a street of grand mansion houses which still runs parallel to the Neva to the south-east of the Winter Palace); Lugovaya (Meadow Street, which ran westwards towards the Admiralty); and the elegant row of merchants' houses along the river to the west of St Isaac's Square (known as the English Line or Quay by the time of Catherine's reign, and subsequently as the English Embankment). These three thoroughfares formed 'a curtain, so to speak' around rows of 'wooden barracks as unpleasant as it is possible to imagine'.[7]

Though this was plainly an attempt to advertise her own glorious achievements in the field of urban reconstruction, there was no disguising the squalor of much of the early eighteenth-century city. Even its palaces were wooden. So were most churches apart from Trezzini's Peter-Paul Cathedral. By the early 1740s, many of St Petersburg's leading buildings had already gone the way of the derelict Holy Trinity, where Tsar Peter had worshipped almost every day when resident in his new capital.[8] Far from admiring the city, foreign visitors were now more likely to highlight the consequences of shoddy construction on marshy soil. According to Carl Reinhold Berch, a Swedish official resident in St Petersburg in 1735–6, careless building methods condemned the city's brick walls to remain damp for years, while the timber in widespread use for roofs, gutters, staircases and vestibules was 'notoriously and readily combustible'. 'Many handsome houses,' Berch complained, 'cannot be reached by even a single carriage, so that one must enter via the back gates or through a breach in the wall on the first floor, in which case the passageway is as high as any triumphal arch: both these methods are utterly disgraceful.'[9] Critics of tsarist despotism had a field day. Following his visit to Russia in 1739, the Venetian savant Francesco Algarotti snidely remarked that:

> If the ground were a little higher and less marshy, if the plans had not been changed so many times, if a Palladio had been the architect and the building materials had been of a better quality and better assembled and, furthermore, if it were inhabited by people who try to live there pleasantly and comfortably, St Petersburg would be surely one of the finest towns in the world.[10]

As it was, he found the Russian capital characterised by 'a kind of bastard architecture' in which Dutch influences predominated over those from Italy and France, and believed that the poor quality of the city's construction reflected the fact that its palaces had been 'built out of obedience rather than choice': 'Their walls are all cracked, quite out of perpendicular, and ready to fall.' Ruins generally formed themselves, Algarotti famously quipped, but at St Petersburg they were built from scratch.[11]

For more than a decade after Peter the Great's death in 1725, the city's growth had indeed lacked direction. The initial impetus was lost when the Court returned to Moscow in 1728, and even when Empress Anna brought it back to St Petersburg four years later, her advisers hesitated to take decisive action for fear of disturbing a volatile populace. Only when fire destroyed hundreds of wooden shacks in the area around the Admiralty in August 1736 did the government contemplate the opportunity for wholesale change, though not before taking instant retribution against three alleged arsonists. John Cook, a visiting Scottish doctor, saw the two men chained to the top of tall masts:

> They stood upon small scaffolds and many thousand billets of wood were built from the ground, so as to form a pyramid round each mast. These pyramids were so high as to reach within two or three fathoms of the little stages on which the men stood in their shirts, and their drawers. They were condemned in this manner to be burnt to powder. But before the pyramids were set on fire, the woman was brought betwixt these masts, and a declaration of their villainy, and the order for their execution, read ... No sooner was the woman's head chopped off, than a link was put to the wooden pyramids, and as the timber was very dry, it formed in an instant a very terrible fire. The men would soon have died had not the wind frequently blown the flames from them; however, they both expired in less than three quarters of an hour, in great torment.[12]

A second fire on Millionnaya and the palace embankment in June 1737 hastened plans for longer-term reconstruction. Led by the first Russian architects to make a serious impact on the new capital – Peter Yeropkin, Mikhail Zemtsov and Ivan Korobov – the Commission for the Construction of St Petersburg, established shortly afterwards, definitively shifted the centre of the city to the south.[13]

It was a logical enough move to make. Although Peter the Great had insisted on locating his main government buildings on Vasilevsky Island, both these and the Peter-Paul Fortress were inconveniently situated on the northern bank of the Neva, accessible in summer only by boat (the sole bridge was a temporary pontoon to the west of the Admiralty, first strung across the river in 1727 and rebuilt annually after 1732).[14] The new commission determined instead to develop three great avenues radiating out from the Admiralty: Voznesensky Prospect, leading to the barracks of the Izmailovsky Guards in the south-west; Gorokhovaya (Pea Street), culminating at the barracks of the Semënovsky Guards to the south; and Nevsky Prospect, then known as the Great Perspective Road, which stretched south-eastward for almost three miles towards the Alexander Nevsky monastery founded by Peter the Great in memory of the thirteenth-century warrior-saint. Though delayed by political upheavals after Anna's death in 1740, these three avenues, linked by a network of semicircular streets between the Moika and Fontanka canals, were soon to give the city the elegant, geometrical ground plan at which visitors still marvel today.[15]

In the early 1750s, Russia's greatest polymath Mikhailo Lomonosov claimed that from the top of any tall building in the capital one could see 'houses that seemed to float on water and streets laid out in lines as straight as regiments on parade'.[16] As if to prove his point, Mikhailo Makhaev spent the late 1740s perched among the city's bell towers and on top of Tsar Peter's *Kunstkamera*, sketching with the assistance of a large optical 'camera'. The machine's wide-angled lens combined with the artist's elevated viewpoint to distort the perspective in such a way that his famous engravings are dominated by the space between buildings rather than by the buildings themselves.[17] But that is not to underestimate the extent to which St Petersburg was transformed in Elizabeth's reign 'from a Europeanized riverfront backed by thousands of native hovels into a Western metropolis'.[18] In a conscious attempt to legitimise her seizure of the throne, the grandest Baroque edifices were built to mark the route she had taken on that fateful night in November 1741.[19] Indeed, so rapidly had those events acquired mythical status, that shortly after her arrival in February 1744, Johanna Elisabeth was taken to retrace the empress's steps, starting from 'the famous barracks of the

Preobrazhensky Guards' where Elizabeth had already laid the foundation stone of a magnificent new cathedral of the Transfiguration. 'It is incomprehensible that Her Majesty should have managed such a long march without being betrayed.'[20]

Since Tsar Peter had intended his new capital to stand as an icon of Russia's aspirations to sophisticated cosmopolitanism, it is all the more striking that the entertainment laid on for fourteen-year-old Princess Sophie should have been unashamedly exotic and emphatically popular. After dinner at the Winter Palace, she was treated to a display by the fourteen elephants which had become familiar figures on the capital's streets following their presentation to Empress Anna by a visiting Turkish embassy. One of the animals on that occasion was said to be draped in King Solomon's tent, a characteristically extravagant notion duly dismissed by Dr Cook: 'It was of silk, very large, and certainly the worse of the wearing, but I scarcely believe it was Solomon's.' Not long afterwards, a bystander lost his life when two beasts bolted from soldiers who had thrown fireworks at their feet in an attempt to make them fight in the snow.[21] Fortunately for her hosts, the show staged in Sophie's honour passed off without incident. Once the elephants had completed their stately pirouettes in the palace courtyard, she was taken out onto the frozen river to see the ice hills that were a prominent feature of the capital at carnival time.[22]

By the time the last of Anna's elephants died in 1765, the elephant house had long been moved from its central location on the Fontanka Canal to a suburban site near the Alexander Nevsky monastery.[23] Ice hills, however, remained popular throughout Catherine's reign, attracting vast crowds of spectators to watch as intrepid revellers descended precipitous slopes at great speed, either upright on skates or seated on wooden trays. She adored the one at Gostilitsy – the suburban estate belonging to Elizabeth's favourite, Aleksey Razumovsky, where the Russian Court regularly paid a visit halfway through Lent – and in 1762 she had Antonio Rinaldi build her own all-weather tobogganing pavilion at the Summer Palace at Oranienbaum, a fantasy of powder-blue and white.[24]

> It consists of steep declivities built of timber, the highest end being ten fathoms above the ground, and borne up on an arch. The impetus acquired by rapidly descending the first forces the carriage up the second, which having turned it is carried up a third and so proceeds in diminishing altitudes, with amazing

velocity. The carriages are made to contain one person, or two seated facing one another, the wheels running in grooves.[25]

A less extravagant wooden sleigh-run at Tsarskoye Selo was demolished in 1777 to make way for a merry-go-round. Even in the last years of her life, Catherine liked to take visitors to play on the ice hills near the Tauride Palace she had built for Potëmkin, where she treated the local populace and donated money to their other entertainments.[26]

In 1744, such pleasures lay in the future, for no sooner had Sophie arrived in St Petersburg than she was whisked off to Moscow, where the Court was in residence and where Elizabeth expected her in time to celebrate Grand Duke Peter's sixteenth birthday on 10 February. Improved in Catherine's own reign by a series of costly schemes, the highway between the two capitals remained in 1744 in much the same state as other Russian roads – a primitive track, constructed from tree-trunks covered with gravel and sand, and passable at speed only when frozen. While it might take the empress's humbler subjects several weeks to complete the 370-mile journey, she herself could cover the distance in a little over three days by racing through the night and changing horses every twelve or fifteen miles. That January, she had spent forty-nine hours on the road and another twenty-six at staging posts along the way.[27] Even Elizabeth had come to regard the price of such speed as prohibitive. When the officer charged with removing snowdrifts, branches and tree stumps from the relatively short section of road between Chudov and Novgorod requested another 1600 men to assist the 400 already assigned to him, he was ordered to dismiss the whole detachment as the decree went out making the owner of each property along the road responsible for clearing it in the following spring.[28] Sophie's entourage encountered a different problem. Shortly after their departure, her mother's sleigh hit a building while cornering too fast in the dark, injuring a sentry and catapulting the driver from his seat. While Johanna Elisabeth described the incident in typically purple prose, implying that they had all had a brush with death, Catherine's memoir was cooler: 'She claimed that she had been grievously injured, though nothing could be seen, not even a bruise.' Nevertheless, they were delayed for several hours, and it was not until the afternoon of 9 February that they approached the outskirts of the old capital to be escorted to the palace at Lefortovo on the Yauza River, not far from the island where relatives of the young Peter I had created a fortress for his play regiments as a way of mobilising support for his candidature for the throne in the 1680s.[29]

Had it been summer, Sophie and her mother would have been greeted by 'rows of clipped yew-trees, long straight canals' and what her own generation, fond of less formal layouts, would dismiss as 'a profusion of preposterous statues': 'every little structure was a pantheon; and every grove was haunted by its Apollos and Dianas'.[30] For the moment, however, the gardens on which Empress Anna had lavished such careful attention were deep in snow, and the Court was resident not in Rastrelli's Summer Palace but at the nearby Winter Annenhof (re-christened the Golovin Palace by imperial decree on 29 February) on the other side of the Yauza.[31] This ornate wooden structure had been transferred in its entirety from the Kremlin in 1736 before being enlarged and embellished six years later in preparation for Elizabeth's coronation. Its interiors were brightly painted in green, yellow and blue – all typical colours for Russian palaces in the first half of the eighteenth century.[32]

Having met the new arrivals at the foot of the ceremonial staircase, Field Marshal the Prince of Hesse-Homburg, a leading member of the pro-Prussian party at Court, offered his arm to Johanna Elisabeth and led them to their apartments. There they were joined by the household of Grand Duke Peter, who apparently burst in on Sophie's mother as she was loosening her head-dress. A little before 10 p.m., another anti-Austrian schemer, the empress's surgeon Armand Lestocq, announced that the empress was ready to receive them. Having been presented to the ladies- and gentlemen-in-waiting in the crowded antechamber, where Johanna Elisabeth was conscious of being scrutinised 'from head to toe', they processed through the state apartments to the audience chamber, where the thirty-five-year-old empress appeared before them on the threshold of her state bedroom.

> On seeing her for the first time, it was impossible not to be struck by her beauty and majestic bearing. She was a large woman who, in spite of being very stout, was neither disfigured by her size, nor embarrassed in her movements; her head, too, was very beautiful.[33]

Sophie would soon come to suspect that Elizabeth's 'good looks and natural sloth had significantly spoiled her character'. 'Her beauty ought to have saved her from the envy and rivalry she exhibited against every woman who wasn't remotely hideous; but in fact, the anxiety not to be outdone by anyone else was the cause of the extreme jealousy which often threw her into bouts of captiousness unworthy of her majesty.'[34] At this first meeting, however, the star-struck girl followed dutifully as Elizabeth, wearing a huge hooped skirt, embroidered in silver and gold, with a black feather to one side of her head and diamonds in her hair, admitted them to the state bedroom. There they spoke in French for about half an hour before retiring to eat, observed incognito by the empress, who dined separately during the Lenten Fast.[35]

Next day, Peter's birthday, Sophie caught her first sight of Aleksey Razumovsky, 'one of the most handsome men I have seen in my life'.[36] He had first been listed among Elizabeth's servants in 1731, when he was recruited to join the ranks of other talented Ukrainian singers in the Court choir. He soon caught the eye of a princess devoted to Orthodox chant, and even when a throat infection ruined his voice, forcing him instead to take up the *bandura* (a large Ukrainian mandolin), his dashing looks were enough to preserve the spell. Before long, he and the tsarevna were sharing a bed. They may even have married in secret in 1742, though neither this ceremony nor persistent rumours of children have ever been substantiated. Still, there is no doubt that the languid Razumovsky – the most equable of men unless roused by drink – was Elizabeth's right-hand man until the end of the 1740s. Revelling in the riches she bestowed upon him, including vast estates at Kozelets in his native Chernigov province, he took no active part in either her coup or her subsequent government. But to judge from the number of petitions he received and the fawning attitude of the empress's ministers, many Russians shared the view of the Saxon envoy that she hung on his every word.[37] Even if such judgements depended on a widespread misapprehension that only men were fit to rule, Aleksey was at his mistress's side on all major Court occasions as Grand Master of the Hunt. Now he was on hand to pass her the insignia of the Order of St Catherine, which she presented to Sophie and her mother 'in a ritual of sorority that simultaneously welcomed them as "princesses of the blood" and placed them formally under Elizabeth'.[38]

Since the empress customarily took her annual communion after confession at the end of the first week of the Lenten Fast, Sophie's first experience of the incense-filled world of the Russian Orthodox Church was one of the most emotional services in the ecclesiastical calendar. In the mocking phrase of a later foreign diplomat, Lent was a time when 'mushrooms, pickled cucumber, prayers and priests succeed to the active dance, the becoming dress, the genial banquet and the gallant officers' and when Court ladies were left with nothing 'to subsist on but faith, hope and meditation – faith in the constancy of their lovers, hope that the same dear delusions may return, and meditation upon pleasures past'.[39] In 1744, however, the conventional routine was broken by a hectic round of social gatherings as the curious Russian elite scrambled to meet the new arrivals and they in their turn settled into the endless games of cards with which the Court passed the time between Lenten vigil services. Elizabeth herself occasionally called on Sophie and her mother as a sign of her satisfaction with them. Indeed, when the empress set out at the beginning of March on one of her frequent pilgrimages to the Trinity monastery, forty miles north-east of the old capital, all seemed set fair for the future.[40]

Disaster struck on the following Tuesday when Sophie suffered an attack of pleurisy, the first serious illness she had ever experienced. Convinced that it must be smallpox, Johanna Elisabeth refused to allow doctors to bleed her daughter, alleging that her brother, Karl Friedrich, had perished under similar treatment in Russia in 1727. While the bickering continued, Sophie lapsed into a state of delirium until the Saturday, when Elizabeth returned to take command. With the agitated Johanna Elisabeth in attendance, she held the girl's head in her arms as a surgeon opened the first vein. Over the following four weeks, while her mother was kept out of the way and the empress offered prayers for her recovery in a variety of Moscow churches, bleedings were repeated with a vengeance, sometimes as often as four times a day. It is hard to be sure of the effects of this treatment. Sophie certainly did not lack for medical expertise. Abraham Boerhaave, Peter's doctor, was related to the celebrated Dutch specialist, Herman Boerhaave, while the empress's personal physician, António Sanches (1699–1783), a baptised Portuguese Jew who had studied with Boerhaave at Leiden, was a specialist in venereal disease who later published a treatise on the curative powers of steam baths.[41] Yet if her memoir is to be believed, it was not until an abscess on one of her inflamed lungs burst of its own accord that their severely weakened patient began to regain her strength. She managed her first tentative steps around her bedroom at the beginning of April. Though this episode is understandably thought to have bequeathed a lifelong suspicion of doctors, it is worth remembering the tribute she paid to Sanches and Abraham Boerhaave in 1771: 'I swear by God that it is to their care that I owe my life.' Soon after she came to the throne, she rewarded Sanches with an annual pension of 1000 roubles.[42]

To Sophie's anxious Prussian sponsors, her recovery came as a blessed relief.[43] The Russian Court expressed its gratefulness with a series of lavish presents, all duly publicised in the official press. Elizabeth had already rewarded the girl's bravery after the first bleeding with earrings and a diamond cluster variously estimated at between 25,000 and 60,000 roubles. Now more jewels and a diamond watch from the grand duke helped to compensate for Sophie's distress at having to appear in public at the ball in honour of her fifteenth birthday. Heavily rouged, at the empress's insistence, she was as 'thin as a skeleton' and miserably conscious that her scalp had been shaven as smooth as her hand. 'I thought I looked frighteningly ugly and was unable to recognise my own features.' The loss of her hair was especially keenly felt at a time when she 'had the finest hair in the world: it curled naturally without being waved or crinkled in any way'.[44]

More damaging for the pro-Prussian party at Court was Johanna Elisabeth's behaviour during Sophie's illness. Well aware that daughters of eighteenth-century princely houses were little more than saleable breeding stock, she had been enterprising in the search for a match for her firstborn. Dizzy with success on arrival in Russia, she failed to grasp that she was bound to lose control of her prized asset as soon as the deal had been done. Instead, still dreaming of a glorious future for herself, she rashly attempted to help topple the pro-Austrian vice chancellor Bestuzhev. Perhaps she had been lulled into thinking that this would be a simple operation by the pro-Prussian courtiers who had watched over her since that first dinner at the Winter Palace.[45] No doubt her pretensions had been further inflated by Frederick the Great's promise to 'do everything in the world to bring what we have begun to a happy conclusion'. For the king, struggling against Austria for mastery of Germany in the wake of his invasion of Silesia in 1740, Bestuzhev's removal seemed 'a *sine qua non*': 'We need a minister at the Russian Court who would compel the empress to do as we wish.'[46] To achieve this aim, which he regarded as the essential precondition for a triple alliance between Prussia, Russia and Sweden, Frederick was prepared to trust even such an inexperienced agent as Johanna Elisabeth. He was amply repaid for his folly. At the beginning of June, when the king was contemplating a desperate attempt to bribe the vice chancellor to switch sides, Bestuzhev presented the empress with more than seventy decoded dispatches revealing Johanna Elisabeth's unguarded conversations with his other main enemy, the former French ambassador, the Marquis de la Chétardie. The consequences could hardly have been more embarrassing. Bestuzhev was promoted Chancellor; Chétardie was arrested and escorted to the border; Johanna Elisabeth's reputation was permanently blackened. Reduced to tears by the empress's 'terrible wrath', she, too, would soon be obliged to return home.[47]

The sole consolation for the pro-Prussian party was their success in persuading Elizabeth not to cancel plans for Sophie's wedding. Though Lestocq had feared the worst when the scandal broke, the empress had invested too much political capital to send the girl packing now. The sooner she married, the sooner

Russia could be rid of her meddlesome mother, and the sooner the succession could be secured. Since the couple were not yet formally engaged, and a crucial precondition of their betrothal was Sophie's conversion to Orthodoxy, it was all the more pressing to complete her induction to the Russian faith. Frederick, who feared that her stubbornness in matters of religion would be the greatest stumbling block to the whole project, was confident that she could be brought round by careful persuasion. To make the task as painless as possible, her conversion was entrusted to Archimandrite Simon (Todorsky), a monk who had studied in Halle, the nerve centre of the Pietist religion in which she had been raised. Only 29 of his 800 books were in Russian, the overwhelming majority being in German, Latin and Greek.[48] At a time when Orthodox theologians depended so heavily on Western scholarship, it was not so difficult to argue that the two faiths were separated more by external rituals than by essential doctrine. Simon assuaged any anxieties on the former score by ascribing the Russian Church's famously flamboyant rites to popular superstition. He probably did not have to work very hard. Sophie's acceptance of Orthodoxy is the first clear sign of her lifelong grasp of the realities of power. Since there was plainly no alternative, she wrote coolly to her father at the beginning of May that because she could detect 'hardly any difference' between Orthodoxy and Lutheranism, she had already resolved to convert.[49]

Following her first visit to the Trinity monastery later that month, she settled down to prepare for her baptism. Like the great majority of the Orthodox episcopate until the 1760s, Simon was a Ukrainian whose pronunciation proved controversial when she came to learn the creed. (The poet and versifier Alexander Sumarokov later blamed the 'shameful' influence of Ukrainian bishops for the 'incorrect and provincial dialect' allegedly adopted by the Russian clergy as a whole.)[50] Sophie, who was given a German translation to ensure that she grasped the meaning, eventually opted to recite the Slavonic text 'parrot-fashion' in the Russian diction recommended by her language tutor, Vasily Adodurov, a likeable writer and grammarian twenty years her senior who was to become a valued friend and confidant. 'Otherwise you will make everyone laugh with your Ukrainian pronunciation,' Peter warned.[51] On the appointed day, Thursday 28 June, Elizabeth had the girl dressed in scarlet and silver to match her own costume and led her in solemn procession through packed antechambers to the chapel of the Summer Annenhof. Sophie was left kneeling at the door while the empress went in search of the abbess of the Novodevichy convent, chosen as the new convert's baptismal sponsor in the face of fierce competition among the Court ladies. (Having already performed this function for her nephew, Elizabeth was unable to repeat the honour for Sophie since by Orthodox tradition those who have the same baptismal witness are unable to marry.) When the ritual finally began, the girl knelt on a red cushion to receive the blessing of Amvrosy (Iushkevich), who had less than a month to live as archbishop of Novgorod. (This was the same 'bigoted or corrupt prelate' to whom Frederick the Great's ambassador, Baron Mardefeld, had offered a bribe of 2000 roubles to overcome the Holy Synod's scruples about a match between two such close relatives, with a promise to 'triple the dose' when the deed was done.)[52] Then Sophie stood to declaim the confession of faith in words that she did not yet understand before reciting the creed from memory to a tearful congregation. If critics detected any failings in her confident performance, then they kept their opinions to themselves. Those who had most to lose were keenest to praise her achievements. Sophie was 'a heroine', Mardefeld declared. Johanna Elisabeth was predictably emotional: 'I was already so overcome in advance that I burst out crying before she had reached the end of the first word.'[53]

On her acceptance into the Russian faith, Princess Sophie Auguste Friderike at last became Yekaterina Alekseyevna, a name chosen by Elizabeth in honour of her own mother, Catherine I. That night, after receiving yet more diamonds from the empress and allowing courtiers to kiss her hand for the first time (a formal ceremony which lasted almost two hours), Catherine and Peter drove incognito across Moscow to the Kremlin in preparation for the following day's betrothal service on the feast of Sts Peter and Paul.[54] After morning prayers in her apartments, they processed through the Palace of Facets and out onto the Red Staircase exactly as she would eighteen years later at her own coronation. Before the liturgy in the Dormition Cathedral began, Elizabeth placed engagement rings on the fingers of her heir and his fiancée. Now Catherine had a new title – grand duchess – as well as a new name. As cannon fired to signal the moment to the expectant crowd, the liturgy began, culminating with a sermon by Metropolitan Arseny of Rostov, the only prelate who protested against her secularisation of the monastic lands twenty years later (he paid the price with lifelong monastic imprisonment). At lunch in the Palace of Facets, Elizabeth sat beneath a canopy at the centre of her customary dais with Peter to her right and Catherine to her left. As always at a Russian banquet, there was a series of elaborate toasts. The empress toasted her heir; he returned the compliment; she toasted his new fiancée before finally raising her glass to all her loyal subjects. More festivities followed in the evening so that it was half past one in the morning before the exhausted couple started the journey back to the Golovin Palace. Elizabeth stayed up even longer to watch the fireworks on the Ivan the Great bell tower.[55] Relieved to hear of the triumphant conclusion of his schemes, Frederick the Great laid on the flattery with a trowel:

> I count it among the finest days of my life to have seen the elevation of Your Imperial Highness to this high rank. I am happy to have contributed to it and pleased to have rendered service to my dear ally, the empress of Russia, and all her vast empire by procuring a princess of your abilities, Madame, as a bedfellow for the Grand Duke.[56]

Though they were not quite yet ready to sleep together, Catherine and Peter seem initially to have got on well enough, and until the Court set out for Kiev at the end of July after celebrating the peace with Sweden, Catherine had seen little of the empress's irascibility.[57] It was only at close quarters on the journey south that cracks in their relationships began to appear. Delayed by inaccurate mileposts, which she insisted must be replaced later that year, Elizabeth was in a foul temper by the time she caught up with the young couple at Razumovsky's estate at Kozelets, where Johanna Elisabeth had her first serious argument with Peter. They relieved the tension by gambling for high stakes for a fortnight.[58]

On arrival at Kiev in the last week of August, Catherine had her first taste of the embarrassment caused by over-eager subjects. When they went to see a theatrical performance staged in the grounds of a nearby convent, where they had to pass through the chapel to reach their seats, it became clear that they were in for a long evening:

> There were prologues, ballets, a comedy, in which Marcus Aurelius hanged his favourite, a battle in which the Cossacks defeated the Poles, a fishing scene on the Boristhène [the River Dnieper], and choruses without end. The empress kept her patience until almost two in the morning, when she sent someone to ask if it might finish soon. She was told that they were not yet half way through, but that if Her Majesty ordered it, they would stop straightaway.

Stop they did, but only to launch a disastrous firework. The first rockets flew straight into the main marquee, causing pandemonium among the imperial party and a stampede of the horses waiting patiently by the nearby carriages.[59]

The main reason for visiting Kiev was to pay tribute to the cradle of Ortho-doxy in the empire, for it was there that Prince Vladimir had accepted the Chris-tian faith in 988. At the Monastery of the Caves, the pious empress was in her element. Though it would soon be possible, with the aid of a telescope, to see back to Kozelets from the top of the Baroque bell tower which she commis-sioned, the monastery's real 'sights' lay within its own walls, in the catacombs and in the ancient Cathedral of the Dormition, where the relics of the great men of Kievan Rus were objects of open veneration (the head of Vladimir himself had been returned to the monastery in 1634).[60] Catherine and her fiancé were forbidden entry to the catacombs in case they caught a chill, but she was much taken by the cathedral. 'I had never been more struck in my life,' she recalled in 1771, 'than I was by the extreme magnificence of that church, where all the icons were covered in gold, silver and jewels. The church itself is spacious and built in the Gothic style of architecture that gives churches a much more majestic appearance than the current ones, where the size and transparency of the windows makes them indistinguishable from a ballroom or a [winter] –garden.'[61]

Back in Moscow for Elizabeth's name day on 5 September, the Court launched into its customary autumn round of celebrations. Although Catherine took dancing lessons with the ballet master Jean-Baptiste Landé, nothing in her expe-rience had prepared her for the cross-dressing balls that so delighted the empress. Elizabeth enjoyed showing off her excellent legs, but no one else took much pleasure from these so-called metamorphoses, at which the men were forced to stumble about the dance floor in huge hooped skirts.[62] They were happier watch-ing the French comedies and German dramas staged at the 5000-seat opera house built near the Golovin Palace for Elizabeth's coronation in 1742.[63] No less important to the life of the Court were its 'theatres of piety' in which the impe-rial family celebrated the major autumn feasts in the Orthodox calendar: the Nativity of the Mother of God on 8 September, the Exaltation of the Honour-able and Life-Giving Cross on 14 September, and the Presentation of the Mother of God in the Temple on 21 November.[64] Since the reign of Empress Anna, this last had been appropriated as the annual celebration of the Semënovsky Guards, so that the day which began with morning service culminated in a banquet and ball.[65] Now there were two new fixtures to add to the list of secular festivities: the birthday of Johanna Elisabeth on 13 October and Catherine's name day on 24 November. The following day was Elizabeth's accession day – the most sig-nificant event in the Court calendar.[66] The sickly Peter missed it all, being confined to bed by a chest infection in October and by chickenpox in November. Only when he seemed well enough to travel did the Court depart for St Petersburg.[67]

Begun by Bartolomeo Rastrelli almost as soon as the Court returned from Moscow in January 1732, the Winter Palace he completed three years later was a highly embellished wooden structure incorporating the mansion which had once belonged to Peter the Great's Admiral Apraksin. Empress Anna's apartments struck visitors as 'rather beautiful' but 'not very imperial', because they were small and dark.[68] Catherine and Peter were to think better of them during their brief occupation in the winter of 1746. This time, however, there was no room in the palace for either of them. While the lower floor was allocated to the small army of servants, actors, musicians and guards who accompanied the Court, the fun-loving Elizabeth was busy converting the upper rooms formerly occupied by her ladies-in-waiting to make space for a new merry-go-round, complete with expensively saddled wooden horses, to replace the dilapidated machine which stood outside the Summer Palace at the time of Catherine's arrival in Russia.[69] She and Johanna Elisabeth were lodged in a neighbouring house, where for the first time they had separate apartments on either side of the main staircase. Catherine had known of Elizabeth's orders in advance. For her status-conscious mother, who had not, it came as a shock:

> As soon as she saw this arrangement, she lost her temper, *primo*, because she thought that my apartment was laid out better than hers; *secondo* because hers was separated from mine by a shared room. In fact, we each had four rooms, two at the front and two overlooking the courtyard, and the rooms were of equal size, furnished in exactly the same blue and red fabric.[70]

Squabbles about precedence were the last thing Catherine needed now that her fiancé had again been taken ill on the journey from Moscow. On learning of this new outbreak of pox, accompanied by a high fever, Elizabeth raced back from St Petersburg to join her nephew at Khotilov, a staging post between Novgorod and Tver where they had all celebrated her birthday on 18 December. Cancelling the New Year's banquet, she stayed with him there until his recovery was assured, having cannon hauled specially from Tver to celebrate Epiphany, though Khotilov was too far from the river to conduct the customary blessing of the waters.[71] By 26 January, empress and heir were safely back at Tsarskoye Selo. When they returned to the capital at the beginning of the following month, Catherine and her mother were taken straight to see Peter in the gloomy great hall of the Winter Palace. Johanna Elisabeth reported to her husband in Zerbst that Providence had granted the youth a miraculous recovery. Catherine remembered the scene differently:

> All of his features were distorted; his face was still completely swollen, and one could see that he was bound to be permanently scarred. As his hair had been cut, he wore a huge wig that disfigured him all the more. He came up to me and asked if I found it difficult to recognise him. I stammered my congratulations on his recovery, but in truth he had become hideous.[72]

At best this was a disconcerting turn of events. Yet there was nothing to be done about it now. While Lent kept her pock-marked fiancé out of the public eye between his birthday and hers, preparations for their marriage continued in earnest.[73]

———

Since Princess Charlotte of Brunswick-Wolfenbüttel, the consort of Peter the Great's ill-fated tsarevich, had been permitted to retain her Lutheran faith, Elizabeth instructed Count Santi, her Master of Ceremonies, to model Catherine's wedding on the marriage of her own elder sister, Anna Petrovna, to Karl Friedrich of Holstein-Gottorp in 1725. On discovering that no records of that occasion survived, Santi had to work partly on oral tradition but above all on the basis of his own researches into the practice of rival European Courts.[74] The plan he presented to the College of Foreign Affairs on 22 March 1745 left plenty for the empress to decide. The seating arrangements for Johanna Elisabeth and her brother, Prince Adolf Friedrich, were a particularly sensitive matter. Unbeknownst to either Catherine or her mother, her uncle had been invited to Russia by Chancellor Bestuzhev, and his arrival on 5 February, motivated by his desire to gain control over the affairs of the duchy of Holstein, caused nothing but trouble.[75] ('His appearance alone did him no favours,' Catherine later commented. 'He was very small and badly proportioned, not at all intelligent, hot tempered, and furthermore governed by his entourage.') Santi, however, had already resolved to dispense with the idea of seating the bride under a canopy so that she could offer wine to the guests who came to congratulate her. Such an 'Oriental' custom might be appropriate for the 'middling sort', declared the haughty

Piedmontese, who had spent the whole of Anna's reign in exile in Siberia, but it was scarcely compatible with 'good practice in the courts of Sovereigns'.[76]

When it came to opulence, there was no question which of these Courts had set the standard. It can hardly have been a coincidence that the official press chose the eve of the announcement of Catherine's nuptials to report on the festivities at Versailles following the Dauphin's marriage to the Spanish Infanta.[77] 'Never has finer magnificence been witnessed than during those three days,' insisted the *St Petersburg News* on 15 March. 'Diamonds worth 250 million were on display, not counting the crown, which is estimated at 70 million. The attire of the Dauphin and his wife alone stretched to 45 million.'[78] To allow them to prepare in suitable style, the leading Russian statesmen (known collectively as the *generalitet* because they ranked with army generals on the top four ranks of Peter the Great's Table) were advanced a full year's salary, normally paid in instalments every four months. Elizabeth issued a personal decree urging each of them to spend the money on 'worthy costumes, as rich as possible, open landaus and other carriages, decorated where possible in silver and gold'. Since the celebrations were to continue for several days, more than one new outfit was permitted for each person, and courtiers were allowed separate carriages for their wives.[79]

Catherine took no pleasure from the prospect. From the moment her marriage was announced, she was barely able to speak of it. Indeed, it is in describing that moment that the final version of her memoirs first mentions the word 'melancholy', or what we might now think of as depression. An earlier version, hinting at much the same symptoms, says that the closer the event approached, the sadder she became, and she 'often burst into tears without really knowing why'.[80] Even if we discount the calculated note of martyrdom, it seems likely that a sense of foreboding took the edge off her first summer in St Petersburg, a romantic time when the river was alive with a flotilla of small craft, and the 'white nights' hummed to the melancholy sound of boatmen's lullabies. The Court enjoyed its cruises too. Resident from 9 May at the new wooden Summer Palace on the Fontanka – one of Rastrelli's most attractive creations, demolished by Tsar Paul to make way for the Mikhailovsky Palace – Catherine and her fiancé sailed by barge to the Peter-Paul Fortress to celebrate his name day on 29 June.[81] The day after the banquet for the Order of the Polish Eagle on 25 July, where she sat between the empress and Adolf Friedrich, they all boarded sloops to Aptekarsky Island in the delta of the Neva.[82] Earlier that week, they had joined Elizabeth and a large group of courtiers on board the Dutch vessel *St Petersburg* to inspect the luxury goods it had brought to Russia.[83]

Behind the scenes, ministers had been preoccupied since April with a particularly expensive and controversial measure: the first census of the male tax-paying population since 1719–23. Because this had raised many of the most awkward problems confronting the Russian government in the eighteenth century – tax evasion by peasants who tried to conceal children born since the previous census; fugitive serfs and soldiers; vagrant clergy, and so on – it is perhaps not surprising that the wedding seems to have been postponed more than once.[84] Peter's doctors had urged that the event be delayed for at least a year to allow him to recover from the pox. By the end of July, however, all eyes were focused on the impending nuptials. 'This Court is at present so busy in preparing for the Great Duke's marriage,' the British ambassador complained, 'that every thing else is at a stand.'[85] When Elizabeth finally gave her formal assent to Santi's plans on 3 August, the ceremony was scheduled for the 18th. The annual celebrations in honour of St Alexander Nevsky, established in the Court calendar the year before, were duly brought forward from 30 August to 17 August, when Catherine made her first visit to the monastery with Peter and the empress.[86] However, when the appointed day passed with only the customary Court reception, Lord Hyndford was unsure what would transpire. 'The marriage, which was to have been solemnised as yesterday, is put off till tomorrow,' he reported on 20 August, 'and some say till Sunday next, or til the weather gets better, for we have lately had great rains here.'[87] He need not have worried. So anxious was the empress to secure the succession and hasten the departure of Johanna Elisabeth that she would brook no further delay. The wedding was at last fixed for 21 August.[88]

Two days before the ceremony, Catherine and Peter moved with the rest of the Court into the Winter Palace, where her mother lectured her on her duties for the future: 'we cried a little and parted very tenderly'.[89] Woken by a canon salute at five on the appointed morning, the bride could see thousands of troops lining up on parade as she presented herself to be dressed in the empress's state bedroom at eight o'clock. Though Elizabeth initially lost her temper with the hairdresser, he was eventually permitted to curl Catherine's dark and unpowdered locks, now fully restored to their luxuriant prime. The empress placed a small crown on her head, leaving her mother to look on as the Court ladies continued their ministrations with her 'awfully heavy' dress, sewn with silver thread and embroidered in silver at the cuffs and hems.[90]

At ten o'clock, the carriages were ready to depart, led by a detachment of 100 Horse Guards. At the head of the procession came members of the *generalitet*, who drove off in order of rank and seniority, kept in line by a mounted officer for every ten coaches. In this status-obsessed society, members of the first two ranks were allowed between eight and twelve lackeys to walk in front of their carriages with a heyduck on either side (a more senior male servant dressed in semi-military costume derived originally from the Hungarian style). Ranks three and four had proportionately smaller retinues, specified in the edict of 16 March. All of them wore richly decorated silk tunics: no velvet, Santi had stipulated.[91] Although Russia's wealthiest aristocrats had spent their salaries (and much more) just as Elizabeth had ordered, many of their coaches remained unoccupied, representing owners who took their places further back in the procession as officers of the Court. One such was Semën Naryshkin, whose empty open landau was made entirely from mirrored glass. 'Even the wheels were covered in mirrors,' Catherine's son learned twenty years later from Count Nikita Panin, who had not forgotten Naryshkin's tunic, embroidered with an elaborate silver tree whose branches and leaves flowed down the sleeves and cuffs.[92]

After the *generalitet* came the empress's ladies-in-waiting and the officers of the Court, led by Aleksey Razumovsky with four huntsmen on either side of his carriage. Immediately behind him came Adolf Friedrich and Johanna Elisabeth, whose state coach was as big as the one allocated to her brother, only newer and finer, as she was naturally keen to stress. In 1706, six years before the Court moved to St Petersburg, 290 of the Muscovite Stable Chancellery's 313 coaches had been built in the Kremlin itself. Some 250 craftsmen were still attached to the palace stables in the new capital in the middle of the eighteenth century. By then, however, demand was so high that the Court had begun to import coaches from Berlin, Vienna, Paris and London – all of them intricately carved and gilded in the Baroque style.[93] To Catherine's impressionable mother, the state coach in which Elizabeth travelled with the bride and groom seemed like 'a small palace' in itself. Preceded by drummers and trumpeters and flanked by the Master of the Horse and two mounted Adjutants General, it was drawn by eight horses, each led by its own groom, with two pages on the running board and six moors and twelve heyducks alongside. All of them wore the new state livery commissioned expressly for the occasion.[94] Resplendent in shiny white boots, the Chevaliers Gardes who rode in front of the empress were allowed wigs or their own hair, done 'in the Spanish fashion'. Whichever they chose, pigtails were banned.[95] Doubtless expecting his dispatch to be opened by Russian officials, Lord Hyndford joined the chorus of diplomatic approval: 'The procession was the most magnificent that ever was known in this country, and infinitely surpassed anything I ever saw.'[96]

So great was the number of coaches – 125 all told – and so deep the ranks of the cheering populace, that it took almost two hours for the procession to lumber barely half a mile down the Great Perspective Road to the wooden church of the Nativity of the Mother of God. Designed by Mikhail Zemtsov and known as the Kazan Church because it housed a miracle-working icon of the Virgin of Kazan, closely associated with Petrine triumphs, the church had its bells decorated with the imperial monogram as a symbol of the sacralisation of tsarist power. Its main function following its consecration in June 1737 had been to hold thanksgiving services to commemorate Russia's ever-lengthening list of military and naval 'victory days'.[97] Now Santi had decreed that 'for the prevention of confusion and overcrowding', all doors were to be guarded by sentries with strict instructions to admit no one without a ticket. While Rastrelli had arranged seating in the body of the church for the empire's highest-ranking officials and the foreign ambassadors, other senior men and their families found places upstairs, though their numbers were limited in advance to prevent the choir loft from collapsing. Only the 'common people' were explicitly refused admission.[98]

At the end of the opening liturgy, the archbishop of Novgorod emerged from the sanctuary to request the empress's permission to conduct the marriage. As Elizabeth led the couple to their places on a dais facing the altar, two more prelates emerged bearing the wedding crowns that according to Orthodox tradition were held over the heads of the bride and groom throughout the blessing (Peter's crown was held by Prince Adolf Friedrich while Aleksey Razumovsky performed the same service for his bride). According to Catherine, who missed no opportunity to highlight the superstitions that penetrated to the apex of Russian society, one of the Court ladies whispered to Peter not to turn round, 'because the one who turns first will be the first to die'. Whether he really told her to 'clear off' cannot be known (it is possible, but it sounds very much like one of Catherine's attempts to besmirch his memory). After the rings had been exchanged, the couple turned to prostrate themselves before the empress, who lifted them to their feet and embraced them as they listened to Simon (Todorsky), now bishop of Pskov, preach a sermon praising Providence for uniting these two offspring of the houses of Anhalt and Holstein.[99] By four in the afternoon, they were all back at the Winter Palace for a banquet. Catherine sat to Elizabeth's left, next to her uncle, Prince Adolf Friedrich. Behind her, in attendance, stood Count Peter Sheremetev; Count Andrey Hendrikov served as her 'carver' for the meal. When the tables were cleared, she was so exhausted by the weight of her crown that she longed to remove it. But since that gave rise to another superstitious worry on the part of her ladies, she was permitted to do so only after anxious consultations with the reluctant empress.[100]

The most theatrical celebration of all came on the following evening. That morning, after Peter had been formally congratulated by the ambassadors and leading statesmen, the Court transferred to the Summer Palace for lunch. While Her Majesty sat on her usual chair, upholstered in emerald green, Their Imperial Highnesses (as Catherine and Peter were to be called for the remainder of Elizabeth's reign) were given trademark red ones embroidered in gold. Catherine was placed opposite her husband, between Elizabeth and Aleksey Razumovsky, who had an exultant Armand Lestocq on his other side. In their absence, the Winter Palace was made ready for a ball that went on until midnight, when the Marshal of the Court led the procession to dinner. While Elizabeth dined with the clergy and her intimates in a neighbouring stateroom, Peter and Catherine presided over a meal for 130 guests in a banqueting hall transformed for the occasion by Rastrelli.[101] Let the architect describe his own fantastic creation:

> Between the first two ledges of the tables another ledge was made, covered with turf, on which were arranged fifty pyramids with Italian flowers in earthenware pots, decorated with gilded carvings with festoons of the same flowers, and between them burned two rows of crystal lamps with candles made from the purest white wax. At the corners of the second table were eight fountains in the form of mushrooms, each three *funts* in diameter. To the side of each fountain stood two marble statues, three *funts* high. The whole of the large upper ledge was covered with glass pyramids burning with candles of various sorts, so that everything around the cascades and the pedestals of the statues was illuminated by some eight thousand flames. With the music that played throughout and the noise of the water flowing through the fountains, it all made for a magnificent spectacle.[102]

Since it was nearly two in the morning by the time fountains and orchestra ceased playing, the Court required a day of rest before the festivities could resume. Among the most colourful events still to come was a ball on 26 August. While lottery tickets were sold at 2 roubles each (there were 15,000 losing numbers and 2,000 winning ones), the guests formed into four quadrilles, each comprising seventeen pairs. Catherine's set was dressed in white and gold, Peter's in rose and silver, Johanna Elisabeth's in light blue and silver, and the last, led by Adolf Friedrich, in yellow and silver. Disconcerted to find that each quadrille had been ordered to stick to its allotted corner of the ballroom, a tearful grand duchess persuaded the Hofmarshal to allow them to mingle, since otherwise she would have been obliged to dance with courtiers as 'lame, gouty and decrepit' as her partner, Field Marshal Lacy. If it was an obvious exaggeration to claim that men such as Peter Shuvalov (b. 1710) were aged 'between sixty and eighty', he and the other senior members of her quadrille, who included Prince Nikita Trubetskoy and Count Mikhail Vorontsov, were no match for a fun-loving princess who had spent most of her first year in Russia playing riotous games with girls of her own age. 'I never saw a more doleful or insipid entertainment,' she recalled in 1791.[103]

Francesco Araja's new opera, *Scipio*, which they had all attended the night before, must have run it close. Handel's version of Scipio's capture of New Carthage, drawn from the Roman historian Livy, had been premiered in London as long ago as 1726. But since his plot of a general exercising his rights of conquest over a beautiful female captive was scarcely appropriate for Catherine's wedding, Araja's librettist, the mediocre Florentine poet, Giuseppe Bonecchi, told a more conventional love story enhanced by his ballet intermezzo 'Cupid and Psyche'. Even if the audience was reassured by the announcement in the extravagantly bound programme that the performance would be 'at least a third shorter than last year's', they do not seem to have enjoyed it much. Though they dutifully sang a hymn in praise of the empress when it finished at half past ten, *Scipio* was reprised only once at Court.[104]

More immediately successful was the firework display on 30 August, the tenth and final day of the celebrations, preserved for posterity in an engraving by Grigory Kalachov. Stretching out behind a flaming obelisk bearing the emblems of the married couple, Elizabeth, and her father, Peter the Great, was a vast colonnade that catered to the empress's anxieties about dynastic legitimacy by sheltering statues not only of Peter and his second wife, Catherine I, but also of his father, Tsar Aleksey Mikhailovich, and Tsar Mikhail Fëdorovich, the founder of the Romanov dynasty in 1613. The whole scene was set on a huge raft on the Neva, surrounded by tritons and all manner of fantastic sea creatures. In the foreground sat Neptune in a chariot drawn by sea horses, next to Venus, the goddess of love, who held two flaming hearts in her hands with two kissing doves behind her as a symbol of conjugal bliss.[105]

There could scarcely have been a less accurate image of the married life that Peter and Catherine were to lead. Although we have only her word for what happened on their wedding night, there seems little doubt that it was a disaster. By the time she came to write her memoirs, Catherine's growing reputation for sexual licence required her to emphasise her childlike innocence.[106] Yet even allowing for a degree of special pleading, there seems no reason to think of her as anything but a virginal novice in 1745. Although sexual teasing was an integral part of life at any eighteenth-century Court, as her experiences with her Uncle Georg had shown, neither she nor Peter had been given any formal advice about 'the difference between the sexes' (her mother, she said, scolded her when asked) and the playful discussion she remembered with her young companions was presumably so laced with myth and folk tales as to be wholly misleading.[107] When Elizabeth led the married couple to their newly prepared apartments after the dancing (in a formal procession led by the Masters of Ceremonies and the Marshal of the Court), the grand duchess's ladies undressed her and put her to bed. She was left alone for more than two hours, 'not knowing what I was expected to do':

Should I get up again? Should I go to sleep? I knew nothing. Eventually, Mme Kruse, my new lady of the bedchamber, came in and announced very gaily that the grand duke was waiting for his supper, which they were about to serve. Having eaten well, His Imperial Highness went to sleep.[108]

The eccentric accommodation decreed by the empress made married life no easier. Peter undressed in his apartments, but in order to reach Catherine's, where the couple slept together, he had first to pass through rooms where his tutors were themselves preparing for bed, and then cross a vestibule at the top of a draughty staircase. Catherine suspected that these nocturnal peregrinations might have been the reason why her husband caught another fever in the spring of 1746, when he was ill for two months, causing renewed anxieties about the succession. Drawing on all her reserves of 'natural sensitivity', she apparently tried to broach the issue with the empress. She trod carefully all the same: 'It always seemed to me that both of them were likely to turn on you, and I was wary of compromising myself with them.'[109]

The truth was that the more they got to know one another, the less compatible Catherine and her husband seemed. While she was intelligent, bookish and eager to learn, sustained thought proved beyond Peter's grasp. Modern historians have gone to great lengths to show that, as a young boy in Holstein being groomed for the Swedish throne, he was exposed to an ambitious and unrelenting curriculum: French, Theology and Latin for three hours in the morning (when Latin, which he hated, eventually gave way to geometry and the study of artillery); dancing, history and geography or jurisprudence for three hours in the late afternoon.[110] Nevertheless, Rulhière (the French diplomat who wrote a controversial account of Catherine's coup) judged right in remarking that Peter's tutors made 'a great mistake in attempting to form their pupil after the grandest models, attending rather to his fortune than to his capacity'.[111] Catherine apparently decided much the same when she first met him at Eutin in 1739: by coercing this 'thin, delicate' child 'to perform as an adult', his entourage had 'inculcated the duplicity in his character'.[112] Though nothing she says about her husband can be taken at face value, and each version of her memoirs presents a slightly different portrait, she was right about the coercion.[113] As he later told his Russian tutor, Jacob Stählin, Peter had been forced to kneel on dried peas (which made it almost impossible for him to walk next day), and public floggings of up to forty strokes of the birch were inflicted with dread ceremony by a masked soldier to the beat of a drum at eight o'clock on a Saturday evening.[114] By tempting him with images from historic coins and medals, Stählin managed to teach Peter to count out the names of the tsars on his fingers. Even so, the grand duke's attention span remained dangerously short. The only academic exercises that excited his interest were those relating to military affairs. For these he had a genuine talent, based on a prodigious memory.[115] But it was not enough to bring him close to Catherine. Deprived of her husband's affections and further isolated by her debt-ridden mother's departure on 28 September, barely a month after her wedding, she faced an uncertain future in the hostile environment of a foreign Court.

CHAPTER THREE

LIVING AND LOVING AT THE COURT OF EMPRESS ELIZABETH
1746–1753

Having been raised as an adult from a comparatively tender age, Catherine now found herself treated as a child just as she was blossoming into maturity. For nine lonely years between her wedding and the birth of her son Paul, she had to negotiate the hazards of a Court shot through with intrigue while coping with an unpredictable empress irritated by her failure to produce a male heir. It was all a far cry from the carefree life she had led at the Court of Brunswick-Wolfenbüttel.

Though Catherine had been provided with young female companions on her arrival in Moscow, it was only after her betrothal that a formal establishment was settled upon her. Peter's household was also expanded on the occasion of the celebration of the peace with Sweden in 1744. Count Zakhar Chernyshëv, one of three gentlemen of the bedchamber appointed to the Young Court (the small entourage settled on the grand duke and duchess), was still among Catherine's closest advisers on his death in 1785. Another, Field Marshal Alexander Golitsyn, was to lead her troops against the Turks in 1768. But if these proved to be early examples of her capacity for lifelong trust, the immediate prospects for lasting friendships looked bleak. Zakhar was soon removed when Johanna Elisabeth feared that he might be pressing his attentions on her daughter and the level of supervision over the Young Court was sharply intensified when Countess Rumy-antseva was replaced as Catherine's leading lady-in-waiting by the empress's cousin, Maria Choglokova.[1]

Only six years older than her new charge, Choglokova was appointed in May 1746 when Elizabeth, alarmed that Catherine had failed to conceive in the early months of her marriage, ordered Bestuzhev to draw up a formal instruction for the Young Court which made 'marital relationships between both Imperial Highnesses' a matter of state significance, second only to the formulaic acknowledgement of Catherine's 'true zeal' in the Orthodox faith.[2] It was widely assumed that the attractive new governess, who had grown up as a maid of honour in Elizabeth's household in the 1730s, had been chosen in the hope that her affection for her equally uxorious spouse might serve as a model for the royal couple.[3] At first, however, Catherine regarded her as 'the most disagreeable and most capricious woman at Court'. Not that her husband was any better. However adorable he may have seemed to Maria, Nikolay Choglokov, who assumed charge of Peter's household, struck the young grand duchess as 'far from loveable'. 'No man in the world was more puffed up with *amour propre*.' 'Fat, stupid, arrogant and contemptuous,' Choglokov was 'at least as unpleasant as his wife, which was saying something.' Faced with the prospect of life under the surveillance of such a ghastly couple, Catherine spent much of the Court's visit to Reval (now Tallinn) in tears and continued to be plagued by headaches and low mood on her return at the end of July.[4]

It would be wrong to paint a picture of unrelieved misery. Over the winter of 1746–7, she and Peter enjoyed living in the 'very comfortable' Winter Palace apartments occupied by Empress Anna in the 1730s and were thrilled by the twice-weekly productions in the large theatre opposite the Kazan Church. 'In a word, that winter was one of the happiest and best arranged that I have spent in my life. We did nothing but laugh and romp about all day long.'[5] Yet the pleasure was shattered in March 1747 by news from Zerbst of the death of Prince Christian August. Catherine had her first taste of the Romanovs' dynastic pretensions when her grieving was cut short by the instruction that 'it was not fitting for a grand duchess to mourn any longer for a father who was not a king'.[6] More misery was to follow when Andrey Chernyshëv was packed off to Orenburg with his cousins Zathar and Ivan at the end of May. So persistent were the whispers of an attraction between him and Catherine that even her confessor was prevailed upon to ask her about it. Although she continued to write to Andrey in exile, smuggling letters out with the help of her faithful 'oracle', the valet Timofey Yevreinov, her friend's departure left Catherine feeling lonelier than ever. As if to emphasise her sense of isolation, she had to undergo the indignity of a visit from the empress herself. It was the first time they had been alone together and Elizabeth took the opportunity to express her disappointment in no uncertain terms, accusing the eighteen-year-old of unfaithfulness, a charge she vehemently denied.[7]

Peter & Cathrine dont like eachother

Over the following autumn, the Choglokovs sought to limit the potential for temptation by restricting access to Peter and Catherine so severely that it seemed they were virtually under house arrest. Yet such crude attempts to drive the young couple into each other's arms merely succeeded in feeding their mutual resentments. Far from producing the universally desired heir, Catherine and her husband already seemed to be leading separate lives. During the pilgrimage to the Trinity monastery while the Court was in Moscow in summer 1749, they rarely met except at table and in bed – and 'he came there after I had fallen asleep and went out before I woke up'.[8]

Seeking solace in private reading, Catherine was often to be found with her head in a book. Shortly before the Court returned to St Petersburg at the end of 1744, Count Henning Adolf Gyllenborg, a Swedish nobleman whom she had first met in Hamburg, had flatteringly suggested that she might draft an autobiographical 'character-sketch of a fifteen-year-old *philosophe*'. As models, he recommended Plutarch's *Lives*, which she tracked down only later, and the life of Cicero, of which she apparently read no more than a couple of pages in German translation. Neither did she finish Montesquieu's short treatise *On the Causes of the Grandeur and Decline of the Roman Republic* (1734): 'it made me yawn'.[9] Even for one so self-consciously 'studious', such works were too demanding. Voltaire's fiction, which she discovered in 1746, was more immediately attractive. Two years later, she had graduated to Brantôme's lubricious memoirs of the sixteenth-century French Court and Péréfixe's life of its most celebrated monarch, Henri IV, who was to remain one of her lifelong heroes. Soon more difficult books came within her range. Before tackling Montesquieu's *The Spirit of the Laws* (1748), the greatest work of political philosophy of the age on which she would later base her own Instruction to the Legislative Commission, she started in 1751 to read Pierre Bayle's *Historical and Critical Dictionary*, a fundamental work of the early Enlightenment. 'Every six months I finished a volume, and from this, one can imagine in what solitude I spent my life.'[10]

––––––––––

Withdrawal was only one of Catherine's strategies for survival. In public she embarked on a concerted campaign to please Elizabeth and her Court, though it was by no means simple to retain the approval of such a volatile monarch. It was particularly fruitless to try to share her developing literary interests with an empress who had inherited her father's volcanic temper with none of his intellectual curiosity. Although the library at St Petersburg's Summer Palace contained almost 600 volumes in French, including classic works by Bayle, Michel Montaigne and Hugo Grotius, Elizabeth had them removed to the Academy of Sciences in 1745, when diplomatic relations between St Petersburg and Versailles were damaged by the disgrace of the French ambassador, the Marquis de Chétardie, and their return five years later seems unlikely to have been connected with her personal tastes in reading.[11] Indeed, as Catherine soon discovered, 'there was a whole raft of subjects that she did not like at all. So, for example, one must not speak of the king of Prussia, nor of Voltaire, illness, the dead, beautiful women, French manners or the sciences; all these subjects displeased her.'[12]

There is no need to accept this verdict on Elizabeth's philistinism at face value. Monarchs are famously difficult to talk to – 'I would rather let people interpret my silence than my words,' remarked the taciturn Louis XVI[13] – and Catherine was understandably cautious about offending the woman whose permission was required every time she wanted to set foot outside the palace. Though there seems little reason to credit the empress with bookish interests, her attitude to death, mocked by Catherine as fearful superstition, was by no means incompatible with rational Enlightened thinking. Nauseated by the smell of corpses on her way to the suburban palace at Yekaterinhof, she ordered more earth to be piled on the graves she could see from her carriage and insisted that future burials be carried out further from the centre of St Petersburg. Still more drastic steps were taken in advance of the Court's visit to Moscow in 1749, when not only were burials banned at churches between the Kremlin and the Golovin Palace, but existing graves were razed to the ground, the tombstones being donated for new church buildings.[14] These were measures which owed something to a growing concern with public hygiene. Meanwhile, Elizabeth had done everything in her power to limit the 'great and useless expense' that her leading subjects insisted on lavishing on their funerals.[15] Whereas Russian nobles continued to regard an elaborate funeral as the ultimate status symbol, their monarch's attitude was more in tune with changing sentiments in Western Europe, where 'grief was becoming more introverted and intense, more private, separated from the formal observances of the corporate hierarchical society'.[16]

Elusive though it remained, privacy was highly prized by Elizabeth, who had a metal grille put up around her box at the opera house in St Petersburg. One of the best-known episodes in Catherine's memoirs describes the empress's splenetic outburst on discovering that Peter had drilled holes through a door so that he could spy on her meals with Aleksey Razumovsky.[17] It was this incident which prompted the reorganisation of the Young Court in 1746. Usually interpreted as evidence of her husband's incurable infantilism (or, at any rate, of Catherine's anxiety to highlight it), it tells us just as much about the empress's yearning to escape the relentless public eye at a Court where the monarch was permanently on display.

Hunting offers another revealing example. Had they known that Louis XV and his entourage had shot more than 1700 partridges on the plain of Saint-Denis on a single day in September 1738, readers of the *St Petersburg News* might have been less impressed to learn that in the six weeks between 10 July and 26 August 1740, Empress Anna had bagged a total of 488 items: 9 stags, each with between 14 and 24 antlers, 16 wild goats, 4 wild boar, a wolf, 374 hares, 68 wild duck and 16 large seabirds.[18] Nevertheless, lists of such achievements were routinely published since success in the field was understood everywhere in Europe as a sign of imperial prowess and international prestige. In September 1751, Elizabeth staged an extravagant hunt at Krasnoye Selo for the Austrian ambassador, who was given one of the best horses from the imperial stables and led by grooms wearing costumes designed expressly for the event at a cost of 20,000 roubles. This hunt took place in the full glare of publicity. Yet when the official press drew attention to the empress's personal passion for hawking later that autumn, she promptly banned all articles referring to the imperial family without her prior approval.[19]

Elizabeth had grown up at the hunting lodge at Tsarskoye Selo and consistently sought to preserve it as a private space. Though it was later to become Catherine's favourite summer residence, she and Peter were invited there a mere eight times before 1762. Only in 1748 were they in residence with the empress herself, to celebrate Bartolomeo Rastrelli's first reconstruction of the palace, and even then Elizabeth often dined alone.[20] For the most part, she preferred private jaunts with Razumovsky and her friends, during which she could most readily resume her father's role as 'the leader of revelry'.[21] For one such bacchanalian expedition, the cellarer at Monplaisir brought out 11 half-flasks of 'Her Majesty's sweet wine' (Hungarian Tokay), 21 bottles of her favourite English beer, 12 bottles of fortified wine, 1 bottle of the 'new sweet wine', 17 bottles of Burgundy, 16 bottles of champagne, 53 bottles of Rhine wine, 6 flasks of Gdansk vodka, 2 flasks of aniseed-flavour vodka, half a flask of lemon vodka and 2 phials of mustard.[22]

While the governors of the Young Court held Peter and Catherine to a clockwork routine, Elizabeth's life was famously irregular. Visitors to Russia in the 1730s had recognised in the attractive young tsarevna a free spirit ill-suited to the constraints of formal ritual. 'She dances better than anyone I have ever seen,' one acknowledged, 'but hates the ceremony of a court.'[23] Even after her accession, she shunned formal society, preferring the earthier company of her far from blue-blooded relatives, the Hendrikovs and the Skavronskys (Maria Choglokova's family). Surrounded by the guards who had brought her to the throne, Elizabeth gave special licence to the new Life Company (her personal bodyguard), the majority of them peasants by origin, who 'committed all imaginable disorders' in the early months of the reign as 'the new noble lieutenants ran through all the dirtiest public-houses, got drunk, and wallowed in the streets. They entered into the houses of the greatest noblemen, demanding money with threats, and took away, without ceremony, whatever they liked.'[24] It was a pardonable exaggeration on the part of the Austrian ambassador. Fourteen men were discharged following disorders at Elizabeth's coronation, and the regimental archives from her reign are peppered with the records of fights, broken windows, and a rich variety of derelictions of duty caused by severe inebriation. One wretched drunk was so hungover that he turned out on guard in his slippers.[25]

Hawking and hunting with hounds were pleasures generally reserved for the period between lunch and dinner; grouse shooting, in autumn and winter, lasted from five or six in the morning until midday. These, however, were almost the only fixed points in Elizabeth's daily regime. Mealtimes were unstable (and often the occasion for the empress to dictate haphazard personal edicts); theatrical performances regularly began late and continued into the small hours so that, until the empress condescended to provide carriages for her musicians late in her reign, they could be seen lumbering through the streets with their bulky instruments in the middle of the night.[26] It was entirely characteristic for Elizabeth to finish the carnival season in 1748 'with a magnificent bal masqué and a supper of a hundred and fifty covers in the opera house, which she honoured with her presence, till three o'clock in the morning'.[27] On less formal occasions, she might retire to bed only as dawn was breaking. Such irregular habits have long been ascribed to Elizabeth's fear of assassination.[28] Yet although the anxieties of a usurper are not to be underestimated, it seems more plausible to interpret her erratic daily timetable as an extreme example of the 'nocturnalisation' of Court life – a move traceable in most European Courts in the century after 1650 away from a dawn-to-dusk regimen towards one in which mealtimes, balls and masquerades moved ever further into the night, when fireworks and Baroque theatrical spectacles acquired even greater powers of illusion under cover of darkness.[29]

———————

The roots of Russia's Baroque Court culture stretched back into seventeenth-century Muscovy, when its image-makers lacked for nothing in intellectual sophistication.[30] Manners were not always so refined. By the time of Catherine's arrival, barely a generation had passed since Peter the Great first introduced women to Russian public society by obliging them in 1718 to attend his 'assemblies' – gatherings inspired by his visit to Paris at which both sexes were obliged to dance, smoke and play cards. Since these were all habits formerly condemned as 'foreign devilishness', the tsar found that the best way of encouraging guests to participate was to post armed guards at the door. If his new forms of sociability were largely alien to the Muscovite elite, then so was the Western dress he imposed in 1702. Decades later, hooped skirts and corsets (the English style laced down the front, the French down the back, rather tighter, to emphasise the waist) still seemed uncomfortable and unwieldy to noblewomen who hankered after the looser garments of a bygone age. Even those who were keen to adapt to new ways of doing things had precious few sources of instruction. First published in 1717, *The Honourable Mirror of Youth, or a guide to social conduct*, an advice book for both sexes based on Erasmus and other Western authorities, remained the only work of its kind in Russia until the mid-1730s and was still being reprinted in 1767, five years into Catherine's own reign.[31]

Peter's efforts to create a refined European society were disrupted by the Court's return to Moscow under his teenage grandson. Even when Anna brought the Court back to St Petersburg in 1732, visitors could expect to find as many rough edges there as in any of the smaller German Courts. 'The richest coat would be sometimes worn together with the vilest uncombed wig,' noted Manstein, the condescending Austrian ambassador, 'or you might see a beautiful piece of stuff spoiled by some botcher of a tailor.'[32] Even Manstein nevertheless had to acknowledge that 'at length, every thing grew to be well regulated' so that by the end of the 1730s St Petersburg could boast many of the attributes of a recognisable Court society.[33] Anna held regular reception days – *kurtagy* was the Russian word, taken from the German *Courtag*; the English called them drawing rooms – where the atmosphere was relatively informal. 'Our drawing-room is more like an assembly,' the English envoy's wife observed. 'There is a circle in form, for about half an hour, then the czarina and the princesses make their party at cards.'[34] By the mid-1740s, when Catherine arrived in Russia, the main ladies' costume at such gatherings was the *shlafrok* (from the German *Schlafrock*), which resembled English informal morning dress. For more formal occasions, there was the *samara*, a loose dress with a pleated back, not unlike the French *contouche*, worn over a corset and a decorated underskirt and supported by a hooped *panier*.[35]

'The Empress is a great lover of English stuffs,' reported the British ambassador in the year of Catherine's wedding, 'particularly white and other light colours with large flowers of gold and silver.'[36] Europe was not the only source of such gorgeous fabrics. Although they never showed much profit, the cumbersome, state-controlled caravans to Peking, sanctioned by the Treaty of Kyakhta in 1727, remained a crucial link in the palace's supply chain. Anna's Court had bought a third of the goods from the 1738 caravan and funds confiscated from her disgraced favourite, Ernst Bühren, helped Elizabeth to take her pick from the next in 1743. Yards of her favourite white velvet headed the list of Chinese silks purchased at auction, where the empress also invested in green, yellow, crimson and scarlet satins, woven with silver and gold thread, a multiplicity of damasks, muslin, gauze and coloured brocades, and some 4117 wire-mounted paper flowers.[37] Diplomats, appalled by Elizabeth's dilatory attitude to business, were irritated to find that she thought nothing of making a trip from one of her summer palaces expressly to examine silks on the market in St Petersburg.[38] Yet there was nothing casual about such visits to an empress who, in common with her fellow European sovereigns, used dress as a political instrument to inculcate loyalty, satisfy vanity and impress the world at large.[39]

Although Elizabeth prided herself on driving a hard bargain, the sums she allocated to her own wardrobe were effectively limitless. The young cavalier assigned to supervise alterations to her furs in 1759 claimed that some 70,000 roubles were spent in less than nine months – more than twice Catherine's total annual allowance of 30,000 roubles and only marginally less than the (grossly inadequate) budget for rebuilding the palace at Tsarskoye Selo in 1744.[40] Manstein calculated that a courtier in the 1730s who 'did not lay out above two or three thousand roubles, or from four to six hundred pounds a year in his dress, made no great figure'.[41] Catherine's expenses were far higher. Though she had to be careful not to outdo a capricious monarch – not long after her arrival in Russia, Elizabeth ordered all her ladies to shave their heads, a fate Catherine escaped only because she was recovering from pleurisy – the grand duchess's wardrobe was expected to range far beyond the standard repertoire. Like the empress, she usually changed costume three times at a public masquerade, and when an outfit attracted praise, it was never worn again because she made it 'a rule that if it had once made a big impact, it could only make a lesser one the second time'. Though indebtedness was a crucial marker of nobility in a culture defined by conspicuous consumption, the grand duchess's need for money would ultimately leave her vulnerable to bribes from foreign Courts. At first, it was Elizabeth who saved her from embarrassment. By the end of Catherine's first year in Russia, only a gift from the empress could prevent her arrears from exceeding 2000 roubles, and her debts kept on mounting thanks to expenditure on jewellery and gambling.[42]

Gift-giving was a central part of Court culture, and although Catherine might occasionally expect to receive presents from visiting royalty, she was usually expected to offer them. On the night of her conversion to Orthodoxy, she had been able to present Peter with a jewel-encrusted hunting knife and a gold cane-head only because Elizabeth had provided them for her. After her marriage, she had to pay for her own presents. The empress set the standard, providing courtiers with new clothes every Easter and bestowing valuable dowries on her maids of honour. Her stepsister Anna Karlovna received 10,000 roubles when she married Chancellor Mikhail Vorontsov in 1742. Sixteen years later, their daughter Anna Mikhailovna in turn received 15,000 roubles along with dresses, silks and bed linen that brought the total value of the gift to more than 25,000 roubles.[43] So we may believe Catherine when she complains of the demands of Countess Rumyantseva – 'the most spendthrift woman in Russia' – and Maria Choglokova, who alone was said to cost her 17,000 roubles a year.[44]

———

Such sums were a drop in the ocean by comparison with the outlay required to sustain a rapidly expanding Court. Though it remained significantly smaller than Versailles or Vienna, the establishment in St Petersburg was beginning to spiral out of control at the time of Catherine's arrival in Russia.[45] In 1748, when a financial crisis prompted officials to compare Elizabeth's household with the establishment under Anna in 1739, seven dwarves provided a reassuring measure of continuity, testifying to the Russian elite's persistent fascination with human freaks. In every other respect, however, the Court had undergone unprecedented growth. Whereas Anna had managed with eight gentlemen-in-waiting, Elizabeth needed twice as many. She employed seven chamber pages, compared to Anna's three, and the number of ordinary pages had increased from eight to fourteen. In

1739, the Court had required but a single cupbearer: nine years later there were six – and fourteen assistants. To manage them, the empress revived a series of offices unknown to Anna but mentioned in documents from previous reigns (among others, her Court now boasted a Chief Cellar-master and Chief Cup-bearer). In view of her passion for clothes, a *maître de garderobe* seemed equally indispensable and Elizabeth duly appointed Vasily Chulkov, a former lackey who had looked after her wardrobe since 1731. Inflation was even more obvious among the burgeoning ranks of coffee-servers, table-cloth layers and table-setters. As for the lesser servants, Anna had made do with four chamber lackeys, forty-eight lackeys, eight heyducks and four messengers. By 1748, their total numbers had more than doubled. All of them had to be kitted out in expensive livery: at 13,000 roubles, Elizabeth's annual bill on this count was more than three times higher than Anna's. Lackeys, drawn mainly from the Ukrainian regiments, wore an outfit based on the standard Russian military uniform: green breeches and tunics with red cuffs and a scarlet cloth blouson. Heyducks dressed in red breeches, like the Hussars, and a fancier tunic, trimmed with lace, loops and large buttons. For state occasions and major religious feast days, the livery was still more extravagant. Below stairs, forty-five cooks manned Elizabeth's kitchens in much the same way as they had done under Anna, but by 1748 they had sixty-eight apprentices to her eighteen. It was only because most of this mushrooming establishment were miserably paid – the eighty stokers each had to survive on 30 roubles a year, half as much again as the twenty grooms – that the increase in the total salary bill could be held at 239,331 roubles in 1748 by comparison with 148,388 in 1739.[46]

The costs of consumption rose faster still. In 1746, the three palace kitchens responsible for preparing food for the empress, the grand ducal couple and the leading courtiers paid 10,721 roubles for wine and fresh vegetables – more than twice as much as Anna had spent. The drinks budget was even higher: 38,830 roubles in 1746 by comparison with 18,163 in the 1730s. (Despite the drunken portrait of her husband presented in Catherine's memoirs, the 13,150 roubles spent on alcohol for her and Peter tell us less about their personal habits than about the central role they played in entertaining the Court and the foreign ambassadors.) Changing fashions led Elizabeth to pay three times as much for coffee as Anna had done, while the bill for sweets rose more than sevenfold to 6389 roubles. It was this 'enormous number of sweets' that contributed to the Russians' lasting reputation for bad breath – 'especially at court' reported a visitor in the early nineteenth century, 'where the ladies not merely chew them all through dinner, but send plates back to their rooms'.[47] All told, the catering budget for the imperial family and the leading courtiers in 1746 came to 83,714 roubles – well over twice as much as Anna's total of 35,388 – and actual expenditure was almost certainly higher.[48]

Although the 1740s was the decade in which Peter the Great's reforms finally began to take root in a number of areas of government, it would have taken a more robust accounting system than any Russia could command to control expansion on this scale. Not long before the national debt peaked in 1748 at around 3.6 million roubles – between a quarter and a third of the empire's annual gross income – the Admiralty College blithely allocated more than 1.5 million roubles to an attempt to rebuild the military harbour at Kronstadt in stone, abandoning the plan three years later only when it learned that even an outlay of 3 million would offer no guarantee of success.[49] The Court's deficit may have been trivial by comparison, but by the time administrators worked it out for themselves, it was already too late. In theory, salaries and catering were accounted for by an annual state grant of 200,000 roubles, to which Elizabeth had added a recurrent supplement of 30,000 roubles in April 1747. Yet although payments were supposed to be made in instalments every four months, the Court Office complained that the money was transferred only 'with great delays, and never in a single issue'. No funds at all were handed over on 1 May 1748, so that officials, already behind with salary payments and facing a formal protest from sentries who had been given no new uniforms for the past three years, now found themselves more than 43,000 roubles in arrears and unable to pay for the 'drinks, Gdansk vodka, vegetables and other provisions without which it is impossible for the Court to manage, either for its ordinary needs or for banquets'. By mid-May, the Court Office's resources were 'utterly exhausted': not only was there no money to buy luxury goods from the foreign vessels expected imminently in St Petersburg; they could not even afford to commission orders from the regular packet-boats that brought cloth and alcohol from Danzig.[50]

———

Expensive as the Court had proved, there was never any question that Elizabeth would rein in her spending. In a political climate in which 'the main currency of imperial competition was cultural achievement', there was nothing self-indulgent about representational display. On the contrary, as Tim Blanning has shown, display was a 'constitutive element of power itself'. And nowhere was it a more vital element than in Russia under the usurper Elizabeth, because the representational culture which radiated across Europe from Versailles was by no means an expression of unbounded confidence: 'On the contrary, the greater the doubts about the stability or legitimacy of a throne, the greater the need for display.'[51]

For a sense of what that meant in practice, consider the magnificent four-poster bed in the state bedroom at Tsarskoye Selo. A shimmering confection of light-blue French damask fringed with silver brocade, this *lit de parade* was the most expensive piece of furniture in the palace. Above it hung a massive canopy decorated with crimson velvet into which a cross and a crown lying on a feather pillow had been embroidered in gold and silver. The interior of the canopy was embroidered with the empress's monogram.[52] No matter that the Russian Court had never adopted the elaborate public rituals of the *lever* and *coucher* practised at Versailles, or that Elizabeth preferred to sleep in a room next to Aleksey Razumovsky's: the state bed's purpose was representational rather than functional. And it was no more than Europe had come to expect. Touring the continent in the early 1750s, the young Demidov brothers, heirs to the precious-metal mines in the Urals, were proudly told that it had taken forty craftsmen twelve years to construct the bed at the Elector of Bavaria's palace in Munich, where a dozen people were required merely to lift the bedspread.[53] A later British visitor learned that the furniture in that bedroom alone had cost £100,000.[54]

For a further representation of the power and prosperity that Elizabeth claimed to have brought to the Russian throne, visitors to Tsarskoye Selo had only to glance up at the ceiling in the Great Hall. In the words of the artist, Giuseppe Valeriani, his painting's allegorical central panel depicted:

> Russia seated amidst the coats of arms of the Kingdoms and Provinces of her Empire, leaning on one where the Crowned Name of Her Imperial Majesty can be seen surrounded by Graces with festoons of flowers; next to her is Abundance, pouring out horns of fruit; on every side there are the Genies of War and Peace.
>
> In the foreground are the Sciences and the Arts, Navigation and Commerce which the Genies of Her Majesty's Magnanimity and Magnificence pour their Horns of Plenty to recompense and encourage the Sciences and the Arts.
>
> In the niches at the four corners are the four parts of the World expressing their just admiration for the heroic virtues of Her Imperial Majesty.[55]

The New Year firework in 1751 represented the northern hemisphere of a colossal globe, where the empress's initials burned at the centre of a vast map of Russia.[56] Writers conveyed similar messages, sometimes in overtly sexual terms. In Lomonosov's anniversary ode for 1748, for example, Russia 'sits and spreads her legs upon the steppe', turning her 'lively eyes' to 'take stock of the prosperity around her, leaning with her elbow on the Caucasus'.[57] Masculine associations were even more frequent. Female rule had been associated with bravery in Russia since Catherine I's legendary role at the battle of the Pruth in 1711, and Elizabeth's clerical mythmakers duly seized on the image to portray their empress as 'Peter's daughter'.[58]

Since no artistic form was better suited to represent heroism than opera, opera libretti, usually published simultaneously in St Petersburg in Russian, Italian and French, added to the chorus. As Jacob Stählin reminded readers of the *St Petersburg News*, everything in opera was 'exaggerated, magnificent and amazing. It contains nothing save high and incomparable deeds, godlike faculties in man, a prosperous world, and portraits of golden ages.'[59] Giuseppe Bonecchi drove the point home by announcing that the hero of Araja's opera *Bellerofont*, staged to commemorate the anniversary of Elizabeth's accession in 1750, was intended to represent 'an image of Her Imperial Majesty, who, gloriously surmounting on that day all the obstacles that injustice and envy had placed in her way, came to the paternal throne, to which she has consistently brought glory, and to which she gives by her virtues more éclat than she receives in return'.[60] Indeed, the very presentation of Italian opera in St Petersburg was widely interpreted as evidence of the civilised blessings that Elizabeth's rule had conferred on her empire. As Voltaire declared in his *Anecdotes on Peter the Great*, published in 1748 to flatter the Russian Court: 'Magnificence and even taste have in every respect replaced barbarity.'[61]

In such a cultural climate, only the monarch mattered. Although Catherine's birthday (21 April) and her name day (24 November) were cause for formal celebration, as were Peter's (10 February and 29 June), these were secondary events, designed more to promote the dynasty than to fete the heir and his wife. Throughout Elizabeth's reign, the most important days in the Court calendar were, in descending order of significance, the empress's accession day (25 November), coronation day (25 April), name day (5 September) and birthday (18 December). It was these that provided the occasions not only for operas and literary commemorations, but also for extravagant banquets culminating in the presentation of intricate allegorical desserts, each of which was a work of art in itself.

By the middle of the eighteenth century, the sugar subtleties first created for medieval Arab potentates had slid far enough down the English social scale to be recommended by Hannah Glasse in *The Art of Cookery* (1747), one of the best-selling books of the age: 'If you make them in pretty little figures, they make a fine little dish.'[62] In Russia, they remained a novelty confined to the Court elite, though a marginally wider group of readers could drool over the descriptions that appeared in the official press. To celebrate one of her triumphs against the Turks in the late 1730s, Anna's Parisian confectioner made a model fortress complete with twelve sugar cannons; on another occasion, the dessert resembled the park and gardens at Peterhof.[63] Under Elizabeth, designs became more ambitious still. At the first coronation-day banquet Catherine attended, shortly after her recovery from illness in April 1744, the dessert took the form of a coronation hall, complete with throne and regalia. 'Among the subtleties at high table,' reported the *St Petersburg News*, 'there were various triumphal gates with avenues, and magnificent buildings with entertainment gardens and *parterres*; incidentally, the chamber of the Imperial Academy of Sciences and the Kunstkamera with its observatory in St Petersburg were also represented, in models done to scale.'[64]

Sheer extravagance was itself a powerful enough symbol of prosperity, and Rastrelli's favourite device, used on many occasions after Catherine's wedding, was a pyramid of fire created by setting light to wax poured through thousands of glass globes.[65] These were merely the centrepiece of fantastic theatrical settings. Fountains played in the banqueting hall, where tables for up to 200 guests were laid out in a single 'figured' sequence, flanked by orange and pomegranate trees. Our earliest description dates from 1738, when the tables were arranged in the shape of a double-headed eagle.[66] Even a genius such as Rastrelli found it hard to keep up this level of inspiration, but Catherine attended banquets where the architect had laid out the tables in the form of her own monogram, or the empress's, or in an echo of the formal palace gardens. One young officer retained a sufficiently vivid memory of a Summer Palace feast to reproduce the table plan in his memoirs: Elizabeth, Catherine and Peter were placed as jewels in a crown, from which four long tassels trailed out, one for each of the guards regiments.[67]

On state occasions, when the tables were arranged in a single sequence like this, Catherine sat to the left of the empress with the Court ladies ranged out alongside her in order of seniority, while her husband was placed on Elizabeth's right next to members of the *generalitet*. At lesser banquets, when the tables were set separately, the heir and his consort were expected to entertain the foreign diplomats and leading courtiers, dining either in their own apartments or in one of the palace staterooms. At the premier of Araja's opera *Mithridates* on 26 April

1747, when Peter and Catherine hosted the ambassadors in the empress's box, dinner was served throughout the performance. There was plenty of time for a banquet: the performance of *Seleucco* on 9 January 1746 lasted more than seven hours.[68] Only Peter's manners left something to be desired. In 1746, Chancellor Bestuzhev felt obliged to instruct the Young Court that the grand duke must refrain from pulling faces and telling vulgar jokes to foreign dignitaries, and that when at table, he must not, for example, 'pour his drinks over the poor servants' heads'.[69]

Such puerile behaviour was doubly embarrassing in church, where Catherine spent a good deal of her time. Elizabeth's reign was a golden age of Baroque church-building. Most of the major monasteries she visited underwent major reconstruction. In and around the old capital, she spent a small fortune rebuilding the Trinity Lavra and the 'New Jerusalem' Ascension monastery, established by Patriarch Nikon in the seventeenth century to represent the Holy Sepulchre in Russia. In St Petersburg, not content with founding the St Nicholas (Naval) Cathedral and the Smolny Cathedral, Elizabeth commissioned Savva Chevakin-sky to build a sumptuous new chapel at Tsarskoye Selo, consecrated in 1756, ten years after the foundation stone was laid.[70] Several of the capital's churches incorporated a 'tsar's place' where she could listen to the liturgy, and some had more than one of these gilded canopies since, as Catherine later recalled, the empress liked to wander about during the service, in the manner of humbler members of the congregation. There was no doubt about the sincerity of her conspicuous piety. It was at Elizabeth's behest, for example, that public floggings were prohibited on religious feast days and a ban was placed on imported porcelain and other items bearing images of the crucifixion.[71] However, in keeping with her quest for privacy, the empress preferred to make her devotions in the seclusion of the smaller of the two Winter Palace chapels, named after St Zachary and the Blessed Elizabeth, where she could emulate her father by 'singing with great grace in the most difficult motets' and 'competing with the strongest choristers'.[72] In her absence, Peter and Catherine, and even Catherine alone, were often left to represent the imperial family in the Great Chapel, not only at regular Sunday services, but also on the major feast days in the Orthodox calendar.

Churches were often perishingly cold. On Christmas Day in 1748, when the Court was in Moscow, Catherine and her husband were already preparing to take the carriage to mass when they were told that Elizabeth had excused them because 'it was twenty-eight or twenty-nine degrees below zero'. It was barely warmer in April, when Catherine returned from the Easter service 'as blue as a prune'.[73] Faced with such icy conditions, courtiers were inclined to stay away, much to the irritation of the empress who accepted only illness as an excuse for their absence (those who failed to attend the blessing of the waters at Epiphany in 1752 were threatened with a ban from Court receptions).[74] Less of an ordeal were the summer sanctification services, which appealed to Catherine's sense of theatre. In her first summer in St Petersburg, she and her mother followed the procession of the cross to a Jordan on the Moika canal. When the ritual was performed at Peterhof – where the upper pond was christened 'the Jordan' to symbolise the flow of 'holy water' through the palace's system of ponds and fountains – Elizabeth occupied a gallery lined with velvet to the left of the Jordan, while the attendant notables took their places in a second stand lined with scarlet cloth.[75]

On fast days the Court dined on fish and vegetables, though the variety of dishes served scarcely amounted to the sacrifice which many common people made and which threatened to undermine the performance of Russian troops in the field. In and around Moscow alone, there were at least sixty-five imperial orchards and kitchen gardens in the first half of the eighteenth century, supplying the Court with their choicest produce and sending the rest to market. Tons of fruit and berries from the orchards at Kolomenskoye, Izmailovo and Vorobëvo were stewed and sweetened at the end of every summer under the direction of the Court's deputy confectioner. The largest operation was at Kolomenskoye, where cabbages (Russian, red and Savoy), beans (Russian and Turkish), peas and cucumbers were also grown in prodigious quantities. In 1737 alone, Kolomenskoye supplied 2500 buckets of chopped cabbage, 500 buckets of shredded cabbage and 2000 buckets of cucumber for the imperial table. Mint, used in cooking since the seventeenth century and also for flavouring vodka, became a particular speciality of the Dmitrovo kitchen gardens, which each year supplied between 400 and 500 poods of mint to the Court by the end of Elizabeth's reign (a pood weighed approximately 36 lb or 16.38 kg).

Gardeners from Kolomenskoye were sent out to advise the winegrowers at Chuguyev; they also travelled to Astrakhan, from where fruit was shipped to Tsaritsyn before beginning the long overland journey to St Petersburg. (In an effort to prevent it from rotting, Elizabeth personally decreed that the posting stations should be no more than thirty versts – around thirty-two kilometres – apart.) Still more Muscovite specialists helped to establish the imperial kitchen gardens in St Petersburg, where several acres of both the Summer Garden and the Italian Garden were given over to orchard and allotments. There were similar establishments at all the suburban palaces, where foreign specialists such as Michelangelo Mass, Justus Riger and Johann Brandt, assisted by Russian apprentices, coaxed radish, cucumbers, lettuce, peas, onions and various sorts of grass and flowers to grow in the orangeries all year round, so that the Court could enjoy them even out of season.[76]

And then there were the fish. 'I have dined with Russians in Lent,' reported an English governess in St Petersburg in the mid-1730s, 'and seen them eat heartily of a sole of salmon raw.'[77] The Court was offered even richer pickings. In the normal run of things, the second upper kitchen served up for Catherine and Peter almost exactly the same daily fare as the first upper kitchen prepared for the empress's table: 3 poods of ham, 1 pood and 20 pounds of mutton, 1 fresh tongue, 1 and a half poods of veal, 4 and a half poods of lamb, 3 pounds of lard, 2 geese, 4 turkeys, 4 duck, 38 Russian hens, 3 suckling pigs, 5 chickens and a selection of grouse and partridge in season. On fast days, these quantities were halved to cater for foreign guests and heterodox courtiers while Orthodox members of the household dined on 6 sterlets (a particular delicacy, generally boiled but sometimes roasted), 14 pike (usually fried), 2 bream, 2 ide-carp, 10 burbots, 16 perch, 10 roach, 3 freshwater salmon, 6 grayling, 2 pike-perch, 1 salmon, 50 ruff fish, 100 crayfish and a variety of salted fish and caviars.[78]

On such a diet, it is no wonder that courtiers were plagued by constipation. But then, as Catherine soon discovered, personal comforts were everywhere subordinated to the relentless requirements of representational display. She grew up surrounded by scaffolding and workmen, ever-present symbols of recurrent alterations to the imperial palaces, usually completed at breakneck speed. If Rastrelli submitted a budget for 200 labourers for a project lasting six months, he was likely to be told to recruit 1200 and complete the job in four weeks, though such a timescale never allowed for the empress's frequent changes of mind over the details, often announced on a whim over lunch.[79] One of the Court architect's first commissions in St Petersburg, the summer house he built for Empress Anna, was simply chopped in two in 1748 and rebuilt on either side of the palace at Yekaterinhof, where the empress stipulated that the trees should not be destroyed.[80] Elsewhere, his pattern was to begin with cosmetic changes before launching into wholesale reconstruction, as at Peterhof.[81] 'This was the work of Penelope,' Catherine remarked of a similar operation at Tsarskoye Selo: 'they pull down tomorrow what has been built today. This house was destroyed and rebuilt six times before it reached its present state.'[82] The result was a restless progress from palace to palace, in which she and Peter scarcely ever returned to the apartments they had previously occupied.

A thirst for splendour was by no means the only reason why they lived in perpetual discomfort. 'The Dutch may brag that Amsterdam is built out of the water,' observed a British visitor in 1741, 'but I insist that Petersburg is built in spite of all the four elements ... the Earth is all a bog, the air is commonly foggy, the Water sometimes fills half the Houses, and the fire burns down half the Town at a time.'[83] Catherine discovered for herself the perils of building on frost-bitten marshland when Aleksey Razumovsky's three-storey country house at Gostilitsy gave way underneath her in May 1748. Having laid a limestone foundation the previous autumn, the architect had departed for Ukraine leaving strict instructions that the beams he had used to support the vestibule were not to be touched. Thinking them unsightly, the steward of the estate nevertheless had them removed, rendering the whole structure unstable as the foundations began to shift in the spring thaw. Comparing the noise of the collapsing building to a ship of the line shuddering down the launch pad, Catherine was careful to stress in her memoirs that her husband had fled to save his own skin while she selflessly paused to rescue a slumbering member of their household. Whatever the truth of that claim, there was no doubt about the scale of the tragedy. While Catherine's maid of honour, Princess Anna Gagarina, was dragged bleeding from the wreckage, three labourers were killed on the ground floor and a further sixteen, employed on the neighbouring sleigh-run, were crushed to death in the basement. The distraught Razumovsky threatened to shoot himself while Catherine, who had only just recovered from measles, was bled to relieve her shock.[84]

Even architects who built to last were frustrated by the Russian climate. 'Because spring and summer together last only three months,' Rastrelli complained, 'it is very hard to achieve perfection in work on the facades, since barely have they been completed than the cold and damp take hold of them and everything cracks up.'[85] Just as much damage was caused by stoves designed to ward off the elements from the inside. Works of art in themselves, these ceramic monsters played havoc with the interior decoration. Catherine complained loudest about water seeping down the panelling of Moscow's wooden palaces.[86] But condensation was everywhere a menace. No sooner had the celebrated Amber Room, a gift to Peter the Great from Frederick William I of Prussia in 1717, finally been installed in the Winter Palace between 1743 and 1745, than the stone started to come unstuck. As cracks appeared across the entire surface of one of the panels, the room was already under restoration by 1746.[87]

In 1750, Peter and Catherine enjoyed a brief return to Peter the Great's summer house while their new rooms in the Summer Palace were being finished. The ground floor at Monplaisir, where they spent part of that summer, was also 'fairly pleasant' because there were windows on both sides. But these were exceptions that proved the rule. It rained so hard that year that the landings at Yekaterinhof were 'covered in pools of water', and the new Summer Palace rooms which had initially promised much, being further from Elizabeth's part of the palace than before, turned out to overlook the Fontanka – dismissed by Catherine as 'nothing but a muddy swamp' before its banks were clad with granite in her own reign – and 'an ugly, narrow little courtyard on the other side'.[88] The apartments they replaced had been even less satisfactory:

> This was an enfilade of double rooms which had only two exits: one via the staircase, through which everyone who came to see us had to pass; and the other adjoining the empress's staterooms, so that our servants were obliged to pass through one or other of these exits with the necessary, and one day it happened that when one of the foreign ministers (I don't remember which) arrived for an audience, the first thing he encountered was a commode being taken away to be emptied.[89]

The only escape from such privations lay at their country estate at Oranienbaum, attractively situated on rising ground overlooking Kronstadt and the Gulf of Finland, four miles west of Peterhof. Here Catherine and Peter had 'more freedom' than in town, though it was to be some time before they could count themselves as masters of their own household.[90] Built in the 1720s for Peter the Great's corrupt favourite, Alexander Menshikov, the palace bore several marks of his insatiable vanity: subtly in the form of a personalised iconostasis, and more brazenly in the form of a monstrous princely crown, carved in stone on top of the main building. After Menshikov's disgrace in 1727, the estate fell rapidly into disrepair. Although Sir Francis Dashwood reckoned Oranienbaum 'with the additions of art very grand', the future founder of the Hellfire Club noted that it was already 'going the way of their other buildings' when he visited it in 1733.[91] Three further years of neglect were to follow before the palace was requisitioned for use as a naval hospital, whose patients were transferred to Kronstadt when Elizabeth granted the estate to Peter in November 1743. By then, serious work was required to make the place inhabitable and it is not surprising that Catherine should have remembered it as being 'in a fairly dilapidated state' when they first began to spend time there in 1746.[92]

At that point, traipsing in the wake of the restless Elizabeth, she and her husband were rarely able to spend more than a week at a time 'in the country'. Perhaps it was just as well. Until 1750, their estate was little more than a building site as thousands of the grand duke's serfs laboured to transform it into a cross between a summer palace and a military encampment. The first project to be completed in 1746 was a small but heavily armed fortress which may have been partly designed by Peter himself. Built near the pond to the south of the palace, the fortress was christened 'Yekaterinburg' in Catherine's honour. Yet her husband's obsession with his soldiers drove her to distraction. Everyone, from the leading courtiers down to the household servants, was forced to march about with muskets on their shoulders, as Peter was finally able to indulge his passion for military drill. While he drove his troops up and down the parade ground, Catherine was left to a 'detestable' life playing shuttlecock with her maids of honour. Reading and hunting were her only consolations.[93]

Prospects temporarily improved in the following spring, when work began on the conversion of Menshikov's stables into an opera house. But this was soon abandoned, apparently because the master stonemason in charge of the works was anxious not to destroy the effect of the façade. An alternative site was approved in August, but progress was delayed by the disaster at Gostilitsy. This prompted a safety inspection of all the imperial palaces in the summer of 1748, forcing Catherine and Peter to move into one of the wings attached to the main building and to dine in a tent in the courtyard. The inspectors' efforts were ultimately in vain, since fire destroyed the new buildings at Oranienbaum in September 1748, along with Menshikov's bell tower.[94] Construction restarted only after the Court had left for Moscow in December and it was not until 25 July 1750 that Peter could celebrate the completion of the first stage by throwing a lavish ball for the empress and 450 guests, including the foreign ambassadors. 'There was also a very fine illumination,' the British Resident reported, 'and Her Imperial Majesty took this occasion to make the great duke a present of sixty thousand roubles to finish the additional buildings and improvements.'[95]

Having enjoyed hunting with Aleksey Razumovsky on the Court's visit to Reval in 1746, Peter acquired a pack of hounds at Oranienbaum the following summer. Catherine, who mocked his sporting prowess in every version of her memoirs, complained that he 'tortured' his dogs and kept them chained up in a room adjoining their palace apartments over the winter of 1747. This, however, was all part of a strategy designed to depict her husband as a brutal ingrate, all the more suspicious for consorting with German huntsmen.[96] While Elizabeth was on her pilgrimage to the Trinity monastery in 1749, Catherine herself rode out into the fields almost every day. So sunburned was she on arrival at Bratov-shchina at the end of June that the empress sent her a rinse made of lemon, egg white and French *eau de vie* to restore her complexion: 'When the skin is over-heated, I know of no better remedy.'[97]

By her own account, however, she took little pleasure from the chase: it was riding that she found exhilarating – 'and the more violent the exercise, the more I enjoyed it'. At Oranienbaum the following summer, she hunted 'every day that God granted, sometimes spending thirteen hours a day on horseback'.[98] Genera-tions of biographers have made much of this passion for riding, seeing it as a means of relief for everything from sexual frustration to premenstrual tension. Perhaps it was. But it is just as plausibly explained as a healthy escape from dank, smoke-filled palaces. Catherine certainly thought so. She told the doctor who inoculated her against smallpox in 1768 that although she had taken asses' milk and spa water for seven years to relieve her weakened lungs in the wake of her illness in 1744, she attributed her recovery largely to riding.[99] In her memoirs, Catherine presented her prowess on horseback somewhat differently, as a symbol of courage and virility. By refusing to ride side-saddle, even when the empress complained that riding astride was unseemly and might prevent her from con-ceiving a child, she could 'keep up with the most determined huntsmen'. Indeed, she liked nothing better than to dress 'from head to toe' in male attire for a day's duck shooting in the reeds of the Oranienbaum canal with an old hunter who sometimes took her further out to risk the open sea.[100]

Catherine liked to hunt & ride horses

Back in St Petersburg for the winter of 1750–51, Elizabeth revived her cross-dressing balls, events for between 150 and 200 guests at which 'most of the women resembled stunted little boys'. As Catherine later complained, 'the eldest had fat, short legs that hardly flattered them'. Only the empress was displayed to advantage: 'She had more beautiful legs than I have ever seen on any man and admirably proportioned feet.'[101] Less bizarre, though scarcely less onerous, were the public masquerades held every autumn and at New Year. Guests arrived between half past six and eight, briefly dropped their masks at the door to establish their noble status, surrendered their weapons (if they had been naïve enough to suppose that daggers were a legitimate part of Turkish costume) and entered a fantasy world that lasted long into the night. No alcohol was served, but liveried pages were on hand to offer tea, coffee, lemonade, *orshad* (a milky drink made with almonds), a variety of luscious fruits and piles of the ubiquitous sweets. Music began at half past seven and continued until the early hours. Dinner was usually served between midnight and two in the morning, when Catherine and her husband sat down with dignitaries of the top two ranks before dancing the night away. It was a test of endurance to survive these entertainments in the first six weeks of the New Year, when up to seven of them were held as little as three or four days apart with theatrical performances sandwiched in between. Since sickness was rife at that time of year, it is perhaps not surprising that only 665 nobles appeared at the first masked ball of 1751, though more than 1400 tickets had been issued and the Academy of Sciences was ordered to publish an attendance of 'as many as 1500 guests' in the newspapers.[102] 'One pretended to be entertained by them,' Catherine later wrote of these balls, 'but in fact one was bored to death.'

To judge from her memoirs, tedium was the dominant feature of Catherine's life by the beginning of the new decade. Bored with the stultifying round of social occasions at Court and even more bored with her husband, who had already embarked on a series of more or less open liaisons with other women, she found her own eyes beginning to wander. There was no shortage of potential suitors now that the ugly duckling from Stettin had begun to mature into an elegant Russian swan. Zakhar Chernyshëv, who returned to Court in the autumn of 1751, told her how much prettier she looked. 'This was the first time in my life that someone had said such a thing to me. I did not find it displeasing.' They secretly exchanged billets-doux, using Anna Gagarina as a reluctant postman. Though Zakhar hoped that the relationship might blossom, Catherine eventually demurred. When he left to rejoin his regiment in the spring, she found herself courted by a new and more persistent admirer.

Two years older than the grand duchess, who celebrated her twenty-fourth birthday around the time of their first meeting, Sergey Saltykov was handsome, intelligent and adept in the courtly arts. He was also married. With characteristic insouciance, he played on Catherine's sympathies by telling her 'that he was paying dearly for a moment of blindness'. Though at first she resisted his advances, she enjoyed his company. Thanks to his friendship with the Choglokovs, he became her almost constant companion throughout the spring and summer of 1752. After a secret tryst during a hunt on Choglokov's island at the mouth of the Neva, she was disconcerted to find that she had begun to lose control of her emotions. Having initially supposed that she could 'govern and elevate both his thoughts and mine', she discovered that it was 'difficult, if not impossible'.[103]

It was not the last time that Catherine would embark on a relationship with such high-minded aspirations – and it was not the last time that the object of her affections would let her down. If we are to believe the jaundiced account in her memoirs, coloured by Sergey's subsequent infidelity, his ardour had already begun to cool by the winter of 1752. As he 'became distracted, and sometimes smug, arrogant, and dissolute', Catherine found it hard to accept that he was merely trying to distract attention from their affair. Even so, she was pregnant by the time the Court departed for Moscow in December. Although she suffered a miscarriage on the journey, the relationship revived when Sergey arrived in the old capital. It was then, according to a passage which censors excised from the first Russian edition of Catherine's memoirs in 1907, that Maria Choglokova seized her chance to secure the succession by encouraging the grand duchess to sleep with him. By May 1753, there were renewed signs of pregnancy, but this too was brought to an end by an early miscarriage. 'I was in great danger for thirteen days because it was suspected that part of the afterbirth had remained inside me. No one told me this. Eventually, on the thirteenth day, it came out of its own accord, without pains or effort. I was made to rest for six weeks in my room because of this complication, during an intolerable heatwave.'[104]

It was to be the beginning of a long year of discomfort. That month, Elizabeth decreed that no further wooden structures were to be allowed near the Kremlin and China Town.[105] Three stokers and another workman had been whipped in January for allowing burning coals to fall from a stove in the palace, setting light to the floor and a panel in the wall of the empress's apartments. Yet although primitive fire equipment was carted from palace to palace in an attempt to limit any conflagration, both capitals became tinderboxes in a hot, dry summer, when it was one of Elizabeth's more melancholy diversions to drive out to witness the destruction of one of her courtier's homes. On 1 November 1753, she experienced the same fate herself.

A mere two days after she had moved into her new Golovin Palace, the whole edifice was reduced to ashes by a fire that began at midday in the heating pipes under the floor of the great hall. 'It was twenty paces from our wing,' Catherine recalled. 'I went into my rooms and found them already full of soldiers and servants, who were removing the furniture and carrying what they could.' Since there was nothing to be done, she retreated to a safe distance in the carriage of the Court *Kapellmeister*, reserving her coolest irony for the passage in her memoirs in which she describes the 'astonishing number of rats and mice' that allegedly 'descended the stairs in single file, without even really hurrying'. For once, Rastrelli's advanced techniques counted against him because it proved impossible, even by firing cannon balls into the burning ruins, to dislodge the iron girders that underpinned the whole structure, and so to isolate the fire in the main staterooms. Flames soon engulfed the entire 400-metre length of the building. By the time they were finally extinguished at six o'clock, only the chapel and the summer apartments remained standing, though a salvage operation managed to rescue the majority of the valuables. The most sensible loss for the empress was her wardrobe, including a dress she had had made from Parisian fabric sent to Catherine as a gift from her mother.[106]

Even as she looked on aghast, Elizabeth boasted to the Dutch ambassador that she would commission a new palace, 'only not in the Italian style, but more in the Russian'.[107] She was as good as her word. Having defiantly returned to the neighbouring theatre to see a French comedy the day after the fire, she ordered that a new palace must be ready in time for her birthday in six weeks' time. Clearance work began on 5 November and building started three days later under the direction of Russian architects working to a new design by Rastrelli. To speed reconstruction, materials were brought from both the Petrovsky palace and the old wooden palace in the Kremlin, dismantled in the spring (the Moscow nobility might have been unnerved to learn of the further order to survey the surrounding area for 'buildings made of good timber belonging to private individuals'). By 10 November, 1018 men were already at work, erecting a new superstructure onto the existing foundations since fresh ones would have threatened a repeat of the disaster at Gostilitsy by sweating through the winter. As all the Court's neighbouring construction projects came to a halt to release the necessary labour force, the total soon reached 6000, including 3000 carpenters and 120 specialist woodcarvers. Fed and housed on site, they worked around the clock to complete the project in time for an architects' inspection on 13 December.[108] Two days later, Elizabeth took possession of her new apartments and on 18 December she duly celebrated her birthday in a richly gilded hall, even larger than its predecessor, lit by twenty-two tall windows. 'There was no court at noon, as usual,' the British resident reported, 'because of the excessive cold, but in the evening there was a ball, illuminations and a magnificent supper at a table which held near three hundred people.'[109] The fact that only 130 guests sat down at a table laid for 160 scarcely diminishes the scale of the achievement. Ambitious state construction projects were by no means a creation of the Stalinist era. At the beginning of the nineteenth century, Count Alexander Vorontsov highlighted the resurrection of the Golovin Palace in his autobiography as an example of 'what can be done in Russia'.[110]

Catherine was less impressed. Though a degree of inconvenience was to be expected in the aftermath of such a disaster, the misery she endured at a nearby courtier's house was insufferable. 'It is hardly possible to be worse off than we were there,' she recalled. 'The wind blew in from all directions, the windows and doors were half rotted, and you could get two or three fingers into the cracks in the floor.' Conditions were little better when she and Peter moved to a former episcopal palace, where they feared being burned alive. Prospects improved only when they were allowed to go to Liuberets, an estate outside Moscow granted to her husband in 1751, where they had initially been obliged to sleep in tents: 'Here we thought we were in paradise. The house was completely new and quite well furnished.'[111]

The first indications of a third pregnancy showed in February 1754. In view of the earlier miscarriages, anxieties about Catherine's health were understandable. The empress herself paid her a visit in Easter week, perhaps to check that Saltykov was not lurking in her apartments. She left after half an hour, having excused the grand duchess from appearing in public on her birthday and on coronation day.[112] That was small relief by comparison with the distress caused by the discovery that Nikolay Choglokov, who collapsed during the Easter service, was terminally ill. It had taken Catherine seven years to bring the Choglokovs round by flattering them and pandering to their weakness for gambling. Now Nikolay had selfishly chosen to die 'just at the point when we had managed, after several years of trouble and effort, to make him less wicked and nasty, and he had become more tractable'. As for his wife, she too 'had changed from a hard-hearted and malevolent Argus into a firm and devoted friend'. Now they were gone, and at the moment of her greatest uncertainty Catherine had to face the future under the supervision of a new governor of the Young Court: Alexander Shuvalov, the head of the Secret Chancellery. Finding it astonishing that 'a man with such a hideous grimace' should have been placed in the company of a pregnant young woman, she cried all the way back to St Petersburg.[113]

CHAPTER FOUR

AMBITION 1754–1759

She gave Birth

W hen Catherine finally gave birth to a son on 20 September 1754, the
Russian Court erupted in an explosion of relief whose tremors were felt
across the continent. The British minister in Florence, Sir Horace Mann, wrote
in December:

> All Europe seems to have agreed for some months past to do nothing worth
> talking of – except the Great Prince of Russia, who has made a little Great
> Prince to exclude forever the lawful Czar [Ivan VI, still imprisoned at Schlüs-
> selburg], and for whose birth the Empress has given such presents, and made
> such rejoicings, both at home and abroad, as quite outdo those on the birth of
> an heir to the French monarchy.[1]

It was a pardonable exaggeration. Among the courtiers who competed to stage
celebrations in Elizabeth's honour in a series of festivities lasting through the New
Year carnival, none could surpass her young favourite, Ivan Shuvalov, who hosted
a public masquerade that lasted for two whole days and nights in the last week of
October, beginning and ending with allegorical fireworks.[2] The scale of the
empress's own accession-day celebrations on 25 November can be judged from the
tally of candles alone. In addition to 4000 plain white sticks for the chandeliers and
300 table candles of unspecified weight, the Court accountants recorded 1642
'semi-banquet' candles and 1505 'ordinary' ones weighing almost 900 lbs. Some
725 of these were used for the seven flaming pyramids designed by Rastrelli, who
excelled himself by requiring 4000 glass bottles for their construction.[3]

In contrast to such unrestrained public rejoicing, Catherine had been abandoned in miserable isolation. On her return from Moscow, she had been disconcerted to find that the apartment being prepared for her confinement was in Elizabeth's wing of the Summer Palace, where she was later to remember two sombre rooms, 'badly done out with crimson damask, and with almost no furniture or comfort of any kind'. The reason for their location was confirmed when her child was taken from her at the end of a difficult labour lasting from two in the morning until midday. Catherine's room was cold and draughty, and since no one dared to change her linen without orders from the empress, she was left to writhe in blood-stained sheets soaked with sweat. At the baptism on 25 September, when the baby was christened Paul, it was the fifty-four-year-old Princess of Hesse-Homburg (née Anna Trubetskaya), flanked by Ober-hofmeister Shepelëv and General Alexander Shuvalov, who carried him into the palace chapel behind Grand Duke Peter and the empress. Catherine could learn of him only 'furtively', because 'asking for news would have been interpreted as casting doubt on the care the empress was taking of him, and would have been very badly received'. By the following Easter, she had seen her son on only three occasions, the first being the forty-day churching ceremony to celebrate the end of her confinement, when she was too weak even to stand for prayers. Paul's upbringing for the first eight years of his life was almost entirely in Elizabeth's hands.[4]

Anxious about the stifling conditions in which the swaddled child was kept, bathed in sweat in a cradle lined with the fur of a silver fox, Catherine descended into post-natal depression. Her mood sank lower still with the news that Sergey Saltykov had been sent abroad on the pretext of announcing Paul's birth to the Court of Stockholm. (Later he was dispatched to Hamburg, showing every sign of having tired of their relationship.) Whether Saltykov was Paul's father is a mystery that will never be resolved. Catherine's memoirs hint strongly that he was, much to the horror of her nineteenth-century descendants who struggled to censor such an explosive revelation, and it is striking that Grand Duke Peter sired no other child, in spite of his many dalliances. Perhaps he was simply infertile. On the other hand, Catherine's memoir may have been a rhetorical way of disinheriting her deposed husband rather than a confident biological claim. Paul certainly grew up to look and behave very much like Peter (puny, snub-nosed and prone to rage) and always revered him as his father. Amid all this circumstantial evidence, one thing is certain: Paul's birth did nothing to reconcile Peter with Catherine. While the grand duke sought comfort in an affair with the unprepossessing Elizabeth Vorontsova, his wife looked out for a new companion of her own.

She found him in Count Stanisław August Poniatowski, a twenty-three-year-old Polish aristocrat who came to Russia in June 1755 in the entourage of the new British ambassador, Sir Charles Hanbury-Williams. Having befriended Stanisław in Berlin in 1750, Williams took him under his wing, introducing him first to the Court at Dresden and later to some of the best company in Europe as together they visited Vienna, Hanover and The Hague in 1753. A classic man of his times, equally at home with the bawdy Hellfire Club and the refinements of Latin verse, Sir Charles set out to polish Stanisław's manners and broaden his mind, grooming his young protégé for the most enlightened circles in Paris. There his admittance was guaranteed thanks to the renown of a father who had fought with Charles XII against Peter the Great at Poltava and was praised by Voltaire as a 'man of extraordinary merit'. At the literary salon presided over by Madame Geoffrin, herself the uneducated daughter of a footman, Stanisław met Montesquieu. And it was Montesquieu's thirty-two-year-old friend Charles Yorke who became his leading companion during his visit to England in 1754, when Williams was distracted by the demands of a Parliamentary election. A Fellow of the Royal Society whose library boasted some of the latest works of the French Enlightenment, Yorke introduced the young Pole to the pleasures of the English landscape and took him to Salisbury, Bath, Oxford and Stowe. With Yakov Sievers, a youthful secretary at the Russian embassy who later became one of Catherine's most influential advisers, he went to the debtors' prison in London to see Theodore I, the deposed self-proclaimed king of Corsica. Having sampled everything in England from Shakespeare to cock fighting, Stanisław arrived in Russia equipped with a cosmopolitan ease of manner in the company of an avuncular ambassador with a talent for gaining the trust of the young.[5]

Catherine instinctively liked them both. While Sir Charles became her confidant (it was for him that she wrote her first memoir), Stanisław became her lover. He offered her a seductive combination of wit, bookishness and sensitivity that her husband so obviously lacked. Hesitant at first – perhaps because he was a virgin (as he later liked to suggest), or more probably because he was understandably wary of the consequences – he eventually succumbed to her advances at the end of December. Like so many royal romances before and since, their affair began with furtive visits to her apartments and continued with secret assignations, fraught with risk, in the houses of complicit friends and courtiers. Catherine had to be smuggled in and out dressed as a man. Such a relationship was too precarious to survive for long, but while it lasted they made each other deliriously happy. 'I did not think that I was made to love women,' Stanisław confessed in the revealing self-portrait he composed at her request. 'I attributed the first attempts I made in that direction to particular circumstance, but then, at last, I found tenderness, and [now] I love with such passion that I feel that were my love to suffer any reverse I should become the most miserable man on earth.'[6] Apart from 'a mouth which seemed to invite kisses', he later remembered the attractions of a mind capable of shifting effortlessly from madcap, childish games to complex arithmetical puzzles. In his handsome company, Catherine found the confidence to build a new life of her own.

———

She first encountered Stanisław at Oranienbaum on 29 June 1755, when 121 guests of the first five ranks were spread across the palace staterooms at the banquet in honour of her husband's name day.[7] Though Peter had to be satisfied with toy soldiers in the winter months, he preferred drilling the real regiments he had been allowed to recruit from Holstein. An elaborate new star-shaped fort was built for their exercises. With its guns trained firmly on Yekaterinburg, Peterstadt was an excellent metaphor for their marriage.[8] To avoid arguments, Catherine had bought all her own furniture for her part of the palace. But her true passion was not so much for interior design as for gardening. We cannot know how far Stanisław discussed the subject with Catherine – on his visit to Stowe, he had risked offending his hosts by criticising 'Capability' Brown's 'natural' landscapes – but by the time of their meeting she had both time and opportunity at Oranienbaum to create a garden of her own. 'I began to make plans to build and plant, and since this was my first venture into building and planting, my plans became very ambitious.'[9]

When it came to ambition, the standard was set by Elizabeth herself. On arrival at St Petersburg, Stanisław had reported home on 'the astonishing prodigality' of a Court which continued to look to Versailles for inspiration. In 1756, in response to requests from the francophile Ivan Shuvalov, Mikhail Vorontsov urged Russian diplomats in Paris to write 'often and in detail', not only about international affairs, but 'especially about the king and his family and their way of life'. The favourite would be particularly interested, the vice chancellor continued, to receive detailed reports on the king's *lever* and the *toilette de la reine*, and also to learn of new plays, operas and comedies, and other Parisian theatrical spectacles.[10] To provide an appropriate setting for such display, his mistress had embarked on several extravagant construction projects. While the Court was in

Moscow, she had initially planned a fundamental restoration of the Winter Palace, masterminded by Rastrelli from May 1753 with a budget of 567,674 roubles. By the following year, however, she had concluded that the existing building was 'inadequate, not only for the reception of foreign ministers and the performance of ritual festivities on the appointed days in accordance with our great Imperial dignity, but also to accommodate us with the necessary servants and possessions'. So instead the Senate was ordered to find 900,000 roubles to build a new stone palace, 'longer, wider, and taller' than the old wooden one.[11] (While the new building was under construction, the Court moved into a temporary wooden structure, erected at characteristically breakneck speed at the junction of the Great Perspective Road with the Moika canal, which probably made it easier for Catherine to conduct her affair with Stanisław.) Meanwhile, in May 1752, the month in which Rastrelli completed his seven-year transformation of Peterhof, Elizabeth had decreed another total reconstruction of the palace at Tsarskoye Selo. The costs will probably never be known. As Catherine later remarked, the surviving accounts totalled some 1.6 million roubles, 'but in addition to that the empress paid a lot more money out of her own pocket of which there are no records'.[12]

Scarcely less fabulous sums were spent by leading courtiers, for the mid-1750s was the heyday of private building projects in St Petersburg. Catherine's architect at Oranienbaum, Antonio Rinaldi, had initially come to Russia to build a palace for Kirill Razumovsky, brother of Aleksey. Rastrelli also accepted numerous private commissions. Delayed by the vice chancellor's debts, it took him more than a decade to complete the Vorontsov Palace on the Fontanka, where the empress herself attended the consecration of the chapel on 23 November 1758, rewarding its exultant (and bankrupt) owner with 40,000 roubles.[13] It was there, over the coming winter, that Catherine first met and befriended his fifteen-year-old niece, the future Princess Dashkova. Between 1753 and 1755, while Vorontsov was struggling to find the money to pay his builders, Elizabeth's largesse to her favourite allowed Savva Chevakinsky to build a palace for Ivan Shuvalov on Italian Street, overlooking the Summer Palace labyrinth.[14] Nearby on the Great Perspective Road, the limitless resources of his family's salt mines allowed Baron Sergey Stroganov to complete his new palace – an innovative design, adapted to the increasing density of building in the city centre by fronting directly onto the street without a garden – in less than two years after its predecessor was destroyed by fire in 1752.[15]

As Prince Mikhail Shcherbatov later complained, 'such examples could not fail to spread to the whole nation, and luxury and voluptuousness everywhere increased'. Nobles who had once been satisfied with tallow candles were now content only with the finest white wax. 'Houses began to be magnificently furnished,' Shcherbatov continued, 'and people were ashamed not to have English furniture. Meals became magnificent, and cooks who were not originally considered the most important servant in the household, began to receive large salaries … Costly and hitherto unknown wines came into use, and not only in the houses of the great.'[16] Tempting though it may be to put such grumbling down to the rhetoric of Russia's most acerbic critic of luxury, it is worth remembering that in 1754–5 alone, the English merchants in St Petersburg imported furniture to the value of 37,000 roubles, far outstripping their continental rivals.[17] And there was no limit to the pretensions of the great. Reputed to be the first private individual in Russia to plant his own pineapple orchard, Elizabeth's principal minister Peter Shuvalov had its fruit fermented into wine and once served a dessert in the form of a mountain studded with precious stones from his own mineralogical collection.[18] Mikhail Vorontsov, who frequently enjoined his nephew Alexander to live within his means, nevertheless sent him orders for expensive clarets, port and madeira from Paris and Madrid: 'P.S. The best chocolate is made in Spain. Buy 100 lbs of it for me, and two or three pounds of the best Spanish snuff.'[19]

Catherine was aware of the competition. Looking back, she dismissed Shuvalov's palace as 'tasteless and ugly, though very richly appointed':

> There were a lot of paintings, but most were copies. One room had been done out in chinar wood, but since chinar does not shine, it had been covered with varnish, which made it yellow, but an unpleasant yellow that made it look nasty. To make up for this, the room was covered in very heavy and richly carved wood, painted in silver. Impressive in itself from the outside, the house was so heavily decorated that its ornamentation resembled ruffles of Alençon lace.[20]

At the time, her tone was less secure. 'I would like to know whether they were pleased,' she wrote plaintively to Sir Charles, following a visit by his compatriots that had made her country estate resemble 'an English colony'. The ambassador was all suave reassurance: 'All the English who returned from Oranienbaum are enchanted. I do not believe in spells. But they are enchanted. They speak of you as if I were speaking myself. That is all there is to say.'[21]

There was more to be said about the costs. Since no account was taken of inflation, Catherine received the same annual allowance in 1761 that Elizabeth herself had been paid as tsarevna thirty years earlier. Though 30,000 roubles seems generous alongside a general's salary of 4118 – and it was a king's ransom by comparison with the 20 roubles paid to the palace grooms – it was never enough to sustain the lifestyle to which the grand duchess aspired. (Vorontsov's account books, kept in his own hand while the Court was in Moscow in 1753, registered an annual turnover of rather more than 35,000 roubles. But the apparently perfect balance between income and expenditure was achieved only because none of his building costs was entered.)[22] Catherine's need for money was an open secret. When Peter requested a subsidy for his German regiments in 1753, the British Resident explained to Whitehall that since the two major generals on his list were none other than the grand duke and his wife, they might not require payment, 'though I can assure Your Grace that they want it as much as the poorest cornet or ensign in the Holstein troops'.[23] Faced with the need to support their outlay, the couple became familiar figures among the foreign communities in St Petersburg, who acted, in the absence of any Russian bank, as the principal source of credit. The British led the field. So well had they cornered the market, indeed, that an envious French diplomat noted at the end of the decade that Peter treated the British merchants 'less as creditors than as friends'.[24]

The most influential figure in such deals was Jacob Wolff, British consul general between 1744 and his death in 1759. Having made his fortune in the 1730s by exporting the 'wondrous drug' rhubarb from Russia and importing British woollen cloth, the Russian-speaking Wolff developed some of the best connections in St Petersburg. The Austrians made him a baron on the strength of it.[25] Wolff even hired out his Italian confectioner to show the Court kitchens how to make ice cream.[26] Mostly, however, he lent money. It was thanks to him that Chancellor Bestuzhev managed to pay for his ornate Baroque mansion on the Neva, where Carlo Rossi's Senate Building now stands. Vorontsov was another desperate client who turned to Ivan Shuvalov only after exhausting his credit with Wolff. In 1754, he mortgaged his Baltic estates to the British consul for 40,000 roubles, repayable over eight years, simultaneously offsetting existing debts of more than 19,000 roubles. And still it was not enough. 'I have already borrowed 5000 roubles from Baron Wolff this month,' he confessed in October 1756, 'and it has all gone to pay my suppliers and labourers; and now I must quickly satisfy these poor people again.'[27]

Catherine was not far behind. She was evidently already indebted to the baron when she asked for 1000 golden ducats at the end of July 1756: 'It is with difficulty that I address myself to you again'. That same month, Williams secretly arranged a much larger loan from the British government for which Wolff was to be the crucial intermediary. Once they had settled a rate of exchange, the ambassador expected to be able to convert the original £10,000 sterling into 42,500 roubles. 'You can count on me to strike a good bargain for you,' he promised.[28] Clearly expecting to gain a hold over the young grand duchess by acting as her personal banker, Sir Charles advised her 'to order me to pay Baron Wolff what is due to him, because that will help to arrange your future credit with him. When I have done that, I shall retain the rest, which I shall pay at any time to your order.'[29] 'Here is the form which the bond should take,' he explained, asking Catherine to insert the date:

> I have received by the hand of the British Ambassador the sum of ten thousand pounds sterling, which I promise to repay to His Majesty, the King of Great Britain, whenever he demands it of me. C.

Since such business methods were evidently foreign to her, he had to explain further in the autumn. 'All money leaving our Treasury pays in the region of 6 per cent to the Treasury officials, which is repaid when the money is returned. So, on the 44,000 roubles, there is around 2600 to be paid, which you will be reimbursed. I have already paid it in London, and I shall be obliged if you will send it to me at your convenience.'[30] But still she did not understand. 'The form of your bond to Wolff is no bond at all,' Sir Charles complained, offering her a further model to follow. 'It would not befit your honour to give a worthless bond as this would convert into a gift what is only a loan. Send word to Wolff to send you your money in gold little by little. He can always find five or six thousand roubles in imperials, and in three or four instalments you will have it all. The sum which you have to send me will amount to 2600 crowns ... This will be returned to you when the debt is paid off.'[31] Once a suitably clandestine means of payment had been arranged – a process that took several months – Wolff delivered the money in person in November.[32] He was only just in time. 'I learned today,' wrote Williams a week later, 'that a Dutch vessel, which arrived at Riga, brought 86,000 gold ducats for [the Austrian ambassador] Count Esterhazy. You see by that, how the Russian trade flourishes!'[33]

Foreign governments would scarcely have been prepared to invest so heavily in Catherine's prospects had they not suspected that Elizabeth's reign might soon come to an end. An empress who spent the summer months 'rambling from one country house to another, as long as the weather will permit' had long tried the ambassadors' patience.[34] 'Their way and manner of proceeding here with respect to every thing that has the name of business, is so extraordinary and shocking, that I am surprised they are not ashamed of it,' complained Britain's Colonel Guy Dickens in 1750. 'But we are so entirely given up to our pleasures, that we are deaf to all remonstrances and declare publicly that we will not be interrupted in the pursuit of them.' He was not the last diplomat to mistake Russian prevarication for idleness. When Bestuzhev seemed, as usual, to have evaporated at the height of a diplomatic crisis, the colonel confessed that the ambassadors knew 'as little, what his mistress and he are doing, as if they were at Japan'.[35] It would probably not have surprised him to learn that the empress had no idea that Britain was an island, or so Dimitry Volkov the secretary of her governing Conference later suggested.[36] There is no need to worry about the literal accuracy of this claim, which merely suggests that some eighteenth-century rulers (like some modern American presidents) had a greater grasp of geography than others. Unlike Maria Theresa, who had succeeded to the Austrian throne a year before her own coup, Elizabeth displayed little interest in the details of day-to-day government. Indeed, her aversion to business became so legendary that by Christmas 1751, Europe's chancelleries were humming with talk of her impending abdication. Following rumours that she might take the veil in the 1730s, an earlier British ambassador had reassured his masters that she had 'not an ounce of the nun's flesh about her'.[37] Now Guy Dickens again poured scorn on the idea. Though it was true that the empress had talked of entering her new Smolny Convent when she reached her sixtieth birthday, there was no prospect of her abdication since 'the first act of her successor's authority, let him be who he will, would be to lock her up in a cloister for the remainder of her life'.[38]

The real question was how long that life could be expected to last. Elizabeth's health was already a cause of serious anxiety. The first scare had come in 1749, soon after the Court's arrival in Moscow, when she was stricken with constipation halfway through the carnival. Catherine learned of the crisis almost immediately from Mme Vladislavova and her valet Yevreinov, but was sworn to secrecy in case her informants lost their jobs.[39] Lord Hyndford reported that, apart from Dr Boerhaave, only Aleksey Razumovsky and his brother Kirill, Bestuzhev and Apraksin were aware of 'the imminent danger'. All four had 'taken proper measures for their security, in case of an accident, for they are by no means in favour with the Great Duke'. Once the worst had been averted, Hyndford hoped that Elizabeth would 'take more care, for altho' she is of a very strong constitution, yet she neglects herself too much'.[40] Hedonism was indeed beginning to take its toll. By the mid-1750s, staircases in all the palaces had been fitted with mechanical chairlifts to allow the increasingly breathless empress to get about. Another was installed in the garden at Peterhof so that she could manoeuvre between the terraces during the summer sanctification ceremonies. Later in the reign, a similar device, operated by a servant in the basement, was even installed at the Alexander Nevsky monastery once the narrow wooden stairs to the upper cathedral proved too steep for Elizabeth to negotiate.[41]

None of these contraptions could save her from further bouts of debilitating illness. Sensing that the end might be near, she took communion twice in 1756: first on Maundy Thursday and again on 6 August, halfway through the Dormition Fast, when she was too ill even to greet the Preobrazhensky Guards on their annual feast day. Three days of celebrations following the consecration of Chevakinsky's new chapel at Tsarskoye Selo on 30 July had left her exhausted.[42] 'A certain person's health is worse than ever,' Catherine confided to Sir Charles on 3 August. 'They say that her leading doctor wishes to leave in three months' time, as the prospect gives him nothing to laugh about. During her stay at M[oscow], she tried witchcraft without his knowledge to cure herself; and an old woman, who was employed, has, it is said, succeeded in putting an end to the discomfort from which she was suffering.' Imploring Catherine to tell him everything she heard about the empress's health, the ambassador assured her that 'There is nothing in the world that interests me so much'.[43]

The extraordinary correspondence into which Catherine and Sir Charles entered over the summer of 1756, while Stanisław Poniatowski had temporarily been recalled to Poland, gives us the first incontrovertible sign of her maturing political aspirations. By her own subsequent account, Catherine survived the years of misery she suffered as Peter's consort through 'ambition alone', sustained by a pervading sense of destiny – '*a je ne sais quoi* that never left me in doubt for a moment that sooner or later I should succeed in becoming sovereign empress of Russia in my own right'.[44] It seems unlikely that such ambitions were very far developed when she first arrived from Zerbst. Although she claimed quickly to have mastered the blacker arts of the Court, she can hardly have 'learned many things' by feigning sleep during her illness in 1744 because at that time she knew scarcely any Russian. There can be no doubt, however, that, in contrast to her husband (a gossip 'as discreet as a cannon-ball'), Catherine soon learned to keep her own counsel while redoubling her efforts 'to gain the affection of everyone, both great and small'. Widely suspected of being a Prussian agent, she understandably claimed to have been no more than 'a very passive spectator' of the great debates on foreign policy when she first arrived in Russia – 'very discreet and more or less indifferent' was how she later described herself.[45] Nevertheless, the frequency of her contact with foreign diplomats gave her plenty of opportunities to develop her political antennae. One of the longest entries in the *Complete Collected Laws of the Russian Empire* describes the ceremonial by which foreign ambassadors presented their credentials to the tsar.[46] Peter and Catherine had a crucial part to play in these audiences and often found themselves in the company of the ambassadors, not only at regular Court reception days, but also on state occasions. While Elizabeth, 'dressed in her regimentals', chose as usual to dine with her intimates at the banquet on Catherine's name day in 1751, it was the grand duchess and her husband who entertained the great officers of the crown and the foreign ministers.[47]

By then, Catherine had become involved in complex (and ultimately fruitless) negotiations over Peter's Holstein possessions. The Holsteiners were represented by the Danish envoy, Count Lynar, a burly redhead with a penchant for lilac and flesh-pink clothes who took such great care of his complexion that he was reputed to wear gloves and face cream in bed. (Lest such behaviour be mistaken for effeminacy, Lynar was swift to boast of his eighteen children, claiming that he had always prepared their wet nurses by getting them pregnant too.)[48] To practical experiences such as these, Catherine added further intellectual reflection. In her self-imposed seclusion after the birth of her son, she read more seriously than ever before. This, it seems, is when she first tackled Montesquieu's *Spirit of the Laws*, the eighteenth century's greatest work of political philosophy, which was later to be the main inspiration for the Instruction (*Nakaz*) she presented to the Legislative Commission she summoned in 1767. She also immersed herself in the *Annals* of Tacitus, and since no reader of Tacitus in Elizabeth's Russia could fail to hear the contemporary echoes of the Praetorian Guards' role in deciding the fate of the Roman emperors, his book produced 'a singular revolution' in Catherine's mind. 'Aided perhaps by my depressed state of mind at the time, I began to see many things in black and searched to find deeper causes for the various events which presented themselves to my sight.'[49]

There was scarcely any limit to her ambitions in the summer of 1756, when she was openly prepared to contemplate the consequences of the empress's demise. Already on 11 August, Catherine's head was 'a jumble of intrigues and negotiations'. A week later, she confided to Sir Charles her remarkable 'dreams':

After being alerted [to Elizabeth's death], and being certain that I am not mistaken, I shall go straight to my son's room. If I meet, or can quickly get hold of, the Grand Master of the Hunt [Aleksey Razumovsky], I shall leave the boy with him and the men under his command. If not, I shall carry him off to my room. I shall also send a man that I can trust to warn five officers of the Guards of whom I am sure, who will each bring me fifty soldiers (this is arranged at the first signal), and though perhaps I may not use them, they will follow me as a reserve in case of difficulty. NB that they will take no orders except from the grand duke or me. I shall send orders to the Chancellor [Bestuzhev], [General] Apraksin and Lieven to come to me, and meanwhile I shall enter the death chamber, where I shall summon the captain of the guard, and shall make him take the oath and keep him at my side. I think that it would be better and safer if the two grand dukes [Peter and Paul] were together, than if only one went with me; also that the rendezvous for my followers should be my antechamber. If I see any commotion, or even the slightest signs of it, I shall secure, either with my own people or with those of the captain of the guard, the Shuvalovs and the Adjutant General of the day. Add to that the fact that, the lower ranking officers of the Life Guards are trustworthy; and though I have had no communication with all of them, I can count sufficiently on two or three, and on having enough means at my disposal to make myself obeyed by everyone who is not bought.[50]

This astonishing letter was followed by a stream of others scarcely less frank, in which Catherine commented in characteristically ironic fashion on everything from Elizabeth's failing health to the plans for Russian troop movements. (As her 'dreams' revealed, she was friendly with the Russian commander-in-chief, General Apraksin, and attempted to persuade him on Sir Charles's behalf to oppose the resumption of diplomatic relations with France.) 'I do not know what I am saying, or what I am doing,' she confessed on 11 September, 'I can truly say that it is the first time in my life that this has happened to me.' Hardly able to believe what he was reading, Sir Charles coaxed her into further indiscretion in terms quite outside the normal diplomatic lexicon:

One word from you is my most sacred law. When I think of you, my duty to my Master [George II] grows less. I am ready to carry out all the orders you can give me, provided they are not dangerous to you; for in that case I shall disobey with a firmness equal to the obedience with which I would carry out all others ... I am yours, yours alone, and all yours. I esteem you, I honour you, I adore you. I shall die convinced that there was never a sweetness, a sound-ness, a face, a heart, a head, to equal yours.

Not to be outdone, the grand duchess replied in kind: 'My head is splendid, when it has one like yours to think for it.'[51]

So long as Elizabeth stubbornly confounded predictions of her demise, there was no opportunity to test the power of such fantasies. Instead, Catherine had to cope with the changed circumstances in which Stanisław Poniatowski made his long awaited return to St Petersburg in January 1757. In that same month, despite all Sir Charles's efforts to prevent it, Russia entered the Seven Years' War against Prussia on the side of France, Austria and Saxony, for whom Stanisław was charged with securing Russian military aid. Since England was Prussia's informal ally, it was no longer possible for the young Pole to consort openly with his mentor, who, amid the debris of his failed diplomacy, was already beginning to show signs of the mental derangement that would kill him two years later. Sir Charles was recalled to London in July. By then, however, Stanisław's love affair with Catherine had resumed in all its passion. Indeed, she was already four months pregnant with his child.

Following her twenty-eighth birthday in April, Catherine retreated to Oranienbaum, where the seating plans for her dinner parties were distributed by lot to avoid the torture of official precedence regulations. A French diplomat's account of the procedure suggests that not everything was left to chance:

Just before we ate, pages came in with gilded vases full of little tickets: these were for us to draw the *valentins*, a custom which overthrows etiquette and removes all the appointed places, even from princes. The seats are numbered 1, 1; 2, 2; etc. The gentleman who has the same number as a lady sits next to her. This put me on the grand duchess's left and Monsieur de Poniatowsky on her right. On my other side, I had the princess of Georgia, who spoke only

Armenian. The grand duchess took pity on my embarrassment, sometimes joining in the conversation.[52]

Anxious to mollify Peter, who was irritated by her refusal to receive his mistress, Elizabeth Vorontsova, Catherine, knowing her husband's love for music, commissioned Rinaldi and Araja to stage a lavish outdoor spectacle at Oranienbaum on 17 July, paid for by a further British loan at a cost of between 10,000 and 15,000 roubles.

We sat down at table, and after the first course the curtain that hid the main avenue was raised and we saw in the distance the rolling orchestra, drawn by twenty oxen decorated with garlands and surrounded by all the male and female dancers I could find. The avenue was so brightly lit that we could make out everything in it. When the chariot came to a halt, chance had it that the moon hung directly overhead, which made an admirable impression and greatly astonished the whole company. Moreover, the weather was the finest in the world. Everyone jumped up from the table to enjoy the beauty of the symphony and the spectacle. When it was over, the curtain was lowered and we returned to the table for the second course. At the end of this, we heard trumpets and drums and a barker cried out: 'Roll up, roll up, ladies and gentlemen, get your free lottery tickets here in my booths!' On both sides of the large curtain, two smaller ones were raised and we saw two brightly lit booths, one of which distributed free tickets for the porcelain lottery, and the other tickets for flowers, ribbons, fans, combs, purses, gloves, sword knots, and other finery of the kind. Once the booths were empty, we went back for dessert, after which we danced until six in the morning.

'In short,' as Catherine wrote in her memoirs, 'on that day people discovered qualities in me that they had not known I possessed, and in this way I disarmed my enemies. That was my aim, but it did not last for long, as we shall see.'[53]

The most disconcerting part of the celebration at Oranienbaum was a fall Catherine suffered when the horse drawing her carriage reared up as she stepped out to inspect the preparations. Fortunately, her pregnancy was unaffected. When her daughter was born at the end of November, she begged Elizabeth to be allowed to choose a name. Instead, the empress pointedly had the child christened Anna Petrovna, in memory of her older sister, Peter's mother. Peter himself rejoiced at Anna's birth, though he was surely not her father. Poniatowski, who was, made clandestine visits to Catherine, who remained in solitary confinement while her baby was removed, as Paul had been before her, to the care of the empress's wet nurses. But worse was still to come for the grand duchess when Chancellor Bestuzhev was arrested, along with Vasily Adodurov and other friends of hers, on the night of 14 February 1758.

When Catherine first arrived in Russia, Bestuzhev had been her greatest enemy. No one had done more to make her life at the Young Court a misery. After the 'diplomatic revolution' of 1756, however, as Russia edged ever closer to an improbable alliance with France (her principal continental rival), the Machiavellian chancellor had come to see the grand duchess as a potential counterbalance to his Francophile rivals at Court, the Shuvalovs and the Vorontsovs. Though he was initially horrified to learn from Sir Charles Hanbury-Williams of Catherine's liaison with Stanisław Poniatowski, he helped her to conceal it, and it was Bestuzhev, remembered by Stanisław as a ghoulish figure 'with a mouth which opened to reveal only four stumps of teeth and a pair of small flashing eyes', who did most to secure the young Pole's return to Russia.[54] The very chancellor who had prevented her from corresponding with her mother in the 1740s now opened up a channel to Johanna Elisabeth. Meanwhile, the empress's failing health prompted him to make his own plans for an alternative regime, drafting a manifesto that would place Peter on the throne with Catherine as his co-ruler. She was flattered to discover that the chancellor regarded her 'as perhaps the only person upon whom at that time the hopes of the public could rest when the empress was no more'.[55]

Precisely when Bestuzhev showed Catherine his plans remains uncertain, but the issue of the succession was brought into focus more sharply than ever before when Elizabeth collapsed in public outside her favourite Church of the Sign at Tsarskoye Selo on 8 September 1757. (For an index of the panic she created, we need look no further than the Court journals, which are blank for the following week.)[56] Faced with the possibility that the pro-Prussian Grand Duke Peter might come to the throne, Russian generals leading the campaign against Frederick the Great were placed in a delicate position. As recently as 19 August, they had scored a famous victory over the king at Gross Jägersdorf, less than a year after Frederick had himself routed the French at Rossbach. In the wake of such a triumph, General Apraksin had been expected to advance on Berlin. Instead, he retreated to Memel. Driven by the fragility of Russia's supply line (his troops had to wait while the grass grew under their feet to feed their horses),[57] Apraksin's decision was taken on 27 August – before the empress's collapse. But in St

Petersburg it could easily be made to seem that he had been motivated by doubts about her health, generated by his treasonable correspondence with Catherine and Bestuzhev. Urged on by the chancellor, Catherine begged Apraksin to reverse his retreat. But by then it was too late. In October, he was removed from his command as Bestuzhev's enemies, profiting from Catherine's withdrawal from the public gaze in the final months of her pregnancy, steadily poisoned Elizabeth's mind against him.[58]

Catherine learned of Bestuzhev's arrest from Stanisław Poniatowski on the morning after it occurred. That evening, as the lovers attended a ball pretending that nothing had happened, she felt 'a dagger in the heart'. While the chancellor fell under a lengthy investigation that was to end in public disgrace and banishment, Catherine faced a crisis more dangerous than the one in 1744, when it could reasonably be claimed that she had been no more than an unwitting accomplice to her mother's clumsy pro-Prussian machinations. Now her complicity was harder to deny and it was vital to limit the damage. Following the chancellor's example, she had burned all her papers as soon as the danger arose. Now, according to the account in her memoirs, which comes closer to her mother's purple prose than her own customarily deadpan style, she prostrated herself in front of Elizabeth on the night of 13 April and pleaded tearfully to be sent back to Zerbst. While her husband berated her as a liar, she stubbornly refused to admit any treasonable intent in her correspondence with Apraksin. Perhaps, as she suggests, her performance was enough to win Elizabeth over. At any rate, she was given a stay of execution until a further audience six weeks later, when she faced more questioning about her letters to the general. Although we cannot know precisely how the matter was resolved – for one thing, her memoirs dramatically break off at this point – Bestuzhev's enemies probably decided (just as he had before them) that Catherine could still be useful to them. While he was eventually committed to house arrest on his estate on 5 April 1759 in a manifesto that highlighted his vain attempts to corrupt both Catherine and Peter – the manifesto was published at the beginning of Passion Week, creating an inescapable association with sinfulness – the Vorontsovs and the Shuvalovs left the grand duchess in place as a pawn on the chessboard of Court politics and began to treat her well.[59]

That, as events were to show, was a serious underestimation of her abilities. But there was no sign of a glorious future for Catherine in the spring of 1759. Poniatowski had gone back to Poland in the previous August; Bestuzhev's disgrace made it impossible for him to return to Russia. The death of her infant daughter on 8 March left her 'inconsolable'. 'It was only her virtue and her complete resignation to the decrees of Providence that could bring her out of her state of shock,' Vorontsov reported to his nephew, enclosing a letter of condolence for Johanna Elisabeth.[60] When Catherine's debt-ridden mother herself died in Paris in May 1760, she was left completely alone. Like everyone else at the Russian Court, all she could do was watch and wait as the ailing empress entered the sixth decade of her life.

CHAPTER FIVE

ASSASSINATION 1759–1762

Modern historians of medicine have stressed that 'virtually no important doctor in the first half of the eighteenth century placed the root of hysteria in the uterus' and that 'all forms of hysteria tended to be seen as the physical manifestations of a specifically mental derangement'.[1] Told that Elizabeth's symptoms had first manifested themselves when colic seemed to threaten the life of the baby Grand Duke Paul, François Poissonnier, the French specialist summoned to examine her at Peterhof in August 1759, declared it 'easy to understand' that fear had unsettled 'all her nerves, and particularly those of the uterus'. Though he could find little wrong with her 'excellent constitution', Elizabeth's lifestyle left much to be desired. The collapse at Tsarskoye Selo had been made the more serious by her refusal to follow her doctors' advice. Observing that with age 'the humours become slower in their circulation', Poissonnier prescribed a purgative intended to induce two or three evacuations every day for a month. To sweeten the pill, the doctor suggested that his tablets should be dipped in marmalade and swallowed with an infusion of lime-blossom tea. He also prescribed coffee at bedtime, flavoured with *liqueur d'Hofmann* mixed with sweetened water or diluted lemonade. 'This liqueur, which resembles nothing one might call a remedy because it is very pleasant, has the singular property of strengthening the nerves without inflaming them.' While he particularly recommended peony, 'whose taste is as good as its effects are salutary', his main aim was to steer Elizabeth away from dairy foods and pastries. 'I realise that Her Imperial Majesty has been accustomed to them since childhood, but when circumstances change, it is equally necessary to alter one's habits.' By the same token, her preference for lettuce, chicory, spinach, sorrel and watercress, cooked in meat juices, was bound to give her constipation. If she persisted with such a damaging diet, then she must accept the enemas he prescribed in return. Her best option, however, was regular exercise. Poissonnier advised her firmly against 'too sedentary a lifestyle, which seems opposed to the vivacity of her character and to the continuous activity in which she engaged until the age of forty-five'.[2]

Whether or not it owed anything to her doctor's prescriptions, Elizabeth's health seemed briefly to improve. In 1758, perhaps haunted by the memory of her collapse in the previous autumn, she had avoided Tsarskoye Selo altogether. Two brief visits are recorded from 1759, and the rhythm of her visits to the summer palaces began to pick up in 1760 – a sure sign that she was feeling stronger. Even so, in these final years of her life she largely withdrew from public life, leaving much of the work of her government in the hands of her sophisticated favourite, Ivan Shuvalov. In retrospect, the continuities between Russian cultural policies of the late 1750s and those of Catherine's own reign are obvious. It was largely thanks to Shuvalov, for example, that the Imperial Academy of Fine Arts was founded in St Petersburg in 1757 (Catherine was later to set it on firmer foundations), and he corresponded with Voltaire.[3] But this burst of activity took place without the grand duchess's involvement. In the wake of Bestuzhev's disgrace, she had little option but to keep a low profile.

By the winter of 1760–61, the Russian Court was once again wreathed in gloom. On 7 January 1761, mourning was imposed for six weeks in memory of Britain's George II.[4] Elizabeth had not been seen in public since the St Andrew's Day banquet at the end of November, where she sat between Peter and Paul.[5] She did not appear again until Easter. At first, the British ambassador reported, it was 'an attack of the tooth-ache which occasioned a swelling in her face'; after Christmas, Ivan Shuvalov told of lengthy nosebleeds.[6] 'Apart from bouts of hysteria, and gradual symptoms of blood loss, and another local disease,' wrote a well-informed French diplomat in the spring, she had been 'suffering for the whole of the current winter with sores in her legs'. Stubbornly refusing to seek a cure, the empress remained 'locked up completely alone', subject to 'frequent attacks of melancholy', and with only Paul and her young Kalmyk servants for company. 'When she admitted society, she could bear the presence of only the most restricted number of courtiers.'[7]

Behind closed doors, however, Elizabeth seemed determined to keep up appearances. A sense of her routine emerges from letters sent by her lady-in-waiting, Countess Anna Vorontsova, to her daughter, who was travelling abroad with her husband ('I am sending you your favourite food, flabby fish: I don't think it will go off ').[8] When a favourite chorister married in January, the empress threw a party followed by dancing until four in the morning. While she was too ill to attend the theatre, the theatre came to her. A French comedy was performed in her apartments at Candlemas and, later that week, Sumarokov's Russian players gave her his tragedy *Sinav and Truvor* (they had been fetched back from Moscow at short notice, prompting tantrums from the notoriously volatile playwright, who resigned shortly afterwards).[9] On 9 February, Elizabeth felt well enough to sit for her portrait.[10] Following Peter Shuvalov's marriage eleven days later, she hosted a banquet in her own apartments. (Further weddings were put off until the autumn: 'Think of the poor couples!') This time there was no dancing, but Shuvalov threw a ball of his own, where Catherine joined Peter on 23 February, the last day of the carnival.[11]

At that time, the Court was enjoying a visit from the French astronomer, the abbé Chappe d'Auteroche, en route to Siberia to see the transit of Venus across the sun. As Vasily Sukhodolsky's attractive genre painting *Astronomy* suggests, this was a subject that interested courtiers of both sexes – indeed, one of the most extravagant purchases made by Peter's mistress Elizabeth Vorontsova from the Court jeweller was a telescope with various figures mounted in gold and set with diamonds at a cost of 1200 roubles.[12] On his return to France, Chappe repaid his hosts for their hospitality with a caustic account of his experiences in which Catherine is portrayed as the victim of a corrupt, despotic regime:

> To all external appearances, the court of Russia seemed more tranquil than it had been for some time: but, on the inside, envy, jealousy, and mistrust swept through this vast palace. The grand duke no longer lived with his wife. The princess of Anhalt-Zerbst, born in a free country and brought up among the muses and the arts, was in no way brought down by this disgrace. Her natural talent and acquired knowledge furnished her with the greatest possible resources. She found tranquillity in the middle of the tumults of this court. Not wishing to remain ignorant of anything, she spent her moments of leisure in cultivating literature, the arts, and the sciences.[13]

In fact, Catherine kept up her duties at Court, attending both the theatre and the chapel in place of the fading empress. She and Peter hosted the Sunday reception days, sometimes together, sometimes separately. Looking back on their customary winter week at Oranienbaum in mid-January, Dashkova contrasted the 'wit, good taste and decorum' that prevailed in Catherine's part of the palace with the cruder entertainments that Peter enjoyed with his Holsteiners at camp or in the Grüne Salle (Green Room), whose walls were draped with pine and fir branches.[14] There, in the company of dancers and singers from his opera troupe, he liked to set off table fireworks in the form of intricately decorated desserts, 'not without inconvenience from the smoke and sulphurous vapours', as Jacob Stählin remarked.[15] A less combative picture of the visit emerges from the account by the Piedmontese Misere. Downstairs, a military band played while the men smoked their pipes. The weather stayed fine until after midnight, but after lunch on the following day, undeterred by snow and wind, Peter and his guests – Count Hendrikov and his wife, the Shafirov family and Prince Dashkov – set out for Catherine's dacha in twelve small sledges. There was 'much pleasure and a lot of laughter' as they tumbled in the snow. The grand duchess herself served Italian liqueurs 'in her beautiful round house at the top of the hill', as they all 'drank coffee and milk from the farm, with black bread and butter'.[16]

By the end of January, Chappe was ready to depart for Siberia, but the Court now found even more entertaining company in the shape of another visitor, King Irakly of Georgia. In a letter to her daughter, Countess Vorontsova listed his gifts with a practised eye for size and value:

> Our Gracious Sovereign was presented with a very pure agate, weighing two zolotniks or more, twenty-three strings of large oriental pearls, and two Persian silver brocades. His Highness [Peter] – a dagger with diamonds and agates; Her Highness [Catherine] – a small mirror with precious stones and two strings of large pearls; and His Highness P[aul] P[etrovich] – a dagger. And he gave Mikhail Larionovich [Vorontsov] a very good dagger, which Shah-Nadir himself had worn, some gilded silver tackle for the horses, and a hookah-pipe with precious stones for smoking tobacco that Pauzié said was worth 2000 roubles. And he gave me a big diamond ring, a string of large pearls and a 15-string pearl bracelet (as big as yours), handmade from Persian silver.[17]

Elizabeth felt sufficiently recovered to appear before her Court on Easter Saturday. 'We were all delighted to see [her] in the great chapel,' reported her relieved lady-in-waiting, 'and everyone was pleased that she permitted them to kiss her hand.' Another important 'first' was achieved when Paul made his debut on the dance floor. 'He is a very handsome child,' reported the dutiful Sir Robert Keith, 'and dances wonderfully well for one of his age.'[18] The Court was glad to see the little boy dance with his mother at the coronation day ceremony. By then, Catherine's birthday banquet celebrations had been followed by an opera on 23 April, which the Georgian king much enjoyed. Pleased to have found an exotic potentate to patronise, Vorontsova told her daughter that it was 'impossible to believe how well he behaves!'[19]

On 11 May, Peter and Catherine travelled to Oranienbaum for what was probably their longest single spell of uninterrupted residence. Although they returned to Peterhof for Peter's name day celebrations at the end of June – and both Catherine and Peter subsequently made separate trips to see their son (in her case for not much more than an hour) – they were to remain 'in the country' until they moved back to the Winter Palace on 9 September.[20] Perhaps it was during this period of relative leisure that Catherine jotted down (or at any rate added to) a series of miscellaneous notes that give a sense of her developing political ideas and ambitions (though they cannot be dated precisely, the notes were made between February 1758 and February 1762, and the final one quotes a French periodical of March 1761).[21] Peace and prosperity were two obvious aims for an empire engaged in an exhausting European war. 'All I hope, all that I wish is that this country in which God has cast me should prosper. God is my witness to that. The glory of this country is my glory.' 'Peace is necessary to this vast empire; we need population, not devastation; we need to populate our great empty spaces as much as possible.' A passage in Bielfeld's Cameralist *Political Instruction* prompted her to reflect on the benefits of enlightened toleration: 'To do nothing without principle or without reason, not to allow one to be led by prejudice, to respect religion, but not to give it any power in State matters, to banish everything that reeks of fanaticism and to draw the best out of every situation for the public good, is the basis of the Chinese Empire, the most durable of all those known on this earth.' A strong sense of justice emerges, prompted by the treatment meted out to Bestuzhev: 'All my life I will remain hostile to the idea of establishing a secret Committee of Inquiry to judge a guilty man. An open trial, the judgement of the Senate, as in France and England, where a peer is tried by his peers, is the only solution.' There was also a strong note of idealism: 'It is against justice and the Christian religion to make slaves out of men, born to be free.'[22]

By the summer of 1761, Catherine was pregnant again, this time by a new lover, Grigory Orlov, the virile guards officer who was to remain by her side until 1773. Wounded at the battle of Zorndorf, Grigory had returned from the war with a reputation for valour. We do not know when their affair began, but here was a type who would subsequently attract her again and again. Though he could boast none of Poniatowski's intellectual accomplishments, Grigory seemed willing to learn (he too was interested in astronomy) and keen to listen to her ideas. As her political ambitions developed, she may well have chosen him for his military connections – he and his four brothers, all gallant and popular officers, could support her in good times and bad. And the Orlovs were not the only people Catherine had begun to cultivate. Nikita Panin, a protégé of Bestuzhev who had survived his master's disgrace and remained on terms with the Vorontsovs during his twelve years as ambassador to Sweden, had returned to St Petersburg in 1760 to take charge of her son's education and allowed her to see more of him than she had previously been able to do. Another occasional visitor to Oranienbaum was Princess Dashkova, a potential source of intelligence on the whole Vorontsov clan.[23]

While Catherine kept out of sight in the country, an increasingly breathless Elizabeth was left to cope with the heat of the summer in St Petersburg. After lunch on 26 May, she drove out to watch the fire that blazed all day in Meshchanskaya Street.[24] June brought the prospect of more pleasurable excursions, as she travelled first to Peter Shuvalov's estate at Pargolovo and then to Peterhof, reliving the old days by dining in Aleksey Razumovsky's rooms while hunting horns serenaded them outside. After another excursion a few days later, it was three in the morning before she returned from Monplaisir, the seaside pavilion at Peterhof. Such a regime was bound to alarm the medics. Dr Condoidi, Elizabeth's Greek physician, himself died of apoplexy the previous August, being replaced by the Scot, James Mounsey, and Dr Schilling. Karl Kruse joined them in June 1761. 'We are rich in doctors here,' Countess Vorontsova told her daughter.[25]

In mid-July 'the Empress caused great anxiety to all her Court' with 'an attack of the hysterical vapours and convulsions which knocked her unconscious for several hours'.[26] It was the beginning of the end. Now that Elizabeth's horizons were shrinking, there was no great ceremony or banquet at the end of August for the knights of the Order of St Alexander Nevsky. Back in St Petersburg, she took her meals at a round table in a corner room of the Summer Palace, overlooking the Fontanka. She still found the energy for the occasional visit to Ivan Shuvalov, but was always back by 10 p.m. The banquet and ball, hosted by Peter and Catherine on Paul's birthday, went ahead without her. After the Court's return to the temporary Winter Palace two days later, the grand ducal couple hosted the Court receptions, too. Elizabeth celebrated with Catherine in the great chapel for the first time that autumn on 26 October to give thanks for the capture of Troppau by Field Marshal Buturlin. On 13 November, they both attended a French comedy. It proved to be the empress's last appearance in public. Only the grand duchess and her son attended the ball on her name day. It was over by eleven. Though the following day, 25 November, was the empress's accession day, the greatest day in the Court calendar, Elizabeth remained closeted in her apartments. Despite the customary 101-gun salute, the servants wore only standard livery. Banquet, music and fanfares were all cancelled on her birthday, 18 December, though there was a salute after the end of the morning liturgy attended on the empress's behalf by Catherine alone.[27]

Mikhail Vorontsov tried to forestall rumours in Europe by sending a circular to the Russian ambassadors on 19 December:

> For several days, all Her Imperial Majesty's faithful subjects have been in a state of general sadness and wild alarm on account of an illness deriving from a fever which at first seemed dangerous because Her Majesty, out of a natural aversion to doctors, was reluctant to see one, and her blood was so inflamed that it caused her to vomit. But as result of two bleedings administered over three days, the fever has so far dropped and the illness so far changed for the better this seventh day of the crisis, that, thank God, the misery into which we were all plunged is now transformed into ravishing transports of joy by the great hope we have that with the aid of Divine Providence, the Empress will soon entirely recover her precious health.[28]

He was hoping against hope. By the time the ambassadors received his message, it was already too late. The Court journal for Elizabeth's reign falls silent on 24 December. She died the next day.

In the event, all Catherine's dreams of seizing the throne came to nothing. Pregnant and politically isolated, she could only stand by as the Shuvalovs and Vorontsovs ensured that all Russia proclaimed the advent of Tsar Peter III – and she became his empress.

———

By the time of her husband's accession, he and Catherine had long been leading separate lives. In that sense, little now changed. The thirty-four-year-old tsar rose at seven and gave his first orders of the day while dressing. By eight, he was in his study to hear the Procurator-General, Alexander Glebov, deliver his reports. Occasionally Peter visited government offices unannounced to keep negligent officials on their toes. Regularly at eleven, he inspected the parade in the square outside the palace. Although he called on his new empress most mornings, they rarely dined together.[29] While she ate with senior courtiers, he preferred to eat with Elizabeth Vorontsova and carouse in the company of Prince Georg Ludwig, the very same uncle who had courted Catherine twenty years earlier and was greeted with great pomp on his arrival at the military encampment Krasnoye Selo on 23 January and later lodged at Ivan Shuvalov's palace.[30] Even on ceremonial occasions, the imperial couple played roles that kept them apart. At the Blessing of the Waters at Epiphany – a ritual revived in all its splendour at the beginning of the new reign – Catherine followed the icon procession to the Jordan on the Moika while the tsar emulated his hero Peter the Great by riding at the head of his troops.[31] Though they were unavoidably brought together for the funeral procession of Peter Shuvalov, which they watched from the balcony of the Stroganov Palace on 21 January, the tsar arrived late and there was little contact between them.[32]

Though Shuvalov's funeral was exactly the sort of elaborate ritual that Elizabeth despised, the most extravagant obsequies were reserved for the late empress herself. The day after her death, the tsar allocated 100,000 roubles to the newly appointed funeral commission which met daily at the mansion of the disgraced Chancellor Bestuzhev. The commission established after Anna's death in 1740 offered the most recent precedent, though it was not to be emulated in every respect. Almost 45,000 roubles of its total budget of 65,000 had been spent on velvet, taffeta and other fabrics, to the neglect of the corpse itself: 'She had lain in state for a month,' a British visitor remarked, 'but not having been rightly embalmed was almost fallen to pieces before her burial.'[33] Now, while work went ahead 'day and night' on Jacob Stählin's designs for an allegorical chamber of mourning in the wooden Winter Palace and an elaborate catafalque in the Peter-Paul Cathedral, leading courtiers gathered on the evening of Monday 14 January to convey the corpse to the stateroom where it was first displayed to the Court. Dressed in her favourite virginal white, the late empress was laid out on a *lit de parade* on a dais covered in white cloth under a canopy trimmed with gold. The walls of the room were also draped in white cloth edged with gold braid.[34]

On Friday 25 January, Elizabeth's corpse was transferred to lie in state in a second chamber of sorrows, where Stählin had gone to elaborate lengths to represent the Russian realm weeping at the tomb of its beloved ruler.[35] At two in the afternoon, the Captains of the Guard formed a new guard of honour in this much darker chamber, draped in black and adorned with festoons of silver brocade. Twelve Chevaliers Gardes placed the coffin, covered with a pall of gold cloth trimmed with Spanish lace, on a raised catafalque beneath a canopy emblazoned with the imperial crown. By its side stood four ladies-in-waiting, dressed in deep mourning, and entirely covered with crepe veils. Two officers, in full dress uniform, stood guard on the first step, while two archimandrites, standing at the foot of the coffin, took it in turn to read aloud from the Bible throughout the day and night.[36]

Yakov Shakhovskoy — a far from sentimental bureaucrat whose memoirs mention his wedding only as a temporary interruption to his work — was overcome with emotion at the sight of his late sovereign.[37] Bowing twice on approaching the corpse, which was now dressed in a silver gown, trimmed with lace sleeves, he joined the procession of Russians who prostrated themselves before it, or rather 'threw themselves face down on the ground in front of the bed' so violently that at least one foreign observer 'feared that they must fracture their skulls'.[38] 'There is a multiplicity of such customs,' the supercilious French ambassador reported, 'full of superstitions at which [Catherine] naturally laughs, but the clergy and the people have faith in her deep grieving over the deceased and rate her feelings very highly.'[39]

According to Pauzié, the Court jeweller, it was Catherine rather than the tsar who summoned him to this 'large room, lit by six thousand candles', where he helped her to place a gold crown on the swollen skull of the deceased. Since Pauzié had 'taken the precaution of placing several screws in the band that gripped the forehead', he was able to use his tweezers to make the crown big enough to fit. But it was not a pleasant operation. 'Despite all the incense and fragrance, the smell of the corpse was so strong that I could hardly stand near it. However, the empress bore all this with amazing fortitude and in this way completely won over the hearts of her subjects.'[40]

Peter made no secret of his impatience with such rituals and visibly chafed against them. Courtiers had been shocked to discover that deep mourning was not immediately prescribed when the empress died.[41] Scarcely had the corpse been transferred to its second chamber of rest than Peter ordered them to abandon mourning dress altogether on future Sundays and feast days. That night, 27 January, he and Catherine dined with Prince Trubetskoy, returning to the palace at three and two in the morning respectively.[42] On Monday 4 February, the tsar was taken incognito to inspect the final preparations at the Peter-Paul Cathedral, promising further funds to ensure that the spectacle lacked nothing in magnificence. (The funeral commission's outstanding expenses of 74,000 roubles were ultimately paid by Catherine shortly after her own accession.) While he spent the evening drinking with Prince Georg until three in the morning, his wife, now six months pregnant with Orlov's child, remained in her apartments in order to be at her most demure for the next day's funeral.[43]

Following a pattern established after her father's death in 1725, Elizabeth's coffin was borne with great pomp to its burial place on the far side of the frozen Neva, where, between the cathedral's four main pillars, Stählin had created a Temple of Sorrow and Remembrance with a life-size half-length portrait of the late empress.[44] The capital's bells began to toll at ten as troops lined the route of the procession. Three hundred guardsmen led the way, followed by an even larger number of priests, processing two by two and chanting hymns. Behind them, in single file, came the gentlemen of the Court, wearing the uniforms of the various orders of chivalry, and each attended by a chamberlain. A single cavalier, armed from head to toe, rode ahead of the coffin on a stately charger held by two equerries. Released from captivity in the fortress by the pro-Prussian Tsar Peter, Count Hård was there to observe the scene:

> The coffin, placed on a sort of chariot, drawn by eight horses and adorned with black velvet festoons, was covered with a black cloth pall richly trimmed with Spanish silver-point lace. A canopy made from the same materials was carried by Generals and Senators, accompanied by several officers of the guards. The Emperor followed immediately behind the coffin, wearing a large black cloak carried by twelve chamberlains, each holding a wax taper in his hand. Prince Georg of Holstein followed the Emperor as his nearest relation; then came the Prince of Holstein-Beck. The Empress followed also on foot, holding a burning taper and clad in a robe carried by all her maids of honour. Three hundred grenadiers brought up the rear of the procession.[45]

Nothing could sound more solemn. Yet, according to Catherine, the tsar behaved in typically unseemly fashion. Irrepressibly cheerful throughout, he indulged in childish games, first lagging behind the hearse and then charging across the ice to catch it up, much to the embarrassment of the courtiers deputed to carry his train. When Count Sheremetev could no longer keep hold of it, it blew about in the wind to Peter's intense amusement.[46]

'Everyone dined privately that day,' Hård recalled, 'and spent the evening in privacy, as if their grief and affliction had been real. But from the following day, no more was said or thought of Elizabeth, than if she had never existed. Such is ever the fate of things in this world: every thing passes; everything is forgotten.'[47] As if to prove his point, the Court travelled to Tsarskoye Selo a mere three days after the funeral to celebrate the tsar's thirty-fourth birthday in style. Before the first dinner in the Picture Gallery, he invested Anna Vorontsova with the Order of St Catherine and announced that Yelena Naryshkina was to take her place as senior lady-in-waiting. In the ensuing banquets, he sat next to Princess Golitsyna and Countess Bruce. Catherine, having travelled separately from St Petersburg, remained in her apartments throughout the weekend, apparently oblivious as the first fireworks to be set off since Elizabeth's death exploded all around her.[48]

Conscious that the new empress had been isolated from the beginning of Peter's reign, diplomats soon realised that she was entirely without influence. The disappointed Austrian ambassador, who had hoped to use her to undermine the tsar's admiration for all things Prussian, assumed that her 'calm exterior' must conceal 'some sort of secret undertakings'. But he had little hope of a plot maturing because, despite her obvious intelligence, Catherine seemed too impetuous to lead a successful conspiracy: 'she lacks caution and fundamental sense, and her somewhat arrogant and lively nature will prevent her from following a premeditated plan'.[49] She, not surprisingly, remembered things differently, telling Poniatowski soon after her accession that the coup had been 'planned for the last six months'. Yet even if it was true that 'propositions' had been made to Catherine from the time of Elizabeth's death, there was little that she could have done to challenge her husband before Easter.[50] For one thing, she was pregnant. For another, the new tsar initially seemed to promise greater things than his detractors had anticipated.

For all his boorishness, Peter was the first adult male to ascend the Russian throne for more than a century. That in itself was cause for widespread jubilation. Further good news followed in February, when he issued an edict emancipating the nobility from the compulsory state service enforced by Peter the Great. Though this was one of the most significant pieces of legislation in eighteenth-century Russia, it is surprisingly difficult to be sure of its origins. Prince Shcherbatov famously claimed that the tsar had locked Dimitry Volkov, one of Elizabeth's leading officials, into a palace stateroom with a great dane and told him to come up with something important overnight while he went off to carouse with Princess Kurakina:

Not knowing the reason for this or what the monarch had in mind, Volkov did not know what to begin writing. But write he must. Being an enterprising man, he remembered the frequent exhortations made by Count Roman Larionovich Vorontsov to the monarch, concerning the freedom of the nobility. Sitting down, he wrote out the manifesto concerning this. In the morning he was released from confinement, and the manifesto was approved by the monarch and promulgated.[51]

Though we cannot be sure precisely how the final compromise was negotiated, or how difficult it was to reach it, the manifesto seems actually to have emerged from a spectrum of interests in Peter's new government, all of which had deeper roots in Elizabeth's reign. Roman Vorontsov was indeed anxious to secure noble property interests in an expanding land market, but his interests had to be balanced against those of the Shuvalovs, who took a more favourable view of the merchants. In the event, the nobles were denied a monopoly of serf ownership and immunity from corporal punishment (privileges that were ultimately confirmed by Catherine's own Charter to the Nobility in 1785), but granted the option of serving voluntarily – no great sacrifice for a government which could already rely on a flourishing central bureaucracy and now wanted nobles to return to their provincial estates.[52] Whatever the precise balance of forces, the decree seemed to presage a more considered approach to government than the tsar's earlier behaviour had led people to expect. As Catherine's first English biographer put it: 'The grand duke had been inconsistent, impetuous and wild: Peter III now shewed himself equitable, patient, and enlightened.'[53]

Easter, however, marked a turning point in the fortunes of both the tsar and his consort. One of Peter's first acts on his accession had been to inspect Rastrelli's stone Winter Palace, whose construction had been delayed by the Seven Years' War. As he and Catherine made another visit on 19 February, workmen laboured day and night to allow them to move in at the end of Lent. With the snow swirling all around, the tsar made a final inspection on Tuesday 2 April, decreeing that everything be made ready for the following Saturday.[54] It was a tall order. A vast swathe of land, stretching south towards the Moika and west beyond the Admiralty, was still a building site, home to a small army of craftsmen housed in primitive wooden shacks, and festooned with the debris of an eight-year construction project. The authorities solved their problem in characteristically imaginative fashion by allowing the populace to take whatever they liked: thousands of scavengers swarmed towards the palace, denuding the surrounding area of timber, stones, bricks, tar and all manner of valuable building materials. The site having been miraculously cleared, Peter duly took possession of his new residence on 6 April.[55]

No ceremony was shown: the tsar entered the palace incognito and only the firing of the guns announced that he had done so. But it was a different story in the week that followed, as celebration followed celebration. There could hardly have been better cover for the final stages of Catherine's pregnancy. On Thursday of Easter week she gave birth to a boy – named Aleksey Grigoryevich in acknowledgement of the paternity of Grigory Orlov – who was promptly spirited away. Peter, who may never have known of his wife's pregnancy (conveniently concealed by the mourning dress she wore throughout his reign), was irritated to discover that she was too ill to attend the banquet in honour of the peace with Prussia held on 29 April, less than three weeks after the birth. While that celebration had to be turned into a men-only affair, the tsar determined to hold another as soon as the ratification papers had been exchanged.[56]

Before he learned of Elizabeth's death, Frederick had begun the New Year nervous of a Russian attack on Berlin and anxious that Europe would self-combust into a general war within six months.[57] The accession of a pro-Prussian tsar in St Petersburg offered the unexpected prospect of delivery for his war-torn state. To escape from his 'moment of great crisis', the king had been unwilling to oppose Peter's ambition to recapture Schleswig for Holstein by invading Denmark. 'There is nothing more pressing for us,' he had written at the end of January, 'than to achieve a prompt reconciliation with Russia to pull us back from the edge of the precipice.' To hinder Peter's plans was to 'risk embittering him and spoiling everything right from the start'.[58] Paradoxically, it would be the tsar who ultimately suffered most from the apparent encouragement of his Prussian hero. Secure in the knowledge that Frederick would not stand in his way, he launched into rash plans to attack the Danes.

Catherine and her friends had aspirations of their own. Left alone since February, when her husband had been appointed as ambassador to Constantinople after a public altercation with the tsar, Princess Dashkova had had plenty of time to mull over her plans for a revolution. It was in April that she later claimed to have begun to sound out contacts in the capital – and it is possible that she did, since the Austrian ambassador reported her in mid-May as an 'intriguer who likes to meddle in affairs'.[59] The signs could hardly have been more promising. If only 'the desire of making improvements' had not made Peter III 'imprudently hazard premature reformations', he might have achieved so much more.[60] As it was, most of the political capital his government had gained by emancipating the nobility was dissipated by more impetuous measures that undermined the security of the governing elite. By substituting his Holsteiners for Elizabeth's trusty Life Guards, and forcing haughty courtiers such as Prince Trubetskoy to parade in front of the Winter Palace at eleven o'clock each morning, Peter ruptured his relationship with the highest civil and military officers. By depriving the Senate of its powers of patronage over lesser government offices and formally forbidding it to declare laws in its own name, he launched 'something in the nature of a constitutional revolution'. And by determining to confiscate the Church's lands in a series of edicts beginning on 21 March, he had alienated the clergy and left himself open to the charge of being an alien ruler determined to undermine the foundations of Russian culture.[61]

Such changes seemed all the more unnerving against a background of financial crisis. Although Russia's annual deficit, having peaked at 3.6 million roubles in 1748, had been reduced to something nearer 1.25 million by 1755, the Seven Years' War had put the treasury under intolerable strain. By the autumn of 1760, no further funds could be found to support a campaign that had already cost some 40 million roubles; a year later Russian troops were owed more than 1.5 million in arrears and deserters were causing havoc with arson and theft. In these circumstances, peace with Prussia was not so much an act of homage to Frederick as a financial necessity.[62] Peter's ministers planned imaginatively for financial reform. But since their measures could only be expected to bear fruit in the medium term (as indeed they did, much to Catherine's subsequent benefit), the short-term options were limited. Since no Russian bid to borrow on the Amsterdam finance markets had yet succeeded, the tsar had more than 2 million roubles minted.[63] But once the Senate learned on 23 May that the deficit stood at 1.1 million, Peter's plan to attack Denmark could hardly be countenanced. A week later, the ten-man council of war, claiming to speak 'on behalf of the nation', unanimously recommended him to reconsider. Even advisers who had initially urged him on were now, as the British ambassador reported, 'throwing pitchforks into the fire to stop the Emperor from going'.[64]

It was at this point, according to his own account, that Nikita Panin began to plan for a bloodless coup. As a former ambassador to Stockholm, the idea of attacking Denmark was particularly abhorrent to him, and everything in Peter's emerging style of government seemed to echo the arbitrary elements of Elizabeth's reign that Panin, a confirmed constitutionalist, was anxious to supersede. Expert in the art of political bribery as a result of his time in Sweden, he set out to buy support for Catherine.[65] Meanwhile, as if to prove that he remained his own worst enemy, Tsar Peter risked further obloquy by publicly humiliating the empress at the second banquet in honour of the peace with Prussia on 9 June. Having placed himself at some distance from his consort in order to sit opposite the Prussian ambassador, he lost his temper when she failed to rise for the toast to the Imperial family (among whom she had in all innocence included herself). Yelling across the table that she was 'a fool', Peter reduced Catherine to floods of tears. This incident understandably caused 'a great sensation in the city'. After it, as Dashkova recalled, 'sympathy for the empress grew in proportion to contempt for her husband'.[66] Barely a week after the coup that soon followed, Sumarokov highlighted the event in his ode on her accession, in which Catherine's tears were made to symbolise the consternation of the whole Russian nation.[67]

By her own subsequent testimony, it was this public humiliation that persuaded Catherine herself to 'lend an ear' to the treasonous plots developing all around her.[68] When Peter, who had never been blessed with sensitive political antennae, departed for Oranienbaum on 12 June, she was left in St Petersburg for a further five days, in constant touch with Dashkova, Grigory Orlov and Panin. It was then that their conspiracy began to take shape.

'If all leaders of conspiracies were to admit how much chance and opportunity had contributed to the success of their various ventures,' Dashkova later observed, 'they would have to descend from a very high scaffold.'[69] She, however, showed little sign of modesty in a notoriously self-serving account that attributed all the major initiatives of Catherine's coup to her own zeal and ingenuity. In fact, she knew nothing of her friend's relationship with Grigory Orlov. He himself apparently took little part in the plotting, fearful that the tsar was having him watched. His brother, Aleksey, was more active in recruiting forty or so of his fellow Guards officers. Though his allegiances remain uncertain, the chief of police, Baron Korf, may also have been at least a tacit supporter. Having once been a firm ally of the tsar, he began to pay more attention to Catherine in June, and his subordinates did nothing to prevent the coup that they were obviously expecting.[70]

Having initially determined to arrest Peter when he returned to St Petersburg to depart for the Danish campaign, the plotters were thrown into action earlier than they had expected when careless talk led to the arrest of one of their supporters, Captain Passek. At dawn on the morning of 28 June, Aleksey Orlov woke Catherine at Peterhof, where Peter was expected later that day to prepare for his name day celebrations. According to her own account, they drove at speed towards St Petersburg. Met by Grigory along the way, they made straight for the barracks of the Izmailovsky Guards where Catherine was immediately proclaimed empress and sovereign of all the Russias. From there, Kirill Razumovsky took her to the Semënovsky Regiment's barracks where they were joined by the Preobrazhensky Guards. The Horse Guards soon followed as Catherine made her way to the Kazan Church where she was again proclaimed sovereign by the clergy. It was barely ten in the morning when she reached the Winter Palace, where Paul, brought from the Summer Palace in his nightclothes by Nikita Panin, was displayed from a balcony to the cheering crowds while Archbishop Dimitry (Sechënov) circulated among the soldiers to administer the oath of loyalty.

By their swift action, the Orlovs had ruthlessly undercut any attempt on Panin's part to have Catherine rule as regent for her son. Now it remained to secure her throne. Although sentries were posted across the city on 30 June to prevent drunken brawls, there was surprisingly little violence in St Petersburg, where quantities of alcohol released from the taverns made the atmosphere seem festive rather than vengeful among soldiers thankful not to be sent to invade Denmark.[71] Instead they attacked the house of the unpopular Prince Georg Ludwig. For Johann Georg Eisen, a Lutheran pastor resident there thanks to the prince's support for his Enlightened agricultural reforms, it was a deeply unnerving experience. 'Those were such days,' wrote Eisen after his return to Estland, 'that the Last Judgment cannot appear any worse. I got back as if saved from a great fire.'[72]

'They who plan a conspiracy', Tooke remarked, 'have always more zeal, more vigilance and activity, than he against whom it is directed.'[73] So it proved in the case of Peter III. For twenty-four hours he remained at Oranienbaum, unaware that he had been overthrown. Only when he found Peterhof deserted on the morning of 29 June did he begin to realise the scale of the disaster. Had the tsar been made of sterner stuff, he might have marched on the capital, as he was urged to do by Field Marshal Münnich, a veteran of Empress Anna's war against the Turks in 1735–9 and the most distinguished of the exiles he had released from Siberia. But since Peter was no hero, this option was rapidly dismissed. Neither was he a coward, however, so he refused to flee to Mitau. Instead, he determined to sail to Kronstadt. Yet for once caution got the better of him, so that by the time he arrived the fortress had fallen to the rebels. When the tsar identified himself to a sentry at the blockaded entrance to the harbour, he was told that Peter III no longer existed. Having successfully repelled his 'guest', Admiral Talyzin wrote anxiously to Panin, asking for reinforcements.[74] He need not have worried. Whatever resolve Peter may initially have possessed had gone. As his galley returned to Oranienbaum, he fainted into the arms of Elizabeth Vorontsova.

Catherine had meanwhile borrowed a Guards uniform, mounted her charger and ridden out with Dashkova to arrest her deposed husband. At the Trinity monastery, on the road to Peterhof, she met the vice chancellor, Prince Alexander Golitsyn, who presented a letter in which Peter offered to negotiate. The missive went without reply as Golitsyn swore allegiance to Catherine. Peter now offered to abdicate in return for safe passage to Holstein with his mistress. After this offer, too, had been refused, he was persuaded to sign an unconditional abdication. At first, he was taken with Vorontsova to Peterhof, where he was arrested after surrendering his sword, and transferred to his country estate, Ropsha. Here he was intended to remain in the custody of Aleksey Orlov, Fëdor Baryatynsky and Peter Passek, until the Schlüsselburg fortress was ready to receive him.

After his first restless night at Ropsha, Peter complained of headaches and wrote a pathetic letter to Catherine, asking her to remove the sentries from the neighbouring room since his own was so small and he was too fastidious to relieve himself in the presence of others. '[Your Majesty] knows that I always pace about in my room. This will make my legs swell up.' That day, 30 June, his favourite bed was brought from Oranienbaum to make him more comfortable. Catherine, however, had no intention of granting his request to be taken to Holstein. As she later explained to Poniatowski, 'he had everything he wanted, except for his freedom'.[75] They made an odd couple, the giant, scar-faced Aleksey Orlov, and the shrivelled, sickly emperor. Only copious quantities of alcohol obscured the artificiality of their situation. This was fully revealed on 2 July, when Peter's health took a turn for the worse. As Orlov reported to Catherine, 'our ugly freak' had fallen 'seriously ill' with 'an unexpected colic'. 'I fear that he might die tonight, but I fear even more that he might live through it. The first fear is caused by the fact that he talks nonsense all the time, which amuses us, and the second fear is that he is really a danger to us all and behaves as though nothing had happened.'[76]

The note of menace was unmistakeable. According to the Danish diplomat

Andreas Schumacher, the end was swift. After refusing a poisoned cocktail made up by Dr Kruse, Peter was murdered on 3 July, so that he was dead by the time Dr Lüders reached Ropsha, and the only remaining job for a medic was the dissection performed by a second physician.[77] The villains of the piece in this version of Peter's demise are Grigory Teplov and Nikita Panin. Indeed, a prominent Russian historian has recently argued on the basis of Schumacher's account that Panin ordered the deposed tsar's murder as a last-ditch attempt to wrest the initiative from Catherine and the Orlovs and to ensure that she ruled as regent for her son.[78]

Ingenious as this reconstruction of events may be, its central assumption remains incredible. Why should Panin, the urbane constitutionalist who had been anxious all along to ensure a bloodless transition of power, suddenly sanction Peter's assassination? It is no more likely that Catherine herself gave explicit orders to kill him. She had proved herself audacious in a crisis, but there was nothing to be gained from making a martyr of her husband. Though a third letter from Aleksey Orlov to Catherine, dated 5 July, survives only in the form of a later copy, there seems no reason to disbelieve its claim that Peter was killed in a drunken scuffle:

> Little Mother, most gracious lady, How can I explain or describe what happened. You will not believe your faithful servant but before God I speak the truth. … Little Mother, he is no more. But it never occurred to anyone, how could anyone think of raising a hand against our sovereign lord. But Sovereign lady, the deed is done. He started struggling with Prince Fëdor [Baryatynsky] at table. We had no time to separate them and he is no more. I don't remember what we did but all of us are guilty and worthy of punishment. Have mercy upon me if only for my brother's sake. I confess it all to you, and there is nothing to investigate. Forgive us, or order an end to be made quickly. Life is not worth living. We have angered you, and lost our souls forever.[79]

Catherine accepted his word. She may not have sanctioned her husband's death, but his survival would surely have imperilled hers. Now she was not only a usurper, but an assassin by association. Peter was given a paltry burial at the Alexander Nevsky monastery. Thirty-four years later, Tsar Paul would make Orlov, Baryatynsky and Passek pay dearly for their treachery. But for the moment, their star was in the ascendant, as Russia's new ruler laid plans for her coronation and for the burst of reforming legislation that was to occupy the first five years of her reign.

CHAPTER SIX

'OUR LADY OF ST PETERSBURG'
1763–1766

A few days before Catherine's return to St Petersburg in the summer of 1763, the foreign ambassadors gathered for supper at the house of the Earl of Buckinghamshire. 'We were all questioning one another, each man doubtful of his own information, yet everyone agreeing that we ought to be prepared for any event.' Convinced from the start of the new regime's inherent instability, they were sure they could scent its imminent collapse. The French attaché and the Austrian ambassador interpreted the desecration of the empress's portrait on one of Moscow's triumphal arches as a symptom of the wider unrest generated by rumours that she was about to marry Grigory Orlov.[1] Catherine herself had unwittingly caused the scare by seeking official approval for a second marriage in case her sickly son died. One supporter of her coup, the Guards Captain Fëdor Khitrovo, was so appalled by the idea that he planned to kill Grigory and his brothers. Arrested at the end of May, Khitrovo caused alarm by claiming that he had been told by Aleksey Orlov that Catherine had accepted the throne only under pressure from his brothers, having initially promised Panin that she would rule as regent for Grand Duke Paul.[2] Though Khitrovo was quietly bundled away to his estates, in a vain attempt to avoid publicity, the security cordon erected in a six-mile radius around Tsarskoye Selo struck the diplomats as a sign of Catherine's lasting nervousness. The Prussian ambassador Count Solms in turn thought her too frantic in her rush to reform. Now that she had quarrelled with Princess Dashkova – 'the sort of woman to attempt a new revolution every week, purely for the pleasure of it' – Solms feared that her reign would last no longer than her husband's. Buckinghamshire was inclined to agree: 'I cannot help feeling for Her Imperial Majesty. Her present distress must be very great, and at the best, Her future prospect a most melancholy one.'[3]

If Catherine shared any of these concerns – and it is difficult to imagine that they wholly escaped her – then she was careful to give no sign of it. Optimistic by nature, she spent her final week in Moscow cementing her links with favoured courtiers by touring their country estates. On 7 June, after lunch at Znamenskoye with the Chief Cup-Bearer, Alexander Naryshkin, she took a stroll through the garden to see the museum where her host preserved a treasured yacht built before the foundation of the Russian fleet in the early 1690s. From there, it was but a short journey to inspect the troops on exercise in the neighbouring fields. Having dined at Pokrovskoye with the Master of the Horse, Lev Naryshkin, she returned to her palace along a route illuminated by extravagant fireworks. Two days later, she drove out to Tsar Boris's ponds, eight miles from the city centre, where she kissed the icons in the local church before watching the fishing. Then it was Peter Sheremetev's turn to entertain her at Kuskovo, one of Russia's most opulent estates, where a magnificent orangery was currently under construction. They sailed on the lake before playing cards; it was two in the morning before she got back to Moscow. There was still time for a final afternoon's hawking before the Court departed for Tsarskoye Selo on Saturday 14 June. After a journey punctuated by the customary visits to churches and monasteries, it was one of Catherine's first priorities to check on the progress of her new dacha at Oranienbaum, where she travelled 'with the smallest possible entourage' on 25 June.[4]

Any residual anxieties were masked by her ceremonial re-entry into the capital on Saturday 28 June, the first anniversary of Catherine's accession. There could hardly have been a greater public display of self-confidence.[5] Bathed in the cool glow of the midsummer 'white nights', more than 11,000 soldiers lined the streets to salute the procession. As her open carriage rolled over the Obukhov bridge at 7 p.m., three cannon fired to signal the start of a carillon across the city. Seventy-one guns roared from the Admiralty and seventy more from the Peter and Paul fortress as the empress and her Court were led past the cheering crowds by a detachment of mounted cavalry. In the Haymarket, at the junction of Pea Street and Garden Street, Savva Yakovlev, an ennobled merchant of fabulous wealth, had hoisted a crown onto the main cupola of his new Church of the Dormition to mark the completion of the exterior in the year of her coronation.[6] When the procession reached the Kazan Church, Catherine descended from her carriage to meet Archbishop Gavriil and paused briefly for prayers while seminarians from the Alexander Nevsky monastery chanted salutations from platforms raised on either side of the great door. Her emergence from the church triggered a second, longer salute as she continued along the Great Perspective Road to meet the city's merchants, who turned out in force at Gostiny dvor, a vast covered market. At the Anichkov Palace, it was the turn of Prince Nikolay Repnin and the Cadet Corps to greet her. Only when she reached the Summer Palace did a final 101-gun salute issue from the fortresses. Three times the cry went up: 'Vivat, Yekaterina: Great Empress!' Then she passed inside to permit the foreign diplomats assembled in the throne room to kiss her hand. [7]

After dining alone, Catherine emerged from her apartments just before midnight to stroll through the Summer Gardens to the riverbank where Colonel Melissino was ready to set off one of Jacob Stählin's most extravagant firework displays. The first rockets went up as soon as she had taken her place in a baroque wooden gallery, built in short order by carpenters from the Admiralty College according to designs sent up from Moscow. [8] 'Vigilance and Virtue' was the theme of the first scene, set in the temple of Pallas, where the goddess fired thunderbolts from her perch in the clouds, brandishing in her left hand a sceptre with the Russian coat of arms and in her right the head of Medusa to ward off her enemies. 'Glory' was the slogan emblazoned on a temple flanked by allegorical figures of Wisdom and Courage; 'Astonishment' the name of an obelisk celebrating Catherine's prowess as a female sovereign. No sooner had the smoke from this first tableau cleared than the scene changed to reveal a forest of luxuriant palm trees on 'the island of scholarship and amusement'. This time the subject was 'Wisdom and Clemency' and the empress was represented as Minerva, the helmeted goddess of wisdom. [9] Even the hostile French attaché had to concede that the whole evening had been 'a very brilliant and well organised spectacle'. [10] And no one could miss its central message: here was a ruler whose maternal gentleness was not to be mistaken for weakness. On the contrary, she had every intention of deploying knowledge and reason in the service of her formidable empire.

Proud and imperturbable in public, Catherine was well aware of the scale of the challenge she faced in restoring order and prosperity to her empire in the aftermath of the Seven Years' War. In the wake of that gruelling conflict, every state in Europe faced a period of tough internal consolidation. Russia was no exception. Over the next few years, Catherine would write several memoranda bemoaning the legacy she had inherited: 'the fleet was derelict, the army in disarray, the fortresses collapsing'; the treasury was in arrears, though no one could tell her by how much; the prisons were overflowing (she secretly arranged for minor debtors to be released); corrupt officials were everywhere despised; and parts of the countryside were in open revolt.[11] No state could have survived for long the massive peasant unrest that characterised Catherine's early years on the throne.[12] Fortunately for her, most Russian peasants had more to gain from violence against each other than from risky attempts to overthrow the authorities. Once the major incidents had been summarily put down, the empress turned her mind to more fundamental change. Although serfdom was far too integral to Russian political culture to allow for wholesale emancipation of the serfs, an audience with Pastor Eisen in October 1763 may have persuaded her to try out his controversial ideas for a free, property-owning peasantry on the crown estate at Bronnaya, beyond Oranienbaum. Though it ultimately proved too small for the purpose, Eisen soon discovered that the greatest obstacle to imperial initiatives was presented by officials hostile to change. 'Not only has Hell in its entirety opened up against me,' he told a fellow pastor in January 1764, 'but devilish extraordinary chance events have occurred which have really put me in the firing line. If the ground underneath me were not so secure, I should long since have broken my neck.'[13]

One excuse offered to Eisen in explanation of the delays was that Catherine was too busy with other projects to attend to his own. There was some truth in that. No sooner had she seized the throne than the pace was set for a sustained burst of reforming energy which on average saw almost twice as many edicts issued each month between 1762 and 1767 as in the reign as a whole.[14] Since her main aim was to change her subjects' hearts and minds, popular education – a subject all the rage in Europe in the wake of Rousseau's *Emile* (1762) – was at the forefront of her priorities. Over the next few years, she commissioned a wide range of projects, many of which drew on the interest in the subject that had flourished in Russia since the end of the previous decade. Daniel Dumaresq, a former chaplain to the British Factory in St Petersburg, returned in 1764 bearing information about a variety of English and Irish institutions, ranging from Moravian boarding schools to the dormitories at Eton. He was personally acquainted with Catherine and spent time with Grand Duke Paul while he devised a 'General Plan of Gymnasia', completed two years later.[15] By that time, however, Catherine had placed her trust in a rival scheme devised by her mother's old paramour, Ivan Betskoy. Authorised to admit destitute and illegitimate children without question, his Moscow Foundling Home, opened on her thirty-fifth birthday in

1764, was intended to foster the creation of a wholly 'new kind of people', raised in isolation from the damaging influence of a backward Russian environment according to an ambitious curriculum set out in Betskoy's *General Plan for the Education of Young People of Both Sexes*. This remarkable document envisaged nothing less than a new generation of Russians imbued with a high moral sense of duty to the fatherland and to their fellow men.[16] Betskoy believed that the empire's greatest need was for the sorts of artisan and craftsman who could supply the 'third estate' that Russia notoriously lacked. He drove the point home to Catherine by giving Paul a carpenter's bench for the Winter Palace, where a French master carpenter was employed to teach him.[17]

Females were to be catered for by the Society for the Education of Young Noblewomen (the Smolny Institute founded in May 1764), another experiment in social engineering designed to produce nothing less than 'a new type of mother in the form of cultured, industrious, proper young women who combined social graces with domesticity, and who would raise the general level of society through their upbringing of children'.[18] Like the foundling home, the Smolny was a charitable organisation rather than a government institution, in which both Catherine and Betskoy invested personal fortunes (his, of course, being ultimately derived from hers). The empress remained devoted to the Institute for the rest of her life, taking several favourite pupils under her wing.[19]

Central to the success of Catherine's various projects were three long-serving state secretaries: Adam Olsufyev, Grigory Teplov and Ivan Yelagin. Since they and their successors probably spent more time in the empress's company than anyone else, it was vital that each of them should know how to respond to her playful imperiousness. All three had demonstrated their loyalty to her during her difficult years as a grand duchess; all three knew how to get things done; and all three were cultivated men – precisely the sorts of educated and industrious individual that Catherine wanted to flourish in her Enlightened empire. They not only dealt with all her confidential business, but were also responsible for responding to the hundreds of petitions that flooded in despite her attempts to deter them (within a week of her coup, she had told the assembled Senate that no petitions whatsoever were to be presented to her in person).[20] In return, she offered them security and material rewards, and was characteristically solicitous for their personal wellbeing.

At the age of thirty-seven, Olsufyev had been chosen in 1758 to head Elizabeth's Closet (*Kabinet*), the personal office responsible for the distribution of imperial funds which acted as the tsars' principal point of contact with other government bodies. Once Catherine reappointed him on 8 July 1762, he was to remain at her side until his death in 1784. As a junior member of Chancellor Bestuzhev's staff, he had earned her lasting trust by helping her to conduct a secret correspondence with her mother in the 1750s. Now, fluent in several languages and generally acknowledged as one of the most erudite and capable men in Russia, he acted as a link between the palace, the College of Foreign Affairs and the Senate.[21]

Widely supposed to be the bastard child of Peter the Great's influential prelate, Feofan (Prokopovich), Teplov was actually the son of a smelter at the Novgorod episcopal palace, which was how he acquired his name, meaning 'warmth'. Aged forty-six when Catherine seized the throne, he had come to prominence by supervising the education of Kirill Razumovsky, touring Europe with him for two years and managing his business when he became president of the Academy of Sciences in 1746 and Ukrainian chieftain (*hetman*) four years later. A competent violinist like Olsufyev, Teplov had translated into Russian the libretti of several operas by Francesco Araja in the 1740s and 1750s. Teplov was also a talented amateur actor who published learned articles on poetics and was familiar with radical Western writings on materialism and atheism. Having been both cuckolded and imprisoned by Peter III, he had every reason to support Catherine's coup. It was Teplov who drafted the most important edicts in the first crucial days of her reign, when it was one of Olsufyev's first duties to pay him a reward of 20,000 roubles. After that, he became the moving force behind numerous major projects, including the reorganisation of the Medical Chancery (one of several reforms motivated by Catherine's determination to preserve and increase the population). He was intimately involved with Dumaresq's abortive plans for urban primary schools, having drawn up proposals for a university at the Ukrainian town of Baturin in 1760. Probably his most important role lay in the Commission on Church Lands, created in November 1762, which was responsible two years later for a wholesale secularisation of monastic property. Since this yielded the state an annual income of almost 1.37 million roubles, of which less than 463,000 was returned to the Church each year between 1764 and 1768, it is not surprising that he remained an influential presence in Catherine's government until his death in 1779.[22]

Ivan Yelagin, the last of the three secretaries to be appointed in July 1762, was another lifelong servant who was still at her side in 1793. Four years older than the empress, he had first encountered her in 1748 as an impoverished acolyte of Elizabeth's favourite, Aleksey Razumovsky. Ten years later, he suffered on Catherine's behalf when he was arrested with Bestuzhev as a friend and correspondent of Stanisław Poniatowski. Notable for his connections to English Masonic lodges, Yelagin was a leading light in Russian Freemasonry, a movement that Catherine held increasingly in contempt. On being shown one of his Masonic manuscripts after his death in 1794, she took it as evidence that her secretary had gone mad. But she always admired his loyalty. 'This was a man of probity whom one could trust,' the empress declared that same year. 'Once one had gained his affection, it was not easily lost; he always demonstrated zeal and a marked liking for me.'[23]

In September 1763, Catherine decided that Teplov should report on Mondays and Wednesdays, Olsufyev on Tuesdays and Thursdays, and Yelagin on Fridays and Saturdays.[24] By the time they arrived at her study at eight in the morning, she had already been up for two hours, writing and reading alone, having lit her own fire. Sketching her routine in a letter to Madame Geoffrin, she explained how a succession of secretaries and advisers trooped in one by one, keeping her busy until eleven, when she dressed for her first public appearance of the day (in the relative privacy of her own apartments Catherine wore a loose-fitting silk gown). On Sundays and feast days she attended mass in the palace chapel, after a vigil service in her rooms. Otherwise, she liked to wander into the Chevaliers Gardes' Room, where visitors lurked in the hope of catching her eye. Lunch was a relatively modest affair, sometimes eaten alone, but usually taken in the company of between ten and twenty courtiers. Since Catherine drank little and was frugal in her culinary tastes, it was by no means an experience to savour: seasoning was limited (pepper was not sold on the capital's markets, though it may have been supplied from the imperial greenhouses), and even some of St Petersburg's poorest people probably ate almost as nourishing food as their empress.[25] After lunch, she retreated to her own rooms, shuttling silken knots while Betskoy kept her company by reading aloud:

> Our reading, when it is not interrupted by parcels of letters and other nui-
> sances, lasts until half-past five, when I either go to the theatre, or I play, or I
> gossip to the first people to arrive before dinner, which is over before eleven
> when I retire to bed in order to do the same again on the following day. And all
> this is ruled out as regularly as musical manuscript paper.[26]

In practice, of course, her life was more varied than this jocular summary implied. The letter studiously avoided any mention of Grigory Orlov, whom she usually entertained after lunch – an hour that gossips were to dub 'the Time of

Mystery' for the rest of her reign.[27] Paul, who lived with his Young Court in a neighbouring part of the palace, was another regular visitor to her rooms, though she rarely spent as much as half an hour with him. He saw her early on Wednesday evenings or after church on Sunday mornings – both were Court reception days when the empress entertained not only her courtiers, but also foreign visitors to the city.[28] Hawking was still a favourite pastime, though Catherine's days in the saddle were all but over, and when the weather permitted, she enjoyed a carriage ride through the streets with a favourite lady-in-waiting. These, however, were distractions from a gruelling week at her desk.

Noticeably missing from the empress's working day was any collective meeting of her advisers. Although she had initially been tempted to accept Panin's proposal for an imperial council of between six and eight aristocrats, she soon rejected the idea as a potential limitation on her own absolute power. While Panin had made his suggestion in December 1762 as a way of preventing a recurrence of the arbitrary favouritism of Elizabeth's time, Catherine almost certainly suspected a bid to enhance his own influence at the expense of the Orlovs. Although the idea was quietly shelved, the membership of the Imperial Assembly, secretly formed in Moscow on 11 February 1763 to determine how to respond to Peter III's manifesto on the nobility, was much the same as Panin had projected for his council. Meeting some twenty-one times before the end of October with the ubiquitous Teplov as its secretary, this informal but highly influential body became, in effect, the Russian government. In a balanced representation of elite political interests, Panin and Grigory Orlov were joined by Bestuzhev, Kirill Razumovsky, Mikhail Vorontsov, Yakov Shakhovskoy and Zakhar Chernyshëv, whom Catherine had put in charge of the College of War. When the Court returned to St Petersburg, the Assembly extended its remit to consider a root-and-branch reform of the Senate, much as Panin had originally intended.[29] Catherine was delighted. At the time of her accession, she later complained, 'the Senate regarded it as excessive to hear state business with a map on the table in front of them', so that 'sometimes they did not know what they were judging. Shameful to say, there was not a single printed map in the Senate, and indeed, being present there, I sent for the first one to be bought from the Academy [of Sciences].' Always a scourge of laziness and inefficiency, she sent the Senators a long list of personal orders that they had failed to fulfil, insisting that they attend their office for four hours every morning and for three afternoons a week until the backlog had been cleared.[30]

In January 1764, Glebov was replaced as the Procurator-General of the Senate by Alexander Vyazemsky, who was to dominate the Russian bureaucracy until his death in 1792. The instruction Catherine sent to him on his appointment is rightly considered as 'one of the most important documents illustrating her conception of statecraft'. Ordering him to remain above and beyond factional conflict and to trust in her alone, she explained what he could expect in return:

> You will find that I have no other view than the greatest welfare and glory of the fatherland, and I wish for nothing but the happiness of my subjects, of whatever order they may be. All my thoughts are directed towards the preservation of external and internal peace, satisfaction and tranquillity. I am very fond of the truth, and you may tell me the truth fearlessly and argue with me without any danger if it leads to good results in affairs. I hear you are regarded as an honest man by all; I hope to show you by experience that people with such qualities do well at Court. And I may add that I require no flattery from you, but only honest behaviour and firmness in affairs.[31]

She was as good as her word. Conscious of the fate that had traditionally befallen most advisers of a disgraced monarch in Russia, Peter III's leading minister, Dimitry Volkov, assumed that his time had come. Yet he, too, found that he had nothing to fear. 'I am always delighted when I see a swift attitude to business and an earnest approach to service in my subjects,' Catherine assured him. 'When subjects wish to see an industrious and solicitous sovereign taking care of their interests, then the sovereign is no less happy to see her subjects helping her. Don't bother about your circumstances: just get on with the job, because your reasoning is good. Upright service will always rectify circumstances, of that you should have no doubt.'[32] Having proved his efficiency as governor of Orenburg, Volkov was recalled to St Petersburg in 1764 to take charge of the College of Manufactures, where he remained until retiring age. Long periods of office were to be the norm in the new reign, even for some of the families whose loyalty Catherine initially had reason to doubt. Since the pool of available talent was limited, she was even prepared to give jobs to the aloof Vorontsovs. Count Alexander Vorontsov, brother of Peter III's mistress, was president of the College of Commerce for twenty years from 1773, his brother Semën a long-serving ambassador in London. 'Tolerate an unpleasant person in your sight,' the empress later exhorted her infant grandson, the future tsar Alexander I, 'and do not glance askance at him: a man who can get on only with people he likes, and not with those he does not, is lacking in wisdom.'[33]

The nerve centre of Catherine's government was the Winter Palace, still under reconstruction when the Court returned from Moscow, though not under the direction of its original architect. Having been close to Peter III, Rastrelli thought it prudent to take temporary leave from Russia shortly after Catherine's coup. When he returned a year later, he found that his circumstances had changed for the worse. Among the petitions forwarded to Yelagin's secretariat in the autumn of 1763 was one from the disgruntled architect:

> Your holy Imperial Highness, I am taking the liberty to inform Your Imperial Majesty with the most humble respect that, having received permission to return to Italy for a year thanks to Your kindness, and having received at that time a gift of 5000 roubles to allow me to complete my journey in the greatest comfort, for which I express my eternal gratitude to Your Imperial Majesty, I would have been happy on my return to continue in Your Imperial Majesty's humble service, on the same basis established by Your august predecessors. However, Your Majesty has ordered the Great Marshal, Count Sievers, to inform me that in future I must depend solely on the Director of the Construction Chancellery and not on the Court. This change has grieved me greatly, since after so many years of service I have found myself deprived of the pleasure of receiving Your precious orders, with which I was always honoured in the past, and this compels me with great sadness to beg humbly for my retirement, since it is impossible for me to agree to subject myself to any other instructions than the ones I have hitherto received. I hope that an old retainer, who has been in service for forty-eight years, and who has always fulfilled his duties across this long period of time, will have the pleasure of receiving from Your Imperial Majesty, by virtue of Her great mercy, instructions about some sort of compensation, so that I may live with my family in our native land and continually pray to the Almighty to preserve the precious lives of Your Majesty and Her most august heir.

> Your holy Imperial Majesty's most humble and obedient servant,
> Count de Rastrelli[34]

Though he was duly granted an annual pension of 1000 roubles, Catherine remained deaf to his pleas to be confirmed in the rank of major general granted to him by Peter III since this would have entitled him to more money. While he continued to be treated respectfully at Court, dining with her in the spring of 1764, it was not long before Rastrelli finally left Russia for good.

It fell to Catherine's contemporary – the Frenchman Jean Baptiste Vallin de la Mothe – to fill Rastrelli's empty shell, and he set to work as soon as she departed for her coronation in Moscow in September 1762. Vallin began by designing neo-classical interiors and furniture for a new bedroom, dressing room, boudoir and study in the west wing, overlooking the Admiralty, where the empress initially intended to live. At that stage his role was restricted largely to decorative detail, but he became more ambitious when she changed her mind at the beginning of 1763 and decided instead to convert the apartments formerly occupied by Peter III in the south-east corner of the palace. Here the architect created a suite of staterooms based on the neoclassical principles he had learned from Jean Blondel at the Parisian École des Arts. Racing to meet the empress's deadlines, Vallin told Stählin that he had 'thrown the internal walls out of the window' and replaced them with wooden partitions.[35] By the time Catherine returned to St Petersburg, the transformation was obvious. As the Prussian ambassador reported in June 1763:

> She is making considerable alterations in the palace of stone. The apartments of the former empress have been turned entirely upside down and rebuilt so differently that they look nothing like they used to do. But since the workers have not been paid for two months, this prompts lines of reasoning which are not favourable to Her Imperial Majesty.[36]

Oblivious to such carping, Catherine forged ahead, inspecting progress over the summer, and finally moving in with great pomp and ceremony on Tuesday 14 October, some three weeks later than planned and more than a year since she had last occupied the Winter Palace.[37] By then, the ceremonial first floor was largely complete, save for the suite of rooms overlooking the River Neva, and Vallin had also finished most of the work on the warren of staircases and corridors that led to the floor above, where Catherine's twenty maids of honour were to live for the remainder of her reign in the western and south-western parts of the building. 'Guess where I've been today!' proclaimed an excited Paul after Grigory Orlov had taken him to visit them. Back downstairs, in the grip of a crush on Vera Choglokova, he immersed himself in the *Encyclopédie* article on 'Amour'.[38]

Vallin's work for Catherine differed from his other private commissions only in

scale. At the heart of his creation for the empress, just as in the house he built for
the Chernyshëvs at much the same time, was a salon – the centre of civility and
sociability – surrounded by a suite of private and semi-public apartments, all conceived as part of a single stylistic whole, and ranged around two inner courtyards
on the western, southern and eastern sides of a large square, whose northern side
was taken up by the great palace chapel. Although these rooms underwent a major
renovation between 1782 and 1784, their layout and use remained essentially
unchanged until the end of Catherine's life.[39] Having ascended the main staircase
near the west door of the chapel, visitors passed through a suite of three antechambers flowing south towards what is now Palace Square, with their windows
facing westwards towards the Admiralty. The central anteroom was a Portrait
Room, hung with portraits of the imperial family as a reminder of Catherine's
dynastic pretensions. Here, sergeants of the guard permitted well-dressed nobles
to enter the Chevaliers Gardes' Room, where the Court gathered on a Sunday
before processing to chapel. To 'pass beyond the Chevaliers Gardes' was to enjoy
privileged access to the empress's own apartments, ranged in a line overlooking
the square to the south. The first of these rooms was also the largest: an audience
chamber some 227 metres square, decorated in green damask, where Catherine
received her ambassadors. Until a permanent throne room was built in 1795, the
audience chamber shared that function with another, overlooking the river, where
banquets were held on state occasions. With her sixty Chevaliers Gardes fanned
out two-by-two on either side of her, the empress sat beneath a huge gilded canopy,
draped in red silk, on a velvet throne raised up against the eastern wall.

Immediately behind this throne lay a green and gold dining room which
doubled as a billiard room in the evenings. Although Catherine was always keen
to enrich the imperial porcelain collection – she paid the Saxon merchant Poggen-
pohl more than 13,000 roubles for a 256-piece service for Tsarskoye Selo in 1762
– banquets were also served on gold and silver tableware dating back to time of
Ivan the Terrible and Mikhail Fëdorovich. Though Paul was bored by a visit to
the storerooms at the foot of the main staircase, where Panin insisted on scruti-
nising every item of his priceless heritage, these historic dinner services offered
a further reminder of a usurper's claims to dynastic legitimacy.[40] Above the din-
ing-room ceiling was a glass lantern, initially placed by Georg Veldten over the
western entrance to the palace, which was large enough to have doors leading to
a balcony. Here Catherine occasionally listened to the liturgy when she failed to
attend the chapel, which was entered via a large gallery leading northwards from
the dining room between the two inner courtyards.

Directly to the east of the dining room was the Diamond Room, so called because the regalia were kept there when not on public display. Though this was formally the state bedroom, equipped with an appropriately imposing *lit de parade* under a canopy in an alcove on the northern wall, it was in effect the empress's salon, furnished with two sofas, four armchairs, two upright chairs and several marble tables, all designed by Vallin de la Mothe in keeping with his neo-classical concept for the palace interior. 'As you know, every piece of furniture is a different colour, even in the same room,' Panin reminded his mistress in 1767.[41] Here the empress was to spend countless evenings at the card table. Beyond lay a dressing room leading to her bedroom, whose panels were decorated in green lacquer. It was there that Catherine heard reports from her advisers each morning, sitting on an upright chair at a small table. (Her secretaries occupied a nearby room, overlooking the inner courtyard and accessible via a private staircase.) Catherine's bedroom led to a small boudoir and from there to her study, at the far south-eastern corner of the palace. This gave access to the last of her private apartments, the library, which stretched northwards towards the chapel until she had it moved upstairs in the mid-1770s, converting the lower apartment to a Mirror Room where in later life she worked every morning from seven until nine. It was in her library that Catherine had scientific experiments set up for visiting ambassadors, using apparatus such as the 'small electrical machine' with which her son enjoyed electrocuting his servants.[42]

Since all these interiors were either lost in subsequent alterations or destroyed by the great fire of December 1837, the achievements of Veldten and Vallin de la Mothe have come down to us only in their plans and correspondence.[43] However, it seems clear that the Winter Palace impressed visitors then, as now, more by its massive proportions than by any claim to elegance or beauty. In its final incarnation, the building could boast 1050 rooms, 117 staircases, 1886 doors and 1945 windows. Its principal cornice was almost two kilometres long.[44] The full extent of such a colossal structure could only be appreciated from the opposite bank of the Neva. To Lord Cathcart, who arrived as British ambassador in 1768, the conception was comparable in both extent and magnificence to 'Inigo Jones's idea for Whitehall, with which it also corresponded in the happy circumstance of being situated on a very noble river'.[45] Nevertheless, as European tastes swung from Baroque exuberance towards classical simplicity, Rastrelli's monster was bound to seem 'very large and very heavy'. And as another traveller pointed out in the mid-1770s, comparing the palace with the work of Britain's most lugubrious Baroque architect, Sir John Vanbrugh, the creator of Blenheim Palace and

Castle Howard, it was still 'not quite finished, like almost everything else in Russia'.[46]

————

Panin, who was negotiating an alliance with the Danes in the autumn of 1764, liked to boast that the Winter Palace had cost twenty times as much as the royal palace in Copenhagen.[47] Magnificent as it seemed as a symbol of Russian power and prosperity, it was too vast and uncomfortable for the relaxed sociability in which Catherine excelled. Not that she found it easy to relax once she had ascended the throne of all the Russias. 'Believe me,' she complained to Madame Geoffrin in 1764, 'there is nothing more unpleasant in the world than greatness':

> When I enter a room, you would say that I had the head of a Medusa: everyone is petrified and they all stiffen up. I often screech like an eagle against such habits. But I can tell you that this isn't the way to stop them because the more I screech, the less people are at their ease. So I employ other expedients.[48]

Courtiers could be forgiven for approaching the empress with caution since, for all her yearning for informality, she was swift to complain when they failed to observe due ceremony. Emerging unexpectedly early from her apartments one Sunday in July 1765, she was furious to find only the senior chamberlain in attendance. Count Sheremetev's subsequent admonishment to his juniors caused 'much whispering' at lunch.[49] By the time the image of Medusa's head recurred in a letter of 1781, Catherine seemed more sympathetic to her courtiers' dilemmas: 'With due respect to my fellow monarchs, I suppose that we must all of us, such as we are, become unbearable people in society ... There are no more than ten or a dozen people who put up with me without constraint.'[50]

One of the pleasures of this more intimate entourage, which remained remarkably constant throughout her life in Russia, was the opportunities it offered to escape the suffocating atmosphere of the palace. Nowhere was etiquette more relaxed than at the aristocratic country houses which had sprung up along the Peterhof road since Peter the Great first laid out regular plots 'like the keys of a giant piano pressed up against the south shore of the Gulf of Finland'. As Derzhavin put it in his poem 'Picnics' in 1776, it was here, in a striking reversal of the bourgeois notion *Stadtluft macht Frei!* (City air makes you free!), that the Russian elite could abandon the social distinctions imposed on them in the capital:

We resolved among friends
To preserve the laws of equality;
To abandon the conceits,
Of wealth, power, and rank.[51]

Ivan Chernyshëv had one such estate by the sea where Catherine occasionally called in on the way to Peterhof and Oranienbaum; Yakov Sievers owned another. Some of their freedoms carried over to Peterhof itself, where she could go fishing and her friends liked to help cook what they had caught. In the heat of the summer, they loved swimming there, too, following the empress into the sea or the pool at Monplaisir until they were up to their necks in water. 'It must be said that they were fully clothed,' recorded Paul's strait-laced tutor, Semën Poroshin, after Yelagin had regaled the Young Court with one such escapade.[52] Alexander Stroganov lived closer in at Chernaya Rechka (Black River) on St Petersburg's Vyborg Side, a favourite hunting ground for Empress Elizabeth. From Colonel Passek's house, Catherine could drive to Stone Island, which she purchased from Bestuzhev in 1765 for the use of her son, to watch the common people at play in the delta of the River Neva.[53]

Along with Zakhar Chernyshëv, Prince Andrey Beloselsky and the Orlov brothers, these were among the empress's closest intimates. She played billiards or cards with them most nights. Gambling presented Catherine with a dilemma. On the one hand, she condemned its pernicious impact on society. 'The noble who has squandered his money,' she warned Moscow's Governor General in 1763, 'will be obliged to sell his village, which other nobles, lacking sufficient resources, will be in no position to buy; and in that case the only remaining purchasers will be manufacturers ... so you are to make very sure that no games of chance are played, and confirm to the police that the published edicts about this are to be precisely enforced.'[54] On the other hand, import duties on foreign playing cards and a tax on Russian-made packs led the College of Commerce to promise her in 1765 a combined annual revenue of 27,000 roubles, which Betskoy persuaded her to donate to the Moscow Foundling Home.[55] The empress's favourite game was ombre, the fashionable Spanish three-hander whose addictive powers were satirised in 1763 by the poet Vasily Maikov.[56] Piquet was another regular pastime. Nothing, however, gave her greater pleasure than her friends' amateur theatricals. In the carnival of 1765, she went to the Sheremetev Palace on the Fontanka to see Stroganov, Beloselsky, Prince Peter Khovansky and the Prussian ambassador, Count Solms, perform *Le philosophe marié* under the direction of Ivan Chernyshëv. His brother Zakhar was the house manager who collected the tickets while Ivan's fiancée played the part of the usher. More than a hundred top-ranking courtiers made up the audience with the foreign ambassadors. Catherine enjoyed herself so much that she returned four days later for a repeat performance.[57]

In private, the company was even more relaxed, and especially so on Christmas Day when they gathered late in the afternoon with Paul and his Young Court to play games in the audience chamber of the Winter Palace. Ribbon dancing and hunt the treasure were particular favourites. In the Russian dances that followed, Catherine was partnered by Panin, who remained on the fringes of her inner circle, never quite a friend. In a mock tribute to the Smolny Institute, and in a curious echo of Elizabeth's cross-dressing masquerades, several of the men, including the beefy Passek and Grigory Orlov, excelled themselves by dressing up as noble girls under the watchful eye of their 'mama', Prince Beloselsky. 'They were all wearing jackets, skirts and bonnets,' Paul's tutor noted warily. 'Only Beloselsky had a scarf, and he was dressed worse than the others.' There was more mischief as they sat down to punch and a cold table, and then the dancing began all over again.[58]

Not all Catherine's leisure pursuits were so mindless. In Alexander Stroganov she had acquired a genuinely cultivated companion who provided an important link to Paul's Young Court. In a ceiling painting at the Stroganov Palace by Giuseppe Valeriani, Alexander's grand tour in the 1750s was represented in the guise of Fénelon's celebrated *Adventures of Télémaque* (1699), in which the young son of Ulysses encounters contrasting models of good and bad kingship as his tutor leads him on a journey through the Mediterranean world.[59] It was an appropriate analogy. While his friends Alexander and Ivan Cherkasov went to Cambridge – 'not a very entertaining place in itself, but pleasant enough in good company' – Stroganov chose Geneva, where, in addition to winning his spurs at the riding school, he learned to play the clavichord, studied Latin and Italian, and launched himself with enthusiasm into courses in natural law, geometry and physics under the direction of Professor Jean Jallabert, an expert in electricity.[60] Ancient history, his favourite subject, was taught by Pastor Jacob Vernet, celebrated for his attempts to steer between revealed religion and Enlightened reason. By the end of the century, Stroganov had produced his own scholarly catalogue of what had become one of the finest private art collections in Europe. Though many of his sixteenth- and seventeenth-century Italian paintings were acquired during his second spell in Paris in the 1770s, Stroganov had bought his first significant work, by Antonio Correggio, as early as 1755.[61] Already a committed bibliophile by the time of his grand tour, he admired a collection belonging to the Elector of Hanover which contained 'the best books now to be found'. Later, he saw the more extensive holdings at Frankfurt am Main and a library that surpassed them both in Cardinal de Soubise's palace at Strasbourg. Above all, he was impressed by access afforded to the public at the royal library in Turin, which was open every day except Thursdays, Sundays and holidays so that 'anyone who wishes may subscribe and read there'.[62] On his return to Russia, Stroganov opened up his own collection, which ran to some 4000 titles in 10,000 volumes. According to the loan book kept in his own hand and dating from the period between Catherine's accession and her coronation, the empress herself borrowed a French play called, appropriately enough, *Le Philosophe*.[63] Stroganov entertained her to an annual banquet lunch in January and his palace became open house to leading courtiers. It was there, in 1766, that a plan was formed to found the Imperial Russian Public Library, of which he was eventually appointed director in 1800.[64]

Stroganov had plenty of time to spend with the empress and her son because his marriage to Anna Vorontsova had fallen apart by the summer of 1765. Their wedding seven years earlier had been sandwiched in between those of Count Buturlin and Lev Naryshkin. According to Catherine, Kirill Razumovsky made a bet with the Danish ambassador as to which of the three grooms would be cuckolded first, and it turned out to be Stroganov, 'whose new wife seemed at the time the ugliest, the most innocent, and the most childish'.[65] By spring 1766, as the British ambassador reported, both partners desired a divorce with equal zeal, 'the only thing in which, it is said, they ever agreed in'.[66] Yet as Catherine had already explained to Count Mikhail Vorontsov, this was a matter over which she had no control:

From your letter of 14 November, I have seen your request about the divorce of your daughter from her husband, to which I can make no other reply than to say that I am very sorry about your considerable domestic sadness over the differences between your daughter and son-in-law; however, divorce does not depend on me, but is solely an ecclesiastical matter, in which I cannot and will not intervene. Count Stroganov sent me a similar request a month ago, but I ordered it to be given back to him with the message that I cannot intervene in this affair because it is spiritual and there are established channels for such a case; secondly, in the absence of his wife and your daughter [who were then abroad], there can be no resolution; and third, I hesitate even more to intervene in this case because of the close relationship between the Counts Skavronsky and my late grandmother of blessed memory, Catherine I.[67]

Only his wife's death could release Stroganov from his misery. It came in 1768, but not before she had caused him further embarrassment by embarking on an open affair with Nikita Panin. Though it had amused Panin to make fun of his friend's marital problems over lunch with Grand Duke Paul, he was disconcerted to find himself the butt of jokes by a public which, as Sir George Macartney remarked, could 'scarce pardon an undisguised boyish passion, in a man of his years, station and experience'.[68]

Not even a failed marriage could dull Stroganov's natural wit: as Catherine's regular 'carver' on state occasions, he had stood behind her chair at the fateful banquet when Peter III denounced her as a fool, comforting her with 'the witty banter of which he was such a master'.[69] However, the real life and soul of the empress's inner circle was Lev Naryshkin. Though his presence at the empress's side doubtless helped to reinforce his family's grip on senior appointments, Lev Aleksandrovich himself played no overt part in either government or the administration of the Court. It became a running joke that he had been made Master of the Horse because he was so rarely to be seen in the saddle ('We must mount him on a donkey,' Catherine quipped).[70] Critics dismissed him as a gadfly – 'a quite intelligent man', as Prince Shcherbatov put it, 'but with the sort of mind that never concentrates, greedy for honours and gain, prone to every luxury, a joker, and, in a word, from his behaviour and his love of joking, more fit to be a court-jester than a grandee'.[71] Yet these were precisely the qualities that Catherine had loved and admired since Naryshkin first lit up the Young Court in the dark years of Elizabeth's reign. Sir Charles Hanbury-Williams had liked him then for his 'good heart and quick understanding'. To Catherine, he was simply 'the most trustworthy person I have among this nation'.[72] As she put it in her memoirs:

He was one of the most singular personages that I have known, and no one ever made me laugh as much. He was a born Harlequin, and had he been of different birth, he could have made a living and a lot of money from his genuinely comic talents. He lacked for nothing in qualities of mind, he had heard tell of everything, and it was all uniquely arranged in his head. He was capable of discoursing on whatever art or science one might wish. He used the relevant technical terms and spoke to you continuously for a quarter hour or more, and when he stopped, neither he nor anyone else could make anything of the stream of words that had flowed from his mouth, and everyone ended up bursting with laughter.[73]

'No serious person could resist him', she said, particularly on the subject of politics. Perhaps only such an accomplished jester could have managed the tightrope act of remaining equally trusted by Peter III and his consort, right down to the very day of Catherine's coup.

Observing that the empress's life was 'a mixture of trifling amusements and intense application to business', Buckinghamshire singled out Countess Bruce as the leading lady in Catherine's 'private party'. Even in her thirties, she remained 'the first ornament of the circle':

> She dresses well, dances tolerably, speaks French with fluency and elegance, has read a dozen plays and as many *brochures*, and has naturally a partiality for a nation to whom she is indebted for all her acquired accomplishments. Not averse to gallantry, but discreet in her choice of those she favours, her affections, ever subservient to her judgement and studiously observant of those of her mistress, fix upon an object so connected with the favourite of the hour as must necessarily introduce her to the confidence of the secrets and the society of the pleasures.[74]

The amorous adventures of Countess Praskovya Bruce were eventually to be her undoing. In 1779, she was banished from Court when Catherine discovered, long after it had become public knowledge, that the countess had 'conceived a violent passion' for her own twenty-four-year-old favourite, Ivan Rimsky-Korsakov.[75] But there was no sign of such indiscretions in the 1760s, when the empress could look back on a friendship lasting more than twenty years. As the second daughter of Countess Rumyantseva, Catherine's first Russian governess in 1744, Praskovya had been introduced to Catherine soon after her arrival in Moscow. They formed an immediate bond. 'At my request, she often slept in my room, and even in my bed, and then the whole night was spent in romping, dancing and frolics. Sometimes it was nearly morning before we went to bed, so great was the racket we made.'[76] Despite the fact that, like Naryshkin, Praskovya later became attached to Peter III in 'heart, body and soul',[77] she recovered Catherine's confidence to the point where 'of all the Ladies she is the one who comes to me most often'. The empress dedicated her first significant memoir to this trusted female 'friend, to whom I can say everything without fear of consequences'.[78] In a Court shot through with rumour and innuendo, that was no mean tribute.

Praskovya had known about Catherine's affair with Grigory Orlov from the moment it began in 1761 and the two of them performed regularly in amateur theatricals.[79] Although there could be no question of a marriage in the aftermath of the Khitrovo fiasco, Catherine had come to rely on Grigory's bear-like support, seeing his intellectual limitations not as a defect but rather as an opportunity for her to bring him on. To the astonishment of the foreign ambassadors, she made no attempt to conceal their shared domestic bliss. He occupied rooms above hers at the Winter Palace, connected to the imperial apartments by a private staircase. There was a similar arrangement at the Summer Palace, where Grigory indulged his passion for astronomy in an observatory occasionally visited by Grand Duke Paul. (They missed the eclipse of the sun in August 1765 because it was too cloudy, though Paul's tutor was no less satisfied with the close-up of the capital's bell towers afforded by Grigory's telescope.[80])

Considered alongside the crucial role the Orlovs had played in Catherine's coup, the widespread eighteenth-century assumption that only a man could hold the reins of power was enough to persuade many foreigners that the empress must be in thrall to her favourite. Nothing could have been further from the truth. Grigory certainly served as an important counterweight to Panin and his acolytes and took an interest in many of Catherine's initiatives. His appointment as president of the Chancellery of Guardianship of Foreigners, opened on 22 July 1763 as a means of attracting foreigners to make more productive use of the vast Russian lands, was a clear indication of the significance she attached to the scheme. This was a big operation – 17,866 potential colonists were dispatched from Lübeck in 1766 alone; the total number of registered arrivals between 1762 and 1775 was 30,623 – and Grigory played an active part in the administration. Indeed, he did more than that. While Catherine apparently visited settlers in transit for the Volga in the barracks built for her husband's Holstein regiments at Oranienbaum, Grigory settled individual colonists at Peter III's old estate at Ropsha (given to him by the empress in 1764), where Pastor Eisen was commissioned to continue his experiments with peasant land-ownership.[81] At his house on Millionnaya, Orlov also hosted meetings of the Free Economic Society, founded in 1765, puffing on his pipe as he listened to learned papers on agronomy. In political terms, he represented Catherine's most personal link to the Guards regiments who had brought her to the throne. Yet he was not a natural man of intrigue. 'He is good natur'd, indolent, unaffected, and unassuming,' Macartney reported in 1767. 'His sudden elevation has neither made him giddy nor ungrateful; and his present friends are the same satellites which attended his course when he moved in a humbler sphere.'[82] While Catherine showered him with expensive gifts of porcelain, decorated with symbols of their mutual love, he made every attempt to entertain her in the manner to which she had become accustomed. On his name day, 25 January 1766, he threw a ball in her honour at which sixty-seven guests sat down to a banquet accompanied not only by Court choristers, but also by table fireworks in the manner preferred by Peter III. Afterwards Grigory was joined in a comedy by his fellow amateurs. Catherine enjoyed herself so much that she stopped out until two in the morning.[83]

She was not so keen to stay up for the mind-numbing round of public masquerades she had hated as a grand duchess. These were now staged with such obvious economy (no food, and only sour milk to drink) that Panin thought it would have been better to abandon them altogether, despite their popularity with the merchantry.[84] More popular still was the theatre, which remained as central to the rhythm of the Court's secular festivities as it had been under Elizabeth. Only the setting was different. A team of twenty-seven artists worked round the clock for two months to allow the theatre in the south-west corner of the Winter Palace to open on 13 December 1763 with a performance of Sumarokov's familiar tragedy, *Sinav and Truvor*. With an auditorium seating 600 in four rows of boxes and the stalls, this was to remain the principal Court stage for the next twenty years.[85] The main imperial box faced the stage, but Catherine also had another one stage-left, immediately opposite her son's (he was often brought to see her after a performance). This was where Paul developed his lifelong delight in French comedies, though he cried if they lasted too long and showed worrying signs of petulance if the audience applauded before he did, a practice that his mother was happy to tolerate.[86]

It was even harder for his tutors to keep Paul amused at gala performances of *opera seria*. The boy enjoyed the battle scene in Manfredini's *Carlo Magno* [*Charlemagne*], staged to commemorate Catherine's name day in 1764, but he was glad when the performance ended at half past eight: 'although Italian operas are bad', he remarked to his tutor, 'this one was good because it finished early'.[87] The adults were no better pleased. Learned as they may have been, Manfredini's intricate arias failed to sustain his audience's attention and Count Sievers determined to secure the services of a more celebrated composer. While the search was on, Manfredini partially redeemed himself with an extravagant musical drama for the third anniversary of Catherine's accession. The Court celebrated the occasion with a week-long military exercise at Krasnoye Selo, where the empress wore nothing but uniform and Paul, who had been dreaming about the event for almost a year, was sick with excitement. *Apollo and Minerva* required an orchestra and two choruses; dinner was served in a marquee to some 365 guests, including the whole *generalitet* and all the Russian staff officers; and the entertainment was brought to a spectacular conclusion at midnight when fireworks were used to blow up an artificial town.[88]

Baldasare Galuppi, who had first attracted the Russian Court's attention in the late 1750s, arrived in St Petersburg, after protracted negotiations with the Venetians, in September 1765. Although Catherine immediately commissioned his *Dido Abandoned* for her name day celebrations in November, the production had to be held over until the following February. Since the opera had been premiered in Modena as early as 1741, the problem lay not with the composer's creativity, but rather in the scale of the production. No fewer than seventy-two boys from the Guards regiments were brought in as extras and Galuppi insisted on additional rehearsals with his new orchestra, berating them in his native dialect until standards improved. On her name day, the empress had to be satisfied with a cantata, 'Virtue emancipated', which was so successful that it was repeated on 26 November with three encores. 'The music is extremely good, massive and pleasant,' commented Semën Poroshin. 'If you listen to it carefully, the heart is rapt with admiration.' Still more delighted with Galuppi's opera when it was finally ready, Catherine gave its composer a diamond-encrusted snuff box and 1000 roubles, accompanied by a characteristically skittish note saying that Dido had bequeathed this present to him in her will.[89]

If these were all developments typical of a Baroque Court, the carousel staged in 1766 was even more of a throwback to Louis XIV's Versailles.[90] This medieval tournament had originally been planned for the summer of 1765, when Catherine visited Elizabeth's old wooden winter palace to inspect the costumes and took part in a full-scale rehearsal.[91] In the event, inclement weather caused it to be postponed until the following year. To raise echoes of the Olympic games in ancient Greece, the medallion struck to commemorate the occasion was engraved with the slogan 'From the banks of the Alfei to the banks of the Neva', and its designers drove home the classical allusions by depicting a cylindrical structure on the model of the Roman coliseum.[92] Rinaldi's wooden amphitheatre in Palace

Square, which Catherine inspected several times during the course of its construction, was actually in the form of a rectangle, 200 yards by 180, in which the empress and her son sat facing each other in boxes on the eastern and western sides. Thomas Newberry, a British instructor in navigation at the Cadet Corps, described the performance on 11 July to the merchant Robert Dingley:

> There were six Rows of Seats on each side, the lowest of which was eight feet from the Ground. All round the Square, there was a path of about 5 yards in breadth and the rest was inclos'd in a handsome manner breast high, and turn'd into the form of an Oval, in the Centre of which sat the Famous old Count Munich, who with his officers, was to judge of the performances and distribute the Prizes. The Knights, Sir, were sixteen, and the Ladies eight, beside an innumerable train of Squires, who carried their Shields &c. They were divided into four Parties call'd Quadrills, and supposed to be of four different Nations, namely the Roman, the Sclavonian, the Turkish, and the Indian, and were all properly and most magnificently Cloath'd in the Habits of the several Countrys.

The knights and their ladies jousted not against each other, but against 'Beasts only, who appeared in the formidable shape of Bears, Lyons, Tygers and Dragons', and afterwards they were all invited to a masquerade, honoured with Catherine's presence. 'Your humble Servant was in a Black Domino, without a Mask, because my views and wishes, Sir, were only to be seen, and taken notice of by Her Majesty.'[93]

'Our carousel was extremely good,' a delighted empress reported after the first performance, though critics later grumbled that the Russian knights 'displayed more magnificence than gallantry, and greater strength than dexterity', so that the tourneys 'were beheld with disapprobation, as frivolous and expensive'.[94] It was true that representational monarchy never came cheap. Its costs rose steeply in the early years of Catherine's reign. The bill for fourteen Turkish costumes for the masquerade in honour of Paul's tenth birthday came to 1950 roubles – half the annual salary of the Court *Kapellmeister*, and almost twice as much as Father Platon (Lëvshin) was paid as tutor in divinity to the grand duke. The annual budget for the Imperial theatres, re-organised under Yelagin's direction in 1766, was set at 138,410 roubles, including pensions and a small theatrical school. But this was never enough to support nine Italian opera singers, a thirty-two-piece orchestra, a ballet company of forty-two and both French and Russian theatre troupes.[95] Formally speaking, the Court's basic operations were still sustained by the same annual grant of 260,000 roubles decreed by Empress Anna in 1733, with a further 6765 roubles 73 and a quarter kopecks for the servants' salaries.[96] Yet this was merely a fiction. By one generally accepted estimate, all told the Court consumed 9.5 per cent of the total state budget in 1763. Six years later, the proportion had risen to 12 per cent and expenditure had almost doubled in absolute terms from 1.64 million roubles to 3 million.[97]

Within two years of his accession to the Habsburg throne in 1765, Joseph II had reduced the number of religious services attended annually by his Court from seventy-eight to thirty-two. Ten more had gone by 1774. As a leading Viennese official noted, the emperor's decision to abolish the Maundy Thursday ritual of washing the feet in 1767 created 'an exceptional sensation'.[98] In St Petersburg, such a move would have been inconceivable. Catherine may have worn her own religion lightly, but she had come to the throne as a defender of Orthodoxy. The number of religious rituals in the Russian Court calendar went up rather than down during her reign as her Court remained knee-deep in holy water.

The very first entry in the Court journals after the coup is from 1 August 1762, when the empress followed an elaborate clerical procession from the chapel at the Summer Palace to the blessing of the waters on the Moika canal at the beginning of the Dormition Fast.[99] A similar ceremony was repeated three times in the 1760s, Catherine sheltering from the rain in 1764 in a specially constructed gallery. That was the year in which the Court clergy first staged an icon procession at mid-Pentecost, the moveable feast halfway between Easter and Trinity Sunday. On 30 August 1762, the empress made a point of processing on foot for more than two miles from the Kazan Church to worship at the relics of St Alexander Nevsky – a severe test of patience for one so sceptical. In later years, she either drove to the Anichkov Palace and processed from there or bypassed the annual icon procession altogether. Not until 1772 was she once again persuaded to complete the full route on foot. It was a similar story at Epiphany. Catherine followed the icons to the Jordan in both 1764 and 1765, while Zakhar Chernyshëv showed the watching Paul a plan of the layout of the 8900 soldiers on parade. After that, she was ill for several days and never again ventured out after being deterred by a severe frost in 1766, when the parade was cancelled and only a single company from each regiment braved the cold to present their standards to be dipped.[100] For the remainder of her reign, Catherine was content to watch the blessing of the waters from the windows of the Winter Palace.

The palace's great chapel had been consecrated on Easter Saturday, 1762, the day that Peter III moved in. Two weeks after her return from Moscow in 1763, Catherine had it re-consecrated in the name of the icon 'not made by human hands' (a version of this celebrated image, made seventy years earlier by F. F. Ukhtomsky and studded with gold and diamonds, was placed by the altar). Rastrelli had originally intended the chapel to extend to the full height of the palace, but eventually opted to place it on the first floor at the same level as the other staterooms so that, exceptionally for a sacred space, there were kitchens and laundries beneath, not to mention the bathhouse where Catherine later spent time with Potëmkin. The chapel remained a 'very lofty and spacious room', lined by 'gilt Ionic pillars' and decorated with icons which one visiting Protestant found 'glaring and ill-executed', but which are now reckoned among the finest examples of collaboration between Russian and Italian artists in the eighteenth century. Much of the plate was taken from the Moscow Armoury to represent a clear line of succession from Catherine's Muscovite 'ancestors', and the chapel also housed treasured relics, including a cross incorporating a fragment of the Life-Giving Cross of Our Lord, an image of the Filermskaya Mother of God, said to be the work of St Luke, and part of the right hand of John the Baptist.[101] In the depth of winter, Paul kept warm by listening to the service from an adjoining room while his mother regularly took her place behind the railing in front of the altar. Here she could listen to her choir, more than fifty strong by the late 1760s, perform works influenced by the Italian style by Western-educated composers such as Maxim Berezovsky. Daily services were accompanied by traditional chants and the occasional motet, but in the empress's presence, on Sundays and lesser feast days, there was always an ornate mass, and the twelve great feasts in the Orthodox calendar were celebrated with a full-scale cantata.[102]

Not that Catherine's worship was confined to her palaces. On Thursday 17 October 1762, she and her entourage made the traditional post-coronation pilgrimage to the Trinity St Sergius monastery. Advised of her visit in August, the monks had lost no time in smartening the place up and preparing gorgeous new vestments. The suite where the empress was to stay was also rejuvenated. Proclaimed on her arrival as a 'second Helen' in piety and 'the image of Judith of Israel' in courage, Catherine was shown the library and took particular pleasure from debates between the pupils of the seminary, organised by its twenty-four-year-old rector, Archimandrite Platon.[103] Father Platon made another favourable impression with a sermon on 'the uses of piety' when the empress returned to the monastery in the following May, on the first leg of her pilgrimage to Rostov.[104] Following the pattern set by Elizabeth, she proceeded in crab-like fashion, covering up to seven miles on foot during the day, and then partially retracing her steps by carriage to spend the night at a favourite staging post. As far as the Trinity monastery, the route was dotted with imperial villages, each of which had its own small wooden 'palace'. At Taininskoye, where the exquisite seventeenth-century church still stands in the shadow of a huge electric power station, a new log cabin had been built alongside the palace to house her suite.[105] She made good progress, completing the journey in eleven days. However, as so often on Catherine's travels, the elements were against her: driving wind and rain turned the roads to mud, 'depriving us of the pleasure we might have taken from the journey in better times'.[106] Pereyaslavl, where she arrived on 21 May, offered 'foul weather and boredom in equal measure'. She stayed with a government official, whose house was 'very large, good, and full of cockroaches'. The empress insisted, against the Church's better wishes, that monasteries should serve some useful purpose by caring not only for the sick, but also for the insane. Less certain about the use of monasteries as gaols, she was appalled to discover a monastic prisoner who had been held captive at Pereyaslavl for fifteen years: 'Find out about him!' she ordered.[107] Peasants had flocked to Rostov in the hope of glimpsing their sovereign and being cured by the saint's relics. 'Yesterday there was another miracle,' reported the sceptical empress. 'A woman was healed and Bishop [Dimitry] Sechënov wants to seal the casket, so that the relics cannot be stolen; however, in order that the common people shouldn't think that the relics had been hidden from me, I requested that they be left out for some time longer.'[108]

Father Platon followed Catherine to St Petersburg at the beginning of August 1763. On Sunday 10 August, the empress travelled to the Trinity hermitage, where she had received representatives of the deposed Peter III on the day after her coup, to hear him preach at the consecration of the Baroque cathedral, begun seven years earlier to a design by Trezzini and completed under the supervision of the ubiquitous Rastrelli.[109] Given rooms in Elizabeth's temporary wooden palace, Platon was to deliver more than thirty sermons to Catherine and her Court over the next two years. In addition to his annual salary of 1000 roubles, he received a further 300 for subsistence, and was supplied not only with fire-wood and candles, but also with beer, more than a litre of vodka each week and a bottle of Rhine wine every day. Although Panin worried that this 'clear-headed' monk might be corrupted by his new surroundings, he remained alert to the dangers of ambition and extravagance. Several of his Lenten sermons touched on the temptations faced by hedonistic courtiers, and on 10 October 1764 he 'spoke with considerable vehemence against those who ruin themselves by squandering their wealth on frivolous and unnecessary things and, consequently, are unable to be of any help to the poor'. 'Father Platon was in a bad mood today,' Catherine remarked afterwards, 'but he spoke extremely well.'[110] Always impressed by the young monk's eloquence, she had been moved to tears by his sermon on the tsarevich's tenth birthday on 20 September. Many in the congregation also wept at the end, when 'the preacher spoke of her Majesty's patience in bearing her labours for the use and safety of the fatherland, on the success of his Highness in the sciences which he was taught, and the resultant hope for Russia'.[111] Catherine had herself attended Paul's first lesson with Platon on 29 August 1763, the Feast of the Beheading of St John the Baptist. Two years later, she stood at her son's side as he faced a carefully rehearsed oral examination on matters of basic dogma in the presence of a large number of courtiers. 'Her Majesty deigned to listen with the greatest attention,' Poroshin recorded. 'The examination lasted for three quarters of an hour. After it was completed, Reverend Father Platon addressed her Majesty in a brief speech. The Sovereign lady deigned to thank him for teaching the Grand Duke, about whom she said: "I thought he would be shy, but not all; he answered very well."'[112]

———

Since religious ritual remained central to the life of every eighteenth-century monarchy, one of the paradoxical effects of Russia's cultural Westernisation was to reinforce its role at the Court of St Petersburg. For many of Catherine's courtiers, there was nothing offensive about that. 'If I am not much mistaken,' remarked the prescient William Richardson, 'there are among them a greater number who affect indifference or disbelief in religious matters, than who really disbelieve. Perhaps, in times of sickness, disgrace, and low-spirits, they have more faith in St Nicholas, than in Voltaire.'[113]

It was different for Catherine herself: her cast of mind was wholly secular, and one reason why Father Platon felt the need to emphasise the difference between (true) spiritual enlightenment and (mere) secular learning was that he knew he was swimming against the prevailing intellectual tide.[114] The empress had lionised Voltaire since reading him in the 1740s and made attempts to cultivate him as soon as she came to the throne. As she insisted from the start, they both had much to gain from the correspondence that began in the autumn of 1763 and continued until Voltaire's death fifteen years later. While her association with him promised to enhance his status as a writer, 'Our lady of St Petersburg', as Voltaire later christened her, realised in turn that his approval could only enhance her reputation in Enlightened circles in Europe.[115] If her letters gave her the chance to show off – 'He: conversation is brilliant', Macartney remarked in 1766, 'perhaps too brilliant for she loves to shine' – then they also gave her the chance to model her prose on one of the greatest stylists of her age. Frederick the Great declared that he liked 'to maintain correspondences with superior minds, with people who are completely cerebral, as if they had no bodies; this is the human elite'.[116] Catherine took a similar view, self-consciously representing herself as a writer with much to learn. She struck the same tone in her correspondence with Jean d'Alembert, the joint editor of the *Encyclopédie*, whom she attempted in vain to lure to Russia. 'I have long owed a letter to Monsieur d'Alembert,' the empress wrote to Mme Geoffrin, 'and I beg you Madame to tell him that I shall shortly send him a notebook … I hope he will be pleased even though it is from the pen of a novice.'[117]

Realising the *philosophes'* difficulties with the French censorship, Catherine tried to help them (and embarrass Louis XV) by offering to print the final volumes of the *Encyclopédie* in Riga even before her coronation. That invitation was refused, but it was impossible for its second impoverished editor, Denis Diderot, to turn down the empress's subsequent offer to purchase his library for 15,000 livres and pay him to look after it for her. The completion of the deal apparently sent him into a state of stupor. Catherine was just as pleased. 'I would never have believed that the purchase of a library would bring me so many compliments,' she wrote disarmingly to Voltaire. 'Everyone is paying me them for buying Monsieur Diderot's. But admit, you to whom humanity owes a debt for the help you have given to innocence and virtue in the persons of the Calas family, that it would have been cruel and unjust to separate a scholar from his books.'[118]

Catherine realised very early on in their correspondence that it would be 'very difficult' to reduce Voltaire's sparkling shafts of wisdom to a practical programme of reform. *Philosophes* who disagreed among themselves never offered a blueprint for government.[119] Nevertheless, the Enlightenment was an important influence on Catherine's legislation right from the start. Motivated primarily by the need for money, her secularisation of the monasteries was greeted with acclaim by *philosophes* who condemned the contemplative life as useless. Celibate monks and nuns were an obvious liability in a world which believed, quite wrongly, that the population had declined since classical times. Sharing the widespread perception that Russia was under-populated, Catherine sent the colonists recruited by the College of Guardianship to a huge new province of New Russia, stretching from the Polish border in the west to the Don Cossack territory in the east. Appointing Count Peter Rumyantsev as its Governor General in November 1764, the empress gave him characteristically explicit instructions in the sort of rational administration she expected:

> First of all, you must proceed to learn about the province that has been entrusted to you in all of its conditions and confines, and, for this purpose, you are to obtain a reliable map of sufficient detail to indicate the location of regiments, towns, settlements, villages, outlying farms, seasonal work camps, monasteries, hermitages, manufactures, and any and all places of human habitation, as well as rivers, lakes, marshes, woods, farmland, steppes, roads, and the location of [all] ... borders.[120]

It was almost certainly the empress who initiated the essay competition set up by the Free Economic Society in November 1766 in the manner of the earlier one sponsored by the Academy of Dijon, which had prompted Rousseau's first *Discourse on the Sciences and the Arts*. The topic she set was squarely linked to the Enlightened utility she had claimed as her watchword in a letter to Voltaire: 'What is most useful for society – that the peasant should own land or only moveable property, and how far should his rights over the one or the other extend?' It was the first public discussion in Russia of the question of serfdom. Of the 164 anonymous entries to the competition, only seven were in Russian. One was in Dutch, another in Swedish; the great majority were in German. Of the twenty French entries, one was by the *philosophe* Le Mercier de la Rivière, who made an unsuccessful visit to Russia, and another by Voltaire himself, under the motto '*si populus dives, rex dives*' (if the people are rich, the king is rich). Voltaire also revealed to Catherine that he was the author of one of three essays submitted in Latin, under the motto '*ex tellure omnia*' (everything from the land). Emancipation was the talk of the French salons. But it was all in vain. When the result of the competition was announced in April 1768, the prize-winning entry, duly published in Russian translation, was by the Frenchman Beardé de l'Abbaye, who was critical of serfdom, but advocated only a very gradual liberation of the serfs.[121]

As the choice of Beardé's essay signalled, Catherine was gradually beginning to realise the difficulties raised by her early reforms. When she first encouraged Eisen to contemplate a property-owning peasantry, she can hardly have grasped the extent to which Russia's imperial expansion had been underwritten by the exploitation of unfree labour since the time of Peter the Great. Her other initiatives were scarcely less ambitious ventures, whose impact could only be judged over the long term. Many of their immediate results were questionable. More than four-fifths of the children admitted to the Moscow Foundling Home in 1764 were dead within a year, and in 1767 the mortality rate reached almost 99 per cent.[122] Not surprisingly, Catherine lost confidence in the more extravagant of Betskoy's schemes, leaving herself open to the charge that she failed to complete what she had begun, and invested only in her personal glory.[123] That accusation was false. Having overcome two serious challenges to her authority – a plot among the Guards to restore Ivan VI to the throne in 1763, and a much more menacing attempt by the guardsman Mirovich to release Ivan from captivity while Catherine and her Court were at Reval in 1764 – she embarked on her most ambitious project of all. 'For the last two months,' she told Madame Geoffrin at the end of March 1765, 'I have spent three hours every morning working on the laws of this empire. It is an immense task.'[124] This was the origin of the great treatise which she intended to present to a new Legislative Commission in Moscow. By the time she was ready to convene it, there was nothing insecure about Catherine's position on the throne. As if to prove it, while the greater part of the Russian political nation gathered in the old capital to prepare for the commission's opening, she herself set sail on a voyage down the Volga to Kazan, a Muslim city 500 miles east of Moscow, conquered by Ivan the Terrible in 1552 as his 'gateway to Siberia'.

CHAPTER 7

PHILOSOPHER ON THE THRONE
1767–1768

As news of Catherine's travel plans leaked out in the summer of 1766, the foreign ambassadors were consumed with curiosity about her motives. 'There has been no other question here for some time,' reported Rossignol, Louis XV's secret envoy, on 13 May. Since the journey would oblige her to exchange her fine Petersburg palaces for 'an old house made of wood', as the king's official ambassador put it, she could hardly be travelling for pleasure. The notion that the journey was intended to quell growing turbulence in Moscow seemed equally improbable. Even if Princess Dashkova was stirring up trouble there, 'distant storms' were unlikely to threaten Catherine and she would scarcely be wise to move closer to a centre of unrest. Rossignol was prepared to believe that the whole expedition might be no more than a stunt on the part of the pretentious Orlovs. But he gave little credence to rumours that the empress intended to marry Grigory: 'I doubt that she still has that idea, if it ever existed, especially since the Synod has come out against this union, which would surely revolt all the great men of this empire.' In the end, he was driven to the reluctant conclusion that Catherine must indeed be intent on the bold experiment that Russians had begun to talk about: 'It is said that the Empress will promulgate a code which she wishes to substitute for the multitude of contradictory edicts which are the only laws of this empire and which serve merely as a resource for the dishonesty of litigants, and even more often for that of judges.'[1]

Despite the title *Code russe*, given to the third French edition in 1775, the Great Instruction (*Bolshoy Nakaz*) on which Catherine had been slaving away since the beginning of 1765 was never intended as a law code. 'Don't let the title frighten you as if it anticipated us,' Jeremy Bentham reassured his brother while working on his own *Introduction to the Principles of Morals and Legislation*: 'It is only a plan for putting the Courts of Justice upon a regular establishment.'[2] In fact, the empress's Instruction was much more than that. She intended it partly as a statement of the theoretical foundations of her own regime, and partly as a guide to the Enlightened principles on which a better government and society might ultimately rest. When she had finished, she told Frederick the Great how hard it had been to take account of present needs without 'closing off the way forward to a more favourable future'.[3] Joking that she hoped she might be forgiven for plagiarism, she made no attempt to disguise her debt to two of the most advanced works of Western political thought: Montesquieu's *On the Spirit of the Laws* (1748) and *On Crimes and Punishments* (1764) by the Milanese jurist Cesare Beccaria. Yet even filleting their books into a slimmer treatise of her own was 'an immense task' in itself, as she told Madame Geoffrin, and it occupied most of her mornings for the best part of eighteen months: 'If providence allows, I hope to put everything in a more natural order, acknowledged by humanity and founded on public and private utility.'[4] Such labours took their toll. When Catherine came to complete a medical questionnaire in advance of her inoculation against smallpox in 1768, she complained of unbearable headaches over the previous two years, caused by tired eyes, 'overwork, and the fact that for three years running I got up at between four and five in the morning'.[5]

The ultimate task of codification could scarcely have been more ambitious. The comprehensive code envisaged by Peter the Great in 1700 had been completed only after his death and was never promulgated. Since then, four further attempts had come to grief. The most recent, inspired by Peter Shuvalov in 1754, had collapsed during the Seven Years' War, though it remained formally in existence in 1766. Although Catherine admired the direct style of the last complete Russian Law Code, issued as long ago as 1649 – 'We listen with pleasure when extracts are quoted from it; no one can mistake the meaning of what he hears; the words in it are understood even by persons of middling capacities'[6] – the catalogue of brutal punishments approved by Tsar Aleksey Mikhailovich scarcely matched her own views on the subject. And since many of the thousands of edicts promulgated in the intervening period remained unpublished, and some were mutually contradictory, there was much to do to bring order out of chaos. This task was to be left to a new Legislative Commission, a consultative body at which elected deputies from the free estates of the Russian empire – nobles, merchants, townsmen and state peasants – were to be encouraged to reveal the needs of provincial society 'from below'. Meanwhile, as her subjects launched themselves into elections set in motion in December 1766, the empress planned to see Russian provincial life for herself.[7] As she explained to Voltaire the following March:

> In June this great assembly will begin its sessions, and it will tell us what it needs. After which we shall work on laws of which, I hope, humanity will not disapprove. From now until then, I shall be making a tour of various provinces the length of the Volga; and perhaps at the moment when you least expect it, you will receive a letter from some little hut in Asia.[8]

Since no imperial journey was undertaken without elaborate preparation, plans for the Volga expedition developed alongside those for the Legislative Commission. They were already well advanced by the time of Catherine's trip to the Ladoga Canal in summer 1765, when Paul was excited to hear from Ivan Chernyshëv of the special vessels being designed for the cruise.[9] To build these boats, at an eventual cost of almost 40,000 roubles, Captain P. I. Pushchin was sent out in December to Tver, the empress's favourite provincial capital, where the adventure was to begin. While a new neoclassical town was rebuilt around him following the great fire of 1763, he oversaw the construction of a luxurious galley for Catherine – in effect, a small floating palace – and a further twenty-four large vessels, including one for a detachment of the imperial hunt. This was the fleet which eventually set sail in April 1767 with Pushchin in command of 23 officers, 779 sailors, and a guard of 345. Further downstream, numberless churches and monasteries were spruced up in anticipation of Catherine's arrival. At every calling point on the river, she moored at a newly built quayside covered with green or red cloth; miles of canvas sheeting kept her feet dry as she walked ashore. While three detachments of Cossacks had been dispatched to ward off the bandit gangs reported to be gathering along the Volga's tributaries in Penza province in the summer of 1766, soldiers were sent in December to all the major towns along the route, partly to maintain order and partly to manage the complex logistics for the return journey overland. Half of the 350 horses required at each of the thirty-three staging posts were to be provided by the Postal Chancellery; the remainder had to be prised out of a less than willing merchantry.[10]

At first, the merchants of Tver proved equally reluctant to pay for the triumphal arch that the provincial governor, Count Villem Fermor, had determined to build as early as November 1765. However, there was no deterring a man who had headed Elizabeth's Construction Chancellery in the heyday of Rastrelli before briefly assuming command of the Russian troops during the Seven Years' War. Having collected the necessary funds by the summer of 1766, Fermor ordered four columns to be driven into the ground before the frost set in for the winter, later sending an extravagantly gilded frame for the empress's monogram and decreeing that Her Majesty's portrait should be placed over the archway, facing her as she entered the town.[11] Similar triumphal arches were built all along the route, where provincial governors competed to stage receptions, each more magnificent than the last, at the expense of local dignitaries gathered for the elections to the Legislative Commission.

While the populace made ready to greet their sovereign, Catherine was doing her homework about the provinces. To prepare her for the journey, the Academy of Sciences drew up a short *Geographical Description of the River Volga*, which also allowed her to chart her progress once the cruise had begun. Great care was taken to ensure the accuracy of this attractive publication, whose first edition was pulped when it turned out to contain significant errors. Dividing the course of the river into sections, it illustrated each one with an engraved map accompanied by four readily referenced columns of text. Here Catherine could look up lists of the churches and principal economic activity of the towns along the route, the distances travelled from Tver, the distances between tributaries (faithfully marked on each bank of the Volga), and the position and direction of bends in the river. Full of the sorts of detail the empress admired, this pamphlet gave a good sense of the variety in store for her along the way. For example, whereas Nizhny Novgorod, at the confluence of the Volga and the Oka, could boast thirty-nine churches, four cathedrals, three monasteries, two convents and a trade in grain and handicrafts, there was but a single church at Kokshaisk, the last sizeable settlement before the old Tatar capital at Kazan, where 'the inhabitants feed themselves entirely from agriculture and cattle-breeding'.[12]

Catherine made her final preparations for the journey in Moscow, chosen as the seat of the Legislative Commission in memory of the ad hoc gatherings, later known as Assemblies of the Land, at which the Muscovite tsars had ritually consulted their leading subjects.[13] 'I prefer Petersburg,' she admitted, rehearsing all her frustrations with the unruly old capital that seemed to represent 'a nasty autumn' by comparison with the new one's 'onset of spring'.[14] If her palace was lacking in comfort, she had only herself to blame. 'The Construction Chancellery has asked me for more than 60,000 roubles for repairing and cleaning the Golovin and Kremlin palaces,' she had complained to the Governor General the previous summer. 'And most of it, as you will see, is purely for decoration and furniture. But since I am going to Moscow not for magnificence but for the good of the state, I have not the slightest need for luxury.' In the end, in one of her first clear rejections of Baroque extravagance, she spent only 7000 roubles on safety measures at the Golovin Palace, where she arrived on 13 February to celebrate the beginning of Lent with typically irreverent gusto.[15] As she explained to the French sculptor Etienne-Maurice Falconet:

> I read yesterday in the *Encyclopédie* article on 'religious orders' that your king, Saint Louis, said that if he could divide himself in two, he would do so, and give one half to the Dominicans and the other to the Franciscans. You can see that this good king would not have much left of his kingdom. *Good king* is the wrong expression: I should have said *good man*, for a good man can tell such stories, whereas a good king does better to keep his kingdom intact, and not to divide it among mendicant monks.[16]

Lent nevertheless had its uses. It gave her an excuse to keep out of the public eye until she had taken the political temperature of a city where she had delayed elections for the Legislative Commission until after her arrival. Occasional Court reception days were held during the Great Fast, shorn of the customary musical accompaniment, and Catherine celebrated the feast of the Annunciation with her cavalry officers. Otherwise, Moscow saw little of its empress until 5 April, when she travelled in state to the Kremlin to take her annual communion at the Cathedral of the Dormition and watch as Archbishop Dimitry performed the Maundy Thursday ritual of the washing of the feet. That weekend, cannon salutes signalled the progress of her nocturnal drives back and forth across the city for the Easter vigil services.[17] Alarmed by the decrepitude of all three Kremlin cathedrals, Catherine ordered Field Marshal Saltykov to call a meeting of all the city's architects to decide how to make them safe. 'PS There's no time to lose with the Archangel cathedral.'[18]

On 21 April, the atmosphere was once again more intimate, as the empress celebrated her thirty-eighth birthday at the little wooden palace at Taininskoye in the company of Alexander Stroganov and other friends.[19] She did not attend the public lecture given two days later at Moscow University by Professor Johann Schaden, who looked forward to the Legislative Commission by discoursing 'On the Spirit of the Laws'.[20] By then, she was almost ready to depart for the Volga. On the evening of 29 April, Fermor and Ivan Chernyshëv were on hand to greet her at Tver with the usual barrage of fireworks. 'We are all well,' she reported to

Panin, who had remained in Moscow with his mistress and Grand Duke Paul: 'the journey was average, the weather very good.'[21]

It stayed fine for the next two days, as Catherine was treated to the sorts of gala reception that were to be repeated again and again over the coming weeks: whole regiments stood on parade, awaiting her inspection; nobles and merchants queued to offer her hospitality; seminarians dressed all in white chanted Russian and Latin verses written expressly for the occasion; hundreds of subjects were permitted to kiss her hand. Braving the cold on 1 May, she spent a couple of hours with Archbishop Gavriil (Petrov) in the garden of his new cathedral. Only after that did the clouds burst. But since the following day was mid-Pentecost, the empress and her suite processed through the rain for almost a mile to a sanctification service at a Jordan on the Volga. Once Grigory Orlov had passed her the customary glass of holy water, they returned to the cathedral where Gavriil had given 'a very good sermon' earlier that morning, and the empress lunched with him before finally boarding her galley, the *Tver*. Thousands thronged the streets in the hope of catching a glimpse of the procession of the cross and Catherine declared it 'impossible to count the people and carriages' blocking the route as she made her way to the quayside. Some women in the crowd rowed out to the *Tver*, at anchor in the river, while other cheering well-wishers sailed in her wake or scampered along the riverbank as the colourful flotilla at last set sail at three in the afternoon.[22]

By seven the following evening, Catherine had reached Prince Dolgoruky's estate almost sixty miles downstream. The rain had stopped, she had plenty of good company – among others, she shared the *Tver* with Grigory and Vladimir Orlov, the Chernyshëv brothers and Alexander Bibikov, the man she was grooming to be Marshal of the Legislative Commission – and she was relieved to report that they had all stayed well, despite the weather. It remained changeable as they sailed on to the Makaryev monastery on 5 May. 'Small but handsome', in Vladimir Orlov's words, this ancient house had once owned more than 60,000 peasants in a single provincial district. Since it also marked the boundary of Gavriil's diocese, it was here that she took leave of her favourite prelate. Local boatmen rowed alongside for several miles, accompanying Catherine with their melancholy songs as she departed for Uglich, where Ivan the Terrible's son, the tsarevich Dimitry, had died from stab wounds in 1591. Both Pushkin and Musorgsky later dramatised the event in a version alleging (almost certainly wrongly) that Boris Godunov had brought destruction upon himself by ordering the assassination of a prince who blocked his own path to the throne. In the light of Peter III's fate, this was one aspect of the Muscovite legacy that no one wanted to highlight in 1767. Catherine cruised on regardless. 'It's very jolly to sail on the water,' she told her own son, adding disingenuously: 'I'm sorry only that you are not with me.'[23]

The routine established in these early days set the pattern for the remainder of the journey. While ashore, Catherine divided her time in the manner anticipated by the *Geographical Description* in a programme guided by the young president of the Academy of Sciences, Vladimir Orlov. Part of it was devoted to inspections of the sorts of prosperous economic enterprise that she wanted to promote in Russia (the head of the College of Manufactures, Dimitry Volkov, was another of her companions on board the *Tver*). A fortnight before leaving Moscow, she had secretly decreed that small, unregistered workshops there should no longer be persecuted by the authorities. Matching her instinctive preference for free labour, this policy was also influenced by Catherine's reading of the Cameralist economist Jacob Bielfeld, who believed that large, privileged manufactories were better suited to the provinces than to a capital city. 'The excessive aggrandizement of a capital which is made at the expense of provincial towns, can never be a sign of a state's prosperity,' Bielfeld insisted, in a passage that played directly into the empress's prejudices against Moscow.[24] Now she planned to inspect some of Russia's largest textile manufactories in the Volga region. Despite this preoccupation with the modern economy, however, by far the greater part of her journey was taken up by visits to monasteries and churches where she could conveniently associate herself with medieval princely glories. Here the clergy could show off their miracle-working icons to a sceptical empress while the populace presented her with the traditional symbols of Russian hospitality: bread and salt (usually delivered on silverware made expressly for the occasion), and fish (preferably still live and wriggling).

While under sail, Catherine's priorities were different again. One of the books that she had set aside for the journey was *Bélisaire*, a political novel by the *philosophe* Jean-François Marmontel, which had been banned in France as openly deist. On 7 May, stuck at anchor in a howling headwind, she found time to thank the author. 'I was enchanted to read it and I wasn't the only one: it is a book that deserves to be translated into every language.' As good as her word, she and her companions whiled away the delay by completing the Russian version begun in Tver. It was dedicated to Archbishop Gavriil, whose virtues, listed in the inscription by Voltaire's friend Count Andrey Shuvalov, were said to include 'gentleness, humility, moderation [and] enlightened devotion'.[25] The empress herself translated the chapter on monarchy which projected the image of a just and tolerant ruler that she hoped to propagate by distributing the book throughout the empire (it was published in the following year).[26] The weather defeated even the maps in the *Geographical Description*. 'I know not where to date my letter from,' she complained, 'since I am on a vessel in the middle of the Volga in some rather nasty weather that many ladies would call a frightful storm.'[27] 'Yesterday was the first boring day,' she confessed to Moscow's Governor General next morning, 'but we are all healthy, and although there are close on two thousand people in my entourage, only five are in hospital, and they are not seriously ill. And although troops have been sent to replace the sick soldiers, those on my galley don't want to leave and say that they are well.'[28]

A flotilla of small craft decked with multicoloured flags came out to greet her at Yaroslavl on 9 May. The town 'could hardly be better situated', she boasted, 'it is very pleasing to everyone'. Not quite: Vladimir Orlov found the place 'very badly built, almost all of peasant huts, the streets are narrow and paved with planks'. He was more impressed by a visit to Ivan Zatrapezny's silk works, which had not only supplied many of the hangings in the imperial palaces, but also exported more than 65,000 yards of cloth to England in the previous year. Having taken coffee and dessert with the proprietor's family, Catherine was briefly shown some of their wares before sailing over to Savva Yakovlev's equally thriving enterprise on the opposite side of the river. Orlov, who returned two days later for a more detailed demonstration, learned that 3000 people worked for Zatrapezny in winter, and since there were 'incomparably more at the Sobakina factory', he could count on a combined winter workforce of up to 10,000. Most of them were serfs belonging to Prince Mikhail Shcherbatov, elected to the Legislative Commission in March as the noble deputy for Yaroslavl. Shcherbatov, the most ardent defender of Russia's ancient aristocracy against the pretensions of the service nobility promoted since the time of Peter the Great, was no less critical of lethargic merchants, but since his serfs would otherwise have remained idle in winter, he released them to the enterprising Zatrapezny in exchange for capital to invest in his own weaving sheds, which in turn supplied semi-finished cloth to the larger manufactories.[29]

Having inspected four such enterprises in and around Yaroslavl, interspersed with visits to local monasteries, Catherine chose to relax as she might have done in St Petersburg. After lunch with the ambassadors, she played cards with them in her apartments and sat down to dinner at a table 'laid with fitting magnificence and decorated with pyramids of flaming crystal bottles, covered with white wax, which looked very handsome'.[30] After such a banquet, Catherine was pleased to report to Panin, 'the diplomatic corps is apparently very happy and will travel to Kostroma, where the nobles are making great preparations for my arrival tomorrow'. The Yaroslavl nobility had already made a good impression when they were presented to her in the archbishop's refectory, built by Patriarch Filaret in 1634 on the model of the Kremlin's Palace of Facets: 'It was all very seemly,' the empress reported. Meanwhile, she asked for more government papers to be sent to her: 'I live idly in the extreme.'[31]

For all her professed inactivity, Catherine looked tired on her first morning in Kostroma. Although the obligatory triumphal arch had been built at the entrance to the cathedral, the town could provide no accommodation fit for an empress and she had been obliged to sleep on her galley.[32] Lunch helped to revive her, and so did reports on the five local textile works, whose rival owners, she was pleased to learn, lived in the sort of harmony she desired for all her subjects. No effort was spared to make Muscovite comparisons explicit, though the aim was always to show that Catherine had surpassed rather than merely imitated past triumphs. Bibikov struck a suitably flattering note by comparing her with Tsar Mikhail Fëdorovich, the founder of the Romanov dynasty who had travelled from the nearby Ipatyevsky monastery to accept the crown in 1613: 'What joy this town experienced in the presence of that Sovereign, and what joy it must feel now, when you take incomparably greater care of our well-being!'[33] For Catherine's visit to the monastery on 15 May, the 'tsar's place' built for Mikhail – an intricately carved canopy almost thirty feet tall which had been stored away since the fire of 1649 – was restored to the Trinity Cathedral and carved with her monogram as a memento for posterity.[34]

Next day, she sailed on to an estate belonging to the family of Bibikov's wife, Anastasia Kozlovskaya. Despite their modest means, the Kozlovskys had not only found the wherewithal for a new quayside, but also built the obligatory triumphal gate opposite the empress's mooring, topped by a crown and with several obelisks to one side. Their investment was rewarded by an invitation to dine on the *Tver*. And there was more to come. On Ascension Day, 17 May, Catherine was greeted by cheering crowds of neighbouring nobles, merchants and clergy as she followed the procession of the cross up a path flanked by prostrate peasants. During the service, Bibikov himself read from the Gospel at her request. At lunch, Catherine was served by the daughters of the family and her hosts proposed a toast on their knees. She, in turn, enrolled Bibikov's seven-year-old son as a junior court official. There could hardly have been a more telling ritual celebration of the mutual bonds between a sovereign and her subjects. Although there was never any question of a formal contract between Catherine and the Russian people, she was fully aware of the implicit bargain represented by the cruise. 'Settlements are very frequent,' she told her son, 'and people are all glad to see me, but I know the proverb "one hand washes the other" and so I behave in the same way towards them.'[35]

No amount of festivity could disguise the harsh realities of Russian provincial society. The Yaroslavl merchants seemed so restive that, on her return to Moscow, Catherine sent a Guards officer to restore order and replaced the provincial governor.[36] The brothers of the Fëdorov monastery at Gorodets irritated her even more. Suspicious of monks as an obstacle to Enlightenment, she had seen more than enough of them by the time she arrived there on 19 May to distinguish a well-run establishment from a disorderly one. As the Synod knew, theft and corruption were familiar problems, sometimes involving hundreds of thousands of roubles.[37] Here, however, the empress encountered troubles of a different order. She could hardly have been welcomed more generously by the crowd who flocked to the quayside: Vladimir Orlov overheard one of the pious women who strewed shawls and silk scarves in her path refer to her as 'a little apple', another as 'a little ray of sunshine' and a third as 'our benefactress'.[38] Yet Catherine felt no warmth for the monks as they consecrated their new stone church. Behind its impressive façade, rebuilt from local funds after a fire in 1765, the monastery left much to be desired. Although it enjoyed a proud reputation as the place where St Alexander Nevsky had died in 1263, Abbot Zosima was too old and too ignorant even to say the liturgy properly and, as Catherine discovered, his disrespectful brothers 'swore loudly while telling him how to do it'. She left them a derisory donation.[39]

Worse still, the local clergy told her they were losing their flock (and with it their income) to the schism, which had put down tenacious roots deep in the forests around Nizhny Novgorod since Patriarch Nikon first split the Orthodox Church in the mid-seventeenth century. In their turn, the Old Believers, who had been outlawed by Tsar Aleksey Mikhailovich for resisting Nikon's reforms to the liturgy, complained to Yelagin that Orthodox priests treated them 'like Muslims' and refused to christen their babies. Faced with such open discord, Catherine realised that there would be no easy route to the 'tranquillity between citizens which prudence is everywhere trying to establish'. Since it was impossible to trust the local bishop – a 'weak' man who surrounded himself with 'equally weak simpletons' rather than seek out 'clean-living clergy, enlightened by learning, and meek of morals' – she secretly urged Archbishop Dimitry to reform the diocese on the models of Novgorod and Tver.[40] Insisting on civilised clerical behaviour in the months after the cruise, she urged punishment for priests who extorted money from the Old Believers by violence. Yet the problem was at least in part one of her own making. While her own relatively generous legislation had alarmed the Synod by stimulating a rise in schismatic numbers in the mid-1760s – the official figure of 10,697 reported by the diocese of Nizhny Novgorod in 1765 was surely an underestimate – none of the older, repressive edicts had been repealed. As a result, aggressive clergy were able to exploit precisely the sort of confused legal position that the Legislative Commission was intended to correct, exposing the limits of Catherine's much-vaunted commitment to religious toleration. Although she continued to condemn the degradation of the Old Believers in the combined causes of humanity and civil tranquillity, she had no intention of undermining the privileged status of the Orthodox Church. As a perceptive *Times* correspondent noted a century later, it was to remain a feature of 'the peculiar relations between Church and State' in Russia that 'the Government vigilantly protects the Church from attack, and at the same time prevents her from attacking her enemies'.[41]

Perhaps it was her experiences at Gorodets that led Catherine to be more critical of Nizhny Novgorod than of the other places she had visited. Perhaps it simply failed to live up to the extravagant billing in the *Geographical Description*. At any rate, the empress found little to please her during her stay in Bishop Feofan (Charnutsky)'s palace. Perched high on a cliff above the Volga, the town's situation was striking enough, and made the more attractive by the sunshine which had finally broken through. However, in an unconscious anticipation of the abbé Chappe d'Auteroche, Catherine declared Nizhny to be 'abominably built'.[42] Vladimir Orlov agreed: though the cathedral seemed in many ways the finest they had yet seen, there was 'almost nothing worthy of remark' in a town whose merchants seemed 'very meagre' in view of their advantageous position at the crossroads of Russian trade.[43] Not content with decreeing the reconstruction of its principal public buildings, Catherine immediately set about founding a new trading company to boost the local economy.[44] News of the impending bankruptcy of the British timber merchant William Gomm seemed to confirm all her suspicions about privileged manufacturers. Demanding 'precise accounts' of his various activities, which ranged from tobacco to iron, she was inclined to 'conclude that all these are sustained out of state money'.[45] One of the few bright spots in the visit was when Orlov introduced her to a local inventor, Ivan Kulibin, the protégé of an Old Believer merchant who delighted her with a microscope and telescope. She would see him again in St Petersburg when he had perfected his clock in the form of a mechanical golden egg.[46]

As her galley weighed anchor on 23 May, Catherine was leaving the longest settled Russian lands for the intersection of the Orthodox and Islamic worlds. She had given her first audience to a Tatar delegation at Kostroma.[47] Now she was entering an area where a brutal missionary campaign, sponsored by Church and state in the early 1740s, had culminated in the forcible mass baptism of some 400,000 Finno-Ugric people: Mordvins, Chuvash and Maris. The driving force behind the attack on 'the vile Mordvin faith' had been none other than Catherine's trusty Archbishop Dimitry, who claimed to have barely escaped with his life when a group of Mordvins attacked his convoy in protest against the razing of a sacred burial ground. This incident led to reprisals by Russian troops and mass flight into the forest on the part of the native population. In the following decade, hundreds of mosques were destroyed, particularly in areas where they might 'seduce' converts to revert to their former ways.[48] Though Orthodox missionary work had continued in a more emollient key under Catherine, who scarcely troubled to conceal her distaste for Elizabeth's methods, violence was still a living memory in the Volga region in 1767. So it is perhaps no coincidence that no converts were presented to the empress at Kozmodemyansk or Cheboksary ('superior to Nizhny Novgorod in every way'), or that she sailed straight past Svyazhsk, where the government office in charge of the conversions had been closed in 1764.[49] A reminder of the deviant potential of popular Orthodoxy came at Kozmodemyansk, where a merchant presented her with an icon of the Holy Trinity with three faces and four eyes. She sent it to the Holy Synod, anxious lest 'senseless icon-painters' succumb to the temptation 'to add several further arms and legs' in the manner of Chinese paintings. Appalled by 'such a ridiculous and unworthy image', the Synod swiftly decreed that no more icons should be painted without the express permission of its own specialist artists. That was 'all very well,' Catherine retorted, but 'scarcely possible in an empire of Russia's dimensions' since 'it could give rise to a lot of pestering'. She required only that 'all bishops be instructed that in future no such indecent images should be permitted in their dioceses'.[50]

Had there been any doubt about the friendliness of the reception she could expect in Tatar territory, it was dispelled when the empress arrived at Kazan on the evening of 26 May. 'All along the way my welcome has been equally affectionate,' she told Adam Olsufyev, 'only here it seems a degree higher owing to the rarity of their seeing me.'[51] Overlooking the point where the Volga carves out a majestic 90-degree turn to the south, Kazan is one of the most attractively situated towns in Russia. The decorations in honour of Catherine's visit were no less impressive. She told Panin that the triumphal arches there were better than any she had so far seen. One of them had been designed by Julius von Canitz, director of the town's high schools, founded at the instigation of Ivan Shuvalov to feed suitably qualified noble and non-noble entrants to Moscow University in 1758 (the poet Derzhavin was the most famous pupil). Struggling against unsympathetic neighbours, who littered the road to the schools with dung, Canitz increased the roll to a peak of 125 between his appointment in 1765 and 1773. But Vladimir Orlov found the institution 'in a very bad condition' in 1767, 'with 12 teachers and only 40 pupils' whose speeches in German, French, Russian and Latin were 'very imperfect'. Catherine did not visit the school, but she encouraged the provincial governor to revive the amateur theatricals that Canitz had instituted there as a way of fostering the 'pleasant address and the *savoir vivre* essential in polite society'.[52]

'Pleasant address' seemed a distant enough prospect at Kazan where the cancellation of Canitz's plays was a symptom of feuding between the governor and local nobles. Such tensions were only to be expected in a provincial society that had only recently begun to break away from patriarchal ways of life, in which the greater part of the nobility, living *en famille* on small estates in circumstances not much different from their own peasants, had been unaccustomed to socialising.[53] Arguments among the Russian elite nevertheless helped to cast a more flattering light on the Tatars. The Orlovs were by no means the last Russians to be impressed by the simplicity of the Muslim service they witnessed at a mosque where the attentive humility of the worshippers contrasted sharply with the disrespectful behaviour of many Orthodox in church.[54] Catherine herself watched with pleasure at a ball on 31 May as 'the Mordvins, Chuvash, Cheremis, Votiaks and Tatars ... all danced according to their custom to the sound of Tatar music and songs'. But it was impossible not to be unnerved by the kaleidoscopic variety she encountered in Kazan. In the course of the week she spent there, the empress saw the Tatar children at the seminary, finally received a delegation of recently baptised converts, greeted the son of the Kazakh khan and was presented to a party of Siberian merchants who had travelled almost 500 miles to petition her.[55] Such experiences impressed upon her as never before the complexity of her multinational empire. Daunted by the challenge facing the Legislative Commission, she sat down to write her promised letter to Voltaire:

These laws about which people talk so much are, in the final analysis, not yet made. And who can answer for their benefits? In truth, it is posterity, and not us, who will have to decide that question. Imagine, I beg you, that they must serve for Asia as well as Europe, and what a difference in climate, peoples, customs, and even ideas! Here I am in Asia; I wanted to see it with my own eyes. There are twenty people of various kinds in this town, who in no way resemble one another. And yet we have to make a coat that will fit them all. It may well be possible to discover general principles, but the details? And what details! I might say that there is almost a whole world to be created, united, preserved. I may never finish it![56]

———

Although Catherine's original intention had been to sail all the way to Astrakhan, the *Geographical Description* allowed for a shorter cruise ending further north, at Dmitrevsk. In the event, to speed her return to Moscow, the empress travelled only as far as Simbirsk, almost 700 miles downstream from Tver and 'one hour eleven minutes and twenty seconds ahead of St Petersburg time'.[57] Here she stayed on an estate belonging to Ivan Orlov. The beauty of the Volga lands was breathtaking. 'These people are spoiled by God,' she wrote to Panin, whose brother Peter owned an estate not far away. 'Everything you can imagine is here in plenty and I do not know what else they could need: everything is available and everything is cheap.'[58] Having taken seven weeks to reach her destination, she raced back to Moscow in seven days, travelling by night and sleeping through the heat of the steppe, pausing only to change horses. Hundreds of subjects who lined the roadside to pay homage were passed by in a blur. When she reached the Golovin Palace at 7 p.m. on Thursday 14 June, she needed two days' rest to recover from the journey.[59]

Though the Court was immediately plunged into mourning – first for Prince Frederick of Prussia and then for Joseph II's unhappy second wife, Josepha, who had fallen victim to smallpox in May – there was nothing gloomy about the empress's mood.[60] While Vasily Maikov celebrated her return with verses hymning the usefulness of her enlightened voyage, the deputies converged on Moscow in readiness for the opening of the Legislative Commission. Once Catherine had put the finishing touches to the protocols, she took the opportunity to relax.[61] Although she had to review the cavalry on exercise in the Petrovsky woods and there were the usual festivities in honour of her accession day and

Paul's name day on 28 and 29 June, she preferred the less formal entertainments to be found on the various imperial estates dotted around the old capital. As soon as she returned from the Volga, she inspected her new apartments and stables at Kolomenskoye. 'There is no need for any sort of rich decorations inside,' she had insisted the previous December, after six months of close involvement with the plans. Though the project had been scheduled for completion by the Feast of St Peter at the end of June, she eventually moved in on 11 July, greeted at the gates by the local clergy in full fig.[62] While waiting for Prince Makulov to finish the work, she found time to play on the new sledging pavilion at Pokrovskoye, to drive to the Sparrow Hills on the far side of the city, and to watch the fishing at Tsar Boris's Ponds.[63] She also inspected the stallions brought up from the provinces for the annual sale at the imperial stud farms at Khoroshevo and Pakhrino, where a huge quadrangular stable for 532 horses, under construction since 1752, had been completed in 1764.[64] Perhaps she saw Gardi, a black stallion bred from Lombard stock in 1766, whose exceptionally luxuriant tail made him one of the most celebrated animals of the age.[65]

Hunting was by far Catherine's most frequent leisure activity. Between 18 June and 15 October, the court journal (by no means necessarily a complete record) registered some thirty-seven separate outings. The detailed breakdown – two grouse shoots, three hare chases and no fewer than thirty-two hawking expeditions – gives a good sense of her personal preferences, already reflected in institutional changes over the previous five years, which had seen the animal hunt cut back while the staff of the bird hunt rose from thirty-nine to forty-nine. As in St Petersburg, the preferred time for hawking was after lunch, at four or five in the afternoon, when Catherine liked to ride out in her carriage with her falconers alongside her to while away the journey.[66] They also accompanied her as far as the palace at Bratovshchina on her pilgrimage to worship at the remains of St Sergii on his feast day, 5 August. For all her reservations about monasticism, the empress had always found at the Trinity *lavra* a scholarly atmosphere quite different from the obscurantism she encountered at the Fëdorov monastery, and it was a pleasure to return to the library she had so admired in 1762.[67]

All this, however, was but a prelude to the ceremonial opening of the Legislative Commission on 30 July. Whereas her predecessors' abortive commissions had been dry, bureaucratic affairs, hidden away in the chancelleries of St Petersburg, Catherine wanted hers to begin in a blaze of publicity. It was launched in the manner of a major Court occasion with a glittering carriage procession from the Golovin Palace to the Kremlin. The deputies assembled in the Monastery of

Miracles before processing with the empress to a liturgy at the Dormition Cathedral at which those who belonged to other faiths remained outside. Afterwards, Catherine, wearing the small crown, stood before the throne in the audience hall of the old Kremlin palace (it does not survive today) with copies of her Instruction on the table beside her. In a notable departure from earlier Muscovite assemblies, only one clerical deputy had been elected. The ubiquitous Archbishop Dimitry, elected on behalf of the Synod, made a speech comparing the empress with Justinian. Replying on her behalf, the vice chancellor Prince Alexander Golitsyn (Alexander Stroganov's friend from their student days in Geneva) stressed her hopes that the deputies would confer glory on themselves and their age by contributing to 'the common good, the happiness of mankind, and the introduction of good manners and humanity, tranquillity, security and happiness to your dear fatherland'. Those who had already gathered in Moscow (some 460 out of the eventual total of 564) were permitted to kiss her hand.[68]

On the following morning, the Commission began its formal proceedings in the Palace of Facets. Once Bibikov had duly been chosen as its marshal, the deputies listened to a public reading of her Instruction by Grigory Orlov. Though Catherine had compiled her treatise in French, each deputy was presented with a copy of the Russian translation by her secretary, Grigory Kozitsky, published simultaneously with a German version on 30 July. 'There is not a foreign word in it,' the empress boasted in a characteristic effort to advertise the richness and subtlety of her adopted language. 'However, the subject matter is not of the simplest, and I hope that no one will mistake one word for another.'[69] Fond of listening to her friends read to her (and conscious of the illiteracy of a good proportion of the Russian elite), Catherine had written her text to be read aloud, giving it 'an urgent rhythm' by imitating Montesquieu's series of 'short, staccato chapters' in 526 laconic paragraphs of her own.[70] Even so, it took a full five sessions of the Commission to hear it out, as Yelagin and Volkov succeeded Orlov on the reader's podium.[71]

Catherine was not an original thinker and the Instruction was not a systematic work. Yet there was nothing conventional about her treatise. It set out her vision of a tolerant, educated society in which her subjects' liberty and property would be protected by unambiguous laws, established by a virtuous absolute sovereign and implemented by judges who were to presume the accused innocent until proved guilty. The widespread nineteenth-century belief that she had suggested that it was better to release ten guilty people than convict a single blameless man prompted Solzhenitsyn to quip that Stalin had reversed the empress's maxim by preferring to incarcerate 999 innocents rather than miss a single genuine spy. Although there is no such passage in the Instruction – it was Diderot, in his critical commentary on the text, who declared that 'for humanity's sake, we should allow a crime to escape unpunished rather than put innocence to death' – the legend says much about the Instruction's reputation as a repository of Enlightened thought.[72] Never had such radical ideas been publicly proclaimed by a Russian ruler.

'Russia is a European State.' Catherine began her first chapter with one of her few original contributions to her treatise, a cultural rather than a geographical claim, designed to challenge the prevailing view of her empire as a slough of oriental backwardness. The same motive underlay her implicit argument that Montesquieu had been wrong to classify Russia as a despotism ruled by fear, the only form of government he thought workable in a very large state and the ultimate insult in the vocabulary of eighteenth-century politics. Catherine instead presented Russia as an absolute monarchy in which the sole ruler voluntarily accepted the limitations imposed by fundamental laws. Historians have argued ever since about the plausibility of this claim, resorting to precisely the sort of semantic debates that the empress hoped to avoid. Her intention was almost certainly not to distort Montesquieu, but rather to adapt the ideas of a writer she admired to Russian circumstances about which he knew little. Even so, there were obvious difficulties with her position. Although contemporary thinkers disagreed about the nature of the fundamental laws by which they set such store, an inviolable law of succession was generally taken to be central. We know from an incomplete draft, written in her own hand and dating from after 1767, that Catherine eventually contemplated such a law. But since it was impossible to promulgate one without admitting that she had taken the throne by force, there was no mention of the subject at the time of the Legislative Commission.[73]

Serfdom was another controversial question on which the final version of the Instruction said little. Prompted partly by her experiences with Pastor Eisen, Catherine had initially been prepared to contemplate ways of 'creating new citizens' (that is, reducing the number of serfs), for example by allowing serfs to accumulate sufficient property to purchase their freedom. But these radical proposals were swiftly dropped after she showed drafts of her treatise to her confidants. Panin famously declared that they were 'maxims to bring down walls'. Catherine was particularly astonished to discover that even Alexander Stroganov – 'a gentle and very humane person' who was 'kind to the point of weakness' – defended 'the cause of slavery with fury and passion': 'There were not twenty people at that time, who thought on that subject like human beings.' In the circumstances, the best that could be done was to condemn the mass enserfment of free men and to restrict abuses by exhorting masters to treat their serfs with humanity. Meanwhile, Chapter 11 of the Instruction left the deputies in no doubt of the virtues of social stability: 'There ought to be some to govern, and others to obey.'[74]

The empress was on surer ground when she turned her practical mind to matters of crime and punishment. Since it was a besetting problem of Russian justice that not even the judges could be sure what the laws actually said, her Instruction identified clarity, precision and uniformity as the key requirements for future legislation. Only if laws were written in plain language and imposed with predictable regularity could her subjects have confidence in the courts. Deterrence was no less important: 'By making the penal laws always clearly intelligible, word by word, every one may calculate truly, and know exactly the inconveniences of a bad action; a knowledge which is absolutely necessary for restraining people from committing it.'[75] Judges were to execute rather than interpret the laws since to interpret a law was almost always to corrupt it and only the sovereign had the right to interpret laws which she had made. Nothing could be so dangerous as the idea that the spirit of the law was more important than the letter. That way, 'we should see the same crimes punished differently, at different times, by the very same court of judicature.' Torture was firmly declared 'contrary to all the dictates of nature and reason; even mankind itself cries out against it'. Catherine was equally opposed to the death penalty: 'The most certain curb upon crimes, is not the severity of the punishment, but the absolute conviction in the people, that delinquents will inevitably be punished.' Even so, it was better to prevent crimes than to punish them, and that made education a clear priority: 'Would you prevent crimes? Order it so that the light of knowledge may be diffused among the people.' But were there enough people? As we have seen, Catherine shared the widespread contemporary anxiety – particularly acute in the vast, empty spaces of the Russian empire – that the world's population had fallen since classical times. The way to increase it was to make people happy: 'The more happily people live under a government the more easily the number of the inhabitants increases.'[76]

Such ideas may have been familiar to Enlightened circles in Western Europe, but to the majority of the empress's humble provincial deputies they came as a bolt from the blue. The Commission itself was an equally stunning phenomenon. As Henry Shirley reported to Whitehall:

The Russians think and talk of nothing else, and in seeing the representatives of several nations, so very different both as to dress, customs, and religion, such as the Samoiedes, Cossacks, Bulgarians, Tartars etc., and whom they suppose to be (perhaps not without foundation) entirely dependants of the Russian Empire, assemble in their capital, they are apt to conclude, that they are now the wisest, the happiest, and the most powerful nation in the universe.[77]

The barely concealed note of sarcasm reflected Shirley's disappointment that Catherine had failed to create an institution on the model of the Westminster Parliament. He was particularly offended by the secret gallery, originally built to allow female members of the Muscovite royal family to observe ambassadorial audiences, 'from whence she can hear every thing that is said, without being seen':

The Russians instead of perceiving how much this takes from the freedom their deputies ought to enjoy, admire this very much, and think it an undoubted proof of their sovereign's love and regard to them. But, to render the farce as complete as possible, the deputies went yesterday in a body to thank Her Imperial Majesty for the instructions she has been pleased to give them, and to offer her the new titles of the Great, the Wise, and the Mother of her country.[78]

In a carefully choreographed performance at the Golovin Palace, Catherine formally refused the honour, saying that it should be left to posterity to judge. The episode nevertheless provided a gratifying ritual confirmation of her own dubious legitimacy – almost certainly the prime motive for convening the Legislative Commission in the first place.[79]

Anxious to avoid debates among 'the blind, the semi-educated, and the half-witted', Catherine made it clear from the start that her own treatise was to be the sole intellectual guide to the Commission's proceedings.[80] Here was another apparent restriction on the deputies' freedom. And yet to think in such terms is surely anachronistic. Since no tsar had ritually consulted his subjects since 1653, the very notion of public discussion in Russia lay beyond living memory. Lacking a tradition of civic responsibility, the deputies needed to learn not only to speak, but, no less importantly, to listen. Catherine, having sought their advice on the condition of the empire, more in the manner of a sixteenth-century Humanist than an eighteenth-century Parliamentarian, needed to provide the conditions in which they could be heard. That was why she paid such close attention to the rules governing behaviour: deputies were forbidden from interrupting one another (one noble was fined and forced to apologise to a non-noble deputy whom he had insulted), no swords were to be worn, and fighting was to be punishable by fines or exclusion from the chamber.[81] Here was an even more fundamental conception of mutual tolerance than the one that the empress sought to convey in a letter to Voltaire:

I think you would be pleased to attend this assembly, where orthodox sits alongside heretic and muslim, and all three listen calmly to a heathen; and all four often confer to make their opinions mutually acceptable. So well have they forgotten the habit of burning one another at the stake, that if anyone were sufficiently ill-advised to suggest to a deputy that he should burn his neighbour to please the supreme being, I can say on behalf of all of them that there is not one who would fail to reply: 'He is a man, just as I am; and according to the first paragraph of her Imperial Majesty's Instruction, we must do one another all the good we can, and no harm.'[82]

While Catherine was pleased to encourage measured discussion among Russia's free population at the Legislative Commission, she was far less tolerant of unsolicited complaints from the serfs. Most of the 600 petitions with which she had been bombarded on the Volga cruise were submitted by soldier-farmers and newly baptised converts bemoaning a shortage of land. These led her to stress the need for the General Survey, begun in 1766, to be extended to this very area. However, as she told the Senate on her return, there were also 'a few unfounded petitions from serfs complaining of their owners' exactions, which were returned to them with the instruction not to submit such petitions in future'. Among them was a petition from serfs on an estate belonging to Adam Olsufyev's family, who not only refused to return to work as she insisted, but paid for a representative to plead their case in Moscow. When an infantry regiment was sent to reward them for their disobedience, 130 peasants were arrested and some were flogged with the knout. Further rioting on estates where peasants had presented petitions to Catherine prompted her to attempt to limit the number of such petitions in future. Her edict of 22 August 1767, which confirmed a range of earlier laws limiting the right of serfs to denounce their masters to the authorities, stopped short of threatening the torture that the Senate had been prepared to contemplate. Nevertheless, it increased the penalty for wrongful petitioning by adding hard labour for life to the list of punishments already decreed in 1765: a month's hard labour in the Siberian mines for the first offence, a year's hard labour for a second offence, and public whipping and perpetual exile for a third. This menacing edict was intended merely as a stopgap until the Legislative Commission could formulate a suitable alternative. Since this was never done, and the edict of 22 August was never repealed, it served both to consolidate the landowners' powers over their serfs for the remainder of the reign and to deter petitioners from all but the noble estate. Not long after becoming Holy Roman Emperor in 1765, Joseph II had rashly aspired to 'give the whole universe freedom' to bring him their complaints and he remained receptive to petitioners from all classes of the population. Catherine strongly disapproved, believing, as she told Baron Grimm after Joseph's death, that he had 'ruined his health with his eternal audiences'.[83]

Her own main personal concern that autumn was the health of Aleksey Orlov. Rendered immobile by a bad back (the result of too many jolting carriage rides), he was believed to be at death's door from chronic stomach pains and jaundice. From an account of his symptoms sent on behalf of the anxious empress, doctors in Vienna, Leiden and Leipzig diagnosed gallstones, recommended a less gargantuan diet and advised their patient to take the waters. But since he was too ill to travel abroad, and unable even to join his four brothers for a private lunch with Catherine on her name day, she and Panin went to visit him after Christmas.[84] If she needed a further *memento mori*, it had come on 18 December, birthday of the late Empress Elizabeth, when Catherine donned mourning dress for a memorial service at the Chrysostom monastery before going on to Andrey Shuvalov's mansion to watch for almost an hour as Archbishop Dimitry's funeral procession crawled along Myasnitskaya Street. To dispel the gloom, she took coffee with her host and his family before returning to the Golovin Palace for a game of billiards.[85]

The discomforts of life in that draughty wooden building had long since exhausted its minimal charms. Already on 12 October she had told Falconet of her intention to return to St Petersburg.[86] Irritated by slow progress in the Legislative Commission, which had laboriously worked through each social estate's submissions without reaching any resolutions, she announced in November that its sessions would be suspended in the middle of the following month. The deputies were to reconvene in St Petersburg in February.[87] She travelled north earlier, setting off through streets lined with cheering subjects after attending the consecration of a new church on the Solyanka on Saturday 19 January. At the end of a fifty-three-hour journey via a sequence of 'nasty' roadside palaces, it was a relief

Peter III's tutor, Jacob Stählin, thought Rotari's portrait of Elizabeth in a black lace mantilla the best likeness of this beautiful, irascible empress. Done in the last years of her life, it passed into the collection of her young favourite, Ivan Shuvalov.

The prevailing myth of a conquering foreign ruler bringing civilization and prosperity to Russia is encapsulated by Vigilius Erichsen's portrait of the uniformed empress astride Brilliant, the charger she rode out towards Oranienbaum the day after her coup.

To ensure that enlightened female rule was not mistaken for weakness, Catherine's image-makers represented her as Minerva, the war-like goddess of Wisdom, from the time of her coronation in 1762. This Parisian snuff-box may well have been made to mark her son's visit to the French capital, twenty years later.

'If ever you catch sight of him, you will see without contradiction the finest man that you have ever encountered in your life.' Embracing putti symbolise Catherine's love for Grigory Orlov on the service she commissioned for him from the Imperial Porcelain Factory sometime between 1762 and 1765.

Completed as she arrived in Russia, Rastrelli's Summer Palace on the Fontanka was an exuberant timber fantasy that survived Catherine's reign, along with many other features of a Baroque Court, before being demolished by order of Paul I.

Exemplified by the Green Dining Room, Charles Cameron's cool interiors at Tsarskoye Selo marked the triumph of the restrained neoclassical style in Russian architecture from the late 1770s.

The empress's comedies and operatic pageants played to select audiences at Giacomo Quarenghi's neoclassical Hermitage Theatre, which opened on 22 November 1785. Catherine entered from the adjoining Hermitage, guests from the granite-clad embankment, itself admired as a 'grand work, which, in regard to utility and magnificence' could not 'be paralleled except among the ruins of ancient Rome'.

Done in Kiev in 1787, Mikhail Shibanov's portrait of the empress in travelling dress combines the image of a maternal ruler with the expansionist ambitions represented by the insignia of three chivalric orders: St Andrew the First Called (founded by Peter I), St George (founded 'for bravery' during the Russo-Turkish war of 1768–74) and St Vladimir (founded in 1782, the year in which the empress outlined her 'Greek Project' in a letter to Joseph II of Austria).

'His rarest quality was a courage of heart, mind and soul which set him completely apart from the rest of humanity.' Potëmkin's outsized personality is well captured in Giovanni Battista Lampi's celebration of his martial valour, painted in the last year of the prince's life.

to be home in time to celebrate Grigory Orlov's name day, 25 January. 'You can't believe how good Tsarskoye Selo is,' she told Panin. Town seemed even better: 'Petersburg is paradise by comparison with Ispahan, and especially the palace.'[88]

––––––––––

Catherine was particularly delighted by the large turnout at her first Court reception day and the celebratory mood continued in the festivities surrounding her thirty-ninth birthday. Galuppi pulled out all the stops for his last opera in Russia. When they met shortly after the composer's return to Venice, the renowned Dr Burney thought him still 'full of genius and fire' and later noted that he seemed 'to have constantly kept pace with all the improvements and refinements of the times, and to have been as modern in his dramatic music, to the last year of his life, as ever'.[89] *Iphigenia in Tauride*, premiered on 27 April after Catherine's private audience with the Austrian ambassador, Prince Lobkowitz, was promptly acclaimed in Russia as 'the strongest of his compositions'. It had a more vigorous plot than most *opera seria*, and the ten basses, thirteen tenors, thirteen altos and fifteen trebles of the chapel choir gave an 'outstanding performance' of its innovative, integral choruses.[90] Catherine had spent the birthday itself at Tsarskoye Selo. After church, she invested Aleksey Orlov with the Order of St Andrew and gave him 200,000 roubles (fifty times Galuppi's annual salary) to pay for his convalescence.[91]

Meanwhile the Court was re-adapting to life in the north after its prolonged stay in the old capital. At the end of his affair with Countess Stroganova, Panin had unexpectedly found happiness (and renewed respectability) with one of Catherine's maids of honour, Countess Anna Sheremeteva. Since he was by no means a rich man, her income of 40,000 roubles and family connections made this, as the Prussian ambassador reported, 'the most eminent match that could be made in Russia'.[92] A less fortunate courtier was forced to appeal to the empress when his mother-in-law refused to allow his wife to accompany him to St Petersburg. Catherine sent an official to fetch the girl, entrusting him with a letter for Moscow's Governor General that combines a sense of legal propriety with unmistakeable hauteur:

If the mother becomes stubborn and wants to travel with her daughter, then prevent the mother from leaving the town by my command and bring the daughter whatever happens. If they say that she is ill, then fetch a doctor to examine her to see whether Lopukhina is fit to travel without endangering her life. If the mother cries out a lot, then you should order her to be silent by my command. So that all this should not strike you as strange, let me explain in confidence that the mother will not allow her daughter to join her husband and that the husband has appealed to me to give him his wife. I found his request so just and so in conformity with the laws that I could not refuse; but the mother is to be told nothing of this. Please give the Court official any assistance he needs: the shorter and less public the scene, the better.[93]

For her own part, it was time to catch up with old friends. Within a couple of days of her return to St Petersburg, she had made an informal visit to the girls at the Smolny Institute. Alexander Stroganov entertained her to lunch in March. After Easter, she received Archbishop Gavriil, elected to the Legislative Commission in place of Dimitry, who was escorted to his audience in the Diamond Room by ten noble deputies.[94] Then tragedy struck when Panin's fiancée died from smallpox. Despite her sympathy for his loss, Catherine was more anxious about the threat to her son. Though his Young Court had always been alert to the danger from urban epidemics, now the menace was closer to home. [95] As the empress secretly admitted to Yelagin, the public would never forgive her if the legitimate heir to the throne were to die in her care. 'I am very worried, not being sure what to do for the best, since everything in this critical situation is bad.'[96] Reduced to flitting from one suburban palace to another in the hope of dodging the disease, she tried to relax on the boats and toboggans at Gatchina, and spent longer than usual at Tsarskoye Selo. 'Here I am with my son for the seventh week running,' she told Saltykov at the end of May, 'and there's such an outbreak of the pox, and that of the worst kind, that I decided it was better to live here. It's grist to my mill to have a pretext to stay in the country.'[97] Nothing, she told Panin, could quite match her favourite summer palace:

Count Nikita Ivanovich. Having parted from you on Thursday, we found ourselves in an autumn zephyr in the hills on the way to Krasnoye Selo, although we had left Tsarskoye Selo in very warm weather. On Friday, we travelled in the rain to Gatchina and came back in such a sharp frost that we all wished we had taken our fur coats. Yesterday was Saturday, and although the skies were grey, we didn't feel the cold and are warm and well at Peterhof. Still, it touches the heart to see everything here so neglected, although I have spent a hundred and eighty thousand on it since 1762, including twenty thousand to pay off the debt on the iron piping alone, and the devil alone knows what has been done with the money if it hasn't been used to repair Peterhof. I think it may have been used to pay off the debts of the Construction Chancellery.[98]

As Catherine knew, the chancellery was still as active as ever. Shortly before leaving Moscow, she had agreed to spend 64,915 roubles on marble from the western shores of Lake Ladoga for a new cathedral in honour of St Isaac of Dalmatia. The total budget, to be paid for from state funds, was almost four times as much.[99] As the empress explained, it was not the first attempt to build such a church, which had 'suffered more tribulations and persecutions than the early Christians'.[100] Peter the Great had been born on St Isaac's feast day – 30 May 1672 – but his own St Isaac's Cathedral, where he married Catherine I in 1712, had burned down five years later and its replacement proved to have been built too close to the river. Chevakinsky was appointed to design a grandiose Baroque successor in the last year of Elizabeth's reign, but by 1768 a revised project was in the hands of Rinaldi, currently building a mansion for the Naryshkins on the western side of St Isaac's Square.[101] Although it was not until the following January that Catherine saw the architect's model of the cathedral – a work of art in itself, promising a riot of jasper, marble and porphyry in the manner of the Marble Palace she had commissioned that same year for Grigory Orlov – by midsummer, it was time for her to lay the foundation stone. She inspected the site on 10 July, following lunch with Betskoy and a brief visit to the Academy of Arts on the other side of the river. After reviewing naval exercises in the Gulf on her yacht, the *Saint Catherine* – 'yesterday and the day before,' she boasted, 'I covered ninety miles by sea' – Catherine went to Oranienbaum for the feast of St Panteleymon the Healer on 27 July and to Peterhof for the customary summer sanctification service four days later. Then, braving her fears of the pox, she was back in St Petersburg for the foundation ceremony on 8 August.[102]

Since this was the first public spectacle witnessed by William Richardson, tutor to the sons of the new British ambassador, Lord Cathcart, let Richardson describe the scene:

All the space to be occupied by the church had been previously railed in; and into this place, only persons of high rank, and those who had a particular permission, were admitted. An immense multitude of people were assembled without. An arch, supported upon eight pillars of the Corinthian order, and adorned with garlands, was raised immediately over the place intended for the altar. Beneath this arch was a table covered with crimson velvet, fringed with gold; upon which was placed a small marble chest, fixed to a pully directly above the table. On a side-table, fixed to one of the pillars, was a large gold plate, two pieces of marble in the form of bricks, a gold plate with mortar, and other two plates of the same metal, in which were two hammers and two trowels of gold.[103]

Although guests had been ordered to take their places by 9.30 a.m., it was not until midday that the carriages bearing the imperial party arrived from the Summer Palace.[104] Paul came first, dressed in naval uniform and attended by Panin. Then, bringing up the rear of a solemn clerical procession, Catherine herself appeared, wearing 'a silver-stuff negligee, the ground pea-green, with purple flowers and silver trimming', and carrying a small, green parasol. She made a powerful impression:

> The Empress of Russia is taller than the middle size, very comely, gracefully formed, but inclined to grow corpulent; and of a fair complexion, which, like every other female in this country, she endeavours to improve by the addition of rouge. She has a fine mouth and teeth; and blue eyes, expressive of scrutiny, something not so good as observation, and not so bad as suspicion. Her features are in general regular and pleasing. Indeed, with regard to her appearance altogether, it would be doing her injustice to say it was masculine, yet it would not be doing her justice to say it was entirely feminine.

After some gold coins had been consecrated by the clergy and laid in the chest, it was closed and raised by the pulley. The table disappeared through a trapdoor, so that the empress could lower the chest into place. Once she had cemented a marble brick on top of it, Paul and the bishops followed suit with trowel and mortar, along with some of the attendant notables and the foreign ambassadors. The ceremony was brought to a close with an oration by Archimandrite Platon. Richardson sensed his eloquence but, having no Russian, failed to understand the distinctly political address in which the preacher heralded a new temple of Solomon with Catherine in the role of King David. She was wise as the king of the Israelites, Platon proclaimed, only more peace-loving (a claim which stood at odds with her increasingly belligerent stance on the Polish question). Singling out the empress's humanitarian Instruction for special praise, Platon portrayed the new cathedral as a monument to Russia's greatness and the empress's personal glory.[105] Timofey Ivanov drove home the point with a commemorative medal, designed on the basis of Rinaldi's model, which quoted from the gospel of St Matthew (22: 21): 'Render therefore to Caesar the things that are Caesar's, and to God the things that are God's.'[106]

No less anxious to pander to the empress's obsession with posterity was the Parisian sculptor Etienne-Maurice Falconet, a friend of Diderot and Prince Dimitry Golitsyn who had recommended him to Catherine as the ideal candidate for the statue of Peter the Great she had determined to commission as early as 1764. Falconet arrived in St Petersburg at the end of October 1766, working from a studio on the site of Elizabeth's temporary wooden palace. 'Diderot,' he exclaimed just three months later, 'you can't imagine how this unusual woman can elevate one's merits and talents.'[107] In June 1768 he told her of a drawing 'that I shall show to no one until Your Majesty has seen it: *Catherine the Second gives laws to her Empire. She deigns to lower her sceptre to propose to her subjects a means of rendering them happier.* If this simple idea is not convenient, I know nothing better nor more glorious.'[108] Catherine agreed that it was a noble idea, 'much better' than his earlier plan to depict her with 'tottering Russia', a reference to the coup of 1762 that was judged 'injurious to Peter III and to Russia': 'You will tell me when it is time for me to come to see the statue and the drawing.'[109] Knowing that she had never previously authorised a statue of herself, Falconet wondered why there should be a problem when it was proposed to strike medallions to commemorate the new law code. Only her own '*delicatesse*' stood in its way, Catherine replied, 'but perhaps the beauty of your drawing will make me forget my previous resolutions'.[110]

Apparently it did not. Though the empress sat for at least two busts and two medallions by Falconet's attractive young pupil Marie-Anne Collot,[111] his own statue was never done, perhaps because Catherine had grown anxious about the progress of the Legislative Commission. Its sessions in the long Winter Palace gallery overlooking the river still seemed active enough, as Lord Cathcart discovered during a break in the proceedings on 18 August:

> The room seemed so full, and the different groups so busy in conversation, that it was impossible to look down upon the assembly without thinking of a beehive. The empress's throne fills one end of the room, the other end and both sides have benches as in the House of Commons; on the left side of the throne is a table of State. At the upper end there was a chair for the Marshal of the commission, and on one side two other chairs, one for the director who

minutes the proceedings, and the other for the procureur-général who is there as commissioner for the empress and who has a right to interpose in her name, in case the standing orders should be attached.[112]

Catherine, however, worried that all this activity seemed to be leading nowhere. In turning to discuss justice and judicial procedure when they reconvened in St Petersburg, the deputies had become lost in a morass of shapeless detail. Only a desperate attempt to revise their procedures had focused their attentions on a draft law on the rights of the nobility at the beginning of July, and even then, no decisions were reached.[113]

The fundamental problem facing the Commission was the unbridgeable gap between Catherine's expectations and the preoccupations of most deputies. Having written in one of her earliest notebooks that 'The thing that is most subject to drawbacks is the making of a new law', she was well aware of the restraining power of custom.[114] Her Instruction followed Montesquieu in stressing the need to prepare people's minds for new legislation – scarcely the philosophy of an intemperate despot. On the other hand, having once embarked on a project, the empress was always impatient for swift results. She had boasted to Voltaire during the Christmas recess that the Russian people were 'an excellent ground in which a good seed will quickly grow'.[115] But this turned out to be wishful thinking. She had misjudged both the amount of preparatory work required to ensure the smooth running of the Commission and the inherent conservatism of the deputies. 'The number of ignorant noblemen,' she later admitted, 'was immeasurably larger than I could ever have supposed.'[116] Living in the company of sophisticated friends, Catherine had presumed that their views were widely shared. Many of them took some part in the Commission: Panin as the author of the submission by the Moscow nobility, Grigory Orlov as a noble deputy for St Petersburg, Andrey Shuvalov as director of the journals recording the proceedings. The young Count Semën Vorontsov read Beccaria just before the Commission convened. But while such men reflected the interests of Russia's educated, Western-oriented elite, the overwhelming majority of the deputies had little interest in either philosophy or national politics. Their interests were selfish and parochial.[117]

We can only guess what might have transpired had the Legislative Commission been allowed to run its course. Its proceedings generated a vast reservoir of information, much of which helped to inform Catherine's subsequent legislation, and its sub-commissions continued to work until around 1774. The gold and silver tabernacle donated by the empress to the Dormition Cathedral on the Commission's tenth anniversary depicted Moses on Mount Sinai receiving the Ten Commandments as a reminder of her status as lawgiver.[118] A skeletal secretariat was still employed at the end of her reign. By then, however, the whole project was little more than a memory. All through the empress's time in Moscow, the international situation had been increasingly destabilised by her support for a group of Orthodox fanatics in overwhelmingly Catholic Poland, a perverted stand in favour of religious toleration which resulted in civil war. When Cossack troops were sent to suppress it in June 1768, they crossed the border into the Ottoman Empire, sacking the little frontier town of Balta and massacring its Jews. In retaliation, the Turks declared war in October by imprisoning the Russian ambassador in Constantinople. Since most deputies were required for military service, Catherine announced the suspension of the Legislative Commission on 18 December. The 203rd and final plenary session was held on 12 January 1769. Now all Europe had another extraordinary prospect to occupy its attention. 'An unsuccessful foreign war tends to impair the authority of all despots,' warned William Richardson, 'and this is the first foreign war she has ever waged.'[119]

CHAPTER EIGHT

IMPERIAL AMBITIONS 1768–1772

Catherine's readiness to provoke a conflict in defence of Orthodoxy occasioned widespread surprise. 'Where bigotry baffles reason, and where fanaticism supplies courage,' Sir George Macartney remarked in 1766, the result was bound to be uncertain: 'A religious war, however justly undertaken, is always of the most odious nature, and of all wars of the most doubtful success.'[1] However, if the empress's cause proved unexpected, then there had never been any doubt of her seething ambition. Having entered the Seven Years' War in 1756 as the junior partner in the anti-Prussian coalition, Russia had emerged by 1763 as 'the arbiter of eastern Europe'.[2] Victories over Frederick the Great at Gross-Jägersdorf and Kunersdorf, not long after he had himself routed the French at Rossbach, had raised memories of the glorious era of Peter the Great. No ambassador accredited to St Petersburg in the early years of her reign could fail to sense Russia's growing self-confidence. 'This Court rises hourly higher and higher in her pride,' Macartney reported in 1765, 'and dazzled by her present prosperity looks with less deference upon other powers and with more admiration on herself.'[3]

Now Catherine was keen to translate isolated military triumphs into lasting diplomatic prestige. As Joseph II discovered during his visit to Russia in 1780, she was closely involved in day-to-day diplomacy. 'Among the conversations in which our guest engaged me hourly,' reported the empress's secretary, Alexander Bezborodko, 'he asked me about Her Imperial Majesty's way of managing business, and was amazed when in answer to his question I said that all the dispatches from our ministry, whether they be sent to our ambassadors or to [foreign] courts, have been approved in draft by the Sovereign herself, so that not a single paper goes out that has not been presented to Her Majesty in the original: he thought that relations or letters were put up to her only in abbreviated form, and only those directly worthy of her attention.'[4] Yet for all her hard work, there was a limit to what Catherine could do. Russia's finances were as badly dented by the war as any other power's, her soldiers remained unpaid, and the empress's position on the throne, though never seriously threatened, even by Mirovich, was sufficiently uncertain to deter any grandiose foreign adventure.

Poland, over which Russia had effectively established a protectorate since 1717, seemed to offer the greatest prospect of gain at the lowest level of risk. In September 1763, the death of King Augustus III (who was also the Elector of Saxony) opened up what Princess Dashkova later described as 'a vast field for political intrigue'.[5] Following the convictions of a lifetime, Chancellor Bestuzhev tried to persuade Catherine to support another Saxon candidate for the Polish throne, acceptable to Austria and France. His failure marked the end of a long career and a decisive moment in Russian foreign policy. Instead the empress decided to support the election of a native Pole – and she knew just who she wanted. Soon after her coup, Catherine had promised Stanisław Poniatowski that she would make him king, just as Sir Charles Hanbury-Williams had once imagined. According to Dashkova, whose husband died while serving with the Russian troops sent to put pressure on the Poles, Grigory Orlov and Zakhar Chernyshëv were appalled by the idea. Neither relished the prospect of a revival of the empress's relationship with her former lover. They need not have worried. When it came to international power politics, Catherine always set personal feelings aside. Now it was up to Nikita Panin, who took charge of Russian foreign policy at the end of October 1763, to realise her manipulative intent.[6]

It was far from easy for Panin to hold the balance of forces at Court. Behind the scenes, Zakhar Chernyshëv was already so eager to annexe Polish territory that on 6 October he outlined a plan, probably hatched earlier in the spring, to redraw the border along a line similar to the one eventually agreed in the first partition of 1772.[7] When the news leaked out, Catherine promptly denied any expansionist ambitions. Claiming that she ruled on the basis of 'justice, equity and humanity', a sanctimonious manifesto of December 1763 declared:

If ever malice and falsehood could invent a rumour absolutely untrue, it is certainly that which people have dared to spread about, that we allegedly decided to press for the election of a Diet simply in order that with its help and connivance, we might facilitate the means of invading certain provinces of the King of Poland and the Grand Duchy of Lithuania, to dismember them and then to appropriate them for ourselves and our Empire. The beginning of our reign alone is enough to destroy at its root this sort of fiction and deprive it of all likelihood and foundation. We hold that the prosperity of a people does not consist in foreign conquests. We are firmly convinced that a ruler is only greater when he directs the springs of government towards the welfare and happiness of his people.[8]

It was true that Russia had little to gain from conquering a state whose overwhelmingly Catholic population, Jewish minority, unruly noble elite, and direct borders with Prussia and Austria would all have been liabilities to St Petersburg (as indeed they proved in the era of the partitions). But that did not mean that Catherine had no ulterior motives in Poland. In fact, Augustus's demise provided her with a perfect opportunity to extend her indirect control over a vital buffer state by installing a pliant ruler and keeping his government weak.[9]

She knew that her rivals had similar ambitions. 'Don't laugh at me because I leapt from my chair when I heard of the death of the king of Poland,' she warned Panin: 'the king of Prussia jumped up from his table.'[10] Fortunately for her, Frederick was even more preoccupied by internal reconstruction than she was and decided that his best option was to collaborate with Russia to frustrate his Austrian rivals. Like the Prussians, the French were stymied by their disastrous performance in the Seven Years' War and without their support the Habsburgs were powerless to intervene. Given this relatively free hand, Catherine was able to engineer Stanisław's election in August 1764.[11] To Panin, she could hardly restrain her delight:

Nikita Ivanovich! I congratulate you on the king we have made. This event greatly increases my trust in you, since I see how faultless all your measures were. I didn't want to miss showing you how pleased I am. My back aches so badly that I cannot hold a pen for long, so would you kindly, having explained the reason, take my place on this occasion and write to Count Keyserling and to Prince Repnin, expressing my pleasure at their work and zeal, through which they have obtained no small glory both for themselves and for us. And order a letter to the new King to be prepared for my signature, in reply to his. Either I have rheumatism in my back or I am dying. I fear that it may be a stone, only after a bath it felt better for the first time, so perhaps it is only a chill.[12]

There was a price to pay for Frederick's collaboration, and it came in the form of a defensive alliance with Prussia, concluded in March 1764. In the unstable balance of power bequeathed by the Seven Years' War, Catherine would have preferred to keep her distance from both Austria and Prussia who were now her main rivals to fill the vacuum created by the decline of French influence in eastern Europe. However, since Austria and Prussia were themselves implacable enemies, competing for the domination of the smaller German states, it was utopian to suppose that Russia could stay neutral for long.[13] Since the Austrians remained allied to the French, who continued to resent Russian policies against their traditional satellites, Sweden, Poland and the Ottoman Empire, an Austrian alliance for Catherine was impossible. Frederick, who made it a principle of Prussian policy 'to seek an alliance with those of one's neighbours capable of delivering the most dangerous blows', was swift to see the opportunity presented by Catherine's ambitions in Poland.[14] Outwitting her inexperienced ambassador in Berlin, he inveigled the empress into an alliance by pretending that he might otherwise strike a wholly improbable deal with the Turks.[15]

Making a virtue from necessity, Panin envisaged the Prussian alliance as the first building block in a new 'Northern System' designed to protect Russia's hegemony in the Baltic. He described what he meant to Ivan Chernyshëv, who set out for London as ambassador in 1768:

By the Northern System we have in mind and mean the largest and closest possible union of northern powers in a direct focal point for our common interest, in order to oppose to the Bourbon and Austrian Houses a firm counter-weight among European Courts, and a northern peace completely free from their influence, which has led so often to harmful effects.[16]

This was easier said than done. Frederick had no interest in an alliance with Britain and was anxious not to be drawn into Russian machinations in Sweden. Willing enough to support such machinations as a way of embarrassing the French, the British saw no reason to support Catherine's ambitions in Poland or the Ottoman Empire. Though the empress renewed the Anglo-Russian trade treaty of 1734 in 1766, on terms favourable to Russia, Macartney failed to conclude a diplomatic alliance because Catherine insisted on unilateral British assistance in the event of war with the Turks. 'This Court has listened to me with the most provoking phlegm and the most stoical indifference,' the ambassador was forced to admit. 'The result of the whole is a flat refusal.'[17] In the end, the only tangible evidence of a wider Northern System was the defensive alliance con-cluded between Russia and Denmark – still a significant naval presence in the Baltic – at the end of February 1765. This scarcely counted as a close union of northern powers. And even if it had, there remained an obvious defect in Panin's Northern System, which left the southern and south-western parts of Russia's extensive borders exposed to precisely the sort of incident that sparked off the Russo-Turkish War in 1768.

Though he remained at Catherine's side until 1781, Panin's authority was never the same again. Against his advice, she decided to direct the war through a newly created council, which bore all the marks of her deft approach to govern-ment. Though the council was a purely advisory body, the empress left its members in no doubt that they were complicit in any decisions that might emerge from their deliberations:

> I intend to carry out all the measures proposed with great firmness, since I take them to be measures which you, moved by zeal, fervour and devotion to me and to your country, have unanimously advised me to take in this important matter: hence, if any one still has any doubts, let him say so without loss of time.[18]

Not content with risking her empire in war with the Turks, Catherine risked her own life in October 1768 by electing to be inoculated against smallpox. As an advocate of fresh air and a wholesome diet, the empress generally maintained a healthy disrespect for doctors – 'charlatans', as she described them on the death of the French king, 'who always do you more harm than good, witness Louis XV, who had ten of them around him and is dead all the same'.[19] Still, faced with two evils, as she emphasised to Frederick the Great, 'every reasonable man' would choose the lesser, 'all other things being equal'.[20] So, rather than relapse into more indecisive shuttling between suburban palaces – her pattern, as we have seen, throughout the summer of 1768 – Catherine determined to submit herself to a controversial treatment. Inoculation had been banned by the Sorbonne as an interference with the workings of Providence and was opposed even in some Enlightened circles on the grounds that it might lead to infection. Provided all went well, she could claim to have acted both rationally and courageously.[21]

The doctor chosen to perform the operation was the fifty-six-year-old Thomas

Dimsdale, whose celebrated treatise on the subject had been published in 1767.[22] When he arrived in St Petersburg at the end of August, Dimsdale found himself 'upon as free and easy a footing in the imperial palace as he could be in the house of any nobleman in England'.[23] Despite his execrable French and Catherine's minimal English, doctor and patient established an immediate rapport (their interpreter, on days when he was not paralysed by gout, was Alexander Cherkasov, who had studied informally at Cambridge in the early 1740s and now headed the Medical College). Understandably nervous about exposing a foreign sovereign to risk, and sharing the widespread belief that diseases varied according to climate and geography, Dimsdale hesitated to operate until he was sure that his treatment would be as effective in Russia as it had been at home. Catherine gave him the confidence to continue, even when tests on impoverished local youths proved equivocal. Adding sauce to an already titillating story, a Scottish merchant in St Petersburg reported that the doctor, whose presence in Russia was an open secret, had 'free access' every morning to the empress's bedroom, where Grigory Orlov often sat on the bedspread beside them.[24] Grigory, however, was away on a hunting expedition when Catherine finally summoned Dimsdale to the Winter Palace in the dead of night on 12 October. Apart from Cherkasov, only two others were present at the inoculation: Panin, the treatment's leading advocate, and Caspar von Saldern, the fixer from Holstein who had attached himself to Paul's household in the 1760s.

Complaining of low mood, Catherine retreated to Tsarskoye Selo on the following day. At first she was able to live relatively normally, chatting and playing cards in the afternoon, taking regular walks outside and even a drive to inspect the new road to Gatchina.[25] As she retired to her apartments over the course of the next few days, Panin let it be known that she continued to work, and that her only reported symptom, other than 'a very favourable eruption of small pox, very few in number', was a mild fever.[26] She also complained of persistent giddiness, 'in a manner according to her like drunkenness', and of mild constipation, which Dimsdale treated with his trusty bedtime laxative made from calomel, crabs' claws and tartar emetic, either crushed into pills or mixed with syrup or jelly. To keep her temperature down, he prescribed the occasional glass of cold water and a stroll in the unheated Great Hall. Having noticed the first marks on her arm on the evening of 19 October, he spent the whole of the following day on watch in her apartments. Catherine woke at seven, having 'sweated considerably in the night'. 'The inflammation of the arms was spread considerably & a number of small pustules were discoverable around the incision.' Only one spot had appeared on her forehead, offering no serious threat to her complexion, and two more on her hand or wrist. 'Her complaints were of stiffness under the arms, particularly the left, of some pain in her back and legs and a sort of general weariness, but not sleepy as yesterday. Upon the whole Her Majesty was very brisk and cheerful the whole afternoon.'[27] Now the danger was past, she began a period of active convalescence, informing Saltykov in Moscow on 27 October that she had not only remained on her feet throughout, but experienced only the sort of minor discomfort that was to be expected. 'I tell you this happy outcome so that you can counter any erroneous rumours.'[28] After another drive and a walk in the fresh air, she felt sufficiently confident to reassure Falconet, who had written to her in mock reproach for defying the Sorbonne, that she had no intention of succumbing to the disease: 'They often decide in favour of absurdities, which in my opinion should have discredited them long ago; after all, the human species are no longer goslings.'[29]

Following Catherine's return to St Petersburg on 1 November, Paul, who might have been inoculated earlier had he not been recovering from chickenpox, was treated next evening after a formal Te Deum in the palace chapel led by Archbishop Gavriil.[30] More than a hundred nobles soon followed suit. 'Starting with me and my son,' Catherine boasted to Ivan Chernyshëv a fortnight later, 'there is not an aristocratic household that does not contain some of the inoculated – and many complain that they had smallpox naturally and so cannot follow the fashion.' Grigory Orlov and Kirill Razumovsky were among the 'countless others' who had 'passed through Mr Dimsdale's hands', including even 'beauties' such as Princess Shcherbatova and Princess Trubetskaya. 'See what setting an example can do! Three months ago, no one wanted to hear of it, and yet now they look on it as salvation.'[31]

Once Paul's survival seemed assured, the next great feast in the Orthodox calendar – the Presentation of the Mother of God in the Temple on 21 November – marked a natural opportunity for a formal service of thanksgiving in the Winter Palace chapel. 'On the inside of a rail which extended across the room,' William Richardson recorded, 'and close by the pillar which was next to the altar, on the south side, stood the Empress and her son; and also on the inside of the rail, and on each side of the altar, was a choir of musicians. All the rest who witnessed, or took part in the solemnity, excepting the priests, stood on the outside of the rail.'[32] This service, commemorated annually at Court until 1795 and perpetuated by the Senate in February 1769 in churches across the empire, was the first of a barrage of measures designed to propagate the image of a selfless and knowledgeable empress conferring benefits on her people. Bells rang out day and night from every church in the capital for the next two days, with fireworks across the city at midnight.[33] No one was more relieved than Dimsdale. 'I shall never forget the care you gave me,' Catherine later wrote to him, 'and the anxiety you experienced in the time following my inoculation and that of my son.'[34] On her name day, 24 November, she invested her doctor as a baron of the Russian empire and rewarded him with £10,000 – an outlandish sum, supplemented by an annual pension of £500 for life.[35] Alexander Markov, the boy who had supplied the necessary infected matter, was ennobled under the unflattering soubriquet 'ospenny' ('Lord Smallpox'). The Court theatre staged an allegorical ballet, *Prejudice Overcome*, in which the Genius of Science (played by the ballet master Angiolini), Minerva (representing Catherine), and Ruthenia (Russia), conquered Superstition and Ignorance with the assistance of Alcind (Paul) and released the common people from their grasp.[36] The commemorative medal, struck in 1772, when inoculations were still being administered in a variety of Russian hospitals, drove home the empress's fundamental message: 'She herself set an example.'[37]

When the children of the Austrian empress were successfully inoculated by another British doctor, Maria Theresa held a feast at Schönbrunn at which the royal family waited on his sixty-five lesser-ranking patients.[38] Obsessed with order and hierarchy, Catherine would never have turned the world upside down. Competitive as ever, she gaily told Voltaire in December 1768 that 'more people have been inoculated here in one month than in eight at Vienna'. For her part, she teased, the best medicine during her convalescence had been to listen to readings from *Candide*, in which the master had written that if two armies of 30,000 men were to meet in battle, two-thirds of the soldiers would be pock-marked: 'After that, it is impossible to feel the slightest bit ill.'[39]

———

To make Catherine feel even better, an extension to her palace was nearing completion. At last she would be able to escape echoing staterooms, indulge her passion for informal entertainment, and exercise her legendary charm to devastating effect. Designed by Veldten and Vallin de la Mothe, the Small Hermitage was built on a narrow plot of land immediately to the east of the Winter Palace, hitherto occupied by dilapidated mansions built for two of Peter the Great's admirals, Cornelius Cruys and Fëdor Golovin. Catherine inspected some early plans while in Moscow after her coronation, work started in 1764, and by the time she returned to the old capital in February 1767, she had seen a magnificent pavilion grow up at the southern end of the site. Grigory Orlov was to live there until 1775 in a suite of rooms linked to her own apartments by a flying bridge. His three reception rooms and a dining room overlooked Millionnaya to the south; to the north, a bedroom, mirrored boudoir and study faced onto a hanging garden. While the empress was preparing to sail the Volga, Cruys's house on the Neva was finally demolished, and work began to extend the garden northwards to a new pavilion overlooking the river, originally known as the orangery after the fruit trees planted in decorative pots on the balustrade. Catherine inspected a wooden model in March 1768 and by the following February the new building was ready to hold the first of many private entertainments – themselves soon christened 'small hermitages' – beginning with a theatrical performance in the neighbouring stables and ending with dinner at the two mechanical tables in the easternmost room.[40]

Soon imitated by leading aristocrats, this device had been pioneered by Elizabeth at Tsarskoye Selo, where it remained a source of merriment in Catherine's time:

> When the plates are changed you pull a string by the side of everybody's right hand which goes underneath the table and rings a bell. Your plate goes down, as all round it is composed of so many divisions like stove holes. You write down upon a slate and pencil which is fixed ready, and what you want immediately comes up. A great diversion was from one table to the other to send something or other that served to laugh.[41]

Towards the end of the carnival, Dr Dimsdale had to be called when Catherine caught a fever that knocked her off her feet 'for six whole days, which was highly inconvenient for someone who loves to bustle about and who hates being stuck in bed'.[42] But this proved to be merely a temporary interruption to her convivial way of life. 'Those who form her society,' Lord Cathcart reported, 'are either young people who are extremely gay, or such as are capable from the vivacity of their disposition to keep pace with those who are younger than themselves.'[43]

While the northern part of the Small Hermitage was under construction, Catherine decided in March 1768 to build a new gallery along the sides of the hanging garden to house her growing art collection. Some of the finest works to be seen in today's Hermitage Museum were acquired in these early years. The foundations of the collection had been laid in 1764 with the purchase of 225 paintings belonging to the Berlin picture dealer, Johann Ernst Gotzkowsky, whose seventeenth-century Flemish Masters included Jan Steen's *Revellers* and Frans Hals's *Young Man Holding a Glove*. In the following year, Prince Dimitry Alekseyevich Golitsyn became Catherine's principal agent in Paris having been appointed ambassador to Versailles at the age of thirty-one. It was thanks to his collaboration with Diderot that the Hermitage acquired Rembrandt's *Return of the Prodigal Son* and a more recent masterpiece by Jean-Baptiste Greuze, *The Paralytic, or the Fruits of a Good Education* (1763). When he moved to The Hague in 1768, Golitsyn negotiated the purchase of about 600 paintings – including works by Rembrandt, Rubens, Wouvermans and Watteau – from the collection of Count Heinrich von Brühl, who had amassed his treasures by stealing from his master, Augustus III of Poland. But Golitsyn had not lost touch with Diderot, who helped him to secure François Tronchin's Genevan collection in 1770 and brokered an even more sensational deal in the following year, when Catherine paid the heirs of the Parisian financier Pierre Crozat 460,000 livres for 500 paintings including Giorgione's *Judith*, Titian's *Danaë* and Raphael's *Holy Family*. Diderot believed that the collection was worth more than twice as much.[44]

It is hard to say what pleasure Catherine took from most of these purchases. Although her charmed circle included the connoisseurs Alexander Stroganov and Ivan Shuvalov, who spent much of the period between 1763 and 1777 in Italy collecting sculptures for himself and the Hermitage, she seems to have revelled in a kind of inverted snobbery that oscillated between dependence on 'expert' opinion and a determination to defy it. She and Lev Naryshkin were 'professional ignoramuses', the empress later declared, 'and we use our ignorance to annoy the Grand Chamberlain Shuvalov and Count Stroganov, who are both members of at least 24 academies'.[45] She clearly took a liking to Jean Huber's innovative cycle of portraits of Voltaire in various intimate, everyday poses, which arrived in St Petersburg at the rate of about one a year after Grimm had announced her commission in the *Correspondance littéraire* in March 1769. 'I had to burst out laughing when I saw the patriarch getting out of bed,' Catherine admitted on re-discovering the paintings hidden away at Tsarksoye Selo in 1776. 'I think that one's original: the vivacity of his character and the impatience of his imagination give him no time to do one thing at once. The kicking horse being corrected by Voltaire is also very good.'[46] However, since her early letters reveal little about her personal tastes, it is tempting to conclude that many of the masterpieces arriving in St Petersburg by the carton-load left her unmoved. The sheer scale of her acquisitions prevented any intimate acquaintance with all of them: she bought some 4000 canvases in the first twenty years of her reign.

Apart from the fact that Catherine liked a bargain, the most important benefit conferred by great works of art was international prestige. Like diplomacy, collecting was a competitive business. And paintings, no less than territory, were best acquired at the expense of weakened rivals. Gotzkowsky's collection was snatched from under the nose of Frederick the Great when financial embarrassments brought about by the Seven Years' War prevented him from fulfilling his promise to buy them for himself. Paradoxically, such triumphs made it harder for the empress's agents to strike a confidential deal once her interest leaked out to journalists hungry for gossip on the Parisian art market. In 1768 Bachaumont's *Mémoires secrets* mocked Diderot's vain attempts to acquire Louis-Jean Gaignat's paintings, which foundered on a will forbidding the sale of the collection as a whole. Forced to compete against the duc de Choiseul at auction in February 1769, he eventually acquired only five pictures, including Murillo's *Rest on the Flight to Egypt*. Falconet told Catherine that it was a painting 'to speak of on one's knees'. As Diderot discovered, to represent an upstart foreign power that threatened to denude France of such treasures was to invite widespread obloquy. Some feared that the greatest Western masterpieces were disappearing into oblivion. 'How sad it is to see going and passing into the hands of the Scythians things that are so precious that ten people at most will admire them in Russia,' complained Jean-Henri Eberts in September 1769. 'Everyone can aspire to the pleasure of seeing the banks of the Seine, but few are curious to visit those of the cold Neva.'[47] Diderot himself was more philosophical. Having initially doubted the empress's ability to collect enough paintings to inspire good taste in art, he gradually acknowledged the changing balance of power. 'We sell our pictures and our statues in the midst of peace, but Catherine buys them in the midst of war,' he remarked in rueful admiration to Falconet in April 1772. 'The sciences, the arts, taste and wisdom climb to the north, and barbarism with its train comes southwards.'[48]

Egged on by Grimm, Diderot's Neapolitan friend, the economist abbé Galiani, later found a philosophical explanation for these developments in an ironic contrast between Catherine and the king of France. If one wanted to know why 'the Russians have climbed so high and the French come tumbling down so low under Catherine and Louis XV', then the causes were to be found 'in the character, conduct and gestures of their sovereigns'. Both monarchs had encouraged luxury and the arts, and yet 'French morals have been corrupted, valour has gone soft, while the opposite has happened to the Russians. The reason is that in France they have encouraged a voluptuous luxury which enervates, and in Russia a magnificent luxury which invigorates.' 'The cause of the decadence of French military power,' Galiani concluded, 'and the aggrandisement of that of the Russians derives from the same principle.' The Russians would never have won their battles had they been covered 'in lace and chiffon'.[49]

Since war was even more expensive than art collecting, its onset led Catherine to tighten her tax policy. She could also draw on a new stream of income because the Russo-Turkish campaign of 1768–74 was the first to be financed by foreign loans, advanced by the Amsterdam finance markets on the strength of her armies' performance in the Seven Years' War. These loans in turn prompted unprecedented financial sophistication within Russia as the empress oversaw the introduction of paper money under the aegis of a new bank, created at the end of December 1768 and headed by Andrey Shuvalov. Whereas Peter III had contemplated five notes in 1762, ranging in value from 10 to 500 roubles, Catherine settled for four denominations: 25, 50, 75 and 100. Before long she faced problems of forgery and inflation. 'I have in my hands a 100-rouble note numbered 80,000', reported the hostile French ambassador in September 1770. 'It is from last year: another indication that this operation is overstretched.' By the end of the war, notes to the value of some 12.7 million roubles were in circulation.[50] There were short-term worries too. While Count Solms, the Prussian ambassador, was anxious that Shuvalov's very name would be sufficient to revive 'disagreeable memories' of his father – Elizabeth's unpopular minister, Peter Shuvalov – who had 'acquired millions at the expense of the state and to the ruin of several individuals', Catherine was more concerned about the change of culture required in her own Court administration.[51] As she complained to Yelagin in April 1769:

It is with the greatest possible surprise that I hear that the palace chancellery is refusing to accept state assignats from private individuals. A peasant presented his papers and was told to bring cash. Can it be that my statutes are not valid in the palace chancellery, or do the clerks steal [coins] for their own loathsome gain, when no accounting errors can be made with assignats? Kindly look into this without delay: I beg you to punish those who have infringed my statutes.[52]

Such tones were always reserved for officials who should have known better. Even so, a degree of tetchiness was understandable as the empress became impatient with the protracted preparations for battle. Although war had been declared in the autumn, it was not until the following spring that campaigning could begin. While more than 50,000 troops were being recruited, Catherine spent the winter of 1768–9 reading herself into a world as far removed from Panin's Northern System as it was possible to imagine. Since there was no prospect of drawing the Italian states into her conflict with the Turks – Naples, she discovered, danced 'to the sound of the French flute, and this flute is not in harmony with the voice of Russia' – she concentrated on trying to support the Corsican revolt against France. Boswell's account of his travels on the island, provided for her by Lord Cathcart, enhanced her admiration for the revolt's leader, General Pasquale Paoli.[53] Judging from the letter she wrote to Ivan Chernyshëv on 14 December, Paoli's buccaneering spirit proved more infectious than the smallpox:

And now the sleeping cat has been awakened; and now the cat is going to chase the mice; and now you will see what you will see; and now they're going to talk about us; and no one will expect all the racket we're going to make; and now the Turks are going to be defeated; and now the French will everywhere be treated as the Corsicans treat them; and now that's quite enough verbiage. Adieu, Monsieur![54]

Meanwhile, spontaneous revolts among the Balkan Slavs seemed to offer the prospect of coordinated resistance against the Turks, and especially in Montenegro, where an Italian bandit calling himself Stephen the Little had publicly declared that he was Peter III, giving Catherine an added incentive to intervene. She employed an Italian aristocrat in a vain attempt to draw the Order of the Knights of Malta into her struggle against the infidel. 'Above all,' as Franco Venturi has shown, 'she created a net of agents and listening posts in Italy and thus set in motion a type of diplomacy quite different from the traditional one.'[55]

Most of this was as much the stuff of fantasy as the ancient prophecy, unexpectedly given renewed credence by Russian designs on Constantinople, that the downfall of the Ottoman Empire would be brought about by a race of blond men.[56] Yet for Catherine the deeds of war were bound to remain a thing of the mind. Unlike the male monarchs of her age, who regularly led their troops into battle, she could experience war only vicariously. For much of the time, she was forced to play a waiting game, not without its stresses for a sovereign accustomed to rapid progress in all her activities. Both her mood and her health fluctuated sharply with the news from the front. Victories were greeted with unrestrained joy, reverses with undisguised irritation. During the anxious intervals in between, her entourage did their best to keep her relaxed and amused.

At the beginning of April 1769, Vladimir Orlov reintroduced her to Ivan Kulibin, the inventor from Nizhny Novgorod whose clock in the form of a mechanical toy egg struck the hour with Easter tunes and opened to reveal a scene of the Resurrection, played out by miniature figures done in gold and silver. Catherine rewarded him with 1000 roubles.[57] God seemed firmly on her side when campaigning opened just before her fortieth birthday. General A. M. Golitsyn was her commander-in-chief, appointed as a compromise between two more distinguished candidates: General Peter Panin (favoured by his brother, Nikita) and General Peter Rumyantsev (supported by Grigory Orlov against the Panins).[58] When news of his first victory at Khotin, the main Turkish fort on the Dniester, reached Tsarskoye Selo on the afternoon of 30 April, Catherine called her courtiers into the dining room to deliver the glad tidings herself. 'The Turkish camp is taken,' she informed Saltykov next day, 'along with a great number of trophies and prisoners. Our losses were almost nil, since the enemy cannon fired over our heads.' That morning, the Court travelled to St Petersburg for a thanksgiving service at the Kazan Church where she made sure Paul was present. A jubilant crowd lined the streets to join the celebrations.[59] Soon there were more. By 10 May, Catherine was delighted to report that Golitsyn had defeated another 30,000-strong Turkish army.[60]

Confident of his further progress, she relaxed at Gatchina, where Rinaldi's building work was advancing apace, and where she and Grigory Orlov strolled through the park to see the pheasants in the menagerie after Lev Naryshkin had played the violin for them in the new wooden apartments on 15 May. Eight days later, Zakhar Chernyshëv and Praskovya Bruce joined the three of them at the dacha at Bronnaya, where they sat up all night playing cards to watch the long-awaited transit of Venus through a telescope set up by Paul's science tutor, Professor Aepinus (the Russian Academy of Sciences played a central part in the world-wide observations of the event).[61] Military matters loomed larger at the beginning of June, when Grigory, acting in his capacity as Master of the Ordinance, took Catherine on a tour of the Liteyny cannon foundry in St Petersburg attended by all her artillery generals. Not that the common people were forgotten. At the accession day celebrations in the Dutch Hall at Monplaisir, the empress made a patriotic gesture by proposing a new toast 'to all her subjects' after the usual toasts to herself and the heir to the throne.[62]

The summer brought more disconcerting news. Catherine's early boasts were made to seem embarrassing when adroit manoeuvring by the Ottomans forced Golitsyn to retreat across the Dniester, abandoning his earlier gains. Yet no sooner had she given orders to sack him on 13 August than he embarrassed her again by retaking Khotin in September. That was a more pardonable offence. 'The tsarina is drunk with joy,' reported the appalled French ambassador. 'Her health, which had been crushed by the reverses, is visibly restored.'[63] Until then, the atmosphere had indeed been tense in St Petersburg, where rumours of conspiracies and mysterious disappearances circulated in the sort of 'confidential whispers' that Richardson attributed to a people 'prohibited from speaking or writing about politics':

> The Empress tells them, that as her maternal care for her dear people keeps her sleepless by night, and busy by day – and I really believe that her nights are as sleepless as her days are busy – they have no occasion to give themselves any further trouble about public affairs, than to act implicitly as she directs ... Happy king of England! who may go about with as much security after a defeat, as after a victory; who has no occasion for a board of spies against his own subjects; and may allow his people to speak, write, and think as they please.[64]

———

Richardson's timing could hardly have been less felicitous. Far from spurning public opinion, Catherine was even keener to nurture it in the aftermath of the abortive Legislative Commission. Now that it was clear that the ideas she had borrowed from Montesquieu and Beccaria were unrecognisable to the majority of Russian nobles, she tried another tack. Posing as 'Granny' (*Babushka*), the benign editorial persona of a new journal, *All Sorts*, at the beginning of 1769, Catherine tried to coax her subjects to improve their manners by mocking their bad habits in light-hearted journalism in the tradition of Addison and Steele's *Spectator*. Much of their material was indeed paraphrased in Catherine's journal, which openly acknowledged its debt to its progenitor: 'There is not a little salt in the English *Spectator*, and *All Sorts* resembles it, so why should it not contain something useful for society?'[65] Although she was still a woman in a hurry – 'We have no doubts regarding the speedy correction of morals and expect an immediate extirpation of all vices', Granny confidently declared – Catherine permitted a degree of playful banter between her own journal and others in the same vein published by Nikolay Novikov, a former minute-taker at the Legislative Commission who was as keen as she was to disperse the clouds of prejudice and injustice.[66] His journal *The Drone* mocked corrupt judges who had unaccountably failed to read Beccaria *On Crimes and Punishments* and understood as little of their own duties as they did of the Syrian and Khaldean languages: 'O enlightenment, heavenly gift, lift the veil of ignorance and cruelty swiftly for the defence of humanity!'[67]

Although it remains a mystery why Catherine chose to encourage public discussion of the defects of Russian society at the start of her war with the Turks, her turn to journalism was entirely of a piece with the first of five aims she had once jotted down under the heading 'Maxims of Administration': 'One must refine the nation one is to govern.'[68] Conscious of the benefits of her own reading, she paid 5000 roubles a year to support a Society for the Translation of Foreign Books, founded in November 1768 under the aegis of her secretary Grigory Kozitsky, a graduate of the Kiev Spiritual Academy who had studied in Leipzig. Kozitsky translated her Instruction into Latin and Ovid's *Metamorphoses* into Russian before committing suicide in December 1775. ('He was in bed with his wife,' Jeremy Bentham learned later, 'who finding herself wet in the morning spoke to her husband, and receiving no answer, drew aside the Cloaths and found him with a penknife in his hand, dead, with upwards of 30 wounds about him.')[69] The Society's life lasted longer. More than forty titles were in print by 1772, and by the time its work was transferred to the newly created Russian Academy in 1783, 112 translations had been published with a further 129 still in progress. Many of the first works to appear were extracts from the *Encyclopédie* which reflected the empress's current interest in Greece and the Mediterranean. Boswell's *Corsica* came out in 1773. Fielding's *Joseph Andrews* and Swift's *Gulliver's Travels* may well have reflected her personal tastes (Catherine read English literature in French and German translation). Corneille and Voltaire were also on the list.[70]

Though she confessed to Voltaire in March 1771 that she was 'too busy fighting' to contemplate a widespread implementation of her Instruction, such a burst of intellectual activity helped to create an atmosphere in which the empress might reasonably think that her treatise had not been in vain. That autumn, Novikov published a number of positive European responses to it in his journal *The Painter*.[71] Archbishop Platon had offered more explicit reassurance in his New

Year sermon, given in her presence at the Winter Palace. 'Our age is the age of enlightenment,' he proclaimed in his most fulsome acknowledgement of the achievements of secular reform, going on to praise impartial judges for bringing clarity to Russian legislation, in words which echoed Catherine's own, and to praise her for stressing the need for moderate punishments. The aim was to destroy vice itself, rather than the unhappy criminal. 'Never, indeed, has a government incorporated so abundantly the spirit of guardianship and philanthropy.'[72] On her forty-second birthday in April, the empress began a memoir designed to highlight the uncivilised features of Elizabeth's Court. So it came as a shock when she discovered in May that her own servants were still being dragged off to the palace candle factory to be flogged, just as they had been when she first arrived in Russia. Since this was an 'evil custom' that she had banned at the beginning of her reign, she expressed outrage that it had been revived. Henceforth, no liveried servant was to be beaten on any account. 'If some of them commit a major crime such as theft, then they should be stripped of their livery and sent to the criminal courts. Attempts should be made to correct drunks, defaulters and the disobedient by: 1) gentleness, and if that doesn't work: 2) detention. 3) The punishment should be 48 hours on bread and water.'[73]

Evidently the empress was unable to rely on books alone in her quest for polite refinement. Many Russian nobles were illiterate and, as Novikov discovered, it was impossible to make a profit from the small number of sophisticated men who subscribed to his journals (many of which were eventually recirculated as haircurlers). Though it sold better than any other Russian journal in the eighteenth century, *The Drone* petered out like the others as print runs slipped. They would scarcely have survived at all without support from Catherine and her Court. Novikov was swift to return the compliment, as part of a new compact between writer and ruler in Russia. When the empress turned to her beloved theatre as the best way of promoting civilised noble values in 1772, Novikov declared *O these times!*, the first, best-known and most successful of the five comedies she wrote that year, worthy of comparison with Molière. The play was modelled on *Die Betschwester* by C. F. Gellert, transposing its plot into a denunciation of superstitious bigotry that must have made uncomfortable viewing for some of her more conspicuously pious courtiers.[74]

It was precisely because she was so keen to eradicate it that Catherine was so prickly in response to condescending foreign verdicts on Russian backwardness. Even so sympathetic a foreigner as Lord Cathcart, who praised the empress for her 'quickness of thought and discernment, an attention to business and a desire to fill her throne with dignity and with utility even to the lowest of her subjects', followed a widespread tendency to dismiss 'the Russians in general' as 'men of no education or principles of any sort, though not without quickness of parts'.[75] Travelling to Russia in 1769, the Lutheran pastor and political thinker Johann Gottfried Herder regarded the Russians' desire to imitate as 'nothing but the healthy disposition of a developing nation – a tendency in the right direction'. But he was equally sure that 'the great work of "civilizing a nation to perfection"' was 'yet to be accomplished' because the Russians had bungled the adoption of everything they had taken from Western Europe, from the art of navigation to French manners.[76] Anxious to counter that her subjects showed 'great natural aptitude' for reasoned behaviour, Catherine attributed their earlier failings to faulty methods on the part of her predecessors. 'I would willingly blame the government for acting clumsily. When this nation is better known in Europe, people will take back many errors and prejudices about Russia.'[77]

No one seemed more prejudiced than Le Mercier de la Rivière, whose visit to St Petersburg, arranged by Diderot in 1768, failed also because he believed that it was the ruler's task to implement immutable geometric laws (a strategy totally at variance with Catherine's flexible cast of mind). She was still complaining in 1774 of the *philosophe* 'who supposed, six years ago, that we walked on four paws, and who very politely gave himself the trouble of coming from Martinique to stand us up on our hind feet'.[78] When the abbé Chappe d'Auteroche's *A Journey into Siberia* (1768) ridiculed her subjects as impoverished alcoholics, superstitious slaves, and lascivious mixed-bathers, Catherine countered with an indignant *Antidote*, published in French in 1770 (almost certainly in St Petersburg, though the title page said Amsterdam) and translated into English two years later. Acknowledging that parents were tempted to marry their sons off too young in order to acquire a working daughter-in-law, the empress insisted that the practice survived only in isolated provinces where her bishops were striving to restrict it. When the common people drank in Russia, they fell into no 'greater excess during the carnival than those of any other nation, where Lent is strictly observed'. Of course Russian peasants were credulous, but they were surely not alone in maintaining absurd beliefs. 'For many centuries,' Catherine reminded the abbé, French queens 'could not be brought to bed without an astrologer being placed in the wardrobe to foretell the good or ill fortune of the new-born child'. In sum, she concluded in the spirit of Enlightened universalism, since Russia was 'inhabited by *men*', people would 'prove the same there as in every other part of the globe'.[79]

After a characteristically hesitant start, her armed forces were certainly proving equal to anything the enemy could throw at them. Reviewing the navy at Kronstadt in July 1769, she had treated Admiral Spiridov and his officers to a glass of champagne. But once the fleet had set sail, its fate was out of her hands.[80] By mid-October, Spiridov had been obliged to put into Hull, seeking treatment for 800 sick sailors. Catherine was undeterred. It was hard to keep anything in perspective when your principal correspondent was Voltaire. 'I believe that my fleet is at Gibraltar, if it has not already passed through the Straits,' wrote an excited empress in mid-December. 'By now you will have news of it sooner than I. May God protect Mustapha!' Reporting the fleet's arrival at Port-Mahon 'in very good order' at the beginning of the New Year, Voltaire renewed his encouragement:

> I cannot refrain from telling Your Majesty once more that your project is the greatest and most astonishing that was ever conceived: Hannibal's scarcely came close to it. I very much hope that yours will be more successful than his. Indeed, how will the Turks be able to resist you? They pass for the worst sailors in Europe, and they currently have very few ships.[81]

So far did it threaten the prevailing maritime balance of power that the appearance of three squadrons of Russian ships in the eastern Mediterranean has been plausibly ranked as 'one of the most spectacular events of the eighteenth century'.[82] Their commander-in-chief was equally extraordinary. While he convalesced from his gallstones, Aleksey Orlov had been swaggering round Tuscany with servants dressed in gold-trimmed livery and two eunuchs taken from a seraglio. Inspirational as a leader of men, he had almost certainly never previously been to sea. So he wisely flew his flag on the 66-gun *Three Bishops*, commanded by Admiral Samuel Greig of Inverkeithing, who had entered Russian service in 1764. It was Greig who masterminded the victory over the 11,000-man Turkish navy on 24–25 June. A total of 523 Russian lives were lost in a two-hour engagement on the first day, when Fëdor Orlov was one of few survivors rescued from the sinking *Saint Evstafy*. The following night, it was a different story as Greig destroyed the enemy, holed up in Chesme harbour, with a bomb-ship and four fire-ships. In a characteristically extravagant gesture, Orlov later blew up one of his own ships to give artists an accurate impression of the devastation he had inflicted.[83] 'Almost a hundred vessels of every kind have been reduced to ashes,'

Catherine boasted to Voltaire. 'I dare not say how many Muslims perished: it may be as many as twenty thousand.'[84] Trumpeting news of her triumphs to Europe was one of her greatest contributions to the war effort. Another was inspiring her commanders. On discovering that Orlov had lost a signet ring with her portrait on it at Chesme, she sent another to spur him on: 'Having lost that ring, you won the battle and destroyed the enemy fleet. On receipt of this new one, you will capture their fortresses.'[85]

That was exactly what General Rumyantsev was doing, in a scarcely less spectacular series of victories in Moldavia and Wallachia that had a far greater impact on the outcome of the war. In July 1770, he led a 25,000-strong army to victory over 150,000 enemy soldiers at the River Larga, emphasising in his reports to the empress the leading roles played by Lieutenant General Potëmkin and by General Bauer, a military engineer who had been close to her through his friendship with Grigory Orlov since entering Russian service the year before.[86] Their troops received simple silver medals inscribed with the date of the battle and a bust of the empress. By mid December 18,000 such medals, minted in St Petersburg in October, had already been delivered to Jassy, and when these proved too few to meet the demand, she authorised 1157 more in the spring of 1772.[87] All her armies' victories were celebrated with an elaborate Te Deum at the Kazan Church in St Petersburg.[88] Yet for Catherine there was always a measure of relief amidst the triumphalism. Tidings of Rumyantsev's next victory at the River Kagul, which reached Tsarskoye Selo on the evening of 1 August, unleashed a migraine that prevented her from writing for three days.[89]

When she had recovered, she composed an ironic letter to Voltaire, reassuring him that there was as yet no prospect of a truce:

> I agree with you that peace is a fine thing: so long as it existed, I thought it the *nec plus ultra* of happiness. Now that I have been at war for almost two years, I see that one can get used to anything. War, it is true, does have some fine moments. The one great fault I find with it is that [in war] one does not love one's neighbour as oneself. I used to think it dishonourable to do people harm; however I console myself somewhat today by saying to Mustapha [like Molière]: 'Georges [Dandin], you wished it on yourself!' And after that reflection, I am at ease, almost as before.[90]

In fact, that same month, Catherine, while planning for the following summer's campaign, permitted Rumyantsev to enter into peace negotiations with the Turks provided that they released her imprisoned ambassador at Constantinople (a condition they refused). What she was not prepared to accept was the repeated offers of mediation made by Austria and Prussia at the instigation of Frederick the Great, who was desperate to prevent Russia from making further unilateral conquests.[91]

Catherine's determination to hold out for maximal gain made it impossible for Prince Henry of Prussia, sent to St Petersburg by Frederick in October 1770, to persuade Russia to settle for peace.[92] It was the first time Catherine had seen him since their youthful dalliance at the Court of Berlin. Small in stature and cold in manner, the king's notoriously ugly younger brother made a poor impression on courtiers who mocked the toupee perched precariously above his unnaturally high forehead. The empress, by contrast, made a great show of warming to him, declaring Henry 'cheerful, honest and humane' and reassuring Frau Johanna Bielke, a friend of her mother's in Hamburg, that 'no visit from a prince could be more agreeable to me than his'. At any rate, as she observed sarcastically to Voltaire, shortly after Henry's departure in January 1771, 'he seemed to enjoy himself here more than the abbé Chappe, who raced along the post-road in an entirely enclosed sleigh, from which he saw everything in Russia.'[93]

Competitive to the core, Catherine had good reason to impress her Prussian rivals. 'You know how patriotic I am,' she reminded Field Marshal Saltykov, who had defeated Frederick at Kunersdorf: 'I wish our nation to shine in all the military and civil virtues and that we should surpass all other nations in every genre.' So she spared no expense to ensure that her guest returned to Potsdam convinced that the Russians were 'sufficiently polite to know how to beat their enemies'.[94] She sent three yachts to meet him at Reval, where she personally arranged for a suitable wine cellar and Court chef to be on hand at the Yekaterintal Palace.[95] Soon after arriving in St Petersburg, Henry attended the thanksgiving prayers for the fall of Bender. Later he was shown captured Turkish standards at the Peter-Paul fortress, where Peter the Great's 'little boat' was on display as a symbol of Russian naval power.[96] Determined to demonstrate that she could outdo even such a virile predecessor, Catherine also took Henry to see the 'thunder-rock', a block of Karelian granite weighing some 3 million pounds on which Falconet planned to mount his statue of Tsar Peter. This massive boulder, so-called because peasants believed that the crack at one corner had been caused by a bolt of lightning, had taken far longer than Henry himself to reach the Russian capital. Selected for the purpose just before the outbreak of war, it began its overland journey from Count Bruce's estate at Konnaya in November 1769, using machinery designed by a Greek engineer. 'Daringly performed' was the inscription on the medal struck to commemorate Catherine's visit to see the rock on 20 January 1770, when it was being rolled along at the rate of approximately a mile per month. For the final part of its journey, it was floated down the Neva on a purpose-built raft, reaching St Petersburg on the eighth anniversary of Catherine's coronation. A few days later, Prince Henry saw it manoeuvred into position at the centre of Senate Square, where it still stands today. Acknowledged across Europe as a stunning feat of engineering, this operation was duly claimed by Catherine's panegyrists as superior to the building of the Egyptian pyramids and the creation of the Colossus of Rhodes.[97]

On 28 October, Henry was driven to Tsarskoye Selo under cover of darkness in a sledge equipped with mirrors so that the snow-covered landscape would seem to stretch to infinity. After a brilliantly lit triumphal arch there followed a series of illuminated pyramids and pleasure gardens in which peasants dressed in national costume could be seen dancing behind newly married couples in an allegorical display of fertility and happiness. Outside the menagerie, Semën Naryshkin had arranged for a Temple of Diana, where his huntsmen played on their distinctive horns.[98] Still more extravagant was the masquerade staged at the Winter Palace on 28 November when some twenty-one staterooms were commandeered to provide dancing and games for 3600 guests. Shortly before nine, a fanfare of trumpets announced the arrival of Apollo with the four seasons and the twelve months of the year, played by boys from the Cadet Corps and girls from the Smolny Convent school for noble girls. Twelve alcoves, each set with a table for ten, had been created in the banqueting hall.[99] The stolid soldier must have needed all the tact he could muster to smile at a Frenchman in parrot costume who squawked '*Henri! Henri! Henri!*' into his ear before vanishing into the crowd. Yet it was hard not to admire the pyrotechnic representation of Russia's recent conquests. For all Catherine's periodic attempts at self-restraint, the Court of St Petersburg had lost none of its fascination for Baroque spectacle:

The various colours, the bright green, and the snowy white, exhibited in these fireworks, were truly astonishing. For the space of twenty minutes, a tree adorned with the loveliest and most verdant foliage, seemed to be waving as with a gentle breeze. It was entirely of fire; and during the whole of this stupendous scene, an arch of fire, by the continued throwing of rockets and fireballs in one direction, formed as it were a suitable canopy.[100]

Literary celebrations of the Russian victories and Catherine's letters of this period betray the ideological foundations of the so-called Greek project which emerged between 1780 and 1782 – the plan to recapture Byzantium and install a Russian ruler on its throne.[101] 'Soon it will be time for me to study the Greeks at some university,' the empress told Voltaire in October 1770, 'until such time as I can translate Homer into Russian.' She made a start by donning Grecian costume for the masquerade in honour of Prince Henry.[102]

So determined was Catherine to advertise the magnificence of this event that she checked several times that Voltaire had received her detailed description of it.[103] Indeed he had, but it was her triumphs at the expense of the Infidel that really sparked his imagination. As she regaled him with Aleksey Orlov's lurid accounts of the waters of Chesme harbour churning with Turkish blood, he responded by picturing himself 'transported' from the eighteenth century 'to the Alps at the time of the foundation of Babylon': 'Monsieur d'Alembert, who is here at Ferney now, is as enthusiastic as I am, and the only difference is that he expresses himself better. We both hate Mustapha just as much.'[104]

Blissfully unaware of the danger he faced, Prince Henry left Moscow only days before Saltykov, the city's Governor General, reported an epidemic on 22 December 1770. Catherine had first referred to the disease at the end of May, when she gave her approval to counter-measures taken by Rumyantsev in the south-west. By the time Kiev succumbed in mid-September, she was already concerned about the threat to the old capital, 'for besides sickness and fires, there is much stupidity there'.[105] Since it was almost certainly Ottoman cloth that carried what she called the 'infectious pestilential distemper' to the heart of the Russian empire, the empress's efforts to blame it on the enemy carried some plausibility. But while Voltaire urged her to 'exterminate the two great scourges on earth, the plague and the Turks',[106] a cure proved elusive as doctors continued to debate the nature of the disease. Though a cold snap in the New Year brought a temporary respite, warmer weather saw a sharp increase in mortality at Moscow's leading woollen manufactory, prompting the police to stage a secret evacuation of the 640-strong workforce on the night of 13 March 1771. Sensing trouble ahead, many nobles fled to their rural estates. Since nothing alarmed Catherine more than indecision, Saltykov was tactfully sidelined at the end of the month to allow Senator Peter Yeropkin to take charge of the anti-plague campaign. At first, his impeccably modern methods suggested little for the authorities to do. Statistics supplied by the parish clergy showed no marked increase in the death rate, and Archbishop Amvrosy sensibly warned that public prayers for deliverance were likely to result only in panic. No one anticipated the scale of the disaster to come, and only a mass evacuation of the city – scarcely a feasible option – would significantly have stemmed the losses that followed in a warm, wet summer which provided the ideal conditions for the spread of plague.[107]

Meanwhile, the empress had problems of her own in St Petersburg, though not quite the ones she had foreseen in the autumn. In the face of her intransigence, the pressure from the German powers had eased. In the intensive debates in Vienna over the winter of 1770–71, it was probably the Russian-born Marshal Lacy, whose father had danced in Catherine's ill-fated wedding quadrille, who did most to convince Austria's rulers of Russia's impregnability. For different reasons, neither the pacific Maria Theresa nor Joseph II supported Chancellor Kaunitz's arguments in favour of a campaign against Catherine. 'I am for a thousand reasons of opinion that we ought never to wage war on our own against Russia,' the emperor wrote in January 1771, 'but that we ought to put ourselves into a condition to profit promptly and without risk from the Russians' moments of weakness, if any present themselves.' Joseph imagined that the most likely way for the Austrians to profit would be from some future partition of the Ottoman Empire.[108] By that time, however, irritated by Austria's incorporation of the Polish enclave of Zips (Spisz) on the Galician border, Frederick the Great had decided that his best hope of compensating Prussia for Russia's Black Sea conquests was to take some Polish territory for himself: 'ointment for the burn' as he described it to Solms in February. From what Prince Henry told him, Catherine was not averse to the idea – 'Why shouldn't we all take something?' she had asked towards the end of his visit, though as usual he found it hard to decide whether she was joking. Playing up the prospect of Austrian aggression, and pretending that he wanted only 'little parcels' of land for himself, Frederick embarked on a determined push for partition. Though Panin tried to warn Stanisław August what was in store, and Austrian hesitations held up the final division of spoils for a further year, the die was effectively cast. On 19 May, after the negotiations with Prussia had been revealed to the Russian Council for the first time, Panin and Solms pored over a map in St Petersburg, discussing precisely which territories Frederick hoped to take.[109]

Thanks to a poor harvest and the impact of plague on both sides, campaigning on the Danube was limited that summer, when Russian forces concentrated on a successful occupation of the Crimea. Even so, not everything went to plan. 'These last two days have not been very happy,' Catherine admitted to Panin on 19 June. 'My son is ill, we have lost Zhurzha [to the Turks], [Admiral] Senyavin has lost a bomb-ship, and on top of that, I have received six different denunciations these past few weeks containing such nonsense that it tries your patience and I have ordered three of the Semnovsky Guards to be flogged on parade.'[110]

Paul's illness – apparently a virulent form of influenza accompanied by persistent diarrhoea – was by far the most serious difficulty. In view of his approaching name day, there could scarcely have been a more awkward time for him to fall sick. 'The grand duke has already been indisposed for ten days,' Catherine continued on 23 June from a damp Peterhof. 'Wouldn't it be better for me to come to town for the celebrations, rather than risk moving him?'[111] 'They are in mortal anguish here about the grand duke,' the French ambassador reported after Paul had failed to appear in public on the appointed day.[112] All the empress could do to deter rumours about the succession was to make a very obvious show of caring for her son. As he took his first uncertain steps around his bedroom at the end of July, she announced his recovery in a studiously lighted-hearted letter to Mme Bielke. 'He has grown a lot during this illness,' she added a month later, 'and his beard has started to sprout. There is a Russian proverb which says that no moustache appears without illness. I don't know whether this saying is just, but on the subject of the grand duke we have had a severe alarm.'[113]

There was worse news to come from Moscow, where the recorded daily death rate peaked at 920 on 15 September, unleashing a riot that lasted for several days. Already unpopular thanks to his attempts to control clerical vagrancy, Archbishop Amvrosy was assassinated by a mob outraged by rumours that he intended to confiscate a renowned miracle-working icon and transfer all the money donated to it to Betskoy's Foundling Home. Yeropkin reported on 18 September that at least 100 had died in the Kremlin, where rioters ransacked the archbishop's residence before hounding him to his death at the Don monastery on the other side of the river. It was not what the empress wanted to hear. 'She is much affected with these calamities,' Cathcart reported on 27 September, 'and cannot, though she endeavours, conceal it.'[114] 'Truly this famous eighteenth century has a lot to be proud of here,' Catherine wrote a week later in describing Amvrosy's fate to Voltaire. 'What wise people we have become.'[115]

By the time Grigory Orlov learned of the riots, he was already en route to the old capital to take over from Saltykov, who had petitioned for his retirement after taking unauthorised (and unforgiven) leave. While he was away, elaborate measures were taken to protect St Petersburg and its palaces from infection. The gates at Tsarskoye Selo were to be kept shut at all times; only Court carriages were permitted on the new road between the menagerie and the toboggan ride at Pulkovo; sentries were posted at the entrance to every village on the estate with instructions to turn away anyone suspected of coming from an infected area.[116] Moscow's government offices were not to reopen until 1 December 1772 after the end of the epidemic had been formally proclaimed by successive Te Deums in both cities.[117] Yet still the war with the Ottomans dragged on, as Catherine concentrated on recording her victories for posterity.

———————

'If this war continues,' she told Voltaire in August 1771, 'my garden at Tsarskoye Selo will soon resemble a game of skittles, because I put up a monument there after each of our glorious battles':

> The battle of Kagul, where seventeen thousand men fought a hundred and fifty thousand, produced an obelisk with an inscription stating only the event and the name of the general. The naval battle at Chesme gave birth to a rostral column in the middle of a large stretch of water. The capture of the Crimea will be preserved by one large column; the descent in the Morea and the capture of Sparta by another. All these are made of the finest marbles one can see, admired by the Italians themselves. Some are found on the shores of Lake Ladoga, the remainder in Yekaterinburg in Siberia, and we use them as you see. They come in nearly every colour. Besides this, in a wood behind my garden, I have had the idea of building a temple of memory to be approached through a triumphal arch. All the important events of the war will be engraved on medallions, with simple and short inscriptions in the language of this country, giving the date and the names of those who took part. I have an excellent Italian architect [Rinaldi], who is drawing up the plans for this building, which will, I hope, be a beautiful one, in good taste, and will relate the history of this war. This idea amuses me greatly and I trust that you will not find it inappropriate.[118]

Falconet had told her that the 'lapidary style is the simplest and best that the Ancients used for the inscriptions on their monuments'. Catherine duly followed his example when she came to specify the inscriptions for the plaques on the

Kagul obelisk. Meanwhile, two Medal Committees, apparently inspired by Louis XIV's *Académie des inscriptions*, set to work between May 1772 and November 1774.[119]

'I wouldn't know how to live in a place where I could neither plant nor build,' Catherine admitted to Frau Bielke in April 1772. 'After that, even the most beautiful place in the world would seem insipid.' As it was, much to the amusement of Grigory Orlov, she was in the grip of a bout of 'plantomania'. That spring, as Orlov departed for the peace talks at Fokshany, he left her in charge of his garden at Gatchina, where she could commit her own 'indiscretions'.[120] She had done so all along. The Scot Charles Sparrow, who designed the widely admired park at Gatchina, had been the first of several British gardeners recruited to Russia by Ivan Chernyshëv in 1769. Soon the Hanoverian Johann Busch (John Bush) joined the list, signing a contract for a salary of 1500 roubles a year in January 1771. Having briefly worked at Oranienbaum, he took charge of landscaping the English park at Tsarskoye Selo, where Vasily Neëlov, who had worked there since the 1740s, was already busy rearranging the paths and bridges. An even more obvious result of Neëlov's six-month visit to England in 1770 was the fashion for all things Chinese. In 1772, he completed the Large Caprice, a Chinese summer house spanning the road to the palace. He also worked on Rinaldi's Chinese Village, a neo-oriental fantasy which comprised some fifteen small houses by the time it was finished by Charles Cameron, connected by a colonnade that cost 41,000 roubles and dominated by a pagoda built for 48,000. *Chinoiserie* was equally prominent in Thomas Whately's influential *Observations on Modern Gardening* (1770), which Catherine acquired in French translation in 1771.[121]

Though the Russian version she planned never appeared in print, Catherine dedicated her adaptation of Whately's book 'To the owners of estates bordering the sea and lying along the Peterhof road ... by one who has seen their natural attractions and capabilities, so that they should be further improved according to the principles herein prescribed.'[122] One such owner was Lev Naryshkin, to whom Novikov dedicated the second printing of *The Drone* on 28 July 1769, the eve of Naryshkin's annual masquerade at Leventhal (Lev's Valley). To Novikov, the estate seemed 'the most perfect Eden', and indeed, three years later, it proved to be the ideal setting for an entertainment that was remembered in Russia long into the nineteenth century.[123] By the time Catherine arrived at 7 p.m. on 29 July 1772, 2000 guests had already spent a pleasant afternoon strolling in her friend's sylvan groves. When two shepherdesses, played by his daughters, Natalia and Katerina, gambolled into view to invite her to their hut on a nearby hillside, it seemed that they were to witness no more than a conventional pastoral idyll. Soon, however, the crowd gasped when the hillside parted, as if by magic, to reveal a magnificent temple of victory, its entrances guarded by statues representing the Russian army and navy. Dressed as the 'genius of victory', Naryshkin's son Dimitry led the empress through a portal emblazoned with the slogan 'CATHERINE II: CONQUEROR'. Inside, he presented her with a laurel wreath and a speech which had been printed (in French) along with plans of the temple in a booklet distributed to all the guests. As she crossed the threshold into a hall adorned with the trophies of war, a cannon salute signalled the first of a series of scenes representing a litany of all her finest triumphs at Khotin, the River Larga, Kagul, Chesme and Bender. Only after reliving the glories of her *annus mirabilis* was she permitted to relax among Naryshkin's colourful Chinese pagodas, where attendants in Chinese costume were on hand to serve her to the accompaniment of Chinese musical instruments. There was still a magnificent banquet to come. Not until three in the morning, an exceptionally late hour, did she finally return to Peterhof.[124]

Although St Petersburg in the early 1770s remained, as a British traveller remarked, 'only an immense outline, which will require future empresses, and almost future ages, to complete', there was no doubt about the scale of Catherine's ambitions in the field of urban reconstruction.[125] 'Augustus said that he had found Rome built of brick and left it built of marble,' she told Frau Bielke in July 1770, 'and I shall say that I found Petersburg almost entirely made of wood and will leave it with buildings decorated in marble. Despite the war and the Welches, we continue to build.'[126] In the light of her determination to press ahead in difficult circumstances, it was all the more frustrating to see hard-earned progress undone. 'I have resembled Job since yesterday', she wrote angrily to Panin, after a fire destroyed part of Vasilevsky Island on 23 May 1771. 'I sent Count Orlov into town with instructions not to return until the last spark is extinguished.' Having initially suspected arson, she soon blamed careless residents.[127] Voltaire received a different explanation: 'There is no doubt that the wind and the excessive heat caused all the damage which will soon be repaired. In Russia we build faster than in any other country in Europe.' She was as good as her word. On 26 July, plans were approved for the development of low-rise stone houses to replace the majority of burnt-out wooden ones.[128]

Designs for Moscow were more grandiose. Vasily Bazhenov had been appointed to oversee a major reconstruction of the Kremlin just before Catherine's departure from the old capital in January 1768 and she kept in close touch with him as he surveyed the foundations. 'Be so good as to open the air-vents,' she instructed Saltykov at the end of May. 'Bazhenov needs to move about the cellars and if the vents won't open he'll be in danger of suffocating.'[129] Warned that even this prestige project would be subject to wartime economies, the architect took advantage of successive delays to develop increasingly ambitious plans. Having originally intended to begin with new government buildings, the empress soon opted instead for a four-storey neoclassical palace with a 700-yard frontage onto the Moscow River.[130] Pandering to her obsession with posterity, Bazhenov planned to glorify her name with a building to rival all the wonders of the world, from the Egyptian pyramids to the Parisian Palais Royal: the main reception hall alone was destined to measure seventy metres by fifty metres. However, as he soon discovered, Catherine was just as preoccupied with more immediate practicalities. After meeting him in St Petersburg in December 1768, she insisted that the kitchens and confectionery should be built side by side for ease of service.[131] And she could barely conceal her irritation on discovering, a year later, that crucial comforts had been neglected. On reviewing the revised plans in February 1770, Grigory Teplov reported that 'Her Majesty made the following observations':

1: Nowhere in the palace is there provision for the necessary, without which it will be impossible for a large number of residents and visitors to remain there, and if this is not taken care of, then there will always be dirtiness and filth in the palace. 2: Nowhere can it be seen how and from where carriages will arrive at the various entrances so that it will not to be too far to walk in case of a severe frost.[132]

Catherine was equally determined that the works should not damage the three great Muscovite cathedrals, monuments of the national heritage that she was proud to show off to Prince Henry along with the university and the foundling home in December 1770.[133] Not satisfied with mere preservation, the empress wanted their priceless frescoes to be restored to their former glory by appropriately qualified 'religious people'. There was no shortage of such experts in the old capital and its monasteries, she reminded Archbishop Amvrosy, instructing him to 'make sure that they carry out their work with the decorum appropriate to God's holy churches'.[134] This was no mere whim. After Amvrosy's assassination, responsibility for the work was transferred to the disciplinarian Samuil (Mislavsky), a favourite Court preacher whom Catherine had appointed to a suffragan see in the diocese of Moscow. Though modern scholars are aghast at the damage done by eighteenth-century 'restoration' methods, she was pleased to learn that the work had been completed over the following two years, first in the Annunciation cathedral and later in the Archangel and Dormition cathedrals.[135]

She was not present at the foundation ceremony for the Kremlin Palace on 1 June 1773, but Bazhenov's speech on that occasion left no doubt about the meaning of his plans. If Catherine had yet to conquer Constantinople, Constantinople must come to her in a classic instance of *translatio imperii*:

> The Eastern Church celebrates the renovation of Tsar-Grad because the pious Constantine transferred his throne from the banks of the Tiber to Byzantium and adorned it with magnificence, and consecrated that place in the spirit of God. On this day Moscow, too, is renewed. You, great Catherine, in the midst of a bloody conflict, and in the midst of the many affairs entrusted to you by God, have not forgotten the adornment of the capital city ... Exult, O Kremlin! On this day, we are laying the first stone of a new temple of Ephesus.[136]

It proved to be a false hope. Before the building could rise from the ground, Bazhenov's project was cancelled. The empress had a more pressing need for a residence in Moscow, where she planned to celebrate her ultimate victory against the Turks. When Elizabeth's Golovin Palace finally burned down in December 1771, Catherine expressed surprise 'only that it had survived for so long, despite my hundredfold prophesies about it'.[137] In the search for a replacement the following autumn, her thoughts turned first to the Menshikov Palace at Lefortovo. As usual, she was closely involved in the design. 'Ask Prince Makulov if he agrees to take on the construction work,' Catherine instructed Prince Volkonsky, Salytkov's successor as Moscow's Governor General, 'and tell him that he will see from my plan that the internal wall of this palace should be rebuilt and pushed out into the courtyard so that we obtain a double room whose width is indicated on the plan.' Only after the architect went to see her in St Petersburg did she concede that her designs were impracticable. 'I see that it is impossible to reconstruct the house at Lefortovo according to my plan and it would be better to knock almost all of it down and start anew. Even then it would be bad since it is near a slope and it would cost up to 900,000 roubles, which I am certainly not prepared to spend on a temporary building.'[138]

In the end, the Menshikov Palace was used to house theatrical staff and Catherine chose to build a new stone residence on the site of the burnt-out palace on the other side of the Yauza River. Noting that it was 'designed to be two or three English miles in circumference', Wraxall observed that there was 'a sort of savage and barbarous grandeur in this taste, which never appears in the edifices and productions of Athenian sculpture or architecture'.[139] So ambitious was the project that the empress never occupied her Catherine Palace, which was completed only in 1796. Since the immediate need for a useable residence remained, Bazhenov's assistant, Matvey Kazakov, returned from St Petersburg at the end of August 1774 with a more modest commission to connect three large houses belonging to the Golitsyns, the Dolgorukys and the Lopukhins. It was in this ramshackle Prechistensky Palace, dismantled shortly afterwards, that Catherine was to celebrate victory over the Turks in 1775. Before then, however, she had not only to defeat the enemy, but also to overcome the most serious internal challenges of her reign.

CHAPTER NINE

PAUL, PUGACHËV AND POTËMKIN
1772–1775

Five years of war and plague would have taken their toll on any eighteenth-century empire. For Catherine, they were particularly ominous. If her son, now rapidly approaching the age of majority, were to become the figurehead for 'patriotic' nobles alarmed by the damage inflicted on their estates by Russian troops en route to the battlefields, the empress's position would be no more secure than Peter III's had been in the face of her own claims to represent the national interest. The plague afflicting Moscow made such dangers all the more acute in a city where Paul's popularity had always been higher than hers.[1] To unsettle her further, Catherine lost faith in Grigory Orlov, her constant companion since the last years of the reign of Elizabeth. Against Panin's better judgement, Grigory had been sent to conduct the peace negotiations at Fokshany in May 1772. Shortly after his departure, Catherine learned that he had been unfaithful. Now the foreign ambassadors, whose reports on the rivalry between Panin and the Orlovs had so far been little more than whistling in the dark, suddenly found themselves at the heart of an extended crisis that was to transform the empress's personal life, and with it the politics of her Court.

The story began to unfold on 1 August 1772, three days after Naryshkin's celebrations at Leventhal. In the heat of the summer, Catherine had been forced to escape 'suffocation' at Tsarskoye Selo by spending longer than usual at the 'detestable, hateful' Peterhof.[2] Courtiers sweetened the pill by staging an amateur performance of her comedy *O, these times!* on 30 July, when 227 tickets were collected at the door of the opera house. This brought to an end a week of festivities by the seaside. Yet even as the atmosphere darkened at the onset of the

Dormition Fast, when the empress followed the icons to a sanctification service on the upper pond, there was news to keep her cheerful.[3] As she sailed that evening to visit a new summer house at Oranienbaum, she left her Court humming at the appointment, as gentleman of the bedchamber, of Alexander Vasilchikov, a previously unnoticed lieutenant in the Horse Guards who had commanded the sentries at Tsarskoye Selo. 'It is true,' Solms reported, 'that to diminish somewhat the surprise of such an extraordinary promotion of a man who has no connection with the Court, the empress has simultaneously appointed four more ... But everyone knows perfectly well that these were merely a bridge for the other to cross.'[4] By the time the Crimean Khan's emissary, Kalga Sultan, came to take his leave on 12 August, the twenty-eight-year-old Vasilchikov was already a fixture in the empress's intimate circle.[5] While they spent the summer at Marly and the Dutch cottage at Peterhof, with the occasional hunt on horseback after the Court had returned to Tsarskoye Selo, Orlov charged back from Moldavia only to find himself diverted to Gatchina on the pretext of quarantine regulations. In any case, he was too late: on 30 August, the feast of St Alexander Nevsky, Vasilchikov was promoted to Adjutant General, the office now firmly associated with the role of favourite. Sometime in early September, he moved into the palace.

As the recently arrived British ambassador straightaway realised, 'the advancement of a new minion' was bound to 'occasion some change'.[6] Yet neither Sir Robert Gunning nor his fellow diplomats fully anticipated what was to follow. They watched transfixed as Grigory held out for a satisfactory redundancy package in negotiations conducted by his brother Ivan. In addition to permission to use the title of Prince of the Holy Roman Empire, conferred on him in 1763, he finally settled at the end of September for an annual pension of 150,000 roubles; a further 100,000 to do out Rinaldi's Marble Palace, still under construction; the run of the empress's other palaces until it was finished; two silver services (one for everyday use, the other for special occasions); and more than double the number of serfs on the estates he owned jointly with his brother Aleksey. For her part, Catherine bore no grudges. Grigory was not to be blamed for the failure of the peace conference, and although she offered, in a veiled reference to his unfaithfulness, to consign 'all that has passed to perpetual oblivion', she vowed never to forget 'how much I owe to your whole clan and the qualities with which you are adorned'.[7] Cynics saw merely a prudent measure of self-preservation. Warning that she would 'do well to be on her guard' against the resentful Orlovs, Frederick the Great thought that if they were all like Aleksey, the menacing giant whom he had met at Potsdam in April 1771, then they must indeed be 'a very enterprising family, capable of achieving the greatest aims'.[8] Gunning could scarcely credit the exit of the man widely assumed to have installed the empress on the throne: 'The successor that has been given him is perhaps the strongest instance of weakness and the greatest blot in the character of her Imperial Majesty, and will lessen the high opinion that was generally and in a great measure deservedly entertained of her.'[9]

There was some force to these charges. Shortly after Grigory's departure for Fokshany, a plot to enthrone Paul had been discovered among the Preobrazhensky Guards in which between thirty and a hundred men, stiffened by a recent mutiny against their officers' cruelty, were said to have taken part. Under interrogation in July, their ringleaders confessed their dream of unseating the Orlovs and consigning Catherine to a convent. One was knouted and committed to hard labour at Nerchinsk; others were flogged and exiled in perpetuity. Though mild by contemporary standards, partly on account of the conspirators' youthfulness (most were non-commissioned officers, aged twenty or less), the sentences reflected the empress's deepening sense of unease. No sooner had one foreign adventure come to fruition with the first partition of Poland on 5 August, than another clouded the horizon three days later. To deter the partitioning powers from casting their acquisitive eyes towards Sweden, Gustav III suspended the constitution of 1720 and restored the monarchy's absolute powers. 'In less than a quarter of an hour,' Catherine complained to Voltaire, Sweden had lost her liberty and gained a king 'as despotic as the one in France'.[10] The real cause of her anxiety, however, was the damage inflicted on her own diplomacy. Backed by the French, Gustav's coup had turned the tables on Russia's long-standing influence in Stockholm and raised the threat of a descent on the empire's Baltic lands.[11] While the empress and her Council were forced to plan for such an attack, there could be no question of purging the rebellious Guards. Vasilchikov's confirmation as the new favourite looked more like an olive branch to the disaffected. Meanwhile, 'no precautions' had been 'neglected to guard against sudden attempts' on her life.[12]

To take her mind off her troubles, Catherine regaled Voltaire with the success of her new comedies. He would enjoy these works by 'an anonymous Russian author', she told him in August, since any weakness in their plots was more than compensated by the liveliness of the characters: 'some of them are really rather good'. Announcing the forthcoming French translation of *O, these times!* two months later, she seemed to be on top form: 'Perhaps you will say after reading it that it is easier to make me laugh than other sovereigns, and you will be right. I am fundamentally an extremely jolly person.'[13] Behind the bravado, however, diplomats in St Petersburg sensed a different mood that autumn. A telltale sign was Catherine's own admission that she had put off a routine reply to Falconet until 'the next day and the next day and the day after that'.[14] 'Hitherto active and industrious,' the Prussian ambassador complained at the end of December, 'she is becoming indolent and slack over business.' Indeed, though she preferred not to dwell to Voltaire on 'the great tragedy' of the Turkish war and the prospect of a more general conflict if Gustav III invaded Norway, Solms thought that these pressures, when combined with the crisis in her love life, had been enough to prompt a spiral of depression that threatened to paralyse her government. 'The empress increasingly displays the strongest of passions for her new favourite,' he reported when Orlov finally left for Reval in January 1773. 'Nevertheless, the departure of the former one made her sad and irritable and for three days she sent back all business.'[15] Vasilchikov, it transpired, was no more than a handsome face, and certainly no substitute for Grigory. 'I have never cried so much since the day I was born as I have over the last eighteen months,' she later admitted to Potëmkin.[16]

Although Panin undoubtedly benefited from the fall of Orlov and did his best to hasten it once the die was cast, there is no evidence that he was responsible for poisoning Catherine's mind against Grigory. Still less did he plot to install Paul on the throne. Conscious of Panin's reputation for sloth, Gunning concluded that the grand duke's future had been entrusted to him 'from a conviction that he has neither abilities, resolution nor creativity enough to attempt placing [the crown] on the head of this young Prince, even if the latter had spirit enough to wear it, which is as yet very problematical'.[17] If that was an underestimate of Panin's intellect, it was a shrewd assessment of the ambitions of both tutor and pupil. Paul himself posed no threat to his mother. Despite his simmering resentment of her treatment of Peter III, she received the same unquestioning loyalty from her heir as he later expected from his subjects. Indeed, at this point they seemed to be united by more than mere duty. Following his recovery from illness in 1771, relations between mother and son sharply improved after a decade in which her lack of affection attracted regular comment from foreign diplomats. Though some saw nothing more in this reconciliation than an arrangement of convenience between two inveterate dissemblers, it was impossible to ignore their newfound fondness for each other's company. 'I will be returning to town on Tuesday,' Catherine told Frau Bielke at the end of August 1772, 'with my son who no longer wants to be a step away from me and whom I have the honour of amusing so well that he sometimes changes his place at table in order to sit beside me.'[18] In the excitement over the negotiations with Orlov, Paul's eighteenth birthday passed without incident. In a private ceremony, attended only by Panin and his Holsteiner associate, Caspar von Saldern, the empress exhorted him on the need to govern justly and with moderation. Though the foreign ministers were entertained at Court to celebrate his Holstein inheritance, no promotions were announced. With luck, his Russian coming-of-age in the following year could be similarly overshadowed by his marriage.[19]

Had either Panin or the grand duke harboured any design of pressing Paul's claim to the throne, they would surely have exploited the opportunity offered by unscrupulous Saldern in the months before the wedding. Though the circumstances remain mysterious, it was apparently the Holsteiner who persuaded Paul that Panin could no longer be relied upon to serve his interests. Cathcart had characterised Saldern in 1769 as 'a man of consummate knowledge in business, great perspicacity, strong expression, and very much the friend or enemy of every system he adopts or opposes and in the same degree of the persons who espouse them'. At that time, he seemed 'a great assertor of the northern system', and it was in that capacity that he was appointed to lead Russia's negotiations in Warsaw in 1771.[20] By the time he returned, embittered by Panin's criticism of his peremptory treatment of the Poles, his loyalties had been reversed. Sometime in late 1772 or early 1773, Saldern talked the grand duke into authorising him to act as his representative in his dealings with the Young Court. Armed with a signed agreement to this effect, he approached Panin with a plan to increase Paul's role in government, allegedly to the point of creating a co-regency on the model of Joseph II and Maria Theresa. Perhaps he was trying on behalf of the Orlovs to discredit his former patron; just as probably, he had mercenary self-interest at heart. Whatever his motives, this time he had overreached himself. Panin destroyed the incriminating paper. While Paul, for the moment, kept silent, Saldern was packed off to Copenhagen, his reputation temporarily intact. Now all eyes turned to the wedding, for which plans were already complete by January 1773.[21]

The search for a bride had been entrusted to Baron von Assebourg, the former Danish minister to the empress's Court, as long ago as 1768. By Easter 1771 he had submitted the results of his preliminary researches, which Catherine considered at Tsarskoye Selo not long before Paul fell ill. Just as Elizabeth had done before her, the empress sought a pliable candidate, no older than the grand duke, from the Protestant 'third Germany' (the Princess of Nassau was explicitly ruled out on grounds of her Catholicism). Princess Louise of Saxe-Gotha had been an early front-runner, not least because her paternal grandmother was first cousin to the late Christian August of Anhalt-Zerbst. On investigation, however, the girl turned out to be too plump and her mother too squeamish about her conversion to Orthodoxy. 'Think no further of the princess of Saxe-Gotha,' Catherine ordered Assebourg: 'She is exactly what it takes to displease us.' Though the empress found it hard to believe that Princess Wilhelmina of Hesse-Darmstadt could be quite so attractive as Assebourg claimed, she seemed worthy of further consideration despite doubts about her temperament and the expense involved in settling an establishment on her siblings. Even so, Catherine still favoured Sophia Dorothea of Württemberg, whose father had been assiduous in his attentions and 'who will be at the end of her twelfth year next October. Her doctor's reflections on her robust health draw me to her'.[22] Panin, however, had already determined that Sophia Dorothea was too young (thirteen was then the age of consent for females in the Orthodox Church) and since his view prevailed, it was Wilhelmina of Hesse-Darmstadt and her sisters, Amalia and Louisa, who eventually travelled to Russia via Berlin, just as Catherine had done almost thirty years earlier, in the company of their mother and with the assistance of Frederick the Great. 'I have intrigued like the very devil to lead things to this point,' the king told Prince Henry, predicting that the alliance would be 'of the greatest possible utility to posterity'.[23]

By the time their party approached the Russian capital on Saturday 15 June 1773, Grigory Orlov had already been back at Court for almost a month, having resumed all his former offices except that of favourite on 20 May. It was he who rode out with General Bauer to meet the girls on their way from Count Karl Sievers' estate at Seltsa. Catherine was waiting for them at Gatchina, where they arrived at two o'clock in time for lunch. Paul caught his first sight of his future wife when they set off for Tsarskoye Selo three hours later. He met them halfway, stepping out of his carriage to pay his respects to their mother, Landgravine Caroline. On reaching the palace, where a small crowd had gathered to greet them at the gates, the guests were given an hour to unwind in their apartments before being taken to the Picture Gallery, lined from floor to ceiling with 130 seventeenth-century masterpieces, mostly Flemish and Dutch, as a way of emphasising Russia's rightful place among the European great powers.[24] At her most resplendent in the insignia of the Order of St Andrew, the empress engaged them in conversation until she retired to bed at ten. At the dinner which followed, protocol dictated that the eldest girl, Amalia, and her mother should sit beside Paul while the seventeen-year-old Wilhelmina found herself sandwiched between Panin and Lev Naryshkin, the leading voice in foreign affairs and the wittiest man at Court.[25] The same pattern followed next day, as banquet followed upon banquet in an effort to overwhelm the guests with the magnificence of Russian power. Sometimes they dined outside on the balcony, on tables made from the finest mahogany; a band played as they strolled through the garden to the grotto. Catherine was delighted to find that Wilhelmina seemed to confirm all her instincts. In view of her evident desire that her son's marriage should be happier than her own, it was even more reassuring that Paul instantly liked the girl (by no means a foregone conclusion, particularly for such a temperamental youth) and she accepted him. At lunch on 17 June, they sat next to each other for the first time.[26] Within four days of her arrival, the deal was done. Soon the young princess was taking instruction in Orthodoxy from Father Platon, now archbishop of Tver, whose *Short Course in Christian Theology* was familiar to her mother in German translation.[27]

Still dreaming of a 'crusade' to Constantinople, Voltaire would have preferred Wilhelmina to be 're-baptised in the church of Saint Sophia, in the presence of the prophet Grimm'.[28] Instead, she was converted at the end of the Dormition Fast on 15 August, taking the name Natalia Alekseyevna. The couple were betrothed next day. At the end of the month, in a further demonstration of Orthodox splendour, Catherine was again persuaded to trudge to the Alexander Nevsky monastery on the saint's feast day, for only the second time since 1762. While Landgravine Caroline looked on from Field Marshal Golitsyn's house near the Kazan Church, Paul and his fiancée joined the empress in the procession. Wearing the small crown and dressed as a knight of the Order of St Alexander, she emerged from the Winter Palace at ten o'clock to be driven to the church, where Grigory Orlov greeted her at the door, resplendent in his silver guards' uniform. Platon and the bishop of Mogilëv, Georgy (Konissky), led a brief service for the knights, already gathered inside the church. Then, flanked by more than fifty liveried servants, banner-carrying clergy set out on foot to the monastery. The knights followed two-by-two in order of seniority. Behind them came Paul, Natalia and Catherine herself, accompanied by senior courtiers. The Horse Guards brought up the rear. Having twice paused for prayers, first at the Anichkov bridge and then opposite the Church of the Entry into Jerusalem, the empress reached the monastery gates just before midday. Archbishop Gavriil led her past the serried ranks of the Izmailovsky Guards to a service conducted by

Innokenty (Nechaev), the bishop of Pskov. Suspending her disbelief during prayers, Catherine kissed the shrine containing the saint's relics. It was three in the afternoon before she returned to the palace, where the customary banquet and ball continued into the small hours.[29]

They returned to the Kazan Church for the wedding on 29 September, nine days after Paul's nineteenth birthday had signalled his coming-of-age in Russia. Just as Catherine's wedding had been, the ceremony was followed by ten days of celebrations, advertised almost immediately in an official guide to the proceedings.[30] Gunning echoed Lord Hyndford's praise in 1745: 'The weather was remarkably fine, which added much to the splendid appearance of the equipages and dresses, the magnificence of which nothing could exceed.'[31] To compensate him for the loss of his tutorship, and with it the direction of the Young Court, Panin was rewarded on coronation day with the rank of field marshal, 10,000 serfs, 100,000 roubles for a house, another 50,000 for a silver service, and an annual pension of 30,000. For eleven years, Catherine had lived in fear that Paul might die before reaching the age of majority. His survival had helped to ensure hers. Relieved that her son's majority had passed without any increase in his political influence, she was not to know that a very different menace was brewing among rebellious Cossacks in the lands east of the Volga. Instead, in the brief interval before disaster struck, she delighted in her first encounter with one of the closest friends of her life and one of the most brilliant minds of the age.

———

Friedrich-Melchior Grimm had edited the *Correspondance littéraire* for twenty years before leaving for Russia in the entourage of Wilhelmina's brother, Ludwig, whose Grand Tour he had been conducting since 1771. D'Alembert, who edited the *Encyclopédie* with Diderot, had recommended this fortnightly manuscript newsletter to Catherine as long ago as 1764. She became a regular subscriber in the following year, joining the elite circle of crowned heads, never more than fifteen in number, who relied on Grimm for a digest of the Parisian journals and an insider's view of the salons. As a member of the philosopher Baron d'Holbach's circle, he was well placed to report on the *philosophes* and pulled no punches in his accounts of their debates. D'Holbach's own *Good Sense*, written in response to critics of his *System of Nature*, was breezily dismissed as 'atheism made easy for chambermaids and wigmakers'.[32] Grimm helped to confirm Catherine's low view of Rousseau (Voltaire was delighted to join in) and steered her towards a more favourable appreciation of Beccaria. He sent her the abbé Galiani's influential treatise on grain prices in 1770. More practically, in his acknowledged role as 'a great friend of humanity',[33] he had not only helped her to acquire Diderot's library and numerous works of art, but also, as a trusted servant of Landgravine Caroline, played a crucial part as matchmaker for Paul and Natalia.

Since Catherine had every reason to admire him, Grimm found himself subjected to a charm offensive almost as soon as he arrived in St Petersburg. Even before the wedding, General Bauer had already made the first attempt to lure him into Russian service; Vladimir Orlov tried again shortly afterwards. Grimm found the courage to refuse in an audience, scheduled to last five minutes, which went on for an hour and a half.[34] Dubbed 'the white tyrant' thanks to his penchant for face powder, he knew that no amount of make-up could conceal the social chasm separating a pastor's son from Regensburg from a reigning empress. Nevertheless, he was determined to try. 'I believe that it is unprecedented that a man of my station should have been treated by the sovereign of one of the most powerful empires with the kindness that I have experienced,' Grimm boasted to Mme Geoffrin. Though protocol kept him well down the table at mealtimes, he was drawn into Catherine's intimate circle after dinner. Predictably, he found her 'a charming woman, the like of whom is not to be found in Paris', admiring the way that she chattered, 'often very gaily about serious things, and very seriously about frivolous things, by virtue of the laws of all good conversation'.[35]

Had Grimm accepted her repeated offers of jobs, either during this first visit or on his return to Russia in 1776, when she hoped he might play a leading role in educational reform, their talks might have lasted for longer. As it was, while he accepted a retainer from the empress from 1777, he chose to preserve a degree of independence by returning to Paris in the service of the duke of Saxe-Gotha (who promptly made him a baron). Now they had to pursue their friendship by other means. Since correspondence formed a natural extension of salon conversation in the eighteenth century, they started to write to one another as soon as he left St Petersburg in the spring of 1774. 'Adieu, monsieur', Catherine concluded her opening salvo on 25 April, 'this letter is beginning to resemble our gossip after eight at Tsarskoye Selo, and the fools who read it after you might find it indecent that people as serious as us should write such letters.'[36] It was worth taking care over compositions that straddled the boundary between private and public spheres. The whole correspondence is punctuated by the sorts of self-conscious literary artifice that characterised all such exchanges at the time.[37] 'For as long as there have been German barons in the world,' ran a typical missive from the empress, 'no one has been so passionately in favour of the post-scriptum as you.' 'For my honour and glory,' she continued on another occasion, 'I have to tell you that everything that was written above on the 20th of September between dinner and the ball is divine in style and inspiration and the promulgation of a divine communication [from Grimm himself] acting on a mortal brain on a day half cloudy, half rainy. You will see that it is vital for you to know all this for the sake of historical understanding. If anyone ever makes a commentary on this letter, I think the price of paper will go up.'[38] Since there could be no more responsible business than writing for posterity, it was crucial that nothing should fall into unscrupulous hands. Appalled in 1787 that Beaumarchais might include her letters in his edition of Voltaire's correspondence, Catherine ordered Grimm to buy up every relevant volume and consign it to the flames. 'And make sure that this objectionable man doesn't keep a copy, so that having sold it to me, he cannot publish it again.' 'Listen, we are all mortal,' she had written earlier that autumn. 'Burn my letters so that they cannot be printed in my lifetime; they are much more sprightly than the ones I wrote to Voltaire, and could do the most awful damage; I insist that you burn them, do you understand? Or that you put them somewhere so safe that no one will unearth them for a hundred years.'[39]

Quite how Grimm managed to inspire her to write such revealing letters remains a mystery. His own are deadly dull. Yet somehow he gave her the confidence to rise above conventional generic pleasantries so that her side of the correspondence not only sparkles, but also takes us to the heart of her sensibility. It was to her Parisian 'whipping-boy' that Catherine confided some of her most intimate thoughts for the remainder of her life. 'I think,' she declared in 1791, 'that it is decreed on high that you and I have been created expressly so that we may each have a pen continually in hand to write to one another without stopping.'[40]

One reason why Catherine felt so secure with Grimm was that he was generally to be found at the least radical end of the Enlightened political spectrum. Whereas Voltaire was uncomfortably aware that by supporting his heroine's campaign against the Turks he was not thinking 'sufficiently as a *philosophe* ought', Grimm regarded war as a good in itself because it channelled man's violent instincts into active, noble virtues. Along with his growing intimacy with Catherine, that was one reason why he was eventually disowned by one of his oldest pacifist collaborators. 'My friend, I no longer recognise you,' sighed Diderot, looking back on their time together in Russia. 'Perhaps without suspecting it, you have become one of the most closet and yet most dangerous *anti-philosophes*. You live among us, yet you hate us.'[41]

Having been the beneficiary of Catherine's largesse since she purchased his library in 1765, Diderot was in no position to refuse her invitation to St Petersburg. His arrival on the eve of Paul's wedding brought the empress into contact with a very different sort of Enlightenment from Grimm's. For a sixty-year-old with no experience of continental travel, the journey had proved predictably gruelling. Illness had delayed him along the way and continued to afflict him for much of his stay (he drank from the infested waters of the River Neva and 'paid them the tribute they obtain from all foreigners').[42] The visit could hardly have got off to a less auspicious start when he discovered, to his distress, that the room promised by his friend Falconet was occupied by the sculptor's artist son, a pupil of Sir Joshua Reynolds. Forced to take refuge at the Naryshkin mansion in St Isaac's Square, Diderot was a fish out of water at Court, turning up for all the dinners and balls in his little black suit to widespread ridicule and suspicion. Etiquette and intrigue were foreign to him; he had virtually no Russian, though he made desultory efforts to learn some over the course of the autumn; and he made little impact on polite or academic society. Although he and Grimm were elected foreign members of the Russian Academy of Sciences on 25 October, that inauguration was the only meeting he attended, even though a further twenty-six were held before he left for Holland in the following March. Grimm told Mme Geoffrin that it was 'the only occasion on which I should have been well disposed to see my name alongside that of Diderot'.[43]

Catherine, however, was fascinated by him. 'And with her he is just as odd, just as original, just as much Diderot, as when with you,' Grimm explained to another Parisian salon hostess, Suzanne Necker. 'He shakes her hand as he takes yours, he shakes her arm as he shakes yours; but in this last point he obeys sovereign orders, and, as you may imagine, a man does not seat himself opposite to Her Majesty unless he is so obliged.'[44] By the end of October, if not before, they were meeting daily at the Winter Palace. So bored was she with Vasilchikov that Diderot was received at the lover's hour, after lunch, when he joined her to discuss the essays he presented to her in advance. Happy to borrow an occasional joke from Lev Naryshkin – 'A capital at the edge of an empire is like an animal with a heart at the tip of its finger' – he kept most of these essays short, out of a self-confessed antipathy to 'purely systematic ideas on serious subjects'. Nevertheless, the empress had encouraged him to write at length and he had no intention of patronising her. Following their disillusion with Frederick the Great, Catherine was the monarch that the *philosophes* had been waiting for. It was for her, Diderot proclaimed, that Montesquieu has written his great book,

The Spirit of the Laws. 'Your Majesty has a strong mind, a great soul, extensive vision.'[45]

A meeting of minds was nevertheless prevented by the recent radicalisation of Diderot's political views. In 1765, when Catherine bought his library, he could still reconcile his materialism with his politics by trusting the superior abilities of the 'great soul' – a wise, absolute ruler surrounded by equally enlightened advisers who could realise the general will by their unique capacity to incorporate in microcosm the social and physiological harmony of the whole species.[46] But that confidence had been severely undermined by Chancellor Maupeou's abolition of the French *parlements* in January 1771. Though Diderot had little respect for these noble-dominated law courts, they played an important constitutional role in registering the king's edicts and their abolition was widely interpreted as an act of tyranny. 'We are on the brink of a crisis which will end in slavery or liberty,' Diderot warned Princess Dashkova in an apocalyptic letter that April, 'and if it is slavery, it will be slavery like that which exists at Morocco or Constantinople.'[47] By the time he arrived in Russia, he was already convinced that liberty could be preserved only by a shift of power away from the monarch and towards a representative national body. 'All arbitrary government is bad,' he insisted to Catherine, not excepting the 'arbitrary government of a good, firm, just and enlightened master'. 'One of the greatest misfortunes that could happen to a free nation,' he continued, in an essay urging the creation of a permanent representative assembly, 'would be two or three consecutive reigns of a just and enlightened despotism. Three sovereigns in a row like Elizabeth, and the English would have been imperceptibly led to a condition of servitude of which no one could predict the end.'[48]

Few monarchs would have listened to such subversive talk. Yet the empress remained unperturbed as Diderot went on to inform her, in the space of that same essay, that resistance was 'a natural right, inalienable and sacred'; that the sovereign was made for the nation and not the other way round; and that any impartial judge of the conflict between the English monarchs and their parliaments would conclude that the king was 'almost always wrong' because he attacked popular liberties.[49] 'I am allowed to say everything that comes into my head,' the astonished *philosophe* explained to Dashkova, 'wise things, perhaps, when I'm feeling stupid, and perhaps very silly things when I'm feeling wise. Ideas transplanted from Paris to Petersburg certainly take on a very different colour.'[50] The most remarkable thing was that Catherine should be prepared to condescend so graciously to a mere writer. 'I swear to you that the empress, this astonishing woman, does all in her power to come down to my level,' Diderot wrote to his wife, 'but it is at moments like these that I find her ten feet tall.'[51]

Catherine was quite right to tell a later French ambassador that if she had placed her faith in Diderot, 'every institution in my empire would have been overturned'.[52] Nevertheless, she was prepared to offer guarded responses to a questionnaire he gave her in search of information on the Russian economy. Since he frankly admitted that the French government hoped to profit from their acquaintance – 'I should be transported by joy to see my nation united with Russia' – it is hardly surprising that sensitive information was held back from the representative of a hostile power.[53] Some of his questions were deflected to offi-cials; others were answered more frankly, particularly when they offered Cather-ine the opportunity to boast about the rich variety of her empire's wildlife; still more received a curt 'I don't know'. The most delicate inquiries were brushed aside with a playfulness she knew he would appreciate:

Q. In which provinces are your woollen manufactories?
A. In every province where there are sheep.
Q. What is the public debt?
A. So modest that I could pay it off in twenty-four hours if I wanted to.[54]

Diderot, it is now clear, took his visit to St Petersburg more seriously than once was thought. Conceiving of Russia as a *tabula rasa* on which an appropri-ately enlightened mind could create a new and glorious civilisation, he saw foreign settlement as a natural way to approach his goal. Though Catherine's colonies on the Volga had been much discussed in the French salons in the 1760s, they had not passed without criticism. Diderot famously proposed that she should 'plant' the seeds of liberty in the form of a colony of Swiss people in Saratov.[55] While scholars have been able to demonstrate the connection between this idea and his broader social and political thought, the empress, who had nothing more than the evidence of their conversations to go on, could be forgiven for dismiss-ing such sallies as utopian. As she became irritated by his impracticality, Diderot was conscious of the danger: 'Nothing is easier than bringing an empire to order with one's head on one's pillow. That way, everything goes as one might wish.'[56] What he could not know, because Catherine did not tell him, was that his visit to Russia had coincided with the emergence of the gravest threat to the order of her empire that she ever faced.

Even as Grimm arrived in St Petersburg on 17 September 1773, an illiterate Don Cossack was issuing his first manifesto to the Yaik Cossack host almost a thousand miles to the south-east: 'As your fathers and grandfathers served previous tsars to the last drop of their blood, so you, my friends, will serve me, the Great Sovereign Emperor Peter Fedaravich.'[57] When the thirty-one-year-old Yemelyan Pugachëv set out to tempt all those who had 'longed for him' with the prospect of land, water, grasses, money, powder and bread, threatening them with his 'just wrath' if they refused to answer his call, the prospects for a rebellion in the territory between the Volga and the Urals could hardly have been more promising.[58] No matter that portraits of Pugachëv made him look more like a lop-sided Peter the Great than Peter III. He had shown off the scrofulous scars on his chest as the authentic 'marks of tsardom' and the forts standing guard over those unruly borderlands were insufficiently manned to repel the heterogeneous band of Cossacks, Old Believers, fugitive serfs, Bashkir and Kazakh tribal leaders (eighteenth-century Russians called them Kirghizians to distinguish them from the Cossacks, *kazaki*) who responded to his appeal to defend their traditional freedoms against the advance of Catherine's Enlightened administration. Not that her bureaucracy presented an indomitable force: Kazan province had only eighty permanent officials for a population of 2.5 million. Famine, plague and war had everywhere taken their toll (the latest levy of one recruit in every hundred souls, decreed on 23 August, was due to begin on 1 October, and by the time it was complete some 323,360 men had been drafted in the space of five years). Once the factory peasants in the metallurgical plants in the Urals had joined him, Pugachëv had the additional advantage of a reliable supply of arms.[59]

By the time General Kar was dispatched to quell the rebellion on 15 October, Catherine already knew of Pugachëv's seizure of Iletsk. A week later, she demanded to see the latest maps of Orenburg province, comprising most of Bashkiria, in order to follow the progress of events. At first she assumed that it was merely a matter of time before Kar sent news of his victory, but this was to underestimate the power of the insurgents. In an area where the Cossacks were in effect the imperial police force, their secession signalled a serious threat to security. Having laid siege to Orenburg on 5 October, Pugachëv set up his own 'College of War' at nearby Berda, where his henchman Zarubin Chika called himself Field Marshal Count Chernyshëv and others among his lieutenants adopted the names of Panin and Orlov. Kar's poorly trained punitive battalion (all that could be spared when the crack troops were in Moldavia and Wallachia) was crushed in early November by a better-disciplined Cossack force more adroit than his own in the use of artillery. News of the disaster reached Tsarskoye Selo on the evening of Catherine's name day, throwing the Court into alarm. The rebels, she was horrified to learn, now numbered several thousand. Suspecting a Turkish conspiracy, she appointed General Bibikov, the former Marshal of the Legislative Commission, to replace the disgraced Kar, whose arrival in Moscow set off a wave of rumours that forced the government to lift its veil of secrecy over the whole affair. 'Probably it will all end on the gallows,' Catherine wrote to Yakov Sievers on 10 December, as Bibikov departed for Kazan, 'but what sort of expectation is that for me, Mr. Governor, who has no love for the gallows? European opinion will relegate us to the time of Tsar Ivan the Terrible!'[60]

Now she had less time for Diderot, who recorded 5 December as the date of their last discussion. Nor was Vasilchikov the man for a crisis. Instead, on 4 December, the empress wrote her first surviving letter to the man who was to supplant him and almost everyone else in her affections for the remainder of his life. The thirty-four-year-old Grigory Potëmkin was at that time besieging the Turks on the Danube:

> Mr Lieutenant-General and Cavalier. You, I imagine, are so firmly focused on Silistria that you have no time to read letters. And although I do not at this moment know whether your bombardment has succeeded, I am certain, nevertheless, that everything you undertake should be ascribed to nothing but your impassioned zeal toward me personally and toward the dear fatherland in general, whose service you love.
>
> But since for my part I very much wish to preserve zealous, brave, intelligent and skilful people, so I ask you not to endanger yourself in vain. Having read this letter, you may put the question: why was it written? To which I can reply: so that you should have confirmation of the way I think about you, for I am always most benevolent toward you.[61]

Confronted with this tantalising summons, Potëmkin promptly sought leave from his camp and headed for St Petersburg.

While she was waiting for him, Catherine attempted to blunt the international impact of Pugachëv's rebellion by making light of it to Frau Bielke. 'There is no revolt at Kazan,' she declared. 'That kingdom is peaceful.' It was true that the 'so-called Peter III' and his 'band of robbers' had 'hanged five hundred people of every age and sex' in their rapacious progress through Orenburg province. Nevertheless, Bibikov had everything in hand 'and it will probably all come to very little'.[62] In the meanwhile, there was no shortage of New Year celebrations to distract her. At a betrothal ceremony before the ball on Epiphany, she placed rings on the fingers of Duke Peter of Courland (the son of Anna's disgraced favourite, Ernst Bühren) and his fiancée Princess Yevdokiya Trubetskaya. And although it was too cold to spend long looking at the model of Bazhenov's new palace in the Kremlin, set up for her inspection in the furthest palace antechamber, she found time to play chess and cards with Grimm and other guests in the Hermitage, having attended a performance of the ballet *Cupid and Psyche*.[63]

Yet even as the carnival continued all around her, the empress failed to match its mood. A placard found at the Winter Palace on New Year's Day, apparently alleging government corruption, was burned in front of the Senate on 11 January when it proved impossible to discover the identity of its anonymous author, a self-styled 'honest man'. Security was stepped up at the palace so that no one below the rank of major could 'pass beyond the Chevaliers Gardes'.[64] With both Orenburg and Ufa under siege, the prospects looked a good deal less certain than Catherine had implied in her letter to Frau Bielke. Even a French comic opera performed by the girls at the Smolny Institute on 20 January was not enough to lift her spirits. After that, she retreated to her apartments for several days. 'The Empress is at present a good deal out of order,' Gunning reported in the middle of this self-imposed seclusion. 'The insurrection in Orenburg, and the height it has been allowed to get to, has certainly given her great uneasiness.'[65] As if to unsettle her further, Paul finally confessed Caspar von Saldern's duplicity to Catherine before the end of the first week in February. This news 'must have been extremely offensive to her', Gunning concluded, 'as, in the passion it threw her into, she declared she would have the wretch tied neck and heels and brought hither'. Only thanks to Panin was she persuaded to allow Saldern to retire, provided that he returned a snuffbox she had given him and renounced all his titles.[66]

Honesty and fidelity were subjects at the forefront of the empress's mind as the turmoil in her personal life matched the chaos in the eastern borderlands. We do not know whether she was already in love with Potëmkin when she wrote to him in December. (Even if she was, it did not prevent her from continuing to lunch with Vasilchikov and Orlov, who can hardly have felt at ease as the only guests at her table apart from Alexander Cherkasov and the duty gentleman-in-waiting.)[67] By the beginning of March, however, there could be no doubt about her new passion. Potëmkin was first presented to the empress at Tsarskoye Selo on 4 February. That morning, she had said farewell in the Amber Room to Prince Dolgoruky, who was returning to Berlin as her ambassador. They were joined for lunch by a regular guest, Admiral Sir Charles Knowles, a seventy-two-year-old veteran of the Royal Navy who, in addition to designing several new men-of-war, had done much to rescue the dilapidated dockyard at Kronstadt since arriving in Russia at the beginning of 1771. Then, late in the afternoon, a very different visitor arrived to be led straight to her private apartments.[68]

Quite how the relationship developed we cannot be sure. But sometime that month, lost in the delirium of their new affair yet painfully conscious of its fragility, Catherine and Potëmkin consummated their passion at the Winter Palace. As a harbinger of the mood-swings to come, he was already jealous of her previous lovers. Concealing herself from public gaze on 21 February, she sent him a list of them in a 'sincere confession' designed to test his faith in her:

> The trouble is that my heart is unwilling to be without love for as long as an hour. They say that people try to hide such vices as if out of kindness, and it may be that such a disposition of the heart is more of a vice than a virtue. Perhaps it is in vain to write this to you, since after this you will fall in love with me or will not want to go back to the army fearing that I shall forget you. However, in truth, I don't think I should do anything so stupid, and if you want to keep me for eternity, then show me as much friendship as love, and above all, love me and tell me the truth.[69]

After all, he had scarcely been celibate himself. 'I'm not surprised that the whole town has credited you with countless women,' she continued two days later. 'No one on earth romps with them more than you do, I imagine.' She asked him only to refrain from criticising Orlov and his brothers: 'He loves you, and they are my friends, and I shan't give them up.'[70]

Despite their attempts to conceal it from prurient eyes, their whirlwind romance was obvious to her closest companions. 'They've all begun to preach to me,' she told her lover on 26 February after a fifth sleepless night alone, 'and I hear them out. But inwardly they don't dislike you, the Prince [Grigory Orlov] above all. I have not admitted to anything. Neither have I justified myself in such a way that they could reproach me for lying.' Now they had only a few days left together before the onset of the Great Fast. 'I shall have to prepare for communion. Ugh! I can hardly contemplate such thoughts without crying.'[71] Aleksey

Orlov, who had come up from Moscow to take stock of developments, twice asked her 'Yes or no?' 'I cannot lie,' she answered, causing him to laugh when she admitted that she had fallen in love: '"And you see each other in the bath-house?" I asked him why he thought so. "Because," he said, "for about four days we have seen a light in the window rather later than usual."' There could be no room for Vasilchikov now. Panin must find some way of sending him away to take the waters. 'Then he could be appointed ambassador somewhere where there isn't much business. He's boring and suffocating.'[72] Meanwhile, on the first day of the Fast, Vasilchikov had to suffer the indignity of lunch in the Diamond Room with the man who had displaced him in Catherine's affections. They sat next to one another again after mass on the following Sunday.[73]

By then it was clear to watching diplomats that the new favourite was cast from a different mould. 'His figure is gigantic and disproportioned,' Gunning reported on 4 March, 'and his countenance far from engaging. From the character I have had of him, he appears to have a great knowledge of mankind, and more of a discriminating faculty that his countrymen in general possess ... and although the profligacy of his manner is notorious, he is the only one who has formed connections with the clergy.'[74] Links with the bishops were a legacy of Potëmkin's time as a student of theology at Moscow University. Though the subject kept its hold on his mercurial mind, he was far too flamboyant to contemplate an ecclesiastical career. Now languid, now brimming with muscular energy, he presented the empress with a fascinating study in contradictions, so different from the colourless creatures who fawned on her at Court. If his intelligence was one part of the attraction, his virility was another, tested and confirmed in action against the Turk. The last time she had seen him in St Petersburg was in the afterglow of the victories at Kagul and Larga, where he had been decorated with the Order of St George, Third Class.[75] Now they launched into a flurry of love letters (she burned his so that only hers survive). 'My dear little dove, *I love you so very much*, you're good, you're clever, you're jolly, and you're amusing: I have no need for anyone else in the world when I'm with you.'[76] And so it went on, now tender, now passionate, and studded throughout with a rich variety of affectionate diminutives: 'sweet darling Grishenka', 'giaour' (an insulting Turkish epithet for non-Muslims), 'Muscovite' and even, in a letter written from the Hermitage on 10 April, 'Mr Yaik Cossack'.[77]

That Catherine felt able to joke about Pugachëv was a sure sign that the crisis in the east had eased. Two days earlier, in fact, Gunning had reported the arrival of a messenger from Bibikov 'with the very agreeable tidings of the rebellion being entirely extinguished by the total defeat and dispersion of the rebel army'. On 22 March, government troops had routed the insurgents at Tatishchevo, at the junction of the roads to Orenburg and Yaitsk, forcing Pugachëv to abandon his headquarters. Most of his confederates were taken prisoner. Having learned of these developments on the morning of 7 April, a relieved Catherine sat down to lunch with Praskovya Bruce, Kirill Razumovsky, Grigory Orlov, Zakhar Cherny-shëv, Alexander Golitsyn and Alexander Vyazemsky. The list reads like a roll-call of her oldest friends. Only Potëmkin was a parvenu. That evening, as her card game drew to a close, she permitted Grimm and Prince Ludwig to kiss her hand on the eve of their departure from Russia.[78]

In fact, the news was not quite so good as it seemed. Bibikov, it emerged soon afterwards, had died of a fever in Kazan on that same day, and it was a mistake to imagine that the revolt was over when its leader was still on the run. Neverthe-less, while Pugachëv was re-grouping in the Ural mountains, Catherine had time to face up to the rivalries stimulated by Potëmkin's meteoric rise. On the Court's return to the Winter Palace on 9 April, he occupied a new suite of apartments on the floor beneath her own. Catherine no longer looked forward to her birthdays. 'I hate that day like the plague,' she complained to Grimm: 'Tell me, truly, wouldn't it be charming if an empress could remain fifteen years old for the whole of her life?'[79] On her forty-fifth birthday, Easter Monday, she invested her new lover with the Order of St Alexander Nevsky.[80] He was appointed to her Council on 5 May and later that month became vice-president of the College of War with the rank of general-in-chief. Though the most obvious casualty of these manoeuvrings was Zakhar Chernyshëv, whose mishandling of the Cos-sacks was held to have left the door open for Pugachëv, it was all too much for Grigory Orlov, who again went abroad after 'a very warm altercation' with Catherine 'which is said to have moved her more than she was ever known to have been'.[81]

Just as Paul was proving a satisfactorily uxorious companion for Natalia, so Catherine herself was by now settling into something approaching married life with Potëmkin. They laughed; they made love; they quarrelled; they may even have been pledged to one another in a secret ceremony. Even now that Paul had reached the age of majority, a formal wedding was no more possible than it had been for Orlov. The best they could hope for was some sort of blessing. No such ritual could take place during Lent, when their passion first ignited; Easter also got in the way. Spring was a time for carriage rides through the streets of the capital, for coffee in the grotto at Tsarskoye Selo, where the Court transferred on

29 April, for picnics in the English garden at Pulkovo, and for relaxing visits to her friends' estates on the Peterhof Road. If it had been difficult for Catherine to sleep with her lover in the early days (the mere sight of his valet was enough to turn her away from his door), it was now even harder to arrange a blessing. The most recent (and most scholarly) Russian editor of Catherine's correspondence with Potëmkin suggests that the likeliest date is Trinity Sunday, 8 June, the annual feast of the Izmailovsky Guards, when the empress allegedly met her lover late in the evening at the Church of St Sampson the Hospitable, founded on the Vyborg Side by Peter the Great to commemorate the saint's day of the battle of Poltava. The evidence could hardly be flimsier. The Court journal records only that Catherine sailed to Yekaterinhof late in the afternoon, spending an hour there before returning via Count Sievers's suburban mansion, where a crowd had gathered to watch. She was back at the Summer Palace by nine. Though the 'white nights' certainly offered the perfect setting for a romantic cruise, there is no proof whatsoever that she took a detour to St Sampson's, still less that a ceremony took place there.[82] It seems just as likely that Catherine's confessor was called upon to bless the couple in the privacy of her own apartments. At any rate, by the time the Court decamped to Peterhof on 16 June, Catherine was already addressing Potëmkin as her husband.

'Dear spouse,' she announced in one such letter, 'there is to be a concert.'[83] Music had always filled the air at the summer celebrations as the wagons of the Court orchestra joined the straggling caravan of carriages that choked the road to the seaside. This year, there was a new star in the firmament: one of the most stunning sopranos in Europe. Catherine liked to tease her faithless 'whipping-boy' that, by reducing him to tears during a recital at Yelagin's house, Caterina Gabrielli had taken him 'half-way to salvation'.[84] Though no less an authority than Mozart judged that 'in the long run, G could not please, for people soon get tired of coloratura passages,' her initial impact was seductive, deriving as much from her charismatic personality as it did from the quality of her voice.[85] One modern writer has seen her as forerunner of the modern prima donna, a fragile proto-Callas who swept from the opera house surrounded by servants carrying her train, her dog, her parrot and her monkey, and who broke free from the semi-servility in which most artists were forced to perform by singing only when it suited her.[86] 'She is indolent and capricious, so there is no depending on her,' Elizabeth Harris complained during a later London season. 'I fancy a good English *hiss* might be of service to her, and most probably in time she may have it.'[87] There was no hissing at Peterhof on 25 June. So captivating was Gabrielli that Catherine, who talked through most concerts, approached the orchestra to listen. Another member of the audience, the English traveller Nathaniel Wraxall, recognised 'a sovereign of a different kind, and perhaps not less despotic or unlimited in her empire': 'I must own I never heard any voice so perfectly sweet, melting, and absolute in its command over the soul: nor can any thing exceed the negligent carelessness apparent in her whole manner, which she employed in this occupation, as if she despised the appearance of exertion or any labor to please.'[88] There was no gainsaying genius. 'Gabrielsha wants to renew her contract,' Catherine told Yelagin the following winter: 'Renew it!'[89] But the singer left for London all the same.

As the festivities continued at Peterhof, good news from the Danube helped to compensate for a shocking report from the Volga. Pugachëv, having escaped capture at Berda in March, had emerged from his hideaway in the Urals and appeared before Kazan at the head of 20,000 troops on 11 July. Next day, nearly three quarters of the 2873 houses in the city were destroyed by fire as the rebels indulged in an orgy of looting and pillage. News of the disaster reached Catherine on Monday 21 July, the day after the feast of the Prophet Elijah. At the Council meeting that morning, she had to be dissuaded from going straight to Moscow to restore confidence in a city whose gaols were overflowing with rebel prisoners. This time, fortune was on her side. Though she learned about it only on 23 July, Rumyantsev had already agreed peace with the Turks at Kuchuk Kainardzhi, not far from Potëmkin's old camp outside Silistria, after Generals Kamensky and Suvorov had finally broken the back of Ottoman resistance at Koludzhi on 9 June. Since the news was better than she had been led to expect, the prayers Catherine offered at a hastily arranged thanksgiving service that afternoon were probably unusually heartfelt. And there was more to come. On the last day of the month, Prince Repnin and Count Semën Vorontsov arrived from Moldavia to explain that, in the treaty signed on 14 July, Rumyantsev had secured the whole of the coast between the Bug and the Dnieper, and an indemnity of 4.5 million roubles. Now she could turn her mind to challenging Pugachëv's final rally.

As Catherine prepared for a Te Deum in honour of the peace treaty at the Kazan Church on Sunday 3 August, the pretender was already carving a swathe through the steppe.[90] Routed by General Mikhelson in a four-hour battle at Kazan on 13 July, he had retreated southwards into an area settled mostly by nobles owning fewer than twenty serfs. These were the plentiful lands that Catherine had so admired on her Volga cruise only seven years earlier. Now, in the last and bloodiest phase of the revolt, the peasants flocked to the rebel cause in increasing numbers, burning their lords' manor houses and slaughtering many of their 'unjust' and 'cruel' occupants. Penza fell to Pugachëv on 1 August, Saratov five days later. But even as he marched towards his native Don Cossack territory, the unsuspecting pretender was finally approaching his nemesis. Shortly after he drew up at the outskirts of Tsaritsyn on 21 August, one of his fellow Cossacks finally recognised him as an illiterate imposter. Once 'the world of suspended belief' in which so many of his followers had lived was shattered, it was only a matter of time before the so-called Peter III was defeated once and for all.[91] On 25 August, while Catherine was lunching with Potëmkin in the Hermitage in preparation for Natalia's name day, Mikhelson inflicted a final devastating defeat.[92] Though Pugachëv again escaped capture, this time his luck was out. On 15 September, the Cossacks betrayed him to the authorities and the greatest revolt of Russia's eighteenth century ended in ignominy.

As the authorities began their interrogation of the pretender, the autumn balls had already begun in St Petersburg. Catherine prepared for the winter by inspecting an array of valuable sables and silks, laid out for her in the Summer Palace much as they had once been for Empress Elizabeth.[93] This time there were no rash announcements about the fate of the rebellion, but two days after Paul's twentieth birthday, she celebrated the twelfth anniversary of her coronation in greater security than she had enjoyed for at least four years.

Potëmkin's incipient rivalry with Nikita Panin was meanwhile being played out at a secondary level in the struggle between their relatives for control over the investigation into the revolt in Kazan. 'Count Panin wants to make his brother the ruler with unlimited powers in the best part of the empire,' Catherine complained, as Peter Panin departed for the Volga at the end of July. Though Catherine was anxious to keep the Panins' pretensions in check, Peter's appointment signalled a noticeable change of policy. Until then, the government had been moderate in its treatment of the rebels. In March Catherine had explicitly urged Bibikov to be cautious in his methods: 'For twelve years the Secret Expedition under my own eyes has not flogged a single person under interrogation, and every single affair has been properly sorted out, and even more came out than we needed to know.' Most of the prisoners taken from the rebels had been released without harm. Now retribution was placed in the hands of Peter Panin, a martinet who calculated that 324 insurgents were executed during his time in charge. A further 399 lost an ear and were knouted; 7000 more were flogged in other ways.[94]

Nothing could compare in Catherine's mind with the damage inflicted by Pugachëv himself. 'There has hardly been anyone so destructive of the human race since Tamerlane,' she spluttered to Voltaire in October. 'He entertains some hope that I might treat him gracefully, saying that he might erase the memory of his past crimes by his courage and future services. If it were only me that he had offended, his reasoning would be just and I would pardon him; however, this is the empire's cause and the empire has laws.'[95] Brought to Moscow in an iron cage on 4 November, Pugachëv was subjected to a secret trial at the Kremlin at the end of December. Vyazemsky was on hand to make sure that no torture was applied. Though the rebel was sentenced to be quartered, Catherine gave orders that his executioner should behead him first, much to the rage of the ghoulish mob that gathered to witness the event on Bolotnaya Square on 10 January.[96] Five days later, as a symbol of her determination to look forward rather than back, she decreed that the Yaik, the name of the river where Pugachëv had begun his revolt, should be changed to the Ural, 'so that the unhappy occurrences on the said Yaik should be forgotten forever'.[97] Her wider ambition was now to consign to the same oblivion the 'blindness, stupidity, ignorance and superstition' that had tempted her subjects into rebellion. And that meant tackling the 'weakness, indolence, carelessness in respect to their duties, idleness, arguments, disagreements, extortions and injustices' perpetrated by her inadequate provincial officials.[98] The task of improving local government was to preoccupy her for much of the following decade.

———

With Pugachëv gone, Moscow was safe to visit, seven years after Catherine had last set foot in the old capital. 'Seven years seems like a whole century to us,' Sumarokov made the populace exclaim in his *Ode to Potëmkin* in 1774. But since the empress was less certain of a rapturous reception, she delayed her departure until news of the pretender's execution had been confirmed, making her formal entry into Moscow on 23 January 1775.[99] Passing two newly erected triumphal arches, commemorating her victories against the Turks, she processed to the customary service at the Dormition Cathedral, and from there to her new palace, where she retired to her apartments. 'The whole passed with scarce any acclamations amongst the populace, or their manifesting the least degree of satisfaction,' Gunning reported secretly to Whitehall. 'The Empress's visit here is far from agreeable to them, and as little so to the nobility. Her Majesty is not ignorant of this, nor of the little affection they bear her; nor are they less acquainted with the unfavourable opinion she entertains of them.'[100]

Inside the porticoed entrance of the Prechistensky Palace, Matvey Kazakov had created a large reception room leading to a throne room, just as big, where Catherine could receive the ambassadors. Beyond that lay a still greater apartment, running the length of the building and divided by columns: she played cards in one half while her courtiers danced in the other.[101] 'To be fair,' as she acknowledged to Grimm, the conversion had been artfully done. But she enjoyed poking fun at the 'labyrinth' connecting the disparate parts of her new palace, portraying her new study as 'a triumph of exits' from which it had taken her two hours to escape. 'I have never seen so many doors in my life. I have already condemned half a dozen of them, and I still have twice as many as I need.'[102]

Thrust into this unfamiliar environment, Catherine and Potëmkin struggled to maintain the explosive intensity of their initial affair, relapsing instead into bickering about the terms of their relationship. It was already clear that they were partners in government. Indeed, when her sulky lover took offence at some corrections she sent him, she assured him that they were 'only guidelines' from which he could make his own choice. While he set to work to ensure that there could never be another Pugachëv, she concentrated on commemorating the defeat of the Turks. At first sight, it was Potëmkin who had the more ambitious task and he set about it with characteristic ruthlessness. Powerless to intervene, Panin watched in horror as the new favourite heaped obloquy on the errant Zaporozhian Cossacks barely twelve years after they had taken a proud role at the empress's coronation. Their host was summarily disbanded on 3 August and its territory assimilated under the regular imperial administration.[103] Meanwhile, Catherine had taken responsibility for an equally visionary piece of legislation. The manifesto commemorating the end of the Turkish war on 17 March 1775 has rightly been accorded 'considerable importance in the history of human rights in Russia' because it offered unprecedented protection to the individual by preventing the arbitrary enserfment of the population by census-takers who had deprived more than 830,000 men of their freedom between 1721 and 1741 alone.[104]

The vagaries of life with Potëmkin help to explain why Easter Sunday found Catherine in wistful mood about Grigory Orlov. 'If ever you catch sight of him,' she wrote to Frau Bielke, 'you will see without contradiction the finest man that you have ever encountered in your life.'[105] Paul and his wife were treated less charitably. Now that Natalia's wilfulness had begun to emerge, the empress's patience was starting to wear thin. She mocked the girl's headstrong profligacy in a letter to Grimm in December: 'we cannot stand this or that; we are indebted beyond twice what we have, and what we have is twice more than anyone else in Europe.'[106] Now that her son had requested a further 20,000 roubles, she grumbled to Potëmkin that there would be 'no end to it': 'If you count everything, including what I have given to them, then more than five hundred thousand has been spent on them this year, and still they want more. But neither thanks nor a penny-worth of gratitude!'[107] On the whole, however, Catherine's mood was positive. Even the obligatory summer pilgrimage to the Trinity monastery, with the Chernyshëvs and Kirill Razumovsky in tow, turned out to be 'very agreeable and a real promenade: we had fine weather and good company and weren't bored for a moment; I returned in perfect health'.[108]

Unfortunately, it was not to last. The peace celebrations had to be postponed when a surfeit of peaches gave her chronic diarrhoea. Onlookers remembered her looking old when she was finally fit to attend having been bled by the medics. On the southern perimeter of the city, fourteen obelisks, each decorated with battle scenes, had been erected to commemorate the greatest victories of the war. From there, the troops marched through the two similarly adorned triumphal arches toward the Kremlin, where Catherine processed down the Red Staircase just as she had at her coronation, only this time in full military uniform. The sound of Slizov's bell 'was so tremendous that it seemed that the Ivan Tower itself trembled', recalled Andrey Bolotov at the beginning of the nineteenth century. 'Many of us feared it would collapse.' Bazhenov had initially proposed temples to Janus, Bacchus and Minerva, but Catherine was having none of it. Classical imagery was deliberately excluded as the empress insisted on a range of neo-Gothic structures, erected on Khodynka field at the north-western edge of the city. All of them found their place on an imaginary map of the Black Sea, where Kerch and Yenikale were made to serve as ballrooms, Kinburn as a theatre, and Azov a huge banqueting hall.[109] Not since the carousel of 1766 had the Court been treated to such a riot of medievalism. The Black Sea transported to a field near Moscow? It was too much even for Voltaire: 'I knew very well that the very great Catherine II was the leading person in the whole world; but I hadn't realised that she was a magician.'[110]

In the midst of this glorious fantasy, the empress had turned her very practical mind to one of the most significant statutes of her reign, the Provincial Reform of November 1775, designed to bring her government closer to the people through a rationalisation of local administration in the wake of the Pugachëv rebellion. Though six surviving drafts in her own hand testify to the depth of

Catherine's commitment to the legislation, the ideas in it came from her advisers. The most influential was Yakov Sievers, who had been brought to Moscow to help her with the reform. 'Work this out with Sievers,' ran a typical note on one of her drafts. 'This is the most stupid article of all,' she confessed at a moment of particular frustration. 'My head hurts from it. This endless rumination is very dry and boring. To tell the truth, I am already at the end of my Latin, and I do not know what to do about the Lower Court, the Board of Public Welfare, and the Conscience Court. One word from your excellency on these subjects would be a ray of light, bringing order out of chaos, as when the world was created.'[111] In November, Sievers was appointed Governor General of Tver, Novgorod, Olonets and Pskov, an area larger than many European states in which he was given the honour of being the first to put the new reform into practice. As a sign that they had been appointed as the empress's personal viceroys, he and Zakhar Chernyshëv in Belorussia were each rewarded with an English silver service weighing over 45 poods. Catherine eventually paid a total of 125,000 roubles for the two services, setting aside a further 42 roubles and 35 kopecks to provide fur coats for officers in the troop which accompanied the final consignment.[112] 'I think these regulations are better than my Instruction for the code,' she told Grimm in January 1776. 'They are being introduced at this moment in the provinces of Tver and Smolensk where they have been received with open arms.'[113]

The Court had returned to St Petersburg in December. It would be another ten years before Catherine saw Moscow again. By then, the city and the surrounding provinces had been transformed almost beyond recognition, at least in part by her own reforming zeal. Yet even that transformation paled by comparison with the turbulence in the empress's personal life.

Small as it was, the palace at
Zerbst provided Catherine's
father, Prince Christian August,
with the quintessentially
cosmopolitan setting of a
Baroque Court in miniature.

Boisterous in private, discreet
and demure in public, the young
Grand Duchess Catherine set
out on her arrival at the Russian
Court 'to please the grand duke,
to please the empress, and to
please the nation'.

Few eighteenth-century princes escaped unscathed at the hands of second-rate artists. Peter III was no exception. The Synodal painter Aleksey Antropov captured something of the fabled vacuity of Catherine's ill-fated husband.

While the empress's memoirs implied that Paul I was the progeny of Sergey Saltykov, her son always regarded Peter III as his father and resembled him strongly in both personality and physique.

Modelling his illustrations of Catherine's coronation on those of the French kings at Reims, Jean-Louis de Veilly transformed the intimate interior of the Cathedral of the Dormition into a cavernous temple.

Elaborate allegorical fireworks were one feature of Baroque Court culture that remained central to Russian ceremonials throughout Catherine's reign. This display, performed on the banks of the Moscow River opposite the Kremlin on 29 September 1762, was intended to confer dynastic legitimacy on a newly-crowned usurper.

Elizabeth's coronation in 1742 served as the model for Catherine's twenty years later. In a scene facing north towards the Cathedral of the Dormition, the cockaigne for the populace on the Kremlin's Cathedral Square is flanked by the Red Staircase and the Ivan the Great bell-tower. Such feasts were still staged in the 1790s, though by then they had long been dismissed as barbaric by Western visitors to Russia.

'From Catherine II to Peter I' was the lapidary motto chosen by Falconet for his statue of the empress's most glorious predecessor. On 7 August 1782 she witnessed the unveiling of the first public monument in Russia from the balcony of the former Bestuzhev mansion on the left of the engraving.

'Apart from seven rooms garnished in jasper, agate, and real and artificial marble, and a garden right at the door of my apartments, I have an immense colonnade which also leads to this garden and which ends in a flight of stairs leading straight to the lake. So, search for me after that, if you can!'

Though Catherine sought to surpass rather than merely imitate Peter I, her declared intention to complete what he had begun was part of her spurious claim to legitimacy. Tsar Peter gazes down approvingly from the heavens in Ferdinand de Meys's allegorical representation of the empress's great journey to the South in 1787.

The first pornographic British caricature of the empress appeared less than two months after Caroline Walker's majestic engraving, done at the outset of the Russo-Turkish War in 1787 from the copy of Alexander Roslin's portrait owned by Catherine's ambassador to London, Count Semën Vorontsov.

Though Platon Zubov liked to pose as a worthy successor to Potëmkin, he was in reality an arrogant upstart who damaged the empress's reputation in her declining years. This version of Lampi's portrait was done by the British engraver, James Walker, resident in Russia between 1784 and 1802.

The caricature in this French version of 'The Imperial Stride', first published in London on 12 April 1791 NS, was the sort of salacious image that corrupted Catherine's reputation among her 19th-century male successors.

Under Russia's last tsar, Nicholas II, it was left to the beholder to imagine the relationship between the bronzed youth and the statuesque empress represented by Lampi's portrait of 1794. Pride of place on the 500-rouble note went to Peter the Great.

CHAPTER TEN

THE SEARCH FOR EMOTIONAL STABILITY 1776–1784

After her accession to the throne, Catherine spent all too little time at Oranienbaum. But had she ever gazed up from the bed in the Damask Room, she would have seen on the ceiling a painting that perfectly encapsulated the tutelary relationship she strove to establish with each of her favourites. *Urania teaching a youth*, by the Venetian artist Domenico Maggiotto, portrayed a bare-breasted goddess looking down at a virile young man who returns her gaze in simple trust.[1] Leonine, earnest and not very bright, Grigory Orlov had fitted the mould to perfection. 'The apprehension of the Empress is extremely quick,' Lord Cathcart observed in 1770, 'that of Mr. Orloff rather slow, but very capable of judging well upon a single proposition, though not of combining many different ideas.'[2] Horace Walpole was typically franker: 'Orlow talks an infinite deal of nonsense,' he remarked during Grigory's visit to London in 1775, 'but parts are not necessary to a royal favourite or to an assassin.'[3]

Potëmkin, by contrast, demanded to be treated not as a pupil, but as an equal, and it made for heated arguments between them in the spring of 1776. 'Sometimes,' Catherine complained, 'to listen to you speak one might think that I was a monster with every possible fault, and especially that of being beastly.' It upset her that he resented her other friends, and flounced off in a temper when she refused to listen: 'We quarrel about power, not about love. That's the truth of it.'[4] Potëmkin, however, had reason to be unnerved. As a sign of Catherine's wavering affections, Rumyantsev's protégé Peter Zavadovsky, who had worked with her on the Provincial Reform, had been promoted Adjutant General on 2 January. This was the favourite's office, still indelibly associated with Grigory Orlov.

Later that month, Orlov himself unexpectedly returned to Russia, where he promptly fell sick, creating a complicated love triangle in which only Catherine herself can have felt fully at ease. A British diplomat reported that 'two visits, which the Empress made to the Prince during his illness, caused a very warm altercation between her and the favourite'. Amidst rumours that he had poisoned Orlov, Potëmkin's downfall was widely predicted, although some acknowledged that this arose 'rather from its being universally wished, than from any actual symptoms'.[5] Meanwhile, Catherine firmly resisted his attempts to persuade her to remove Zavadovsky. Quite apart from the 'injustice and persecution' the dismissal would inflict on 'an innocent man', there was her own reputation to consider: 'If I fulfil this request, my glory will suffer in every possible way.'[6] Instead, her affair with Zavadovsky was publicly confirmed when he was promoted major general and granted 20,000 roubles and 1000 serfs on 28 June, the fourteenth anniversary of the empress's accession. In an attempt to appease Potëmkin, she appealed to his vanity by presenting him with the Anichkov Palace and 100,000 roubles to decorate it as he pleased. Most of all, however, she appealed to his conscience, reassuring him that even as her passion had cooled, her friendship remained unquestioned: 'I dare say that there is no more faithful friend than me. But what is friendship? Mutual trust, I have always thought. For my part, it is total.'[7] There is no reason to think this insincere, but she had meant it just as much when she insisted in an earlier note that 'the first sign of loyalty is obedience'.[8] True equality remained beyond reach in any relationship with an absolute monarch.

Such rapid changes of scene in the empress's bedchamber prompted persistent rumours in the autumn of 1776 that she had taken yet another lover. Rumyantsev's name was mentioned. 'The leading actor of the German comedy is also spoken of,' noted the venomous French chargé, the chevalier de Corberon: 'It wouldn't be surprising, but I doubt it.'[9] In the event, Zavadovsky was to remain in place until May 1777, a month before Orlov finally married his teenage cousin, Elizabeth Zinovyev. While Catherine bombarded 'Petrushinka' with passionate billets-doux, the stolid Ukrainian struggled to keep up his working relationship with her, sulking that she had so little time to spend on him. Increasingly conscious that Icarus was an impossible part to play, Zavadovsky discovered that politics was a topic best avoided: 'If you had thought as much about despotism as I have,' Catherine warned him, 'you would not mention it much.' Soon she was urging him to exchange his insecurity for trust and playfulness: 'all this feeds love, which without amusement is dead, like faith without kind deeds'.[10] In the end, it was he who tearfully begged the empress to release him from his misery. As Catherine told Potëmkin, 'the whole conversation lasted less than five minutes'.[11] Zavadovsky would soon return to a long career at Court, forgiven and befriended like all her former lovers. For the moment, however, he retired smarting to his Ukrainian estate at Lyalichi (later rechristened Ekaterinindar – 'Catherine's Gift').[12] 'Amid hope, amid passion full of feelings, my fortunate lot has been broken, like the wind, like a dream which one cannot halt; [her] love for me has vanished.'[13]

No sooner had Zavadovsky faded from the scene than a more colourful lover emerged to take his place. This was Potëmkin's Serbian-born adjutant, Semën Zorich, a swarthy hussar sixteen years younger than Catherine. 'What a funny creature you have introduced to me!'[14] Having been imprisoned by the Turks after distinguishing himself in action, Zorich seemed less likely than Zavadovsky to suffer from hypochondria. Yet it was no easier for him to cope with the mercurial presence of his patron, who remained the guiding influence in the empress's life.[15] In May 1778, when Potëmkin humiliated him by presenting a handsome young officer to Catherine on her way to the theatre at Tsarskoye Selo, Zorich could no longer control himself. 'As soon as Her Imperial Majesty was gone, he fell upon Potemkin in a very violent manner, made use of the strongest expressions of abuse, and insisted on his fighting him.' Irritated by such a 'fuss about nothing', Catherine forced the rivals to shake hands over dinner in St Petersburg, but it was only a temporary rapprochement. 'Potemkin is determined to have him dismissed,' reported the recently arrived British ambassador, James Harris, 'and Zoritz is determined to cut the throat of his successor. Judge of the tenour of the whole Court from this anecdote.'[16]

Insensitive to the anguish the empress suffered in her search for a stable, loving relationship – she blamed her recurrent headaches on her recent bout of 'legislomania' – Harris regarded the 'scene of dissipation and inattention' presented by the Court of St Petersburg as the inevitable consequence of unnatural female rule. 'Age does not deaden the passions, they rather quicken with years: and on a closer approach I find report had magnified the eminent qualities, and diminished the foibles, of one of the greatest ladies in Europe.'[17] Two years later, after Catherine had exchanged the favours of Zorich's unfaithful successor, Ivan Rimsky-Korsakov, for those of another strapping young guards officer, Alexander Lanskoy, Corberon came to much the same conclusion:

If this sovereign were led, as she could be, by a man of genius, the greatest and best things might be achieved: but this man is not to be found, and by deluding each of her favourites, doing away with them and renewing them one by one, this woman's successive weaknesses become innumerable and their consequences appalling. With the greatest of visions and the best of intentions, Catherine is destroying her country through her morals, ruining it by her expenditure, and will end up being judged a weak and romantic woman.[18]

Generally the preserve of foreigners, and provoked most often by the failure of a particular ambassador's diplomacy at St Petersburg, such verdicts owed more to stereotypical assumptions about female rule than to the realities of Catherine's reign. The political impact of her sex was felt less in her relationship with her favourites than in her treatment of her two grandsons. They were not, however, to be born in the way that she had originally anticipated when the pregnant Natalia was rushed back from Moscow in the summer of 1775. The grand duchess went into labour early in the morning of 10 April 1776, at the height of the crisis between Catherine and Potëmkin. At first there seemed no reason to panic, but when it emerged that the birth canal was too narrow – 'four fingers wide,' as the watching empress subsequently described it to Frau Bielke, 'when the baby's shoulders measured eight' – the midwife left Natalia to writhe in agony for forty-eight hours before calling a surgeon. The unborn child, a large boy, may already have been dead before forceps were used in a vain attempt to save his mother. The cause of the obstruction, a deformation of her spine, was revealed only at the autopsy. Natalia died on 15 April, leaving Paul inconsolable for three days. Even the annual cannon salute to herald the breaking of the ice on the Neva was cancelled as a mark of respect.[19] Dressed 'very richly in white satin', with her dead infant at her feet, the grand duchess lay in state at the Alexander Nevsky monastery, where mourners 'might go and see them, walk up to the coffin, kiss her hand, and then walk round on the other side, but were not suffered to stop, and were obliged to go out again immediately'.[20] Corberon, who blamed Catherine for Natalia's negligent treatment, noted that she 'gave the impression of crying' at the funeral. 'But I give no credence to her tears: her heart is too dry.'[21]

The empress certainly did not linger over her disappointment. As she explained to Voltaire on 25 June: 'We are currently very busy recouping our losses.'[22] That meant finding a new wife for Paul and there was only one serious candidate: the sixteen-year-old Princess Sophia Dorothea of Württemberg, passed over in 1773 only because she was too young. Ruthless in a crisis, Catherine bought off her existing fiancé Prince Ludwig of Hesse-Darmstadt – 'I never want to see him again,' she told Grimm – and cunningly soured Paul's memory of Natalia by revealing her dalliance with Andrey Razumovsky. While Field Marshal Rumyantsev and Prince Henry of Prussia, visiting St Petersburg for the second time, escorted Paul to Berlin for an audience with his hero, Frederick the Great, the empress made arrangements to welcome Sophia to Russia.[23] Having ordered twelve dresses and plenty of Dutch bedlinen, she turned her attentions to the apartments in the Winter Palace, marking out the position of new stoves on the plans and dictating a revised colour scheme for the furnishings: pink and white for the bedroom, with columns of blue glass; blue and gold for the state bedroom, with a new *lit de parade* and a drawing of Raphael's loggias in the Vatican 'which I will give you'; cushions for the sofa in the sitting room 'in gold fabric which I shall supply'. All the rooms were to be hung with tapestries of a specified colour and type, and 'the second ante-chamber should be decorated in stucco or artificial marble with ornaments as pretty as they are rich'.[24]

When Paul returned with his new consort at the end of August 1776, barely four months after the death of his first wife, Catherine promptly declared herself 'crazy' about a girl who seemed to have everything Natalia had lacked. 'She is exactly what I had hoped for: the figure of a nymph; the colour of lilies and roses; the finest complexion in the world; tall and broad-shouldered, yet slight.'[25] Whereas Natalia's progress in the Russian language had been maddeningly slow, Sophia had already begun to master the Cyrillic alphabet in Berlin. Catherine sent a tutor to 'lessen the task of learning' on the journey.[26] She need not have worried: re-baptised Grand Duchess Maria Fëdorovna on her conversion to Orthodoxy, Sophia was to prove the most dutiful of consorts. When the empress led the couple to the altar on 26 September, Grigory Orlov held a crown above Paul's head after the Orthodox custom. Betskoy, now in his seventies, performed the same service for the bride, his hand trembling with the effort. Why had this honour been granted to such a grizzled courtier? 'Because bastards are lucky,' grumbled Corberon, who left the ceremony early finding the crowded chapel uncomfortably warm. Dinner was more agreeable, and much the same in form as Catherine's own wedding feast thirty-one years earlier. Seated between bride and groom, she dined under a canopy with Alexander and Lev Naryshkin in attendance, facing four tables for statesmen of the first four ranks and their wives:

The gallery above was packed with people and occupied by the orchestra, to whom no one listened. The famous Nolly [the violinist, Antonio Lolli, who had given four public concerts to great acclaim in the spring] played well to no purpose amidst this brouhaha and the fanfare that followed the toast to Her Imperial Majesty. The tables were narrow and served *en filet*; they were placed underneath the orange trees, which poked their rounded heads out over the guests and made a very fine effect.[27]

In the tradition established by Peter the Great, there followed ten days of celebrations, including the obligatory firework display and a reprise of the opera *Armida* ('I saw and heard little because I was talking,' Corberon confessed, 'but the music was feeble, so they say, and only one duet gave me pleasure').[28] For once, such public festivities were not the prelude to personal disaster. Only mildly offended by the tone of Paul's written instructions urging thrift, regularity and obedience, his spouse devoted herself to the difficult task of pleasing both her husband and the empress.[29] In time, the couple would irritate Catherine with their profligacy and her son's eye would begin to wander. In the short term, however, his personal life proved noticeably less volatile than hers. As a waspish Harris noted in February 1778, 'The great duke and duchess live indeed on the best terms, and offer an example they neither receive, nor can get imitated.'[30]

By then the Court had launched into another round of lavish celebrations following the birth of the couple's first son on 12 December 1777. Potëmkin hosted a dinner reputed to have cost 50,000 roubles and the ambassadors were invited to inspect the table decorations for Catherine's banquet for top-ranking Russians, 'set out with jewels to the amount of upwards of two millions sterling'.[31] There was more to this than mere magnificence. In christening her grandson Alexander, the empress associated him with both Alexander of Macedon and St Alexander Nevsky, the medieval warrior saint adopted by Peter the Great as the protector of his new capital. As Catherine explained to Grimm, Nevsky 'was respected by the Tatars, the republic of Novgorod submitted to him out of respect for his virtues, he gave the Swedes a good thrashing, and the title of grand duke was conferred upon him thanks to his reputation'.[32] At 8 a.m. on 30 August 1778, the empress solemnly initiated the infant as a knight of the Order of St Alexander and processed in her carriage to the monastery for the annual liturgy. It was not a ritual dear to Catherine's heart – 'You stand there like a dog,' she had once complained to Potëmkin, 'and no one thanks you for it'[33] – but this year she had the consolation of laying the foundation stone for the massive neoclassical Trinity Cathedral commissioned from Ivan Starov in November 1774. He had set to work while the Court was in Moscow and in February 1776 Catherine had confirmed his designs with a budget of half a million roubles. For the foundation ceremony, a yellow canvas awning, emblazoned with the warrior saint's monogram, had been stretched out above a wooden gallery, decorated by Corinthian columns, built out over the foundations. To the accompaniment of cannon and choristers, Catherine ceremonially lowered into the ground a silver shrine containing the remains of Peter the Great's patron saint, St Andrew the First-Called, and a silver salver engraved in commemoration of the event.[34]

Despite such symbol-laden spectacle, it was in private that the empress's maternal instincts were finally allowed to blossom at the age of forty-eight. 'The infant instinctively likes me,' she boasted to Grimm, and indeed to anyone else who would listen. Gustav III, whose heir had been born not long before, was a natural target for her ideas about child rearing and soon received a detailed description of Alexander's nursery, evidently designed to provide the cool, natural environment denied to her own son in 1754:

> The balustrade prevents too many people from approaching the child at once. Care is taken to ensure that only a few of his entourage are allowed in the room at the same time, and only a couple of candles are lit in the evening so that the air around him doesn't get stuffy. Monsieur Alexander's bed, for he knows neither rocker nor cradle, is made of iron and has no curtains; he sleeps on a leather-covered mattress covered with a sheet. He has a pillow and his English bedspread is very light. He is not roused by ear-splitting alarms, but by the same token neither are voices lowered in his room, even when he is asleep. No sort of noise is prohibited in the corridors above and below his room. Cannon are fired from the bastions of the Admiralty, opposite his window, which has made him afraid of nothing [legend had it that this was the cause of his subsequent deafness]. Great care has been taken to ensure that the thermometers in his room do not rise above fourteen or fifteen degrees. Every morning, while his room is swept, whether it be winter or summer, he is taken to another apartment while his own windows are opened to let in fresh air.[35]

A second grandson, Constantine, born eighteen months later, was similarly taken over, though he could never compare with Alexander in Catherine's eyes. Dr Dimsdale was re-called to Russia to inoculate both boys at seven o'clock on the evening of 27 August 1781. She was surprised that Gustav should be so reluctant to offer his own son the same treatment: 'If you yourself were in any danger, then it was assuredly the fault of the method by which you were inoculated.' The king should send a doctor to St Petersburg to learn Dimsdale's method, 'without contradiction, the best'.[36]

As Catherine later explained to Paul and Maria Fëdorovna, 'your children belong to you, to me, and to the state. From their earliest childhood I have made it a duty and a pleasure to take the most tender care of them.'[37] She aimed to nurture not only healthy boys, but also rational children of the Enlightenment. While tears were forbidden, as a sign of stubbornness or undue sensitivity, inquisitiveness was encouraged.[38] By the time of his fourth birthday, Alexander was already said to be 'a determined questioner', just like his grandmother.[39] He could point out Vienna, Kiev and St Petersburg on the globe and willingly devoted two or three hours a day to his ABC. 'If he continues like this,' Catherine boasted to his mother, 'there is no doubt that he will be reading by the spring.'[40] Anticipating the need, she had prepared her own *Russian primer to teach young people to read*, a series of maxims written 'even while legislating' in the spring of 1780.[41] 'No child is born learned,' the empress declared at the outset: 'the parent's duty is to give learning to the child.' Then she moved on to a series of moral injunctions based on her own brand of secularised Protestantism – 'the law requires a man to love his neighbour as himself'; 'do as you would be done by' – before concluding with a definition of citizenship highlighting her favourite virtues: obedience and exactitude. 'Question: what is a good citizen? Answer: A good citizen is he who fulfils precisely all the duties of a citizen.'[42]

Such ideas were soon to be given wider application in the empire thanks to the efforts of an advisory commission on education, set up in 1782 under the aegis of Paul's old science tutor, Professor Aepinus. It was partly on his advice that Catherine adopted the Austrian model of village, urban and provincial schools, using a teaching system initially introduced in Prussian Silesia by the Augustinian abbot Johann Ignaz von Felbiger. Though Felbiger's emphasis on rote learning was a far cry from the permissive methods advocated by Betskoy in the 1760s, it seemed better suited to the needs of a diverse multinational empire. F. I. Jankovich de Mirjevo, who had been responsible for introducing the Habsburg reforms to the predominantly Orthodox population of his native Serbia, arrived in St Petersburg on 4 September 1782. Three days later Zavadovsky was appointed to head a new Commission of National Schools. In the following year, the empress sponsored the publication of *The Book On the Duties of a Man and Citizen*, a textbook based on a work by Felbiger which emphasised society's duty to obey an appropriately enlightened monarch. Pupils were to be taught to believe that 'those who give orders know what is useful to the state, their subjects and all civil society in general, that they do not wish for anything but that which is generally recognised as useful to society'.[43]

Not until August 1786 was a statute promulgated to put these maxims into action in schools at provincial and district level (rural schools, mentioned in earlier drafts were dropped from the final legislation). Meanwhile, although the *Russian primer* was also intended for a wider readership – Catherine improbably claimed that the published version sold 20,000 copies in barely a fortnight – she had eyes only for Alexander, whose progress continued to delight her. By January 1782, she claimed that he could divide the map of Russia into provinces and count to a thousand, 'beginning with two times two'.[44] A month later, she revealed that she was compiling a suitable reader for a child who 'seizes every [book] he finds'.[45] Catherine's *Tale of Tsarevich Khlor* was the first children's story to be written in the Russian language. Sure enough, these 'dozen tales, wise and not so wise' were soon judged to have had 'an excellent effect: he reads and re-reads them and follows them afterwards; he is polite, obedient, and jolly, like Constantine; this one imitates his brother and has a very pleasant personality'.[46]

Whether the grand dukes were really the paragons that their proud grand-mother described, we cannot tell. Yet there is no doubt about the purpose of their education. While Alexander was being groomed to inherit the Russian throne, Constantine (as his name proclaimed) was destined for Constantinople. That was why Catherine's *Russian primer* incorporated a section on the Greek alphabet and why Richard Brompton's saccharine portrait of the two boys, completed in July 1781, depicts Alexander cutting the Gordian knot on the altar of Zeus while Con-stantine holds a flag topped with a victory cross ('With this sign you will conquer').[47] Potëmkin, who had celebrated Constantine's birth with a stylised Greek festival at his country estate at Ozerki, wanted both boys to concentrate on Greek as the foundation of all other languages: 'One can scarcely credit what learning and delicacy of style it has given to so many writers who are distorted in translation, not so much by the translators as by the weakness of other languages.'[48]

Reporting Potëmkin's obsession 'with the idea of raising an Empire in the east', Harris noted that 'he has so far infected the Empress with these sentiments, that she has been chimerical enough to christen the new born Grand Duke, Con-stantine; to give him a Greek nurse, whose name was Helen, and to talk in her private society, of placing him on the throne of the Eastern Empire. In the mean-while, she is building a town at Czarsco Zelo, to be called Constantingorod.'[49]

The new town was in fact named, no less emblematically, Sofia, with a cathedral resembling Hagia Sophia visible across the great pond in an echo of the Bosphorus.[50] Though Catherine denied any expansionist ambitions, she spoke at length to Harris 'on the ancient Greeks, of their alacrity and the superiority of their genius, and the same character being still extant in the modern ones, and of the possibility of their again becoming the first people, if properly assisted and seconded. She told me she talked this language to me as she knew my father was an admirer of the Greeks, and that she hoped I inherited his predilection.'[51] James Harris senior, who had presented Catherine with a copy of his celebrated universal grammar, *Hermes* (1751), was indeed delighted. When his daughter-in-law sent him the Greek chorus, sung at Peterhof at the end of June 1779 to celebrate Constantine's birth, he spent the next two years badgering his son for a copy of the score by Paisiello, one of his favourite composers.[52]

Catherine's so-called Greek project – a visionary plan to recreate the Byzantine empire under Russian domination, first formulated in detail between 1780 and 1782 – was the logical culmination of a foreign policy whose intellectual foundations had been laid more than a decade earlier during Russia's war against the Ottomans. Whereas the Prussian alliance (still formally in existence) had been the linchpin of Panin's Northern System, this reorientation towards the south dictated the need for a rapprochement with Austria, a policy firmly supported by Potëmkin. So when Joseph II suggested a meeting in 1780 as an extension of his tour of Galicia, Catherine readily accepted. Her journey to Mogilëv in Belorussia would not only build bridges with her southern neighbour, but also give her the opportunity to test the impact of her Provincial Reform in lands acquired in the first partition of Poland and governed since 1775 by her old friend Zakhar Chernyshëv.[53]

Accompanied by Alexander Lanskoy, she set off from Tsarskoye Selo supported by an entourage including her secretary, Alexander Bezborodko, the rising star of her administration, and Alexander Stroganov, who had returned from France in December 1779 talking about nothing but Paris.[54] Even such a small suite was expensive. As Elizabeth Dimsdale learned from Catherine's apothecary, 'at every stage they had four hundred and forty horses and twenty coaches besides other carriages'. There were fifty-two of those, drawn by animals requisitioned from some 177 provincial towns. More than 60,000 roubles had been spent on sprucing up the wooden 'palaces' along the route.[55]

The expedition got off to a bad start at Pskov, a medieval stronghold now in terminal decline. 'Inoculate someone with your talent for development and send him here,' Catherine appealed to Grimm: 'Perhaps he will be able to bring on its industry.'[56] 'Tomorrow we move on,' Bezborodko noted on 15 May, 'having seen much that is not good among the nobles, merchants and others.'[57] As they advanced south-westward towards Poland, another disconcerting phenomenon was revealed at Polotsk: 'Jesuits and Dominicans etc., and Jews all lined up on parade.' To Catherine, the Jews looked 'horribly filthy' while the others made 'an august masquerade' to greet her ceremonial entry to the town.[58] 'Everyone lives jumbled together here,' she observed, unwittingly encapsulating one of the most awkward problems facing her administrators' attempts to standardise the government of the empire: 'Orthodox, Catholics, Uniates, Jews etc., Russians, Poles, Finns, Germans, Courlanders – there are not two people dressed the same who speak the same language correctly.'[59] Stroganov, who had started out with a terrible cold, improved after being purged in Polotsk. His 'main task in each town', as he explained to his son's tutor on 20 May, was to discover from the local authorities 'and even the simple citizens' what their needs were, how justice was administered and about 'the unfortunates who languish in prison':

> As soon as I have informed the empress, if the crimes are not capital, the prison doors open and her largesse is distributed to all those in genuine need. Apart from here, where the schools are on a fairly good footing thanks to the Jesuits, education is everywhere badly neglected. The empress wants to take effective measures to repair this deficiency which requires a prompt remedy.[60]

At lunch on 21 May, Zakhar Chernyshëv brought out the treasured silver service presented to him as Governor General after the Provincial Reform. That evening he threw a ball for 500 guests: 'I should never finish if I named them all,' Catherine boasted to Paul and Maria Fëdorovna.[61] Next morning, she was up early for the sixty-mile drive to Sennoye, where she realised that the emperor had already beaten her in the mock race for Mogilëv: 'When he learned that I had lopped off four days from my schedule to overtake him, he ran night and day and overtook me by two days.'[62] Suppressing the urge to join him immediately, Catherine stuck to her schedule. On 23 May she drove through a landscape resembling one of her favourite English gardens to meet Field Marshal Rumyantsev at Shklov, the estate to which Zorich had retired to dispense hospitality on a heroic scale. Guests came from as far away as the two capitals to act in his theatre and there was always a place at his table for 'Frenchmen, Italians, Germans, Serbs, Greeks, Moldavians, Turks – in a word, every kind of riff-raff and tramp'.[63] To greet this exceptional vagrant, he had built his own triumphal arch, where he formally welcomed the empress at 6 p.m. But Zorich's day had passed. Catherine may never even have set eyes on the Saxon dinner service on which he was said to have spent 50,000 roubles since she retired early to write to her 'loving friend', Potëmkin. Leaving her entourage to indulge themselves (and their host) at Zorich's ball and banquet, she drifted off to sleep to the sound of fireworks exploding on an obelisk inside the house and music from a Jewish band dressed in Turkish costume.[64]

Next morning, leaving her deflated former lover clutching at nothing more than the promise of a return visit, Catherine set off to face a potentially tricky week at Mogilëv. Joseph had as always insisted on travelling without ceremony, and his eccentric incognito posed troubling problems of etiquette:

I don't know how best to arrange a meeting without others present because, when I get back from mass, people will be milling all around me. To postpone it again until after dinner would be discourteous. Perhaps he could come when everyone is at mass with me, so that when I get back to my inner apartments – those before my bedroom, that is – I shall find him already there. Tell me if you find a better way, though this one seems clever enough. Since Count Rumyantsev writes that our guest doesn't wish to dine anywhere, I can only conclude that he doesn't even want to eat with me at the high table; I shall wait to be informed about this.[65]

In the event, though disconcerted to find that Joseph looked nothing like his portraits, she found him as determined to please her as she was to admire him. In spite of the weather – there had been thunder in the air since she left Polotsk and the fireworks had to be cancelled because of the rain – Chernyshëv had spared no expense to impress his guests, fetching Caterina Bonafini from St Petersburg to sing in the new theatre.[66] Disappointed to find that Joseph did not know the abbé Galiani, Catherine nevertheless recognised that he was 'clever' and liked to talk.[67] Conscious that all Europe was hanging on their every word, she teased Grimm that the emperor had said many things worth publishing that would have to remain confidential. One topic for serious discussion was elementary schooling (it was Joseph, acting on the recommendation of Abbot Felbiger, who sent Jankovich to Russia in 1782). During mass at the Catholic cathedral, however, the two monarchs behaved with characteristic irreverence, 'laughing and talking more than we listened, with him as the cicerone and me as the gaping tourist'.[68] 'You will find him less boring than the king of Sweden, mark my words,' Catherine assured her son.[69]

Though she became less respectful towards 'Caesar' when he proved to be a feeble general, it suited her to cast herself in a supporting role in 1780. As Harris reported from St Petersburg, 'the amiable qualities of the emperor seem particularly calculated to suit a sovereign, who possesses the art of pleasing in so eminent a degree'.[70] Alarmed by the progress of events, the Prussians redoubled their efforts to discredit Joseph in Catherine's eyes. She was not to be taken in. 'You would do very little justice to the character of the empress of Russia,' Harris commented, 'if you supposed she admitted all this trash to dwell upon her mind, or that she was not enlightened enough to see the motives of such a language.'[71] The visit of the Prussian Crown Prince also backfired. Though he provided Catherine with a welcome excuse to absent herself from the Alexander Nevsky liturgy for the first time in her reign, Frederick William was otherwise a resounding flop – cold, awkward and hard to like, even when he lost 500 roubles at a single game of cards. 'If his uncle ever went wrong in his political speculations,' Bezborodko remarked, 'then he should count this visit among his greatest mistakes.'[72] By contrast, Count Cobenzl had found a perfect advocate for the Habsburg cause in the forty-five-year-old Prince de Ligne, a rakish cosmopolitan charmer with a penchant for the sorts of contrived witticism that Catherine loved best. Ligne, she duly reported to Grimm, was 'one of the easiest and most agreeable beings I have ever met; he is truly original, thinks profoundly and performs follies like a child'.[73]

Once the death of Maria Theresa in November 1780 had removed the last major obstacle to a formal alliance between Austria and Russia, it was delayed only by a dispute over protocol. Joseph, as Holy Roman Emperor, was unable to accept Catherine's status-conscious demand to sign first. She resolved the impasse by proposing an exchange of private letters in place of a conventional treaty. In a secret exchange in May and June 1781, each vowed to support the other in the event of a Turkish attack. As soon as the little grand dukes had recovered from their inoculation, Paul and his wife were packed off to Vienna on 19 September in an attempt to bring them round to Catherine's way of thinking. In such a political climate, there was no further room for the disappointed advocate of the Northern System. Panin had not been taken to Mogilëv and had failed in his attempts to prevent Paul's Grand Tour: three days after the departure of his former pupil, he was unceremoniously sacked.[74]

'The big noise has arrived,' Mozart reported to his father when Paul reached Vienna in November. 'I have been looking about for Russian popular songs, so as to be able to play variations on them.'[75] Though at first the grand duke made a poor impression, scarcely troubling to conceal his preference for Berlin, Joseph brought his visitor round by balancing a series of magnificent Court balls with a tantalising glimpse of his own working methods. He even showed the grand duke his secret correspondence with Catherine.[76] After six weeks as his guests, Paul and Maria Fëdorovna moved on to Italy, travelling semi-incognito as the count and countess of the North. After visiting Venice, Rome and Naples, they reached Florence as guests of Joseph's brother. Having been irritated by Paul's enthusiasm for the Venetian republic – it was easy enough for such a tiny state to put its affairs in order, she told him – Catherine was relieved to learn of his admiration for Archduke Leopold's enlightened regime in Tuscany.[77] Throughout their tour, which reached its climax with an adulatory reception in Paris at the beginning of May 1782, she kept in regular touch with her children, regaling them with news of their sons' progress in her care. No less revealing are the letters sent to a member of Paul's entourage, Prince Kurakin, by his former tutor, which tell us much about the rhythms of life at Court over the winter of 1781–2.[78]

In political terms, the autumn was uneventful. Despite public expectations of changes in the wake of Panin's dismissal, there were no civic or military promotions either on Catherine's name day or on St Andrew's Day. For once the empress had resisted what Bezborodko called 'her habit of making alterations'.[79] He himself proved the only exception to the rule, continuing his inexorable rise by being placed in charge of the postal service on 1 December.

Meanwhile, the empress's 'hermitages' continued on Thursdays and Sundays, despite a scare in late October when a lackey discovered three intruders under some matting in a vacant room. One turned out to be a deserter from the army, another a fugitive serf from Moscow. While the third escaped the guards, Catherine ordered her two prisoners to be handed over to the police to face the criminal courts. Her concern with justice remained undimmed. In an attempt to evade the delays about which delegates to the Legislative Commission had complained, the Provincial Reform had created 'conscience courts'. The empress boasted to Grimm in 1776 that they were already 'working wonders' and would prove 'the tomb of chicanery'.[80] If that was a triumph of hope over expectation, new courts were soon hard at work as far away as Bashkiria, more in the manner of modern arbitration tribunals than of the English equity courts on which they may have been based. 'Only those with no conscience would refuse to serve in a conscience court,' Catherine insisted to her secretary in April 1782. And again in July: 'The conscience court is the pulse showing the morals of each province.'[81] To reinforce those morals, she had promulgated a lengthy Police Ordinance on 8 April – literally a 'statute of good order' – which not only determined the procedures and punitive powers of urban police boards, but also embodied the Cameralist conception of 'police' as a rational, creative force for shaping her subjects' behaviour. To that end, police boards were provided with a characteristic instruction, 'The Mirror of the Police', incorporating moral injunctions reminiscent of the empress's *Russian primer*: 'do not unto others what you would not wish to be done unto you'.[82]

While Catherine was at work on this new statute, the Court had embarked on its usual round of formal entertainments. Panin's dismissal had cleared the way for Potëmkin to arrange suitable marriages for his nieces in the autumn of 1781. Not that he ever released his hold over them. Count Skavronsky soon discovered that his wedding on 5 September to Catherine Engelhardt had not ended her incestuous relationship with her uncle. Alexandra, who had replaced Praskovya Bruce in the empress's affections, was married off to the forty-nine-year-old Count Branicki as a way of staking Potëmkin's claims in Poland.[83] No banquets followed these weddings, much to the irritation of the more elderly relatives, who were displeased to find old customs ignored. As a further sign of the passing of the generations, the ageing Hofmeisterin Countess Maria Rumyantseva, who had once danced with Peter the Great, was chosen to partner little Alexander at the ball on Catherine's name day. Rumours that the Engelhardts' eleven-year-old sister would be made a maid of honour turned out to be false. The St George's Day ceremony was notable mainly for Catherine's anger when Princess Repnin was the sole Court lady to appear in chapel. Already irritated by the low turnout earlier in the month – when her maids of honour had been happy to watch the banquet for the Semënovsky officers from the gallery, but not to attend mass – Catherine instructed the Hofmarshal to fine future absentees ten roubles. In that respect, she was no different from the Empress Elizabeth.

There was no difficulty in persuading courtiers to attend the theatre. Molière's *Georges Dandin* was given on the main court stage on 2 November, a week after being performed in the Hermitage. Catherine did not attend the revival of Paisiello's *I filosofi immaginari*, one of the few operas she had enjoyed. 'It is full of sublime follies,' she wrote after the first performance in 1779: 'you can't imagine what this musician does to gain the attention of organs which are the least sensitive to music and those organs are mine'.[84] She was happier now with Ablesimov's comic opera *The Miller-Sorcerer, Cheat and Matchmaker*, a by-product of the increased interest in the peasant question provoked by Pugachëv. Derived from Rousseau's *Le devin du village*, this overtly folksy piece had been the most popular work in the Russian repertoire for two years by the time it was given at the Hermitage on 21 October.[85] That same month, a new public theatre opened opposite the Summer Garden for performances of Russian tragedy. As Picart reported to Kurakin:

> The theatre is built in the new style, hitherto completely unknown in this country. The stage is very wide and high, whereas the hall for the spectators is made of three-quarters of a circle. There are no boxes, but apart from the benches in the stalls, there are three balconies, one above the other and running around the auditorium without interruption. The paintings are very beautiful and the view excellent when, on entering, you see the audience, sitting, as in ancient times, in an amphitheatre. Apart from the main entrance there are six more very roomy exits, built in such a way that the public can get out in a matter of minutes in case of fire. Everyone is very pleased with this exceptional and spacious new place of entertainment, which they owe to General Betskoy.[86]

Though the autumn of 1781 was one of the warmest in living memory, winter finally set in with a vengeance at the end of November. In the following week, it was so cold that Catherine had to close the imperial theatres and cancel her gatherings at the Hermitage. On 20 December, two coachmen were found dead in more than thirty degrees of frost. Nor was this the final trick that the weather had up its sleeve. Within a week of an unseasonal thaw in mid-January, the Court apothecary had dispensed medicine to more than 500 victims of a flu epidemic. Catherine herself succumbed at the end of the month, bringing the Court to a standstill for several days. Though she felt well enough on 3 February to attend her annual lunch with Stroganov, who had returned from Siberia in December with two ancient silver vases, dug up from his own salt mines, she did not linger long.[87] Yet any thoughts of a permanent slowdown in middle age were soon dispelled. At Peterhof to celebrate the twentieth anniversary of her accession to the throne in June, she had lost none of her energy, as she emphasised to Grimm:

> Would you like to know what I did the day I arrived here? I ran like a hare and

at 11 o'clock, I duly went to mass, as if it were a Sunday. Then I gave an audience to M. de la Torre, whom I count among my old acquaintances, and to M. de la Hererra and Count Lacy, and then to the minister of Saxony. After that, I walked the length of the garden to the quayside in search of my lunch with M. Betskoy. After lunch, I took a launch to the admiralty; there I took some tar and gave three strokes of the hammer to each of two new 100-gun vessels that I had ordered to be built; then I got onto a ship with 74 guns which I ordered to be launched into the water once I was aboard. It took us towards the bridge over the Neva. There, having dropped anchor, we disembarked and got back into the launch to return to the admiralty, where we walked across to find a carriage to take us to the Master of the Horse's country estate [Leventhal on the Peterhof road]. Having walked through his woods and his promenades, we dined and then arrived here at half-past midnight. So what do you say of a day like that? Wasn't it packed? I assure you that everyone apart from me was exhausted.[88]

As if to symbolise her indomitable drive, Catherine finally unveiled Falconet's statue of Peter the Great on 7 August 1782, a hundred years after his accession to the throne. Only the clergy were absent, perhaps still smarting that the Church had been unable to register its objections to the superhuman figure, twice as big as the tsar himself.[89] 'From Catherine II to Peter I' was the lapidary motto, inscribed in Latin on the west-facing side of the pedestal and in Russian on the side facing east. Harris grasped the unspoken comparison immediately: 'I could not avoid, during this ceremony, reflecting how impossible it was that any successor of Her Imperial Majesty who might, in some future day, erect a statue in commemoration of her great actions, ever should be so much superior to her, as she herself is superior to Peter the Great, both in the art of governing, and in that of making her people respected and happy.'[90]

———

If Tsar Peter remained the single most powerful symbol of Russia's superhuman potential, then the great flood of 1777 had offered a salutary reminder of the fragility of man's triumph over nature. Woken by a gale at five o'clock on the morning of 10 September, Catherine gazed out from the Hermitage onto a scene resembling 'the destruction of Jerusalem'.[91] Rising almost eleven feet above its normal level, the swollen Neva had dumped a fleet of merchant vessels onto the embankment, leaving a forest of tangled masts prey to scavengers for timber. It subsequently emerged that the storm had felled hundreds of trees at both the Summer Palace and Peterhof; the Winter Palace cellars were flooded and its roof damaged; and dozens of the capital's grandest buildings were severely disfigured.[92] Though her first thought had been to summon her sentries to safety, more than a hundred of Catherine's subjects lost their lives that night. 'Where am I going to put the 100 gaolbirds taken prisoner by the water?' she mused to Potëmkin. 'In the House of Quarantine, I say, but I don't know whether it is strong enough. The canals are alive, and fifteen faithful soldiers have sunk into them.'[93]

Even as it overflowed, the river was gradually being enclosed by granite embankments designed by Georg Veldten. Begun in 1763, this extraordinary project had reached the Summer Garden by 1770 but was still incomplete in 1777. Four years later, as her carriage snaked between the boulders littering the English Embankment, Elizabeth Dimsdale expressed a common prejudice by doubting that it would ever be finished: 'the Russians are with great truth remarked to begin things with great spirit and for a little time go on very rapidly, then leave for some other object'.[94] She did Catherine an injustice. In January 1780, the empress had charged General Bauer with dredging and redecorating the Fontanka with a budget of 2,372,650 roubles, payable in ten annual instalments. By 1787, much of the canal had been clad in stone under her watchful eye, despite a disconcerting demonstration by 400 peasant labourers, protesting against the miseries imposed on them by the merchant contractor.[95] Ultimately, only the Admiralty wharf interrupted an elegant promenade stretching ten feet above the normal water line for several miles along the left bank of the Neva. Widely admired as 'one of the most sumptuous ornaments of the city', the embankment was praised by foreign visitors as a 'grand work, which, in regard to utility and magnificence' could not 'be paralleled except among the ruins of ancient Rome'.[96]

Classical models were no less prominent in Catherine's mind in planning the redesign of Tsarskoye Selo, where she had advertised her intention 'to summarise the age of the Caesars, the Augustuses, the Ciceros and such patrons as Maecenas and to create a building where it would be possible to find all these people in one'.[97] In 1773, she had hoped that Charles-Louis Clérisseau would draw on his long residence in Rome to design a classical *maison du jardin*, but he disappointed her by proposing a gargantuan structure on the scale of Bazhenov's abortive plans for the Moscow Kremlin.[98] The architect ultimately entrusted with her dreams was Charles Cameron, a barely tested Londoner of Scottish descent who came to Russia to make his fortune in 1779. Over the next few years, Cameron and a small army of Russian and Scottish labourers created an elegant neoclassical gallery above the Roman baths on which he had written a treatise. 'To drive you wild, monsieur le chevalier,' Catherine boasted to Grimm in 1786, 'I have to tell you that you will no longer be able to find me here after dinner, because apart from seven rooms garnished in jasper, agate, and real and artificial marble, and a garden right at the door of my apartments, I have an immense colonnade which also leads to this garden and which ends in a flight of stairs leading straight to the lake. So, search for me after that, if you can!'[99]

As this letter shows, Rastrelli's Baroque interiors were also transformed in these years. Once the main staircase had been moved in 1778 from the southern end of the palace to the centre where it now stands, Catherine had the southern wing converted into a series of cool, neoclassical rooms, no longer extant. Cameron produced at least three variations for the décor of the Lyon room, ultimately said to have cost 201,250 roubles, or £40,250, not including the lapis lazuli. Measuring thirty-six by thirty-two feet, the room was twenty-eight feet high and took its name from the French silks hanging between twelve mirrors, thirteen feet long by four feet wide. It was almost complete by the time the Court returned to St Petersburg at the end of September 1781. Three further apartments were already finished: the Chinese room, decorated 'with prodigious fine China jarrs'; the Arabesque room, where Catherine was to enjoy countless games of cards and chess; and her tiny study, which appeared to Elizabeth Dimsdale 'like an enchanted place, the sides of it inlaid with foil red and green so that it dazzled ones eyes to look at it'.[100] Equally delighted by Cameron's 'superlative' interiors, the ever-competitive empress announced to Grimm that 'no one has seen anything to match them: I can tell you that I have done nothing but look at them for the last nine weeks'.[101] Paul's departure for Vienna allowed Cameron to start on his northern part of the palace, between the staircase and the chapel. 'Every Sunday I pass your apartments,' Catherine reported to Maria Fëdorovna shortly after her fifty-third birthday in 1782, 'which currently have neither windows nor doors and are full of workmen.'[102]

The grand duchess was even keener to hear of progress at the new palace at nearby Pavlovsk, the estate presented to the heir on the birth of his first son. There was still snow on the ground when Catherine made an impromptu visit on 29 April, much to the alarm of the steward, who had only recently taken delivery of 3.5 million bricks. Catching up with the empress while she was still inside the house, he accompanied her on a characteristically demanding tour of the park:

From the ruin Her Majesty wanted to go down to the right of the temple where the paths are not yet made ... I prayed M. Nelidinsky to go by a better path but Her Majesty wished to continue ... Before arriving [at the cascade] she asked several questions about the water, which I had to answer as no one could explain it sufficiently to Her Majesty. She stopped a moment at the cascade, and passed to the chalet, asking me questions from time to time. She sat a moment at the chalet and asked me several questions about the colonnade then took the path to the edge of the garden.[103]

'Building is a devilish thing,' Catherine confessed to Grimm in one of her periodic excursions into her native German. 'It devours money, and the more one builds, the more one wants to go on. It is a sickness, like drinking, and a sort of habit.'[104] So powerful was that habit that it was not only her favourite summer palace that she had 'turned upside down, so to speak':

You wouldn't recognise my bedroom here in town ... I used to have a niche: I have it no longer. My bed is facing the windows and, so that I don't have the light in my eyes, there is a mirror facing the windows at the foot of the bed, under which is a canopy that barely covers the bed. On both sides of the bed, I have some banquettes which go around the alcove. It's charming, and this invention by your humble servant is currently being adopted in all the houses in Petersburg. Besides, my bed is not at all in the imperial style: it has only curtains.[105]

———

Much more in the imperial style was the empress's growing art collection. When Potëmkin first took Corberon to the Hermitage in January 1776, he found 'a lot of pictures, badly displayed':

The gallery is too narrow; there is not enough space to see them and the windows don't reach high enough, or rather, they descend too low. These are ordinary casements, unlike those in the gallery at Kassel. Here I noticed, with sorrow, Greuze's *Paralytic*: it has lost its colour and its effect; it is diminished now.[106]

The answer was to build a bigger gallery – the Large Hermitage – and to keep on making acquisitions to fill it. Catherine's most significant purchase in these years was from the bankrupt descendants of Sir Robert Walpole at Houghton Hall, where a formal portrait of the empress, offered in part exchange, still dominates the saloon. The Walpole collection, which included Rembrandt's *Abraham and Isaac*, was so important that John Wilkes had proposed to Parliament that it be purchased from public funds as the basis for a new National Gallery. George Walpole, the third earl, had other ideas. As Horace Walpole reported in December 1778, 'the mad master' had 'sent his final demand of forty-five thousand pounds to the Empress of Russia'. In the end, she paid £40,555 in a sale negotiated by her ambassador in London. 'Russia is sacking our palaces and museums,' moaned Josiah Wedgwood.[107]

Despite her support for the Imperial Academy of Arts at St Petersburg, Russian painters scarcely figured in her collection. For the lucky neoclassical artists who impressed her foreign agents – Grimm in Paris and Johann Friedrich Reiffenstein in Rome – Catherine's patronage offered a potential bonanza. Anton Raphael Mengs was already approaching the end of a life of service to the Courts of Dresden and Madrid when she first expressed interest in his work in 1776. By the time *Perseus and Andromeda* (1777) arrived in the Hermitage, shortly after the departure of Joseph II, he had been dead for a year. 'The fever takes hold of me, too, when I think of the state Mengs is in,' Catherine told Grimm during the artist's final illness. 'I hope all the great men of our century are not destined to die before the year 1780.'[108] Clérisseau, whose drawings of Rome arrived in the same consignment as the Mengs, was still very much alive, having recovered from his earlier embarrassment to trade so openly on the empress's fondness for his work that a scandal erupted when Paul inadvertently snubbed him in Paris.[109] It was there that Alexander Stroganov showed off the bust of Catherine commissioned from Jean-Antoine Houdon. She herself had ordered a bust of Voltaire, whose death in 1778 at the beginning of her infatuation for Rimsky-Korsakov had made her feel 'a very great contempt for all the things of this world'.[110] All Europe echoed Jeremy Bentham's mock awe at her well-publicised aspiration to build a replica of Ferney: 'Kitty you will find is going to erect a monument to him, in the middle of Petersburgh and to have a model of his house in her park at Czarskozelo.'[111] In the end, she settled for buying his library for the Hermitage. It arrived in 1779, seven years before Diderot's books finally made their way to St Petersburg, to be placed in the care of A. I. Luzhkov, still not thirty, who had translated the *Encyclopédie* article on 'political economy' for Catherine's Society of Translators.[112] Yet by no means all her purchases pleased her. Returning to town with the newly inoculated grand dukes in September 1781, shortly after their parents' departure for Vienna, Catherine complained to Grimm about the latest delivery from Rome. It was if the rain had somehow obscured her vision:

> To my great astonishment, except for the Mengs and a few other trifles, all the rest, except for the Raphael loggias, are nasty daubs: I have told Martinelli, the painter who takes care of my gallery, to choose [the best] and send the daubs to auction for the benefit of the civic hospital. Heavens above! It is incredible how the divine one [Reiffenstein] has allowed himself to go wrong this time: I beg you to ask him expressly to buy no more from Monsieur Jenkins. It is scandalous to pass off such banalities under the name of this or the other painter. My guests at the Hermitage were ashamed to go in there ahead of me.[113]

Some reasonably assumed that there must be no end to Catherine's resources. When a French craftsman set his price in 1776 for a writing desk to commemorate the victory at Chesme, Grimm thought the sum 'so ridiculous' that he expected the deal to be cancelled. Yet, as he later explained to the French foreign minister, 'it turned out otherwise. The empress, who likes to encourage artists in extraordinary projects – and who perhaps intended this escritoire as a mark of her munificence – ordered me to have it done.'[114] In reality, even Catherine's budget was overstretched. In 1778, she had her ambassador in Paris commission a 744-piece Sèvres service. (It was a gift for 'my dear, beloved Prince Potëmkin, but so that it should be all the finer, I have said that it is for me'.) Each plate was priced at 242 livres, the sugar bowls at 1410 livres, and the liqueur decanter at 2236 livres, making a grand total of 328,188 livres (roughly 41,000 roubles at the rate of exchange given by Bentham in June 1778). But when it emerged in the following year that the full amount had not been paid, part of the service was held back in compensation and it was not until 1857 that officials acting on behalf of her youngest grandson, Nicholas I, acquired the missing pieces.[115] The tension between ambition and economy remained unresolved in many of Catherine's commissions. No one was to learn this sooner than Giacomo Quarenghi, one of two Italians recommended by Grimm in 1779 when the empress complained that Rinaldi and her other architects were 'too old, or too blind, or too slow, or too lazy, or too young, or too slothful, or too much the grand seigneur, or too rich, or too respectable, or too stale'.[116] Having been ordered to design new bronze doors for her bedroom at Tsarskoye Selo in 1784, Quarenghi warned Betskoy that 'although Her Majesty desires that these doors should be as sumptuous as possible, if Your Excellency finds the price rising too high, bronze could be used only for the locks and the doorframes'.[117] Most of his subsequent designs were supplied with alternative specifications, allowing for variations in cost.

It had cost Catherine more than 7 million roubles to keep Khan Shagin Girey on the Crimean throne since 1774 and by the end of the decade she was beginning to question the value of her investment. The revolt that broke out in the khanate in the winter of 1780–81 threatened to topple her handsome puppet altogether. By May 1782, he had been forced to flee to the Russian port of Kerch, at the mouth of the Sea of Azov. After Potëmkin had been sent to quell the rebellion on 1 September, Catherine outlined the clearest statement so far of the 'Greek Project' in a letter to Joseph II contemplating joint Austro-Russian action to deliver Europe from the Turk. But there was no hope of achieving her grandest ambitions just yet. Though her partner returned from the Crimea in late October convinced of the need for outright annexation – diplomats noticed that he was now a man with a mission – Catherine remained hesitant, anxious about the reaction of rival powers. She was brought round to his way of thinking in the spring of 1783. So long as France and Britain were paralysed by the War of American Independence, Russia had little to fear. The preliminary peace the two powers had signed in January was an added incentive not to delay. On 8 April, the empress issued a manifesto signalling her intention to annexe the strategically significant peninsula. That same month, her partner returned to the South, exasperating her this time by his prevarication. 'I expected that the Crimea would be occupied by the middle of May,' she complained, 'and now here we are in the middle of July and I know nothing more about it than the Pope in Rome.'[118]

She did not have long to wait. Five days before this impatient letter was written, Potëmkin had already secured the prize. As usual, his jubilation was soon followed by physical collapse, prompting renewed anxieties in Catherine's heart. It was to be November before he returned to St Petersburg. There, far from receiving a hero's welcome, he found that his triumphs had merely intensified his rivals' jealousies. Their resentments seemed to affect the empress, who treated him with unanticipated coolness. From then on, he was to spend more and more time in the South. On 2 February 1784, Catherine appointed him Governor General of the new province of the Tauride, incorporating the former Crimean khanate. The tensions between her and the prince were partially resolved by a division of spoils which made him the effective ruler of some of the most productive lands in her empire.

No sooner had this crucial relationship been resolved than another old friendship, potentially no less difficult to handle, was reignited. After a long period of residence in Europe, during which her son had studied at the University of Edinburgh, Princess Dashkova returned to St Petersburg. Her reception at Tsarskoye Selo on 10 July 1782 marked the beginning of a renaissance at Court that lasted, with varying degress of intensity, for the remainder of the decade.[119] On 24 January 1783 Dashkova was unexpectedly named as director of the Academy of Sciences in succession to the ineffectual Sergey Domashnëv. As Isabel de Madariaga has written, 'it was a tribute to Catherine's perception and to her disregard for current prejudices, that she appointed a woman to take charge of an institution regarded as a male preserve. It was also a way of keeping a busybody busy.'[120] Lacking nothing in nerve and determination, Dashkova set to work with her customary tactless vim. Led into the hall by the mathematician Leonhard Euler, the most distinguished scientist to work in eighteenth-century Russia, then in the final year of his life, she presided over her first meeting less than a week after her appointment. It took all the organisational ability she could muster to tackle the Academy's mounting debts, revitalise its publishing activity, organise public lectures and reform its creaking administration.[121] Impressed by the rapid results, Catherine appointed her later in the year to preside over a new Russian Academy tasked with producing a dictionary of the Russian language (its first six volumes were published between 1789 and 1794). It was in Dashkova's new journal, *The Companion of Lovers of Russian Literature* (1783–4), that the empress published her first essays on Russian history, a subject that was to remain a more or less constant preoccupation for the rest of her life. But it was too much to hope that Dashkova's return would be trouble free. It was not long before her ambitions for her son put her at loggerheads with Alexander Lanskoy.

En route to Mogilëv in 1780, Cobenzl had reassured Joseph II that Lanskoy belonged to 'that species of favourite, who are frequently subject to change, have no influence on affairs, and who limit themselves to making their fortune and that of all those who belong to them'.[122] The twenty-two-year-old major general certainly relished the trappings of office, strutting about at Court 'dressed most magnificently with a shoulder knot of fine brilliant diamonds'. True to form, he 'leapt like a hind' when he learned that Gustav III planned to invest him with the Grand Cross of the Order of the Polar Star.[123] To Catherine, however, the dashing young Sashinka was no mere trinket. Her relationship with him was the closest she came to repeating her experience with Grigory Orlov, except that Lanskoy lacked Orlov's streak of ruthless courage and both she and Potëmkin always treated him like a child in a gilded cage.

After Catherine's roller-coaster ride with Potëmkin – 'the leading nail-biter in the universe'[124] – life with Sasha Lanskoy must have seemed reassuringly undemanding. It was certainly less competitive. Catherine's illegitimate son, Aleksey Bobrinsky, who paid regular visits to the Winter Palace during his time at the Cadet Corps, caught the prevailing balance of power in a note on a game of billiards in 1782: 'She won the game, then started another one and began to win again. She told me to finish the game for her, and I won it.'[125] Dashkova recalled a scene in which a petulant favourite allegedly tried to deter the empress from giving her a treasured bust he regarded as his own: '"But this bust is mine," exclaimed Lanskoy in protest. "It belongs to me."'[126] Sasha, however, was a 'golden individual', accustomed to such 'sacrifices'. It was presumably easier to regard them with equanimity when Quarenghi was not only designing a house for him at Sofia, but also working on a grandiose palace at Velë, the estate Catherine had bought for him in Pskov province. Sent there to plan the park, the Scot James Meader, who had designed the English Park at Peterhof, found that 'the spot where the gardens are to be is very fine laid & planted by nature so that it only wants a little polishing & planting to complete it'.[127] Lanskoy was just as keen to share the empress's passion for engraved gemstones. She tried to stimulate his literary interests, too. As the sceptical French *chargé* noted in September 1780, 'He has just been bought a library for 10,000 roubles, which he certainly will not read.'[128]

Lanskoy's support was more emotional than intellectual. As she approached her mid-fifties, Catherine faced the loss of some of her closest companions. When she learned of General Bauer's fatal illness in the autumn of 1782, she complained to Dr Rogerson that 'there was scarcely a doctor who knew how to cure even the bite of a bed-bug'. Bauer's death on 11 February prompted 'great floods of tears for many days'.[129] Though the carnival continued all around her – 3130 nobles and merchants attended the masked ball at the Winter Palace on 17 February – it was almost three weeks before the empress could bear to break the news to Grimm, a sure sign of the depression which often afflicted her at times of personal despair.[130] Before making her annual confession at the end of the first week of the Great Fast, she quipped bleakly to her *souffre-douleur* that the 'bovine medics' had seen off 'yet another person who has been close to me for thirty-three years'. Only Monsieur Tom, a favourite greyhound, was safe – 'he who has no use for any doctor'.[131] At the end of March, Panin, who had had 'one foot in the grave' since his sacking in 1781, finally breathed his last. And worse was to come. Since the autumn, the empress had been nursing Grigory Orlov, whose descent into insanity after the death of his wife disturbed all who witnessed it. 'One cannot see him in this state without pity,' Zavadovsky admitted.[132] Refusing to have her patient confined, Catherine tended him with unfailing compassion. 'His wild and incoherent discourse ever affect her to tears,' Harris learned, 'and discompose her so entirely, that for the remainder of the day she can enjoy neither pleasure nor business.'[133] Though the end, when it came in Moscow on 11 April, was a blessed release, it was no less shocking for that. On hearing the news at Tsarskoye Selo just before her fifty-fourth birthday, Catherine confessed 'the most acute affliction' to Grimm. In Orlov, she had lost 'a friend and the man to whom I have the greatest obligations in the world ... General Lanskoy is tearing himself apart to help me bear my grief, but that makes me melt even more.'[134] 'It has been a black year for me,' she admitted to Potëmkin when Field Marshal Golitsyn went to his grave in October: 'It seems that whoever falls into Rogerson's hands is already a dead man.'[135]

The one loss for which nothing had prepared her was the death of Lanskoy himself. In her mind, at least, everything seemed set fair for a long and happy future. Plunged into 'the most acute grief' by her bereavement, she made one of her frankest admissions to Grimm:

> I thought I myself would die as a result of the irreparable loss I sustained, just eight days ago, of my best friend. I hoped that he would be my support in my old age: he applied himself, he profited, he acquired all my tastes. This was a young man whom I brought up myself, who was grateful, sweet and honest. He shared my troubles when I had them and rejoiced in my happiness. In a word, I have the misfortune to tell you, sobbing as I am, that General Lanskoy is no more.[136]

Not yet twenty-six, Lanskoy died of what was probably diphtheria on Tuesday 25 June 1784. The tragedy rapidly became the stuff of legend. Following a raucous dinner in 1792 at which the guests cracked crude jokes about the empress's insatiable

sexual appetite, John Parkinson, an Oxford don conducting a young English nobleman on the Grand Tour, wrote a 'Note on Lanskoy' that gives a fine sense of the
fecundity of the Petersburg rumour-mill in the last years of Catherine's life:

> It is certain that after his death his legs dropped off. The stench was also insuf-
> ferable. The boy who gave him his coffee disappeared or died I believe the day
> after. All these circumstances lead [one] to suppose that he was poisoned. The
> Empress was inconsolable for his loss. No person but her faithful valet de
> chambre was suffered to approach her. Grief and the loss of sleep occasioned
> some spots to appear on her breasts which led her to fancy that she had caught
> the putrid fever of which they made her believe that L[anskoy] died. For four
> months afterwards, she kept herself shut up at Peterhoff. Her first reappear-
> ance was on occasion of the Polish Deputies; which gave Nariskin occasion to
> say 'A plague on these Polish Deputies, I have not sat down to one of these
> murderous dinners before for an age.'[137]

Apparently inspired by Quarenghi, and demonstrably inaccurate in almost every
respect, such a tissue of invention tells us little about the events of summer 1784.
Yet, along with Princess Dashkova's claim that Lanskoy's 'stomach burst open'
after his death, it has helped to prompt some impossibly romanticised accounts
of the favourite's demise.[138] His corpse, it is alleged, was left to rot in the heat of
the summer because Catherine could not bear to see it buried for more than a
month.[139] The truth is more prosaic, but none the less touching for that.

The favourite's lifeless body was taken from the palace at Tsarskoye Selo to
the house Quarenghi had designed for him in Sofia. From there it was borne 'with
due honour' to Cameron's new cathedral on the morning of Thursday 27 June
and immediately interred in the neighbouring cemetery following a funeral
service conducted by Metropolitan Gavriil.[140] Bezborodko's attempts not to
trouble the empress with the details were thwarted by typically persistent questioning which, as he pointed out, 'only made her grief the greater'. Catherine did
not attend, having been confined to her apartments since Sunday. She, too, had
developed alarming symptoms – a sore throat and a high fever – which prompted
Dr Rogerson to draw two cups of 'extremely inflamed' blood on the day of the
funeral. By then, he decided, she was out of danger. Prescribing salt to relieve the
indigestion that had prevented her from sleeping, he confidently predicted a full
recovery.[141] In physical terms, he was right. Emotionally, however, Catherine
took longer to recuperate. She shunned most visitors. Sasha's mother, who

arrived in response to the empress's letter of condolence in the hope of securing her family's favour, was deflected onto a lady-in-waiting.[142] Though Catherine could hardly refuse to receive Paul and his wife on Paul's name day, the audience was brief and the subdued celebrations went ahead without her. Servants were confined to their everyday livery and the customary salute, music and toasts were all cancelled as a mark of respect.[143]

Soon the wider implications of the crisis were on everyone's lips. Princess Dashkova would scarcely mourn the favourite, observed her younger sister: 'They hated one another.'[144] Personalities were scarcely the point, countered Alexander Vorontsov. Even those who had no connection with Lanskoy must regret his passing when they learned of its impact on Catherine: 'The preservation of the empress is too interesting to us all.'[145] Riding to the rescue from Kremenchug, Potëmkin arrived at Tsarskoye Selo on 10 July, having covered 760 miles in barely a week. He and Fëdor Orlov went straight to comfort their bereaved sovereign. On the following Sunday, they were joined briefly by Bruce, Osterman, Kirill Razumovsky, Ivan Chernyshëv and Lev Naryshkin. Catherine was persuaded to ride out in her carriage with a favourite lady-in-waiting, Maria Perekusikhina, but not even such close friends could draw her out of her self-imposed seclusion. She continued to dine alone, seeing few apart from Bezborodko, Potëmkin, Orlov and her confessor. Though she received further brief visits from Paul and Maria Fëdorovna, she avoided the traditional rituals during the Dormition Fast. By 18 August, she felt well enough to write a jocular letter to the Prince de Ligne, explaining (without mentioning Lanskoy) that she had immersed herself in work on her universal etymological dictionary. Anticipating Ligne's next visit to Russia, she teased him about his son's abortive flight in the Montgolfier balloon that tore open in mid-air on 19 January:

> If you arrive here by balloon, my Prince, I shall reconcile myself to this fine invention, which I have banned for fear of increasing the danger of fire among the wooden buildings of which we have too many in our territories. The crash of the balloon at Lyon has not caused this new method of travel to be believed in here.[146]

Yet it was one thing to joke to a friend, another to face her Court. While the feast of St Alexander Nevsky on 30 August brought a welcome opportunity to see her elder grandson, the annual celebrations, transferred from the monastery to Tsarskoye Selo, were conducted in her absence. To deepen her misery, a courier arrived from Moscow next day to announce the death of Zakhar Chernyshëv. At the time of their dalliance in 1751, Catherine had been unable to imagine paradise without her dashing cavalier; now he had got there before her. [147]

Having initially intended to remain in the country until 10 September, she returned to town five days early, travelling in a simple two-seater with a favourite lady-in-waiting, Anna Protasova, and sleeping in the Hermitage. The rooms she had occupied with Lanskoy carried too many memories, and it was not until the following spring that she returned to her usual Winter Palace apartments. Looking back, Catherine remembered the summer of 1784 as a perpetual series of battles to recover her equilibrium: 'one to be fought, one to be won, one to be lost.'[148] Only on 8 September did she finally summon the courage to appear in public on the feast of the Nativity of the Virgin. After mass, she endured a lengthy hand-kissing ceremony before retiring to the Hermitage for lunch with Potëmkin, a handful of friends, and Prince Repnin, who had come to request her permission to take his sick daughter abroad.[149] 'In truth,' Catherine confessed to Grimm, 'it was such a big effort that on returning to my bedroom, I felt so exhausted that anyone else would have fainted, something which has never happened to me in my life.' 'If you want to know my true state,' she continued a fortnight later:

> I will tell you that for three months from yesterday I have been inconsolable over the irreparable loss I have sustained, that the sole improvement is that I have got used to human faces again, that otherwise my heart still bleeds just as it did at that first moment, that I do my duty and try to do it well, but that my grief is extreme, and such as I have never felt in my life, and it is now three months that I have been in this cruel situation, suffering like the damned.[150]

Count Cobenzl was more interested in the political consequences of such 'immoderate grief'. Mercifully for a supporter of the Austrian alliance, they had proved to be minimal. For all Catherine's emotional turbulence, the direction of her government had remained firm:

> There has been not a single sort of discord within the Court. On the contrary, I believe that there have been few epochs where there has been so much unity and so little jealousy between the people to whom the management of affairs is entrusted. There is no question of a new favourite, and many people are beginning to believe that there won't be one. If the health of the Empress is not altered by this change, it will certainly do more good than harm.[151]

CHAPTER ELEVEN

ZENITH 1785–1790

In the event, the interval between favourites, though longer than usual, proved to be only temporary. During the celebrations surrounding Catherine's fifty-sixth birthday on Easter Monday 1785, a new shooting star emerged. Introduced to the empress by Potëmkin, the thirty-one-year-old Lieutenant Alexander Yermolov was first mentioned in the Court journal on 22 April. His presence among the five guests at lunch on the following day suggests that the relationship may have begun during Lent, a time of greater privacy than any other for the empress.[1] Although Potëmkin dubbed him the 'white negro' on account of his unusually flat nose, it was Yermolov's flat-footedness in politics that led to his rapid downfall. Drawn into business in April 1786 by his appointment to a commission to restructure the assignat bank, he struggled, as his friend Bezborodko had predicted, to cope with machinations at Court. After being inveigled into an intrigue against Potëmkin that may have been inspired by Zavadovsky and Alexander Vorontsov, Yermolov was dismissed in July with the now customary redundancy package – the Polish Order of the White Eagle, 4300 serfs in Belorussia, 130,000 roubles in cash and a silver dinner service – and sent abroad. In the following year, he embarrassed Semën Vorontsov, Catherine's ambassador in London, by demanding to be presented to George III. 'The king has always found it ridiculous that in Russia one can be promoted from sergeant to major general in the space of two years without serving at all.'[2]

By comparison with Yermolov's extended 'retirement' (he died in Vienna at the age of eighty in 1834), the empress's infatuation was brief indeed. While it lasted, however, it served its purpose, as Cobenzl noted, by staving off melancholy and stimulating her natural *joie de vivre*. During the long months of misery after Lanskoy's death, she had been consoled by a treatise sent to her by the Court physician at Hanover, Dr Johann Zimmerman. *Solitude considered with respect to its influence on the mind and the heart* was eventually published in Russian translation in 1791. For the moment, Catherine acknowledged the support of the new favourite and her other faithful friends: 'My inner self has regained its calm and serenity.'[3] Restored to health and happiness, she had launched into a new bout of 'legislomania', capping a decade of fundamental domestic reform by promulgating the Charter to the Nobility and the Charter to the Towns on her birthday, 21 April 1785.

Though Catherine had no intention of inflating the pretensions of the nobility as a whole – it was part of the compact by which her empire was governed that nobles should abdicate corporate political ambitions in return for virtually unlimited social and economic control over their serfs – she wanted to boost the nobles' *esprit de corps* in order to convert them into a civilised instrument for the transmission of her Enlightened policies. Whereas most European sovereigns were anxious to limit noble status, Catherine was keen to enhance it in the interests of her empire. Far from being a concession to noble pressure, the Charter of 1785 represented a consolidation and development of Peter III's 'emancipation' manifesto of 1762. Corporate rights granted to the noble estate as a whole – including the right to attend provincial assemblies and elect a provincial marshal – were linked to the assumption that individuals would continue to serve voluntarily in the provinces: those who failed to serve could play no part in the assemblies. The charter confirmed nobles' property rights and personal security (they could not be flogged; they were permitted to petition the empress direct; they could be tried only by their peers; and they could be deprived of their nobility only by decision of the Senate, confirmed by Catherine herself). The legislation also attempted to regulate membership of the noble estate by making provincial assemblies responsible for registering six different groups of nobles, defined for the first time according to the antiquity and origins of their titles.[4]

The Charter to the Towns similarly divided the merchantry and urban-dwellers into six categories, defined according to wealth and occupation. As part of the hierarchical social order Catherine strove to create, they too were given rights of personal security and property (to a lesser degree than the nobles) and the institutional modernisation begun in the Provincial Reform of 1775 was capped by the creation of an even more elaborate system of urban government, based on a representative town council (*duma*). Although the empress contemplated an equally rational approach to social engineering in a draft charter to the state peasantry, this was never published, perhaps because of its unsettling implications for the serfs. Symmetrical in form, obsessively detailed in content, and increasingly prescriptive as they descended the social scale, the charters stand as a monument to Catherine's confidence in the reforming power of legislation.[5] Although some of that confidence was misplaced, since it took too little notice of prevailing social realities, there was no doubt about her commitment to the development of a vigorous urban economy. On Saturday 24 May 1785, she set out from Tsarskoye Selo without escort in a small suite of twenty carriages to inspect the progress that had been made in the decade since the Provincial Reform.

Passing through the staging posts immortalised five years later in Alexander Radishchev's sentimentalist *Journey from St Petersburg to Moscow*, Catherine had no eyes for the rural misery he was soon to depict. Her immediate purpose was to inspect the newly enlarged locks at Vyshny Volochëk, the pivot of the system of inland waterways built by forced labour under Peter the Great which carried 216,000 tons of freight a year to St Petersburg by the 1750s. Soon after arriving in the little town, she looked on as some thirty barges passed through its new stone locks, loaded with grain and iron.[6]

The empress had originally planned to be away for no longer than a month.[7] But while she was at Vyshny, Count Bruce persuaded her to divert briefly to Moscow in order to quell rumours of potential unrest. Although the road between the two capitals was probably the only one in Russia smooth enough to attempt at short notice, only the most entertaining of company could have persuaded her to face such a punishing schedule with equanimity (in the following year she approved a comprehensive programme of improvements to the road, scheduled for completion in 1790 at a total cost of 4 million roubles).[8] Her sixteen-strong entourage included not only Potëmkin and Lev Naryshkin, but also three 'very easy-going, very clever, NB. very jolly' travelling companions in Cobenzl, Alleyne Fitzherbert and Count Ségur, the 'pocket ministers' who took turns to share her six-seater with Yermolov. They relieved the tedium by playing word games devised by Ségur, who seemed particularly 'pleased to be with us and is as jolly as a chaffinch'.[9] 'The journey is doing me a lot of good,' Catherine reported to her grandsons' governor from Torzhok.[10]

Seen through such rose-tinted spectacles, even the old capital seemed to have something to recommend it. She told Paul and Maria Fëdorovna that General Bauer's aqueduct at Rostokino, built in imitation of Roman models to channel water into the city from the springs at Mytishchi and completed only in 1803, was already 'the best building in Moscow: it seems as light as a feather'.[11] If the city itself was 'far better than it used to be', as Catherine was prepared to acknowledge on the return journey, then so were the villages on the main Petersburg road, rebuilt in stone as a consequence of the Provincial Reform.[12] While the ancient settlements along the route had sunk into decline – 'No place,' Coxe admitted in 1778, 'ever filled me with more melancholy ideas of fallen grandeur than the town of Novgorod' – the new and recently restored towns showed signs of genuine vigour. Enlivened by a 'rising spirit of commerce', Tver itself promised to be 'no inconsiderable ornament to the most opulent and civilized country'.[13] Although such rapid improvements could hardly have been achieved without the active involvement of merchants who shared the Charter to the Towns' aspirations towards a prosperous civic society protected by law, Catherine took legitimate pride in having inspired them under the energetic direction of Tver's Protestant governor, Yakov Sievers.[14] 'I am told that this is a consequence of the arrangements I put in place and which have been followed to the letter for ten years: and seeing all that, I say that I am well pleased.'[15]

Although the main aim of her travels was to publicise the benefits of modern technology and administration, the rituals that punctuated the journey spoke of the resilience of an older cultural world. To celebrate their recently granted charters, nobles and townsmen flocked to pay homage to their sovereign. The merchants of Torzhok presented her with leather bags and slippers, embroidered with golden thread, which she promptly sent back to St Petersburg as a gift for Constantine and Alexander.[16] As befitted an expedition resembling a medieval monarch's progress, the tone of the proceedings remained overwhelmingly religious. Catherine attended cathedral services at every major calling point, kissing the holy relics in several more churches along the way and permitting a succession of bishops, abbots and abbesses, themselves attended by countless clergy, monks and nuns, to kiss her hand.[17] Yet even the religious aspect of the journey was given a distinctive new colouring. After dining in Moscow with Archbishop Platon and his brother, Alexander, archpriest of the Dormition Cathedral, the empress made a parting gesture towards toleration by receiving a delegation of registered Old Believers at the Petrovsky Palace on 5 June.[18] Four days later, on the feast of the Holy Spirit, she laid the foundation stone for Prince Nikolay Lvov's monumental neoclassical cathedral at the Torzhok monastery of Boris and Gleb. (The Scottish stonemason Adam Menelaws had left Tsarskoye Selo a week ahead of her to begin work there.)[19]

The final part of the return journey was completed by water from Borovichy on 11 June. One of the large galleys manned by the 674 sailors under Vice Admiral Pushchin's command was devoted entirely to the preparation of lunch, another was responsible for dinner. Catherine shared her craft with Yermolov and her favourite ladies-in-waiting, Anna Protasova and Maria Perekusikhina.[20] As Ségur later recalled, Lake Ilmen, a 'sort of calm and limpid sea' south of Novgorod, 'was covered with a number of boats of all sizes, adorned with painted sails, and garlands of flowers':

> The numerous bodies of boatmen, peasants and peasant girls who were on board of them, strove with each other to approach our splendid flotilla, and made the air resound with their musical instruments and loud shouts, and at the close of day, with their melodious but rather plaintive songs.[21]

Catherine's company was more raucous. As always, she had taken plenty of work with her, chivvying Prince Vyazemsky about a series of unresolved criminal cases in St Petersburg province. In the evenings, however, she and her entourage relaxed by compiling a fantastic story about the revolution that had failed to materialise in Moscow. No wonder 'Prince Potëmkin died of laughing throughout the journey'.[22]

Though the wide range of personal and public funds used to subsidise the empress's travels makes it impossible to determine their total costs, the following accounts, issued by the Court administration, give some estimate of the types of expenditure involved:

Rewards:	30,368 r.
Fees for horses at staging posts betweenTsarskoye Selo and Moscow and back to Borovichy	81,535 r. 6k.
To the Court Office for various duties connected with the journey	12,000 r.
For construction of vessels here and at Borovichy	5,060 r. 12.5k.
For boatmen and workmen on the boats during the cruise and other necessities	18,335 r.
For repairing the road and bridges to Moscow	2,000 r.

For schools, almshouses and hospitals in Moscow, Novgorod   27,900 r.
and Tver provinces
For the building of homes for the homeless, in Novgorod,   8,000 r.
6,000 and in Klin, 2,000
For things used on the journey   36,305 r.
Total: 231,493 r 18.5k.[23]

Back at Peterhof for the twenty-third anniversary of her coup, Catherine boasted to Grimm about the comparative etymological dictionary on which she had been working since the death of Lanskoy: 'It is perhaps the most useful thing that has ever been done for all languages and every dictionary, and namely for the Russian language, of which the Russian Academy has undertaken to produce a dictionary, and for which, if the truth be told, it totally lacked the requisite knowledge.'[24] Requests for information were sent across Europe, and also to both South and North America. Invited to contribute lists of Native American words by the marquis de Lafayette, George Washington replied in May 1786 that he would do his best to help Catherine, 'but she must have a little patience – the Indian tribes on the Ohio are numerous, dispersed & distant from those who are most likely to do the business properly'.[25] She forged ahead regardless. *Linguarum totius orbis, vocabularia comparativa* was published in 1787 with a title page in Russian and Latin. Since the empress's contribution depended more on enthusiasm than expertise, the scholarly value of the work owed most to Peter Simon Pallas, the leader of the Academy of Sciences' expeditions to the steppes. However, her own patriotic instincts were reflected in a determination to detect Slavonic influences in many of the world's languages.[26]

Unlike her etymological dictionary, another of Catherine's projects in the summer of 1785 was still incomplete in 1796 when her son decided to dismantle it. By that time, she had spent at least 823,389 roubles on the monumental neoclassical Pella Palace, designed by Ivan Starov overlooking a bend in the River Neva to the east of St Petersburg. Here, opposite Potëmkin's estate at Ostrovki, she could watch the barges from Vyshny Volochëk gliding silently towards the capital and indulge her passion for garden design. 'It's a beautiful situation,' she had told Grimm in April, 'with a variety of views and it will be good to enhance it all with an English park.' Having commissioned three white marble columns for her garden when she returned from Moscow, she confided the 'fantasy that took hold of me three days ago, when I had a sort of fever for these three columns that I wish to see executed in all their grandeur and beauty'.[27]

———

Only one false note had been struck on the visit to Moscow, and it was possibly a significant one. Although she reacted favourably to most of the new buildings there, Catherine angrily rejected the interiors at suburban Tsaritsyno, declaring the palace uninhabitable as it stood.[28] Bazhenov, who had kept her secretaries in close touch with his plans since being commissioned in 1776, had evidently failed to prepare the empress for the results.[29] She was not the only critic of his stunning neo-Gothic extravaganza. An English visitor in 1792, who found the buildings at Tsaritsyno 'crowded together in such manner, that one could fancy it the object of the architect to shut out as much as possible the beauties of the situation', noted that the external embellishments were 'stuck all over in such profusion that we compared the ground on which they were stuck to a larded chicken'.[30] Yet perhaps there was a more ideological reason for the empress's irritation. Though she did not say so, it has often been supposed that she was offended above all by the Masonic symbolism of Bazhenov's designs.

Catherine had certainly lost patience with Freemasonry by the time of her visit to the old capital. Unable to distinguish between philanthropic Rosicrucians devoted to the inner life and the revolutionary mysticism of the 'illuminati' and Saint Martin, she was excluded from the movement by her sex and suspicious of it as a Prussian-dominated espionage network with the potential to ensnare her son. (Though it seems doubtful that Paul ever belonged to a Masonic lodge, it emerged in 1792 that Bazhenov himself had delivered a parcel of mystical and devotional literature to the grand duke on behalf of the publisher Nikolay Novikov.)[31] Having been nauseated by the visit to St Petersburg in 1779 of Count Cagliostro – the Sicilian charlatan Giuseppe Balsamo, who was a pseudo-alchemist rather than a Freemason – Catherine condemned Freemasonry to Grimm as 'one of the greatest extravagances ever in fashion among the human species'.[32] Cagliostro was resurrected in the guise of Kalifalkzherston, a character who embezzles gold from gullible victims in Catherine's play *The Deceiver*, one of three anti-Masonic dramas dating from 1785–6 that she claimed proved a 'prodigious success' with her audience.[33]

Governor General Bruce had been expressing anxiety about unregulated publishing for more than a year by December 1785, when the empress ordered him to investigate some of the books published by Novikov's Moscow university press so that she could be sure that they contained no Masonic 'ravings'. In March 1786, warning Bezborodko that he faced 'complete ruin' from the sequestration of his stock, Novikov implored Catherine's secretary to intervene on his behalf. Shortly afterwards, she banned only six Masonic texts, including the Rosicrucian *New Chrysomander* and the *Chemical Psalter*, a pseudo-Paracelsus. Sent to test the publisher's faith, the sympathetic Archbishop Platon could find no contradiction between his Freemasonry and his Christian beliefs. Nevertheless, the empress's suspicions continued to be fuelled by her confessor, Father Ioann Pamfilov, in cahoots with one of Platon's most influential enemies, Archpriest Peter Alekseyev of the Archangel Cathedral in Moscow. Although no further systematic censorship was imposed, Bruce and these clerics led her to worry that her 1783 edict permitting private publishers had generated not only the sorts of 'useful' book she was keen to propagate, but also a lot of dangerous and potentially subversive nonsense. Though she was pleased to learn that Dr Zimmerman admired her final anti-Masonic drama, *The Shaman of Siberia*, 'because I like that play very much', she feared that it was likely to 'correct no one: absurdities are tenacious and these particular absurdities have become fashionable. The majority of German princes think it good form to bow their heads to all these illusionists'.[34]

While Novikov's books were impounded, Catherine continued her own voracious reading. Necker's *Compte rendu* reminded her that Louis XVI's finances were 'in general, completely disgusting'.[35] The long-awaited arrival of Diderot's library and manuscripts in the autumn of 1785 unnerved her more. Nothing had prepared her for the shock of finding his critical 'Observations' on her *Nakaz*, which remained unpublished in his lifetime. Directing his treatise as much against Montesquieu as against the empress, Diderot had been able to see 'only a formal difference' between despotism and pure monarchy: 'It is the spirit of pure monarchy which has dictated the Instruction of Catherine II. Pure monarchy remains as it is or reverts to despotism, according to the character of the monarch. It is therefore a bad sort of government.' His verdict on serfdom was equally uncompromising: 'There is only one way to avoid the abuses of serfdom and prevent its dangers: and that is to abolish serfdom and rule only over free men.'[36] 'This essay,' the empress retorted, 'is utter drizzle in which one finds neither an understanding of things, nor prudence, nor foresight.' Observing that 'criticism is easy, but art is difficult', she insisted to Grimm that her *Nakaz* had been 'not only good, but even excellent, and well adapted to circumstances' because 'everyone benefits from the principles established by this Instruction'.[37]

The benefits of Quarenghi's Hermitage theatre were destined to be enjoyed by a much narrower circle. When the space above the stables in the courtyard of the Small Hermitage proved too small for the purpose, it was decided to build on the river on the site of Peter the Great's Winter Palace. 'I shall not need the theatre this winter,' Catherine commented in response to the plans the architect sent her in 1784. 'Therefore you may quietly proceed with the drying and painting, since it won't be used until the winter of 1785, that is, you have a full 14–15 months ahead of you.'[38]

Meanwhile, Quarenghi had plenty of other projects to occupy his time. He had written without exaggeration in 1783 that he had 'so much work' that he scarcely had 'time to eat and sleep'. Two years later, he sent another Italian correspondent a staggering list of commissions which were soon to transform not only the urban landscape in St Petersburg, but also many provincial towns and estates:

> ... three pavilions in the new garden at Peterhof ...; the Stock Market; a large building for the State bank; a very large two-storey block of shops for the fair in Irkutsk; a church with a hospital attached for their imperial highnesses at Pavlovsk; a building ... to accommodate the copies of Raphael's loggias; ... a façade for the colleges and church in Polotsk; the façade for the governor's residence in Smolensk; a palace and stables for General Zavadovsky in Ukraine; the Hermitage theatre ... on the model of the ancients; the façade of the new imperial palace in Moscow ...; a marble gallery for the palace of Her Imperial Majesty, which I have begun and which I must bring to order and re-do, and which, when finished, may be considered the richest gallery in the whole of the North; the façade of the College of Foreign Affairs; shops for silversmiths ...; . ... five churches; ... a large group of buildings and a stock-exchange for the fair at Kursk; a house belonging to the late General Lanskoy in the town of St Sophia; a building for public shops, the press and professors' apartments at the Academy of Sciences; a manege, stables, a great staircase and many internal decorations at the late General Lanskoy's palace [at Velë in Polotsk province]; and equally the reconstruction of the whole of this aforementioned palace and three large gates in marble and bronze for the big square; two iron and bronze bridges for her imperial majesty's garden at Tsarskoye Selo; the renovation and enlargement of the governor's residence at Voronezh, and also the

archbishop's palace, the seminary and its bell-tower, houses for the choristers, the provincial administration, and many other renovations and façades for a lot of public buildings in the town; a pavilion with a large hall for music, two rooms and an open temple, dedicated to the goddess Ceres, with a ruin nearby in the ancient style in the aforementioned garden. All these buildings are part complete, part in the process of being finished.[39]

Amidst this flurry of activity, Quarenghi pressed ahead with his theatre, modelled on the Palladian theatre at Vicenza, itself inspired by classical Rome. It opened on schedule on 22 November 1785 with a performance of Ablesimov's ever-popular comic opera *Miller-Sorcerer, Cheat and Matchmaker* at which Cobenzl was the guest of honour.[40] Some months later, the architect proclaimed that he had tried to give his semicircular auditorium 'an ancient appearance, while making it simultaneously correspond to contemporary requirements ... All the seats are equivalent, and each may sit wherever he judges best'.[41] It was here amidst the pink marble columns that a select audience celebrated the empress's fifty-seventh birthday in 1786 with the first two performances of *Fevei*, an opera for which she herself had written the libretto.[42] As the French émigré Prince Esterhazy later observed, Vasily Pashkevich's music was entirely based on 'ancient local chants':

The production was magnificent. The action takes place in Russia in ancient times. All the costumes were made with the greatest luxury from Turkish fabrics, exactly as they wore then. There was an embassy of Kalmyks, singing and dancing in the Tatar manner, and Kamchadals, dressed in national costume, who likewise perform the dances of central Asia. The ballet with which the opera ends was performed by Picquet, Madame Rosa, and other good dancers. Represented in it are all the different peoples who populate the empire, each in its own national dress. I never saw a more magnificent or more varied spectacle: there were more than five hundred people on stage! However, there were fewer than fifty of us in the audience: so uncompromising is the empress with regard to access to her Hermitage.[43]

Nervous about the quality of her theatrical compositions, Catherine recruited her secretary, Alexander Khrapovitsky, to work through the night to correct her grammar and spelling. In 1789, she asked Lev Naryshkin to shorten her comedy *The Misunderstanding*, complaining that it had been the cause of 'more labour than laughter'.[44] By then, she had turned her hand to innovative historical dramas inspired by Shakespeare. *Ryurik*, written in August 1786 but never performed, was an allegory intended to glorify the benefits of a benevolent foreign ruler. Its sequel was Catherine's libretto for *The Beginning of Oleg's Reign*, an operatic pageant celebrating the union of Greek and Russian cultures, published in 1787 and eventually premiered in a lavish production in the autumn of 1790 to commemorate her empire's victories in the Russo-Turkish War of 1787–91.[45]

Contemporary imperial developments were indeed as fantastic as any opera plot. In October 1786 Potëmkin requested more money to fund his insatiable ambitions in the South. Not content with plans for a university at Yekaterinoslav (now Dnipropetrovsk in Ukraine), he envisaged a cathedral grand enough to rival St Peter's in Rome and 'dedicated to the Transfiguration of the Lord as a sign that your labours have transfigured this land from a barren steppe into an abundant garden, and the abode of beasts into a favourable refuge for immigrants from all countries'.[46] Catherine had already trumpeted his claims to Dr Zimmerman:

'In the Tauride the main thing must probably be agriculture, and also silk-worms, and after that plantations of mulberry-trees. We could manufacture cloth there, though the wool is not of the best quality, and it would be good to make cheese too (NB hardly any cheese is made in the whole of Russia). A further key objective in the Tauride might be gardens, and especially botanical gardens.'[47]

It remained only to see this paradise for herself in the company of her handsome new favourite. The twenty-six-year-old guards officer Alexander Dmitryev-Mamonov, nicknamed 'Redcoat' by the empress, had been installed by Potëmkin in July. Describing this latest paragon to Grimm in December, she praised his heart, his honesty and his intelligence: 'in a word, he is as sound in his inner self as his dextrous, strong and brilliant exterior'.[48] Though the same optimistic tone could always be heard at the start of each new relationship, this time there was a grain of truth in the hyperbole. Mamonov shared many of Catherine's interests and delighted a select audience at the Hermitage Theatre in 1788 with his comedy *L'Insouciant*, written in mock tribute to Lev Naryshkin.[49]

As the empress cleared her desk at the Winter Palace on New Year's Day 1787, a range of scandals was brewing among her closest circle. Bezborodko had fallen for an attractive dancer and set her up in a house next to his own, depositing 10,000 roubles in her name at the foundling home.[50] More menacingly, Prince Frederick of Württemberg had returned to Germany, having abandoned his long-suffering wife, Zelmira (Princess Auguste of Brunswick), the sister-in-law of Maria Fëdorovna. 'The Prince of Württemberg's thrashings have finally forced his wife to withdraw to my apartments because she was actually in danger for her life,' the empress reported to Potëmkin. As her secretary noted with typical understatement, 'various consequences transpired which took up a lot of time'. Despite the empress's support for Zelmira, the dispute remained unresolved at the princess's death in September 1788.[51] For the moment, all Catherine could do was to try to put such troubles behind her as she left for Tsarskoye Selo on 2 January to prepare for the greatest journey of her life.

It had been long enough in the planning. Four years earlier, Zavadovsky had told Field Marshal Rumyantsev of the empress's secret intention to travel via Smolensk and Kiev for a meeting with Joseph II at Kherson.[52] Orders went out in September 1784 that all the dams on the Dnieper and its tributaries be cleared to allow 'navigation from their very sources' in the following spring. Court officials were urged to do everything possible to economise and limit the number of horses required.[53] Later that autumn, however, the renewed threat of plague in the South threw the whole project into doubt – in the aftermath of Lanskoy's death, the Vorontsovs were not the only ones opposed to the idea of exposing Catherine to unnecessary risk – and by the time she returned from Moscow in summer 1785 it had already been decided to postpone her great venture until January 1787.[54]

When her cavalcade left Tsarskoye Selo on 7 January Catherine and her suite sheltered under bearskins inside their carriages while their servants' faces were exposed to driving sleet and wind. She had to stop for three days at Smolensk while their eyes recovered and Dr Rogerson administered St James's powders to the feverish 'Redcoat'. Archdeacon Coxe, who passed through Smolensk in the summer of 1778, thought it 'by far the most singular town' he had ever seen. 'The walls stretching over the uneven sides of the hills till they reach the banks of the Dnieper, their ancient style of architecture, their grotesque towers, the spires of churches shooting above the trees, which are so numerous as almost to conceal the buildings from view, the appearance of meadows and the arable ground, all these objects blended together exhibit a scene of the most singular and contrasted kind.'[55] The empress liked the place better. Though far from enchanted by the populace who thronged to catch a glimpse of her – 'they'd gather in fistfuls to see a bear, too'[56] – she was so impressed by the local nobility that she staged an impromptu ball and congratulated the Governor General and his staff on 'their zeal for the common good and the precision with which each fulfilled his duties'.[57]

At Smolensk, Catherine worshipped in the Dormition Cathedral, a huge, five-domed edifice completed in 1772 almost a century after the foundation stone had been laid.[58] At Chernigov, she admired an altogether more ancient foundation, the tenth-century cathedral founded by Mstislav Vladimirovich, while privately singling out Bishop Feofil for his 'stupidity'. Archimandrite Dorofey made a better impression at Kozelsk, receiving 500 roubles for a pleasing sermon.[59] But it was left to one of her favourite preachers, Bishop Georgy of Mogilëv, to greet the empress at Mstislavl with an oration studded with the sorts of leaden bon mot she most admired: 'Let us leave it to the astronomers to prove that the earth revolves around the sun: our Sun travels around us, and travels in order that we may rest in prosperity.'[60]

The 'palace' in which Catherine slept at Potëmkin's estate at Krichëv on 19 January was in reality a large wooden house similar to those built at every staging post on the journey. Here the sentries fell under the command of the twenty-one-year-old Lev Nikolayevich Engelhardt, a relative of the prince who spent most of the night scurrying round in search of buckets of water to guard against fire.[61] Staying nearby was Jeremy Bentham, on a visit to his brother, Samuel, who had been in Potëmkin's service since 1784. Bentham, who preferred to be 'inquired after' rather than seen, learned that the empress had processed through fir-strewn streets 'illuminated with tar barrels, alternating with rows of lamps, formed by earthen-pots filled with tallow and a candle wick in the middle'. Though it was hard not to be impressed by her cavalcade, Bentham derived a jaundiced view of the proceedings from Alleyne Fitzherbert, who was 'sick of the excursion' having 'got something the matter with his liver':

> The same company, the same furniture, the same victuals: it is only Petersburg carried up and down the empire. Natives have too much awe to furnish any conversation: if it were not for the diplomatic people, she would have been dead with ennui.[62]

Back in St Petersburg, Zavadovsky was just as cynical, telling Alexander Vorontsov that those 'eternal companions of the court – baseness, meanness, hypocrisy, flattery, lies and cunning' had merely 'migrated from the banks of the

Neva to the stream of the Dnieper'.[63] Yet in a characteristic triumph of hope over experience Catherine was enjoying herself in the company of the 'pocket ministers' who took turns to share her carriage, just as they had on the journey to Moscow in 1785.

Effervescent as ever, Ségur kept boredom at bay by devising word games with which a delighted empress could later regale Grimm (only the occasional risqué joke backfired – Catherine was never bawdy in public). Unlike Fitzherbert, Ségur recognised her talent for eliciting useful information from her subjects:

'More is to be learned,' she said to me one day, 'by speaking to ignorant persons about their own affairs, than by talking with the learned, who have nothing but theories, and who would be ashamed not to answer you by ridiculous observations on subjects of which they have no positive knowledge. How I pity these poor *savans*! They never dare to pronounce these four words, *I do not know*, which we ignorant people find so convenient, and which often prevent us from adopting dangerous decisions, for, in a doubtful case, it is much better to do nothing than to do wrong.'[64]

Montesquieu would have been proud of her.

Though Kiev lay under 20 degrees of frost when the empress arrived on 29 January, she was amazed to discover that neither her ears nor her nose had frozen: 'that would be impossible in Petersburg, but here the air is softer'.[65] The weather, which remained a topic of conversation throughout the journey, was not the only surprise in store. Not long after her arrival, Catherine complained that although she had seen 'two fortresses and their suburbs', she couldn't yet 'find the town'. From the 'scattered dwellings they call Kiev', she could only conclude that it had shrunk since her first visit in 1744.[66] This was indeed a city in decline. 'Of its former splendour', she wrote to Dr Zimmerman, 'only some rich churches remain.' 'Straggling' and 'extremely badly built', Kiev was ill-equipped to accommodate the unprecedented crowd of cosmopolitan visitors who descended in the empress's wake, plagued by crowds of beggars in a city whose almshouses provided for only 136 paupers.[67] Conscious that 'illusion is always more attractive than reality', Ségur famously declared that the city had been transformed into 'a magic theatre, where ancient and modern times seemed to be mingled and confounded with one another, where civilization went hand in hand with barbarism'.[68] No less aware of the theatrical aspect of her journey, which she described to Grimm as a 'continuous series of fêtes', Catherine was more brutal: 'We have here four Spanish counts, numberless imperial princes, a crowd of Poles, English, Americans, French, Germans, ... more heathens than I have ever seen, including even Kirghizians [i.e. Kazakhs], and they are all living in Kievan shacks, and one cannot understand how there is room for them.'[69]

Affecting not to know what had attracted such a crowd, the empress attributed the influx to reports in the foreign press that she planned to provoke the Turks by staging a second coronation in New Russia 'of which there was never any question'.[70] 'Half Poland' had come to bend her ear before she renewed her acquaintance with her former lover, Stanisław Poniatowski, and a good number of his nobles had to be turned away from her apartments: 'I think they wanted to see me and had come to keep me company.' The king's American secretary, Lewis Littlepage, was there to keep an eye on the Poles; Potëmkin, stretched languidly on his divan at the Monastery of the Caves, wove his own web of intrigue.[71] In such a feverish atmosphere, a hectic round of social engagements served to raise the sexual stakes. Field Marshal Rumyantsev could think of 'no better representation of temptation' than the low-cut dress worn by Countess Natalia Sollogub to Cobenzl's ball.[72] If we are to believe the South American Francisco de Miranda, who let it be thought that the empress herself had been one of his conquests, the whole company descended into hedonistic excess: one of his Russian friends claimed to have won 28,000 roubles at cards since leaving St Petersburg.[73]

While her entourage indulged themselves, Catherine found more improving relaxation. Deprived of the attentions of Alexander and Constantine, whom she had reluctantly left behind in St Petersburg when they were stricken with illness just before her departure, she all but adopted a surrogate grandson: the five-year-old child of Potëmkin's niece, Alexandra Branicka. 'His mother, having seen how the grand dukes behave, follows my regulations precisely.' According to Catherine, the boy duly responded in kind: 'healthy, agile, not stubborn, and so free in his manner that it is as though he had lived with us for a century: far from wild, not timid, but clever and happy, so that anyone who sees him is devoted to him'. She had him inoculated against smallpox in mid-March.[74]

Though the enervating round of balls and masquerades had by then been brought to an end by the onset of Lent, the relief proved short-lived as Catherine immersed herself in an equally exhausting series of religious rituals. Expecting the Dnieper to thaw before Easter, she chose to observe the first week of the Great Fast. On 7 February, she returned from a liturgy at the New Maiden Convent complaining about the canting hypocrisy of the abbess, a former lady-in-waiting at Court.[75] She confessed at the Monastery of the Caves on the following Saturday. Sunday was set aside for communion. Next day, Catherine returned to inspect the relics buried deep in the catacombs, emerging coated in sweat 'as if from the bath-house'.[76] Passing through narrow underground passages, she was greeted by a scene as macabre as the one that Baedeker advertised to tourists at the beginning of the twentieth century:

> No fewer than 73 saints are buried here in niches, the bodies lying like mummies in open coffins and enveloped in costly garments ... Another curiosity is a head projecting from the ground, and covered with a mitre said to have been worn by John the Longsuffering, who had himself buried in the earth up to his neck and is said to have lived so for 30 years, while his dead body was afterwards preserved in the same position (Twelfth Cent.).[77]

Although Aleksey Bobrinsky's tutor had been told in 1783 that the ceilings had been raised to allow Empress Elizabeth to walk without stooping, the catacombs remained so constricted that many courtiers in Catherine's entourage were forced to turn back when their candles filled the tunnels with smoke and condensation.[78] Despite such a 'terrible promenade', she herself remained 'as nimble as a bird' as she boasted to Count Bruce in her ninth letter on the following morning. The visit had 'lasted at least two hours because we went all over, in both the highest and the deepest catacombs, and everywhere on foot, and the monk who accompanied us could not have been more ignorant'.[79] Such mockery was common enough among the more sceptical members of Russia's westernised elite. In public, however, the empress took care to demonstrate her reverence for the cradle of Orthodoxy, donating 24,000 roubles for building work, gold candelabra studded with diamonds for the relics of St Vladimir, and new silk shrouds for the other saints' remains.[80]

As so often, Catherine presented her religious observances as a form of physical endurance from which it was a relief to settle down to work. Amidst the routine letters of congratulation to efficient subordinates, there was time to catch up with artistic purchases ranging from antique gemstones to furniture. On 29 June, she handed over to Grimm the largest single payment of the reign: 100,000 roubles, roughly a third of the total paid to him in Russian coin between 1765 and 1797. Meanwhile, she was as anxious as ever to achieve value for money, warning him not to buy at a public sale: 'make sure you get the best possible price so that Prince Vyazemsky [in charge of the state budget] doesn't choke'.[81] Much time was spent completing the manifesto on duels, an ultimately ineffective piece of legislation inspired by the *Encyclopédie*. While confirming her earlier prohibition on duelling, regarded by Catherine as dishonourable, it introduced milder penalties for a crime against the individual.[82] When this manifesto was finished, she returned to Blackstone. All her notes on the British jurist had been taken on the journey, along with a copy of her own Instruction, so that she could work on further constitutional reform, which never came to fruition.[83]

By early April, even Catherine's patience was wearing thin. To an absolute monarch who regarded her own travel plans as 'almost faultless', it was vexing to be delayed first by the weather and then by Potëmkin. Yet the prince had good reason to prevaricate. Although the prospect of an imperial visit had given renewed urgency to all sorts of dormant provincial projects (the municipal *duma* at Kharkov was one), not all of them were ready on schedule. Along the route, officials complained about the difficulty of finding sober servants for the empress's palaces and the impossibility of completing the necessary building work. Pleading for more time on 31 March, the major general in charge of the palace at Kremenchug, where Potëmkin had his headquarters, reported that it was so cold that the pitch was freezing on the roofs.[84] Embarrassed by such problems, the prince held Catherine off as long as he could, adamant in his desire to display New Russia in all its glory. But when some of the foreigners in Kiev began to drift away in search of Stanisław and Joseph II, she determined to leave for the South.[85]

On 22 April, the day after publishing her manifesto on duels on her fifty-eighth birthday, Catherine set out at four in the afternoon on board a Roman-style galley, commissioned by Potëmkin, designed by Samuel Bentham and decked out in red and gold. On 16 May, Vice Admiral Peter Ivanovich Pushchin, who had masterminded every one of her cruises since 1767, was invested with the Order of St Alexander Nevsky.[86]

Wending its leisurely way downriver toward the cataracts, the flotilla made frequent stops at picturesque settlements where the empress was greeted by crowds of well-dressed peasants, all carefully stage-managed by Potëmkin and his lieutenants. But it would be wrong to suppose that these 'Potëmkin villages'—a byword ever since for fraudulent attainments—were cardboard silhouettes, deliberately erected to hoodwink a gullible empress. That was a rumour circulated by the prince's enemies even before her departure from St Petersburg.[87] In fact, Catherine was fully complicit in the theatricality of the cruise, conscious of being the star of an elaborate show.

Naturally there were signs of haste in many of the new buildings she saw, but most of her companions chose, like Ségur, to emphasise the scale of the achievements that had been made in a short time. The empress caught the balance nicely by describing Kherson – then a town of 1200 stone buildings and a population of around 50,000, including 5000 convicts – as 'very fine, for a six-year-old adolescent'.[88] It was certainly a different scene from the one that had greeted Bobrinsky and his tutor in 1783, when there had been 'very few buildings in the town itself'.[89]

Catherine reached her principal naval base on the Dnieper estuary on 12 May. There had apparently been no stirring of emotion at her meeting with her former lover, Stanisław Poniatowski. To the king's evident chagrin, their interview at Kaniev on 25 April was brief indeed. She not only refused the Polish alliance that Potëmkin had wanted her to make, but determined to press on with her journey without even attending the ball on which Poniatowski had lavished a small fortune. It was more than twenty-five years since they had seen each other. Now, urged on by Potëmkin's most influential critic, Alexander Vorontsov, she had a more important ally to impress.[90]

While the Caucausus reminded Joseph II of the Alps, Catherine and her image-makers invented complex layers of overlapping symbolism which portrayed the Crimean peninsula simultaneously as an Edenic paradise, an exotic Orient and a new Greece, complete with Greek place names and Greek Orthodox bishops, with Catherine cast in the role of Iphigenia in Tauride.[91] At the khan's palace at Bakhchisaray, she heard the imams calling the faithful to prayer five times a day. At Inkerman, overlooking the harbour at Sevastopol, she reviewed the fleet with the emperor. Simferopol and Karazubazar were further exotic destinations on their itinerary. Catherine contributed to the prevailing atmosphere of unreality by collaborating on an 'Authentic relation of a journey overseas that Sir Léon the Grand Equerry would have undertaken in the opinion of some of his friends'. Written before her departure from St Petersburg, this was a fantasy in which Lev Naryshkin, blown ashore off Constantinople in the sort of preposterous storm that featured widely in eighteenth-century adventure stories, met the Sultan before sailing back to Kronstadt, where he narrowly escaped drowning and had to be rescued by Admiral Greig's Newfoundland dogs.[92]

Catherine herself returned to St Petersburg by land, making the long trek north in the heat of the summer via Poltava, where Potëmkin, who was henceforth allowed to call himself 'Tavrichesky' ('of the Tauride'), staged a re-enactment of Peter the Great's victory over the Swedes in 1709. Then came Kharkov, Kursk, Orël and Tula, where the empress was too exhausted to attend the nobles' ball.[93] Having arrived at Kolomenskoye late on 23 June, she made her entry into the old capital on the eve of the twenty-fifth anniversary of her accession. Tuesday 29 June, the feast of SS Peter and Paul, was Archbishop Platon's fiftieth birthday. During the service at the Dormition Cathedral, the empress surprised him by instructing her confessor to address him as 'metropolitan', the most senior office in the Russian Orthodox Church. Platon emerged from the altar to bow to her in acknowledgement of his unexpected promotion.[94] Next morning, she drove out to Kuskovo to be fêted by Count Nikolay Sheremetev, Count Peter's son and heir, who had been planning her reception since the previous autumn. 'The money is flowing like water,' he told his St Petersburg estate manager on 17 May, announcing that he was 'building quite a lot'. Apart from the obligatory triumphal arches, the most elaborate project was a new 150-seat theatre, designed by Charles de Wailly, the architect of the French royal opera at Versailles, in conjunction with Louis XVI's chief theatrical machinist. Catherine sat on a gilded throne in the count's box for a performance of Grétry's neoclassical comic opera *The Marriage of the Samnites*, a celebration of heroic virtue and loyalty to family and state. The heroine was played by Sheremetev's wife, the former serf Praskovya Kovalyova, who was presented to the empress at the end. Conscious of the effort her host had made, Catherine reassured the expectant Sheremetev that it was the most magnificent performance she had ever seen.[95]

Six months later, the voyage to the South seemed no more than 'a dream'.[96] Aggravated by Potëmkin's aggressive posturing in the Crimea, the Turks had imprisoned Catherine's ambassador in Constantinople soon after her return to St Petersburg. This was the traditional Ottoman way of declaring war. Fortified by her implacable faith in Potëmkin, Catherine expected her troops to make a better start to the campaign than they had in 1768. But her partner was in no fit state to lead the charge. Exhausted by the summer's celebrations and alarmed by a diarrhoea epidemic at Kherson (Catherine ordered him to cure the sick with rice and a tot of fortified wine), he sank into a debilitating bout of hypochondria. 'In truth, I'm not sure I can stand this for long,' he warned on 16 September. 'I can neither sleep nor eat ... When can I retire or cut myself off so that the world will hear of me no more?!' Eight days later, when a storm threatened to destroy his precious fleet at Sevastopol, he seemed a broken man: 'My mind and spirit are gone. I have requested that my command be transferred to another.' Catherine initially responded to such wailing with a combination of encouragement and reassurance that prompted the prince to acknowledge that 'you genuinely write to me like my own mother'. By early October, however, tolerance had given way to irritation. Her affairs demanded unshakeable patience, she chided him, whereas he was 'as impatient as a five-year-old'. She was far from serene herself: 'There is one way to lessen my anxiety,' she declared on 9 October: 'write more often and inform me about the state of affairs. I await the promised details with impatience. And don't forget to write to me about Kinburn.'[97]

In the event, the details were unexpectedly encouraging. Potëmkin recovered both his health and his energy; his fleet, though damaged, had escaped destruction; and, thanks to General Suvorov, Kinburn, the Russian fort at the mouth of the Dnieper, successfully resisted the bombardment to which it had been subjected since August. The respite, however, was only temporary. Now it was Catherine's turn to suffer: she complained of sickness and headaches throughout the winter and was so ill in the spring that on 11 April 1788, just before her fifty-ninth birthday, *The Times* prematurely announced her death. Neither the Russians nor the Austrians, who belatedly came to Catherine's aid in February 1788, made much progress that summer. Joseph II proved a limited general and his troops were stymied by disease. The mercurial Potëmkin had to be dissuaded from abandoning the Crimea to the Turks: 'When you are sitting on a horse,' Catherine pointed out, 'there is no point in dismounting and holding on by the tail.' Instead, he committed himself to a lengthy siege of Ochakov, the Turkish fort opposite Kinburn, whose 24,000-strong garrison trapped the Russian fleet in the Dnieper estuary. Thanks to an attack by gunboats armed by Samuel Bentham, the Turks lost fifteen ships in two days in June (Catherine donned naval uniform for the exultant Te Deum at Tsarskoye Selo). Yet attempts in the following month to blockade the fort proved inconclusive and heavy snow in November prevented Potëmkin from delivering Ochakov to the empress as a gift on her name day. Not until 6 December did he launch a full-scale attack. Ten days later, Catherine learned of the fall of the fortress, the main aim of her strategy since the beginning of the conflict. 'I grasp you by the ears with both hands and kiss you in my thoughts, dearest friend.'[98]

Plagued with headaches, she had been sleepless for days. Now she caught a chill at the Te Deum in celebration of the victory, complaining to Khrapovitsky of an unbearable backache that left her tossing and turning until four in the morning.[99] It had not been an easy year. That summer, while Catherine was diverted by her campaign against the Turks, Gustav III had grasped the opportunity to limit Russian interference in Swedish politics by bombarding the Russian fort at Nyslott on 22 June. (Since his constitution prevented him from appearing to be the aggressor, the attack was launched in pseudo-retaliation against a raid into Swedish territory by a 'Cossack' band from Russian Finland, alleged at the time to be Swedish troops wearing costumes borrowed from the royal opera in Stockholm.)[100] Admiral Greig came to the rescue for one last time by holding off the Swedish fleet at a brutal stalemate off the island of Hogland on 6 July. Catherine, who sent Dr Rogerson to minister to her feverish admiral, mourned Greig's death at Reval on 15 October as a 'great loss to the state' and paid for his funeral. By then, she herself had survived one of her nerviest summers under threat of a Swedish descent on her palace. St Petersburg resembled an armed camp as regiment after regiment assembled for its defence. 'This is a difficult time for me,' Catherine admitted to Potëmkin on 3 July. Yet even an enervating heatwave failed to blunt her competitive edge. 'The heat was so great here,' she wrote a fortnight later, 'that the thermometer registered over 39 and a half degrees in the sun. In Portugal they can't remember anything higher than 44.'[101]

Over the following winter, a tearful empress faced divisions within her own Council, as her determination to maintain the Austrian alliance and to prop up King Stanisław in Poland (a policy supported by Bezborodko, Zavadovsky and Alexander Vorontsov) came under pressure from those who favoured a compromise with Prussia at the Poles' expense. By far the most important of these was Potëmkin himself, who had built up his Polish estates to the point where he owned 112,000 serfs. In the spring of 1789, having sent Catherine a map outlining his plans for the occupation of three Polish provinces (Bratslav, Kiev and Podolia), he travelled to St Petersburg in a vain attempt to persuade Catherine to change her course. While he returned to the South in May, the empress renewed her Austrian alliance in a further exchange of letters with Joseph II.[102]

She did so against a background of personal crisis when it emerged that 'Redcoat' Mamonov had betrayed her with one of her maids of honour, Princess Darya Shcherbatova. As her courtiers noticed, the cracks had been opening in Catherine's relationship with her favourite for some months, prompting tears and bad temper. She spent her sixtieth birthday – one of the most significant state occasions in the Court calendar – closeted in her rooms.[103] Mamonov's request for permission to marry his lover was the ultimate blow. As she confessed in a self-styled 'apophthegm' to Potëmkin on 29 June, 'I nearly fell over, so great was my surprise, and had still not recovered when he came into my room, fell at my feet and confessed his whole intrigue.'[104] Despite copious tears, meticulously recorded by Mamonov's friend Alexander Khrapovitsky, Catherine betrothed the couple herself and sent them to Moscow. This time there was to be no lonely interlude between lovers. On the day of Mamonov's dismissal, her friend Anna Naryshkina introduced her to the young man who was to be her last and youngest favourite. The swarthy Platon Zubov, thirty-eight years Catherine's junior, was promptly dubbed 'the little black one' in the apophthegm to Potëmkin, which outlined all the usual virtues of gentleness, eagerness and modesty (a singular misapprehension of the new favourite's nature).

It was in Zubov's company that the empress faced the outbreak of the French Revolution in July 1789. Though no friend of sedition, Catherine initially had little reason to fear events in Paris, and indeed could reasonably hope to profit from French weakness in the international arena. Her subjects could read about the fall of the Bastille in the Russian newspapers (whose circulation increased in response to such exciting developments), and many also had access to the range of French revolutionary pamphlets and news-sheets which circulated freely in St Petersburg and Moscow.[105] One reason for the empress's confidence was the good news she received from the Southern front, where Potëmkin and General Suvorov were enjoying a triumphant summer on the Bug and the Dniester. After 15,000 Turks were slaughtered on the River Rymnik on 11 September, Suvorov was made a count of both the Russian Empire and the Holy Roman Empire, and allowed to call himself 'Rymniksky' at Potëmkin's suggestion.[106] Wider European developments, however, prevented Catherine from converting military victories into a peaceful settlement on her own terms. British hostility was an increasing hazard for her, and so were Prussia's ambitions in Poland. 'We are stroking the Prussians,' she told Potëmkin in October 1789, 'but how our heart can endure their words and deeds which are filled with rudeness and abuse, God alone knows.'[107]

Russia's international position was still critical when Radishchev's *Journey from St Petersburg to Moscow* appeared in May 1790. A book that criticised 'the murder called war' was bound to catch Catherine on the raw. 'What do they want?' she asked in a splenetic marginal comment. 'To be left defenceless to fall captive to the Turks and Tatars, or to be conquered by the Swedes?' A noble writer twenty years her junior, Radishchev had grown up as a page at the empress's Court and had been one of the first Russian students selected to study at Leipzig at her government's expense.[108] Now he had betrayed her trust with a fictional travelogue in the mould of Sterne's *Sentimental Journey*. His book launched a stinging attack on the evils of favouritism and a bitter critique of the inhumanity of slavery, derived from Radishchev's reading of Raynal's *History of the Two Indies* and now applied to Russian serfdom in particular. The empress was appalled. 'The purpose of this book is clear on every page,' she retorted in notes which subsequently provided the basis for the interrogation conducted by Sheshkovsky, the prosecutor who later investigated Novikov. 'Its author, infected and full of the French madness, is trying in every possible way to break down respect for authority and for the authorities, to stir up in the people indignation against their superiors and against the government.' If Radishchev's views on serfdom made him a rebel worse than Pugachëv, then the chapter on corruption, levelled primarily at Potëmkin (identifiable by his craving for oysters), revealed the purpose of the whole book: 'It is a safe bet that the author's motive in writing it was this, that *he does not have entrée to the palace.* Maybe he had it once and lost it, but since he does not have it now but does have an evil and consequently ungrateful heart, he is struggling for it now with his pen.' As Catherine sensed, the point of Radishchev's book could be derived from the very direction of travel of his fictional narrator – towards the heart of old Muscovy and away from the false foreign values of her northern *Residenzstadt.* 'Our babbler is timid. If he stood closer to the sovereign, he would pipe a different tune. We have seen a lot of such humbugs, especially among the schismatics.'[109] Although Catherine eventually commuted Radishchev's death sentence to exile in Siberia, where his passage was smoothed by his embarrassed patron, Alexander Vorontsov, no one could miss the increasing signs of a significant change of heart on the empress's part – a mounting hostility to the intellectual independence of the very writers whom she had done so much to encourage in the earlier part of her reign. Its twilight years would be recalled as a period of intellectual repression.

CHAPTER TWELVE

END OF AN ERA 1790–1796

The Swedish menace evaporated as suddenly as it had appeared after a period of rising alarm in the spring of 1790. When a courier arrived at Tsarskoye Selo on 4 May to announce the capture of an enemy man-of-war off Reval, Catherine hastily announced thanksgiving prayers: she had scarcely slept in anticipation of an adverse result.[1] When Admiral Chichagov nevertheless failed to block the Swedish fleet's course toward the Russian capital, her nerves stretched tauter still. From dawn on 23 May, 'a terrible cannonade' echoed all day, rattling windows from St Petersburg to the summer residence. 'Anxiety' was Khrapovitsky's laconic comment.[2] While Catherine tried to ease the tension by boating on the lake, the implications for the conflict on the Danube were inescapable. 'Everyone is sick of the war,' Zavadovsky told Field Marshal Rumyantsev on 14 June. 'Any peace would be desirable and useful in our state of complete exhaustion.'[3] Subsequent developments were even more disturbing. Although the Russian galley fleet under Prince Nassau Siegen captured seven Swedish ships of the line at Vyborg on 22 June, it proved to be a pyrrhic victory. Even as the empress was boasting about it in a letter to Potëmkin on the twenty-eighth anniversary of her coup, a disastrous encounter was taking place off Svensksund in which Nassau Siegen lost a total of sixty-four ships and more than 7300 men, most of them taken prisoner. Magnanimous as ever, Catherine refused to blame her distraught commander. 'It was not the king of Sweden or even his fleet that defeated the prince of Nassau,' she suggested to Grimm. 'It was the high wind and people who thought themselves invincible out of an excess of ardour.'[4] She was fortunate that Gustav III, deprived of the British subsidies that might have kept him in the war, was as keen as she was to sue for peace. At the price of Russia's tacit abdication from further interference in Swedish politics, a settlement was reached at the small town of Verela on 3 August. 'We have dragged one paw out of the mud,' a relieved empress told Potëmkin. 'When we drag the other out, we'll sing Hallelujah.'[5]

While Potëmkin contemplated ways to bring the Turkish war to a triumphant conclusion – by no means a predictable outcome to pessimists such as Zavadovsky – Catherine prepared to commemorate the peace with Sweden with festivities out of all proportion to Russia's achievements (the peace was announced with a glittering procession to the Kazan Church at the end of the Dormition Fast on 15 August and commemorated with sixteen days of celebrations beginning on the next great feast in the Orthodox calendar, the Feast of the Nativity of the Mother of God on 8 September). Meanwhile, neither Radishchev's trial nor the exceptionally wet weather could dampen her mood. After an enjoyable summer in the company of Platon Zubov, playing cards in the Arabesque Room and strolling through the park at Tsarskoye Selo, she even managed to express enthusiasm for the annual celebrations at the Alexander Nevsky monastery, where echoes of her imperial ambitions sounded loud and clear. On 30 August, Giuseppe Sarti's *Te Deum*, commissioned by Potëmkin to celebrate the fall of Ochakov and incorporating the sound of cannon fire, was sung to full orchestral accompaniment at the banquet following the consecration of Starov's Trinity Cathedral ('it is a pity it cannot be sung in church because of the instruments').[6] That morning, Catherine had processed with Grand Duke Paul and his sons as the silver casket containing St Alexander's relics was borne to its ultimate resting place. Metropolitan Gavriil was assisted at the service by Bishop Innokenty of Pskov and another of the empress's favourite prelates, the seventy-three-year-old Greek, Eugenios Voulgaris, recently retired as the first bishop of Kherson and now in the last stages of his translation of Virgil's *Aeneid* into Greek (it was published in 1791–2 by the Academy of Sciences in St Petersburg).[7] The day before, she had presented Gavriil with 'an extremely fine' emerald-studded panageia to wear round his neck alongside his pectoral cross 'as a sign of his contribution to the building of the church'.[8]

As it transpired, these high spirits were only temporary. At the end of September, Baron Stedingk, the new Swedish ambassador, reported that Catherine had not been seen since 'the day of the firework that brought the peace celebrations to an end, thank God'. Soaked by persistent rain, she had developed 'a bad cold and was exhausted with all these fêtes, though that did not prevent her from going into her garden in the evening after the firework, so eager was she to appear at every rejoicing'.[9] In fact, her colic had put her in such a bad mood that when told of the costs of the display on the meadow in front of Rastrelli's Summer Palace, she demanded a full account from Colonel Melissino, whose pyrotechnics had 'resembled a comic puppet show'. In this weakened state, it became a chore even to sign a decree ('it was easier for Empress Anna: her name was shorter'), and she was irritated by all manner of setbacks, not least the slow progress of elementary education in Moscow ('I shall have to go and live there for a year').[10] The same gallows humour was shared with Grimm once she had retired to bed to cure her cough: 'In six weeks time I hope to read in the papers that I am at death's door.'[11] Her comedies might have been expected to lift her spirits – 'tragedies are never given at the Hermitage,' Stedingk remarked later, 'the empress being unable to endure the emotions of a tragedian' – but these had been playing to an increasingly select company. 'Often there are only four or five in the audience,' the Swede was told, 'which drives the actors to despair.' At larger gatherings, 'which are very rare', she was content with a hand of boston if there was no theatrical performance. 'It is all over by nine o'clock. The empress goes to bed and a small company of the men dine with Mr Zubov.'[12] Early in the New Year, Stedingk reported the creation of a new institution – 'middling-size Hermitages', with a guest list of about sixty. In the first half of October, however, illness kept Catherine out of the public eye. When she appeared at Court on the morning of Maria Fëdorovna's birthday, it was the first time she had been seen for three weeks.[13]

The triumphant premiere of her operatic pageant *The Beginning of Oleg's Reign* on 22 October signalled a change of mood. At the large Hermitage two days later, the empress danced the polonaise and stayed up for the ball and dinner.[14] For Count Nikolay Saltykov's masked ball at the Vorontsov palace, she wore 'a white satin dress in the Russian style' with a 'cocked hat à la Henri IV, decorated with a plume of white feathers and a glittering diamond solitaire'. 'The costume was fine, simple and grand,' reported the secretary of the Swedish embassy.[15] In November, the knights of the orders of St George and St Andrew were able to celebrate with due ceremony in Catherine's company; Princess Dashkova sat beside her at the banquet on her name day.[16] Meanwhile she had resumed her efforts to charm the foreign diplomats. Invited to inspect Voltaire's library, Stedingk and the Prussian ambassador 'spent a part of the day, as one might say, with Voltaire himself. The remarks he scribbled in the margins of his books while he was reading perhaps paint a better picture of this extraordinary man than his works themselves. His spirit, his gaiety, his humour and his caprices appear in their true light.'[17]

Something of the empress's own capacity for whimsy was revealed when she surprised her courtiers at a masquerade on 10 November. The event was a mixture between Elizabeth's cross-dressing balls and the entertainment staged for Grand Duke Peter at Oranienbaum in 1757. Ordered in advance not to wear hooped underskirts, her guests at the Hermitage found themselves steered towards stalls manned by actors from the French theatre, who sold them (on credit) the costumes she had chosen – a mixture of Turkish, Persian and Egyptian dress, all designed for a quick change. 'Everyone was very happy,' Khrapovitsky commented.[18] Flushed with success, Catherine became noticeably more relaxed as winter set in. 'Her Majesty gladly speaks of education in general,' Stedingk noted, 'and those of her grandsons in particular.' The voyage to the South was another favoured subject: '"I have never felt better than I did on that journey," the empress said to me, "and what amused me greatly was that all the newspapers announced that I was dying." "Fortunately, madame, the newspapers almost never tell the truth."'[19]

By the end of the year, she had a new topic of conversation, widely reported in the European press. Potëmkin's autumn advances along the Danube had been thwarted at Ismail, a 265-gun fortress on the northern bank of the river defended by an exceptionally large garrison of 35,000 Turks. But on 29 December, the favourite's younger brother Valerian Zubov arrived in St Petersburg with news that even this seemingly impregnable stronghold had fallen. Summoned expressly for the task, Suvorov had stormed the ramparts in swirling mists in the early hours of the morning of 11 December. While six columns of men attacked the walls – built with the assistance of French military engineers, four miles in circumference and protected by moats fifty feet wide and twenty feet deep – a galley flotilla invaded from the river under the command of the Neapolitan adventurer José de Ribas.[20] 'The most horrible carnage followed,' recalled the Comte de Damas, 'the most unequalled butchery. It is no exaggeration to say that the gutters of the town were dyed with blood.' Immortalised by Byron in *Don Juan*, the fighting took on a romantic hue from the start. 'The walls and people of Ismail fell at the foot of Her Imperial Majesty's throne,' Suvorov announced to Potëmkin at the end of the day. 'The assault was prolonged and bloody. Ismail is taken, thank God!'[21] 'We are assured that 20,000 Turks perished in this affair,' Stedingk reported, 'and 11,000 were taken prisoner, though the assailants numbered no more than 18,000 so they say. The Russians lost 2000 men and a further 4000 injured.' That was almost certainly an understatement. Though the precise casualties may never be known, the Turks are thought to have lost 26,000 men and the Russians somewhere between 4000 and 8000.[22]

While Potëmkin had been plotting the defeat of the Sultan, Catherine had been faced with a crisis in the Court theatre. It erupted at the Hermitage on 11 February 1791 when the leading lady threw herself at the empress's feet at the end of a performance of her latest comic opera, *Fedul and his children*. Once interpreted as a young lover's struggle against the arbitrary tsarist regime, Yelizaveta Uranova's plea to be released from the attentions of the debauched Count Bezborodko seems more likely to have been staged by the empress as a way of embarrassing Khrapovitsky and the count. Assuming that she would be distracted by the pressures of international events, Bezborodko had defied Catherine's earlier decision to permit Uranova to marry her fiancé, the actor Silu Sandunov, who had been dismissed after demanding more money. Now it was the count's turn to be humiliated when the empress not only granted Uranova's petition, but reinstated Sandunov at a higher salary than before (though not quite the rate he had himself requested). The seemingly vacuous plot of *Fedul and his children* has been revealed by Andrey Zorin as an allegory of the transfer of the direction of the Court theatre to the sovereign from Khrapovitsky, who was removed from his position immediately after the performance. Part of Catherine's concern lay with the lax behaviour of his voluptuous young actresses, many of whom were drawn into covert prostitution. But her earlier warning to her secretary that France had been undone by a decline in morals pointed to a significantly wider anxiety.[23]

Beyond the walls of her own palace, few regarded the empress as a plausible guardian of morality of any kind. Now that the storming of Ismail had reinforced the European stereotype of the Russians as a primitive people led by bloodthirsty savages, Catherine's international rivals drew increasingly explicit parallels between her apparently insatiable appetite for imperial expansion and her notorious sexual rapaciousness. In the age of Gillray and Rowlandson, English caricaturists were in their element. The first semi-pornographic engraving to feature the empress had appeared on 24 October 1787 NS, two months after the beginning of the Turkish war. Backed by a cowering Joseph II complete with dunce's cap, Catherine appears as 'The Christian Amazon' as a simian Louis XVI lobs towards her two grenades that form testicles to the phallic symbol of the Turk's bayonet.[24] The great majority of such satirical prints, however, date from the spring of 1791. One of the most explicit – 'The Imperial Stride', published anonymously on 12 April NS – features a colossal figure of the empress with one foot in Russia and the other stretched out to Constantinople. Beneath her, ten diminished European rulers gaze up into her skirts in awe: 'By Saint Jago,' declares the king of Spain, 'I'll strip her of her fur!' George III splutters his trademark 'What! What! What! What a prodigious expansion!', and the Sultan reluctantly admits that 'The whole Turkish army wouldn't satisfy her.'[25]

This sudden rash of derogatory images signalled that Anglo-Russian relations had reached an all-time low. Irritated by the Franco-Russian commercial treaty of 1787 that undermined Britain's longstanding domination of the Russia trade, William Pitt had been further alarmed by the empress's gains at the Turks' expense. In January 1791, spurred on by his ambassador in Berlin, the prime minister demanded an end to the war and a return to the status quo ante by which Russia would have been forced to relinquish Ochakov, whose capture had been interpreted as a harbinger of the dismemberment of the Ottoman Empire.[26] In March, when Catherine refused to capitulate, Pitt threatened to send a fleet to the Baltic with Prussian support. As King Frederick William II mobilised 88,000 troops in preparation for an attack on his eastern neighbour, both Bezborodko and Potëmkin urged concessions. Catherine was clearly disturbed: 'Anxiety about Prussia,' Khrapovitsky recorded in his diary on 15 March. 'It has gone on a long time. She cried.'[27]

As so often in her declining years, nervousness led to exhaustion and lapses in concentration. 'The empress is not what she was,' Stedingk reported privately to Gustav III at the end of the month. 'Age and the inconveniences it brings render her less capable of doing business.'[28] But there was never anything pathetic about Catherine. 'Angry,' her secretary noted on 7 April, 'obstinacy will lead to a new war.' Since it is not always clear whose words Khrapovitsky is recording, it is hard to be sure whether this was the voice of Potëmkin, irritated by her refusal to appease the Prussians, or an expression of the empress's own exasperation at the sabre-rattling in Whitehall and Potsdam.[29] Whichever it was, Catherine held her nerve and was vindicated when British public opinion, encouraged by her ambassador, Semën Vorontsov, and her admirer, Pitt's rival Charles James Fox, helped to force the prime minister to back down.[30] On 14 September NS, William Dent's cartoon 'Black Carlo's White Bust, or The Party's Plenipo in Catherine's Closet' portrayed the playwright Sheridan urging Fox to visit Russia: 'your fortune is made – she has certainly heard of your fine parts.' Indeed she had, though not in the way the cartoonist's innuendo implied. When the Hermitage had taken delivery of a marble bust of Fox by Joseph Nollekens, a bronze copy was placed between Demosthenes and Cicero in the Cameron Gallery at Tsarskoye Selo. There it stayed until 1793, when Fox doubly disgraced himself in the empress's eyes by supporting the Poles and expressing sympathy for the revolution in France. At that stage, the visiting English tutor John Parkinson was told that she was prepared to sell the bust, 'but that it was not worth while, for that she could not get thirty roubles for it'.[31]

According to a leading historian of international relations, the 'Ochakov crisis' of spring 1791 was 'not just a clash over peace terms with Turkey or a contest of wills between Pitt and Catherine, but a wider contest between the two relatively invulnerable flank powers over which of them would lead Europe and control the balance of power'.[32] For the moment, it was the Russians who were in the ascendant and they saw no reason to conceal their glee. 'General Suvorov has been here for a fortnight,' Stedingk reported on 14 March. '480 flags and regimental colours, along with several Pashas' tails and other tokens of dignity, carried off from the Turks at Ismail and solemnly paraded on Sunday to the church in the fortress [the Peter-Paul Cathedral], constitute a eulogy to this general far more eloquent than any panegyric.' Catherine watched the parade from the windows of the Winter Palace.[33] The whole city had come to a standstill in anticipation of Potëmkin's arrival at the end of February. On 28 April he staged his own glorification of the fall of Ismail at his new residence, later christened the Tauride Palace in his memory, complete with choruses by Derzhavin: 'Thunder of victory, resound!'

'Like all his other plans,' remarked Catherine's first Western biographer, this entertainment 'was extraordinary and great. A whole month was consumed in preparations: artists of all kinds were employed; whole shops and warehouses were emptied to supply the necessaries of the occasion; several hundred persons were daily assembled in making previous rehearsals for the final execution; and each of these days was of itself a grand spectacle.'[34] On the appointed evening, Catherine found herself serenaded by Potëmkin's private orchestra as Alexander and Constantine – their very names redolent of Russia's imperial ambitions in the South – opened the dancing with a stylish quadrille. Then the company moved to the Gobelins Room, where, amidst the tapestries, their host had prepared a typical conceit: a life-size mechanical elephant studded with emeralds and rubies. 'The Persian who conducted him struck upon a bell, and this was the signal for another change: A curtain flew up as if by magic, and opened to view a magnificently decorated theatre, where two ballets and a dramatical piece afforded entertainment to the spectators with their extraordinary excellence.' One of the pieces performed was a version of Nicolas Chamfort's *The Merchant of Smyrna*, staged in celebration of the deliverance of Russia's southern provinces from Turkish rule. Indeed, though the pouring rain obliged them to suspend their disbelief, Potëmkin's guests found themselves transported throughout the evening to an exotic southern paradise, complete with luscious fruits in the brilliantly lit Winter Garden designed by his English gardener, William Gould.[35] 'Whichever way the spectator turned his eye, the magnificent illumination struck him with amazement. The walls and columns all seemed to glow with various-coloured fire: large mirrors, here and there judiciously fixed to the sides of the apartments, or made to form pyramids and grottos, multiplied the effect of this singular exhibition, and even made the whole enclosure from top to bottom, seem to be composed of sparkling stones.'[36]

At the centre of the entertainment, both physically and rhetorically, was Catherine herself. 'Before her,' Derzhavin proclaimed in a celebrated description of the event, 'everything becomes more alive, everything takes on greater radiance ... Her bright face encourages smiles, dances, charades, games. This is the image of a mother, this is a monarch surrounded by glory, love, magnificence.'[37] Intended for her sixty-second birthday on Easter Monday, the entertainment was delayed only by the scale of its host's ambition. Once he had persuaded the empress to send Suvorov to Finland on 25 April, as a way of putting pressure on the Swedes, Potëmkin could pose as the sole victor of Ismail. By the time he was ready to greet her, resplendent in his new crimson velvet tailcoat, his private party resembled a state occasion in almost every detail, down to the cockaigne for the populace in the square outside.[38] For Catherine, the event brought to an end an exceptionally stressful week, in which her pleasure at the news of Pitt's growing difficulties in Parliament was balanced by the need for preparations at Kronstadt in case the threatened British squadron materialised. She was later to pay for her excitement with an attack of the colic, but for now she celebrated her relief by staying at the Tauride Palace until two in the morning. 'There you are, monsieur,' she boasted to Grimm on her return to her apartments: 'That is how we conduct ourselves in Petersburg in the midst of trouble and war and the threats of dictators.'[39]

In one crucial respect, Potëmkin's entertainment missed its mark. It failed to dislodge Platon Zubov and his relations, the only prominent Russians left off the 3000-strong guest list. Diplomats heard that the empress was privately critical of the prince's extravagance and irritated by his machinations against her favourite. Certainly his appearances at Court were few in May and June. Since Radishchev had reminded Catherine of the damage that Potëmkin's reputation for corruption could do, a measure of hesitation was understandable. But it was never enough to rupture the trust between them. As Isabel de Madariaga puts it, 'there was a solidity in the link between the two which could be ruffled, but not broken by a Zubov'.[40]

That was just as well, since before Potëmkin left for the South on 24 July, he and Catherine had to agree on their response to the latest developments in Warsaw. The Poles had already taken advantage of the Russo-Turkish war to operate free from Russian influence through the sovereign Diet that began its four-year term in 1788.[41] On 3 May 1791 NS, the week before the entertainment at the Tauride Palace, King Stanisław August and a group of royalist conspirators, acting in temporary alliance with Ignacy Potocki and the Patriot Party, forced through the Diet a new constitution promising a major overhaul of the Polish political system. By abolishing the *liberum veto*, by which a single objection could de-rail proposed legislation, they sought to replace Poland's anarchic 'republic of nobles' with a more orderly bi-cameral legislature backed by executive royal authority ('Experience has taught us that the neglect of this essential part of government has overwhelmed Poland with disasters').[42] The Constitution of 3 May was doubly offensive to Catherine: not only did it threaten the prospect of a permanently stronger Western neighbour, but to a sovereign unable to distinguish between electoral reform and revolutionary Jacobinism, it seemed to signal the advance of the French contagion towards the borders of her own empire. For as long as the Turkish war continued, there could be no question of direct intervention against the Poles. So the empress satisfied herself by signalling her determination to overthrow the new constitution in the name of the old order. 'This,' Paul Schroeder has suggested, 'was a serious, middle-of-the-road kind of programme for dealing with the Polish problem, stabilising Central and Eastern Europe, and making the European system work – about as good a one as the eighteenth century could offer.' And it had the further advantage of leaving open two more radical options for the future: once the new constitution had been pushed aside, Poland could either be preserved as a Russian satellite or partitioned once more by a Russian-dominated coalition.[43]

Events in Poland obliged Catherine to cast her eye towards France with new urgency. Not long after Louis XVI's abortive flight to Varennes in June 1791, she made a secret loan of 500,000 roubles 'for use in French affairs'.[44] Yet much as she might urge Sweden, Prussia and Austria to intervene against the Revolution, her aim was always to embroil them while retaining a free hand (not until 1798 did Russia join the anti-French coalition, with disastrous results for Tsar Paul). As the leading French émigré Count Valentin Esterhazy discovered, Catherine's methods were at once more subtle and less risky. Soon after arriving in St Petersburg at the end of August, the count was entertained to dinner by Alexander Stroganov, an old acquaintance from Paris:

> There were thirty of us. I ate several Russian dishes, sterlet soup, mushroom paté and other nourishing ragouts which are good when they are prepared by good cooks, excepting, however, an iced soup which was detestable and a drink whose name I have forgotten, made with flour, which was no better.[45]

Yet even Stroganov's hospitality paled into insignificance alongside Catherine's determination to woo the émigrés. 'I work on the feelings of everyone of that ilk who falls into my hands,' she admitted to Grimm. 'I do not know in what state they return, but I cover them with fur as far as I can, and I tell them to seek their plans and their measures in the conduct of Henri IV.' Catherine knew full well that Louis XVI was no Henri IV. Still, treating Esterhazy 'entirely without ceremony', she thought he seemed 'fairly pleased' with her. In fact, he was bowled over. After Catherine had shown off her paintings during the interval at his first 'small Hermitage', the astonished count told his wife that it was the sort of tour he might have taken 'at the country estate of a private individual who was kind enough to show me round his house'.[46] Formal occasions were stunning in a different way. 'The empress was in white,' Esterhazy reported after chapel one Sunday, 'with a sky-blue, sleeveless Russian robe and a broad, blue sash, tied in front of her skirt. She wore gauze on her head and a pendant with two enormous diamonds, diamond clusters in each ear and a pretty bracelet.' On the twenty-ninth anniversary of Catherine's coronation, he kissed her hand and dined at the house of Count Osterman, the vice chancellor, with a hundred others at the Court's expense. That night, more than a thousand carriages were ranged across the square for the dress ball at the Winter Palace.[47]

Behind the façade, Catherine was deeply troubled. Although the summer had brought good news from the Danube, where the Turks, weakened by the fall of Ismail, had sued for peace in the wake of defeats inflicted by Prince Nikolay Repnin, the preliminary treaty agreed at Jassy on 1 August was unsatisfactory. Despite securing the swathe of land between the Bug and the Dnieper, including Ochakov, Repnin had conceded the Turkish demand that the conquered territory should remain unfortified, and also agreed to an eight-month armistice which

Potëmkin regarded as no more than a ruse to postpone the final treaty, thereby hampering Russia intervention in Poland.[48] Worse was to come when the prince contracted a fatal fever while trying to negotiate a better settlement. News of his illness reached the empress at the end of August and fluctuating reports of his health left her increasingly agitated. 'My true friend Prince Grigory Aleksandrovich,' she wrote on 16 September. 'I have received your letters of 29 August and 6 September. The first greatly cheered me, since I could see you were better, whereas the second only made me more anxious, seeing that for four days you had an uninterrupted fever and a headache. I beg God to give you strength ... I, thank God, am well, and the colic has completely gone, which I put down to the girdle and the Hungarian wine you recommended.' At the end of the month, she sent him a little fur coat and a homily: 'For Christ's sake, if need be, take whatever the doctors prescribe to bring you relief. And after taking it I beg you to avoid any food and drink that might counteract the medicine.'[49] (The prince's appetite exceeded even his disdain for the medical profession: 'his ordinary breakfast was the greater part of a smoke-dried goose from Hamburgh' washed down by 'a prodigious quantity of wine and Dantzick-liqueurs'.)[50] On 3 October, Catherine was in tears on hearing that he had been given the last rites. Still hoping against hope, she wrote a final note of encouragement, reassuring him that his physicians were sure he was improving. Potëmkin never saw it. On 4 October, he confessed that he could no longer bear his suffering. Next day, the man with whom she had shared more than any other was laid out on the road to Jassy and died in a coma soon after his fifty-second birthday.[51]

'Between you and me,' Esterhazy confided to his wife not long afterwards, 'I believe the empress has not missed Potëmkin much. He rather abused the sway he had over her and I am assured that she received complaints against him every day.'[52] This was the voice of the prince's enemies, led by Repnin and the governor of Alexander's Young Court, Count Nikolay Saltykov, who had drawn General Suvorov into their ambit by arranging protection at Court for his daughter, a pupil at the Smolny Institute. Anxious not to be associated too publicly with critics of his late patron, Suvorov claimed that his conscience was clear 'before God and my Great Empress'. Even so, he privately described Bezborodko, who had replaced Potëmkin in the peace negotiations at Jassy, as 'wise, like the deceased, only less treacherous'.[53]

In fact, though conscious of the mistrust he inspired, Catherine never lost her faith in her 'pupil, friend and almost idol'. So devastated was she by Potëmkin's death that her doctors insisted she be bled as soon as she heard the news on the afternoon of 12 October. Sleepless with grief, she poured out her feelings to Grimm in the early hours of the following morning, telling him of the 'bludgeoning blow' her mind had just sustained:

> You can have no idea of my state of affliction! He combined an excellent heart with a rare understanding and an extraordinary breadth of spirit; his views were always great and magnanimous; he was very humane, full of knowledge, singularly loveable, and his ideas were always original; no other man had his gift for *bons mots* and apt remarks; his military genius during this war must have been striking, because he never missed a blow on land or sea. No one in the world was less easily led than he; he also had a particular talent for knowing how to use the people around him. In a word, he was a statesman in both counsel and action; he was passionately and zealously attached to me; scolding and getting angry when he believed I might have done better; with age and experience he was correcting his faults ... But his rarest quality was a courage of heart, mind and soul which set him completely apart from the rest of humanity, and which meant that we understood each other perfectly and could allow those who understood less to babble as much as they liked. I regard Prince Potëmkin as a very great man, who did not fulfil half of what was in his grasp.[54]

It took almost year to settle the prince's affairs. On 20 August 1792, Catherine signed a decree at Tsarskoye Selo paying his testators a total of 2,611,144 roubles and 1 kopeck for his property and possessions. The Tauride Palace, built mainly at her own expense for almost 400,000 roubles between 1782 and 1790, was valued at more than twice as much, mostly on the basis of alterations made in the last summer of Potëmkin's life. His art collection, purchased from the Duchess of Kingston among others, included paintings by Leonardo da Vinci, Raphael, Rubens, van Dyck, Murillo, Poussin and Watteau. His library amounted to some 1065 foreign-language titles, many in multiple volumes, and 106 in Russian. She gave the books he had purchased from Eugenios Voulgaris, including nearly 150 Greek works dating from the early sixteenth century, to the Department of Public Welfare in Yekaterinoslav (Potëmkin's plans for a university there had never borne fruit). Among his jewels and treasures, valued at well over a million roubles in total, were a diamond ring set in pink foil (20,000 r), two marble vases

(10,000 r), 176 porcelain vases, urns and dolls (17,600 r), sixty-five hunting horns (1500 r), a large mahogany organ (3460 r); a lacquered commode, mounted in bronze (4000 r) and another decorated with gilded mirrors (2500 r); a bronze oak tree covered with mechanical birds (11,000 r); four pieces of topaz, one of which weighed almost 500 lbs (2300 r); and no fewer than seventy-three of his trademark pearl-encrusted kaftans (13,505 r). By comparison, the white marble bust of Her Majesty was a mere bagatelle at 1000 roubles.[55]

Once the war with the Turks had finally been settled at the peace of Jassy in January 1792, Catherine herself planned to spend more time at the Tauride Palace. Though at first she was conscious of the shade of her late partner, it was convenient, as she grew less mobile, to have everything on one level, right down to the pond for the summer sanctification ceremonies. 'This palace is the height of fashion,' she boasted to Grimm in 1794, 'since it is all on the ground floor, with a large and beautiful garden, right in the middle of the barracks on the bank of the Neva, the cavalry to the right, the artillery to the left, and the Preobrazhensky [Guards] behind the garden. There is nowhere better for the spring and autumn.'[56] Designed by Ivan Starov in the restrained neoclassical style she had come to prefer, there was nothing modest about the palace's dimensions: as an English visitor remarked in 1790, its apartments were as 'immense' as Potëmkin himself.[57] The colonnade hall in which he had entertained the empress in April 1791 was reputed to be the largest in Europe. The prince had dined in the semicircular bow at one end while his orchestra played at the other; the empress preferred to eat in the centre of the room.[58] From there she could see into Gould's Winter Garden, beyond the temple containing Fëdor Shubin's statue of Catherine the Legislatrix. Having lost none of her enthusiasm for building, she commissioned a Palladian villa for Gould in the palace grounds in 1793.[59] But before she herself could embark on long periods of residence there, the palace required significant restoration. In January 1793, Catherine approved a long list of repairs to be completed by 20 March. The wooden partitions erected in her private apartments the year before were to be strengthened; beams were to be replaced 'in all those places where danger is most foreseen'; the porcelain stoves were to be stripped to their foundations so that the panels behind them could be replaced in brick to prevent a conflagration; and all 'doubtful places' near the theatre were to be reinforced. Further work, including a safety inspection of the cupola, was planned for the summer while the Court was at Tsarskoye Selo.[60]

The structural deficiencies that Catherine strove to correct at the Tauride Palace were not so different from the ones she mocked in her description of

Elizabeth's draughty residences in the final version of her memoir, written in 1794. But this was a text designed to highlight contrasts rather than similarities between the two eras. In later life Catherine liked to boast how much more orderly her own Court had become by comparison with the chaos she had experienced as a grand duchess (failures of protocol on the part of her officials were treated with corresponding severity).[61] Modelled on Plutarch's *Lives*, her memoirs pursued the same theme in more subtle form. Platon Zubov had been obliged to construe Plutarch with her while waiting for news from the Danube in the spring of 1790, when they translated his biographies of Alcibiades and Coriolanus ('it fortifies my soul'). After that, the author first recommended to her by Count Gyllenborg in Hamburg was never far from her mind (in February 1796, an eighteen-volume edition of his works was among her last purchases for her library at Tsarskoye Selo).[62] Plutarch's pairing of lives of the great men of ancient Greece with those of ancient Rome suggested to Catherine a way of comparing herself with her murdered husband. Like her classical mentor, she concentrated primarily on questions of character and personal virtue, implying that she, and not Peter III, was the worthier successor to Elizabeth.[63]

Unable to read her confidential memoirs, contemporaries struggled to match Catherine's claims to orderliness with the reality of Russia in the early 1790s. Though it came as no surprise at the end of a degenerative illness that had rendered him 'useless for four years', the death of Prince Vyazemsky on 8 January 1793 significantly destabilised her regime. 'You can't imagine what a state he's in,' Catherine had warned Zubov after seeing her ailing Senate Procurator in 1792. 'As he says himself, he neither eats nor sleeps. His heart races almost continually; his head is so weak that it drops on his shoulder when he sits down; seated in his chair, he rocks from side to side out of feebleness; he says that every movement is unbearable and that fresh air leaves him breathless.'[64] Such was the nature of Russia's patronage system that Vyazemsky's demise signalled far more than the loss of a single experienced administrator. Between the onset of the prince's illness in 1791 and his death, nearly half the empire's senior provincial offices changed hands. The political implications of this merry-go-round were all the more unsettling because Catherine's reforms had left provincial bodies responsible for many of her government's most important functions. And among her newly appointed provincial governors and their staff were men who had begun to wonder where the new centre of gravity would lie in the absence of Vyazemsky and Potëmkin.[65]

If some of them understandably looked sidelong towards Gatchina, where Grand Duke Paul was waiting impatiently in the wings, the one thing that united most prominent courtiers and officials was the conviction that Platon Zubov was unsuited to fill the void. Since an age gap of thirty-eight years between the empress and her favourite was bound to excite comment, John Parkinson found the Russian capital alive with prurient gossip in 1792–3. This was the atmosphere in which the fabulist Ivan Krylov could venture to publish (anonymously) suggestive verses about 'The dying coquette' that owed something to the libertine tradition of pornographic journalism rampant in late eighteenth-century France.[66] But if Catherine's increasingly desperate search for comfort and companionship threatened to desacralise the monarchy, Zubov's inflated ambitions were even more damaging to her reputation. While she tirelessly advertised his virtues to Grimm, St Petersburg remained unconvinced. Ivan Shuvalov, the leading influence behind Russia's cultural efflorescence in the late 1750s, had shown what could be done by an intelligent favourite operating under the aegis of an ailing empress. Zubov was a mere cipher by comparison. Here was an avaricious upstart who had achieved nothing and yet pretended to everything. Making a pun on '*zub*', the Russian word for tooth, Potëmkin had likened Catherine's latest protégé to an irritating molar that ought to be removed. Released from his rivalry with Potëmkin, whose enemy Saltykov became Zubov's firmest ally at Court, the new favourite interfered in both domestic and foreign policy, relentlessly acquiring offices in the army and New Russia in a vain attempt to inherit the master's mantle. On the day before her sixty-seventh birthday in 1796, Catherine rewarded his service to the state with 100,000 roubles; in January 1792, she had given him his own chancery; he even held his own elaborate *lever* in his palace apartments. 'This Zeuboff has the character of being an active little man,' Parkinson remarked, 'who however behaves with no small degree of hauteur, which in a person from the dust as he is gives no small offence.'[67]

The exposure of the corrupt Court banker in 1791 symbolised the cracks that had begun to open up in Catherine's administration. Living in style on the English Line as the scion of a prominent shipbuilding family, Richard Sutherland had acquired a reputation for wheeler-dealing that led Catherine to trust him with her finances and invest him, as she had Dr Dimsdale, as a baron of the Russian empire in 1788. Three years later, when she began to hear complaints about his activities, Derzhavin, whom Zubov had helped to appoint as one of her secretaries, was ordered to investigate. Frustrated to discover that almost all the leading figures in the government were as indebted to Sutherland as he was himself, Derzhavin was unable to complete his inquiry before the banker died on 4 October 1791, the day before Potëmkin. Nevertheless, a further probe in the following spring revealed that he had embezzled more than 2 million roubles. The prince, who had been borrowing from Sutherland since 1783, owed 800,000; Zubov's influential protégé, Arkady Morkov, owed 42,000; Vyazemsky and Grand Duke Paul were also deeply in debt. Infuriated by her son's behaviour, Catherine had no option but to order the treasury to absorb the largest debts.[68]

A different investigation was begun in the following year when Nikolay Novikov again fell under suspicion. After the raids on his shops in 1787, the cautious publisher had issued very few radical occult books and spent more time at his family estate at Avdotino, forty miles east of Moscow. But since his efforts at famine relief were combined with a determination to improve the profitability of the estate, critics accused him of using Masonic philanthropy as a smokescreen for the exploitation of his peasants. Though Catherine initially wanted Novikov to defend himself against such charges in a court of law, the Governor General of Moscow, Prince Prozorovsky, persuaded her to have him sent under armed guard to the fortress at Schlüsselburg. There he was questioned by the widely feared prosecutor Sheshkovsky and sentenced to fifteen years' imprisonment on 1 August 1792. Although the interrogation was based on twelve points raised by the empress herself, her motivation remains uncertain. Was it pressure from the Holy Synod that inclined her to make an example of this Rosicrucian heretic? Was it his links with the Prussian-based Masons who surrounded Grand Duke Paul? Why was it that Novikov, rather than his many collaborators, was singled out for persecution?[69]

In the absence of definitive answers to such questions, Novikov's arrest and imprisonment seem best interpreted as part of a wider pattern of increasingly visceral (and increasingly erratic) responses to the challenges of the revolutionary era. It was not an easy time for Europe's sovereigns. Joseph II had died in 1790; his brother, Leopold II, unexpectedly followed him to the grave two years later. Within less than a month, Catherine was horrified to learn that Gustav III of Sweden had been shot by a disgruntled aristocrat at a masked ball on 5 March 1792 (the incident inspired Verdi's *Un ballo in maschera*). Small as her respect for Louis XVI had been, she was completely disconcerted by his execution on 21 January 1793NS – by a macabre coincidence, the anniversary of the execution of Pugachëv in 1775. After retiring to bed, Catherine remained out of the public eye until 1 February, when she emerged to proclaim six weeks of mourning at Court. All relations with the revolutionary regime in Paris were broken off.[70]

The empress's inveterate English critic Horace Walpole was sure that the wrong monarch had died:

Oh! that Catherine Slay-Czar had been Queen of France in the room of Antoi-nette – I do not say it would have been any security for her *husband's* life; but it would have saved thousands and thousands of other lives, and preserved the late new, amiable and disinterested Constitution of Poland – Well, that Fury of the North has barefaced her own hypocrisy – She pretended to give a code of laws to her ruffians, and to emancipate their slaves; and now plunges the poor Poles again into vassalage under a vile system.[71]

Although the Polish question remained in most respects as complex as ever – not least as a result of the confessional heterogeneity of some parts of the popula-tion[72] – there was one sense in which Catherine's options had been simplified by Potëmkin's demise. By the end of his life, there were almost a quarter of a million people on his Polish estates around Śmiła, on the River Dnieper, which he was widely suspected of wanting to transform into a feudal principality. After his death, Catherine could pursue his ambitions for a further partition without fear of a rival power base.[73] Having signalled her intention to intervene in Poland in February 1792, she seized her chance in May when a group of Polish reactionar-ies, with Russian support, appealed to her to restore Polish liberties at the Con-federation of Targowica, a town in eastern Poland. As many as 100,000 Russian troops soon overwhelmed the Polish resistance that helped to justify their inter-vention. Now the way was open for a second partition, shared between Russia and Prussia. 'My part is sung,' wrote Catherine to Rumyantsev when the Prus-sian alliance was sealed in November, 'It is an example of how it is not impossible to attain an end and to succeed if one really wills it.'[74] Handicapped by the French declaration of war in August 1792, the Austrians, having unwisely consented to Prussian gains in Poland in the false hope of exchanging Belgium for Bavaria, were left to seek compensation from France by the deal agreed in January 1793 which gave Russia most of eastern Poland and a further 3 million subjects, includ-ing, for the first time, a significant number of Jews.[75] Now that Stanisław August's dreams of autonomy had been shattered, the final dismemberment of his kingdom could not be long postponed. When Tadeusz Kościusko led an insurrection against the Russian plenipotentiary in March 1794, all three eastern powers com-bined to suppress it. Initially delayed by the threat of another war with the Turks, Catherine sent Suvorov into Poland in August. On 4 November, he stormed Praga, a suburb of Warsaw, butchering between 13,000 and 20,000 Poles. After that, Zavadovsky predicted to Rumyantsev that 'the impending partition' would be straightforward enough: 'Our neighbours, in their current exhaustion, are in no state to swagger.'[76] So it proved. On 24 December 1794, the third partition removed the name of Poland from the map of Europe, giving the Russians 120,000 square kilometres of new territory, by comparison with 48,000 for Prussia and 47,000 for Austria. In celebration, Catherine granted 107,000 Polish serfs to her closest advisers, 13,199 of them to Platon Zubov.[77]

Though the empress never totally rejected French ideas – a luxurious edition of Bayle's *Dictionary*, which she had first read at the beginning of the 1750s, was on the list with Plutarch among her last orders from Johann Weitbrecht, the leading bookseller in St Petersburg – she did little to conceal her growing pessimism.[78] Faced with revolutionary death threats from France in April 1792, she complained to Grimm that 'it is apparently a good thing to assassinate people at the end of the eighteenth century, and I am told that it is Voltaire who preached this. See how they dare to cast calumnies on people: I think Voltaire would rather stay where he is buried than find himself in the company of Mirabeau'. By February 1794, however, she told Grimm that he had been right to distance himself from the *philosophes*, whose work had 'served only to destroy'. In April she went further: 'I remembered yesterday something you have said to me more than once: that this century has been a century of preparation.' Now that preparation seemed only to have led to 'filth' of every kind, with the prospect of 'calamities without end and innumerable wretched people'.[79] In such a climate, the moderate Russian writers whose careers Catherine had done so much to foster found themselves under increasing suspicion. A year after the assassination of Louis XVI, even Shakespeare's *Julius Caesar* was removed from the bookshops because it dealt with regicide. Catherine's last significant piece of legislation was the edict of 11 October 1796 which revoked the right of individuals to operate private presses, granted in 1783. Anxious as she had been to propagate improving ideas, an empress obsessed with obedience not only baulked at the growth of independent publishing but was unable to conceive of an orderly system of censorship for the private presses. Twelve of the sixteen closed overnight. Whereas 320 secular books had been published in Russia in 1796, only 212 appeared in the first year of Tsar Paul's reign, the lowest total since 1777.[80]

Although the empress's view of the Enlightenment had undergone a marked transformation since her patronage of Voltaire and Diderot in the 1760s, little in her daily routine had changed. Sitting in her study every morning, she continued to dispatch business just as she had done throughout her reign. One of her secretaries' jobs was to process the petitions submitted in her name. Of the 1920 submitted to the chancellery directed by Dimitry Troshchinsky and Adrian Gribovsky between January 1795 and 4 November 1796, two thirds (1036) were from nobles. Merchants (119) constituted the next largest group; 85 came from non-noble officials and army officers; 66 were from peasants, 46 from foreigners and 12 from the empress's own Court servants. Of the noble petitions, the greatest number (147) concerned disputes over estates, with 56 more to do with squabbles over land. Few such documents reached the empress as a result of the draconian legislation against false petitions and official attempts to limit their number – on her trip to the South in 1787, the archbishop of Yekaterinoslav had strictly forbidden his clergy from daring to appeal to her directly (they were not to go near the palace, still less lurk outside her windows).[81] Of those petitions she scrutinised, however, a fair number seem to have received a positive response: of the 133 requests for aid in these two years, 74 were granted and so were 48 of the 61 requests for pensions.[82]

Another of her secretaries' functions was to dispense her largesse as Catherine allocated funds from the Closet and other sources to favoured friends and advisers. As a sop for Zubov's inexorable rise, Bezborodko received 50,000 roubles from the postal taxes on New Year's Day 1795, with a pension of 10,000. On 18 April, another 50,000 was sent to Suvorov in Warsaw. (When he stayed at the Tauride Palace later in the year, wandering about in various states of undress, the empress thought him 'a very strange individual. He is very erudite, and naturally very talented, but infinitely eccentric, in ways which do him no good.') There were the customary Easter presents for courtiers and servants, mostly in the form of new uniforms and dresses at a cost of 21,900 roubles (by 1796, the price had risen to 25,300 roubles). Property had always been one of the empress's greatest gifts. In January, she bought Count Osterman's house on Millionnaya for 150,000 roubles and gave it to Prince Repnin; in April she paid 160,000 roubles for Andrey Shuvalov's house on the Moika and presented it to Alexandra Branicka, furnished and fitted out with new mirrors from Potëmkin's glassworks. Foreign dignitaries were given more intricate treasures. In July she sent a snuffbox with her portrait on it, valued at 11,656 roubles, to Prime Minister Pitt; the Austrian foreign minister Baron Thugut received another worth 14,000 roubles in September. Aleksey Orlov had been sent a more personalised gift in July: 'I would have put in it snuff from tobacco grown in my own garden, for I take no other, but I was worried that it would dry out on the journey.' Meanwhile she had paid for the transport of a Herschel telescope, presented to her by George III, and given another 3229 roubles to Ivan Kulibin, the inventor from Nizhny Novgorod to whom she had first been introduced on the Volga cruise in 1767. Fëdor Shubin received 3000 roubles for a waxwork of Joseph II. [83]

For an ageing empress, the length and frequency of Orthodox services was an increasing irritation, especially in Lent when she might spend up to eight hours a day in the palace chapel.[84] The Church nevertheless had its uses as a bastion against revolutionary excess: 'for my part,' Catherine proclaimed tongue in cheek to Grimm in February 1794, 'I propose that all the Protestant powers should embrace the Greek religion to preserve themselves against this irreligious, immoral, anarchical, evil and diabolical plague, the enemy of throne and altar. It is the sole apostolic and truly Christian [faith]'.[85] In the circumstances, it was all the more important to continue to make lavish donations as a public expression of her religious commitment. In 1790, she commissioned two sets of liturgical plate from Iver Buch, the son of a Danish goldsmith who had worked in Russia since 1776. Each set was studded with diamonds from the treasury and 'antique stones' from her own collection in the Hermitage. While one was sent to the Dormition Cathedral in Moscow, the other was presented to the Trinity Cathedral at the Alexander Nevsky monastery at the annual celebrations on 30 August 1791.[86] Further internal gilding there, costing over 24,000 roubles, was paid for by February 1795, and in May of that year she spent another 90,000 roubles on marble to rebuild the ageing Kazan Church.[87]

Although the upkeep of the palaces constituted another drain on the imperial purse – in June 1795, 68,193 roubles had to be set aside to repair General Bauer's water-supply system at Tsarskoye Selo – Catherine was as usual more parsimonious with her own accommodation.[88] The secretary with responsibility for the royal residences was Suvorov's old comrade Peter Turchaninov, 'a little slip of a man, and so addicted to bowing and scraping that he only seemed half as high as he was'.[89] In preparation for the empress's visit to Tsarskoye Selo after Easter 1795, he instructed the Court administration on 8 April to furnish the Chinese pagodas with curtains and leather chairs. Twelve days later came a characteristic amplification: '1) do not make fringes and tassels for the curtains; 2) only hang the smallest icons; 3) mirrors at 25 roubles each; 4) use old dressing-tables and commodes and buy only what cannot be supplied from these; 5) black leather chairs are much cheaper, on no account purchase any armchairs; 6) also use old stone wash-basins'. 'Listen,' Catherine once told Grimm, 'the thing I like least in the world is to speak about finances.' Still, she was anxious that the Court had been running a 2-million-rouble deficit on an annual turnover of 3 million since 1789.

Caution even came through in the autumn preparations for Constantine's wedding to Princess Juliana Henrietta of Sachsen-Coburg. The upper floor of the Marble Palace was to be furnished for the empress and several guests, but only 'for the shortest possible time' so that everything could be taken 'back to where it belongs'. Even so, 118,528 roubles were set aside over the course of 1796 and 1797 to convert new Winter Palace apartments for the groom.[90]

Though Constantine's wedding had to be postponed when the bride was struck down by toothache, it went ahead in February 1796 with all the customary banquets, balls and fireworks. 'So far I am very well,' Catherine reported to Grimm in the middle of the whirl, after being told that she seemed as merry as a lark: 'and that is a very good compliment I have been given at the age of sixty-seven'.[91] Alexander had already married the fourteen-year-old Princess Louise of Baden-Durlach in September 1793 ('everyone said that it was two angels who were betrothed').[92] The empress had always revelled in the preparations for such nuptials, and these were especially important as they seemed to presage a happy and glorious future for the two boys she had brought up as her own. Other family news was less welcome. She scarcely troubled to conceal her disappointment when Maria Fëdorovna gave birth to another girl, Olga, on 11 July 1792. Fretting that a clutch of expensive grand duchesses would be left on the shelf, the empress resented everything from the costs of their upkeep (from jewels for the newborn child down to the single rouble given to each of the palace sentries) to the complications their birthdays and name days would bring to an over-crowded Court calendar. Even so, she was distraught when Olga died less than three years later. While teething, the child had 'developed such a hunger that she wanted to eat all the time,' Catherine explained to Grimm on 16 January 1795. 'After sixteen weeks of suffering and a slow consumptive fever came 24 hours of terrible agony.' Four days later, dressed in deep mourning, the empress braved the cold to travel to the funeral at the Alexander Nevsky monastery, accompanied in her carriage by her two eldest granddaughters Alexandra and Yelena. Though it was greeted by rejoicings at Court, the birth on 7 January of a sixth granddaughter, Anna, was scant compensation.[93] Not until her last grandchild, the future Nicholas I, came into the world on 25 June 1796, did the prospects for the dynasty seem to improve. 'His brothers will prove to be dwarfs before this colossus,' Catherine boasted to Grimm: 'his hands are only a bit smaller than my own.'[94]

By then her own horizons were already shrinking. 'I am old, too,' she had confessed as she grieved for Potëmkin in October 1791.[95] Six months later, Khrapovitsky found among her papers an undated will in her own hand, specifying various burial grounds depending on her place of death. Should it occur at Tsar-skoye Selo, she wanted to be interred (alongside the unmentioned Alexander Lanskoy) in the cemetery at Sofia; if she died in St Petersburg, then she must be buried in the Alexander Nevsky monastery. Its Trinity Cathedral, as a later note made clear, had been 'built by me': there was no mention of the imperial necrop-olis at the Peter-Paul Cathedral, indelibly associated with Peter the Great. 'Lay out my corpse dressed in white, with a golden crown on my head, and on it inscribe my Christian name. Mourning dress is to be worn for six months, and no longer: the shorter the better.'[96] Increasingly conscious of the passage of time, she observed mordantly to Grimm in February 1794, the fiftieth anniversary of her arrival in Russia, that there were now barely a dozen people who could remember the event, one of whom was Lev Naryshkin, who denied it for fear of appearing aged, and another Ivan Shuvalov, 'who scarcely leaves his house as a result of his decrepitude'.[97] That same month, William Gould told John Parkin-son that 'though the empress looks very well when made up, she appears very much otherwise in dishabille, indeed with strong symptoms of old age'.[98] In public, Catherine wore 'a great deal of rouge, for she was still desirous to prevent the impressions of time from being visible on her face'.[99] In the relative privacy of her own apartments, she received ambassadors in a simple white negligee, using spectacles and a magnifying glass for reading. Her hair was worn low, a simple old-fashioned style, with curls behind the ears.[100] It was an image of vul-nerability soon to be attacked by her Western detractors. In his controversial *Secret Memoirs of Russia*, published in Paris soon after her death, Charles Masson described the allegedly toothless empress as 'fat to the point of deformity', mocking her faith in a Greek client of Zubov, the piratical Colonel Lambro-Kochoni, who prescribed seawater for the ulcers that disfigured her legs.[101]

Though the infirmities of old age had done nothing to dull her mind – in addi-tion to her memoirs, she was still at work on a history of Russia in the last years of her life – they made it harder for Catherine to cope with the stresses of Court cer-emonial. The arrival in August 1796 of a 140-strong Swedish delegation was bound to take its toll. Led by the duke of Sudermania, the brother of the late Gustav III, the Swedes had come to secure the betrothal of the empress's eldest granddaugh-ter, Alexandra, to the uncrowned Gustav IV. All the magnificence of the Russian Court was laid out to impress the young king, but on 11 September, when the cer-emony was due to take place, he refused to appear, objecting to Catherine's insist-ence on a written guarantee that Alexandra would be allowed to practise the Orthodox faith in Lutheran Sweden. Whether or not the empress suffered the mild seizure rumoured by one contemporary, she was irritated and exhausted by such a public failure.[102] Although she summoned the energy to celebrate the thirty-fourth anniversary of her coronation at a ball in the St George's Hall of the Winter Palace, the throne room completed by Quarenghi in 1792, public appearances were now infrequent. At lunch in the Diamond Room on Friday 31 October, Arkady Morkov, the negotiator who had struggled in vain to satisfy the Swedes, sat beside companions of much longer standing. Catherine had known Ivan Shuvalov even before he became Elizabeth's favourite in 1749; the Marshal of her Court, Prince Fëdor Baryatinsky, had guarded her husband at Ropsha on the fateful night in 1762 when Peter III was assassinated; soon afterwards, the faithful Anna Protasova had joined the Court ladies at the behest of Aleksey Orlov (according to Countess Golovina, she was nicknamed 'la reine', because she was as dusky as the queen of Tahiti). Later that evening, these intimates were joined at the Hermitage by the empress's grandsons and granddaughters, as the empress watched a French comedy incognito in the presence of her Court and the whole *generalitet*.[103]

That, it transpired, was the last entry in the Court journals for Catherine's reign. The end, when it came, took everyone by surprise. On the morning of Wednesday 5 November, she settled down to her papers after her customary morning coffee. But when the duty chamberlain arrived sometime after nine, he found her palpitating body, barely conscious, on the floor of the neighbouring dressing room. Despite his efforts to revive her, she lapsed into a coma from which she never recovered. Six men were required to lift her into the bedroom, where Dr Rogerson, having diagnosed a stroke, tried in vain to bring her round. Soon Catherine's confessor was summoned; Metropolitan Gavriil arrived that afternoon. Tended by Protasova and Maria Perekusikhina, their sovereign was vomiting so much blood that it was only when the flow briefly abated that she could be given communion and anointed with holy oil. Count Nikolay Zubov was sent to Gatchina to fetch Grand Duke Paul, who had dreamed the night before of being visited by a mysterious, unknown force. Though he rushed to take charge at the Winter Palace, there was little he could do. Informed at dawn next morning that all hope was lost, he ordered that Catherine be given the last rites. Now he could only watch and wait as his mother's pulse gradually faded. Not until a quarter to ten on the evening of 6 November 1796 did the most famous woman in Europe finally breathe her last.[104]

THE AFTERLIFE OF AN EMPRESS

After thirty-four years on the throne, Catherine had become synonymous with Russian rule. Most of her subjects could remember no other monarch. Finding it impossible to imagine anyone else in her place, the Court was stunned by her unexpected demise. 'No one knew what to do,' admitted Platon Zubov's dwarf amanuensis, Ivan Yakubovsky: 'The mind could not grasp that this time had come.'[1] It did not take them long to realise, however, that in an intensely personal monarchy such as the Russian empire, the accession of a new ruler could immediately signal a radical reversal of regime. By the time that shocked courtiers arrived at the Winter Palace on the morning after Catherine's death, 'the change was so great that it looked like nothing other than an enemy invasion'.[2] All the empress's 'brilliance' seemed to have vanished into thin air as her successor staged the first of the military parades that were to dominate life at his Court. Not for nothing did the poet Derzhavin refer to Tsar Paul's accession as an act of conquest: armed soldiers were everywhere. 'The ease and tranquillity of the late Reign are lost with Her from whom they deriv'd,' the British ambassador reported barely a fortnight after Catherine's death. 'A most severe and exact discipline is introduced into every department both civil and military, and this with such a degree of rigour, as has even absolutely chang'd the face of society.'[3]

The Russian succession in 1796 was in practice no more controversial than it had been in December 1761 on the death of Elizabeth. In accordance with Peter the Great's succession law of 1722, Catherine had nominated her Russian-born son as her heir immediately after her coup. Although her growing dissatisfaction with Paul prompted her to investigate the history of the regulations governing the succession when she returned from the Crimea in 1787, and rumours circulated after 1791 that she intended to disinherit him in favour of her grandson Alexander, it seems unlikely that she would ever have taken such a fateful step. Alexander's Swiss tutor claimed to have suffered 'the two most unpleasant hours' of his life at an audience in 1793, in which the empress, without raising the subject directly, apparently tried to persuade him to broach the idea with his pupil. Paul certainly lived in trepidation that his mother might disinherit him, and some historians believe that he found and destroyed a draft law of succession on the night of 6 November. Yet the circumstances of Catherine's own accession surely ruled out any open discussion of the subject while she was alive. To issue a law of succession would have been to advertise her status as a usurper.[4]

In any case, no prominent actor at the Court of St Petersburg seriously doubted that Paul would inherit the throne. The only uncertainty lay in what he would do once he finally had power within his grasp. It was obvious to all that his natural impatience had been intensified by years of waiting in the wings. While the grand duke remained isolated at Gatchina, endlessly parading his troops, the cream of Russian society had been anxious for some time about what lay in store for them. After Potëmkin's death threw into question the future of his extensive network of clients, John Parkinson was told in 1792 that Paul's accession was to be 'feared' because he was 'anxious to make alterations and regulations which would make it more difficult to commit abuses'. The following year, Parkinson was again warned that 'all may not go well, perhaps' at the empress's death.[5] No one, however, had fully anticipated the speed and determination with which the new tsar would reject everything his mother had stood for. 'The most important practices of the Court were changed,' recalled Countess Varvara Golovina, 'and with the wave of a baton he destroyed what had taken a glorious reign of thirty-four years to consolidate.'[6]

Appalled by the paltry burial that Catherine had given to Peter III, whom he always regarded as his father, Paul initially intended to consign the empress to an equally anonymous grave in the cemetery at the Alexander Nevsky monastery. There would have been no clearer way of declaring that his mother had no right to rule. Only when he was persuaded that this was politically impossible did he consent to funeral arrangements that followed the pattern established for Russia's rulers since the death of Peter the Great.[7] Catherine's corpse was embalmed on 8 November and carried on 15 November from her bedroom to the audience chamber of the Winter Palace. It was an emotional scene for the courtiers who had been closest to her. According to Countess Golovina, who recalled the ceremony in openly sentimental terms, the occasion was stage-managed by the new empress, Maria Fëdorovna, whose officious approach to the proceedings 'cut me to the heart'. The countess herself claimed more in common with the melancholy scene she observed through the door of the Chevaliers Gardes' Room, which was draped from floor to ceiling in swathes of black silk and lit only by the flickering flames in the hearth. 'A mournful silence reigned in the apartment, interrupted only by sobs and sighs,' as the Chevaliers, dressed in their red capes and silver helmets, stood listlessly about, 'some leaning on their carbines, others lying on chairs'. Only the sound of the approaching funeral chant roused the countess from the 'depression' into which this 'mournful sight' had plunged her:

> I saw the clergy appear, then the candle-bearers, the choristers, and the Imperial family, and lastly the corpse, which was carried on a magnificent bier covered with the Imperial mantle, the ends of which were borne by persons holding the highest offices at Court. When I caught sight of my sovereign, I began to tremble all over and ceased to weep, while my sobs changed to involuntary little cries.

Six gentlemen of the bedchamber carried the train while ten chamberlains bore the corpse to a raised bed covered with red velvet fringed with gold. At the end of the ceremony, the whole imperial family 'prostrated themselves in turn in front of the body and kissed the hand of her deceased Majesty'. Once they had withdrawn, a priest began to read from the Bible, while six Chevaliers Gardes formed a guard of honour around the bed. The countess returned home 'after being in attendance twenty-four hours, exhausted both in mind and body'.[8]

Ten days later, Catherine was laid to rest in a coffin done out in gold fabric decorated with Russian imperial crests and taken to a chamber of mourning in the palace's Grand Gallery. Familiar to the Court as the site of its glittering balls and masquerades, the gallery had been transformed by the erection of an elaborate chamber of sorrows designed by Antonio Rinaldi. This dome-shaped structure, supported by classical pillars and topped by a bronze statue of the imperial eagle, enclosed the coffin on a raised platform beneath a canopy draped in black velvet with silver fringes. The corpse was dressed in a robe of silver brocade. A gold brocade mantle trimmed with ermine and silver tassels was placed at its feet. As leading courtiers stood in vigil over their late sovereign, and bishops and archimandrites chanted requiem services around the clock, only badly dressed peasants were refused admission to the lying-in-state as the public flocked in to pay their respects with a final kissing of hands.[9]

Paul agreed to such pomp and ceremony only in order to undermine it by extraordinary means. Three days after his mother's death, the tsar announced plans for a joint funeral at the Peter-Paul Cathedral, in which Peter III, rather than Catherine, was bound to be the focal point of attention. The point, he sardonically remarked, was merely to remedy her 'oversight' in failing to accord her husband a proper burial: 'My mother, having been called to the throne by the voice of the people, was too busy to arrange for my father's last rites.'[10] On 10 November, after paying their respects to Catherine's corpse, the imperial family were ordered to attend a requiem service for Peter III in Rastrelli's Winter Palace chapel. On 19 November, Peter's remains were exhumed from their anonymous grave and opened in the tsar's presence at the Cathedral of the Annunciation at the Alexander Nevsky monastery. Since the corpse had never been embalmed, the remains were severely corrupted. Paul nevertheless insisted on kissing them, and returned to the monastery on 25 November to place a crown on top of a new golden coffin, in posthumous compensation for the coronation that his father had never staged. The casket was transferred to the Winter Palace on a hearse drawn by eight horses on the morning of 2 December. The procession, which lasted two and a half hours and was followed by the whole Court, was described by the Swedish ambassador as 'the most august, melancholy, and in every respect compelling ceremony I have ever experienced'.[11] Officials permitted it to proceed only provided that the temperature did not drop 'below 15 degrees of frost'.[12] In a particularly macabre gesture, the tsar humiliated the eighty-year-old Aleksey Orlov, the last surviving participant in the dreadful events at Ropsha in 1762, by ordering him to carry the large crown in the procession. (An allegorical engraving of the exhumation by Nicolas Ancelin portrayed Orlov alone reacting in horror.) One memoirist favourable to Paul recalled that Orlov broke down in the cathedral and took the crown with trembling hands. Two more surviving conspirators from 1762 – Peter Passek, the Governor General of Belorussia, and Prince Fëdor Baryatinsky, the recently dismissed Marshal of the Court – were forced to do penance by carrying the corners of the pall-cloth.[13]

On arrival at the Winter Palace, Peter's coffin was placed alongside Catherine's in Rinaldi's chamber of mourning. But there was no sense that the two were to be seen as equals. To make the point that Paul ruled by right as Peter's son, the large crown was placed on Peter's casket; Catherine's bore only the small crown as a symbol of her posthumous dethronement. Their funeral was held on 5

December, following the customary procession across the ice to the cathedral, where the two coffins were placed side by side on a catafalque designed by Vincenzo Brenna.[14] Only after two further weeks of vigil and requiem masses were they lowered side by side into the vault. The tsar even prevented Metropolitan Amvrosy (Podobedov) from reading a graveside oration in memory of his mother. Amvrosy, who had lauded Catherine for the 'security, peace and glory' she had brought to Russia as recently as the anniversary of her coronation in September 1796, was not to mention her name in public again until the thanksgiving service for the peace with Sweden in 1809.[15]

Everything Paul did seemed to signal his contempt for his mother's claims to immortality. He converted her treasured Tauride Palace into stables and had Charles Cameron's unfinished Temple of Memory at Tsarskoye Selo, built to celebrate her victory over the Turks in 1792, pulled to the ground five years later.[16] Although Catherine had ensured that Paul received an Enlightened education from Nikita Panin and Father Platon, her son unaccountably developed an obsession with medieval chivalry. The tsar was elected Grand Master of the Knights of Jerusalem in 1798. Metropolitan Platon was horrified to learn that he even contemplated extending the Russian orders of chivalry to the Orthodox episcopate. In a welter of legislation – by one estimate, Paul issued 48,000 orders in the first year of his reign alone – he reversed Catherine's trend towards civilian government, imposing an overwhelmingly military ethos modelled on the regimes of Peter III and Frederick the Great. In such a hostile climate, prudent admirers of the late empress understandably thought discretion the better part of valour. Some may have contemplated symbolic ways to commemorate her, as Prince Nikolay Lvov seems to have done in designing a statue of Minerva for Bezborodko's Moscow estate in 1797, but it was not until the accession of Alexander I in 1801 that the prospects for a public revival of her reputation improved.[17]

In the event, Paul's reign lasted less than five years. In his anxiety to discipline his subjects, he went too far too fast, alienating the elite with a series of measures that undermined the privileges Catherine had granted to them in the Charter to the Nobility – not content with limiting their freedom of expression and freeing their serfs from Sunday labour, the tsar himself lashed out at nobles with his cane. On 1 February 1801, the imperial family moved into the new Mikhailovsky Palace, a fortress built on the site of Rastrelli's wooden Summer Palace, which Paul had ordered to be demolished. Less than six weeks later, he enjoyed his last meal in the company of nineteen relations and courtiers. Many of them would have been familiar to his mother. Alexander and Constantine were both present with their wives; so were Alexander Stroganov, Alexander Naryshkin and Nikolay Yusupov. Later that night, 11 March 1801, he was strangled in his apartments by a group of disaffected officers coordinated by St Petersburg's Governor General, General Count Peter von der Pahlen. With fitting symmetry, Paul's brief reign ended, like that of Peter III, in cold-blooded assassination. However his successor might rule, he could never openly imitate Paul's example.[18]

———————

Instead, the new tsar, Alexander I, promised in his accession manifesto that he would rule according to his grandmother's 'heart and laws'.[19] Delighted by the prospect, Princess Dashkova anticipated an opportunity to bask in Catherine's reflected glory. Although their tempestuous relationship had ended in tears – as early as 1792, John Parkinson found that 'her conversation evidently savoured of disaffection to the empress' – the princess was never less than effusive after Catherine's death, relishing the opportunity to regale visitors such as Martha and Catherine Wilmot with tales of 'the wonderful scenes of the revolution in which she acted *so* wonderful a part at the age of 18'.[20] Noting that Dashkova always pronounced Catherine's name 'with rapture', one of her Russian acquaintances suggested that her oratory was so mesmerising that her 'audience unwittingly submitted to her attractive eloquence'.[21] That was stretching the truth. Catherine Wilmot felt uncomfortable in the face of the princess's stories: 'These subjects as ripping up a life that is almost past gives [*sic*] a powerful sort of agitated animation to her Countenance, & I long till it is over.'[22] But Dashkova was undeterred. Apparently oblivious to such reactions, she sought a wider readership by sending anecdotes about Catherine to the new journals that sprang up under Alexander I, and in 1806 published a volume of anecdotes of her own, praising the empress's 'most kind and affectionate love for humanity, a love that rarely dwells in the hearts of rulers'.[23]

Nor was the princess alone in seeking to publicise her heroine's glorious achievements. Documents about Catherine accounted for almost four-fifths of the historical material published in Russian journals in the first five years of the nineteenth century.[24] Within months of Alexander's accession, Catherine's own historical works had been republished alongside a translation of her correspondence with Dr Zimmerman. Editions of some of her plays and multiple Russian versions of her correspondence with Voltaire and Field Marshal Rumyantsev soon followed.[25] As a bandwagon of publications in praise of the late empress

began to roll, Nikolay Karamzin set the tone in 1802 with a paean of praise eulo-
gising the formative role of the ruler in Russian history.[26] Sponsored by seventy
subscribers, including Maria Perekusikhina and Metropolitan Amvrosy, Peter
Kolotov published a six-volume chronology of Catherine's reign in 1811, drawing
on material he had been collecting for the past twenty years.[27] Three years later,
Ivan Sreznevsky published a collection of short anecdotes declaring it 'desirable
that all the works of the Great Catherine, having glorified and magnified Russia,
should be made known to everyone'.[28]

'Every circumstance attending Katherine's Time begins to bear a sacred stamp
already,' noted Martha Wilmot following a visit to Tsarskoye Selo in 1808: 'The
grounds are not remarkable for beauty nor the Contrary; they interest one as
being often *walk'd* by Katherine.'[29] Nor was it only at Tsarskoye Selo that Catherine had left her indelible imprint. 'Without Catherine,' one memoirist claimed, St
Petersburg 'would soon have sunk back into the bog from which it emerged'.[30]
The capital, however, was Peter the Great's shrine. To reach a territory that was
distinctively Catherine's, it was necessary to radiate outwards to Tver, where the
triumphal gates marking the empress's visit in 1767 still stood, or to that other
favourite city of hers, Kazan, where Peter Sumarokov 'bowed his head with
heartfelt feeling' to the berth in Catherine's cabin on her galley in 1838.[31]

Among the military men who proved especially susceptible to the mixture of
nostalgia and self-importance that characterised Catherine's posthumous admirers, none was more gallant than Denis Davydov, hero of 1812 and hero-
worshipper of Field Marshal Suvorov. Horrified that 'the immortal Catherine'
should be subjected to 'lampoons about her private life', Davydov praised her
reign in 1831 as 'most brilliant, most triumphant', and no less useful to Russia
than that of Peter the Great. Many fellow veterans shared in his veneration of
Catherine's 'miraculous age'.[32] It was partly among such circles of 'old people,
officers of the Guards in Catherine's time' that the young Alexander Herzen
grew up in Moscow in the 1830s.[33] For all their importance as mythmakers,
however, soldiers were ultimately outranked by salon hostesses. Though Alexandra Branicka, Potëmkin's eldest niece and one of Catherine's closest friends,
remained closeted on her husband's estate at Belaya Tserkov, there was no shortage of female relics of Catherine's reign who continued to proclaim it as their
finest hour. Catherine's last maid of honour, Praskovia Myatleva (née Saltykova), lived until 1859, when the cream of Petersburg society processed down
Nevsky Prospect behind her catafalque.[34] The most flamboyant was Platon
Zubov's elder sister, Olga Zherebtsova, who became a legend in her own right as

a former lover of the British ambassador Charles Whitworth, an alleged lynchpin in the conspiracy to assassinate Tsar Paul. Steeped as deeply as her heroine in the works of the French *philosophes*, Zherebtsova struck Herzen, who met her in her seventies, as 'a strange, eccentric ruin of another age, surrounded by degenerate successors that had sprung up on the mean and barren soil of Petersburg court life.'[35] But she was far from the only Russian noblewoman to delight in reminiscing about her gilded youth in the shadow of the empress. Alexandra Shishkova hung a full-length portrait of Catherine in her bedroom alongside another of Christ and was said never to wear any other blouse than those she had purchased from the empress's wardrobe. Maria Kikina, daughter of a leading Court official, also preserved her sitting room as a shrine to Catherine.[36]

Even a chance encounter with the empress was enough to infuse a lasting glow in those who outlived her. Yet the sense that hers had been a golden age was by no means confined to subjects who were prominent enough to revel in the memory of personal contact. On the contrary, these few members of the elite merely personified the strong tide of popular sentiment that swelled demand for Nikolay Utkin's engraving of Borovikovsky's *Lady with a dog*, commissioned in 1826 by Count Nikolay Rumyantsev and printed in the following year.[37] A whole generation of Russians grew up, like the writer Apollon Grigoryev, at the feet of grandfathers who reminisced about Catherine and her times as the smoke from their pipes curled into the night.[38] Many, it seemed, still succumbed to the mood of nostalgia which engulfed the 'babbling old Widow' the Wilmot sisters met at Tsarskoye Selo in 1808, 'who has been talking of the days that were pass'd till she was obliged to wipe her eyes in the sleeve of her gown'.[39]

While the modern eye might not detect anything sinister in any of this, the tsar was understandably wary of attempts to veil intemperate demands on his own regime under praise for aspects of Catherine's, and he could hardly have been expected to approve of attempts to manipulate the past as a means of reproaching the present. 'Happily for us,' wrote a canny contributor to Karamzin's *Messenger of Europe* in 1804, 'everything demonstrates the particular resemblance in heart and soul between Alexander and Catherine – favourite grandson of his adored grandmother.'[40] Writers were particularly keen to urge the tsar to reject his father's philistinism and return to the more tolerant atmosphere of the 1760s and 1770s. Before the reign of Alexander II in the mid-nineteenth century, no one paid much attention to Catherine's own literary achievements. The point was that by joining the ranks of the writers, she had radically improved the status of their emergent profession. Without the empress's personal interest and protection, the argument ran, there would have been no Fonvizin, no Derzhavin, and none of the other 'immortal' literary figures who emerged in her reign.[41] 'Talents perish like spring flowers from stormy winds and frost,' warned Nikolay Grech in a lecture at the Imperial Public Library in 1817, 'but in Russia there are no such obstacles ... Catherine gave her subjects the freedom to express their thoughts freely both in print and in speech.'[42] Catherine had loved scholarship for scholarship's sake, Grech told readers of his history of Russian literature. Others took up the refrain. 'Here, at every step,' wrote Konstantin Batyushkov of the Academy of Sciences, 'the enlightened patriot should bless the memory of the monarch who deserves to be called "great and wise" by posterity not so much on account of her victories as for the useful institutions' she established.[43] It was impossible not to notice the veiled criticism of the tsar who had conquered Napoleon. In his speech to the Russian Academy in 1818, Karamzin offered another tactful reminder to Alexander that Catherine had loved 'both the glory of victory and the glory of reason', accepting 'this happy fruit of the Academy's work with the same flattering favour with which she succeeded in rewarding everything praiseworthy and which she bequeathed to you, gracious Tsar, as an unforgettable, precious memory'.[44] The note of reproach sounded rather more obviously in the Decembrist journal *Polar Star*, which looked back on Catherine's reign in 1823 as a 'golden age for literary scholars': 'All our best writers arose or were educated under her dominion.'[45] 'The Age of Catherine is the age of encouragement,' Pushkin remarked in 1825. 'In that respect it is no worse than any others.'[46] In private, scholars were more openly critical. Already in 1810, the American ambassador John Quincy Adams met an official at the Academy of Sciences who complained 'of the neglect of the sciences in the present day. The Age of Catherine is past.'[47]

The fate of the empress's Instruction in the new century seemed to confirm the point. At first, the signs seemed optimistic. Appointing her former favourite, Peter Zavadovsky, to chair a new commission to codify the laws in 1801, the tsar considered it 'almost superfluous to note ... that the suppositions in the *Nakaz* by my Most Kind Grandmother, the Empress Catherine II ... may cast great light on the commission's work. You know this better than anyone else.'[48] For some, such as the poet Derzhavin, the treatise had always remained an object of veneration. While the Russian transcript had been sent to the Senate in 1777, the French original had been placed in a bronze casket at the Kunstkammer, where it was exhibited to foreign visitors and taken to meetings of the Academy of Sciences. The casket and its priceless contents remained on the table at the Academy at its centenary celebrations in 1826.[49] Neither did Catherine's treatise lack practical application. Predictably ignored in the reign of Tsar Paul, it was quoted in at least forty-one court cases under Alexander I.[50] Turning to the *Nakaz* in the context of the proposed codification of the laws, the liberal Alexander Turgenev remarked that though it may only have been a work of theory, it had done more to educate and enlighten the conscience of Russian judges than twenty reprints of the Muscovite law codes. For all this enthusiasm, however, few people seem to have read the *Nakaz*. By 1817, the fiftieth anniversary of the Legislative Commission, Nikolay Turgenev was urging another of his brothers to read Bibikov's memoirs to discover that the empress's efforts were 'not so risible as people generally think'. In the following year, 1421 copies of the empress's treatise were pulped at 4 roubles 5 kopecks per pood.[51]

However promising an official revival of Catherine's principles may have seemed in 1801, the opportunity had evaporated almost as soon as it emerged. Although his grandmother's name appeared in a number of edicts promulgated by Alexander I between his accession and his coronation, it subsequently disappeared from view. In practice, his early reference to Catherine's 'heart and soul' was no more than a rhetorical disavowal of his father's arbitrariness. Early in the new reign, Dashkova was disturbed to learn that 'for all the disagreement among the people surrounding the emperor, they were unanimous in disparaging the reign of Catherine II and instilling in the young monarch the idea that a woman could never govern an empire.'[52] To attempt to turn the clock back would have been hard enough even had the tsar had no aspirations of his own. But his determination to take an ethical approach to both foreign and domestic affairs was in itself sufficient to question Catherine's morals, as Karamzin doubtless realised when criticising the personal 'foibles' that made him 'blush for mankind' in his *Memoir on Ancient and Modern Russia*, written in 1810–11.[53] Mikhail Speransky, the tsar's leading minister between 1808 and 1812, was a genuine constitutionalist with little time for Catherine's style of absolutism. Dismissing her gurus Montesquieu and Blackstone as 'superficial minds', Speransky was scathing about her attempts simultaneously 'to enjoy all the benefits of despotism with all the honour of philosophical conceptions': 'Comparing her instructions and various economical and juridical institutions with the unlimited power and accountability of the administrators, one might say that our laws were written in Athens or England, and our mode of government borrowed from Turkey.'[54]

The empress's fascination with the French Enlightenment seemed equally suspect to a generation which had been taught by French émigré propaganda and the dictates of international politics to regard the *philosophes* as perfidious mentors. 'Posterity judges, and will judge, Catherine with all human prejudice,' wrote Countess Golovina. 'The new philosophy, by which she was unfortunately influenced, and which was the mainspring of her failings, covered as with a thick veil her great and fine qualities.'[55] The Napoleonic invasion of Russia in 1812 understandably made such anxieties more urgent. Ascribing 'all our mistakes' to 'the French alone', Ivan Muravëv-Apostol blamed the *philosophes* for the decline of French morals from the time of Louis XIV. It was then, he declared, that 'the light of true enlightenment begins to fade; talents are employed as a weapon of depravity, and that most dangerous of sophists, the false-sage of Ferney [Voltaire], strains every nerve of his extraordinary mind over the course of half a century to strew with flowers the cup of hemlock he prepared to poison future generations'. The poet Konstantin Batyushkov could only watch in horror as the fall of Moscow set the seal on a catalogue of French treachery: 'And this nation of monsters dared to speak of freedom, of philosophy, of humanity! And we were so blind that we imitated them like apes! How well they have repaid us!'[56] Once Alexander had made his own glory by defeating Napoleon, any lingering need to cling to his grandmother's skirts was finally removed. Celebrating the tsar's 'subjugation of Paris' in 1814, when he rode down the Champs Elysées at the head of his troops on a magnificent white charger, Derzhavin was led to wonder whether even 'Peter and Catherine were as great as you'.[57]

———

Nicholas I, who succeeded his brother in 1825, was certainly not the man to restore Catherine's reputation. Born in the year of her death, nineteen years younger than Alexander, he had no personal memory of his grandmother. So notorious did Nicholas's hostility to her memory become that in 1885 a set of miniature portraits of the tsars was identified as his on the grounds that only Catherine's and his own were missing. Devoted, like his father, to the martial image of Peter the Great, and exuding the same uncompromising masculinity, Nicholas did little to hide his contempt for Catherine's legacy. Even before her beloved Russian Academy was absorbed into the Academy of Sciences in 1841, the Chesme Palace was converted into a dilapidated home for invalids, while the palace at Tsaritsyno became a barracks, the ultimate symbol of the Nicolaevan regime.

It cannot have been an unmitigated pleasure for Nicholas to be reminded in 1826 that Catherine's armies, 'less numerous and less well trained than now', nevertheless achieved 'great feats, worthy of Greece and Rome'.[58] Neither can the tsar's hypersensitive ear have failed to detect the reproachful overtones emitted by a chronicler of the Cadet Corps who proclaimed Catherine's 'glorious' reign as 'unforgettable', and went on to praise Count Anhalt, the director of the Corps between 1786 and 1794, for an Enlightened regime whose values could scarcely have been further removed from Nicholas's militarism.[59] Even under Nicholas, Catherine's name continued to be raised in defence of intellectual independence. Nikolay Polevoy reminded readers of his *Moscow Telegraph* how well she had understood the loss to her reign 'had poetry, art and sciences not added their voices and their glory to the thunder of military victories and the dazzle of courtly magnificence'.[60] In a memorandum of 1833 'On the silence of the Russian press', Prince Peter Vyazemsky stressed that an unmuzzled European press had been Catherine's 'brave and faithful servant'.[61] And the Decembrist Alexander Kornilovich mused from his confinement in the Peter-Paul fortress that 'Catherine loved Russian literature, and Derzhavin, Dmitriev and Karamzin appeared. They could be found now, if only they were sought out.'[62]

In the light of the Russian elite's experiences under Tsar Paul, Catherine's generosity towards her subordinates seemed even more deserving of praise. Anecdotes about the empress published in the first three decades of the nineteenth century portrayed a ruler who was equally well disposed towards each of her subjects, generous in her mercy, just in her punishments, tolerant of human weaknesses and severe only towards herself.[63] Catherine, in other words, had been an autocrat, but not a despot. Sumarokov claimed that not a single instance of 'cruelty, vengeance, the intensification of punishments or menacing autocracy' was to be found in the whole of her reign. For all her superhuman energy – following Perekusikhina he suggested that the empress had been blessed with 'miraculous quantities of static electricity' – Catherine was a model of self-control whose heart never dominated her head. 'He who can govern himself in this way is worthy to rule the universe.'[64] Remembering how the empress had protected him from intrigue, Prince Dolgorukov observed that 'with such a tsaritsa' every subject could 'labour with pleasure' and relax in the knowledge that he was trusted. Under Catherine, 'fools were not frightening and scoundrels were not dangerous'.[65] Such a tolerant monarch could not only forgive her servants their every misdemeanour, but would also respect loyal ministers even when she did not admire them. Repeated in anecdote after anecdote, this point was driven home by Pushkin in his *History of Pugachëv*. Catherine, he reminded the notoriously mistrustful Nicholas I, 'knew how to overcome her prejudices'.[66]

Faced with the possibility that his grandmother might become an icon to inspire his critics, Nicholas instinctively tried to prevent them from learning too much about her. He may have allowed Pushkin access to the archives on the Pugachëv rebellion, but he had no intention of permitting the publication of potentially damaging testimony from Catherine's time. Apart from the empress's own memoirs, Khrapovitsky's diary was pre-eminent. 'No single book,' judged his friend Ivan Dmitriev, 'could give a better understanding of Catherine's mind, character and life.'[67] Like Dmitriev, Alexander Turgenev recognised that Catherine's secretary, having 'recorded *ipsissima verba* everything that he saw and heard', offered an unparalleled guide to her 'inner life' and the morals of her Court.[68] Yet such titillating detail was anathema to the tsar. When Pavel Svinin, who had already published fragments of the diary, proposed a complete annotated edition in 1833, the president of the main censorship committee responded on the tsar's behalf that it was 'politically speaking premature' to publish a text which revealed 'a certain weakening in governmental power, some incongruity in the relationships and behaviour of people close to the Court, and vacillation in the authorities of state'.[69] Turgenev was soon to experience a similar frustration when he sought to publish 'all the gossip' about Catherine's Court that he had unearthed in the French diplomatic archives. Nicholas personally retorted that such sources were 'offensive to Russia and of no historical importance'.[70] Catherine's own memoirs, which implied that all the nineteenth-century Romanovs were descended from Sergey Saltykov, were so incendiary that they remained unpublished in Russia until 1907.

Yet the harder the censors tried to restrict the available information, the more Russians yearned to taste the forbidden fruit. And it was by no means impossible for the well-connected to do so. Catherine's own memoirs circulated in copies from the manuscript version cherished by Turgenev as 'the apple of his eye'. The copy that Pushkin lent to the grand duchess Yelena Pavlovna sent her 'out of her mind'.[71] Natalia Zagryazhskaya, the favourite daughter of the Ukrainian *hetman* Kirill Razumovsky, was a further source of titillating information. Marked down by Catherine herself as 'an adventuress' in 1787, Natalia rapidly gained the reputation of one who was exciting but dangerous to know. Pushkin was introduced to her in 1830 on his engagement to her great-niece, and became captivated, like other members of his circle, by this living link with a recent but disappearing past. In the absence of authoritative written sources, it became all the more important to record her anecdotes for posterity. They supplied most of the information for Pushkin's 'Table-Talk', compiled in 1835–6.[72]

To the untutored eye, paeans of praise to the late empress might seem no more than saccharine effusions. However, the Catherine myth is better regarded as a series of pointed attempts to reshape the pattern of autocracy. The code was transparent enough. To her idolaters, Catherine's name stood for liberty of expression, moderation in government, and respectful treatment of loyal subordinates. To her immediate successors, however, she came to personify unnatural female rule, unethical territorial expansion, and an unnerving flirtation with juridical reform and intellectual speculation. As a result, once the first flush of enthusiasm for a revival of Catherine's ideals had evaporated early in the reign of Alexander I, her devotees made little progress in the first half of the nineteenth century in their attempt to convert their private fascination for the empress into the public adoration they thought she deserved. It was only in the 1860s, once Herzen had published in London the memoirs that Nicholas I had suppressed, that some of the tsarist regime's most intelligent supporters appreciated that by disowning Catherine and all that she stood for, they had inadvertently handed their radical opponents a powerful weapon. The last four decades of the nineteenth century therefore witnessed a concerted attempt to claw back the empress for the establishment.

As the secretary of the Russian Historical Society later confirmed, the 'fundamental idea' underlying its establishment in 1866 was the assumption that the past would seem the 'more attractive' the better it became known. Not for nothing did Alexander II's foreign minister Prince Gorchakov christen the society and its publications a 'patriotic enterprise'.[73] Catherine was at the heart of the venture. When its patron, the future tsar Alexander III, conferred imperial status on the society in 1873, he expressed pleasure that its work had been directed mainly to the preservation of documents concerning her 'praiseworthy actions, tending to the well-being of Russia'.[74] Together with monthly historical journals such as *Russian Archive*, whose founder-editor worked from an office dominated by a portrait of the empress, the society published a voluminous series of sources that ultimately permitted a new generation of scholars to give the empress a new lease of life.[75]

Historical fiction reached an even wider readership. A year after he retired as a senior official at the Ministry of Education, G. P. Danilevsky wrote his first novella, *Catherine the Great on the Dnieper*. Twenty years later, it was followed by another, *Potëmkin on the Danube*. By that time, the author was deputy editor-in-chief of the government newspaper, whose staff was dragooned into publishing a trilogy of more substantial novels about Catherine's reign. *Mirovich* and *Princess Tarakanova* were both based on authentic sources. So was the last and longest of the novels, which continued the theme of rebellion by discussing Pugachëv.[76] In 1890, the last year of Danilevsky's life, he set St Petersburg society alight by delivering a lecture claiming, plausibly enough, that Catherine had married Potëmkin.[77] Works such as these helped to lift Catherine's public profile higher by the centenary of her death than at any time since the reign of Alexander I. According to an American tourist, her picture greeted the visitor 'everywhere, in every variety of costume and position'. Indeed, the honours were divided with Peter the Great, for both were ubiquitous 'in effigy or picture or memorial or legend or belongings'. 'They made Russia what it is', he went on, 'but their remembrance is not so fragrant as Washington or Lincoln'.[78]

On 24 November 1873, Alexander II inaugurated M. O. Mikeshin's majestic monument to Catherine in the square outside the St Petersburg Public Library. The tsar had followed every step of its development as the budget almost doubled from the original estimate in 1865 to a total cost of 456,896 roubles.[79] At a meeting in his presence on the following day, Academician Grot, who edited Catherine's correspondence with Grimm for the Imperial Russian Historical Society, claimed that it was now possible to see the empress in a new perspective:

> A whole century separates us from that glorious era; passions have cooled; the time has come for the unbiased judgement of history, that unhypocritical judgement which, by means of factual enrichment, is reconstructing the attractive, majestic image of Catherine II more clearly and more brightly as each day passes.[80]

In similar fashion, the great Russian historian Vasily Klyuchevsky argued at the centenary of her death in 1896 that 'posterity's accounts' had by then been settled. The empress, he said, had become 'merely a subject for study' who could be safely consigned to the 'remoteness of history' now that she no longer served as either scapegoat or inspiration.[81]

Grot and Klyuchevsky were both mistaken. Unfortunately for those who sought to sanitise Catherine's image, it proved impossible to focus solely on her glorious achievements. On the contrary, a campaign designed primarily to drape Catherine in the Russian flag served rather to enliven interest in her personality.

Biographers, in particular, found it hard to detach her patriotic 'virtues' from her chequered morals. The liberal journalist Vasily Bilbasov managed to complete only the first part of a projected twelve-volume work before running into trouble with the censors. They objected to his quotations from Catherine's memoirs, to a reference to her illegitimate son, Aleksey Bobrinsky, and to his discussion of the vexed question of Tsar Paul's paternity. The book was published thanks to the intervention of Alexander III, who insisted on raising the price to a prohibitive five roubles, but the censors had the last laugh when the tsar discovered that Bilbasov was the same 'swine' who edited the liberal newspaper *The Voice*.[82] Bilbasov's second volume had to be published in Berlin. Russians nevertheless found ways of reading it, and the demand for titillating information about Catherine never abated.

In 1897, the teenage poet Alexander Blok declared that Catherine was his favourite heroine in history on a visit to Bad Neuheim during which, by a delicious coincidence, he lost his virginity to a woman more than twice his age, described by his biographer as 'his type: big, spontaneous, and talented rather than intellectual'.[83] Though it was only after the revolution of 1905 that salacious stories of the empress's 'intimate life' could be published in Russia, Catherine's admirers found their own way of celebrating her memory.[84] Thanks to the patronage of Grand Duke Nikolay Mikhaylovich, a circle of antiquarians including the snuffbox connoisseur S. N. Kaznakov, and Grigory Orlov's biographer, Alexander Golombiyevsky, staged an exhibition of imperial portraits at the Tauride Palace in spring 1905. Between February and May, undeterred by revolutionary unrest, some 45,000 visitors marvelled at forty-four paintings of Catherine, displayed alongside thirty-five of Peter the Great and Alexander I in the palace she had built for Potëmkin. (Shortly afterwards the great colonnade where he had entertained her in April 1791 became the outer hall of Russia's first national representative assembly, the State Duma.)[85] The exhibition's guiding force was Sergey Dyaghilev, whose collaborators in the predominantly homosexual 'World of Art' group experienced their own scandalous frisson by gathering in 1906 to examine what they believed to be a wax model of Potëmkin's phallus, allegedly commissioned by Catherine 'for the edification of diminished successors', and smuggled out of the Hermitage by a curator at the behest of his son, the erotic artist Konstantin Somov.

One reason why the empress continued to have such a profound resonance at the beginning of the twentieth century was the presence at the Court of St Petersburg, throughout the reigns of the last two tsars, of a woman who deliberately modelled herself on Catherine the Great. This was the grand duchess Maria Pav-lovna, wife of Alexander III's brother, Grand Duke Vladimir Aleksandrovich, born Princess Marie of Mecklenburg-Schwerin. Gossips claimed that this 'debauched German' led a 'dissolute life' by holding 'small orgies' at her resi-dence along the embankment from the Winter Palace. A scandal at the Cubat Frères restaurant in 1889 prompted rumours that she would be forced to emi-grate.[86] Shortly afterwards, the customarily humourless Alexander III joked at a fisheries trade fair that a stand featuring semi-naked peasant women dressed as mermaids might inspire Maria Pavlovna's next costumed ball.[87] Recalling Cather-ine's own mistreatment under Elizabeth and Peter III, friends of the grand duchess attributed such sniping to envy of her intelligence and beauty.[88] To her critics, however, she personified the reasons why Catherine's reign symbolised not the golden age of the Romanov dynasty, but rather, to quote Richard Wortman, its 'reprehensible past' in which the empress herself, 'possessed by ambition, flagrant in her inconstancy and indifference to the family, seemed threatening to the very notion of nineteenth-century legitimacy'.[89] The British ambassador Sir George Buchanan outlined the more attractive characteristics that raised echoes of Catherine the Great:

> A *grande dame* in the best sense of that term, but without any pretensions as regards the strict observation of Court etiquette, the Grand Duchess was admirably fitted to play the part of the hostess and to do the honours of the Court. With great conversational gifts, she was not only herself full of verve and entrain, but possessed the art of inspiring them in others. Her entertain-ments, no matter what form they took, were never dull, and no one was ever bored. At her dinners and receptions one met many of the younger members of the Imperial family and the elite of Russian society, more especially the 'smart set', as well as a sprinkling of the official and artistic worlds.[90]

While an uninterrupted male line of succession in Prussia permitted succes-sive Hohenzollerns to draw inspiration from the heroic image of Frederick the Great – as, indeed, did Bismarck, Hitler and Goebbels – no nineteenth-century Romanov tsar could comfortably model himself on Catherine. Major General Sir John Hanbury Williams thought he could still detect in 1914 the shadows of that 'halo of mystery' attaching to the days when Catherine addressed letters to his ancestor Sir Charles 'as "Madame" and he to her as "Monsieur"'. But the more historians emphasised Catherine's contribution to Russia's great power status, the less likely her latest successor seemed to be able to sustain it. One need only recall Hanbury Williams' doleful comment after an interview with the tsar at his Mogilëv headquarters in October 1915: 'Catherine was a wonderful ruler of Russia, but these are not the days of Catherine.'[91]

'True glory cannot be sought,' General Suvorov reminded Admiral Ribas in November 1790, 'it comes from the sacrifice that one makes to the utility of the public good.'[92] Catherine was aware of the tension. Regularly reaffirming her commitment to the common good, she was nevertheless obsessed with her own posthumous reputation. It would have delighted her to know that, after her death, Academician Peter Pallas re-christened one of the steppe grasses he had discovered '*Catharinaea sublimis*'.[93] 'She loves glory and is assiduous in her pursuit of it,' Prince Shcherbatov wrote in 1786–7.[94] Those were years in which she embarked on a major renovation of the road from St Petersburg to Moscow, recommended to her by Diderot in 1773 as a good way of securing immortality. This, indeed, was one subject on which Catherine was particularly anxious to assure the approbation of the *philosophes*.[95] She offered her own self-assessment to Grimm in 1778:

> Here lies Catherine the Second, born at Stettin on 21 April 1729. She came to Russia in 1744 to marry Peter III. At the age of fourteen, she conceived the triple ambition of pleasing her husband, Elizabeth and the nation. She overlooked nothing to achieve this. In eighteen years of boredom and solitude she read many books. Once she had reached the throne of Russia, she wanted only good and sought to procure happiness, freedom and property for her subjects. She forgave with ease and hated no one; indulgent, happy to be alive, cheerful by nature, with a republican soul and a good heart, she had friends; work was easy for her, company and the arts pleased her.[96]

That was not how contemporary critics saw her. Shcherbatov complained in a treatise written only for the eyes of his family that 'true friendship never resided in her heart, and she is ready to betray her best friend and servant in order to please her lover'. According to him, the empress's obsessive quest for immortality had left her vulnerable to a series of cunning flatterers – Betskoy, Yelagin, Vyazemsky and Bezborodko prominent among them. Too many of her projects, founded ostensibly 'for the good of the nation' were in fact 'simply symbols of her love of glory, for if she really had the nation's interest at heart, she would, after founding them, have also paid attention to their progress'. This was the voice of a scholarly aristocrat who had once enjoyed Catherine's patronage as an historian but now found himself permanently excluded from her inner circle. Although she had always tried to balance one adviser against another, never allowing anyone to think that his ideas had no prospect of being accepted, this proved an increasingly difficult balance to hold. To those outside her charmed circle, Potëmkin had come to epitomise the corrupting influence of favouritism in the last decade of her reign: 'love of power, ostentation, pandering to all his desires, gluttony and hence luxury at table, flattery, avarice, rapaciousness, and it may be said, all the other vices known in the world, with which he himself is full and with which he fills his supporters, and so on throughout the empire'. [97]

In April 1790, the chief of the St Petersburg police entered Catherine's inner sanctum to present her with Denis, a four-year-old boy of unknown origin found wandering the streets. Since no one had yet answered advertisements for his parents, the empress adopted him at the Court's expense and placed him in the care of a courtier living close by the Hermitage. [98] She was capable of demonstrative acts of kindness to those who had no right to expect them. Yet she was certainly no saint. Despite her idealised view of the Russian people as a whole, she took a dim view of many of the individuals she met on her travels, reserving some of her cattiest remarks for the earnest merchants' wives who served her at table. Though her legislation allowed for a limited degree of social mobility, her policy was always to encourage her subjects to seek satisfaction in the station into which they had been born. As befitted a believer in a rigid social hierarchy, she relaxed only in the privacy of a narrow circle of aristocratic friends which remained remarkably constant throughout her fifty-two years in Russia (Ivan Betskoy, one of her first contacts at Elizabeth's Court, died at the age of ninety-three in August 1795). Having begun her reign as a usurper, she sought a degree of legitimacy by portraying many of her early edicts as an attempt to complete the work of Peter the Great. But she was never a slavish imitator. [99] On the contrary, having sought throughout to exceed the achievements of her glorious predecessor, she ended her life surrounded by images of her own triumphs on the European stage: paintings commemorating the battle of Chesme by the English artist Richard Paton were originally hung in the Hermitage but significantly moved in 1779 to the throne room at Peter's own summer residence, Peterhof. [100] Catherine had presided over the greatest expansion of Russian territory since the mid-sixteenth century and seen her empire's economy grow in proportion. She had shown at least as great a commitment to the power of ideas as Peter I. But since she had ultimately been unable to trust the Enlightenment's fundamental belief in self-development, a reign which began by fostering a degree of intellectual independence ended by enveloping some of Russia's most interesting writers in clouds of suspicion. Catherine had not succeeded in her aim of establishing a firm rule of law, and the rational bureaucratic institutions she had worked so hard to establish never emasculated the informal patronage networks by which Russia has long been governed. Although she had offered her subjects the example of a tolerant and trusting ruler, her gentle methods have rarely been adopted by her successors. For them, the empress's conduct has most often been an anti-model, not least because it has served as a subtle form of ammunition for their critics for most of the two centuries since her death.

ABBREVIATIONS

AKV: *Arkhiv kniaʒ'ia Vorontsova*, ed. P.I. Bartenev, 40 vols. (M, 1870–95).

Beer and Fiedler: A. Beer and J. Ritter von Fiedler, eds, *Joseph II. und Graf Ludwig Cobenʒl: Ihr Briefwechsel*, 2 vols. (Vienna, 1901).

Benois, *Tsarskoe selo*: Aleksandr Benua, *Tsarskoe Selo v tsarstvovanie Imperatritsy Elisavety Petrovny* (SPb, 1910).

Bentham: *The Correspondence of Jeremy Bentham*, vol. 2 (London, 1968), ed. T. L. S. Sprigge; vol. 3 (London, 1971), ed. I. R. Christie; vol. 4 (London, 1981), ed. A. T. Milne.

Bessarabova: N. V. Bessarabova, *Puteshestviia Ekateriny II po Rossii* (M, 2005).

Best: Voltaire, *Correspondence and Related Documents*, ed. Theodore Besterman, *The Complete Works of Voltaire*, vols. 85–135 (Banbury and Oxford, 1968–77).

Bezborodko: 'Pis'ma A. A. Bezborodka k grafu Petru Aleksandrovichu Rumiantsevu', *Starina i noviʒna*, 3 (1900), 160–370.

Bil'basov: V. A. Bil'basov, *Istoriia Ekateriny Vtoroi*, 2 vols. (Berlin, n.d.).

British Art Treasures: *British Art Treasures from Russian Imperial Collections in the Hermitage*, eds. B. Allen and L. Dukelskaya (New Haven, CT, 1996).

C.: Catherine II

CASS: *Canadian American Slavic Studies*

ChIOIDR: *Chteniia v Imperatorskom Obshchestve istorii i drevnostei Rossiiskikh pri Moskovskom Universitete.*

Corberon: *Un diplomate français à la cour de Catherine II 1775–1780: Journal intime du chevalier de Corberon, chargé d'affaires de France en Russie*, ed. L.-H. Labande, 2 vols. (Paris, 1901).

Correspondance: *Correspondance de Catherine Alexéievna, Grande-Duchesse de Russie, et de Sir Charles H. Williams, Ambassadeur d'Angleterre*, 1756 et 1757, ed. S. Goriaïnow (M, 1909).

Coxe: William Coxe, *Travels into Poland, Russia, Sweden, and Denmark*, 2 vols. (London, 1784).

Cross: Anthony Cross, *By the Banks of the Neva: Chapters from the Lives and Careers of the British in Eighteenth-Century Russia* (Cambridge, 1997).

Despatches: *The Despatches and Correspondence of John, Second Earl of Buckinghamshire, Ambassador to the Court of Catherine II. Of Russia 1762–1765*, ed. A. d'A. Collyer, 2 vols. (London, 1900–01).

Dimsdale: *An English Lady at the Court of Catherine the Great: The Journal of Baroness Elizabeth Dimsdale, 1781*, ed. A. G. Cross (Cambridge, 1989).

Engelhardt: L. N. Engel'gardt, *Zapiski*, ed. I. I. Fediukin (M, 1997).

Falconet: *Correspondance de Falconet avec Catherine II 1767–1778*, ed. Louis Réau (Paris, 1921)

Grimm: 'Pis'ma Imperatritsy Ekateriny II k Grimmu (1774–1796)', ed. Ia. Grot, *SIRIO*, vol. 23 (SPb, 1878).

Harris Diaries: *Diaries and Correspondence of James Harris, First Earl of Malmesbury*, edited by his grandson, 4 vols. (London, 1844).

Harris Papers: *Music and Theatre in Handel's World: The Family Papers of James Harris, 1732–1780*, eds. Donald Burrows and Rosemary Dunhill (Oxford, 2002).

KfZh: *Kamer-fur'erskie zhurnaly, 1696–1816* (SPb, 1853–1917).

Khrapovitskii: *Dnevnik A.V. Khrapovitskago 1782–1793*, ed. N. Barsukov (SPb, 1874).

Kutepov, *Tsarskaia okhota*: Nikolai Kutepov, *Tsarskaia i imperatorskaia okhota na Rusi: Konets XVII-go i XVIII-i vek: Istoricheskii ocherk* vol. 3 (SPb, 1900)

Lettere: *Nikolai Ivanovic, la vostra lettera …: Lettere di Caterina II Romanov a N. I. Saltykov (1773–1793), Catalogo della Mostra 3 Novembre 2005–18 Febbraio 2006* (Milan, 2005).

Lopatin: *Ekaterina II i G. A. Potemkin: lichnaia perepiska*, ed. V. S. Lopatin (M, 1997).

M: Moscow

MP: *Muzykal'yni Peterburg: Entsiklopedicheskii slovar' XVIII vek*, ed. A. L. Porfir'eva, 6 vols. in progress (SPb, 1996–).

McGrew: Roderick E. McGrew, *Paul I of Russia 1754–1801* (Oxford, 1992).

Madariaga: Isabel de Madariaga, *Russia in the Age of Catherine the Great* (London, 1981).

Madariaga, *Short History*: Isabel de Madariaga, *Catherine the Great: A short history* (New Haven, CT, 1990).

Montefiore: Simon Sebag-Montefiore, *Prince of Princes: A Life of Potemkin* (London, 2000).

Omel'chenko: O.A Omel'chenko, *'Zakonnaia monarkhiia' Ekateriny II: Prosveschennyi absoliutizm v Rossii* (M, 1993).

Opisanie: *Obstoiatel'noe opisanie torzhestvennykh poriadkov blagopoluchnago vshestviia v imperatorskuiu drevniuiu rezidentskkiu bogospasaemyi grad Moskvu i osviashchenneishago koronovaniia … Ekateriny Vtoryia, samoderzhitsy vserossiiskiia, materi i izbavitel'nitsy otechestva … 1762 goda*, published as appendix to *KfZh*, 1762 (SPb, 1855).

PKNO: *Pamiatniki kul'tury: novye otkrytiia*.

Parkinson: John Parkinson, *A Tour of Russia, Siberia, and the Crimea 1792–1794*, ed. W. Collier (London, 1971).

PSZ: *Polnoe sobranie zakonov Rossiiskoi Imperii*, 1st series, 46 vols. (SPb, 1830).

Poroshin: S.A. Poroshin, 'Zapiski', in *Russkii Gamlet*, ed. A. Skorobogatov (M, 2004).

Proschwitz: *Catherine II et Gustav III: Une correspondence retrouvée*, ed. Gunnar von Proschwitz (Stockholm, 1998).

Quarenghi: Giacomo Quarenghi, *Architetto a Pietroburgo: Lettere e altri scritti*, ed. Vanni Zanella (Venice, 1988).

Richardson: [William Richardson], *Anecdotes of the Russian Empire. In a series of letters written, a few years ago, from St Petersburg* (London, 1784).

RA: *Russkii arkhiv*

RBS: *Russkii biograficheskii slovar'*

RS: *Russkaia starina*

SK: *Svodyni katalog russkoi grazhdanskoi pechati XVIII veka, 1725–1800*, 5 vols. (M, 1962–7).

Shcherbatov: Prince M. M. Shcherbatov, *On the Corruption of Morals in Russia*, trans. and ed. Antony Lentin (Cambridge, 1969).

Ségur: *Memoirs and Recollections of Count Segur, Ambassador from France to the Courts of Russia and Prussia &c. &c.* Written by himself, 3 vols. (London, 1825–27).

SEER: Slavonic and East European Review.

SIRIO: Sbornik Imperatorskago Russkago Istoricheskago Obshchestva, 148 vols. (SPb, 1867–1916).

Sochineniia: Sochineniia Imperatritsy Ekateriny II, ed. A. N. Pypin , vols. 1–5, 7–12 (SPb, 1901–07).

SPb: St Petersburg

Shtelin, *Muzyka:* Iakob Shtelin, *Muzyka i balet v Rossii XVIII veka* (SPb, 2002).

Shtelin, *Zapiski:* 'Zapiski Shtelina o Petre Tret'em, Imperatore Vserossiiskom', *ChIOIDR*, 1866, bk 4, 67–118.

Starikova: *Teatral'naia zhizn' Rossii v epokhu Elizavety Petrovny: Dokumental'naia khronika 1741–1750*, 2 parts (M, 2003–05).

Stedingk: *Un ambassadeur de Suède à la cour de Catherine II. Feld-Maréchal Comte de Stedingk: Choix de dépêches diplomatiques, rapports secrets et letters particulières de 1790 à 1796*, ed. La Comtesse Brevern de la Gardie, 2 vols. (Stockholm, 1919).

Storch: *The Picture of Petersburgh*, from the German of Henry Storch (London, 1801).

Tooke: [William Tooke], *The Life of Catharine II. Empress of Russia*, An enlarged translation from the French, 3 vols. (London, 1798).

Zapiski Shtelina: Zapiski Iakoba Shtelina ob iziashchnykh iskusstvakh v Rossii, ed. K. V. Malinovskii, 2 vols. (M, 1990).

Zavadovskii: 'Pis'ma grafa P. V. Zavadovskago k fel'dmarshalu grafu P. A. Rumiantsevu', *Starina i novizna*, vol. 4 (1901), 223–382.

Zimmerman: M. Semevskii, ed., 'Imperatritsa Ekaterina II v eia neizdannykh ne vpolne pis'makh k I.G. Tsimmermannu', *RS*, 55, 3 (1887), 239–79.

NOTES

Prologue

1. *The Military, Historical and Political Memories of the Count de Hordt*, 2 vols. (London, 1805–6), II: 72. On the new capital's bells, see I. A. Chudinova, *Penie, zvony, ritual: Topografiia tserkovno-muzykal'noi kul'tury Peterburga* (SPb, 1994), 26–36.

2. I. A. Chudinova, 'Kolokol'nye zvony', *MP*, II: 75; W. F. Ryan, *The Bathhouse at Midnight: An historical survey of magic and divination in Russia* (Stroud, 1999), 240–1.

3. E. V. Williams, *The Bells of Russia: History and Technology* (Princeton, NJ, 1985), 148–65; J. M. R. Lenz, *Moskauer Schriften und Briefe*, ed. H. Tommek, 2 vols. (Berlin, 2007), Textband, 35, 460–6, reviewed by R. Bartlett in *SGECRN*, 37 (2007). The cracked bell is now a major tourist attraction in the Kremlin.

4. Williams, *Bells of Russia*, 166, translation marginally amended.

5. *Opisanie*, 58.

6. *Opisanie*, 51, 56; E. Clarke (1800), quoted in Williams, *Bells of Russia*, 166–7. Slizov's bell smashed to the ground during the Napoleonic invasion of 1812.

7. 'Zamechatel'nye liudi iz russkago belago dukhovenstva v XVIII stoletiia', *Strannik*, Feb. 1897, 261–2.

8. *SIRIO*, VII: 121; Bil'basov, II: 145, n. 3.

9. *KfZh* (1745), 62. The others were Count Ivan Chernyshëv, Count Sergei Iaguzhinskii, Peter Naryshkin, Mikhail Budlianskoi, Count Peter Buturlin and Count Andrei Shuvalov: *Opisanie*, 68.

10. *Opisanie*, 51–2.

11. R. Wortman, 'The Russian Coronation: Rite and Representation', *The Court Historian*, 9 (2004), 23.

12. *Opisanie*, 29–36.

13. Giving no source, Montefiore, 52, puts Potëmkin at the coronation, though he was too junior to be mentioned by name in *Opisanie*.

14. M. A. Alekseeva, *Mikhailo Makhaev: master vidovogo risunka XVIII veka* (SPb, 2003), 185–6.

15. Quoted in D. Beales, *Joseph II, vol. 1: In the shadow of Maria Theresa, 1741–1780* (Cambridge, 1987), 435.

16. Coxe, I: 264.
17. On Moscow in this period, see J. T. Alexander, *Bubonic Plague in Early Modern Russia: Public Health and Urban Disaster* (Baltimore, MD, 1980), ch. 2, esp. 70–1.
18. *Opisanie*, 13.
19. Coxe, I: 265.
20. *Opisanie*, 252–86, lists more than 200 members of the commission and their responsibilities. The architects included Prince Dmitrii Ukhtomskii and Matvei Kazakov, ibid., 258–62.
21. *RA*, 1870, nos. 4–5, 748, C. to I. I. Melissino, 8 Nov. 1765, enclosing a petition from Antropov; *Opisanie*, 255. On earlier triumphal arches, see E. A. Tiukhmeneva, *Iskusstvo triumfal'nykh vrat v Rossii pervoi poloviny XVIII veka* (M, 2005).
22. *Opisanie*, 26–35. N. A. Ogarkova, *Tseremonii, prazdnestva, muzyka russkogo dvora XVIII-nachalo XIX veka* (SPb, 2004), 264–6, reprints the chant with musical notation.
23. *RA*, 1884, no. 2, 253, C. to I. I. Nepliuev, 16 Sept. 1762.
24. *Despatches*, I: 73, Buckinghamshire to Grenville, 24 Sept. 1762 NS.
25. Bil'basov, II: 148; Alexander, 63–5; G. L. Freeze, 'Subversive piety: religion and political crisis in late imperial Russia', *Journal of Modern History*, 68 (1996), 324–5.
26. *Opisanie*, 50–1.
27. Ibid., 228–33.
28. Ogarkova, *Tseremonii*, 19–20, 191, n. 23.
29. For the walkway, missing from de Veilly's illustrations, see *Opisanie*, 49–50, 182.
30. Ibid., 58–9. I. L. Buseva-Davydova, *Khramy Moskovskogo Kremlia: sviatyni i drevnosti* (Moscow, 1997), 38, mistakenly suggests that the west door was used for coronations.
31. Cross, 41, 70–1.
32. *Opisanie*, 59–67.
33. Ibid., 67–9.
34. On canopies in Western Europe, see J. Adamson, 'The making of the ancien-régime Court, 1500–1700', in Adamson, ed., *The Princely Courts of Europe, 1500–1700* (London, 1999), 29.
35. *Despatches*, I: 100, undated 'Russian Memoranda', probably 1763–4.
36. *KfZh* (1753), 20–5, 25 Apr. On this occasion, no alterations were made to the interior of the cathedral.
37. *Sochineniia*, XII: 323.
38. *Sochineniia*, XII: 641–2, 'Réflexions sur Pétersbourg et sur Moscou'.
39. Wortman, 'The Russian Coronation', 21, 31.
40. *Pis'ma gosudaryni imperatritsy Ekateriny Velikoi k Feld'marshalu grafu P.S. Saltykovu* (M, 1886), 9, 29 June 1762, 'the day after our accession to the throne'.
41. *Annual Register*, July 1762, quoted by J. T. Alexander, 'Catherine II's efforts at liberalization and their aftermath', in R. O. Crummey, ed., *Reform in Russia and the USSR* (Urbana, IL, 1989), 73.
42. *PSZ*, XVI: 11,598 (Manifest o koronatsii Imperatritsy Ekateriny Vtoroi); 11,599 (Manifest o konchine Imperatora Petra III).
43. Compare D. Cannadine and S. Price, eds., *Rituals of Royalty: Power and Ceremonial in Traditional Societies* (Cambridge, 1985), 8, 40.
44. D. L. Ransel, *The Politics of Catherinian Russia: The Panin Party* (New Haven, CT, 1975), 65–8.
45. Quoted in L. Hughes, *Sophia: Regent of Russia 1657–1704* (New Haven, CT, 1990), 268.
46. R. A. Jackson, *Vive le roi! A History of the French Coronation from Charles V to Charles X* (Chapel Hill and London, 1984), 11.

47. Bil'basov, II: 144–5; *SIRIO*, CXL: 91, Breteuil to Choiseul, 9 Oct. 1762 NS.

48. *Sochineniia*, XII: 161.

49. Bil'basov, II: 171–84.

50. *Opisanie*, 73; *SIRIO*, CXL: 82, Breteuil to Louis XV, 5 Oct. 1762 NS.

51. Quoted in S. L. Baehr, *The Paradise Myth in Eighteenth-Century Russia* (Stanford, CA, 1991), 39.

52. *Opisanie*, 194–9.

53. J. P. LeDonne, 'Ruling families in the Russian political order, 1689–1825', *Cahiers du monde russe et soviétique*, 28 (1987), 233–322; G. Hosking, 'Patronage and the Russian State', *SEER*, 78 (2000), 301–20.

54. *Sochineniia*, XII: 696.

55. *Obstoiatel'noe opisanie Torzhestvennykh Poriadkov Blagopoluchnago Vshestviia v tsarstvuiushchii grad Moskvu i Sviashchenneishago Koronovaniia ... Imperatritsy Elisaveta Petrovny* (SPb, 1744), 74; *Opisanie*, 65, 176. The important account of C.'s coronation in R. S. Wortman, *Scenarios of Power: Myth and Ceremony in Russian Monarchy, 1: From Peter I to Nicholas I* (Princeton, NJ, 1995), 115, inadvertently suggests that Talyzin carried the state banner, another of Elizabeth's innovations, depicting a double-headed eagle clutching both orb and sceptre in its fearful claws.

56. *Despatches*, I: 98.

57. M. Lepekine, 'Catherine II et l'Eglise', in *Catherine II et l'Europe*, ed. A. Davidenkoff (Paris, 1997), 179.

58. Madariaga, 114.

59. *SIRIO*, CXL: 83, Breteuil to Choiseul, 9 Oct. 1762 NS.

60. *Opisanie*, 48–9.

61. Ibid., 45–7.

62. *Zapiski Shtelina*, I: 78–9.

63. J. McManners, *Church and Society in Eighteenth-Century France, Vol. 1: The Clerical Establishment and its Social Ramifications* (Oxford, 1998), 8.

64. *Opisanie*, 54.

65. 'Mémoires de la Princess Dashkaw, d'après le manuscrit revu et corrigé par l'auteur', *AKV*, XXI: 101–4 (104).

66. *Opisanie*, 75. This is psalm 100 in the Orthodox psalter.

67. See below, pp. 212–3.

68. The Dormition Cathedral contains the earliest known panel icon of the Apocalypse in the Byzantine world: M. S. Flier, 'Till the End of Time: The Apocalypse in Russian Historical Experience Before 1500', in *Orthodox Russia: Belief and Practice under the Tsars*, eds. V. A. Kivelson and R. H. Greene (Philadelphia, PA, 2003), 140–3.

69. See *Khristianskie relikvii v Moskovskom kremle*, ed. A. M. Lidov (M, 2001).

70. Baehr, *Paradise Myth*, 30–1, 38–40.

71. *SIRIO*, CXL: 57, Louis XV to Breteuil, 10 Sept. 1762 NS.

72. Beales, *Joseph II*, 36.

73. *Opisanie*, 78.

74. *Correspondance*, 88, 27 Aug. 1756.

75. *Opisanie*, 84.

76. Wortman, *Scenarios*, 115; *Opisanie*, 234.

77. Bil'basov, II: 146.

78. *Opisanie*, 86–9.

79. 'Mémoires de la Princess Dashkaw', 61.
80. Quoted in Wortman, *Scenarios*, 116.
81. Wortman, 'The Russian Coronation', 19.
82. B. A. Uspenskii, *Tsar' i Patriarkh: Khariẓma vlasti v Rossii (Viẓantiiskaia model' i ee russkoe pereosmyslenie)* (M, 1998).
83. *Sochineniia*, XII: 615; *Opisanie*, 102.
84. *SIRIO*, CXL: 85, Breteuil to Choiseul, 9 Oct. 1762 NS.
85. Bil'basov, II: 146.
86. I. V. Kurukin, *Epokha 'dvorskikh bur': Ocherki politicheskoi istorii poslepetrovskoi Rossii, 1725–1762 gg.* (Riazan, 2003), 415–7.
87. *Opisanie*, 213–9. A second document, perhaps an earlier plan, gives an alternative layout, catering for 358 guests served by 130 lackeys: ibid., 235.
88. D. A. Rovinskii, *Oboẓrenie ikonopisaniia v Rossii do kontsa XVII veka: opisanie feierverkov i illiuminatsii* (SPb, 1903).
89. *SIRIO*, XLVIII: 13, C. to Keyserling, 25 Sept. 1762.
90. *Opisanie*, 157, 291.
91. *Despatches*, I: 88, Buckinghamshire to Countess of Suffolk, 9 Nov. 1762 NS.
92. Plans for the pageant had been laid as early as 10 July 1762: see Iu. A. Dmitriev, ed., *F. G. Volkov i Russkii teatr ego vremeni* (M, 1953), 149–50. Sumarokov's text is at p. 188.
93. Baehr, *Paradise Myth*, 40.
94. *Sochineniia*, XII: 625.

Chapter 1

1. W. H. Meyer, *Stettin in alter und neuer Zeit* (Stettin, 1887), 108–9, 238.
2. Bil'basov, I: 4–5; *Sochineniia*, XII: 5.
3. S. Peller, 'Births and deaths among Europe's ruling families since 1500', in *Population in History: Essays in Historical Demography*, eds. D. V. Glass and D. E. C. Eversley (London, 1965), 91, table 2.
4. T. Blanning, *The Pursuit of Glory: Europe 1648–1815* (London, 2007), 62–3.
5. *SIRIO*, XX: 246, C. to Frederick II, 5 Dec. 1768.
6. *Sochineniia*, XII: 8.
7. *A Full Account of the Situation, Former State and Late Siege of Stetin* (London, 1678), 4–5; J. M. Piskorski, et al, *A Short History of Sẓcẓecin*, trans. K. Wilson (Poznań, 2002), 91–106.
8. M. Völkel, 'The Hohenzollern Court 1535–1740', in *Princely Courts of Europe*, ed. Adamson, 215.
9. *Deutsche Geschichte im Osten Europas: Pommern*, ed. W. Bucholz (Berlin, 1999), 237–85, 341–52; D. McKay and H. M. Scott, *The Rise of the Great Powers 1648–1815* (London, 1983), 10–14.
10. On the castle's changing fortunes through the ages, see E. Cnotliwy, *Zamek książęcy w Sẓcẓecinie* (Szczecin, 1992) and J. Kochanowska et al, *Zamek Książąt Pomorskich w Sẓcẓecinie* (Szczecin, 2002).
11. C. M. Clark, 'When culture meets power: the Prussian coronation of 1701', in *Cultures of Power in Europe during the Long Eighteenth Century*, eds. H. Scott and B. Simms (Cambridge, 2007), 17.
12. V. Bauer, *Die höfische Gesellschaft in Deutschland von der Mitte des 17. bis ẓum Ausgang des 18. Jahrhunderts: Versuch einer Typologie* (Tübingen, 1993), 69.

13. *Les lettres de Catherine II au Prince de Ligne (1780–1796)* (Brussels and Paris, 1924), 104, 2 Dec. 1788.

14. Grimm, 51, 29 July 1776; Bil'basov, I: 5–6.

15. C. Scharf, *Katharina II.: Deutschland und die Deutschen* (Mainz, 1995), 66–7; *Sochineniia*, XII: 223.

16. *Sochineniia*, XII: (6), 11; Scharf, *Katharina II*, 87–90.

17. M. Fulbrook, *Piety and politics: Religion and the rise of absolutism in England, Württemberg and Prussia* (Cambridge, 1983), 9, 167; C. Hinrichs, *Preußentum und Pietismus in Brandenburg-Preußen als religiös-soziale Reformbewegung* (Göttingen, 1971), 148.

18. *Sochineniia*, XII: 9.

19. Grimm, 88, 16 May 1778.

20. Fulbrook, *Piety and Politics*, 31; *Sochineniia*, XII: 10.

21. *Sochineniia*, XII: 6, 11.

22. *Sochineniia*, XII: 17; M. Greenleaf, 'Performing Autobiography: The Multiple Memoirs of Catherine the Great (1756–96)', *Russian Review*, 63 (2004), 411–3.

23. *Sochineniia*, 8–9, (15).

24. Lopatin, 14, C. to Potëmkin, undated.

25. Grimm, 41, 20 Jan. 1776.

26. Grimm, 361, 22 Aug. 1785; O. I. Eliseeva, *Perepiska Ekateriny II i G. A. Potemkina perioda vtoroi Russko-Turetskoi voiny (1787–1791): Istochnikovedcheskoe issledovanie* (M, 1997), 23.

27. Grimm, 212, 8 July 1781.

28. *Sochineniia*, XII: 19, 6–7. Here C. says her distress was caused by an emotional heroine, whereas in an earlier memoir (p. 441), dating from 1756, she attributes it to a battle scene.

29. Scharf, *Katharina II.*, 69.

30. *Sochineniia*, XII: 442.

31. *The Memoirs of Charles-Lewis, Baron de Pollnitz*, 5 vols. (Dublin, 1738), I: 80.

32. H. Reuther, 'Das Gebäude der Herzog August Bibliothek zu Wolfenbüttel und ihr Oberbibliothekar Gottfried Wilhelm Leibniz', in *Leibniz: sein Leben, sein Wirken, seine Welt*, eds. W. Totok and C. Haase (Hanover, 1966), 349–60.

33. P. Albrecht, et al, *Hermann Korb und seine Zeit: Barockes Bauen in Fürstentum Braunschweig-Wolfenbüttel* (Brunswick, 2006), esp. 112–4; H.-H. Grote, *Schloss Wolfenbüttel: Residenz der Herzögen zu Braunschweig und Lüneberg* (Brunswick, 2005).

34. E. Vehse, *Geschichte der Höfe des Hauses Braunschweig in Deutschland und England*, 5 vols. (Hamburg, 1853), V: 227–60.

35. Bauer, *Die höfische Gesellschaft*, 75.

36. *Sochineniia*, XII: 12–14. In an earlier memoir (p. 442), she claimed to have spent two months of the year in Brunswick.

37. A. Fauchier-Magnan, *The Small German Courts in the Eighteenth Century*, trans. M. Savill (London, 1958), 27.

38. Ibid., 43, 46, 48, 145, 37 and *passim*.

39. J. A. Vann, *The Making of a State: Württemberg, 1593–1793* (Ithaca, NY, 1984), 190.

40. R. Wilkinson, *Louis XIV* (London, 2007), 102.

41. H. Watanabe O'Kelly, *Court Culture in Dresden: From Renaissance to Baroque* (Basingstoke, 2002), 205. See also the magnificent catalogue, *Eine gute Figur machen: Kostüm und Fest am Dresdner Hof*, eds. C. Schnitzer and P. Hölscher (Dresden, 2000).

42. Vann, *Making of a State*, 259.

43. The indispensable work is J. Habermas, *The Structural Transformation of the Public Sphere*, trans. T. Burger (Cambridge, 1989).

44. P. Burke, *The Fabrication of Louis XIV* (New Haven, 1992), 17–18.

45. T. C. W. Blanning, *The Power of Culture and the Culture of Power* (Oxford, 2002), 59, is the essential historical commentary on Habermas (see note 43, above).

46. *Sochineniia*, XII: 24.

47. C. Wolff, *Johann Sebastian Bach: The Learned Musician* (Oxford, 2000), 187–235.

48. M. Umbach, 'Visual Culture, Scientific Images and German Small-State Politics in the Late Enlightenment', *Past and Present*, 158 (1998), 110–45.

49. H. Dauer, *Schloßbaukunst des Barock von Anhalt-Zerbst* (Cologne, 1999), 36–95; A. Erdmuter, et al, *Anhaltische Schlösser in Geschichte und Kunst* (Bindlach, 1994), 88–90.

50. J. Duindam, *Vienna and Versailles: The Courts of Europe's Dynastic Rivals, 1550–1780* (Cambridge, 2003); S. J. Klingensmith, *The Utility of Splendor: Ceremony, Social Life, and Architecture at the Court of Bavaria, 1600–1800* (Chicago, 1993).

51. Bauer, *Die höfische Gesellschaft*, 90–1, attempts tabular comparisons of the major German Courts.

52. A rich cosmopolitan literature can be reached via *Princes, Patronage, and the Nobility: The Court at the Beginning of the Modern Age c. 1450–1650*, eds. R. G. Asch and A. M. Birke (Oxford, 1991), and Adamson, 'Making of the ancien-régime Court', 7–41. See also H. Smith, 'Court Studies and the Courts of Early Modern Europe', *Historical Journal*, 49, 4 (2006), 1229–38.

53. *Sochineniia*, XII: 18; Dauer, *Schloßbaukunst*, 243–50.

54. *Sochineniia*, XII: 26.

55. *Sochineniia*, XII: 22–3, 443.

56. *Sochineniia*, XII: 17–18.

57. Madariaga, 2–4; Bil'basov, I: 13–22, 30–7.

58. *Sochineniia*, XII: 30; ibid., 443, gives 6 Jan.

59. *PCFG*, II: 494–5, Frederick to Johanna Elisabeth, 30 Dec. 1743.

60. Beales, *Joseph II*, 69–82 (72).

61. Poroshin, 47, 12 Oct. 1764.

62. M. Bregnsbo, 'Danish Absolutism and Queenship: Louisa, Caroline, Matilda, and Juliana Maria', in *Queenship in Europe: The Role of the Consort 1660–1815*, ed. C. Campell Orr (Cambridge, 2004), 354–5, 357–9.

63. C. C. Noel, '"Bárbara succeeds Elizabeth ...": The feminisation and domestication of politics in the Spanish Monarchy, 1701–1759', in *Queenship*, ed. Campbell Orr, 155–85.

64. T. Biskup, 'The Hidden Queen: Elisabeth Christine of Prussia and Hohenzollern Queenship in the Eighteenth Century', in *Queenship*, ed. Campbell Orr, 306–9, 313, 315.

65. *Sochineniia*, XII: 446.

66. Bil'basov, I: 45–6.

67. D. Blackbourn, *The conquest of nature: Water, landscape and the making of modern Germany* (London, 2006), 22–70 (30).

68. *Sochineniia*, XII: 446.

69. *SIRIO*, VII: 1–2.

70. Edward Finch, quoted in J. Black, *The British Abroad: The Grand Tour in the Eighteenth Century* (Stroud, 2003 edn), 68.

71. *Sochineniia*, XII: 35; R. J. M. Olson and J. M. Pasachoff, *Fire in the Sky: Comets and Meteors, the Decisive Centuries, in British Art and Science* (Cambridge, 1998), 49–51.

72. 'A Letter from the Rev. Mr. Joseph Betts M.A. and Fellow of University College Oxon. To Martin Folkes, Esq.', *Philosophical Transactions of the Royal Society, 1683–1775*, XLIII: 94. See also G. Smith, *A Treatise of Comets* (London, 1744), and Smith's letter in *The Gentleman's Magazine*, XIV: 86, 14 Feb. 1744.

73. S. Schaffer, 'Comets and the world's end', in *Predicting the Future*, eds. L. Howe and A. Wain (Cambridge, 1993), 52–76; Ryan, *Bathhouse at Midnight*, 374–5.

74. *Correspondance*, 1756. The comet of 1757 prompted [F. Aepinus], 'Razmyshleniia o vozvrate komet, s kratkim izvestiem o nyne iavivsheisia komete', *Ezhemesiachniaia sochineniia* (Oct. 1757), 329–48.

75. Poroshin, 265, 29 Aug. 1765.

76. *SIRIO*, VII: 15.

77. *Sochineniia*, XII: 36–7; *SIRIO*, VII: 16–17.

78. E. C. Thaden, *Russia's Western Borderlands, 1710–1870* (Princeton, NJ, 1984), 5, n. 1; *Sochineniia*, XII: 37.

Chapter 2

1. R. Milner-Gulland, '16 May 1703: The Petersburg Foundation-Myth', in *Days from the reigns of eighteenth-century Russian rulers*, ed. A. Cross (Cambridge, SGECRN, 2007), I: 37–48.

2. Quoted in A. M. Wilson, *Diderot* (New York, 1972), 645.

3. J. Cracraft, *The Petrine Revolution in Russian Architecture* (Chicago, IL, 1988), 175–9.

4. F. C. Weber, *The Present State of Russia*, 2 vols. (London, 1723), I: 297–8.

5. V. Berelowitch, 'Europe ou Asie? Saint-Pétersbourg dans les relations de voyage occidentaux', in *Le Mirage russe au XVIIIe siècle*, eds. S. Karp and L. Wolff (Ferney-Voltaire, 2001), 62–7, esp. p. 66.

6. L. Hughes, *Russia in the Age of Peter the Great* (New Haven, CT, 1998), 211–2.

7. *Sochineniia*, XII: 79; A. G. Cross, 'The English Embankment', in *St Petersburg, 1703–1825*, ed. Cross (Basingstoke, 2003), 65.

8. I. S. B., 'K istorii postroiki S.-Peterburgskago Troitskago Sobora', *RS*, Nov. 1911, 426.

9. Iu. N. Bespiatykh, *Peterburg Anny Ioannovny v inostrannykh opisaniiakh* (SPb, 1997), 175.

10. M. di Salvo, 'A Venice of the North? Italian Views of St Petersburg', in *St Petersburg*, ed. Cross, 73–4.

11. *Letters from Count Algarotti to Lord Harvey and the Marquis Scipio Maffei* (Glasgow, 1770), 50.

12. J. Cook, *Voyages and Travels through the Russian Empire, Tartary, and Part of the Kingdom of Persia*, 2 vols. (Edinburgh 1770), I: 96–7.

13. The incident led to a general preoccupation with fire: see *PSZ*, X: 7270, 7275, 7290, 7295.

14. Bespiatykh, *Peterburg Anny Ioannovny*, 72, n. 22.

15. W. B. Lincoln, *Sunlight at Midnight: St Petersburg and the Rise of Modern Russia* (Oxford, 2001), 33–4.

16. M. V. Lomonosov, *Polnoe sobranie sochinenii*, 9 vols. (M, 1950–55).

17. G. Kaganov, *Images of Space: St. Petersburg in the Visual and Verbal Arts*, trans. S. Monas (Stanford, CA, 1997), 19–22, 26–8.

18. Lincoln, *Sunlight at Midnight*, 38.

19. G. Z. Kaganov, *Peterburg v kontekste barokko* (SPb, 2002).

20. *SIRIO*, VII: 20.

21. Cook, *Voyages and Travels*, I: 446–8.

22. *Sochineniia*, XII: 37–8.

23. For the premises on the Fontanka, extended in 1741, see *Vnutrennii byt Russkago gosudarstva s 17 oktiabria 1740 goda po 25-e noiabria 1741 goda* (M, 1880), I: 326–41. Anna decreed an annual fodder budget of 2369r. 71k. on 6 July 1737 (p. 327).

24. *Sochineniia*, XII: 118; A. Orloff and D. Shvidkovsky, *St Petersburg: Architecture of the Tsars* (New York, 1996), 266–7.

25. Storch, 68–9.

26. I. Iakovkin, *Opisanie sela tsarskago* (SPb, 1830), 118–9; *KfZh* (1795), 175, 10 Feb.; appendix II: 121, 132 (grants of 200 and 947 roubles for the residents of the Okhta district). Storch, 419–20, suggests that by then, the well-born had largely abandoned the pastime as too dangerous. The location of earlier ice hills is unknown.

27. *KfZh* (1744), 3–6.

28. *PSZ*, XII: 8851, 9 Jan. 1744.

29. *SIRIO*, VII: 22–3; *Sochineniia*, XII: 39; E. A. Zitser, *The Transfigured Kingdom: Sacred Parody and Charismatic Authority at the Court of Peter the Great* (Ithaca, NY, 2004), 52–5.

30. Coxe, I: 269–70 (visiting in 1778).

31. *PSZ*, XII: 8882, 29 Feb. 1744.

32. O. S. Evangulova, *Dvortsovo-parkovye ansambli Moskvy: pervoi poloviny XVIII veka* (M, 1969), 44–84, 12–24.

33. *SIRIO*, VII: 25; *Sochineniia*, XII: 40.

34. *Sochineniia*, XII: 530.

35. *SIRIO*, VII: 25–7.

36. *Sochineniia*, XII: 41.

37. E. V. Anisimov, *Rossiia v seredine XVIII veka: Bor'ba za nasledie Petra* (M, 1986), 183–6; *idem*, *Elizaveta Petrovna* (M, 1999), 189–204 (192, Saxon envoy).

38. G. Marker, *Imperial Saint: The Cult of St. Catherine and the Dawn of Female Rule in Russia* (DeKalb, IL, 2007), 140.

39. *Despatches*, II: 223, Buckinghamshire to Countess of Suffolk, 14 Feb. 1763.

40. *Sochineniia*, XII: 42. *KfZh* (1744), 7–11, gives 3–8 Mar. as the dates of the pilgrimage. The dates given in C's memoirs are notoriously unreliable.

41. D. Willemse, *Antonio Nunes Ribeiro Sanches, elève de Boerhaave, et son importance pour la Russie* (Leiden, 1966).

42. *Sochineniia*, XII: (43), 203–4; Bil'basov, I: 90–1; Alexander, 81.

43. *PCFG*, III: 94, Frederick to Johanna Elisabeth, 14 Apr. 1744 NS, and subsequent letters to his ambassador, Baron Mardefeld.

44. *KfZh* (1744), 34–6; Bil'basov, I: 95–7; *Sochineniia*, XII: 43, 95, 205.

45. Shortly after the dinner, General Johann-Ludwig Lübras von Pott, the newly appointed Russian ambassador to Sweden, demonstrated his allegiance by travelling to Stockholm via Potsdam, where he reassured Frederick that there was no prospect of another revolution in Russia: *Sochineniia*, XII: 37; *PCFG*, III: 200, Frederick to Mardefeld, 3 July 1744 NS.

46. *PCFG*, III: 48, Frederick to Johanna Elisabeth, 29 Feb. 1744 NS; ibid., 118, Frederick to Mardefeld, 1744.

47. *PCFG*, III: 169, Frederick to Mardefeld, 4 June 1744 NS; *Sochineniia*, XII: 46–8; Anisimov, *Rossiia v seredine XVIII veka*, 86–7, 95–6. For a detailed guide to the diplomacy of these years, see F.-D. Lishtenan, *Rossiia vkhodit v Evropu* (M, 2000).

48. P. I. Khoteev, *Kniga v Rossii v seredine XVIII v.: Chastnye knizhnye sobraniia* (Leningrad, 1989), 45–6.

49. Bil'basov, I: 113–9; *SIRIO*, VII: 4, C. to Christian August, 3 May 1744. In her memoirs, she claimed that Pastor Wagner had taught her that she was free to choose her confession until the time of her first communion: *Sochineniia*, XII: 45–6.

50. A. P. Sumarokov, 'O pravopisanie', in *Polnoe sobranie vsekh sochinenii*, 2nd ed. (M, 1787), X: 24.

51. *Sochineniia*, XII: 48–9. On Adodurov, see A. M. Panchenko, et al, *Slovar' russkikh pisatelei XVIII veka* (Leningrad, 1988), vol. I (A-I), 21–3.

52. Bil'basov, I: 58, n. 1; *PCFG*, II: 488, Frederick to Mardefeld, 16 Dec. 1743 NS.

53. *KfZh* (1744), 56–9; *Sochineniia*, XII: 49; Bil'basov, I: 119–21.

54. Bil'basov, I: 121–4.

55. *KfZh* (1744), 59–67.

56. *PCFG*, III: 239, Frederick to C., 5 Aug. 1744 NS.

57. For the peace celebrations on 15–17 July, see *KfZh* (1744), 69–86.

58. On mileposts, *PSZ*, XII: 9016, 16 Aug. 1744; 9073, 27 Nov.; 9092, 17 Dec.

59. *Sochineniia*, XII: 53–4.

60. M. Berlinskii, *Kratkoe opisanie Kieva* (SPb, 1820), 39–41.

61. *Sochineniia*, XII: 53. C. was then developing an interest in the Gothic, which here seems to mean simply 'medieval'.

62. *Sochineniia*, XII: 55–6.

63. For its construction, see Starikova, doc. 519, pp. 551–86.

64. The phrase 'theatres of piety' is John Adamson's: see 'Making of the ancien-regime Court', in *Princely Courts of Europe*, ed. Adamson, 24–7.

65. S. Dixon, 'Religious Ritual at the Russian Court', in *Monarchy and Religion: The Transformation of Royal Culture in Eighteenth-Century Europe*, ed. M. Schaich (Oxford, 2007), 229–30.

66. *KfZh* (1744), 91–3, 103–12.

67. On 15 Dec.: *KfZh* (1744), 24.

68. Bespiatykh, *Peterburg Anny Ioannovny*, 140 (C. R. Berch).

69. Starikova, doc. 265 (servants' accommodation); docs 970–6 (merry-go-round).

70. *Sochineniia*, XII: 214

71. *KfZh* (1745), I, 153–4.

72. Bil'basov, I: 145, n. 2; *Sochineniia*, XII: 213 (216).

73. *KfZh* (1745), 2–10.

74. P. Keenan, 'Creating a "public" in St Petersburg, 1703–1761', unpublished Ph.D. thesis, University of London, 2005, 107–9.

75. *KfZh* (1744), I and *passim*, refers to him throughout as Prince August.

76. *Sochineniia*, XII: 218; Keenan, 'Creating a "public"', 108.

77. For French celebrations, see e.g. the earlier *Description des festes données par la ville de Paris: à l'occasion du mariage de madame Louise-Elisabeth de France, de dom Philippe, infant & grand amiral d'Espagne, les vingt-neuviéme & trentiéme août mil sept cent trente-neuf* (Paris, 1740).

78. Starikova, doc. 754.

79. *PSZ*, XII: 9123–4, 16 Mar. 1745.

80. *Sochineniia*, XII: 227, 63, 67.

81. *KfZh* (1745), 27 (9 May); 29–32.

82. *KfZh* (1745), 39–42 (39); 43.

83. *KfZh* (1745), 36–7.

84. See, in particular, *PSZ*, XII: 9136–40; 9144–7; 9149; 9154–6; 9174.

85. Bil´basov, I: 164, n. 1, 166, 168.
86. *KfZh* (1745), 187, 51.
87. *KfZh* (1745), 51; *SIRIO*, CII: 320, Hyndford to Harrington, 20 Aug. 1745.
88. Bil´basov, I: 167–70.
89. *Sochineniia*, XII: 67.
90. *Sochineniia*, XII: 68.
91. My account of the wedding celebrations relies on *KfZh* (1745), 52–92 (52–60), and on Santi's order of ceremonies, ibid., 187–222 (195).
92. Poroshin, 24, 1 Oct. 1764. Naryshkin's empty landau was between Prince Aleksei Golitsyn and Count Efim Raguzinskii in the procession; Panin's carriage, also empty, was further forward: *KfZh* (1745), 55. See 194, 223–9, for an indicative list of the empty carriages.
93. L. Kirillova, *Moskovskii Kreml': Starinnye ekipazhi* (M, 1999), 10, 17 and *passim*.
94. *SIRIO*, VII: 50–2. See also *KfZh* (1745), 200.
95. *KfZh* (1745), 193.
96. *SIRIO*, CII: 321, Hyndford to Harrington, 24 Aug. 1745.
97. Chudinova, *Penie*, 33; *KfZh* (1737), 22–3, 32; victory days listed at *PSZ*, IX: 6832, 29 Oct. 1735.
98. *KfZh* (1745), 187–8.
99. *SIRIO*, VII: 53–4; *Sochineniia*, XII: 68; Bil´basov, I: 171–2.
100. *KfZh* (1745), 62; *Sochineniia*, XII: 69.
101. *KfZh* (1745), 64–70.
102. Quoted by N. V. Sipovskaia, 'Obedy "k sluchaiu": Nastol´nye ukrasheniia XVIII veka', in *Razvlekatel'naia kul'tura Rossii XVIII–XIX vv.*, ed. E. V. Dukov (SPb, 2000), 161–2. *KfZh* (1745), 69, claimed 10,000 candles.
103. *SIRIO*, VII: 64; *KfZh* (1745), 77–8, 80; *Sochineniia*, XII: 73–4.
104. S. Sadie, ed., *The New Grove Dictionary of Opera* (London, 1992), IV: 269–70; *MP*, I: 144–6 (Bonecchi); Starikova, doc. 32 (programme and synopsis); Mooser, I: 219–20; *KfZh* (1745), 75.
105. *Zapiski Shtelina*, I: 248; Rovinskii, *Obozrenie ikonopisaniia*, 237–8.
106. The impressive analysis of C's approach to sexuality in Greenleaf, 'Performing Autobiography' may well exaggerate the empress's literary sophistication.
107. *Sochineniia*, XII: 66.
108. *Sochineniia*, XII: 69.
109. *Sochineniia*, XII: 80, 82.
110. G. V. Kalashnikov, 'Zametki ob obrazovanii budushchego imperatora Petra III', *Arkheograficheskii ezhegodnik za 2003 goda* (M, 2004), 131–48 (135).
111. Rulhière, 19–20.
112. *Sochineniia*, XII: 199.
113. O. A. Ivanov, *Ekaterina II i Petr III: istoriia tragicheskogo konflikta* (M, 2007), more inclined to take C.'s memoirs at face value, offers an exhaustive comparison of the passages on Peter.
114. Kalashnikov, 'Zametki', 144.
115. Shtelin, *Zapiski*, 74–5, 79.

Chapter 3

1. *Sochineniia*, XII: 236.
2. Bil´basov, I: 219–22, 227–8.
3. P. F. Karabanov, 'Stats-damy i freiliny russkago dvora XVIII v.', *RS*, 2 (1870), 445–6.
4. *Sochineniia*, XII: 84–5, 89, 91.

5. *Sochineniia*, XII: 245.

6. *Sochineniia*, XII: 245–6.

7. *Sochineniia*, XII: 243–4.

8. *Sochineniia*, XII: 27.

9. *Sochineniia*, XII: 215, 60–1.

10. *Sochineniia*, XII: 329.

11. Khoteev, *Kniga v Rossii v seredine XVIII v.*, 7–9.

12. *Sochineniia*, XII: 532.

13. J. Hardman, *Louis XVI* (New Haven, CT, 1993), vii.

14. *PSZ*, XII: 9276, 10 Apr. 1746; N. Rozanov, *Istoriia Moskovskago Eparkhial'nago Upravleniia so vremeni uchrezhdenii Sv. Sinoda, 1721–1821* (M, 1869), II: 1, 153, 159, n. 370.

15. *PSZ*, XII: 9286, 15 May 1746; XIII: 9860, 11 June 1751.

16. J. McManners, *Death and the Enlightenment* (Oxford, 1981), 302.

17. *Sochineniia*, XII: 232–5.

18. P. Salvadori, *La chasse sous l'ancien régime* (Paris, 1996), 207; Kutepov, *Tsarskaia okhota*, 30.

19. Kutepov, *Tsarskaia okhota*, 64; *KfZh* (1751), 92–5; *PSZ*, XIII: 9903, 3 Nov. 1751.

20. *Sochineniia*, XII: 117.

21. Wortman, *Scenarios*, 107.

22. *AKV*, XXXIV: appendix, n.p, undated. A flask (*shtof*) measured 1.23 litres.

23. Mrs Vigor, *Letters from a lady, who resided some years in Russia, to her friend in England* (London, 1775), 73. See also Bespiatykh, *Peterburg Anny Ioannovny*, 145 (C. R. Berch).

24. C. von Manstein, *Memoirs of Russia, historical, political and military, from the year M DCC XXVII, to M DCC XLIV* (London, 1770), 248.

25. S. Panchulidzev, *Istoriia Kavalergardov 1724–1799–1899*, 4 vols. (SPb, 1899), I: 254–68, at p. 260.

26. Decree of 5 May 1758, quoted in N. Findeizen, *History of Music in Russia from Antiquity to 1800, 2: The Eighteenth Century*, trans. S. W. Pring, eds. M. Velimirovií and C. R. Jensen (Bloomington, IN, 2008), 30.

27. *SIRIO*, CIII: 552, Hyndford to Chesterfield, 23 Feb. 1748.

28. Anisimov, *Elizaveta Petrovna*, 132–3, notes a tradition dating back to the empress's contemporaries.

29. C. Koslofsky, 'Princes of Darkness: The Night at Court, 1650–1750', *Journal of Modern History*, 79, 2 (2007), 236, 244, 251ff., 258ff.

30. See Zitser, *Transfigured Kingdom*, passim.

31. Hughes, *Russia in the Age of Peter the Great*, 267–9; P. Keenan, 'The Function of Fashion: Women and Clothing at the Russian Court (1700–1762)', in *Women in Russian Culture and Society, 1700–1825*, eds. W. Rosslyn and A. Tosi (Basingstoke, 2007), 127–9.

32. Manstein, *Memoirs*, 319.

33. Manstein, *Memoirs*, 248–9.

34. Vigor, *Letters*, 75.

35. Keenan, 'The Function of Fashion', 132–3.

36. Bil'basov, I: 166, n. 2.

37. C. M. Foust, *Muscovite and Mandarin: Russia's trade with China and its setting, 1727–1805* (Chapel Hill, NC, 1969), 105–63 (esp. 139–41), 357; 'Kitaiskie tovary v Rossii XVIII v.', *Istoricheskii arkhiv*, 2006:4, 197–200.

38. *SIRIO*, CXLVIII: 104, Guy Dickens to Newcastle, 17/28 July 1750.

39. P. Mansel, *Dressed to Rule: Royal and Court Costume from Louis XIV to Elizabeth II* (New Haven, CT, 2005), xiii–xiv and *passim*.

40. *Sbornik Biografii Kavalergardov 1724–1762*, ed. S. Panchulidzev (SPb, 1901), 342 (I. I. Babaev); Benois, *Tsarskoe Selo*, 31.

41. Manstein, *Memoirs*, 248.

42. *Sochineniia*, XII: 211; *Russkii pridvornyi kostium ot Petra I do Nikolaia II iz sobraniia Gosudarstvennogo Ermitazha Sankt-Peterburg* (M, 1999), 28–31.

43. N. Iu. Bolotina, 'Zhenshchiny roda Vorontsovykh v povsednevnoi zhizni imperatorskogo dvora XVIII v.', in *E.R. Dashkova i zolotoi vek Ekateriny*, ed. L. Tychinina (M, 2006), 142, 150–3.

44. *Sochineniia*, XII: 301, 211–2, 252–4.

45. For comparisons, see Duindam, *Vienna and Versailles*, ch. 3.

46. *KfZh* (1748), suppl., 120–32, 149 (these figures are almost certainly underestimates); K. Pisarenko, *Povsednevnaia zhizn' russkogo dvora v tsarstvovanie Elizavety Petrovny* (M, 2003), 47–64, esp. 49, 59–60. On titles, see O. G. Ageeva, *Evropeizatsiia russkogo dvora 1700–1796 gg.* (M, 2006), 81–96.

47. C. de Wassenaer, *A Visit to St Petersburg, 1824–1825*, trans. and ed. I. Vinogradoff (Norwich, 1994), 58.

48. *KfZh* (1748), suppl., 140–9.

49. S. M. Troitskii, *Finansovaia politika russkogo absoliutizma v XVIII veke* (M, 1966), 246; *PSZ*, XIII: 9757, 2 June 1750.

50. *KfZh* (1748), suppl., 106–8.

51. Blanning, *Power of Culture*, 59, 32.

52. Benois, *Tsarskoe Selo*, 65–6, 68.

53. *Puteshestvie brat'ev Demidovykh po Evrope: Pis'ma i podnevnye Zhurnaly 1750–1761 gody*, ed. G. A. Pobedimova (M, 2006), 101.

54. N. W. Wraxall, *Memoirs of the Courts of Berlin, Dresden, Warsaw and Vienna in the years 1777, 1778 and 1779*, 2 vols. (London, 1806), II: 213.

55. Benois, *Tsarskoe Selo*, 104–5.

56. A. I. Uspenskii, *Imperatorskie dvortsy*, I: 34, *Zapiski Imperatorskago Moskovskago Arkhaeologicheskago Instituta*, XXIII (M, 1913).

57. I. Reyfman, *Vasilii Trediakovsky: The fool of the 'new' Russian literature* (Stanford, CA, 1990), 239.

58. Marker, *Imperial Saint*, 216–8 and *passim*.

59. Quoted in Anisimov, *Rossiia bez Petra*, 73.

60. Mooser, I: 247.

61. Quoted in K. Ospovat, 'Towards a cultural history of the Court of Elizaveta Petrovna', *SGECRN*, 35 (2007), 38.

62. S. W. Mintz, *Sweetness and power: The place of sugar in modern history* (Harmondsworth, 1986), 88–94.

63. Sipovskaia, 'Obedy', 161.

64. Starikova, doc. 936; N. Kazakevich, *Tsarskie zastol'ia v XVIII veke: Tseremonial i dekorativnoe oformlenie paradnykh stolov pri dvore imperatrits Elizavety i Ekateriny II* (SPb, 2003), 22–4.

65. E.g., *KfZh* (1753), 27, C.'s birthday; 74, Elizabeth's birthday.

66. P. Stolpianskii, 'V starom Peterburge: Banketnye stoly', *Starye gody*, Mar. 1913, 28–32.

67. *KfZh* (1745), Zhurnal banketnyi, 19; *KfZh* (1748), 14–15, 32–3; Iu. Denisov and A. Petrov, *Zodchii Rastrelli* (Leningrad, 1973), 148–9, 187–8; *Zapiski Vasiliia Aleksandrovicha Nashchokina* (SPb, 1842), 101.

68. Starikova, doc.; Mooser, I: 221; *KfZh* (1746), 11.

69. *AKV*, II: 109.

70. G. M. Zelenskaia, *Novyi ierusalim: putevoditel'* (M, 2003), 44–51.

71. *PSZ*, XIII: 9646, 10 July 1749; 9803, 3 Oct. 1750.

72. Shtelin, *Muzyka*, 54–5, para. 6.

73. *Sochineniia*, XII: 265, 150.

74. *KfZh* (1752), 5–6.

75. *KfZh* (1757), 68.

76. E. I. Indova, *Dvortsovoe khoziaistvo v Rossii: Pervaia polovina XVIII veka*, (M, 1964), 202–15, *passim*. For fruit from Astrakhan, see PSZ, XII: 8997, 20 July 1744; 9186, 8 July 1745.

77. E. Justice, *A Voyage to Russia* (York, 1739), 16.

78. Pisarenko, *Povsednevnaia zhizn'*, 515–20; the list probably dates from 1747. For information relating to 1740–1, see *Vnutrennii byt Russkago gosudarstva*, I: 366–402.

79. Bespiatykh, *Peterburg Anny Ioannovny*, 141 (C. R. Berch).

80. *PSZ*, XII: 9161, 27 May 1745; N. I. Batorevich, *Ekateringof: Istoriia dvortsovo-parkovogo ansamblia* (SPb, 2006), 83–9.

81. Benois, *Tsarskoe Selo*, 76–7.

82. *Sochineniia*, XII: 117.

83. I. Vinogradoff, 'Russian Missions to London, 1711–1789: Further Extracts from the Cottrell Papers', *Oxford Slavonic Papers*, NS 15 (1982), 71, C. to R. Cottrell, 1741.

84. *Sochineniia*, XII: 254–7.

85. Iu. Ovsiannikov, *Franchesko Bartolomeo Rastrelli* (Leningrad, 1982), 74.

86. *Sochineniia*, XII: 320.

87. A. A. Kedrintsev, 'Iantarnyi zal v Sankt-Peterburge', in I. P. Sautov, et al, *Iantarnaia komnata: Tri veka istorii* (SPb, 2003), 110–6. The Amber Room was later transferred to Tsarskoe Selo.

88. *Sochineniia*, XII: 241, 291.

89. *Sochineniia*, XII: 181.

90. *Sochineniia*, XII: 183.

91. B. Kemp, 'Sir Francis Dashwood's Diary of his Visit to St Petersburg in 1733', *SEER*, 38 (1959–60), 201.

92. *PSZ*, XI: 8820, 16 Nov. 1743; *Sochineniia*, XII: 106.

93. S. B. Gorbatenko, *Petergofskaia doroga: Oranienbaumskii istoriko-landshaftnyi kompleks* (SPb, 2001), 194; *Sochineniia*, XII: 92–3; 244–5.

94. Gorbatenko, *Petergofskaia doroga*, 197, 199; *Sochineniia*, XII: 127.

95. *SIRIO*, CLXVIII: 111, Guy Dickens to Newcastle, 29 July 1750.

96. *Sochineniia*, XII: 157.

97. *Sochineniia*, XII: 273.

98. *Sochineniia*, XII: 293–4.

99. R. Dimsdale, '20 October 1768: Doctor Dimsdale Spends a Day with the Empress', in *Days from the Reigns*, ed. Cross, II: 190.

100. *Sochineniia*, XII: 260–1.

101. *Sochineniia*, XII: 296.

102. *KfZh* (1751), 4–15.

103. *Sochineniia*, XII: 309, 313–5 (315).
104. *Sochineniia*, XII: 325.
105. *KfZh* (1753), 93; *PSZ*, XIII: 10,103, 27 May 1753.
106. *KfZh* (1753), 65–6; *Sochineniia*, XII: 328–30; *SIRIO*, CXLVIII: 519–20, Guy Dickens to Newcastle, 4/15 Nov. 1753.
107. *AKV*, XXXIII: 466–9, 'O pozhare moskovskago dvortsa'.
108. A. Mikhailov, *Arkhitektor D.V. Ukhtomskii: Ego shkola* (M, 1954), 171–3.
109. *SIRIO*, CXLVIII: 542, Guy Dickens to Newcastle, 20/31 Dec. 1753.
110. *KfZh* (1753), 74–5; *AKV*, V, 17.
111. *Sochineniia*, XII: 329, 332, 324.
112. *Sochineniia*, XII: 336–7.
113. *Sochineniia*, XII: 338–9.

Chapter 4

1. *Walpole Correspondence*, XX: 457–8, Sir H. Mann to Walpole, 13 Dec. 1754 NS.
2. Rovinskii, *Obozrenie ikonopisaniia*, 244–6.
3. *KfZh* (1754), 121–4.
4. *Sochineniia*, XII: 341–7 (341, 345); *KfZh* (1754), 78–9; McGrew, 29–31.
5. R. Butterwick, *Poland's Last King and English Culture: Stanisław August Poniatowski 1732–1798* (Oxford, 1998), 86–100; A. Zamoyski, *The Last King of Poland* (London, 1992), 41–53.
6. Quoted *in extenso* by Zamoyski, *Last King*, 58.
7. *KfZh* (1755), 68–70: 77 men and 44 women were present.
8. V. A. Korentsvit, 'Krepost' Peterstadt v Oranienbaume', in *Pamiatniki istorii i kul'tury Peterburga*, ed. A. V. Pozdnukhov (SPb, 1994), 208–22.
9. *Sochineniia*, XII: 307, 355–6.
10. *AKV*, XXXIII: 83, M. L. Vorontsov to F. D. Bekhteev, 15 June 1756.
11. Uspenskii, *Imperatorskie dvortsy*, I: 38–9, 41; *PSZ*: 10,246, 16 June 1754.
12. *Sochineniia*, XII: 117; Benois, *Tsarskoe Selo*, 78.
13. *AKV*, XXXI: 86, M. L. to A. R. Vorontsov, 19 Dec. 1758.
14. A. N. Petrov, *Savva Chevakinskii* (Leningrad, 1983), 72, 75–6, 79.
15. Iu. V. Trubinov, *Stroganovskii dvorets* (SPb, 1996), 38–61.
16. Shcherbatov, 223, 225.
17. A. V. Dëmkin, *Britanskoe kupechestvo v Rossii XVIII veka* (M, 1998), 70.
18. Sipovskaia, 'Obedy', 162–3.
19. *AKV*, XXXI: 83, M. L. Vorontsov to M. P. Bestuzhev-Riumin, Feb 1758; 101, M. L. to A. R. Vorontsov, undated (Jan/Feb 1760); 105, 4/15 Apr. 1760; 110, 24 Oct. 1760.
20. *Sochineniia*, XII: 391–2.
21. *Correspondance*, 70, 23 Aug. 1756; 81, 24 Aug.
22. *AKV*, XXXIII: 32–48. By the same token, no account was taken of Vorontsov's artistic expenses, for which see S. O. Androsov, 'Zabytyi russkii metsenat – Graf Mikhail Vorontsov', *PKNO*, 2000 (M, 2001), 246–77.
23. *SIRIO*, CLXVIII: 466, Guy Dickens to Newcastle, 7 July 1753.
24. [J-L Favier], 'Russkii dvor v 1761 godu', *RS*, Oct. 1878.
25. Cross, 55–8; Dëmkin, *Britanskoe kupechestvo*, 128–35.
26. Kazakevich, *Tsarskie zastol'ia*, 24.

27. *AKV*, XXXIII: 50, 'Zapiska prikhodu i raskhodu den 'gam na 1754 god'; XXXII: 19, M. L. Vorontsov to I. I. Shuvalov, 27 Oct. 1756.

28. *Correspondance*, 82, 24 Aug. 1756.

29. *Correspondance*, 55, 20 Aug. 1756. See also, p. 74, 23 Aug. (cf. 124, 6 Sept.)

30. *Correspondance*, 197, 6 Oct. 1756.

31. *Correspondance*, 255, undated, Nov. 1756.

32. *SIRIO*, VII: 73, C. to Wolff, 11 Nov. 1756.

33. *Correspondance*, 272, 17 Nov. 1756.

34. *SIRIO*, CXLVIII: 118, Guy Dickens to Newcastle, 8 Sept. 1750.

35. *SIRIO*, CXLVIII: 113, Guy Dickens to Newcastle, 11 Aug. 1750.

36. Shcherbatov, 195.

37. C. Marsden, *Palmyra of the North: The First Days of St Petersburg* (London, 1942), 130.

38. *SIRIO*, CXLVIII: 321–2, 28 Jan. 1752; ibid., 332, 7 Mar., prompted by ibid., 309, Newcastle to Guy Dickens, 27 Dec. 1751 NS.

39. *Sochineniia*, XII: 266.

40. *SIRIO*, CX: 292–3, Hyndford to Newcastle, 2 Feb. 1749.

41. *Correspondance*, 121, 6 Sept; *KfZh* (1758), 112.

42. *KfZh* (1756), 51, 102; Benois, *Tsarskoe Selo*, 246–8.

43. *Correspondance*, 4, 3 Aug. 1756.

44. *Sochineniia*, XII: 227.

45. *Sochineniia*, XII: 224, 219, 225.

46. *PSZ*, XII: 8908, 3 Apr. 1744.

47. *SIRIO*, CXLVIII: 295, Guy Dickens to Newcastle, 26 Nov. 1751; *KfZh* (1751), 108–9.

48. *Sochineniia*, XII: 288–9.

49. *Sochineniia*, XII: 348.

50. *Correspondance*, 34, 11 Aug. 1756; 45, 18 Aug.

51. *Correspondance*, 145, 11 Sept. 1756.

52. Frotier de la Messelière, *Voyage à Pétersbourg, ou nouveaux mémoires sur la Russie* (Paris, 1803), 217–8, punctuation adjusted.

53. *Sochineniia*, XII: 393–5, where the event is misdated to 1758. The mistake recurs in A. L. Porfir 'eva, 'Muzykal 'nye razvlecheniia Petra Fedorovicha v Oranienbaume', in *Archivo Russo–Italiano*, IV, eds. Daniela Rizzi and A. Shishkin (Salerno, 2005), 340, and also in *The Memoirs of Catherine the Great*, eds. M. Cruse and H. Hoogenboom (New York, 2005), 178. Alexander, 51, gives 17 June 1757. The chronology of this period in C.'s memoirs is especially unreliable.

54. Zamoyski, *Last King*, 55.

55. Quoted in Alexander, 51.

56. *KfZh* (1757), 83.

57. J. L. H. Keep, 'Feeding the Troops: Russian Army Supply Policies during the Seven Years' War', *Canadian Slavonic Papers*, 28–31 (1987).

58. Bil basov, I: 332–46.

59. *PSZ*, XV: 10,940, 5 Apr. 1759, para. 5; *KfZh* (1759), 42; *Sochineniia*, XII: 407, 423; Alexander, 53–5.

60. *AKV*, XXXI: 88, M. L. to A. R. Vorontsov, 10 Mar. 1759; *PSZ*, XV: 10,930, 9 Mar. 1759.

Chapter 5

1. G. S. Rousseau, ' "A strange pathology": Hysteria in the Early Modern World', in S. L. Gilman, et al, *Hysteria beyond Freud* (Berkeley, 1993), 157; L. Brockliss and C. Jones, *The Medical World of Early Modern France* (Oxford, 1997), 444.

2. *AKV*, II: 633–6.

3. See E. V. Anisimov, 'I. I. Shuvalov–deiatel' rossiiskogo Prosveshcheniia', *Voprosy istorii*, 1985, no. 7, 94–104.

4. *KfZh* (1761), 7.

5. *KfZh* (1760), 175.

6. Alexander, 'Ivan Shuvalov', 8.

7. 'Russkii dvor', .

8. *AKV*, IV: 461, 20 Feb. 1761.

9. F.G. *Volkov i russkii teatr ego vremeni*, 138–43.

10. *KfZh* (1761), 22. The artist's name is not given.

11. *AKV*, IV: 461, 20 Feb. 1761; 462, 23 Feb.

12. Ia. V. Bruk, *U istokov russkogo zhanra: XVIII vek* (M, 1990), 45, pl. 53–5; *AKV*, XXXIV: 129.

13. Chappe d'Auteroche, *Voyage en Sibérie*, ed. M. Mervaud, II: 344–5, *SVEC*, 2004:04.

14. *KfZh* (1761), 3–4, 7, 10; *AKV*, XXI: 84.

15. *Zapiski Shtelina*, I: 261.

16. 'Dnevnik statskogo sovetnika Misere', in *Ekaterina: put' k vlasti*, eds. M. Lavrinovich and A. Liberman (M, 2003), 54.

17. *AKV*, IV: 464, 10 Apr. 1761, A. K. Vorontsova to her daughter, Anna Mikhailovna.

18. *AKV*, IV: 464–5, 17 Apr. 1761; *KfZh* (1761); Alexander, 'Ivan Shuvalov', 9.

19. *AKV*, IV: 465, 24 Apr. and 30 Apr. 1761.

20. *KfZh* (1761), 76, 94, 99, 102, 109, 122.

21. *Sochineniia*, XII: 785–6.

22. *Sochineniia*, XII: 613–27, *passim*.

23. Alexander, 55–7.

24. *KfZh* (1761), 79–80. For further fires see AKV, IV: 476, 6 July.

25. *AKV*, IV: 474, 15 June 1761.

26. Bil'basov, I: 418, n. 5, quoting the French ambassador Breteuil. Elizabeth had spent most of the week before at her devotions in her private chapel: *KfZh* (1761), 100–1.

27. *KfZh* (1761).

28. *AKV*: XXXI: 151, circular from M. L. Vorontsov, 19 Dec. 1761.

29. Shtelin, *Zapiski*, 97; *KfZh* (1762), 9–10.

30. For daily lists of their respective dining companions in Jan. and Feb., see *KfZh* (1762), 54–118, 1st pagn.

31. *KfZh* (1762), 3, 1st pagn.

32. *KfZh* (1762), 12, 1st pagn; *Sochineniia*, XII: 506–7.

33. Vinogradov, 'Russian Mission', 71. For Anna's funeral commission, see *Vnutrennii byt Russkago gosudarstva*, I: 431–94 (438–9).

34. Shtelin, *Zapiski*, 96; *KfZh* (1762), 6–7, 1st pagn; L. Hughes, 'Royal Funerals in Eighteenth-Century Russia', in *Monarchy and Religion*, ed. Schaich, 411–2.

35. *Sochineniia*, XII: 508, has misled generations of historians by giving 25 Jan. as the date of Elizabeth's funeral.

36. *KfZh* (1762), 16–17, 1st pagn.

37. Ya. P. Shakhovskoy, *Zapiski, 1709–1777*, ed. R. E. Jones (Newtonville, MA, 1974), iii, 183.
38. *Anecdotes russes, ou letters d'un officier allemand a un gentilhomme livonien, écrites de Pétersbourg en 1762* (London [The Hague], 1765), 32–4.
39. Bil'basov, I: 424.
40. 'Zapiski pridvornago bril'iantshchika Poz'e', *RS*, March 1870, 201–3.
41. *AKV*, XXXI: 153, M. L. to A. R. Vorontsov, 28 Dec. 1761. It was imposed that day: *KfZh* (1761), suppl., 4–5.
42. *KfZh* (1762), 19, 1st pagn, 27 Feb.
43. Shtelin, *Zapiski*, 97; *KfZh* (1762), 25, 1st pagn, 4 Feb.; *SIRIO*, VII: 121, 7 July 1762.
44. Hughes, 'Royal funerals', 413. The coffin was lowered into the vault only on 27 Feb., when neither Peter nor C. was present: *KfZh* (1762), 46, 1st pagn.
45. *Mémoires du Comte de Hordt* (Paris, 1784), 267–8.
46. *Sochineniia*, XII: 508–9.
47. *Mémoires du Comte de Hordt*, 267–8. In point of fact, C. was to attend memorial services for Elizabeth for the rest of her life.
48. *KfZh* (1762), 28–34, 1st pagn; 'Dnevnik statskogo sovetnika Mizere', 57; Benois, *Tsarskoe Selo*, 106, 111, 260–3.
49. *SIRIO*, XVIII: 83, 143, Mercy to Kaunitz, 1 Feb. and 26 Feb. 1762 NS.
50. *Sochineniia*, XII: 547, C. to Poniatowski, 2 Aug. 1762.
51. Shcherbatov, 233.
52. C. S. Leonard, *Reform and Regicide: The Reign of Peter III of Russia* (Bloomington, IN, 1993), 42–5; 48–57. For a penetrating discussion, see E. A. Marasinova, 'Manifest o vol'nosti dvorianstva (k voprosu o mekhanizmakh sotsial'nogo kontrolia)', in *E.R. Dashkova i zolotoi vek Ekateriny*, ed. L. V. Tychinina, et al (M, 2006), 84–108.
53. Tooke, I: 219.
54. *KfZh* (1762), 39, 1st pagn; 'Dnevnik statskogo sovetnika Mizere', 59.
55. Bolotov, II: 108–11.
56. Bil'basov, I: 423–4; 428–9.
57. *PCFG*, XXI: 164, Frederick to Prince Henry, 3 Jan. 1762; 175, to Finckelstein, 11 Jan. 1761 NS.
58. Ibid., 194, 22 Jan.; (210), 29 Jan.; (212), 31 Jan.
59. *AKV*, XXI: 46–7; *SIRIO*, XVIII: 361, Mercy to Kaunitz, 28 May 1762 NS. Prince Dashkov reached Kiev before being recalled by Catherine.
60. Tooke, I: 239.
61. Ransel, *Politics*, 59–61 (61).
62. Troitskii, *Finansovaia politika*, 246–7; Leonard, *Reform and Regicide*, 122.
63. Kurukin, *Epokha 'dvorskikh bur'*, 385–92.
64. Leonard, *Reform and Regicide*, 136.
65. Madariaga, 27–8.
66. *AKV*, XXI: 49.
67. R. Vroon, '9 June 1762: The tears of an empress, or the toast that toppled an emperor', in *Days from the Reigns*, ed. Cross, II: 129–30.
68. *Sochineniia*, XII: 547, C. to Poniatowski, 2 Aug. 1762.
69. *AKV*, XXI: 68.
70. The following draws on Madariaga, 29–32, and Alexander, 3–16.
71. *PSZ*, XVI: 11,585.

72. R. Bartlett, '30 October 1763: The Beginning of Abolitionism in Russia', in *Days from the Reigns*, ed. Cross, II: 138.

73. Tooke, I: 292.

74. *Osmnadtsatyi vek*, 2 (1869), 634, Talyzin to Panin, 29 June 1762.

75. *Perevorot 1762 goda* (M, 1908), 141; Bil'basov, II: 104–6.

76. *Sochineniia*, XII: .

77. A. Schumacher, *Geschichte der Thronentsetzung und des Tode Peter des Dritten* (Hamburg, 1858).

78. K. A. Pisarenko, 'Neskol'ko dnei iz istorii "uedinennogo i priiatnogo mestechka" ', in O. A. Ivanov, V. S. Lopatin and K. A. Pisarenko, *Zagadki russkoi istorii: XVIII vek* (M, 2000), 253–398.

79. Madariaga, 32.

Chapter 6

1. *SIRIO*, XII: 113, Buckinghamshire to Halifax, 28 June 1763 NS; CXL: 205, Bérenger to Praslin, 28 June and 8 July; XLVI: 538–40, Mercy to Kaunitz, 28 June.

2. Alexander, 74–5.

3. *SIRIO*, XXII: 66, 75, Solms to Frederick II; 7/18 June 1763; XII: 113, Buckinghamshire to Halifax, 28 June 1763 NS.

4. *KfZh* (1763), 109–11, 112–4, 117, 129; I. V. Kapustina, 'Usad'ba Kuskovo v kontekste evropeiskikh paradnykh rezidentsii XVIII veka', *Russkaia usad'ba*, 9 (2003), 163–81; *Pis'ma Saltykovu*, 14, 25 June 1763.

5. *KfZh* (1763), 131–42.

6. M. I. Pyliaev, *Staryi Peterburg* (SPb, 2007 edn.), 260. Begun in 1753, the church survived until 1961 when it was demolished during Khrushchev's anti-religious campaign to make way for the *Sennaia ploshchad'* metro station.

7. *SIRIO*, CXL: 206–7, Bérenger to Praslin, 12 July 1763 NS.

8. *Zapiski Shtelina*, I: 209; M. F. Korshunova, *Iurii Fel'ten* (Leningrad, 1988), 28. The gallery was demolished in 1766 as part of the scheme to clad the Neva's banks in granite.

9. Rovinskii, *Obozrenie ikonopisaniia*, 279–80; *Zapiski Shtelina*, I: 256.

10. *SIRIO*, CXL: 206, Bérenger to Praslin, 12 July 1763 NS.

11. The longest of these memoranda is at *SIRIO*, X: 380–1, 20 Sept. 1769.

12. Madariaga, 123–32.

13. Bartlett, 30 October 1763, 139–40. See the same author's 'The Question of Serfdom: Catherine II, the Russian Debate and the View from the Baltic Periphery', in *Russia in the Age of the Enlightenment*, eds. R. Bartlett and J. M. Hartley (London, 1990), 142–66, and his 'Serfdom and state power in Imperial Russia', *European History Quarterly*, 33 (2003), 38–9.

14. A. Kamenskii, *Ot Petra I do Pavla I: Reformy v Rossii XVIII veka* (M, 1999), 330.

15. R. Bartlett, 'Educational Projects in the First Decade of the Reign of Catherine II', in *Russische Aufklärungsrezeption im Kontext offizieller Bildungskonzepte (1700–1825)*, ed. G. Lehmann-Carli, et al. (Berlin, 2001), 109–24.

16. D. L. Ransel, *Mothers of Misery: Child Abandonment in Russia* (Princeton, NJ, 1988), 31–45.

17. Poroshin, 20, 29 Sept. 1764; 117, 9 Dec.; 133, 20 Dec; and *passim*.

18. W. Rosslyn, '5 May 1764: The Foundation of the Smol'nyi Institute', in *Days from the Reigns*, ed. Cross, II: 149.

19. See, in particular, her letters to 'Dusky Levushka' (Princess Cherkasskaia), from *c.* 1770: 'Chetyre pis'ma Ekateriny II-y k kniagine A. P. Cherkasskoi', *RA*, 1870, no. 3, 529–39.

20. *PSZ*, XVI: 11,606, 12 July 1762, referring to the Senate meeting on 3 July.

21. J. P. LeDonne, *Ruling Russia: Politics and Administration in the Age of Absolutism 1762–1796* (Princeton, NJ, 1984), 27–30; L. G. Kisliagina, 'Kantseliariia stats-sekretarei pri Ekaterine II', in *Gosudarstvennye uchrezhdeniia Rossii XVI–XVIII vv.* (M, 1991), 171.

22. W. Daniel, *Grigorii Teplov: A Statesman at the Court of Catherine the Great* (Newtonville, MA, 1991); *MP*, III: 144–53.

23. R. Faggionato, *A Rosicrucian Utopia in Eighteenth-Century Russia: The Masonic circle of N.I. Novikov* (Amsterdam, 2005), 16–21; *Sochineniia*, XII: 298, (406).

24. Kisliagina, 'Kantseliariia', 172–5; *SIRIO*, VII: 319, Teplov to Elagin, 12 Sept. 1763.

25. G. E. Munro, 'Food in Catherinian St. Petersburg', in *Food in Russian History and Culture*, eds. M. Glants and J. Toomre (Bloomington, IN, 1997), 31–48. Panin and Elagin reminisced about the imperial table in earlier eras: Poroshin, 23 Dec. 1764.

26. *SIRIO*, I: 261–2, C. to Mme Geoffrin, 4 Nov. 1763.

27. Parkinson, 48, 29 Nov. 1792.

28. Poroshin, 265, 28 Aug. 1765, records a visit of thirty minutes at Tsarskoe Selo: most apparently lasted about fifteen minutes.

29. O. A. Omel'chenko, *Imperatorskoe Sobranie 1763 goda (Komissiia o vol'nosti dvorianskoi)* (M, 2001), 13–48.

30. *SIRIO*, X: 381, 20 Sept. 1769; Madariaga, 43–7. Counting the backlog of Senate business became an annual obsession.

31. Quoted in Madariaga, 58.

32. *RS*, Nov. 1874, 494, C. to Volkov, June 1763.

33. *Ekaterina II: Babushkina azbuka*, ed. L.V. Tychinina (M, 2004), para. 45.

34. Ovsiannikov, *Rastrelli*, 173.

35. *Ermitazh: Istoriia stroitelstva i arkhitektura zdanii*, ed. B. B. Piotrovskii (Leningrad, 1989), 99–102; O. Medvedkova, 'Catherine II et l'architecture à la francaise: le cas de Vallin de la Mothe', in *Catherine II et l'Europe*, ed. Davidenkoff, 39–40; *Zapiski Shtelina*, I: 207.

36. *SIRIO*, XXII: 77, Solms to Frederick II, 3 June 1763.

37. *KfZh* (1763), 213.

38. Poroshin, 305–6, 8 Oct. 1765; McGrew, 56.

39. The following depends on G. N. Komelova, 'Apartamenty Ekateriny II v Zimnem dvortse', in *Zimnii dvorets: Ocherki zhizni imperatorskoi rezidentsii, 1: XVIII-pervaia tret' XIX veka* (SPb, 2000), 44–73.

40. Benois, *Tsarskoe Selo*, 125; Poroshin, 307, 10 Oct. 1765.

41. *AKV*, XXXIV: 358, Panin to Anna Vorontsova, 11 Jan. 1767.

42. Poroshin, 54–5, 15 and 16 Oct. 1764; 192, 20 Feb. 1765. The machine was probably an electrostatic generator donated by Paul's new science tutor, Franz Aepinus, a first-class scientist from Rostock whose treatise on electricity and magnetism had been published in St Petersburg in 1759. See R. W. Home, *Electricity and Experimental Physics in Eighteenth-Century Europe* (Hampshire, 1992), chs. XIV and XV.

43. The rooms formerly occupied by C. are now largely given over to the Hermitage Museum's collection of French painting of the fifteenth to eighteenth centuries and German drawing of the fifteenth to nineteenth centuries.

44. V. Shvarts, *Leningrad: Art and Architecture* (Leningrad, 1986), 54.

45. *SIRIO*, XII: 257, Cathcart to Weymouth, 19 Aug. 1768.

46. Wraxall, 241.

47. Poroshin, 76, 2 Nov. 1764.

48. *SIRIO*, I: 260, C. to Mme Geoffrin, 6 Nov. 1764.

49. Poroshin, 240, 31 July 1765.

50. *Lettres au Prince de Ligne*, 40, 9 Mar. 1781.

51. S. Lovell, *Summerfolk: A History of the Dacha, 1710–2000* (Ithaca, NY, 2003), 9 (piano keys), 11 (Derzhavin translation).

52. *KfZh* (1766), 12; (1765), 92, 10 June; Poroshin, 230–1, 22 July 1765.

53. *KfZh* (1766), 12, 36, 37.

54. *Pis'ma Saltykovu*, 15, 7 July 1763.

55. V. V. Shevtsov, *Kartochnaia igra v Rossii (konets XVI – nachalo XX v.): Istoriia igry i istoriia obshchestva* (Tomsk, 2005), 27–30, summarises C's subsequent legislation.

56. V. Maikov, 'Igrok lombera' (1763), in *Izbrannye proizvedeniia*, ed. A.V. Zapadov (Leningrad, 1966), 55–71.

57. *KfZh* (1765), 18–21, 23–4; Poroshin, 169–70, 1 Feb. 1765.

58. Poroshin, 365–6, 25 Dec. 1765.

59. M. S. Konopleva, *Teatral'nyi zhivopisets Dzhuseppe Valeriani: Materialy k biografii i istorii tvorchestva* (Leningrad, 1948), 22–3.

60. K. A. Pisarenko, ed., 'Pis'ma Barona A.S. Stroganova ottsu iz-za granitsei', *Rossiiskii arkhiv: Istoriia Otechestva v svidetel'stvakh i dokumentakh XVIII–XX vv.*, New Series, 14 (M, 2005), 28 (Cambridge), and *passim*.

61. R. P. Gray, *Russian Genre Painting in the Nineteenth Century* (Oxford, 2000), 23–4.

62. 'Pis'ma Barona A. S. Stroganova', 13–14, 16, 17, (36).

63. V. A. Somov, 'Krug chteniia Peterburgskogo obshchestva v nachale 1760-kh godov (iz istorii biblioteki grafa A. S. Stroganova)', *XVIII vek*, 22 (SPb, 2002), 200–34.

64. Idem, ' "Kabinet dlia chteniia grafa Stroganova" (inostrannyi fond)', in *Vek Prosveshcheniia, 1: Prostranstvo evropeiskoi kul'tury v epokhu Ekateriny II* (M, 2006), 234–5.

65. *Sochineniia*, XII: 404.

66. *SIRIO*, XII: 256–7, Macartney to Grafton 4/15 Apr. 1766.

67. *AKV*, XXXI: 331–2, C. to M. L. Vorontsov, 2 Dec. 1765. Stroganov's divorce petition, dated 2 July 1765, is at *AKV*, XXXIV: 351–2. On the Synod's growing interest in such matters, see G. L. Freeze, 'Bringing order to the Russian family: marriage and divorce in imperial Russia, 1760–1860', *Journal of Modern History*, 62 (1990), 709–48.

68. Poroshin, 167, 22 Feb. 1765; 177, 27 Feb.; *SIRIO*, XII: 257, 4/15 Apr. 1766.

69. *AKV*, XXI: 48. Stroganov also attended C. at her coronation day banquets in 1764 and 1765: Poroshin, 14, 22 Sept. 1764; 288, 22 Sept. 1765.

70. Proschwitz, 147, C. to Gustav III, 6 May 1780; Khrapovitskii, 11, 26 June 1786.

71. Shcherbatov, 231.

72. *Correspondance*, 85, Williams to C., 26 Aug. 1756; 8 Aug., C. to Williams.

73. *Sochineniia*, XII: 305–6.

74. *Despatches*, II: 224 (Russian memoranda).

75. Harris Diaries, I: 227, 20 Jan. 1779.

76. *Sochineniia*, XII: 56.

77. Ibid., 557, C. to Poniatowski, 9 Aug. 1762.

78. *SIRIO*, XII: 126, Buckinghamshire to Halifax, 22 Aug. 1763 NS; ibid., I: 266, C. to Mme Geoffrin, 20 Feb. 1765; *Sochineniia*, XII: 5.

79. See, for example, *Despatches*, II: 221, Buckinghamshire to Halifax, 10 Feb. 1763 NS.

80. Poroshin, 245–6, 5 Aug. 1765. For a similar observatory at the Winter Palace, ibid., 305–6, 9 Oct. 1765.
81. R. P. Bartlett, *Human Capital: The settlement of foreigners in Russia, 1762–1804* (Cambridge, 1979), 42–3 (C.'s initiative), 47, 66–8, 91–4, 99–102.
82. Quoted in Alexander, 98.
83. *KfZh* (1766), 17–18.
84. Poroshin, 56, 16 Oct. 1764, *passim*.
85. I. Petrovskaia, V. Somina, *Teatral'nyi Peterburg: Nachalo XVIII veka-Oktiabr' 1917 goda* (SPb, 1994), 53–64.
86. Poroshin, 56, 16 Oct. 1764 and *passim*.
87. Poroshin, 102, 25 Nov. 1764.
88. Shtelin, *Muzyka*, 222, para. 65; J. T. Alexander, 'Catherine the Great and the Theatre', in *Russian Society and Culture and the Long Eighteenth Century: Essays in Honour of Anthony Cross*, eds. R. Bartlett and L. Hughes (Münster, 2004), 121.
89. Shtelin, *Muzyka*, 218–9, para. 63; *MP*, I: 228; Poroshin, 347, 26 Nov. 1765.
90. On the proliferation of such spectacles, see H. Watanabe O'Kelly, *Triumphall Shews: Tournaments at German-speaking Courts in their European Context, 1560–1730* (Berlin, 1992).
91. Poroshin, 157, 12 Jan. 1765; 225, 11 July.
92. E. S. Shchukina, *Dva veka russkoi medali* (M, 2000), 76; Alekseeva, *Mikhailo Makhaev*, 221–3.
93. A. Cross, 'Professor Thomas Newberry's Letter from St Petersburg, 1766, on the Grand Carousel and Other Matters', *SEER*, 76 (1998), 490–2. On the literary context of the carousel, V. Proskurina, *Mify imperii: Literatura i vlast' v epokhu Ekateriny II* (M, 2006), 11–19.
94. *Pis'ma Saltykovu*, 47, 1 July 1766; Tooke, II: 79.
95. Poroshin, 18, 27 Sept. 1764; Alexander, 'Catherine the Great and the Theatre', 121–2.
96. *PSZ*, XVI: 11, 631, 3 Aug. 1762.
97. N. D. Chechulin, *Ocherki po istorii russkikh finansov v tsarstvovanie Ekateriny II* (SPb, 1906), 281–3 (283).
98. Beales, *Joseph II*, 157–8.
99. For detailed references to this section, see my 'Religious Ritual at the Eighteenth-Century Russian Court', in *Monarchy and Religion*, ed. M. Schaich, 217–48.
100. Poroshin, 6 Jan. 1765; 9, 12 Jan. (illness); 371, 6 Jan. 1766.
101. P. Klimov, ed., *Religioznyi Peterburg* (SPb, 2004), 73–87; Dixon, 'Religious Ritual', 226–7.
102. Poroshin, 336, 13 Nov. 1765; Shtelin, *Muzyka*, 55, 57–8, paras 6–7.
103. Bilbasov, II: 156–8; Wortman, *Scenarios*, 120–1; K. A. Papmehl, *Metropolitan Platon of Moscow (Petr Levshin, 1737–1812)* (Newtonville MA, 1983), 8–9.
104. Bilbasov, II: 165–7; *KfZh* (1763), 86–107, 'Pokhodnyi zhurnal puteshestviia Eia Imperatorskago Velichestva v Rostov'.
105. N. I. Zav'ialova, 'Usad'ba Taininskoe: Istoriia Dvortsovaia ostrova i nekotorye problemy ego sokhraneniia', *Russkaia usad'ba*, 7 (2001), 306–23, photo at p. 315.
106. *SIRIO*, VII: 287, C. to Panin, 22 May 1763.
107. Ibid., 288, same to same, May 1763; J. Hartley, 'Philanthropy in the Reign of Catherine the Great', in Bartlett and Hartley, eds., *Russia in the Age of the Enlightenment*, 176.
108. *SIRIO*, VII: 288, C. to Panin, undated.
109. *KfZh* (1763), 172–3; Klimov, ed., *Religioznyi Peterburg*, 74–5.
110. Papmehl, *Metropolitan Platon*, 13, quoting Poroshin.

111. P. Bushkovitch, 'The Clergy at the Russian Court, 1689–1796', in *Monarchy and Religion*, ed. Schaich, 124, quoting Poroshin.

112. Papmehl, *Metropolitan Platon*, 10–11. The examination was on 12 Sept. following a private 'rehearsal' four days earlier.

113. Richardson, 225.

114. See E. Kimerling Wirtschafter, '20 September 1765: Tsesarevich Paul's Eleventh Birthday and Father Platon's "Sermon on Learning" ', in *Days from the Reigns*, ed. Cross, II: 163–71.

115. Best, D17844, 1 Aug. 1772 NS.

116. Quoted in G. MacDonogh, *Frederick the Great* (London, 1999), 116.

117. *SIRIO*, I: 272, C. to Mme Geoffrin, 17 May 1765.

118. Best. D13032, C. to Voltaire, 28 Nov. 1765; Wilson, *Diderot*, 466–7.

119. Best. D13433, C. to Voltaire, 9 July 1766; Madariaga, *Politics and Culture in Eighteenth-Century Russia* (London, 1998), 215–35.

120. Quoted in W. Sunderland, *Taming the Wild Field: Colonization and Empire on the Russian Steppe* (Ithaca, NY, 2004), 79–80.

121. R. Bartlett, 'The Free Economic Society: The Foundation Years and the Prize Essay Competition of 1766 on Peasant Property', in *Russland zur Zeit Katharinas II: Absolutismus, Aufklärung, Pragmatismus*, eds. E. Hübner, J. Kusber, P. Nitsche (Cologne, 1998), 181–3, 186, 197. The extent of Voltaire's involvement is revealed by V. A. Somov, 'Dva otveta Vol'tera na peterburgskom konkurse o krest'ianskoi sobstvennosti', in *Evropeiskoe Prosveshchenie i tsivilizatsiia Rossii*, ed. S. Ia. Karp (M, 2004), 150–65.

122. Ransel, *Mothers of Misery*, 45.

123. Shcherbatov, 251, 253.

124. *SIRIO* I: 268, C. to Geoffrin, 28 Mar. 1765.

Chapter 7

1. *SIRIO*, CLXI: 73, Bausset to Praslin, 9 May 1766; 73, Rossignol to Louis XV, 13 May; 83, Bausset to Choiseul, 27 May.

2. Bentham, II: 124, J. Bentham to S. Bentham, 3 June 1778.

3. Quoted in Madariaga, 151.

4. *SIRIO*, I: 268–9, C. to Mme Geoffrin, 28 Mar. 1765.

5. Dimsdale, '20 October 1768', in *Days from the Reigns*, ed. Cross, II: 185–6.

6. *Documents of Catherine the Great: The Correspondence with Voltaire and the* Instruction *of 1767 in the English text of 1768*, ed. W. F. Reddaway (Cambridge, 1931), 284, art. 457.

7. On the elections, see Madariaga, 140–9.

8. Best. D14091, C. to Voltaire, 26 Mar. 1767.

9. Poroshin, 239, 29 July 1765; 251, 10 Aug.

10. G. V. Ibneeva, *Puteshestviia Ekateriny II: Opyt 'osvoeniia' imperskogo prostranstva* (Kazan', 2006), 80; Bessarabova, 58, 43; Kutepov, *Tsarskaia okhota*, 70–1.

11. A. V. Gorbunova, 'Triumfal'nye vorota Tverskoi gubernii vo II polovine XVIII v.', in *Russkaia kul'tura XVII–XX vv.*, 3 (Tver', 2005), 30–2.

12. [I. I. Stafengagen], *Geograficheskoe opisanie reki Volgi ot Tveri do Dmitrevska dlia puteshestviia Eia Imperatorskago Velichestva po onoi reke* (St Petersburg, n.d. [1767]), unpaginated, *SK*, 6847. The Academy also prepared more detailed maps.

13. D. Ostrowski, 'The Assembly of the Land (*Zemskii sobor*) as a representative institution', in *Modernizing Muscovy: Reform and social change in seventeenth-century Russia*, eds. J. Kotilaine

and M. Poe (London 2004), 117–42, suggests that these assemblies were adapted from the Tatar khanates' *quriltai*.

14. *SIRIO*, X: 180, C. to Bielke, 28 Apr. 1767; Falconet, 14, C. to Falconet, 27 Mar.

15. *Pis'ma Saltykovu*, 47, 19 July 1766; 48, 6 Aug.

16. Falconet, 5, C. to Falconet, 18 Feb. 1767.

17. *KfZh* (1767), 42–87.

18. *Pis'ma Saltykovu*, 56, 24 Apr. 1767.

19. *KfZh* (1767), 83.

20. *Slovo o dushe zakonov v publichnom sobranii Imperatorskago Moskovskago Universiteta Aprelia 23. dnia, 1767. goda govorennoe Iogannom Matfiem Shadenom* (M, 1767).

21. *KfZh* (1767), 92; *SIRIO*, X: 183, C. to Panin, 30 Apr. 1767.

22. Ibid., 186, C. to Panin, 3 May 1767; Orlov, 'Dnevnik', 26; *KfZh* (1767), 98–101.

23. *KfZh* (1767), 103–6; *SIRIO*, XLII: 353, C. to Paul, 5 May 1767.

24. Alexander, 105.

25. Quoted in V. M Zhivov, *Razyskaniia v oblasti istorii i predistorii russkoi kul'tury* (M, 2002), 449.

26. *Sochineniia*, V: 1–29; Ibneeva, *Puteshestviia Ekateriny*, 220–9; F.-X. Coquin, 'Un inédit de Marmontel: épître à Sa Majesté Catherine II', in *La France et les français à Saint-Petersbourg XVIII–XIX siècles* (SPb, 2005), 11–25.

27. *SIRIO*, X: 187, C. to Marmontel, 7 May 1767.

28. *Pis'ma Saltykovu*, 59, 8 May 1767.

29. *KfZh* (1767), 123–5; Orlov, 'Dnevnik', 30–3; W. Daniel, 'Conflict between Economic Vision and Economic Reality: The Case of M. M. Shcherbatov', *SEER*, 67 (1989), 60–4.

30. *KfZh* (1767), 129–30.

31. *SIRIO*, X: 190, C. to Panin, 13 May 1767. The 51 nobles presented on 10 May are listed at *KfZh* (1767), 394–6.

32. I. Syrtsov, *Arkhipastyri kostromskoi eparkhii za 150 let eia sushchestvovaniia (1745–1898 gg.)* (Kostroma, 1898), 16–19, 21–2; *KfZh* (1767), 137, 147; Orlov, 'Dnevnik', 35.

33. *KfZh* (1767), 137–47; Orlov, 'Dnevnik', 35.

34. G. V. Lukomskii, *Kostroma: Istoricheskii ocherk* (SPb, 1913), 171–2. *KfZh* (1767), 139, says that a new tsar's place was built.

35. L. I. Zoziula and E. G. Shcheboleva, 'Ekaterina v usad'be Kniazei Kozlovskikh', in *Mir russkoi usad'by*, ed. L. V. Ivanova (M, 1995), 141–2; *KfZh* (1767), 148–51, Orlov, 'Dnevnik', 37; *SIRIO*, XLII: 354, C. to Paul, 18 May 1767.

36. Alexander, 108.

37. See *AKV*, XXXIV: 32–5, for the case of the Pyskorskii monastery in the 1750s.

38. Orlov, 'Dnevnik', 38.

39. *SIRIO*, X: 199–200, C. to Dimtrii, 22 May 1767; *KfZh* (1767), 155–6; [Arkhimandrit Feodosii], *Istoricheskoe opisanie Feodorovskago monastyria* (Nizhnii Novgorod, 1890), 20–1, 33–4.

40. *SIRIO*, X: 199–200, C. to Dimtrii, 22 May 1767.

41. D. Mackenzie Wallace, *Russia* (London, 1912 edn.), 304. Ibneeva, *Puteshestvie Ekateriny*, 87–110, has significant new material on the schism.

42. *SIRIO*, X: 201, C. to Panin, 22 May 1767. cf. Chappe d'Auteroche, *Voyage en Sibérie*, ed. Mervaud, II: 275: 'La ville est aussi désagréable par la façon dont elle est batie, qu'agréable par sa situation.'

43. Orlov, 'Dnevnik', 39–40.

44. *KfZh* (1767), 158–68.

45. *SIRIO*, x: 192–3; Cross, 74–9 (77).
46. V. N. Pinunirov, N. M. Raskin, *Ivan Petrovich Kulibin 1735–1818* (Leningrad, 1986), 30–45.
47. *KfZh* (1767), 145.
48. P. W. Werth, 'Armed Defiance and Biblical Appropriation: Assimilation and the Transformation of Mordvin Resistance, 1740–1814', *Nationalities Papers*, 27 (1999), 249–55; idem, *At the Margins of Orthodoxy: Mission, Governance and Confessional Politics in Russia's Volga-Kama Region, 1827–1905* (Ithaca, NY, 2002), 22–35.
49. *KfZh* (1767), 170–2; *SIRIO*, x: 202, 207, C. to Panin, 25 May and 3 June 1767.
50. *RA* (1870), nos. 4–5, 758–63, C. to I. I. Melissino, 24 May and 4 June 1767.
51. *Pis'ma Ekateriny II k Adamu Vasil'evichu Olsuf'evu, 1762–1783* (M, 1863), 81, 30 May 1767.
52. R. P. Bartlett, 'Julius von Canitz and the Kazan' *Gimnazii* in the Eighteenth Century', *CASS*, 14 (1980), 343–4, 358–9; Orlov, 'Dnevnik', 44.
53. N. D. Chechulin, *Russkoe provintsial'noe obshchestvo* (SPb, 1889), 27–34, 60–2, remains the only general study.
54. Orlov, 'Dnevnik', 43.
55. *KfZh* (1767), 185, 191, 193.
56. Best. D14219, C. to Voltaire, 29 May 1767.
57. *Geograficheskoe opisanie*, n.p.
58. Quoted in Bartlett, *Human Capital*, 94.
59. *KfZh* (1767), 231.
60. Ibid., 231–2.
61. Maikov, *Izbrannye proizvedeniia*, 292–5; *SIRIO*, x: 221–34.
62. *Pis'ma Saltykovu*, 47, 1 July 1766; 49, 10 Aug., 1 Sept.; (54), 29 Dec.; 59–60, 30 May 1767; *KfZh* (1767), 259.
63. *KfZh* (1767), 233–4, 262.
64. Ibid., 234–5, 266; E. N. Savinova, 'Dvortsovaia votchina Pakhrino XVII – seredina XIX v.', *Russkaia usad'ba*, 7 (2001), 296, 301.
65. V. O. Vitt, *Iz istorii russkogo konnozavodstva: Sozdanie novykh porod loshadei na rubezhe XVIII– XIX stoletii* (M, 1952), 16.
66. Kutepov, *Tsarskaia okhota*, 71, 94–5.
67. *KfZh* (1767), 247–55, esp. 253.
68. Ibid., 273–6; Alexander, 112–3; Omel'chenko, 114–5.
69. Falconet, 25, C. to Falconet, 12 Oct. 1767.
70. W. G. Jones, 'The Spirit of the *Nakaz*: Catherine II's Literary Debt to Montesquieu', *SEER*, 76 (1998), 662.
71. P. Dukes, *Catherine the Great and the Russian Nobility* (Cambridge, 1967), 80.
72. Dixon, 'Posthumous Reputation', 673; Diderot, 'Observations sur le *Nakaz*', in *Oeuvres*, ed. L. Versini (Paris, 1995), III: 537, para. 57.
73. Madariaga, *Politics and Culture*, 231, 235–61; Ransel, *Politics*, 178–84.
74. Madariaga, 156, 158–9, 554.
75. This point was echoed in Maikov's 'Ode on the occasion of the election of deputies to compose a new Code of Laws in 1767', *Izbrannye sochineniia*, 201, stanza 12.
76. *Documents of Catherine the Great*, ed. Reddaway, arts. 156, 123, 222, 240, 245, 265.
77. *SIRIO*, XII: 304–5, Shirley to Conway, 13/24 Aug. 1767.
78. Ibid., 307.
79. Madariaga, 161–2, 166.

80. Omel'chenko, 134.

81. Madariaga, 165. Phil Withington generously discussed this point with me.

82. Best. D14611, C. to Voltaire, c. 22 Dec. 1767.

83. *SIRIO*, x: 216; Madariaga, *Politics and Culture*, 137–43; D. Beales, 'Joseph II, petitions and the public sphere', in *Cultures of Power in Europe during the Long Eighteenth Century*, eds. H. Scott and B. Simms (Cambridge, 2007), 257.

84. O. A. Ivanov, *Graf Aleksei Grigor'evich Orlov-Chesmenskii v Moskve* (M, 2002), 33–40; *SIRIO*, XII: 302, Shirley to Conway, 28 May 1767; *KfZh* (1767), 375–6.

85. *KfZh* (1767), 367–8.

86. Falconet, 25, C. to Falconet, 12 Oct. 1767.

87. Omel'chenko, 118–24.

88. *KfZh* (1768), 20–2, 32; *SIRIO*, x: 277, 279, C. to Panin, 24, 27, 28 Jan. 1768.

89. C. Burney, *A General History of Music from the Earliest Ages to the Present Period*, 4 vols. (London, 1789), IV: 540.

90. *KfZh* (1768), 74–8; Shtelin, *Muzyka*, 57–9, 234. *MP*, I: 231–2, has the date wrong.

91. *KfZh* (1768), 80–1. Betskoy was also promoted: see N. N. Bantysh-Kamenskii, *Spiski kavalerov Rossiiskikh Imperatorskikh ordenov* (M, 2006 edn.), 90.

92. *SIRIO*, XXXVI: 139, Solms to Frederick, 22 Feb. 1768.

93. *SIRIO*, x: 282–3, C. to Saltykov, 6 Mar. 1768.

94. *KfZh* (1768), 36, 54, 70.

95. See, for example, Poroshin, 313, 19 Oct. 1765.

96. *SIRIO*, x: C. to Elagin, 5 May 1768.

97. *KfZh* (1768), 83–4, 87–8, 96, 99–104; *Pis'ma Saltykovu*, 69, 31 May 1768.

98. *SIRIO*, x: 295, C. to Panin, 8 June 1768.

99. *PSZ*, XVIII: 13,066, 19 Jan. 1768.

100. Falconet, 59, C. to Falconet, 14 July 1768.

101. *Religioznyi Peterburg*, ed. Klimov, 128–31; Iu. I. Kitner, 'K istorii stroitel'stva tserkvi Isaakiia Dalmatskogo v Peterburge', *PKNO*, 1993 (M, 1994), 449–53; A. Buccaro, et al, *Antonio Rinaldi: architetto vanvitelliano a San Pietroburgo* (Milan, 2003), 74–6, 122–5.

102. *KfZh* (1768), 132–8; (1769), 9, 7 Jan.; Falconet, 63–4, C. to Falconet, 17 July 1768; A. E. Ukhnalev, *Mramornyi dvorets v Sankt-Peterburge: Vek vosemnadtsatyi* (SPb, 2002).

103. Richardson, 16–17.

104. *KfZh* (1768), 154, 156–67.

105. Richardson, 19. [Platon], *Pouchitel'nye slova pri Vysochaishem Dvore Eia Imperatorskago Velichestva ... s 1763 goda po 1780 god* (M, 1780), II: 183–4, 189.

106. A. Cross, '8 August 1768: The Laying of the Foundation Stone of Rinaldi's St Isaac's Cathedral', in *Days from the Reigns*, ed. Cross, II: 178, 184.

107. Quoted in A. M. Schenker, *The Bronze Horseman: Falconet's Monument to Peter the Great* (New Haven, CT, 2003), 102.

108. Falconet, 48, Falconet to C., 13 June 1768.

109. Ibid., 52, C. to Falconet, 14 June 1768.

110. Ibid., 56–7, C. to Falconet, 1 July 1768.

111. Schenker, *Bronze Horseman*, 114–5.

112. *SIRIO*, XII: 360, Cathcart to Weymouth, 19 Aug. 1767.

113. Madariaga, 167–78.

114. *Sochineniia*, XII: 617.

115. Best. D14611, C. to Voltaire, *c*. 22 Dec. 1767.
116. *Sochineniia*, XII: 170.
117. Madariaga, 170–83; Ransel, *Politics*, 186–90; W. R. Augustine, 'Notes toward a Portrait of the Eighteenth-Century Nobility', *Canadian Slavic Studies*, 4 (1970).
118. L. Hughes, 'Seeing the Sights in Eighteenth-Century Russia: the Moscow Kremlin', in *Eighteenth-Century Russia: Society, Culture, Economy*, eds. R. Bartlett and G. Lehmann-Carli (Münster, 2007), 326.
119. Richardson, 76; Madariaga, 168, 203–4.

Chapter 8

1. *SIRIO*, XII: 289–90, Macartney to Conway, 28 Nov. 1766.
2. The standard account is H. M. Scott, *The Emergence of the Eastern Powers, 1756–1775* (Cambridge, 2001), here 43–4.
3. *SIRIO*, XII: 232, Macartney to Grafton, 5 Nov. 1765.
4. *AKV*, XIII: 19, A. A. Bezborodko to R. L. Vorontsov, Smolensk, 3 July 1780.
5. *AKV*, XXI: 112.
6. Madariaga, 188–9.
7. The most detailed treatment of these developments is now B. V. Nosov, *Ustanovlenie rossiiskogo gospodstva v Rechi Pospolitoi, 1756–1768 gg.* (M, 2004), here 98–102, 119, which underscores the scale of Chernyshëv's ambitions later in the decade.
8. Translated in A. Lentin, *Enlightened Absolutism (1760–1790): A Documentary Sourcebook* (Newcastle-upon-Tyne, 1985), 220.
9. Scott, *Emergence*, 104–5.
10. *SIRIO*, VII: 321.
11. H. M. Scott, 'France and the Polish Throne, 1763–1764', *SEER*, 53 (1975), 370–88.
12. *SIRIO*, VII: 373–4.
13. Scott, *Emergence*, 65–7; Madariaga, 192.
14. T. Schieder, *Frederick the Great*, ed. and trans. S. Berkeley and H. M. Scott (London, 2000), 151.
15. H. M. Scott, 'Frederick II, the Ottoman Empire and the origins of the Russo-Prussian alliance of April 1764', *European Studies Review* 7 (1977), 153–75.
16. Quoted in Scott, *Emergence*, 121. The ship carrying Chernyshëv's uninsured possessions on his return in the following year sank off Kronstadt with an estimated loss of 200,000 roubles. Only his English horses were saved: *SIRIO*, CLXIII: 71, Sabatier to Choiseul, 15 Dec. 1769.
17. *SIRIO*, XII: 244, Macartney to Grafton, 11 Feb. 1766; Madariaga, 193–4.
18. Madariaga, 206.
19. *SIRIO*, XIII: 408, C. to Grimm, 19 June 1774; Alexander, 143–5.
20. *SIRIO*, XX: 246, C. to Frederick II, 5 Dec. 1768.
21. R. P. Bartlett, 'Russia in the Eighteenth-Century European Adoption of Inoculation for Smallpox', in *Russia and the World of the Eighteenth Century*, eds. R. P. Bartlett, A. G. Cross and K. Rasmussen (Columbus, OH, 1988), 193–213; D. Beales, 'Social Forces and Enlightened Policies', in *Enlightened Absolutism*, ed. H. M. Scott (London, 1990), 49–50.
22. Cross, 137–41.
23. *SIRIO*, XII: 363, Cathcart to Weymouth, 29 Aug. 1768.
24. John Thomson, quoted in Cross, 138.
25. *KfZh* (1768), 206–12.

26. *SIRIO*, XII: 391, Cathcart to Weymouth, 21 Oct. 1768. C. herself subsequently referred to a 'period when I was forbidden to conduct business': *Pis'ma Saltykovu*, 73, 9 Nov.

27. R. Dimsdale, '20 October 1768: Doctor Dimsdale Spends a Day with the Empress', in *Days from the Reigns*, ed. Cross, II: 186–9, reproduces his ancestor's invaluable notes.

28. *Pis'ma Saltykovu*, 73, 27 Oct. 1768.

29. Falconet, 68–9, C. to Falconet, 30 Oct. 1768.

30. *KfZh* (1768), 212–5.

31. 'Pis'ma imperatritsy Ekateriny II k grafu Ivanu Grigor'evichu Chernyshevu (1764–1773)', *RA*, 9 (1871), 1319, 17 Nov. 1768.

32. Richardson, 33–4.

33. *KfZh* (1768), 233.

34. *SIRIO*, XIII: 126, C. to Dimsdale, June 1771.

35. *SIRIO*, XII: 405–6, Cathcart to Rochford, 25 Nov. 1768.

36. Shtelin, *Muzyka*, 284–91; not mentioned in *KfZh*.

37. Bartlett, 'Smallpox', 203.

38. Beales, *Joseph II*, 158.

39. Best. D15396, Dec. 1768.

40. *Ermitazh*, ed. Piotrovskii, 316–23. Korshunova, *Iurii Fel'ten*, 29–31, says the model was sent to Moscow, but C. had returned to St Petersburg in Jan. 1768. The first mention of the Hermitage in the Court journals is *KfZh* (1769), 23, 1 Feb.

41. E. Maxtone Graham, *The Beautiful Mrs Graham and the Cathcart Circle* (London, 1927), quoting Lady Cathcart to Mrs Walkinshaw of Barrowfield, 8 Feb. 1768. For the Sheremetevs' table at Kuskovo, see Parkinson, 213.

42. *SIRIO*, X: 332, C. to Bielke, 4 Mar. 1769; see also *Pis'ma Saltykovu*, 78, 5 Mar.

43. *SIRIO*, XII: 428, Cathcart to Rochford, 17 Mar. 1769.

44. Gray, *Russian Genre Painting*, 14–16.

45. Grimm, 367, 1–2 Nov. 1785.

46. G. Apgar, *L'Art singulier de Jean Huber: Voir Voltaire* (Paris, 1995), 16, 96–8, 106–7 (98), a reference to *Le Patriarche en colère faisant une correction à coups de pied à un cheval qui rue*. The Hermitage now holds eight paintings from the series; there may have been four more.

47. C. Frank, 'Secret deals and public art: Catherine II's cultural patronage in Bachaumont's *Mémoires secrets* (1762–1786)', in *Vek prosvescheniia I: Prostranstvo evropeiskoi kul'tury v epokhu Ekateriny II*, ed. S. Ia. Karp (M, 2006), 55–9, (60).

48. G. Dulac, 'La question des beaux-arts dans les relations de Diderot avec la Russie: Les réflexions d'un philosophe (1765–1780)', in *Vek prosvescheniia, I:* 10.

49. Letter of 1777, quoted in R. Davison, *Diderot et Galiani: étude d'une amitié philosophique*, *SVEC*: 237 (1985), 98–9.

50. B. V. Anan'ich, et al, *Kredit i banki v Rossii do nachala XX veka: Sankt-Peterburg i Moskva* (SPb, 2005), 72–80 (73, 75); *PSZ*, XV: 11,550, 25 May 1762; *SIRIO*, CLXIII: 183–4, Sabatier to Choiseul, 7 Sept. 1770.

51. *SIRIO*, XXXVII: 214, Solms to Frederick, 3 Feb. 1769.

52. *SIRIO*, X: 334, C. to Elagin, 1 Apr. 1769.

53. F. Venturi, *The End of the Old Regime in Europe, 1768–1776*, trans. R. B. Litchfield (Princeton, NJ, 1989), 7–9.

54. 'Pis'ma Chernyshevu', 1325, 14 Dec. 1768.

55. Venturi, *End of the Old Regime*, 10–12, 15 (7).

56. Ibid., 27.
57. *KfZh* (1769), 44; T. Kudriavtseva and H. Whitbeck, *Russian Imperial Porcelain Easter Eggs* (London, 2001), 13.
58. Madariaga, 206.
59. *KfZh* (1769), 69, 70–5; *Pis'ma Saltykovu*, 79, 1 May 1769.
60. *SIRIO*, X: 337, C. to Panin, 10 May 1769.
61. *KfZh* (1769), 86–9, 96–9.
62. *KfZh* (1769), 104–6, 124–6.
63. *SIRIO*, CXLIII: 36, Sabatier to Choiseul, 3 Oct. 1769.
64. Richardson, 103–4.
65. Quoted in W. G. Jones, *Nikolay Novikov: Enlightener of Russia* (Cambridge, 1984), 22.
66. Catherine's *babushka* persona quoted in K. J. McKenna, 'Empress behind the mask: the personae of Md. Vsiakaia Vsiachina in Catherine the Great's periodical essays on manners and morals', *Neophilologus*, 74 (1990), 3.
67. *Satiricheskie zhurnaly N.I. Novikova*, ed. P. N. Berkov (Moscow-Leningrad, 1951), 92, *Truten'*, 21 July 1769.
68. *Sochineniia*, XII: 636.
69. Bentham, II: 126, J. Bentham to S. Bentham, 18 June 1778; *RBS*, 'Knappe-Kiukhel'bekher' (SPb, 1903), 39–40.
70. Madariaga, *Short History*, 95.
71. Best. D17127, C. to Voltaire, 26 Mar. 1771; Jones, *Nikolay Novikov*, 65.
72. Platon, *Pouchitel'nye slova*, II: 310–11.
73. *PSZ*, XIX: 13,603, 6 May 1771.
74. Jones, *Nikolay Novikov*, 20 (curlers), 61–3; P. N. Berkov, *Istoriia russkoi komedii XVIII v.* (Leningrad, 1977), 144.
75. *SIRIO*, XII: 427, Cathcart to Rochford, 17 Mar. 1769.
76. *Herder on Social and Political Culture*, ed. F. M. Barnard (Cambridge 1969), 87, 'Journal of my Voyage in 1769'.
77. Best. D16286, C. to Voltaire, 31 Mar. 1770.
78. Letter to Voltaire, quoted in L. Wolff, *Inventing Eastern Europe: The Map of Civilization on the Mind of the Enlightenment* (Stanford, CA, 1994), 223; Madariaga, 337.
79. *The Antidote; or an enquiry into the merits of a book, entitled A Journey into Siberia* (London, 1772), 22, 76, 25.
80. *KfZh* (1769), 142–4.
81. Madariaga, 210; Best. D16057, C. to Voltaire, 13 Dec. 1769; D16071, Voltaire to C., 2 Jan. 1770 NS.
82. M. S. Anderson, 'Great Britain and the Russo-Turkish War of 1768–1774', *English Historical Review*, 69 (1954), 44.
83. Cross, 185–8; E. V. Tarle, *Chesmenskii boi i pervaia russkaia ekspeditsiia v arkhipelag* (Moscow-Leningrad, 1945), 45–53; Venturi, *End of the Old Regime*, 74.The latest scholarly study is G. A. Grebenshchikova, *Baltiiskii flot v period pravleniia Ekateriny II: dokumenty, fakty, issledovaniia* (SPb, 2007).
84. Best. D16670, C. to Voltaire, 16 Sept. 1770. Turkish losses were probably closer to 10,000.
85. *SIRIO*, I: 62, C. to A. G. Orlov, 3 Oct. 1770.
86. *Fel'dmarshal Rumiantsev: Dokumenty, pis'ma, vospominaniia*, ed. A. P. Kapitonov (M, 2001), 108–22, Rumiantsev to C., 20 June and 31 July 1770.

87. D. I. Peters, *Nagradnye medali Rossii vtoroi poloviny XVIII stoletiia* (M, 1999), 64–71.

88. E.g., *KfZh* (1770), 162–4, 20 July, the Feast of the Prophet Elijah.

89. *KfZh* (1770), 171–2; Falconet, 136, C. to Falconet, 18 Aug. 1770.

90. Best. D16604, C to Voltaire, 9/20 Aug. 1770.

91. Madariaga, 219–20.

92. J. Lukowski, *The Partitions of Poland, 1772, 1793, 1795* (London, 1999), 61.

93. *SIRIO*, XIII: 59, C. to Bielke, 12 Jan. 1771; Best. D16999, C. to Voltaire, 23 Jan. 1771.

94. *Pis'ma Salytkovu*, 85, 23 Nov. 1770.

95. *SIRIO*, X: 433–4.

96. *Zhurnal bytnosti v Rossii Ego Korolevsago Vysochestva Printsa Prusskago Genrikha* (SPb, n.d., supplement to *KfZh* 1770), 12, 30–1.

97. Schenker, *Bronze Horseman*, 135–61, esp. 157–8.

98. *Mémoirs du Comte de Hordt, Gentilhomme Suédois*, etc., 2 vols. (Berlin, 1789), II: 225–6; *Zhurnal bytnosti*, 50–4.

99. *Sochineniia*, IV: 149–63.

100. Richardson, 328, 330–1.

101. A. Zorin, *Kormia dvuglavogo orla* (M, 2001) 33–94.

102. Best. D16711, C. to Voltaire, 7/18 Oct. 1770; Richardson, 327.

103. Best. D16825, C. to Voltaire, 4/15 Dec. 1770; D17081, 3/14 Mar. 1771. For Voltaire's reply, see D16984, 22 Jan. 1771 NS.

104. Best. D16683, Voltaire to C., 2 Oct. 1770 NS.

105. Alexander, *Bubonic Plague*, 101–2, 107, 115, 118.

106. Best., D17443, Voltaire to C., 12 Nov. 1771 NS. See also D16747, 6 Nov. 1770 NS.

107. Alexander, *Bubonic Plague*, 150–61 and *passim*.

108. Beales, *Joseph II*, 286–94 (289).

109. Beales, *Joseph II*, 282–4; Madariaga, 221–3 (222); Lukowski, *Partitions of Poland* (64), 68–74.

110. *SIRIO*, XIII: 116, C. to Panin, 19 June 1771. This was barely six weeks after the edict banning corporal punishment for liveried servants, suggesting a clear distinction between the two groups in C.'s mind.

111. Ibid., 117, C. to Panin, 23 June.

112. *SIRIO*, CLXIII: 309, Sabatier to Aiguillon, 12 July NS.

113. *SIRIO*, XIII: 142, C. to Bielke, 30 July 1770; 149, 29 Aug. See also CLXIII: 321, Sabatier to Aiguillon, 9 Aug. NS.

114. Alexander, *Bubonic Plague*, 186–201 (204).

115. Best. D17407, C. to Voltaire, 6/17 Oct. 1771.

116. *PSZ*, XIX: 13,689, 26 Oct. 1771.

117. Alexander, *Bubonic Plague*, 253.

118. Best. D17341, C. to Voltaire, 14/25 Aug. 1771. The temple of memory was ultimately designed by Charles Cameron and destroyed by order of Paul I in 1797.

119. Falconet, 134, Falconet to C., 14 Aug. 1770; *SIRIO*, X: 431; Shchukina, *Dva veka russkoi medali*, 65–70.

120. *SIRIO*, XIII: 238, C. to Bielke, 28 Apr. 1772.

121. Cross, 266–73; D. Shvidkovsky, *The Empress and the Architect: British Architecture and Gardens at the Court of Catherine the Great* (New Haven, CT, 1996), 172–81; I. Iakovkin, *Opisanie sela tsarskago* (SPb, 1830), 32–4.

122. Cross, 269.

123. *Satiricheskie zhurnaly*, 96, 28 July 1769.The second edition of *The Drone* was dedicated to Naryshkin: see ibid., 45, and *SK*, IV: 202.

124. *Sovremennik*, 38 (1853), 96–101; *KfZh* (1772), 297–302. For an earlier entertainment at Leventhal, see *KfZh* (1770), 157–60.

125. N. Wraxall, *A Tour through some of the Northern Parts of Europe*, 3rd edn. (London, 1776), 213.

126. *SIRIO*, XIII: 23, C. to Bielke, 13 July 1770.

127. *SIRIO*, XIII: 99–100, C. to Panin, 24–25 May, 1771. See also *SIRIO*, CXLIII: 291–2, Sabatier to Vrillière, 7 June NS.

128. Best. D17322, 22 July/3 Aug. 1771; *PSZ*, XIX: 13,651, 26 July.

129. *Pis'ma Saltykovu*, 69, 31 May 1768.

130. A. I. Mikhailov, *Bazhenov* (M, 1951), 50–7, 60.

131. Ibid., 61; Iu. Ia. Gerchuk, ed., *Vasilii Ivanovich Bazhenov* (M, 2001), 73–5, 'Kratkoe rassuzhdenie o kremlevskom stroenii'.

132. Gerchuk, *Bazhenov*, 80, Teplov to Bazhenov, 15 Feb. 1770.

133. *Pis'ma Saltykovu*, 91, 23 Nov. 1770; *Zhurnal bytnosti*, 98, 100. *PSZ*, XIX: 13,581, 15 Mar. 1771, decreed that though the city wall was to be demolished along the Moscow River from the Annunciation Cathedral to the Church of Peter the Metropolitan, neither was to be damaged.

134. Hughes, 'Seeing the Sights', in *Eighteenth-Century Russia*, eds. Bartlett and Lehmann-Carli, 325–6.

135. F. Rozhdestvenskii, *Samuil Mislavskii, Mitropolit Kievskii* (Kiev, 1877), 50–1. C.'s letters to Samuil are at appendix iii–vii. cf. G. I. Vzdornov, *Istoriia otktrytiia izucheniia russkoi srednevekovoi zhivopisi XIX veka* (M, 1986), 16–17.

136. V. I. Bazhenov, 'Slovo na zalozhenie kremlevskogo dvortsa', in S. Razgonov, *V. I. Bazhenov* (M, 1985), 164–5.

137. Volkonskii, 93, 10 Jan. 1772.

138. Letters to Volkonskii quoted *in extenso* by V. P. Iailenko, *Ocherki po istorii i arkhitekture Lefortovo XVII–XVIII vekov* (M, 2004), 159–62.

139. Wraxall, *A Tour*, 231.

Chapter 9

1. R. E. Jones, 'Opposition to War and Expansion in Late Eighteenth-Century Russia', *Jahrbücher für Geschichte Osteuropas*, 32 (1984), 38–44.

2. *SIRIO*, XIII: 259, C. to Mme Bielke, 25 June 1772; 261, 9 Aug.

3. *KfZh* (1772), 302, 306–9.

4. *SIRIO*, LXXII: 227, Solms to Frederick, 3 Aug. 1772.

5. *KfZh* (1772), 323–31 (330).

6. *SIRIO*, XIX: 314, Gunning to Suffolk, 4 Sept. 1772.

7. *SIRIO*, XIII: 270–2, draft letter in C.'s hand; L. Hughes, *The Romanovs* (London, 2008), 108.

8. *PCFG*, XXXII: 527, Frederick to Solms, 1 Oct. 1772 NS.

9. *SIRIO*, XIX: 327–8, Gunning to Suffolk, 27 Sept. 1772.

10. Best. D17929, C. to Voltaire, 12 Sept. 1772. Panin presented Gustav's emissary to C. at Tsarskoe Selo on 17 Aug., *KfZh* (1772), 338.

11. Madariaga, 227.

12. *SIRIO*, XIX: 297, Gunning to Suffolk, 28 July 1772; XIII: 259, C. to Mme Bielke, 25 June 1772; 261, 9 Aug. The Court moved to Tsarskoe Selo on Monday 13 Aug: *KfZh* (1772), 330.

13. Best. D17877, C. to Voltaire, 11 Aug. 1772; D17983, 17 Oct. See also D18090, 5 Dec.

14. Falconet, 185, C. to Falconet, 9 Oct. 1772.

15. Best. D18062, C. to Voltaire, 22 Nov. 1772; *SIRIO*, LXII: 305, Solms to Frederick, II, 25 Dec. 1772; 311, 8 Jan. 1773; Ransel, *Politics*, 235–6.

16. Lopatin, 9, 21 Feb. 1774.

17. *SIRIO*, XIX: 298, Gunning to Suffolk, 28 July 1772.

18. McGrew, 70–1; *SIRIO*, XIII: 265–6, C. to Mme Bielke, 24 Aug. 1772.

19. *KfZh* (1772), 404–7. McGrew, 78, 82, may underestimate the level of public celebration.

20. *SIRIO*, XIX: 14, Cathcart to Rochford, 29 Dec. 1769.

21. Ransel, *Politics*, 242–6, offers the most confident account of the episode; McGrew, 81–2, is more cautious.

22. *SIRIO*, XIII: 91–2, C. to Assebourg, 14 May 1771.

23. Ibid., 85, Panin to Assebourg, 10 May 1771; *PCFG*, XXXIII: 142, Frederick to Henry, 19 Dec. 1772 NS.

24. The gallery was done out in 1755–6: see V. Lemus and L. Lapina, *The Catherine Palace-Museum in Pushkin: Picture Hall* (Leningrad, 1990).

25. *KfZh* (1773), 271–81.

26. *KfZh* (1773), 281–93. The wining and dining continued throughout the summer.

27. McGrew, 83–4; Papmehl, *Metropolitan Platon*, 28–9.

28. Best. D18605, Voltaire to C., 1 Nov. 1773.

29. Dixon, 'Religious Ritual', 234–5.

30. *Opisanie torzhestva vysokobrakosochetaniia Ego Imperatorskago Vysochestva Velikago Kniazia Pavla Petrovicha s Ee Imperatorskim Vysochestvom Velikoiu Kniagieneiu Natalieiu Alekseevnoiu* (SPb, 1773). See also D. Kobeko, *Tsesarevich Pavel Petrovich (1754–1796): Istoricheskoe issledovanie* (SPb, 2001 edn.), 75–7.

31. Quoted in Wilson, *Diderot*, 631.

32. Quoted in N. Cronk, 'Hobbes and Hume: determining voices in *Jacques le fataliste et son maître*', in *Diderot and European Culture*, eds. F. Ogée and A. Strugnell (*SVEC*, 2006:09), 179.

33. E. Anderson, ed., *The Letters of Mozart and His Family*, Third edn. (London, 1989), 43, L. Mozart to L. Hagenauer, 1 Apr. 1764 NS.

34. Grimm told his own story in *SIRIO*, II: 325–93, 'Mémoire historique sur l'origine et les suites de mon attachement pour l'Imperatrice Catherine II, jusqu'au décès de S.M.I.'.

35. S. Karp, 'Grimm à Pétersbourg', in *Deutsch-Russische Beziehungen im 18. Jahrhundert: Kultur, Wissenschaft und Diplomatie*, eds. C. Grau, S. Karp, J. Voss (Wiesbaden, 1997), 294.

36. Grimm, 1–2, 25 Apr. 1774.

37. D. Goodman, *The Republic of Letters: A Cultural History of the French Enlightenment* (Ithaca, NY, 1994), ch. 4; A. Chamayou, *L'Esprit de la lettre (XVIIIe siècle)* (Paris, 1999).

38. Grimm, 97, 17 Aug. 1778; 188, 20 Sept. 1780.

39. Grimm, 421–2, 25 Nov. 1787; ibid. 436, 28 Dec. On the subsequent fate of the letters, see S. Ia. Karp, 'Perepiska Ekaterina II s Fridrikhom Mel'khiorom Grimmom: Iz istorii rukopisei', *Vek Prosveshcheniia:* I, 30–49.

40. Grimm, 543, 1 June 1791.

41. S. Dixon, *Catherine the Great* (Harlow, 2001), 81–2; Diderot, *Oeuvres philosophiques*, ed. P. Vernière (Paris, 1961), 630.

42. Diderot, *Correspondance*, 142, 30 Dec. 1773 NS, to Mmes Diderot and Vandeul.

43. Wilson, *Diderot*, 630–1, 633; Diderot, *Correspondance*, 103, Grimm to Geoffrin, 10 Nov. 1773 NS.

44. Wilson, *Diderot*, 632.

45. Diderot, *Mémoires pour Catherine II*, ed. P. Vernière (Paris, 1966), 199, 178, 10, prints the revised text of the essays following discussion with C.

46. A. Strugnell, *Diderot's Politics* (The Hague, 1973), 25–6.

47. Wilson, *Diderot*, 598.

48. Strugnell, *Diderot's Politics*, 135–8; Diderot, *Mémoires*, 117, 118; Wilson, *Diderot*, 635.

49. Diderot, *Mémoires*, 117, 121, 122.

50. Diderot, *Correspondance*, 135–6, Diderot to Dashkova, 24 Dec. 1773 NS.

51. Quoted in Jones, *Nikolay Novikov*, 65.

52. Quoted in Wilson, *Diderot*, 640.

53. Diderot, *Mémoires*, 44.

54. S. Karp, 'Le questionnaire de Diderot adressé à Catherine II: quelques précisions', *Recherches sur Diderot et sur l'Encyclopédie*, 33 (2002), 47, 55.

55. See, in particular, G. Dulac, 'Diderot et le "mirage russe": quelques preliminaires à l'étude de son travail politique de Pétersbourg', in *Le Mirage russe au XVIIIe siècle*, eds. Karp and Wolff, 149–92, and G. Goggi, 'Diderot et la Russie: colonisation et civilisation. Projets et experience directe', in *Diderot and European Culture*, eds. Ogée and Strugnell, 57–76.

56. Diderot, *Mémoires*, 35.

57. R. V. Ovchinnikov, ed., *Dokumenty stavki E.I. Pugacheva* (M, 1975), 23. See 24–32 for similar manifestos to different interest groups through Oct. 1773.

58. Under interrogation in Moscow in Nov. 1774, Pugachëv claimed to be in his thirty-third year: see R. V. Ovchinnikov, ed., *Emel'ian Pugachev nad sledstvii* (M, 1997), 127.

59. M. Raeff, 'Pugachev's Rebellion', in *Preconditions of Revolution in Early Modern Europe*, eds. R. Forster and J. P. Greene (Baltimore, MD, 1970), 161–202; Madariaga, 233, 243.

60. Madariaga, 239–55; J. P. LeDonne, *The Grand Strategy of the Russian Empire, 1650–1831* (Oxford, 2004), 115; J. T. Alexander, *Autocratic Politics in a National Crisis: The Imperial Russian Government and the Pugachev Revolt, 1773–1775* (Bloomington, IN, 1969), 76.

61. Lopatin, 7, 4 Dec. 1773.

62. *SIRIO*, XIII: C. to Mme. Bielke, 16 Jan. 1774.

63. *KfZh* (1774), 18–19, 22, 25, 28.

64. Alexander, *Autocratic Politics*, 112–3.

65. *KfZh* (1774), 43–7; Gunning to Suffolk, 24 Jan. 1774, quoted in Wilson, 'Diderot in Russia', 190.

66. *SIRIO*, XIX: 399–400, Gunning to Suffolk, 11 Feb. 1774; 401, 14 Feb. See also LXXII: 490–2, Solms to Frederick, 7 Feb.

67. *KfZh* (1774), 15, 26.

68. *KfZh* (1774), 59–60. On Knowles, see Cross, 192–5 and *passim*.

69. *KfZh* (1774), 82–3; Lopatin, 10, 21 Feb. 1774.

70. Lopatin, 12, 28 Feb. 1774.

71. Lopatin, 10, 26 Feb. 1774; 12, 28 Feb.

72. Lopatin, 13–14, 1 Mar. 1774. Aleksey Orlov first appeared at Court on 27 Feb.: *KfZh* (1773), 97.

73. *KfZh* (1774), 103, 110–12.

74. Gunning to Suffolk, 4 Mar. 1774, quoted in Montefiore, 110.

75. Montefiore, 83, 85.

76. Lopatin, 14, after 1 Mar. 1775.

77. Lopatin, 22, 10 Apr. 1774.

78. *SIRIO*, XIX: 409, Gunning to Suffolk, 8 Apr. 1774; Madariaga 248; *KfZh* (1774), 147.

79. Grimm, 1, 25 Apr. 1774.

80. *KfZh* (1774), 172–8.

81. *SIRIO*, XIX: 416, Gunning to Suffolk, 13 June 1774; Alexander, *Autocratic Politics*, 132; Madariaga, 263.

82. *KfZh* (1774), 281–6; Lopatin, 513–5; Madariaga, 344.

83. Lopatin, 34, 22 July 1774.

84. Grimm, 137, 7 May 1779.

85. *Letters of Mozart*, ed. Anderson, 486, 19 Feb. 1778 NS.

86. J. Rosselli, *Singers of Italian Opera: The History of a Profession* (Cambridge, 1992), 66 and *passim*.

87. Harris Papers, 879, Elizabeth Harris to James Harris, jr., 16 Feb. 1776 NS.

88. *KfZh* (1774), 324–5; Wraxall, *A Tour*, 201, 204; Livanova, II: 412.

89. *SIRIO*, XXVII: 39, C. to Elagin, 19 May 1775.

90. C. rode in an open carriage from the Summer Palace while an officer bearing laurel wreaths led a troop of 100 Horse Guards to accompany the Senate official who made five public proclamations of the peace: in front of the Summer Palace; at the Haymarket; in front of the Senate; in front of the Twelve Colleges on Vasilevsky Island; and on the Petersburg side of the city: *KfZh* (1774), 429–39.

91. Madariaga, 254.

92. *KfZh* (1774), 474–5.

93. *KfZh* (1774), 507, 3 Sept.

94. Madariaga, 249, 266.

95. Best. D19188, C. to Voltaire, 2 Nov. 1774.

96. Madariaga, 267–8.

97. *PSZ*, XX: 14,235, 15 Jan. 1775.

98. Quoted in Sunderland, *Taming the Wild Field*, 58.

99. *SIRIO*, XXVII: 23, C. to Mme Bielke, 5 Jan. 1775.

100. *SIRIO*, XIX: 448–9, Gunning to Suffolk, 26 Jan. 1775.

101. Corberon, I: 80–1.

102. Grimm, 15, 30 Jan. 1775.

103. Only later was the host rehabilitated, under a different name, the Black Sea Host: see Madariaga, 359–60; Ransel, *Politics*, 250–1.

104. Madariaga, 553.

105. *SIRIO*, XXVII: 36, C. to Mme Bielke, 12 Apr. 1775.

106. McGrew, 86.

107. Lopatin, 71, C. to Potemkin, after 21 Apr. 1775.

108. *SIRIO*, XXVII: 48, C. to Mme Bielke, 24 July 1775.

109. Shvidkovsky, *The Empress and the Architect*, 192–3.

110. Best. D19712, Voltaire to C., 18 Oct. 1775 NS.

111. R. E. Jones, *The Emancipation of the Russian Nobility, 1762–1785* (Princeton, NJ, 1973), 210–20 (216).

112. M. Lopato, 'English Silver in St Petersburg', in *British Art Treasures*, 131.

113. Grimm, 42, 20 Jan. 1776.

Chapter 10

1. A. Raskin, *Gorod Lomonosova: Dvortsovo-parkovye ansambli XVIII veka* (Leningrad, 1983), 112–3.
2. *SIRIO*, xix: 133, Cathcart to Rochford, 29 Oct. 1770.
3. Quoted in A. G. Cross, *'By the Banks of the Thames': Russians in Eighteenth-Century Britain* (Newtonville, MA, 1980), 241.
4. Lopatin, 92–3, undated, Feb.–Mar. 1776.
5. *SIRIO*, xix: 513, R. Oakes to W. Eden, 8 Mar. 1776.
6. Lopatin, 103, undated, May–June 1776.
7. Lopatin, 106, 22 June 1776; 105, undated, 7–21 June; D. Smith, ed., *Love and Conquest: Personal Correspondence of Catherine the Great and Prince Grigory Potemkin* (DeKalb, IL, 2004), 69–72.
8. Lopatin, 91, undated, Feb.–Mar. 1776.
9. Corberon, ii: 37, 68; 27 Oct. and 8 Dec. 1776 NS.
10. C.'s undated love letters to Zavadovskii are translated in Alexander, 342–53 (here pp. 344–5).
11. Lopatin, 115, before 14 May 1777.
12. Zavadovskii, 263, 14 Aug. 1781. On the estate in Poltava province, presented to him on 10 July 1775 in celebration of the Peace of Kuchuk Kainardzhi, see N. Makarenko, 'Lialichi', *Starye gody*, July–Sept. 1910, 131–51.
13. Alexander, 206–14 (212).
14. Lopatin, 115, before 10 June 1777; I. I. Leshchilovskaia, 'Semen Zorich', in *Vek Ekateriny II: Rossiia i Balkany* (M, 1998), 129–38; M. I. Meshcherskii, 'Semen Gavrilovich Zorich', *RA*, 1879, no. 5, 37–65.
15. Montefiore, 179–84.
16. Harris Diaries, i: 198–9, Harris to Fraser, 16/27 May 1778.
17. Ibid. On headaches, see Grimm, 79, 14 Feb. 1778; 87, 16 May.
18. Corberon, ii: 330, 4 Sept. 1780 NS.
19. McGrew, 91–3; *SIRIO*, xxvii: 81, C. to Mme Bielke, 28 Apr. 1776; Corberon, i: 224–30, 25–6 Apr. NS.
20. Dimsdale, 46, informed by W. Tooke.
21. Corberon, i: 248, 7 May 1776 NS.
22. Best. D20207, C. to Voltaire, 25 June 1776.
23. McGrew, 93–8; Zavadovskii, 242–3, Apr. 1776.
24. *SIRIO*, xxvii: 115–6, in C.'s own hand.
25. *SIRIO*, xxvii: 117–8, C. to Mme Bielke, 5 Sept. 1776.
26. *SIRIO*, xxvii: 109, C. to Paul, early Aug. 1776.
27. Corberon, ii: 7–9, 7 Oct. 1776 NS.
28. Corberon, ii: 20, 13 Oct. 1776 NS. The second performance was 'very badly attended': ibid., 22.
29. McGrew, 99–103.
30. Harris Diaries, i: 174, Harris to Yorke, 2/13 Feb. 1778.
31. Harris Diaries, i: 178–79, Harris to Suffolk, 7/18 Mar. 1778.
32. Grimm, 83, 2–4 Mar. 1778.
33. Lopatin, 39 [30 Aug. 1774].
34. S. G. Runkevich, *Sviato-Troitskaia Aleksandro-Nevskaia Lavra, 1713–1913*, 2 vols. (SPb, 2001 edn.), ii: 134–5, 137–8; N. Belekhov and A. Petrov, *Ivan Starov: Materialy k izucheniiu tvorchestva* (M, 1950), 67–8; *KfZh* (1778), 537–47.

35. Proschwitz, 131–2, C. to Gustav III, 2 Sept. 1778.
36. *KfZh* (1781), 525–6; Proschwitz, 159, 15 Dec. 1781.
37. *SIRIO*, XV: 39, C. to Paul and Maria Fëdorovna, undated.
38. On tears, see *SIRIO*, XXVII: 308, C's instruction to Saltykov.
39. Proschwitz, 159, C. to Gustav III, 15 Dec. 1781.
40. *SIRIO*, IX: 97, C. to Maria Fëdorovna, 7 Dec. 1781
41. Grimm, 176, 14 May 1780; see also 190, 2 Oct.
42. M. Okenfuss, *The Discovery of Childhood in Russia* (Newtonville, MA, 1980), 58–62.
43. Madariaga, 495–8 (497–8). The 'Book On the Duties of Man and Citizen' is translated by E. Gorky in J. L. Black, *Citizens for the Fatherland: Education, educators, and pedagogical ideals in eighteenth-century Russia* (Boulder, CO, 1979), 209–66.
44. *SIRIO*, IX: 110, C. to Maria Fëdorovna, 4 Jan. 1782.
45. Ibid., 124, 25 Feb. 1782.
46. Ibid., 127, 10 Mar. 1782.
47. E. P. Renne, 'Kartiny Bromptona v Ermitazhe', in *Zapadno-Evropeiskoe iskusstvo XVIII veka: Publikatsii i issledovaniia* (Leningrad, 1987), 57–8. On Brompton – 'a harum-scarum artist' to Jeremy Bentham, yet to C. a second Van Dyck – see Cross, 308–12.
48. Lopatin, 189, early 1784; Zorin, *Kormia dvuglavogo orla*, 130–1.
49. Harris Diaries, I: 236, Harris to Weymouth, 24 May/4 June 1779.
50. Shvidkovsky, *The empress and the architect*, 105.
51. Harris Diaries, I: 237–8, Harris to Weymouth, 24 May/4 June 1779.
52. Harris Papers, 1036, G. Harris to E. Harris, 2/13 July 1779. On *Hermes*, see C. T. Probyn, *The sociable Humanist: The life and works of James Harris* (Oxford, 1991), ch. 5.
53. The following draws on 'Zhurnal vysochaishago puteshestviia v gorod Mogilev 1780 g.', *KfZh* (1780), 267–432; 'Dnevnaia zapiska puteshestviia Eia Imperatorskago Velichestva chrez Pskov i Polotsk v Mogilev', *SIRIO*, I: 384–420; and C.'s letters to Paul and Maria Fëdorovna, *SIRIO*, IX: 39–63. See also Beales, *Joseph II*, 431–8 and N. V. Bessarabova, 'Iosif II i Ekaterina II v puteshestviiakh po Rossii', in *Nemtsy v Rossii: rossiisko-nemetskii dialog*, ed. G. I. Smagina (SPb, 2001), 461–9.
54. Grimm, 166, 7 Dec. 1779.
55. Dimsdale, 71; Bessarabova, 38, 45–6.
56. Grimm, 178, 16 May 1780.
57. *AKV*, XIII: 16.
58. *SIRIO*, IX: 49, 19 May 1780.
59. *SIRIO*, IX: 48, 18 May 1780.
60. Grand Duke Nikolai Mikhailovich, *Graf Pavel Aleksandrovich Stroganov (1774–1817)*, 3 vols. (SPb, 1903), I: 237–8, A. S. Stroganov to G. Romme. A total of 300 noble pupils and 130 children of townspeople were enrolled in the six schools in Polotsk province in 1780, when Mogilëv province had 34 schools with 858 pupils: Madariaga, 494.
61. *SIRIO*, IX: 51, 22 May 1780; *KfZh* (1780), 329. On the *namestniki*'s silver services, see above, p. 240.
62. Grimm, 180, 25 May 1780.
63. Engelhardt, 33–6 (33). On the landscape, see ibid., p. 28, and *SIRIO*, IX: 53, 24 May 1780.
64. *KfZh* (1780), 336–9; Lopatin, 140, C. to Potemkin, 23 May 1780.
65. Lopatin, 139, 22 May 1780.
66. Engelhardt, 26–31; Montefiore, 225.

67. Grimm, 181, 27 May 1780; ibid., 208, 23 June 1781.
68. Grimm, 181, 190, 27 May and 2 Oct. 1780.
69. *SIRIO*, IX: 59, 1 June 1780.
70. Harris Diaries, I: 313, Harris to Elliot (at Berlin), 2/13 June 1780.
71. Harris Diaries, I: 314, Harris to Keith (at Vienna), June 1780.
72. Bezborodko, 231, 17 Oct. 1780.
73. P. Mansel, *Prince of Europe: The life of Charles-Joseph de Ligne* (London, 2003), 101.
74. I. de Madariaga, 'The secret Austro-Russian treaty of 1781', *SEER*, 38 (1959), 114–45; Ransel, *Politics*, 254–5.
75. Anderson, ed., *Letters of Mozart*, 780, 24 Nov. 1781 NS.
76. McGrew, 120.
77. McGrew, 112–42; N. I. Stadnichuk, 'Puteshestvie grafa i grafini severnykh v neapolitanskoe korolevstvo', *PKNO*: 2004 (M, 2006), 398–431.
78. The following draws on 'Peterburgskoe obshchestvo v 1781 g., pis'ma Pikara k kn. A.B. Kurakinu', *RS*, Apr. 1870, 297–321; 'S.-Peterburg v 1782 godu: izvestiia Pikara o sobytiiakh v gorode i pri dvore', *RS*, May 1878, 39–66.
79. Bezborodko, 253, 25 Nov. 1781.
80. Grimm, 47, 18 Apr. 1776.
81. Khrapovitskii, 1–2, 18 Apr. and 25 July 1782; J. M. Hartley, 'Catherine's conscience court – an English equity court?', in *Russia and the West in the Eighteenth Century*, ed. A. G. Cross (Newtonville, MA, 1981).
82. Madariaga, 292–5.
83. Montefiore, 237–8, gives different dates.
84. Grimm, 152, 14 July 1779.
85. *KfZh* (1781), 654.
86. 'Peterburgskoe obshchestvo', 300, 12 Oct. 1781.
87. *KfZh* (1782), 50.
88. Grimm, 242–3, 28 June 1782.
89. Falconet, 130, C. to Falconet, 1 June 1770, records the complaint of the 'scandalised' Chebyshev, chief procurator of the Holy Synod. cf. Schenker, *Bronze Horseman*, 249–51.
90. Harris to Grantham, 9 Aug. 1782, quoted in C. Frank, ' "A man more jealous of glory than of wealth": Houdon's dealings with Russia', in *Jean-Antoine Houdon: Sculptor of the Enlightenment*, ed. A. L. Poulet (Washington, D.C., 2003), 56.
91. Grimm, 64–5, 10 Sept. 1777.
92. Corberon, II: 177–80, 21–22 Sept. NS; Proschwitz, 93, C. to Gustav III, 29 Sept. 1777.
93. Lopatin, 118, after 10 Sept. 1777. C. remembered the precise height of the waters in 1777 when the river rose again (by only seven feet) in 1794: Grimm, 603, 21 Apr. 1794.
94. Dimsdale, 41.
95. *PSZ*, XX: 14,968, 14 Jan. 1780. For an inspection, see *KfZh* (1786), 371–4. On the dispute in 1787, see Alexander, 261.
96. Storch, 15. See also, Stedingk, I: 40.
97. Quoted in Shvidkovsky, *The Empress and the Architect*, 45.
98. V. Shevchenko, 'Proekt "antichnogo doma" dlia Ekateriny II. Mify i real'nost', in L. Tedeschi and N. Navone, eds., *Ot mifa k proektu: Vliianie ital'ianskikh i tichinskikh arkhitektorov v Rossii epokhi klassitsizma* (SPb, 2004), 76–9.
99. Grimm, 379, 7 July 1786; Shvidkovsky, *The Empress and the Architect*, 61–9.

100. Shvidkovsky, *The Empress and the Architect*, 85; Dimsdale, 53. See also Grimm, 239, 2 June 1782.

101. Grimm, 207–8, 22 June 1781.

102. *SIRIO*, IX: 140, C. to Maria Fëdorovna, 23 Apr. 1782.

103. Quoted in S. Massie, *Pavlovsk: The Life of a Russian Palace* (London, 1990), 32–3, where the visit is dated 11 May, presumably the NS date of K. Kiukhel'beker's letter to Maria Fëdorovna. Compare *SIRIO*, IX: 145–7, C. to Mariia Fedorovna, 2 May 1782; *KfZh* (1782), 186, 29 Apr.

104. Grimm, 157, 23 Aug. 1779.

105. Grimm, 255, 15 Nov. 1782.

106. Corberon, I: 156, 4 Feb. 1776 NS.

107. A. Moore, 'The Houghton Sale', in *British Art Treasures*, 46–55; J. Conlin, *The Nation's Mantelpiece: A history of the National Gallery* (London, 2006), 21–8.

108. Grimm, 47, 18 Apr. 1776; 145, 18 June 1779. See also C. Frank, ' "Plus il y en aura, mieux ce sera" – Caterina II di Russia e Anton Raphael Mengs. Suo ruolo degli agenti 'cesarei' Grimm e Reiffenstein', in *Mengs: La Scoperta del Neoclassico*, ed. S. Roettgen (Padua, 2001), 86–95.

109. Grimm, 167, 2 Jan. 1780; 253, 14 Nov. 1782; McGrew, 134; *Charles-Louis Clérisseau (1721–1820): Dessins du musée de l'Ermitage Saint-Pétersbourg* (Paris, 1995).

110. Grimm, 93, 21 June 1778; Frank, ' "A man more jealous of glory than wealth" ', in *Jean-Antoine Houdon*, ed. Poulet, 54–5.

111. Bentham, II: 201, J. Bentham to S. Bentham, 20–21 Dec. 1778.

112. M. P. Alekseev, 'Biblioteka Vol'tera v Rossii', in *Biblioteka Vol'tera: Katalog knig* (Leningrad, 1961), 9, 26.

113. Grimm, 221, 27 Sept. 1781.

114. S. Ia. Karp, 'Perepiska Grimma s Verzhennom (1775–1777)', in *Russko-frantsuzskie kul'turnye sviazi v epokhu Prosveshcheniia: Materialy i issledovaniia* (M, 2001), 137–8, Grimm to Vergennes, 15 Feb. 1777. De Mailly's piece was delivered, to general acclamation, in June 1778: see Grimm, 95.

115. Grimm, 84, 2–4 Mar. 1778; N. Rotshtein, 'Novyia knigi po keramiki', *Starye gody*, Apr. 1909, 219. 'A Rouble is 5 French livres', Bentham, II: 126, J. Bentham to S. Bentham, 18 June 1778.

116. Grimm, 135, 16 Apr. 1779.

117. Quarenghi, 58, to Betskoy, July 1784.

118. Madariaga, 387–9; Smith, *Love and Conquest*, 115–20; Montefiore, 246–9, 252–9; Lopatin, 176, 15 July 1783.

119. L. V. Tychinina and N. B. Bessarabova, *Kniaginia Dashkova i imperatorskii dvor* (M, 2006), 40–63, summarises the evidence of *KfZh*.

120. Madariaga, 535.

121. G. I. Smagina, 'Kniaginia Ekaterina Romanovna Dashkova: Shtrikhi k portretu', in E. R. Dashkova, *O smysle slova 'vospitanie': sochineniia, pis'ma, dokumenty* (M, 2001), 56–63, 71–2.

122. Beer and Fiedler, I: 20, Cobenzl to Joseph II, 5 May 1780 NS.

123. Dimsdale, 57; Proschwitz, 196, C. to Gustav III, 10 Jul. 1783.

124. Grimm, 84, 2–4 Mar. 1778. See also, Parkinson, 27, 11 Nov. 1792.

125. 'Dnevnik grafa Bobrinskago', *RA*, Oct. 1877, 135, 23 Feb. 1782.

126. *AKV*, XXI: 264.

127. V. I. Piliavskii, *Dzhakomo Kvarengi* (Leningrad, 1981), 63, 73–4; Cross, 282, where the ownership of the estate is unidentified.

128. Corberon, II: 330, 4 Sept. 1780 NS.

129. Grimm, 253, 15 Nov. 1782; Zavadovskii, 279, n.d. [Feb. 1783].

130. *KfZh* (1783), 59. Of these, 2640 were nobles and 490 merchants. 8170 tickets had been issued: 7100 to nobles and 1070 to merchants.
131. Grimm, 268, 3 Mar. 1783; *KfZh* (1783), 78–9.
132. Zavadovskii, 275, 25 Nov. 1782.
133. Harris Diaries, II: 11–12.
134. Grimm, 274–5, 20 Apr. 1783.
135. Lopatin, 186, 16 Oct. 1783.
136. Grimm, 316–7, 7 July 1784.
137. Parkinson, 49–50; see also 45–6.
138. *AKV*, XXI: 284, n.
139. Alexander, 216–7, is misled by *SIRIO*, XXVI: 281, where Bezborodko's letter to Potëmkin, reporting that the funeral took place 'yesterday', is misdated 28 July 1784. The letter's contents, and the collateral evidence of *KfZh*, place it at 28 June. Montefiore, 553, n. 3, unaccountably dates it 29 June, which invalidates his account of a funeral on 27 July, pp. 312–4.
140. *KfZh* (1784), 380.
141. *SIRIO*, XXVI: 281, Bezborodko to Potëmkin [28 June 1784].
142. *RS* (Sept. 1879), 151, C. to U. Ia. Lanskaia, oddly dated 25 June rather than 26 June.
143. *KfZh* (1784), 382–4.
144. *AKV*, XXI: 462, E. Polianskaia to S. R. Vorontsov, 6 July 1784.
145. *AKV*, XXXI: 444, A. R. to S. R. Vorontsov, 21 July 1784.
146. *Lettres au Prince de Ligne*, 47, 18 Aug. 1784; J. T. Alexander, 'Aeromania, "fire balloons", and Catherine the Great's ban of 1784', *The Historian*, 58 (1996).
147. *KfZh* (1784), 396, 398–9, 442–7; *Sochineniia*, XII: .
148. Grimm, 337, 25 Apr. 1785; *AKV*, XXXI: 448, A. R. to S. R. Vorontsov, 29 Aug. 1784; *KfZh* (1784), 452–4.
149. *KfZh* (1784), 456–9.
150. Grimm, 318, 322, 9 and 26 Sept. 1784.
151. Beer and Fiedler, I: 482, 484, Cobenzl to Joseph, 3 Nov. 1784.

Chapter 11

1. *KfZh* (1785), 221–2.
2. Madariaga, 484; Alexander, 218; Cross, *'By the Banks of the Thames'*, 243, quoting S. R. Vorontsov.
3. Beer and Fiedler, II: 37, Cobenzl to Joseph, 14 May 1785; Alexander, 217; Grimm, 336, 24 Apr. 1785.
4. Jones, *Emancipation of the Russian Nobility*, ch. 8; Madariaga, 295–9.
5. D. Griffiths and G. Munro, eds., *Catherine II's Charters of 1785 to the Nobility and the Towns* (Bakersfield, CA, 1991), *passim*, esp. p. lxiv, introduction by Griffiths.
6. *KfZh* (1785), 281, 307; Coxe, II: 290–5; Ségur, II: 262–3.
7. Zavadovskii, 289, 28 Apr. 1785.
8. *PSZ*, XXII: 16,381, 28 Apr. 1786.
9. Grimm, 342, 1 June 1785.
10. *Lettere*, 162, 31 May 1785.
11. *SIRIO*, XV: 23, C. to Paul and Maria Fëdorovna, 16 June 1785.
12. *Lettere*, 162, 8 June 1785.
13. Coxe, I: 444, 424, 422.

14. R. E. Jones, *Provincial development in Russia: Catherine II and Jakob Sievers* (New Brunswick, NJ, 1984); N. V. Sereda, *Reformy upravleniia Ekateriny Vtoroi* (Moscow, 2004). A. Jones, 'A Russian bourgeois's Arctic Enlightenment', *Historical Journal*, 48 (2005), 623–46, shows that merchant civic involvement was not confined to the central provinces.

15. Grimm, 343, 20 June 1785.

16. *KfZh* (1785), 311; *Lettere*, 162, 31 May 1785.

17. *KfZh* (1785), 281–360, *passim*.

18. *KfZh* (1785), 340.

19. *KfZh* (1785), 354–5; Cross, 298.

20. *KfZh* (1785), 363–7.

21. Ségur, II: 265–6.

22. D. V. Tsvetaev, 'Ukazy i pis'ma Imperatritsy Ekateriny Velikoi', *Zhurnal ministerstva iustitsii* (Dec. 1915), 195, C. to Viazemskii, 16 June 1785; Grimm, 342, 14 June.

23. *KfZh* (1785), appendix, 45.

24. Grimm, 344, 28 June 1785.

25. Letter to the Marquis de Lafayette, 10 May 1786 NS, quoted in M. R. Key, *Catherine the Great's Linguistic Contribution* (Carbondale, IL, 1980), 62, an odd but not wholly negligible book.

26. *SK*, 6812; Madariaga, *Short History*, 99.

27. Belekhov and Petrov, *Ivan Starov*, 103–14.

28. *SIRIO*, XV: 23, C. to Paul and Maria Fëdorovna, 8 June 1785.

29. Gerchuk, *Bazhenov*, 123–63.

30. Parkinson, 212, 19 Nov. 1792.

31. Madariaga, 524–5; McGrew, 195–6.

32. Grimm, 167, 2 Jan. 1780.

33. Zimmerman, 245–6, 17 Apr. 1786.

34. *Pis'ma N.I. Novikova*, eds. M. V. Reizin, et al (SPb, 1994), 42; Jones, *Nikolay Novikov*, 185–91; Marker, *Publishing*, 220–6; Zimmerman, 247, 22 Apr. 1787.

35. Grimm, 372, 10 Nov. 1785.

36. Diderot, *Oeuvres*, ed. L. Versini (Paris, 1995), III: 515, 546 (paras VIII, LXXV).

37. Grimm, 372–3, 23 Nov. 1785.

38. Piliavskii, *Kvarengi*, 121.

39. Ibid., 64.

40. *KfZh* (1785), 704.

41. Piliavskii, *Kvarengi*, 122.

42. Khrapovitskii, 19 and 21 Apr. 1786.

43. *MP*, II: 343; G. Seaman, 'The national element in early Russian opera ', *Music and Letters*, 42 (1961), 260–1. *Lettres de Cte Valetin Esterhazy a sa femme 1784–1792*, ed. E. Daudet (Paris, 1907), 318–9.

44. G. Moracci, ' "Bolee truda nezheli smekha": Pis'mo Ekateriny II L'vu Aleskandrovichu Naryshkinu', *Russian Literature*, 52 (2002), 243–9.

45. L. D. O'Malley, *The dramatic works of Catherine the Great: Theatre and politics in eighteenth-century Russia* (Aldershot, 2006), 140–67.

46. Lopatin, 209, Potëmkin to C., 6 Oct. 1786.

47. Zimmerman, 244, C. to Dr Zimmerman, 10 Jan. 1786.

48. Grimm, 328, 17 Dec. 1786.

49. *Sochineniia*, IV: appendix, 189–219; Khrapovitskii, 163, 29 Sept. 1788; 167, 5 Oct.; 174, 15 Oct.

50. *AKV*, XXI: 467, Elisaveta Polianskaia to S. R. Vorontsov, 1 Jan. 1787.

51. Krapovitskii, 21, 17 Dec. 1786; Lopatin, 212, C. to Potëmkin, 18 Dec.; A. G. Brikner, 'Zel'mira: epizod iz istorii tsarstvovaniia imperatritsy Ekateriny II', *Istoricheskii vestnik* (1890), 277–303; 551–72.

52. Zavadovskii, 276–7, 26 Jan. 1783.

53. Bentham, III: 310, S. Bentham to J. Bentham, 6/17 Sept. 1784; *KfZh* (1784), appendix, 71, 26 Sept.

54. 'Pis'ma grafa A.R. Vorontsova k bratu ego grafu Semenu Romanovichu i ego supruge, 1783–1785', *AKV*, XXXI: 463–4, 24 Oct., 1 Nov. 1784; Bezborodko, 279, 23 July 1785; Grimm, 333, 15 Apr. 1785.

55. Coxe, I: 245.

56. Khrapovitskii, 23, 17 Jan. 1787.

57. *KfZh* (1787), appendix: 5, C. to Ia. A. Brius, 17 Jan. 1787; Bychkov, 166, C. to N. V. Repnin, 16 Jan. 1787.

58. *Istoricheskii ocherk Smolenska* (SPb, 1894), 55–7.

59. Khrapovitskii, 23–4.

60. *Slova i rechi Georgiia Koniiskago, Arkhiepiskopa Mogilevskago* (Mogilev, 1892), 242.

61. Engelhgardt, 54.

62. Bentham, III: 523, 525–6, J. Bentham to G. Wilson, 9/20 Feb. 1787.

63. *AKV*, XII: 35, P. V. Zavadovskii to A. R. Vorontsov, 8 Mar. 1787.

64. Ségur, III: 31.

65. *Lettere*, 166, 30 Jan 1787.

66. *Lettere*, 167, 6 Feb. 1787.

67. Zimmerman, 247, 22 Apr. 1787; V. S. Ikonnikov, 'Kiev v 1654–1855 gg.', *Kievskaia starina* (Sept. 1904), 273.

68. Quoted in L. Wolff, *Inventing Eastern Europe*, 127, 130.

69. *Lettere*, 175, 15 Mar. 1787.

70. Zimmerman, 247, 22 Apr. 1787.

71. Grimm, 393, 8 Feb. 1787; Khrapovitskii, 28, 20 Mar.; Montefiore, 357–62.

72. Khrapovitskii, 26, 22 Feb. 1787.

73. *Archivo del General Miranda, Viajes: Diarios 1785–1787* (Caracas, 1929), II: 256, 11 Feb. 1787.

74. *Lettere*, 170, 20 Feb. 1787; 175, 15 Mar.

75. Khrapovitskii, 24, 7 Feb. 1787. The abbess was the former Countess Anna Pavlovna Iaguzhinskaia.

76. *Lettere*, 169, 16 Feb. 1787.

77. *Baedeker's Russia 1914* (London, 1971 edn.), 381.

78. N. Ia. Ozeretskovskii, *Puteshestvie po Rossii 1782–1783*, ed. S. Kozlov (SPb, 1996), 135, diary, 12 June 1783; *Archivo del General Miranda*, II: 259, 15 Feb. 1787.

79. *KfZh* (1787), appendix.

80. Ibneeva, *Puteshestviia Ekateriny*, 145–6.

81. *SIRIO*, 23: 396, 2 Apr. 1787; ibid., 703–5, 'Vedomost' o den'gakh, perevodimykh k statskomu sovetniku baronu Grimmu'.

82. Khrapovitskii, 25–32, 15 Feb.– 21 Apr. 1787; I. Reyfman, *Ritualized violence Russian style: The duel in Russian culture and literature* (Stanford, CA, 1999), 52–3.

83. Khrapovitskii, 32, 16 Apr. 1787; Madariaga, *Short History*, 207–8.

84. Ibneeva, *Puteshestviia Ekateriny*, 140–4 (142).

85. *Lettere*, 179, 1 Apr. 1787; Khrapovitskii, 30, 4 Apr.
86. Bantysh-Kamenskii, *Spiski*, 159.
87. A. M. Panchenko, 'Potemkinskie derevni kak kul'turnyi mif', *XVIII vek*, 14 (1983), 93–104.
88. *SIRIO*, XV: 105, C. to Paul and Maria Fëdorovna, 14 May 1787; Madariaga, 373. Kherson had actually been founded in 1778.
89. Ozeretskovskii, *Puteshestvie*, 131, diary, 22 May 1783.
90. O. I. Eliseeva, *Geopoliticheskie proekty G. A. Potemkina* (M, 2000), 191–216.
91. Zorin, *Kormia dvuglavogo orla*, ch. 4; A. Schönle, 'Garden of the Empire: Catherine's appropriation of the Crimea', *Slavic Review*, 60 (2001), 1–23.
92. S. Dickinson, 'Russia's First "Orient": Characterizing the Crimea in 1787', *Kritika*, 3 (2002), 22–4; Khrapovitskii, 28, 14 Mar. 1787.
93. Khrapovitskii, 38–9, 8 June 1787; 40, 21 June.
94. Papmehl, *Metropolitan Platon*, 48–9.
95. D. Smith, *The Pearl: A true tale of forbidden love in Catherine the Great's Russia* (New Haven, CT, 2008), 75–84 (75).
96. Zimmerman, 251, 3 Dec. 1787.
97. Lopatin, 223, C. to Potëmkin, 24 Aug. 1787; 229–30, Potëmkin to C., 16 Sept; 232, Potëmkin to C., 24 Sept; 238, C. to Potëmkin, 2 Oct.; 240, C. to Potëmkin, 9 Oct.
98. Alexander, 264, 269; Madariaga, 396–405; Lopatin, 329, 16 Dec. 1788.
99. Khrapovitskii, 215, 18 Dec. 1788.
100. Madariaga, 401.
101. Lopatin, 300, C. to Potëmkin, 3 July 1788; 303, 17 July.
102. Madariaga 399–400, Montefiore, 360–1.
103. Khrapovitskii, 277, 21 Apr. 1789; Alexander, 219–21.
104. Lopatin, 355, C. to Potëmkin, 29 June 1789.
105. Madariaga, 540–1.
106. Lopatin, 372, Potëmkin to C., 22 Sept. 1789.
107. Lopatin, 379, C. to Potëmkin, 18 Oct. 1789.
108. A. Iu. Andreev, *Russkie studenty v nemetskikh universitetakh XVIII – pervoi poloviny XIX veka* (M, 2005), 182–208.
109. Madariaga, 541–5; C.'s notes in A. N. Radishchev, A *Journey from St Petersburg to Moscow*, trans. L. Wiener, ed. R. P. Thaler (Cambridge, MA, 1958), 239–40, emphasis in the original.

Chapter 12

1. Khrapovitskii, 331, 3–4 May 1790; *KfZh* (1790), 217.
2. Khrapovitskii, 333, 23 May 1790.
3. *KfZh* (1790), 269; Zavadovskii, 329–30, 14 June 1790.
4. *KfZh* (1790), 301–2, 26 June 1790; Lopatin, 419, 28 June; Grimm, 493, 12 Sept.
5. Alexander, 281–2; Madariaga, 413–4; Lopatin, 426, 9 Aug. 1790.
6. Lopatin, 426, 9 Aug. 1790; *KfZh* (1790), 425–43; *MP*, III: 83–4.
7. Runkevich, *Aleksandro-Nevskaia Lavra*, II: 146; S. K. Batalden, *Catherine II's Greek Prelate: Eugenios Voulgaris in Russia, 1771–1806* (New York, 1982), 79–80 and *passim*.
8. Lopatin, 429, 29 Aug. 1790.
9. Stedingk, 21, 10 Oct. 1790 NS.
10. Khrapovitskii, 349, 1–5, 7 Oct. 1790.
11. Grimm, 500, 27 Sept. 1790.

12. Stedingk, 99, 17 Mar. 1791 NS; 23, 10 Oct 1790 NS.

13. Stedingk, 78, 8 Feb. 1791 NS; 33, 18/27 Oct. 1790.

14. Khrapovitskii, 350, 24 Oct. 1790.

15. Stedingk, 40, J. J. Jennings to G. de Franc, 13 Nov. 1790 NS.

16. *KfZh* (1790), 614.

17. Stedingk, 44–5, 26 Nov. 1790 NS.

18. *SIRIO*, XLII, 123–4; Stedingk, 45, 26 Nov. 1790 NS; Khrapovitskii, 350–1, 25, 29, 31 Oct., 1, 5, 6, 10 Nov. 1790.

19. Stedingk, 57–8, 29 Dec. 1790 NS.

20. V. S. Lopatin, *Potemkin i Suvorov* (M, 1992), 187–97; P. Longworth, *The art of victory: The life and achievements of Field-Marshal Suvorov* (London, 1965), 165–74.

21. Montefiore, 450 (Damas); A. V. Suvorov, *Pis'ma*, ed. V. S. Lopatin (M, 1986), 207, Suvorov to Potëmkin, 11 Dec. 1790.

22. Montefiore, 580, n. 22; Stedingk, 65, 14 Jan. 1791 NS.

23. A. Zorin, 'Redkaia veshch': 'sandunovskii skandal' i russkii dvor vremen Frantsuzskoi revoliutsii', *Novoe literaturnoe obozrenie*, 80 (2006), 91–110. See also, W. Rosslyn, 'Petersburg actresses on and off stage (1775–1825)', in *St Petersburg 1703–1825*, ed. Cross, esp. 122, 140.

24. M. Duffy, *The Englishman and the foreigner* (London, 1986), 40, pl. 86.

25. A. Cross, 'Catherine in British caricature', in *Catherine the Great and the British: A pot-pourri of essays* (Nottingham, 2001), 33–8; Alexander, 289.

26. J. Black, *British foreign policy in an age of revolutions, 1783–1793* (Cambridge, 1994), 285–91.

27. Khrapovitskii, 359, 15 Mar. 1791; Madariaga, 417–9.

28. Stedingk, 112, 8 Apr. NS.

29. Khrapovitskii, 361, 7–8 Apr. 1791. Lopatin, *Potemkin i Suvorov*, 228, ascribes these words to Potëmkin.

30. M. S. Anderson, *Britain's discovery of Russia 1553–1815* (London, 1958), 154–85.

31. Alexander, 289; Parkinson quoted in Cross, 328.

32. P. Schroeder, *The Transformation of European politics 1763–1848* (Oxford, 1994), 81.

33. Stedingk, 103–4, 25 Mar. 1791 NS; Lopatin, *Potemkin i Suvorov*, 215.

34. Tooke, III: 365. On this influential work, see D. Griffiths, 'Castéra-Tooke: the first Western biographer(s) of Catherine II', *SGECRN*, 10 (1982), 50–62.

35. Zorin, *Kormia dvuglavogo orla*, 138–41.

36. Tooke, III: 367–8.

37. Quoted in Wortman, *Scenarios*, 145.

38. Zorin, *Kormia dvuglavogo orla*, 126–7.

39. Stedingk, 137, 18 May 1791 NS; Grimm, 519, 29 Apr. 1791.

40. Zorin, *Kormia dvuglavogo orla*, 128–30; Madariaga, 424.

41. See R. Butterwick, 'Political discourses of the Polish Revolution, 1788–1792', *English Historical Review*, 120 (2005), 695–731.

42. Constitution quoted in J. Michalski, 'The meaning of the Constitution of 3 May', in *Constitution and reform in eighteenth-century Poland*, ed. S. Fiszman (Bloomington, IN, 1997), 271.

43. Madariaga, 420–44; Schroeder, *Transformation of European politics*, 83–6 (86).

44. Khrapovitskii, 371–2, 16 Aug. 1791.

45. *Lettres de Cte Valentin Esterhazy a sa femme 1784–1792*, ed. E. Daudet (Paris, 1907), 305, 12 Sept. 1791.

46. *Lettres de Esterhazy*, 288, 4 Sept. 1791; Grimm, 558, 16 Sept.; 560, 23 Sept; Khrapovitskii, 374–5, 16 Sept.

47. *Lettres de Esterhazy*, 301, 9 Sept. 1791.

48. Madariaga, 425–6.

49. Lopatin, C. to Potëmkin, 468, 16 Sept. 1791; 470, 30 Sept.

50. Tooke, III, 385.

51. Lopatin, 470, C. to Potëmkin, 3 Oct; Potëmkin to C., 4 Oct.; Khrapovitskii, 374–6; Montefiore, 481–6.

52. *Lettres de Esterhazy*, 347, 29 Oct. 1791.

53. Suvorov, *Pis'ma*, 226–7, to D. I. Khvostov, [30 Oct.] and 12 Dec. 1791; Lopatin, *Potemkin i Suvorov*, 224–7.

54. Khrapovitskii, 377, 12 Oct. 1791; Grimm, 561, 13 Oct.

55. *Obshchii arkhiv Ministerstva Imperatorskago Dvora: Opisi domov i dvizhimago imushchestva kniazia Potemkina-Tavricheskago, kuplennykh u naslednikov ego Imperatritseiu Ekaterinoiu II* (M, 1892), *passim*; Montefiore, 344; Batalden, *Catherine II's Greek Prelate*, 75–6.

56. Grimm, 605, 27 Aug. 1794.

57. Belekhov and Petrov, *Ivan Starov*, 81–102; A. G. Cross, 'British sources for Catherine's Russia: 1) Lionel Colmore's Letters from St Petersburg, 1790–91', *SGECRN*, 17 (1989), 31.

58. Parkinson, 37, 17 Nov. 1792.

59. Cross, 274–6.

60. *SIRIO*, XLII, 19 Jan. 1793.

61. Khrapovitskii, 346, 2 Sept. 1790; 405, 22 July 1792.

62. Madariaga, 412; Alexander, 281; *KfZh* (1796), appendix II, 'Vypiski iz arkhivnykh del', 18. Catherine translated Plutarch into Russian from the Latin, probably using one of the widely available Greek-Latin parallel editions of his work: see Khrapovitskii, 325, 331, 559.

63. *The Memoirs of Catherine the Great*, ed. and trans. Cruse and Hoogenboom, xlix–liv, 'Introduction' by Hoogenboom.

64. Grimm, 609, 29 Aug. 1794; *SIRIO*, XLII: 320–21, undated, 1792.

65. J. P. LeDonne, *Absolutism and ruling class: The formation of the Russian political order 1700–1825* (New York, 1991), 21; *idem, Ruling Russia*, 350.

66. Proskurina, *Mify imperii*, 279–314.

67. Alexander, 286, 294–5, 321; Madariaga, 565–7; Parkinson, 48, 1 Dec. 1792 NS.

68. Cross, 79–81; Montefiore, 436–7, 576, n. 43; Khrapovitskii, 403, 6 July 1792.

69. Faggionato, *Rosicrucian Utopia*, 208–16; Madariaga, 527–30; Jones, *Nikolay Novikov*, 203–15.

70. Alexander, 305.

71. A. Cross, 'Condemned by correspondence: Horace Walpole and Catherine "Slay-Czar"', in Cross, *Catherine the Great and the British*, 25.

72. See, for example, R. Butterwick, 'Deconfessionalization? The policy of the Polish Revolution towards Ruthenia, 1788–1792', *Central Europe*, 6 (2008), 91–121.

73. R. H. Lord, *The second partition of Poland: A study in diplomatic history* (Cambridge, MA, 1915), 84–7, 512–16, remains the classic work. See also Eliseeva, *Geopoliticheskie proekty*, 272–89.

74. Quoted in Lord, *Second partition*, 307.

75. Schroeder, *Transformation of European politics*, 96, 104–5, 122–3.

76. Zavadovskii, 340, 15 Nov. 1794.

77. Schroeder, *Transformation of European politics*, 144–50; Madariaga, 441–51; Alexander, 319.

78. *KfZh* (1796), appendix II, 'Vypiski iz arkhivnykh del', 18.

79. Grimm, 565, 14 Apr. 1792; 593, 11 Feb. 1794; 601, 3 Apr.

80. Marker, *Publishing*, 226–9.

81. 'Kak gotovilos' ekaterinoslavskoe dukhovenstvo k vstreche imper. Ekateriny II', *Kievskaia starina*, 1887, no. 4, 797–8.

82. L. G. Kisliagina, 'Kantseliariia stats-sekretarei pri Ekaterine II', in *Gosudarstvennye uchrezhdeniia Rossii XVI–XVIII vv.*, ed. N. B. Golikova (M, 1991), 185–9.

83. *KfZh* (1795), appendix II, 'Vypiski iz arkhivnykh del', *passim*, quoted at 193–4 (Orlov); Grimm, 644, 25 Aug. 1795 (Suvorov); *SIRIO*, XLII: 256–7 (telescope).

84. Khrapovitskii, 328, 18 Mar. 1790.

85. Grimm, 597, 14 Feb. 1794.

86. A. Odom and L. P. Arend, *A Taste for Splendour: Russian Imperial and European treasures from the Hillwood Museum* (Alexandria, VA, 1998), 212–4.

87. *KfZh* (1795), appendix II, 122, 173, 175.

88. *KfZh* (1795), appendix II, 185–6.

89. *Memoirs of Countess Golovine: A lady at the Court of Catherine II*, trans. G. M. Fox-Davies (London, 1910), 129.

90. Alexander, 321; Grimm, 570, 13 Aug. 1792; *KfZh* (1795), appendix II, 234, 246, 248; ibid. (1796), 34.

91. Grimm, 669, 18 Feb. 1796.

92. Grimm, 583, 14 May 1793.

93. Khrapovitskii, 404, 9–11 July 1792; Grimm, 618, 16 Jan. 1795; *KfZh* (1795), 65–80, 89–90.

94. Quoted in W. B. Lincoln, *Nicholas I: Emperor and autocrat of all the Russias* (London, 1978), 49.

95. Khrapovitskii, 378, 16 Oct. 1791.

96. *Sochineniia*, XII: 702; *SIRIO*, XLII: 267. Cf. Alexander, 297–9.

97. Grimm, 591, 11 Feb. 1794.

98. Parkinson, 226, 18 Feb. 1794.

99. Tooke, III: 434.

100. Stedingk, 81–2, 14 Feb. 1791 NS; A. Gribovskii, *Zapiski o Imperatritse Ekaterine Velikoi*, 2nd edn. (M, 1864), 29.

101. C. F. P. Masson, *Mémoires secrets sur la russie pendant les règnes de Catherine II et de Paul Ier* (Paris, 1863), 70–1.

102. Alexander, 322–4.

103. *KfZh* (1796), 667–76; 724–5; *RBS*, Pritits-Reis (SPb 1910), 'Anna Protasova'.

104. Alexander, 324–5; McGrew, 187–9; *KfZh* (1796), 736–48.

Epilogue

1. *Karlik favorita: Istoriia zhizni Ivana Iakubovskago*, ed. V. P. Zubov (Munich, 1968), 41.

2. *Zapiski, mneniia i perepiska admiral A. S. Shishkova*, 2 vols. (Berlin, 1870), I: 9–10.

3. Wortman, *Scenarios*, 171–2; McGrew, 210.

4. Madariaga, 569–70; McGrew, 184–5, 190, and ch. 6 *passim*.

5. Parkinson, 22–3, 143.

6. *Memoirs of Countess Golovine*, 129.

7. See Hughes, 'The funerals of the Russian emperors and empresses', 395–419.

8. *Memoirs of Countess Golovine*, 130–2.

9. M. B. Asvarishch, et al, *Tsareubiistvo 11 Marta 1801 goda* (SPb, 2001), 69, no. 24.

10. McGrew, 194.

11. Asvarishch, *Tsareubiistvo*, 24–32.

12. Asvarishch, *Tsareubiistvo*, 67, no. 28.

13. Wortman, *Scenarios*, 172–3; M. Safonov, *Zaveshchanie Ekateriny II: Roman-issledovanie* (SPb, 2002), 216–26; Asvarishch, *Tsareubiistvo*, 23, no. 22.

14. Asvarishch, *Tsareubiistvo*, 69, no. 25.

15. *Zapiski A. A. Iakovleva, byvshego v 1803 godu ober-prokurorom Sv. Sinoda*, ed. V. A. Andreev (M, 1915), 36, note; *Sobranie rechei … Amvrosiem Mitropolitom Novgorodskim i Sanktpeterburgskim* (M, 1810), 17, 66–7.

16. P. Hayden, 'Tsarskoe Selo: The History of the Ekaterininskii and Aleksandrovskii Parks', in *A sense of place: Tsarskoe Selo and its poets*, eds. L. Loseff and B. Scherr (Columbus, OH, 1993), 28.

17. A. Makhrov, 'Architecture and politics: Catherine the Great's "Greek Project" in the works of Nikolai L'vov', *SGECRN*, 26 (1998), 12; Wortman, *Scenarios*, 153, 160, 172–3.

18. McGrew, ch. 10.

19. *PSZ*, XXVI: 19,779, 12 Mar. 1801. This section draws in revised form on materials first discussed in my article, 'The posthumous reputation of Catherine II in Russia, 1797–1837', *SEER*, 77 (1999), 646–79, where further references may be found.

20. A. G. Cross, 'Contemporary responses (1762–1810) to the personality and career of Princess Ekaterina Romanovna Dashkova', *Oxford Slavonic Papers*, NS 27 (1994), 56; *The Russian Journals of Martha and Catherine Wilmot*, ed. the Marchioness of Londonderry and H.M. Hyde (London, 1935), 52, Martha's Journal, 23 Sept. 1803.

21. A. Malinovskii, 'Svedeniia dlia zhizneopisaniia Kniagini Ekateriny Romanovny Dashkovoi', appendix to S. R. Dolgova, 'E.R.Dashkova i sem'ia Malinovskikh', in *Ekaterina Romanovna Dashkova: Issledovaniia i materialy* (SPb, 1996), 78.

22. *Russian Journals*, 206, Catherine to her sister, Alicia, 2 Dec. 1805.

23. K[niaginia] D[ashkova] and A. K., *Podlinnye Anekdoty Imperatritsy Ekateriny Velikoi Premudroi Materi Otechestva* (M, 1806), iii.

24. V. Iu. Afiani, 'Stanovlenie zhurnal'noi arkheografii v Rossii v pervoi treti XIX v.', *Arkheograficheskii ezhegodnik za 1989 god* (M, 1990), 30.

25. *Zapiski kasatel'no Rossiiskoi Istorii: Sochineniia Gosudaryni Imperatritsy Ekateriny II*, 6 parts (SPb, 1801); *Filosoficheskaia i politicheskaia perepiska Imperatritsy s Doktorom Tsimermannom* etc. (SPb, 1801); *Ermitazhnyi Teatr Velikiia Ekateriny* etc. etc. (M, 1802); *Perepiska Rossiiskoi Imperatritsy Ekateriny II s gospodiny Vol'tera* etc., 2 parts (M, 1803).

26. [N.M. Karamzin], *Pokhval'noe slovo Ekaterine Vtoroi* (M, 1802).

27. P. Kolotov, *Deianiia Ekateriny, Imperatritsy i Samoderzhitsy Vserossiiskiia*, 6 parts (SPb, 1811).

28. I. S[reznevskii], *Dukh Ekateriny Velikiia* etc. etc. (SPb, 1814), foreword, n.p.

29. *Russian Journals*, 386, 388, Martha's Journal, 7 Oct. 1808.

30. F. F. Vigel, *Zapiski*, ed. S. Ia. Straikh, 2 vols. (M, 1928), I: 100.

31. P. Sumarokov, *Progulka po 12-ti guberniiam s istoricheskimi i statisticheskimi zamecheniiami v 1838 godu* (SPb, 1839), 202.

32. D. Davydov, *Voennye zapiski*, ed. V. Orlov (M, 1940), 415; idem, *Sochineniia* (M, 1985), 129.

33. A. I. Gertsen, *Sobranie sochinenii*, 30 vols. (M, 1954–65), VII: 53; A. Herzen, *My past and thoughts*, trans. C. Garnett, 4 vols. (London, 1968), II: 531.

34. *1857–1861: Perepiska Imperatora Aleksandra II s Velikim Kniazem Konstantinom Nikolaevichem; Dnevnik Velikago Kniazia Konstantina Nikolaevicha*, eds. L. G. Zakharova and L. I. Tiutiunnik (M, 1994), 212, diary, 13 Dec. 1859.

35. Herzen, *My past and thoughts*, II: 448.

36. A. P. Kern, *Vospominaniia, dnevniki, perepiska* (M, 1989), 115; *Zapiski Sverbeeva*, I: 242-4; II: 283-4.

37. T. A. Alekseeva, *Vladimir Lukich Borovikovskii i russkaia kul'tura na rubezhe 18-19 vekov* (M, 1975), 105-6.

38. A. Grigor'ev, *Vospominaniia*, ed. B. F. Egorov (M, 1988), 37.

39. *Russian Journals*, 386, Martha's Journal, 7 Oct. 1808.

40. K. Sh-v, 'Tsaritsyno', *Vestnik Evropy*, 11 (1804), July, 219-22.

41. P. A. Viazemskii, *Polnoe sobranie sochinenii*, V: 127-8; A. F. Merzliakov, 'Rassuzhdenie o Rossiiskom slovesnoti v nyneshnem ee sostoianii (1812)' reprinted in *Literaturnaia kritika 1800-1820-kh godov*, ed. L. G. Frizman (M, 1980), 125.

42. *Sochineniia Nikolaia Grecha*, 3 vols. (SPb, 1855), III: 320-1.

43. K. N. Batiushkov, *Opyty i stikakh v proze*, ed. I. M. Semenko (M, 1977), 80.

44. *Literaturnaia kritika*, ed. Frizman, 36-7, 43.

45. *Poliarnaia zvezda*, eds. V. A. Arkhipov et al (Moscow-Leningrad, 1960), 15.

46. Pushkin, *Polnoe sobranie sochinenii*, XIII: 178, to A. A. Bestuzhev, late May/early June 1825.

47. *Memoirs of John Quincy Adams*, 12 vols. (Philadelphia, PA, 1874-7), II: 115.

48. *PSZ*, XXVI: 19,904, 5 June 1801.

49. Parkinson, 61; V. Khodasevich, *Derzhavin: A biography*, trans. A. Brantlinger (Madison, WI, 2007), 93-4; N. Riasanovsky, *Nicholas I and Official Nationality 1825-1855* (Berkeley, CA, 1969), 116-7.

50. M. V. Klochkov, 'Nakaz imperatritsy Ekateriny II v sudebnoi praktike', *Sbornik statei v chesti M. K. Liubavskago* (Petrograd, 1917), 1-18.

51. *Arkhiv brat'ev Turgenevykh, vyp. 6: Perepiska Aleksandra Ivanovicha Turgeneva s kn. Petrom Aleksandrovichom Viazemskim, chast' I: 1814-1833 gody* (Petrograd, 1921), 295, Aug. 1833; *Dekabrist N. I. Turgenev: Pis'ma k bratu S. I. Turgenevu*, ed. N. G. Svirin (M, 1936), 245, 15 Dec. 1817; Madariaga, *Politics and Culture*, 236.

52. *AKV*, XXI: 361.

53. *Karamzin's Memoir on Ancient and Modern Russia*, ed. and trans. R. Pipes (New York, 1972), 133.

54. M. M. Speranskii, *Proekty i zapiski*, ed. S. N. Valk (Moscow-Leningrad, 1961), 20, 140.

55. *Memoirs of Countess Golovine*, 35.

56. For detailed references, see my essay '"Prosveshchenie": Enlightenment in Eighteenth-Century Russia', in *Peripheries of the Enlightenment*, eds. R. Butterwick, S. Davies and G. Sanchez-Espinoza, *Studies on Voltaire and the Eighteenth Century* (2008:01).

57. *Sochineniia Derzhavina*, ed. Grot, III: 211-3.

58. 'O nravstvennom sostoianii voisk Rossiiskoi imperii i v osobennosti Gvardeiskogo korpusa', ed. N. A. Kargopolova, *Reka vremen*, 1 (1995), 40.

59. A. Viskovatov, *Kratkaia istoriia Pervago Kadetskago Korpusa* (SPb, 1832), 35, 38, 46-8.

60. Polevoi, *Literaturnaia kritika*, 168-9.

61. M. A. Gillel'son, *P. A. Viazemskii: zhizn' i tvorchestva* (Leningrad, 1969), 225-8.

62. A.I. Kornilovich, *Sochineniia i pis'ma* (Moscow-Leningrad, 1957), 211.

63. Shishkov, 'Dostopamiatnye skazaniia', 20; M. Al'tshuller, *Predtechi slavianofil'stva v russkoi literature: Obshchestvo 'Beseda liubitelei russkogo slova'* (Ann Arbor, MI, 1984), 36-7.

64. Sumarokov, *Cherty Ekateriny Velikiia*, xix, 46, 48-9.

65. Dolgorukov, *Kapishche moego serdtsa*, 235.

66. A. S. Pushkin, *Polnoe sobranie sochinenii*, 17 vols. (M, 1937-59), IX: 32, note.

67. I. I. Dmitriev, *Vzgliad na moiu zhizn'* (SPb, 1895), 161.

68. *Ostaf'evskii arkhiv kniazei Viazemskikh, t. 2: Perepiska P.A. Viazemskago s A.I. Turgenvym 1820–1823* (SPb, 1899), 45–6, 11 Aug. 1820.

69. A. G. Tartakovskii, *Russkaia memuaristika XVIII-pervoi polovine XIX v.: Ot rukopisi k knige* (M, 1991), 215, 218–9.

70. M. Mokrousova, 'A. I. Turgenev – sobiratel'istochnikov po istorii Rossii', *Sovetskie arkhivy*, 1974: 4, 40–1.

71. See S. Dixon, 'Pushkin and history', *The Cambridge Companion to Pushkin*, ed. A. Kahn (Cambridge, 2006).

72. Khrapovitskii, 31, 13 Apr. 1787. See also A.A. Vasil'chikov, *Semeistvo Razumovskikh*, vol. V (SPb, 1894), 1–35; L. Maikov, *Pushkin: Biograficheskie materialy i istoriko-literaturnye ocherki* (SPb, 1899), 397–413.

73. *Imperatorskoe russkoe istoricheskoe obshchestvo, 1866–1916* (Petrograd, 1916), 4–5, 60.

74. *SIRIO*, XIII: i.

75. This section draws, in revised form, on sources first discussed in my 'Catherine the Great and the Romanov Dynasty: The case of the Grand Duchess Mariia Pavlovna (1854–1920)', in *Russian Society and Culture and the Long Eighteenth Century*, eds. Bartlett and Hughes (Münster, 2004), 195–208, where further references may be found.

76. S. S. Trubachev, 'G.P. Danilevskii: biograficheskii ocherk', in G.P. Danilevskii, *Polnoe sobranie sochinenii*, 8th edn., 24 vols. (SPb, 1901), I: 44, 46, 61, 79–88; 'Vospominaniia E. N. Opochinina', ed. E. V. Bronnikova, *Vstrechi v proshlym*, 7 (M, 1990), 65; *M. M. Stasiulevich i ego sovremenniki v ikh perepiske*, ed. M. K. Lemke, 5 vols. (SPb, 1911–13), V: 326–7.

77. A. Bogdanovich, *Tri poslednikh samoderzhtsa* (M, 1990 edn.), 133, 27 Jan. 1890.

78. C.A. Stoddard, *Across Russia: From the Baltic to the Danube* (London, 1892), 74, 40.

79. F.-X. Coquin, 'Le monument de Catherine II à Saint-Pétersbourg', in *Catherine II et L'Europe*, ed. Davidenkoff, 21–2.

80. *SIRIO*, XIII: xii-xiii.

81. V.O. Kliuchevsky, *Sochineniia*, 8 vols. (M, 1956–9), V: 309–11.

82. Bil'basov, *passim*; *Dnevnik gosudarstvennogo sekretaria A. A. Polovtsova*, ed. P. A. Zaionchkovskii, 2 vols. (M, 1966), II: 260, 15 Jan. 1890; 341, 8 Jan. 1891; P. A. Zaionchkovskii, *Rossiiskoe samoderzhavie v kontse XIX stoletiia: Politicheskaia reaktsiia 80-kh – nachala 90-kh godov* (M, 1970), 285–6.

83. See A. Pyman, *The life of Aleksandr Blok: I, The distant thunder, 1880–1908* (Oxford, 1978), 51.

84. For example, L. Zhdanov [L. G. Gel'man], *V setiakh intriga: Dva potoka. Istoricheskii roman vremeni Ekateriny II* (SPb, 1912); M. Evgeniia, *Liubovniki Ekateriny* (M, 1917).

85. Velikii kniaz' Nikolai Mikhailovich, *Russkie portrety XVIII i XIX stoletii*, 5 vols. (SPb, 1905–9); J. E. Bowlt, *The silver age: Russian art in the early twentieth century and the 'World of Art' group* (Newtonville, MA, 1979), 166–7; R. Buckle, *Diaghilev* (London, 1979), 84–8.

86. *Dnevnik V. N. Lamzdorfa (1886–1890)*, ed. F. A. Rotshtein (Leningrad, 1926), 93–4, 15 Jan. 1888; 203, 24 Mar. 1889.

87. *Dnevnik Polovtsova*, II: 203, 31 May 1889.

88. N. Notovich, *L'Empereur Alexandre III et son entourage* (Paris, 1893), 93.

89. R. Wortman, 'The Russian empress as mother', in *The family in imperial Russia: New lines of historical research*, ed. D. L. Ransel (Urbana, IL, 1978), 61.

90. Sir G. Buchanan, *My mission to Russia and other diplomatic memories*, 2 vols. (London, 1923), I: 175–6.

91. John Hanbury-Williams, *The Emperor Nicholas II: As I knew him* (London, 1922) 58, diary, 4 Oct. 1915.
92. Suvorov, *Pis'ma*, 204, to I. M. [José] Ribas.
93. The plant's formal name was *cardamine nivalis*: see A. K. Sytin, 'P. S. Pallas, P. I. Shangin i Ekaterina Velikaia', *Voprosy istorii estestvoznaniia i tekhniki*, 2 (1997), 124.
94. Shcherbatov, 235.
95. Diderot, *Mémoires pour Catherine II*, ed. P. Vernière (Paris, 1966), 197–8; D. Griffiths, 'To live forever: Catherine II, Voltaire and the pursuit of immortality', in *Russia and the World of the Eighteenth Century*, eds. Bartlett, Cross, Rasmussen, 446–68.
96. Grimm, 77, 2 Feb. 1778.
97. Shcherbatov, 255, 241–5, 251–3, (241). Compare Martha Wilmot's reflections on a present given to Princess Dashkova: 'It was the first present she ever receiv'd from Katherine the Second, & certainly serv'd to recall the most interesting period of a friendship which *then* existed assuredly, as Katherine was only a Grand Dutchess; but for which sentiment *they say* a Crown very very rarely leaves room & I doubt whether the Great Katherine form'd an exception to the general observation.' *Russian Journals*, 159, Martha's Journal, 1 Dec. 1805 NS.
98. *KfZh* (1790), 160.
99. See K. Rasmussen, 'Catherine II and the image of Peter I', *Slavic Review*, 37 (1978), 51–69.
100. Cross, 322–3.

LIST OF ILLUSTRATIONS

Colour plates

1. Empress Elizabeth Petrovna (1709–61) by Pietro Antonio Rotari (1707–62): State Russian Museum, St. Petersburg, Russia/ The Bridgeman Art Library
2. Equestrian Portrait of Catherine II (1729–96) the Great of Russia by Vigilius Erichsen (1722–82): Musée des Beaux-Arts, Chartres, France/ The Bridgeman Art Library
3. Round snuff-box showing Catherine as Minerva, Paris 1781–2 (gold, verre églomisé, silver): Hillwood Estate, Museum & Gardens; Bequest of Marjorie Merriweather Post, 1973, photo by Ed Owen
4. Tea caddy, coffeepot, and teapot from the Orlov Service, St. Petersburg, Imperial Porcelain Factory, 1762–5: Hillwood Estate, Museum & Gardens; Bequest of Marjorie Merriweather Post, 1973, photo by Ed Owen
5. The Summer Palace, St. Petersburg, Russian School (18th century): State Russian Museum, St. Petersburg, Russia/ Giraudon/ The Bridgeman Art Library
6. Summer Palace, Tsarskoye Selo, Green Dining Room, designed by Charles Cameron, 1784–91: Bridgeman Art Library, London
7. The Hermitage Theatre seen from Vasilevsky Island, 1822 (colour lithograph), Russian School (19th century): Pushkin Museum, Moscow, Russia/ The Bridgeman Art Library
8. Catherine II in a travelling costume, 1787 by Mikhail Shibanov (fl.1783–89): State Russian Museum, St. Petersburg, Russia/ The Bridgeman Art Library
9. Prince Grigory Aleksandrovich Potëmkin (1739–91), c.1790 by Johann Baptist I Lampi(1751–1830): Hermitage, St. Petersburg, Russia/ The Bridgeman Art Library

Black and white plates

1. The Schloss at Zerbst
2. The young Grand Duchess Catherine soon after her marriage, after Grooth
3. Peter III, engraving after A. P. Antropov
4. Paul I, English engraving of the 1790s
5. Catherine's coronation: nineteenth-century engraving after J. L. de Veilly
6. Coronation fireworks , 1762: A. K. Melnikov from an engraving by E. G. Yinogradov
7. Elizabeth's coronation feast in the Kremlin Square, 1742: engraving of 1744
8. The unveiling of Falconet's monument to Peter the Great: engraving by A. K. Lemnikov after A. P. Davydov, 1782
9. The Cameron Gallery, Tsarskoye Selo: aquatint engraving by J. G. de Mayr, 1793
10. Catherine's journey to the south, 1787: allegorical engraving by Ferdinand de Meys, courtesy of Dr James Cutshall
11. Catherine II, engraving by Caroline Walker after Roslin, London, 1787
12. Prince Platon Zubov, engraving by James Walker after Lampi, St Petersburg, 1798
13. 'L'Enjambée impériale', French cartoon of 1791
14. 100 rouble note of 1910

Maps

1. European Russia up to 1801, adapted from Hugh Seton Watson, *The Russian Empire 1801–1917* (Oxford, 1967)
2. St Petersburg and the Gulf of Finland, adapted from Isabel de Madariaga, *Russia in the Age of Catherine the Great* (Weidenfeld and Nicolson, 1981)
3. The Pugachëv revolt 1773–4, adapted from John T. Alexander, *Autocratic Politics in a National Crisis* (Indiana University Press, 1970)
4. The Russo-Turkish Wars of 1768–74 and 1787–91, adapted from Isabel de Madariaga, *Russia in the Age of Catherine the Great* (Weidenfeld and Nicolson, 1981)
5. St Petersburg in 1776
6. The Partitions of Poland, 1772, 1793 and 1795, adapted from John Doyle Klier, *Russia Gathers her Jews: The origins of the 'Jewish question' in Russia 1772–1825* (Northern Illinois University Press, 1986)

FURTHER READING

There is no shortage of primary material in translation to guide the English-speaking reader straight to the heart of Catherine's sensibility. The latest edition of *The Memoirs of Catherine the Great*, ed. and trans. Mark Cruse and Hilde Hoogenboom (New York: Random House, 2005), also offers a perceptive introduction to the circumstances of their composition. No less entrancing is *Love & Conquest: Personal Correspondence of Catherine the Great and Prince Grigory Potemkin*, ed. and trans. Douglas Smith (DeKalb: Northern Illinois University Press, 2004). *Correspondence of Catherine the Great when Grand-Duchess, with Sir Charles Hanbury-Williams and Letters from Count Poniatowski*, ed. and trans. the Earl of Ilchester and Mrs Langford Brooke (London: Thornton Butterworth, 1928), gives a unique insight into Catherine's political ambitions at the Court of Empress Elizabeth. Unfortunately it has not been reprinted. Neither is there a modern translation of the empress's *Nakaz*, though two contemporary English versions have been published by W. F. Reddaway, ed., *Documents of Catherine the Great* (Cambridge: Cambridge University Press, 1931), and Paul Dukes, ed., *Russia Under Catherine the Great: Volume 2 Catherine the Great's Instruction (NAKAZ) to the Legislative Commission, 1767* (Newtonville, MA: Oriental Research Partners, 1977). Diderot's pungent 'Observations on the *Nakaz*' are translated in Diderot, *Political Writings*, ed. John Hope Mason and Robert Wokler (Cambridge: Cambridge University Press, 1992). While Antony Lentin, ed., *Catherine the Great and Voltaire* (Newtonville, MA: Oriental Research Partners), offers a selection of their correspondence in translation, the French originals are readily available in the magisterial edition by Theodore Besterman, published by the Voltaire Foundation.

Among the few Russian memoirs available in English, one of the most attractive and informative is the *Memoirs of Countess Golovine: A Lady at the Court of Catherine II*, trans. G. M. Fox-Davies (London: David Nutt, 1910), which covers the latter part of the reign. Far more self-absorbed are *The Memoirs of Princess Dashkova*, trans. and ed. Kyril Fitzlyon, recently reissued with an introduction by Jehanne M. Geith (Durham, NC: Duke University Press, 1995). A sense of the riches buried in British archives can be gathered from three very different published journals: *Diaries and Correspondence of James Harris, First Earl of Malmesbury*, ed. Third Earl of Malmesbury, 4 vols. (London: Richard Bentley, 1844); *A Lady at the Court of Catherine the Great: The Journal of Baroness Eliʒabeth Dimsdale, 1781*, ed. Anthony Cross (Cambridge: Crest Publications, 1989); and John Parkinson, *A Tour of Russia, Siberia and the Crimea, 1792–1794*, ed. William Collier (London: Frank Cass, 1971). Each offers unique insights into Catherine and her times. The Russian experiences of Dimsdale and Parkinson, along with hundreds of others, are explored in Anthony Cross, *By the Banks of the Neva: Chapters from the Lives and Careers of the British in Eighteenth-Century Russia* (Cambridge: Cambridge University Press, 1997). The same author's companion volume, *By the Banks of the Thames: Russians in Eighteenth-Century Britain* (Newtonville, MA: Oriental Research Partners, 1980), brings to life the Russians who journeyed in the opposite direction. Much the most sophisticated of these was Nikolai Karamzin, whose *Letters of a Russian Traveller* has been published in an excellent translation by Andrew Kahn in *Studies on Voltaire and the Eighteenth Century*, 2003:04 (Oxford: Voltaire Foundation, 2003). For the broader context, see Sara Dickinson, *Breaking Ground: Travel and National Culture in Russia from Peter I to the Era of Pushkin* (Amsterdam: Rodopi, 2006).

The most important (and appropriately weighty) study of Catherine's reign in any language remains Isabel de Madariaga, *Russia in the Age of Catherine the Great* (London: Weidenfeld and Nicolson, 1981), which has been reprinted several times. My debts to this book and its author are profound. No less incisive are the essays collected in Isabel de Madariaga, *Politics and Culture in Eighteenth-Century Russia* (London: Longman, 1998). John T. Alexander, *Catherine the Great: Life and Legend* (Oxford: Oxford University Press, 1989) ranks as the first modern scholarly biography, particularly interesting on medical matters and also strong on social history. Roderick E. McGrew, *Paul I of Russia 1754–1801* (Oxford: Clarendon Press, 1992) explores the troubled life of Catherine's son. Like its subject, Simon Sebag Montefiore, *Prince of Princes: The Life of Potemkin* (London, 2000) is scintillating, wayward and occasionally overblown: but it is packed with insight on the fluctuations of Court politics and remains obligatory reading on the 1780s. The need for a modern scholarly biography of Princess Dashkova is only partly fulfilled by A. Woronzoff-Dashkoff, *Dashkova: A Life of Influence and Exile* (*Transactions of the American Philosophical Society*, 97, 3 (2008)). The best starting-point in English is Sue Ann Prince, ed., *The Princess and the Patriot: Ekaterina Dashkova, Benjamin Franklin, and the Age of Enlightenment* (Philadelphia, PA: American Philosophical Society, 2006).

Having celebrated its tricentenary in 2003, Catherine's capital city is famous primarily as a glittering icon of secular cosmopolitanism. It is not always easy to recall that much of it was a building site in the eighteenth century. For a helpful reminder, see Christopher Marsden, *Palmyra of the North: The First Days of St Petersburg* (London: Faber and Faber, 1942), which wears its learning lightly. W. Bruce Lincoln, *Sunlight at Midnight: St Petersburg and the Rise of Modern Russia* (Oxford: Perseus Press, 2001) offers a more up-to-date treatment, as do the contributors to Anthony Cross, ed., *St Petersburg, 1703–1825* (London: Palgrave Macmillan, 2003). Dmitry Shvidkovsky, *The Empress and the Architect: British Architecture and Gardens at the Court of Catherine the Great* (New Haven, CT: Yale University Press, 1996) brings together in a single, beautifully illustrated volume the author's outstanding essays on Tsarskoye Selo and Pavlovsk. Though it is full of fascinating information about the fate of Pavlovsk in Soviet times, Suzanne Massie's tantalising *Pavlovsk: The Life of a Palace* (London: Hodder and Stoughton, 1990) never quite tells you what you want to know about its early history. An exhaustive and very well-illustrated study of Falconet's monument is provided by Alexander M. Schenker, *The Bronze Horseman: Falconet's Monument to Peter the Great* (New Haven, CT: Yale University Press, 2003), though he makes the fractious sculptor seem more saintly than he was by needlessly blackening the reputation of Ivan Betskoy. Geraldine Norman, *The Hermitage: The Biography of a Great Museum* (London: Jonathan Cape, 1997) breathes life into a unique institution, and very engagingly too.

Although the religious side of Catherine's Court is harder to penetrate, there are helpful essays in Michael Schaich, ed., *Monarchy and Religion: The Transformation of Royal Culture in Eighteenth-Century Europe* (Oxford: Oxford University Press, 2007). Exhibition catalogues tell us a great deal about this and almost every other aspect of the empress's life and reign. Among the informative English-language editions published in recent years is *Catherine the Great: Treasures of Imperial Russia from the State Hermitage Museum, Leningrad* (London: Booth-Clibborn Editions, 1990). Fuller still are *Treasures of Catherine the Great* (London:

Hermitage Rooms at Somerset House, 2000) and *Catherine the Great & Gustav III* (Helsingborg: Nationalmuseum, 1999). Both Cynthia Hyla Whittaker, ed., *Russia Engages the World, 1453–1825* (Cambridge, MA: Harvard University Press, 2004) and *An Imperial Collection: Women Artists from the State Hermitage Museum* (London: Merrell, 2003) have plenty to say about Catherine. So does *British Art Treasures from Russian Imperial Collections in the Hermitage*, eds. Brian Allen and Larissa Dukelskaya (New Haven, CT: Yale University Press, 1996). Among permanent exhibits, Hillwood Museum stands out: anyone within reach of Washington D.C. should make the pilgrimage and purchase the exemplary catalogue by Ann Odom and Liana Paredes Arend, *A Taste for Splendor: Russian Imperial and European Treasures from the Hillwood Museum* (Alexandria, VA: Art Services International, 1998).

Although books written for scholars can sometimes seem hard going, even to the initiated, the best work on Catherine's Russia is stylish and penetrating. Richard S. Wortman, *Scenarios of Power: Myth and Ceremony in Russian Monarchy, vol. 1: From Peter the Great to the Death of Nicholas I* (Princeton, NJ: Princeton University Press, 1995) is a brilliant study of the ways in which the ritual presentation of the monarchy inspired the loyalty of its leading subjects. Whereas Wortman emphasises the secularising influence of classical Roman models, Gary Marker, *Imperial Saint: The Cult of St Catherine and the Dawn of Female Rule in Russia* (DeKalb, IL: Northern Illinois University Press, 2007), reveals the persistence of religious symbolism in Court culture, focusing on Catherine I in an interpretation which carries broader implications for the remainder of the eighteenth century. John LeDonne, *Ruling Russia: Politics and Administration in the Age of Absolutism, 1762–1796* (Princeton, NJ: Princeton University Press, 1984) is a powerful study of patronage. David L. Ransel explores a key interest group in *The Politics of Catherinian Russia: The Panin Party* (New Haven, CT: Yale University Press, 1976). Complementary studies of the nobility are offered by Robert E. Jones, *The Emancipation of the Russian Nobility, 1762–1785* (Princeton, NJ: Princeton University Press, 1973), and Paul Dukes, *Catherine the Great and the Russian Nobility: A Study Based on the Materials of the Legislative Commission of 1767* (Cambridge: Cambridge University Press, 1967). One gets a good sense of the ways in which nobles assimilated and imitated Court culture from Priscilla Roosevelt, *Life on the Russian Country Estate: A Social and Cultural History* (New Haven, CT: Yale University Press, 1995), and from Douglas Smith, *The Pearl: A True Tale of Forbidden Love in Catherine the Great's Russia* (New Haven, CT: Yale University Press, 2008), an imaginative recreation of Count Nikolay

Sheremetev's marriage to a serf actress, particularly good on the setting in which they lived. John T. Alexander, *Bubonic Plague in Early Modern Russia: Public Health and Urban Disaster* (Baltimore, MD: Johns Hopkins University Press, 1980) is a first-class social history of Moscow in the early 1770s. Catriona Kelly, *Refining Russia: Advice Literature, Polite Culture and Gender from Catherine to Yeltsin* (Oxford: Oxford University Press, 2001) offers a brilliant (and often very funny) way into the history of Russian manners. Rafaella Faggionato, *A Rosicrucian Utopia in Eighteenth-Century Russia: The Masonic Circle of N.I. Novikov* (Amsterdam: Springer, 2005) is the most significant recent study of Freemasonry, though the English translation is inelegant. W. Gareth Jones, *Nikolay Novikov: Enlightener of Russia* (Cambridge: Cambridge University Press, 1984) remains the single most important study of the Enlightenment in Russia, a subject which awaits a full-scale treatment. See also *Russia in the Age of the Enlightenment: Essays in Honour of Isabel de Madariaga* (London: Macmillan, 1990) and my own essay '"Prosveshchenie": Enlightenment in Eighteenth-Century Russia', in *Peripheries of the Enlightenment*, eds. Richard Butterwick, Simon Davies and Gabriel Sanchez-Espinoza, *Studies on Voltaire and the Eighteenth Century*, 2008:01. On the wider context, try Larry Wolff, *Inventing Eastern Europe: The Map of Civilization on the Mind of the Enlightenment* (Stanford, CA: Stanford University Press, 1994), a clever book which may overestimate the extent to which the Poles and Russians needed the *philosophes* to alert them to the problem of their own backwardness. Foreign policy is expertly covered by H. M. Scott, *The Emergence of the Eastern Powers* 1756–1773 (Cambridge: Cambridge University Press, 2001) and Isabel de Madariaga, *Britain, Russia and the Armed Neutrality of 1780: Sir James Harris's Mission to St Petersburg during the American Revolution* (London: Hollis and Carter, 1962), which ranges much more widely than its title might imply. I have commented on some of these scholars' conclusions in two earlier attempts to set Catherine and her reign in the broader context of the history of eighteenth-century Europe: *The Modernisation of Russia, 1696–1825* (Cambridge: Cambridge University Press, 1999) and *Catherine the Great: Profile in Power* (Harlow: Longman, 2001). Both these books give lists of further reading.

Readers of Russian will learn much from attractively written books by Evgenii Anisimov, *Zhenshchiny na rossiiskom prestole* (St Petersburg: Norint, 1998), and Aleksandr Kamenskii, *Pod seniiu Ekateriny: Vtoraia polovina XVIII veka* (Moscow: 1992), the first study of Catherine's reign to be published in Russia since the Bolshevik revolution in 1917. Despite its title, V. S. Lopatin, *Potemkin i Suvorov* (Moscow: Nauka, 1992) has just as much to say about Catherine: this book's rehabilitation of Potëmkin, based on the author's excellent editions of the correspondence of the two men, underpins the argument of Montefiore's English biography. More specialised are the work of the legal scholar, O. A. Omel'chenko, *'Zakonnaia monarkhiia' Ekateriny II: Prosveschennyi absoliutizm v Rossii* (Moscow, 1993), and two studies of the relationship between literature and politics by Andrei Zorin, *Kormia dvuglavogo orla: Literatura i gosudarstvennaia ideologiia v Rossii v polednei treti XVIII – pervoi treti XIX vek* (Moscow: Novoe literaturnoe obozrenie, 2001), and Vera Proskurina, *Mify imperii: literatura i vlast' v epokhu Ekateriny II* (Moscow: Novoe literaturnoe obozrenie, 2005), who is not always quite so convincing. In the late 1880s, V. A. Bilbasov completed only two volumes of what promised to be a massive biography before running into trouble with the censors. His *Istoriia Ekateriny Vtoroi*, 2 vols (SPb-Berlin, 1890–91), remains the most detailed study of Catherine's life before 1763. The troubled relationship between Catherine and her husband is explored in unprecedented detail by O. A. Ivanov, *Ekaterina II i Petr III: istoriia tragicheskogo konflikta* (Moscow: Tsentrpoligraf, 2007), a book which reached me just as my own went to press. *Ekaterina II: Annotirovannaia bibliografiia publikatsii*, eds. I. V. Babich, M. V. Babich and T. A. Lapteva (Moscow: Rosspen, 2004), is an invaluable guide to the voluminous published sources on Catherine and her reign. Students of St Petersburg will find a very helpful bibliography of Russian work by A. M. Konechnyi in *Europa Orientalis* (1997, no. 1). No less crucial for the history of eighteenth-century Russian painting is the illustrated catalogue of the State Russian Museum in St Petersburg – Gosudarstvennyi russkii muzei, *Zhivopis': XVIII vek*, ed. Grigorii Goldovskii (St Petersburg: Palace Editions, 1998) – which carries a limited amount of summary information in English.

ACKNOWLEDGEMENTS

I t may never be possible to acknowledge all the influences which lie behind the publication of a book such as this. I certainly cannot do so here. But I should never have begun it without help from Jon Jackson and Sam Johnson, and I could not have finished it without support from Catherine Beaumont. Much of it was written while I was chairman of the School of History at the University of Leeds, and I am deeply indebted to all my former colleagues there for their tolerance and encouragement. In particular, I received invaluable bibliographical advice from Simon Burrows, John Chartres, Emilia Jamroziak and Phil Withington (now of Christ's College, Cambridge), and unstinting support from John Childs, Gordon Forster, John Gooch, Katrina Honeyman, Kevin Linch, Graham Loud, Angela Softley, Edward Spiers, Andrew Thompson, Ian Wood and Anthony Wright. Richard Davies is an incomparable fount of wisdom in the Special Collections Department of the Brotherton Library, which boasts some of the most impressive Russian holdings in the United Kingdom. Among friends and colleagues in the international Study Group on Eighteenth-Century Russia, Paul Keenan generously permitted me to quote from his unpublished doctoral thesis, and I owe a continuing and mounting debt to Roger Bartlett, Anthony Cross, Elise Kimerling Wirtschafter, Joachim Klein, Isabel de Madariaga, Gary Marker, Gareth Jones, Patrick O'Meara, Viktor Zhivov and Andrei Zorin. For all its imperfections, this book would have been much the weaker without their help and example.

Though I have made regular journeys to Moscow and St Petersburg in recent years, much of the reading for this book was done in the Cambridge University Library, the British Library and the National Library of Finland on visits made possible by the University of Leeds. In Helsinki, I owe a profound debt to Marina Vituhnovskaja, Timo Vihavainen, Irina Lukka and her colleagues. In Cambridge, my friends Derek Beales and Tim Blanning still inspire just as much awe and respect as they did when they taught me thirty years ago. In London, my late friend Lindsey Hughes and her husband Jim Cutshall gave me some of the most memorable evenings of my life and much more besides. If there were any justice in the world, Lindsey would occupy the chair I now hold.

Three special obligations remain. Peter Carson has been an unfailingly patient publisher, even when he had grounds to be apoplectic. At home, Stephanie, Oliver and Rachel have been equally uncomplaining, even when the writing took longer than they had any reason to expect. The dedication acknowledges a debt that I shall never be able to repay, to two people who have sustained me for as long as I can remember. I owe them everything.

Simon Dixon
London, October 2008

INDEX

A

Ablesimov, Alexander: *The Miller-Sorcerer, Cheat and Matchmaker* 256, 279

Académie des inscriptions 210

Academy of Dijon 154

Academy of Sciences, St Petersburg, 264

Adams, John Quincy 324

Addison, Joseph 198

Admiralty, St Petersburg 43, 44, 127, 258

Admiralty College, St Petersburg 75, 128

Adodurov, Vasily 51, 105

Adolf Friedrich, Prince Bishop of Lübeck, King of Sweden 35, 56, 57, 59, 60

Aepinus, Professor Franz 197, 248

Alcibiades 306

Aleksey Mikhailovich, Tsar of Russia 13, 19, 62, 157, 165

Alekseyev, Archpriest Peter 277

Alexander I, Tsar of Russia 134, 273, 284, 299, 317, 320, 320–21, 329
  birth (1777) 246
  C's love for him 247, 249, 268, 323
  education 248, 249
  personality 249
  marries Princess Louise 313
  promises to rule according to C's 'heart and laws' 321, 325
  portraits of 331

Alexander II, Tsar of Russia 323, 329, 330

Alexander III, Tsar of Russia 2, 329, 331, 332

Alexander Nevsky monastery, St Petersburg 44, 45, 100, 125, 127, 221, 244, 253, 294, 313, 314, 317
  Church of the Annunciation 319

Alexander of Macedon 246

Alexandra, Grand Duchess 313, 314

Algarotti, Francesco 42–3

All Sorts (journal) 198–9

Amsterdam 82, 195

Amvrosy, Archbishop 207, 208, 212
Amvrosy, Metropolitan *see*
  Podobedov
Ancelin, Nicolas 319
Andrew, St, Apostle 17, 247
Angiolini, Gasparo 191
Anglo-Russian trade treaty (1734,
  renewed 1766) 187
Anhalt, Count 327
Anhalt-Dessau, Prince Leopold of 26
Anhalt-Dessau, Leopold III Friedrich
  Franz of 32
Anhalt-Dessau, princes of 33
Anhalt-Köthen, Leopold, Prince of 32
Anhalt-Zerbst, Auguste Christine
  Charlotte, Princess of (C's sister) 26
Anhalt-Zerbst, Christian August,
  Prince of (C's father) 220
  marries Johanna Elisabeth (1727) 29
  military service 23, 25, 35
  birth of C 23
  personality 25
  representational display 32
  private apartments at Zerbst 33–4
  separation from C 37
  exhorts C to keep her religious
    beliefs 38
  death (1747) 66
Anhalt-Zerbst, Elisabeth, Princess of
  (C's sister) 26
Anhalt-Zerbst, Friedrich August,
  Prince of (C's brother) 26, 33
Anhalt-Zerbst, Johanna Elisabeth,
  Princess of (née Holstein-Gottorp;
  C's mother) 44–5, 46, 88, 105
  marries Christian August (1727) 29
  birth of C 23
  her other children 26

visits her relatives 28–9, 30
match-making for C 34–5
travels with C to Russia 39–40
meets Empress Elizabeth 47
behaviour during C's illness 49, 50
Bestuzhev affair 50
C's baptism 52
first serious argument with Grand
  Duke Peter 53
birthday 54
status-consciousness 55
C's wedding 56, 58, 59, 61–2
leaves the Russian Court 64
death (1760) 107
Anhalt-Zerbst, Sophie Auguste
  Friderike, Princess of *see* Catherine
  II the Great, Empress of Russia
Anhalt-Zerbst, Wilhelm Christian
  Friedrich, Prince of (C's brother)
  26, 27
Anichkov Palace, St Petersburg 128,
  149, 242
Anna, Empress of Russia 3, 8, 14, 43,
  44, 45, 47, 54, 55, 56, 66, 69, 71–5, 78,
  81, 115, 123, 149, 230, 295
Anna Petrovna, Grand Duchess (C's
  illegitimate daughter) 104–5, 106
Anna Petrovna (sister of Elizabeth,
  Empress of Russia) *see* Holstein-
  Gottorp, Anna Petrovna, Duchess of
Antropov, Aleksey 7
Apraksin, Admiral 55, 99–100, 102,
  105–6
Aptekarsky Island 57
Araja, Francesco 104
  Bellerofont 77
  Mithridates 79
  Scipio 62

architecture
  a golden age of Baroque church-
    building 79
  recurrent alterations to imperial
    palaces 81
  disaster at Gostilitsy 82, 84
  effects of the Russian climate 82–3
  resurrection of the Golovin Palace
    88–9
  heyday of private building projects
    in St Petersburg 95
  C's ambitions for urban
    reconstruction 211–14
Arseny, Metropolitan, of Rostov 52
Assebourg, Baron von 219, 220
Assemblies of the Land 159
Astrakhan 169
Augustus, Emperor 211
Augustus III, King of Poland 185, 186
Augustus the Strong, Elector of
  Saxony 31
Austria
  diplomatic alliance with Russia
    (1726) 35
  implacable enemy of Prussia 187
  incorporation of the Polish enclave
    of Zips 207
  education model 248
  Russia's need for a rapprochement
    with 250
  formal alliance with Russia (1781)
    253, 269, 290
Avdotino estate, near Moscow 308
Azov 239

B
Bach, Johann Sebastian
  Brandenburg Concertos 32
  Well-Tempered Clavier 32
Bachaumont, Louis Petit de: *Mémoires
  secrets* 194
Bad Neuheim 331
Baden-Durlach, Louise, Princess of
  313
Baedeker, Karl 25
Bakhchisaray 287
Balkan Slavs 196
Balta, sacking of (1768) 183
Baltic lands 9, 40, 217
Baroque style 59, 160, 179, 205, 259
Baryatinsky, Prince Fëdor 124, 125,
  315, 319
Bashkir tribal leaders 228
Bashkiria 228, 254
Basil the Great, St 17
Batyushkov, Konstantin 324, 326
Bauer, General 203, 220, 223, 258, 265,
  273
Bayle, Pierre 68
  Historical and Critical Dictionary 67,
    310
Bazhenov, Vasily 212, 213, 214, 230,
  239, 258, 276
Beardé de l'Abbaye, M. 154–5
Beaumarchais, Pierre 224
Beccaria, Cesare 182, 198, 223
  On Crimes and Punishments 157,
    199
Belaya Tserkov estate 322
Belorussia 270
Beloselsky, Prince Andrey 140, 141
Bender 204, 211
Bentham, Jeremy 156–7, 199, 261, 282
  *Introduction to the Principles of
    Morals and Legislation* 157
Bentham, Samuel 282, 286

Bentinck, Countess 34
Berch, Carl Reinhold 42
Berda 228, 235
Berezovsky, Maxim 150
Berlin 29, 37, 231, 245, 254
   Court of 25, 30, 204
Bestuzhev-Ryumin, Count Aleksey
   Petrovich 14, 35, 50, 56, 66, 79, 97,
   99–100, 102, 105, 109, 113, 115, 132,
   133, 140, 185
Betskoy, Ivan 129, 132, 140, 155, 179,
   208, 245, 256, 257, 262–3, 333, 334
   General Plan for the Education of
      Young People of Both Sexes 130
Bezborodko, Alexander 184–5, 250,
   251, 253, 254, 268, 270, 277, 281, 290,
   298, 311, 320, 333
Bibikov, Alexander 161, 164, 171, 229,
   230, 232, 233, 236, 325
Bielfeld, Jakob Friedrich, Freiherr von
   162
   Political Instruction 112
Bielke, Frau Johanna 204, 208, 210,
   211, 218, 229, 230, 238, 244
Bilbasov, Vasily 1–2, 331
Bismarck, Prince Otto von 332
Blackstone, William 286, 325
Blanning, Tim 32, 75–6
Blessing of the Waters at Epiphany
   115, 149–50
Blok, Alexander 331
Blondel, Jean 136
Board of Public Welfare 240
Bobrinsky, Aleksey Grigoryevich (C's
   illegitimate son) 6, 120, 265, 285,
   287, 331
Boerhaave, Abraham 49, 99
Boerhaave, Herman 49

Bolotov, Andrey 239
Bonecchi, Giuseppe 62, 77
Book on the Duties of a Man and
   Citizen, The 248
Boris Godunov, Tsar of Russia 15
Borovichy 274
Boswell, James: Corsica 196, 199
Bourbon kings 31
Brandenburg-Prussia 24
Brandt, Johann 81
Branicka, Countess Alexandra (née
   Engelhardt) 255, 284, 311, 322
Branicki, Count 255
Brantôme, Pierre de Bourdeille,
   seigneur de 67
Bratovshchina 85, 170
Bratslav 290
Brenna, Vincenzo 320
Breteuil, Louis-Auguste de Tonnelier,
   baron de 20
Britain
   and War of American
      Independence (1775–83) 263
   Anglo-Russian relations at an all-
      time low 298
Brompton, Richard 249
Bronnaya crown estate 129, 197
Brown, Lancelot 'Capability' 94
Bruce, Count 204, 268, 272, 276–7,
   285
Bruce, Countess Praskovya 118, 144–
   5, 197, 233, 255
   Buckinghamshire on 144
   C's trusted friend 144–5
   banished from Court (1779) 144
Brühl, Count Heinrich von 193
Brummer, Grand Marshal 36
Brunswick, dukes of 30

Brunswick-Lüneburg, Elisabeth
Sophie Marie, Dowager Duchess of 29
Brunswick-Wolfenbüttel, Juliana
Maria, Duchess of, Queen of
Denmark 37
Brunswick-Wolfenbüttel, Lower
Saxony, Court of 29, 30, 65
Buch, Iver 312
Buchanan, Sir George 332
Buckinghamshire, John, 2nd earl 7, 10,
22, 126–7, 144
Bühren, Ernst 72, 230
Bulgarians 174
Burney, Dr Charles 177
Busch, Johann (John Bush) 210
Butler, Martin 9
Buturlin, Count Peter 142
Buturlin, Field Marshal 114
Byron, George Gordon, Lord: *Don
Juan* 296
Byzantine calendar 17
Byzantine empire 250
Byzantium 206

C

Cadet Corps 128, 148, 205, 265, 327
Cagliostro, Count (Giuseppe
Balsamo) 276
Calas family 153
Cameron, Charles 210, 258–9, 320
Canitz, Julius von 168
Cardel, Elisabeth (Babet) 26, 27, 28,
34
Cardel, Magdalena 26
Caroline, Landgravine 220, 221
Catharinaea sublimis 333
Cathcart, Lord 138, 179, 181–2, 192,
196, 200–201, 208, 219, 241

Cathedral of St Isaac, St Petersburg
179, 180–81
Cathedral of the Annunciation,
Moscow 5, 20, 213
Cathedral of the Archangel Michael,
Moscow 5, 20, 213, 277
Cathedral of the Dormition, Kiev 54
Cathedral of the Dormition, Moscow
4, 5, 7, 9, 13–17, 52, 160, 171, 183,
213, 237, 273, 288
Cathedral of the Dormition,
Smolensk 282
Cathedral of the Dormition, Vladimir
15
Cathedral Square, Moscow 8, 9, 10,
14, 20
Catherine I, Empress of Russia 5, 52,
62, 77, 143, 179
Catherine II the Great, Empress of
Russia
birth (21 April 1729; as Princess
Sophie Auguste Friderike of
Anhalt-Zerbst) 4, 23, 333
appearance 10, 27, 49, 58, 180, 302,
314, 332
health 24, 49, 72, 82, 85, 89, 149,
157, 192, 239, 243, 267, 289–90,
294–5, 303
childhood 24, 28–9
education 26–7, 28
journeys to Russia (1744) 37–40
meets Empress Elizabeth 47–8
accepted into the Russian faith 51–2
engaged to Grand Duke Peter 10,
52
name day (24 November) 54, 77,
101, 147, 191, 254, 255
marries Peter (1745) 56–63

mounting debts 73, 97–8
birthday 77, 89, 112, 160, 177, 233,
    266, 270, 271, 279, 289, 290, 300,
    307
relationship with Zakhar
    Chernyshëv 86, 269
pregnancies by Sergey Saltykov 87
third pregnancy 89
birth of Paul 91–2
affair with Poniatowski 93–4, 95, 103
maturing political aspirations 100–
    103, 112, 113
pregnant by Poniatowski 103, 106
birth of Anna Petrovna 104–5
and Bestuzhev's arrest 106
death of Anna Petrovna 106
pregnant by Orlov 112, 114, 117,
    118, 120
birth of Aleksey Grigoryevich 6,
    120
Peter III insults her at a banquet
    122, 143
coup (1762) 11–14, 20, 22, 118,
    122–4, 316
ceremonial re-entry into the capital
    127–8
early reforms 125, 129–30, 155
long-serving state secretaries
    130–32
coronation (1762) 4–22, 125, 136
correspondence with Voltaire 28,
    153, 154, 158, 168–9, 175, 182, 191,
    202, 203, 204, 206, 208, 209, 211,
    217, 218, 224, 237, 244, 321
Volga expedition 155, 156, 158–69,
    175, 235
accession anniversaries 169–70,
    242, 256, 288

denies any expansionist ambitions
    185–6, 250
and Poniatowski's election as king
    of Poland 186
inoculation against smallpox 24,
    188–90
art collection 192–4, 260–63
Greek project 206, 250, 263
'plantomania' 210
urban reconstruction 211–14
Vasilchikov becomes her new
    favourite 216, 217
improved relations with Paul
    218–19
correspondence with Grimm 25,
    223–4, 238–9, 245, 246, 247,
    251–4, 256–7, 259–62, 265, 266,
    269, 275, 277, 280, 283–4, 293,
    295, 302, 304, 305, 310, 312, 313,
    314, 330, 333
relationship with Grigory Potëmkin
    6, 27, 229, 231–2, 234, 238, 241
Provincial Reform 239–40, 250,
    254, 271
relationship with Zavadovsky 28,
    241, 242–3
relationship with Zorich 243, 252
buys off Sophia Dorothea's fiancé
    245
love for grandson Alexander 247,
    249, 268, 323
and education issue 248, 252, 295, 296
visits Mogilëv 250–53
secret correspondence with Joseph
    253, 254, 276
busts of 261, 305
deaths of General Bauer and
    Lanskoy 265–9

relationship with Yermolov 270–71
passion for garden design 94, 275–6
visits Kiev 281–6
journeys South 286–8
her last and youngest favourite,
   Zubov 291, 294
coronation anniversaries 302, 315,
   320
and Potëmkin's death 303–4
and the second partition of Poland
   309
opposes independent publishing 310
daily routine 132–3, 310–11
gifts given by 311–12
will 313–14
death (6 November 1796) 1, 315, 316
succession 316–17
lies in state 317–19
burial 318–20
publications on her 321–29
and exhibition of imperial portraits
   (1905) 331
self-assessment 333
contemporary criticism of 333–4
achievements 334–5
personality
   bookishness 63, 67
   competitiveness 204, 265
   courage 18
   eagerness to learn 63
   fashions her own persona 27
   impetuous nature 118
   intelligence 63
   joie de vivre 271
   obsessed by the value of time 11
   obsessed with her posthumous
      reputation 174, 181, 205, 209,
      212, 333

optimism 127
scepticism 4
secretiveness 27–8
values precision 5, 133, 273
values trustfulness 134, 231
work ethic 28, 134, 184–5
works
   The Antidote 12, 201
   'Authentic relation of a journey
      overseas that Sir Léon the
      Grand Equerry would have
      undertaken in the opinion of
      some of his friends' 287
   The Beginning of Oleg's Reign
      (libretto) 280, 295
   The Deceiver 276
   Fedul and his children 297
   Great Instruction (*Bolshoy
      Nakaz*) 67, 101, 156–7, 171–5,
      182, 199, 277, 324, 325
   *Linguarum totius orbis,
      vocabularia comparativa* 268, 275
   memoirs 26, 27, 28, 30, 34, 35,
      36, 46, 63, 68, 74, 82, 85–8, 92,
      104, 106, 143–5, 200, 306, 314,
      328, 329
   The Misunderstanding 279–80
   O, these times! 200, 215, 217–18
   *Russian primer to teach young
      people to read* 248, 249, 255
   Ryurik 280
   The Shaman of Siberia 277
   Tale of Tsarevich Khlor 249
Catherine Palace, Tsarskoye Selo 214
censorship 310, 328, 331
census (1745) 58
Chamfort, Nicolas: *The Merchant of
   Smyrna* 300

Chancellery of Guardianship of
Foreigners 145
Chappe d'Auteroche, abbé 110, 111,
166, 204
A Journey into Siberia 201
Charles XII, King of Sweden 35, 93
Charnutsky, Bishop Feofan 166
Charter to the Nobility (1785) 119,
271, 320
Charter to the Towns (1785) 271, 273
Cheboksary 167
Chemical Psalter (Masonic text) 277
Cheremis 168
Cherkasov, Alexander 141, 189, 230
Cherkasov, Ivan 141
Chernigov 282
Chernyshëv, Andrey 66
Chernyshëv, Ivan 140, 141, 158, 160,
187, 196, 210, 268
Chernyshëv, Count Zakhar 66, 140,
141, 149, 185, 197, 233, 240
a gentleman of the bedchamber 65
relationship with C 86, 269
at the College of War 133
mishandling of the Cossacks 233
governs lands acquired in first
partition of Poland 250
lavish entertainment of guests 251,
252
death 269
Chernyshëv family 137, 161, 239
Chesme naval battle of (1770) 202–3,
206, 209, 211, 262, 334
Chesme Palace, St Petersburg 326
Chétardie, Marquis de la 50, 68
Chevakinsky, Savva 79, 95, 100
Chevaliers Gardes 9, 59, 116, 132, 137,
230, 318

Chichagov, Admiral 293
Chika, Zarubin 228
Chinese Village, Tsarskoye Selo 210,
312
Chinoiserie 210
Choglokov, Nikolay 66, 67, 87, 89
Choglokova, Maria 67, 70, 73
appointed C's leading lady-in-
waiting 65, 66
initially disliked by C 66
and C's relationship with Sergey
Saltykov 87
becomes a friend to C 89
Choglokova, Vera 136
Choiseul, duc de 194
Chrysostom, St John 17
Chrysostom monastery, Moscow 176
Chuguyev 80
Chulkov, Vasily 74
Church of St Sampson the Hospitable,
St Petersburg 234
Church of the Annunciation,
Alexander Nevsky monastery 319
Church of the Dormition, St
Petersburg 127
Church of the Sign, Tsarskoye Selo 105
Chuvash 168
Cicero 65, 299
Clérisseau, Charles-Louis 258, 261
Cobenzl, Count 253, 264–5, 269, 270,
272, 279, 284
College of Commerce, St Petersburg
134, 140
College of Foreign Affairs, Moscow
9, 56, 278
College of Guardianship 154
College of Manufactures, St
Petersburg 134, 162

College of War 133, 233
Collot, Marie-Anne 181
comet (1744) 38–9
Commission on Church Lands 131
Commission of National Schools 248
Companion of Lovers of Russian Literature, The (journal) 264
Complete Collected Laws of the Russian Empire 101
Condoidi, Dr 113
Confederation of Targowica 309
conscience court 240, 254–5
Constantine Pavlovich, Grand Duke 273, 284, 299, 320–21
  birth (1779) 247, 250
  personality 249
  wedding to Princess Juliana Henrietta 313
Constantingorod 249
Constantinople 196, 213, 298
  falls to the Turks (1453) 17
  Russian ambassador imprisoned in (1768) 183, 204
  Constantine destined for 249
  Russian ambassador imprisoned again (1787) 288
Construction Chancellery 158, 159, 179
Cook, John 43
Copenhagen 219
Corberon, chevalier de 242, 243–4, 245, 246, 260, 265
Coriolanus 306
Coronation Commission 7
Correggio, Antonio 142
Correspondance littéraire 193, 222
Corsica 196
Cossacks 158, 174, 183, 222, 228, 229, 233, 236

Court Office 75, 274
Coxe, Archdeacon William 6, 273, 281
crime and punishment 173, 175–6, 200, 236, 251
Crimea 208, 209, 263, 287, 288, 289, 317
Crozat, Pierre 193
Cruys, Cornelius 191, 192
currency 195

D
d'Alembert, Jean 153, 206, 222
Damas, Comte de 296
Danilevsky, G.P.
  Catherine the Great on the Dnieper 329
  Mirovich 330
  Potëmkin on the Danube 330
  Princess Tarakanova 330
Danube River 207, 293, 296, 302, 306
Dashkov, Prince 111, 120, 185
Dashkova, Princess 16, 95, 110–11, 113, 120, 122, 124, 126, 156, 185, 226, 264, 265, 267, 295, 321, 325
Dashwood, Sir Francis 84
Dauphin of France 57
Davydov, Denis 322
death penalty 173
Demidov brothers 76
Demosthenes 299
Denis (a foundling adopted by C) 334
Denmark
  Swedish pressure on 24
  Peter III prepares to attack the Danes 120, 121
  Panin negotiates an alliance with 139
  defensive alliance with Russia (1765) 188

Dent, William 298
Department of Public Welfare,
    Yekaterinoslav 304
Derzhavin, Gavriil Romanovich 299,
    300, 307, 316, 324, 326, 327
    'Picnics' 139–40
D'Holbach, Baron
    Good Sense 222
    System of Nature 222
Diderot, Denis 41, 153, 172, 181, 193,
    194, 201, 222, 224–7, 229, 261, 277,
    310, 333
Dimitry, Tsarevich 161
Dimsdale, Elizabeth 250, 258, 259
Dimsdale, Dr Thomas 85, 188–92,
    247, 248, 307
Dingley, Robert 148
Dmitrevsk 169
Dmitriev, Ivan 327, 328
Dmitrovo kitchen gardens 80
Dmitryev-Mamonov, Alexander
    ('Redcoat') 280, 281, 290–91
    L'Insouciant 280
Dnieper River 281, 283, 284, 289, 309
Dolgorukov, Prince 327
Dolgoruky, Prince 161, 231
Dolgoruky family 214
Domashnëv, Sergey 264
Dominicans 251
Don Cossacks 9, 228
Dornburg on the Elbe 34
Dorofey, Archimandrite 282
Dorpat (now Tartu, Estonia) 40
Dresden, Court of 30, 31, 93, 261
Drone, The (journal) 199, 200, 210
Dubyansky, Archpriest Fëdor 4
Duke August Library, Wolfenbüttel
    29

duma (town council) 271, 286
Dumaresq, Daniel 129
Dyaghilev, Sergey 331

E
Eastern Empire 249
Eberts, Jean-Henri 194
École des Arts, Paris 136
Edinburgh, University of 264
education 248–9, 252, 295, 296
    advisory committee on 248
Eisen, Pastor Johann Georg 123, 129,
    145, 155, 172
Elisabeth Christine, Queen of Prussia
    30, 37
Elizabeth, Empress of Russia 18, 45,
    200, 255, 296, 332
    coup (1741) 35, 44, 48
    coronation 14, 47, 54
    invites C to Russia 35–6
    her favourite, Razumovsky 45, 48
    meets C 47–8
    personality 5, 47, 55, 67, 70
    appearance 47, 48, 86
    birthday 55, 77, 89, 114, 176
    C's wedding 56, 58–62
    irritated at C's failure to produce a
        male heir 65–6
    taboo subjects 68
    prizes her privacy 68–9
    daily life 70
    spending of 73–8
    accession day 77, 114
    coronation day 10–11, 77, 89, 112
    name day 77
    a golden age of Baroque church-
        building 79
    and Paul's early years 92

aversion to business 99
health 99–100, 105–9, 111, 113, 114
death 114
funeral 115–18
parallels shown between her and
   C 13
Encyclopédie 136, 153, 160, 199, 222,
   261, 286
Engelhardt, Lev Nikolayevich 282
Enlightenment 67, 68, 165
   C as a celebrated patron 28
   an important influence on C's
      legislation 153
   and C's Instruction 172, 173, 199–
      200
   and Grimm 224, 225
   C aims to nurture rational children
      of the Enlightenment 248
   C's Enlightened policies and the
      nobility 271
   suspicion of C's fascination with
      the French Enlightenment 325–6
   fundamental belief in self-
      development 335
equity courts 255
Erasmus, Desiderius 71
Esterhazy, Count 98
Esterhazy, Count Valentin 302, 303
Estland 9, 40
Euler, Leonhard 264
Eutin 35, 36, 64

F
Falconet, Etienne-Maurice 160, 176,
   181, 190, 194, 204, 209, 218, 225, 257
Farnese, Elizabeth 37
Fauchier-Magnan, Adrien 30, 31
Fëdorov monastery, Gorodets 165

Felbiger, Abbot Johann Ignaz von
   248, 252
Fénelon, François de Salignac de la
   Mothe: *Adventures of Télémaque* 141
Feofan, Bishop *see* Charnutsky
Feofil, Bishop 282
Ferdinand, Prince 30
Fermor, Count Villem 158–9, 160
Ferney 206, 261
Fielding, Henry: *Joseph Andrews* 199
Filaret, Patriarch 164
Finland 300
   Russian 9
Finno-Ugric people 167
Fioravanti, Aristotele 5, 15
Fitzherbert, Alleyne 272, 282, 283
Florence 254
Fokshany peace negotiations, 210, 215,
   217
Fonvizin, Denis 324
Fox, Charles James 298–9
France
   stranglehold on European
      diplomacy 24–5
   and War of American
      Independence (1775–83) 263
   commercial treaty with Russia
      (1787) 298
   Russia joins the anti-French
      coalition (1798) 301–2
   pornographic journalism 307
Francis I, Holy Roman Emperor 18
Frederick, Elector of Brandenburg 25
Frederick II, King of Prussia
   (Frederick the Great) 24, 36, 68, 105,
      153, 157, 184, 188, 320
   marriage to Elisabeth Christine 30
   promotes C's father 35

dislike of the Court 37
Enlightened administration 38
Bestuzhev affair 50
pleased at C's engagement 53
and Peter III's plans to attack the
Danes 120
preoccupied by internal
reconstruction 186
and Poniatowski's election as king
of Poland 186, 187
financial embarrassments of the
Seven Years' War 194
and the Russo-Turkish War 204
aims to take Polish territories 207
on the Orlovs 216–17
and Paul's potential bride 220
philosophes disillusioned with 225
Paul's audience with him 245
Frederick William I, King of Prussia
23, 25, 37, 38, 83
Frederick William II, King of Prussia
253, 298
Free Economic Society 145, 154
Freemasonry 132, 276, 277, 308
French Revolution (1789–99) 291,
299, 301
Friedel, Johann Friedrich 33
Fronde, the 12

G
Gabrielli, Caterina 234–5
Gagarina, Princess Anna 82, 86
Gaignat, Louis-Jean 194
Galiani, abbé 194–5, 252
Galicia 250
Galuppi, Baldasare
Dido Abandoned 147
Iphigenia in Tauride 177

Gardi (celebrated black stallion) 170
Gatchina 178, 189, 197, 210, 216, 220,
306, 315, 317
Gavriil, Metropolitan *see* Petrov,
Metropolitan Gavriil
Gellert, C.F.: *Die Betschwester* 200
General Survey 175
generalitet 57, 58, 59, 78, 147, 315
Geoffrin, Madame 93, 132, 139, 153,
155, 157, 223, 225
George II, King 109
George III, King 270, 298, 311
German Courts 31, 33, 71
Gillray, James 297
Giorgione: *Judith* 193
Girey, Khan Shagin 263
Glasse, Hannah: *The Art of Cookery* 78
Glebov, Alexander 115, 133
Godunov, Boris 161
Goebbels, Joseph 332
Goethe, Johann Wolfgang von 31
Golitsyn, Field Marshal A.M. 65, 197,
198, 266
Golitsyn, Prince Alexander 124, 171,
233
Golitsyn, Prince Dimitry 181, 193
Golitsyna, Princess 118
Golitsyn family 214
Golombiyevsky, Alexander 331
Golovin, Fëdor 191
Golovin Palace, Moscow 53, 54, 68,
88–9, 159, 160, 169, 170, 174, 176, 213
Golovina, Countess Varvara 315, 317,
318, 326
Gomm, William 166
Gorchakov, Prince A. M. 329
Gorodets 166
Gostilitsy 45, 82, 84, 88

Gostiny dvor, St Petersburg 128
Gotzkowsky, Johann Ernest 193, 194
Gould, William 300, 305, 314
Great Instruction (*Bolshoy Nakaz*) 67, 101, 156–7, 171–5, 182, 199, 266, 324, 325
Great Northern War (1700–21) 9, 25, 40
Grech, Nikolay 324
Greek project 206, 250, 263
Greeks, ancient 250
Greig, Admiral Samuel 202, 287, 290
Grétry, André: *The Marriage of the Samnites* 288
Greuze, Jean-Baptiste: *The Paralytic, or the Fruits of a Good Education* 193, 260
Gribovsky, Adrian 311
Grigoryev, Apollon 323
Grimm, Baron Melchior 26, 28, 176, 193, 194, 221, 230, 233, 261
  correspondence with C *see under* Catherine II the Great
  edits the *Correspondance littéraire* 222
  a member of d'Holbach's circle 222
  matchmaker for Paul and Natalia 223
  C's repeated offers of jobs 223
  C's artistic purchases 262, 285
Gross Jägersdorf, battle of (1757) 105, 184
Grotius, Hugo 68
Grot, Academician 330
Gunning, Sir Robert 216, 217, 218, 222, 230, 232–3, 237–8
Gustav III, King of Sweden 217, 218, 247–8, 253, 265, 290, 293–4, 298, 308, 314

Gustav IV, King of Sweden 314
Guy Dickens, Colonel 99
Gyllenborg, Count Henning Adolf 67, 306

H
Habsburg family 33, 186
Hagia Sophia, Constantinople 250
Halle 51
Hals, Frans: *Young Man Holding a Glove* 193
Hamburg 28, 39, 92, 306
Hanbury-Williams, Sir Charles 18, 93, 96, 98, 100, 102, 103, 105, 143, 185, 332
Hanbury-Williams, Major General Sir John 332, 333
Handel, George Frideric: *Scipio* 62
Hanover, Elector of 142
Hård, Count Johann 3, 117–18
Hardouin Péréfixe de Beaumont, Paul Philippe 67
Hare Island, St Petersburg 41
Harris, Elizabeth 234
Harris, James 243, 246, 250, 253, 257, 266
Harris, James, senior: *Hermes* 250
hawking 69, 70, 133, 170
Helen (Alexander's Greek nurse) 249
Hellfire Club 84, 93
Hendrikov, Count Andrey 60, 111
Hendrikov family 70
Henri IV, King of France 67, 302
Henry, Prince, of Prussia 34, 204–7, 212, 245
Herder, Johann Gottfried 32, 201
Hermitage, St Petersburg
  Hermitage Museum, St Petersburg 192–3

Hermitage Theatre 278, 280, 295, 297
Large Hermitage 260–61, 295
Small Hermitage 191–2, 230, 232, 236, 255, 256, 257, 260, 261, 269, 298, 302, 312, 334
Herrera, M. de la 257
Herzen, Alexander 322, 323, 329
Hesse-Darmstadt, Amalia of 220, 221
Hesse-Darmstadt, Louisa of 220
Hesse-Darmstadt, Prince Ludwig of 222, 245
Hesse-Homburg, Field Marshal the Prince of 47
Hesse-Homburg, Princess of (née Anna Trubetskaya) 92
Hitler, Adolf 332
Hofburg, Vienna 33
Hogland island 290
Hohenzollerns 332
Holstein, duchy of 56, 63, 101, 120, 124
Holstein-Beck, Prince of 117
Holstein-Gottorp, Anna Petrovna, Duchess of 35, 56, 104
Holstein-Gottorp, Georg Ludwig, Prince of (C's uncle) 34, 35, 63, 115, 117, 123
Holstein-Gottorp, Karl August 35
Holstein-Gottorp, Karl Friedrich, Duke of 35, 49, 56
Holstein-Gottorp, Karl Peter Ulrich, Duke of 35
Holy Synod 21, 156, 165, 166, 167, 171, 308
Holy Trinity Cathedral, St Petersburg 42
Honourable Mirror of Youth, or a guide to social conduct, The 71

Horse Guards 6, 58, 123, 216, 221
Houdon, Jean-Antoine 261
Houghton Hall, Norfolk 261
House of Anhalt 25, 32, 60
House of Anhalt-Zerbst 33
House of Holstein 60
House of Holstein-Gottorp 35
House of Quarantine, St Petersburg 258
Huber, Jean 193
Hull, east Yorkshire 202
hunting 69, 70, 85, 170
Hyndford, Lord 58, 59, 99, 100, 222

I
ice hills 45–6
Iletsk 228
Imperial Academy of Fine Arts, St Petersburg 15, 109, 179, 261
Imperial Academy of Sciences, St Petersburg 68, 78, 86, 133, 162, 197, 225, 264, 275, 278, 294, 324–5, 326
Geographical Description of the River Volga 159, 162, 163, 166, 169
Imperial Assembly 133
Imperial Russian Historical Society 329, 330
Imperial Russian Public Library 133, 142
infant mortality 23
Inkerman 287
Ipatyevsky monastery 164
Irakly, King of Georgia 111, 112
Irkutsk 278
Isaac of Dalmatia, St 179
Isabella of Parma, Princess 36, 37
Ismail, Bessarabia, storming of (1790) 296, 297, 299, 300, 302

Istanbul *see* Constantinople

Iushkevich, Amvrosy, Archbishop of Novgorod 52

Ivan III, Grand Prince of Moscow 5

Ivan IV the Terrible, Tsar of Russia 5, 17, 18, 137, 155, 161, 229

Ivan V, Tsar of Russia 12

Ivan VI, Emperor of Russia 11–12, 13, 35, 91, 155

Ivanov, Timofey 181

Ivanov Square, Moscow 20

Izmailovo 80

Izmailovsky Guards 44, 123, 221, 234

J

Jacobinism 301

Jallabert, Professor Jean 141

Jankovich de Mirjevo, F.I. 248, 252

Jassy, Moldavia 203
    peace of (1792) 203, 302, 303, 305

Jesuits 251

Jews
    massacre of (Balta, 1768) 183
    at Polotsk 251
    Russia gains a significant number of Jewish subjects 309

John the Baptist, St 17, 150

John the Longsuffering 285

Jones, Inigo 138

Joseph II, Holy Roman Emperor 6, 36, 37, 149, 169, 176, 184, 207, 219, 250, 252–3, 254, 261, 263, 264, 281, 286, 287, 289, 297, 308, 312

Juliana Maria of Brunswick, Queen of Denmark 30

Julius, Duke Heinrich 29

Justinian, Emperor 171

K

Kagul, battle of (1770) 209, 210, 211, 232

Kalachov, Grigory 62

Kalga Sultan 216

Kalmyks 279

Kamchadals 279

Kamensky, General 235

Kangxi, Emperor of China 19

Kaniev 287

Kant, Immanuel 38

Kar, General 228–9

Karamzin, Nikolay 322, 323, 327
    Memoir on Ancient and Modern Russia 325

Karazubazar 287

Karl I, Duke of Brunswick-Wolfenbüttel 29, 30, 31

Karl Eugen, Duke of Württemberg 31

Kassel 260

Kaunitz, Chancellor 207

Kazakhs (Kirghizians) 228, 284

Kazakov, Matvey 214, 238

Kazan 17, 155, 159, 168, 233, 235, 322

Kazan Church (church of the Nativity of the Mother of God), St Petersburg 60, 66, 123, 127–8, 149, 197, 203, 221, 222, 235, 294

Kazan province 228, 229

Kaznakov, S.N. 331

Keith, Sir Robert 111–12

Kerch 239, 263

Keyserling, Count 186

Kharkov 286, 288

Kheraskov, Mikhail 7

Kherson 281, 287, 288, 294

Khitrovo, Guards Captain Fëdor 126, 145

Khodynka field, Moscow 239
Khoroshevo 170
Khotilov 55
Khotin 197, 198, 211
Khovansky, Prince Peter 140
Khrapovitsky, Alexander 279, 289, 291, 293, 296, 297, 298, 313, 328
Kiel 36
Kiev 53–4, 206, 281, 283–4, 286, 290
Kikina, Maria 323
Kinburn 239, 289
Kingston, Duchess of 304
Kirghizians see Kazakhs
Klin 275
Klyuchevsky, Vasily 330
Knowles, Admiral Sir Charles 231
Kokshaisk 159
Kolomenskoye 80, 170, 288
Kolotov, Peter 322
Koludzhi 235
Königsberg, Prussia (later Kaliningrad, Russia) 25, 38
Konissky, Georgy, bishop of Mogilëv 221, 282
Konnaya estate 204
Korb, Hermann 29
Korf, Baron 122
Kornilovich, Alexander 327
Korobov, Ivan 44
Kosciuszko, Tadeusz 309
Kostroma 164, 167
Kovalyova, Praskovya 288
Kozelets, Chernigov province 48, 53
Kozelsk 282
Kozitsky, Grigory 171, 199
Kozlovskaya, Anastasia 164
Kozmodemyansk 167
Krasnoye Selo 69, 115, 147, 178

Kremenchug 268, 286
Kremlin, Moscow 3–6, 8, 10, 11, 47, 52, 59, 68, 88, 160, 170, 171, 230
    Arsenal 7
    archbishop's residence 208
    Bazhenov's abortive plans 212, 258
    Pugachëv's secret trial 237
Krichëv 282
Kronstadt 14, 75, 84, 123–4, 202, 300
Kruse, Dr Karl 113, 125
Krylov, Ivan 307
Kuchuk Kainardzhi 235
Kulibin, Ivan 166–7, 197, 312
Kunersdorf, battle of (1759) 184, 204
Kunstkamera, St Petersburg 78
Kurakin, Prince 254, 256
Kurakina, Princess 118
Kursk 278, 288
Kuskovo 127, 288
Kyakhta, Treaty of (1727) 72

L

Lacy, Count 257
Lacy, Field Marshal 62, 207
Lacy, Marshal 207
Ladoga Canal 158
Lafayette, marquis de 275
Lake Ilmen 274
Lake Ladoga 179, 209
Lambro-Kochoni, Colonel 314
Landé, Jean-Baptiste 54
Lanskoy, Alexander 243, 250, 264–9, 271, 278, 281, 314
Larga River, battle of (1770) 203, 211, 232
Large Caprice, Tsarskoye Selo 210
Le Mercier de la Rivière, Pierre-Paul 154, 201

Lefortovo palace *see* Menshikov Palace

Legislative Commission 65, 155, 157–8, 159, 161, 166, 168, 176, 199, 254
  elections to 158, 159, 160, 163
  opening of 169, 170
  Instruction to the 67, 101, 156–7, 171–5, 182, 199, 277, 324, 325
  slow progress of 176, 181–2
  proceedings generate a vast reservoir of information 182
  sub-committees 182
  suspended 183, 198

Leibniz, Gottfried Wilhelm 29

Leonardo da Vinci 304

Leopold, Archduke 254

Leopold II, Holy Roman Emperor 308

Lessing, Gotthold 29

Lestocq, Armand 47, 50, 61

Leventhal (Lev's Valley) 210–11, 215, 257

Lëvshin, Alexander 273

Lëvshin, Metropolitan Platon 148, 151, 152, 180–81, 199–200, 221, 273, 277, 288, 320
  Short Course in Christian Theology 221

Lieven, General 102

Life Company 70

Life Guards 102, 121

Ligne, Prince de 25, 253, 268

Liteyny cannon foundry, St Petersburg 197

Little Russia (Ukraine) 9

Littlepage, Lewis 284

Liuberets estate 89

Livland 9, 40

Livy 62

Lobkowitz, Prince 177

Lolli, Antonio 246

Lomonosov, Mikhailo 44, 77
  'Ode on the Accession of Catherine II' 13

Lopukhin family 214

Lords Commissioners for Trade 9

Louis XIV, King of France 12, 17, 25, 31, 32, 147, 210

Louis XV, King of France 18, 69, 153, 188, 194

Louis XVI, King of France 68, 277, 288, 297, 301, 302, 308, 310

Lüders, Dr 125

Ludwig, Prince, of Brunswick 30

Luke, St 150

Luther, Martin 29

Lutheranism 19, 51

Luzhkov, A.I. 261

Lvov, Prince Nikolay 273, 320

Lyalichi estate 243

Lynar, Count 101

Lyon, France 268

M

Macartney, Sir George 143, 145–6, 153, 184, 187

Madariaga, Isabel de 264, 301

Madrid, Court of 261

Maggiotto, Domenico: *Urania teaching a youth* 241

Maikov, Vasily 140, 169

Maintenon, Madame de 31

Makaryev monastery 161

Makhaev, Mikhailo 44

Makulov, Prince 213

Manfredini, Vincenzo
  Apollo and Minerva 147

Carlo Magno [*Charlemagne*] 146
Mann, Sir Horace 91
Manstein (Austrian ambassador) 71, 72
Manteufel, Count 30
Marble Palace 179, 216, 313
Mardefeld, Baron 52
Maria Fëdorovna, Grand Duchess
  (Princess Sophia Dorothea of
  Wurttemberg) 268, 281
  health 220
  becomes Paul's dutiful second
    consort 244–5
  on Paul's Grand Tour 254
  birthday 295
  births 313
  and C's lying-in-state 318
Maria Josepha of Bavaria, Consort of
  Joseph II 169
Maria Theresa, Empress of Austria 18,
  99, 191, 207, 219, 253
Maria Theresa, Infanta 57
Markov, Alexander 191
Marmontel, Jean-François: *Bélisaire*
  162–3
Mary, Blessed Virgin, the
  female Russian monarchs associated
    with 17
  Marian imagery prominent in
    Moscow 17
Mass, Michelangelo 81
Masson, Charles: *Secret Memoirs of
  Russia* 314
Matveyev, Artamon 13
Maundy Thursday 100, 149, 160
Maupeou, Chancellor 226
Medal Committees 210
Melissino, Colonel 128, 295
Memel, East Prussia 105

Menelaws, Adam 274
Mengs, Anton Raphael: *Perseus and
  Andromeda* 261, 262
Menshikov, Alexander 83, 84
Menshikov Palace, Lefortovo 46, 213,
  214
Messenger of Europe (journal) 323
Mikeshin, M.O. 330
Mikhail Fëdorovich, Tsar of Russia
  62, 137, 164
Mikhailovsky Palace, St Petersburg
  57, 320
Mikhelson, General 235, 236
Minetti, Francesco 33
Mirabeau, Honoré Riqueti, comte de
  310
Miranda, Francisco de 284
Mirovich, guardsman 155
'Mirror of the Police, The' 255
Misere (a Piedmontese) 111
Mislavsky, Samuil 213
Mogilëv, Belorussia 250–53, 264, 333
Moldavia 203, 229, 235
Molière 200
  Georges Dandin 203, 255
monarchy
  intensely personal in Russia 20
  exercise of power in early-modern
    Europe 31–2, 75–9
  cultural rivalry between monarchs
    32
  French kings' daily life 33
  Austrian emperors' comparative
    seclusion 33
  in C's Instruction 172
  pure monarchy 277
Monastery of Miracles, Moscow
  170–71

Monastery of the Caves, Kiev 54, 284–5

monastic lands 52, 131, 153–4

Monomakh, Vladimir 18

Monplaisir, Peterhof 69, 83, 113, 140, 197–8

Monsieur Tom (a favourite greyhound) 266

Montaigne, Michel 68

Montenegro 196

Montesquieu, Charles-Louis de Secondat, baron de 93, 172, 182, 198, 277, 283, 325
  On the Causes of the Grandeur and Decline of the Roman Republic 67
  On the Spirit of the Laws 67, 101, 157, 225–6

Montgolfier balloon (Joseph-Michael and Jacques-Étienne Montgolfier) 268

Mordvins 168

Morkov, Arkady 308, 315

Moscow
  described 6–7
  C's triumphal entry into (1762) 6, 7, 11
  C's dislike for 11, 159
  Marian imagery in 17
  Plague of 1771 206, 215
  C's 1775 visit 237–8
  C's 1785 visit 272–6, 281
  fall of (1812) 326

Moscow Armoury 150

Moscow Foundling Home 129–30, 140, 155, 208, 212, 281

Moscow River 212

Moscow Telegraph 327

Moscow University 7, 160, 232

Mounsey, Dr James 113

Mozart, Wolfgang Amadeus 234, 254

Mstislav Vladimirovich 282

Mstislavl 282

Munich: Elector of Bavaria's palace 76

Münnich, Field Marshal 123

Muravëv-Apostol, Ivan 326

Murillo, Bartolomé Esteban 304
  Rest on the Flight to Egypt 194

Musorgsky, Modest 161

Myatleva, Praskovia (née Saltykova) 322

Mytishchi 273

N

Naples 6, 196, 254

Napoleon Bonaparte 326

Narva 40

Naryshkin, Alexander 127, 245, 321

Naryshkin, Dimitry 211

Naryshkin, Lev 14, 127, 142, 179, 193, 197, 210, 215, 221, 225, 245, 268, 272, 279, 280, 287, 314
  C on 143–4

Naryshkin, Peter 14

Naryshkin, Semën
  guides C into the Russian empire 39, 40
  a future Marshal of Elizabeth's Court 39
  C's wedding 59
  Temple of Diana at Tsarskoye Selo 205

Naryshkin family 14

Naryshkina, Anna 291

Naryshkina, Katerina 210

Naryshkina, Natalia 210

Naryshkina, Yelena 18–19, 118

Nassau, Princess of 220
Natalia Alekseyevna, Grand Duchess
  (previously Princess Wilhelmina of
  Hesse-Darmstadt) 220, 221–2, 233,
  236, 238–9, 244, 245
Nechaev, Innokenty, bishop of Pskov
  222, 292
Necker, Jacques: *Compte rendu* 277
Necker, Suzanne 225
Neëlov, Vasily 210
Nelidinsky, M. 260
Neplyuev, Ivan 7
Nerchinsk 217
Neva River 62, 205, 225, 244, 257–8,
  275, 282–3, 305
Nevsky, St Alexander 58, 149, 165, 216,
  246, 247, 294
New Chrysomander (Masonic text) 277
'New Jerusalem' Ascension monastery
  79
New Maiden Convent, Kiev 284
New Russia 154, 284, 307
New Style (Gregorian) calendar viii
Newberry, Thomas 148
Nicholas, St 152
Nicholas I, Tsar 262, 313, 326–8, 329
Nicholas II, Tsar of Russia 8
Nikolay Mikhailovich, Grand Duke 331
Nikolsky Gate, Moscow 7
Nikon, Patriarch 79, 165
Nizhny Novgorod 159, 165, 166, 167,
  197, 312
nobility
  compulsory state service 118
  emancipated from state service
    118–19, 121, 133, 271
  C's Charter to the Nobility (1785)
    119, 271, 320

flight to their estates during Plague
  of 1771 206
Poland's 'republic of nobles' 301
Nollekens, Joseph 298
Northern System 187, 188, 196, 250, 253
Novgorod 166, 246, 273, 275
  archbishop of 60
Novikov, Nikolay 199, 200, 210, 276,
  277, 292, 308
Novodevichy convent, Moscow 51
Nyslott fort 290

O
Ochakov 289, 298, 302
  1791 crisis 299
Oder River 24
Oka River 159
Old Believers 165, 166, 167, 228, 273
Old Style (Julian) calendar viii
Olsufyev, Adam 130–31, 132, 167
Oranienbaum 45, 83–4, 85, 94, 95, 96,
  103, 104, 110–11, 112, 122, 123, 124,
  127, 145, 179, 210, 216, 296
  Damask Room 241
  Grüne Salle (Green Room) 111
Order of St Alexander Nevsky 113,
  221, 233, 246, 286
Order of St Andrew the First Called
  18, 177, 220, 295
Order of St Catherine 16, 118
Order of St George 232, 295
Order of the Knights of Malta 196
Order of the Polish Eagle 57
Orël 288
Orenburg province 66, 228, 230
Orlov, Count Aleksey 20, 122–5, 126,
  176, 177, 202, 203, 206, 216–17,
  231–2, 311, 315, 319

Orlov, Elizabeth (née Zinovyev) 242
Orlov, Count Fëdor 20, 202, 268
Orlov, Count Grigory 141, 185, 197,
    203, 230, 231, 233, 331
    relationship with C 6, 13, 112–13,
        122, 126, 132–3, 145, 156
    reputation for valour 112
    a keen amateur astronomer 39, 113,
        145
    military connections 113
    C has an illegitimate son by him
        (1762) 6, 120
    conspiracy to overthrow Peter III
        11, 122, 123
    Macartney on 145–6
    name day 146, 177
    the Volga journey 161
    public reading of C's Instruction
        171
    a noble deputy for St Petersburg
        182
    smallpox inoculation 189, 190
    the Small Hermitage 192
    and Moscow plague 208
    peace talks at Fokshany 210, 215,
        216, 217
    C's urban reconstruction 211
    C's split with him (1772) 20, 215,
        216, 218, 233
    and Paul's future wife 220, 221
    C praises 238
    personality 241, 265
    health 242
    marries his cousin 242
    and Paul's marriage to Maria
        Fëdorovna 245
    insanity 266
Orlov, Count Ivan 20, 169, 216

Orlov, Count Vladimir 20, 161, 162,
    163, 165, 166, 168, 197, 223
Orlov family 16, 113, 123, 125, 126,
    133, 140, 145, 156, 168, 215, 216–17,
    219, 231
Osterman, Count 268, 302, 311
Ostrovki estate 275
Ottoman Empire 183, 187, 196, 207,
    298
Our Lady of Vladimir icon 17
Ovid: *Metamorphoses* 199
Ozerki estate 249

P
Pahlen, General Count Peter von der
    321
Painter, The (journal) 199
Paisiello, Giovanni 250
    I filosofi immaginari 255–6
Pakhrino 170
Palace of Facets, Moscow 4, 8, 16, 20,
    21, 52, 164, 171
Pallas, Peter Simon 275, 333
Pamfilov, Father Ioann 277
Panin, Count Nikita 59, 138, 141, 145,
    146, 152, 161, 168, 169, 180, 197
    a protégé of Bestuzhev 113
    ambassador to Sweden 113, 121
    Paul's tutor 12, 113
    a confirmed constitutionalist 121,
        125
    and C's coup 121–2, 123, 125
    imperial council suggestion 133
    negotiates an alliance with the
        Danes 139
    affair with Countess Stroganova
        143, 177
    and C's radical proposals 172

engagement to Countess Anna
  Sheremeteva 177, 178
author of submission by Moscow
  nobility 182
in charge of Russian foreign policy
  185
Northern System 187, 196, 250, 253
loss of authority 188
rivalry with the Orlovs 215
reputation for sloth 218
and Saldern 219, 230
and Paul's potential bride 220, 221
and Vasilchikov 232
and Potëmkin 236, 238
dismissal 253, 254, 255, 266
death 266
Panin, General Peter 169, 197, 236
Paoli, General Pasquale 196
Pargolovo estate 113
Paris 250, 254, 261, 291, 308, 326
Parkinson, John 299, 307, 314, 317, 321
  'Note on Lanskoy' 267
Pashkevich, Vasily: *Fevei* 279
Passek, Peter 123, 124, 125, 140, 141,
  319
Paton, Richard 334
Patriot Party 301
patronage 14, 121, 261, 310, 331, 334
Paul I, Tsar of Russia 143, 161, 268,
  294
  birth 91–2
  early upbringing 92, 105
  question of his paternity 92, 331
  appearance 92, 111
  health 11, 108, 126, 208, 218
  C expected to rule as regent for him
    12
  debut on the dance floor 111–12

education 12, 113, 152, 197
and C's coup 123
and C's coronation 15, 20
visits the reconstructed Winter
  Palace 136, 137
lifelong delight in French comedies
  146
birthday 148, 219, 222
name day 169–70, 268
and the Cathedral of St Isaac 180
smallpox inoculation 190
popularity in Moscow 215
plot to enthrone him 217
resentment of C's treatment of
  Peter III 218
improved relations with C 218–19
Saldern's plan 219
the search for a bride 219–20
marriage to Natalia Alekseyevna
  221–2, 233
death of Natalia 244, 245
marriage to Maria Fëdorovna
  245–6
Grand Tour 253
in Vienna 254
inadvertently snubs Clérisseau 261
and Freemasonry 276, 308
consequences of Russia joining the
  anti-French coalition 302
waits impatiently in the wings 306
deeply in debt 308
death of C 315
military ethos 316, 320
the succession 316–17
alienates the elite 320
assassinated 321, 323
Pauzié, Gérémie 19, 111, 116
Pavlovna, Grand Duchess Anna 313

Pavlovna, Grand Duchess Maria (Princess Marie of Mecklenburg-Schwerin) 332
Pavlovna, Grand Duchess Olga 313
Pavlovna, Grand Duchess Yelena 313, 328
Pavlovsk Palace 259–60
Pella Palace 275
Penza 236
Perekusikhina, Maria 268, 274, 322, 327
Pereyaslavl 151
Peter I the Great, Tsar of Russia 13, 35, 40, 62, 83, 93, 115, 139, 184, 234, 255, 314, 322, 330, 335
  born on St Isaac's feast day 179
  his play regiments 46
  installed as de facto sole ruler 12
  and St Petersburg 41, 42, 44, 45
  in the Great Northern War 9, 288
  Table of Ranks (1722) 15
  succession law (1722) 316
  crowns his second wife (1724) 5
  and the Dormition Cathedral 16
  Russian orders of chivalry 18
  introduces women to Russian public society 71
  reforms 75
  'emancipation' of the nobility (1762) 118, 271
  envisaged comprehensive code 157
  death (1725) 43
  statue commissioned by C 181, 204, 257
  his 'little boat' displayed 204
  and St Alexander Nevsky 246
  single most powerful symbol of Russia's superhuman potential 257
  portraits of 331
  and C's attempts to legitimise her reign 334
Peter III, Tsar of Russia 16, 17, 22, 36, 47, 49, 73, 195, 215, 296, 320, 332
  Elizabeth declares him her heir 35
  education 63–4
  sixteenth birthday 46, 48
  engaged to C 10, 52
  first serious argument with Johanna Elisabeth 53
  health 54–6, 58, 63, 124
  appearance 56
  marries C (1745) 56–63
  birthday 77, 118
  name day 77, 112, 123
  puerile behaviour 79, 117
  question of Paul's paternity 92
  relationship with Elizabeth Vorontsova 92, 104, 115, 124
  C's misery as his consort 100
  and Anna Petrovna's birth 104
  accession 114
  daily routine 114–15
  and Elizabeth's funeral 116–17
  pro-Prussian 117, 118, 120
  emancipates nobility from compulsory state service 118–19
  plans to attack the Danes 120, 121
  insults C at a banquet 122, 143
  overthrown and assassinated 4, 11–14, 123–5, 161, 315, 321
  paltry burial 317, 319
  Paul's resentment of C's treatment of him 218, 319
  requiem service at the Winter Palace 319
  funeral with C 319–20

Peter of Courland, Duke 230
Peter-Paul Cathedral, St Petersburg 3,
  5, 42, 115, 116, 299, 314, 319
Peter-Paul Fortress, St Petersburg 3,
  44, 57, 127, 204, 327
Peterhof, near St Petersburg 78, 82,
  95, 100, 108, 112, 113, 123, 124, 140,
  178–9, 208, 211, 215, 216, 234, 235,
  250, 256, 258, 267, 275, 278, 334
  English Park 265
Petrov, Metropolitan Gavriil 127, 161,
  162, 178, 221, 267, 294, 315
Petrov, Vasily 17–18
Petrovsky Palace, Moscow 88, 273
Petrovsky woods 169
Philip II, Duke, of Pomerania-Stettin
  24
Philip V, King of Spain 37
philosophes 153, 154, 162, 201, 222, 224,
  310, 323, 326, 333
Picart, Pieter 256
Picquet (dancer) 279
Pietism 26, 27, 28, 38, 51
Pitt, William, the Younger 298, 299,
  311
Plague of 1771 206–7, 209, 215
Plutarch 310
  Lives 67, 306
Podobedov, Metropolitan Amvrosy
  320, 322
Podolia 290
Poissonnier, François 108–9
Pokrovskoye 127
Poland
  C's support for Orthdox fanatics
    in 183
  Chernyshëv eager to annexe Polish
    territory 185

C's ambitions in 186, 187
Frederick the Great's ambitions
  186, 207
first partition 217, 250
Potëmkin's claims in 255
Potëmkin builds up his estates in
  290
Fox's support 299
new constitution 301
complexity of the Polish question
  309
second partition 309
massacre of Poles at Praga 309
third partition 309–10
Polar Star (Decembrist journal) 324
Polevoy, Nikolay 327
police boards 255
Police Ordinance 255
Polish Deputies 267
Pöllnitz, Baron 29
Polotsk 251, 252, 278
Poltava 287
  battle of (1709) 41, 93
Pomerania 24
Poniatowski, Count Stanisław August
  100, 106, 113, 118, 132, 286
  Hanbury-Williams' protégé 93
  as C's lover 93–4, 95, 103
  personality 93
  and birth of Anna Petrovna 104–5
  returns to Poland 106
  C promises to make him king 185
  elected King of Poland (1764) 186
  C renews her acquaintanceship with
    him 284, 287
  and the new Polish constitution 301
  shattering of his dreams of
    autonomy 309

Poroshin, Semën 140, 147, 152
Postal Chancellery 8, 158
Potëmkin, Grigory 6, 203, 236, 246, 252, 260, 269, 291, 306
   relationship with C 6, 27, 229, 231–2, 234, 238, 241, 265, 301
   besieges the Turks on the Danube 229
   supplants Vasilchikov 229
   first presented to C 230–31
   appearance 232
   links with the clergy 232
   incipient rivalry with Panin 236
   and Orlov's illness 242
   and Anichkov Palace 242
   and Zorich 243
   celebration of Constantine's birth 249
   obsession 'with the idea of raising an Empire in the east' 249
   supports a rapprochement with Austria 250
   arranges marriages for his nieces 255
   C's gift of a Sèvres service 262
   and Crimean rebellion 263
   Governor General of the Tauride 263–4
   comforts the bereaved C 268
   and Yermolov 270
   visits Moscow with C 272, 274
   insatiable ambitions in the South 280
   and Dmitryev-Mamonov 280
   and Samuel Bentham 282
   headquarters at Kremenchug 286
   re-enactment of Peter the Great's victory over the Swedes (1709) 287–8
   hypochondria 288–9
   his Polish estates 290, 309
   and Radishchev's book 292
   and the second Russo-Turkish War 288–9, 291, 294, 296, 297, 303
   and Tauride Palace 46, 299, 331
   reputation for corruption 301, 334
   on Zubov 307
   death 303–4, 309, 317
   his estate 304–5
   glassworks 311
   Danilevsky's claim 330
'Potëmkin villages' 286
Potocki, Ignacy 301
Potsdam 33, 37, 204, 217
Poussin, Nicolas 304
Praga, Warsaw 309
Prechistensky Palace, Moscow 214, 238
Prejudice Overcome (allegorical ballet) 191
Preobrazhensky Guards 44–5, 100, 123, 217, 305
Prokopovich, Feofan 131
Protasova, Anna 269, 274, 315
Protestantism 248, 312
Provincial Reform 239–40, 241, 250, 251, 254, 271, 273
Prozorovsky, Prince 308
Prussia
   defensive alliance with Russia 187, 250
   implacable enemy of Austria 187
Prussian army: 8th infantry regiment 25
Pruth, battle of the (1711) 77
Pskov 251, 265
publishing, independent 277, 310

Pugachëv, Yemelyan 238, 239, 256,
328, 330
    appearance 228
    seizure of Iletsk 228
    sets up 'College of War' at Berda
    228
    C makes light of his rebellion 229,
    232
    forced to abandon his headquarters
    233
    regroups in the Urals 233
    final rally 235, 236
    betrayed by the Cossacks 236
    trial and execution 237, 308
Pulkovo 209, 234
Pushchin, Vice Admiral Peter
    Ivanovich 158, 274, 286
Pushkin, Alexander 161, 324, 328
    History of Pugachëv 327
    'Table-Talk' 328

Q
Quarenghi, Giacomo 262–3, 265, 267,
278–9, 315

R
Radishchev, Alexander 292, 294,
300–301
    Journey from St Petersburg to
    Moscow 272, 291–2
Raphael 304
    Holy Family 193
    loggias 245, 262, 278
Rastrelli, Francesco Bartolomeo 47,
69, 138, 150, 151, 158, 259, 295, 319
    designs the stone Winter Palace 55
    demolition of his Summer Palace
    57, 320

and C's wedding 60, 61
pyramid of fire device 78, 91
St Petersburg summer house 81–2
Golovin Palace resurrection 88
completes transformation of
    Peterhof 95
temporary leave from Russia 135
fails to be confirmed in the rank of
    major general 135–6
leaves Russia for good 136
Raynal, Guillaume: History of the Two
    Indies 292
Razumovsky, Aleksey 69, 76, 85, 95,
99–100, 113
    a Ukrainian of Cossack extraction
    14
    Elizabeth's lover 14
    Elizabeth's Grand Master of the
    Hunt 14, 48
    Gostilitsy estate 45, 82
    appearance 48
    Kozelets estate 53
    and C's marriage 59, 60, 61
    and C's coronation 14, 19
    and Yelagin 131
Razumovsky, Andrey 245
Razumovsky, Kirill 95, 99–100, 123,
133, 142, 190, 233, 239, 268, 328
Red Square, Moscow 6, 17
Red Staircase, Moscow 8, 9, 10, 13, 21,
52, 239
Reiffenstein, Johann Friedrich 261
Reims Cathedral 16
Rembrandt van Rijn 193
    Abraham and Isaac 261
    Return of the Prodigal Son 193
Repnin, Prince Nikolay 128, 186, 235,
269, 302–3, 311

Repnin, Princess 255
Reval 85, 155, 204, 218, 290, 293
Reynolds, Sir Joshua 225
Ribas, Admiral 333
Ribas, José de 296
Richardson, William 152, 179–80, 183, 190, 198
Riga, Latvia 39, 153
Riger, Justus 81
Rimsky-Korsakov, Ivan 144, 243, 261
Rinaldi, Antonio 45, 104, 147–8, 179, 181, 197, 209, 210, 216, 262, 318, 319
Rogerson, Dr John 265, 266, 267, 281, 290, 315
Romanov dynasty
  founded (1613) 62, 164
  dynastic pretensions 66
  Saltykovs and Naryshkins marry into 14
Rome 6, 254, 258, 261, 279, 306
Ropsha country estate 124, 125, 145, 315
Rosa, Madame 279
Rosicrucians 276, 277, 308
Rossbach, battle of (1757) 105, 184
Rossi, Carlo 97
Rossignol, Antoine 156
Rostokino 273
Rostov 151
Rousseau, Jean-Jacques 32, 222
  Le devin du village 256
  Discourse on the Sciences and the Arts [The First Discourse] 154
  Emile 129
Rowlandson, Thomas 297
Royal Society, London 23–4
Rubens, Peter Paul 193, 304
Rulhière, Claude Carloman de 64

Rumyantsev, Count Nikolay 323
Rumyantsev, Count Peter 154, 197, 203–4, 206, 235, 241, 242, 245, 251, 252, 281, 284, 293, 309, 321
Rumyantseva, Countess Maria 65, 73, 144, 255
Rus 54
Russia
  the second emergent power in the Baltic 25
  diplomatic alliance with Austria (1726) 35
  C journeys to (1744) 37–40
  celebrates peace with Sweden (1744) 65
  financial problems 75, 121, 129
  aftermath of Seven Years' War 128–9
  cultural Westernisation 152, 201
  defensive alliance with Prussia (1764) 187, 250
  defensive alliance with Denmark (1765) 188
  C defends criticism of citizens 201
  Black Sea conquests 207
  conceived by Diderot as a tabula rasa 227
  formal alliance with Austria (1781) 253, 269, 290
  Anglo-Russian relations at an all-time low 298
  commercial treaty with France (1787) 298
  joins anti-French coalition (1798) 301–2
Russian Academy 199, 264, 275, 324, 326
Russian Archive (journal) 329

Russian Court 35
  the roots of Russia's Baroque Court
    culture 71
  in Moscow 10, 43, 46
  ceremonials in church 16, 79–80
  visits Gostilitsy 45
  the Court choir 48, 150, 294
  lavish presents to C on her recovery
    from pleurisy 49
  shot through with intrigue 65
  'nocturnalisation' of Court life
    70–71
  assemblies 71
  dress 71, 72–3, 74
  reception days 71–2
  gift-giving 73
  financial matters 73–5
  food 80–81
  Baroque survivals in C's reign
    147–8, 205, 299–300
Russian fleet 202, 287, 289, 293
Russian Law Code (1649) 157
Russian Orthodox Church
  split in mid-seventeenth century
    165
  Peter III's determination to
    confiscate Church lands 121
  C's coronation 15–16
  monastic property 52, 131, 153–4
  Potëmkin's links with the clergy 232
Russian Orthodoxy
  C's first experience of 48
  C's loyalty to 12, 14, 18, 149–52,
    273, 312
  Peter III's contempt for Orthodox
    tradition 12
  and C's coronation 19, 22
  C's acceptance into 51–2, 73

a golden age of Baroque church-
    building 79
  Elizabeth's piety 79
  services and feast days 79–80
  C ready to provoke a conflict in its
    defence 183, 184
  the cradle of Orthodoxy 285
Russian Revolution (1905) 331
Russo-Swedish War (1741–43) 35
Russo-Swedish War (1788–90) 290,
  291, 293–4
Russo-Swedish War (1808–9) 320
Russo-Turkish War (1768–74) 183,
  188, 195–9, 202–4, 206–11, 213, 214,
  218, 224, 232, 235, 237, 238, 239, 250
Russo-Turkish War (1787–91) 280,
  288–91, 294, 296–303
Ryckwaert, Cornelis 33
Rymnik River 291
Rzhevsky, Aleksey: 'Birthday Ode' 22

S
Sachsen-Coburg, Princess Juliana
  Henrietta of 313
St Basil's Cathedral (Cathedral of the
  Protecting Veil of the Mother of
  God), Moscow 17
Saint Catherine (yacht) 179
Saint Evstafy (ship) 202
St Martin
St Nicholas (Naval) Cathedral, St
  Petersburg 79
St Petersburg 82, 322
  origins 41
  geometrically regimented 7
  granite embankments 258
  as Residenzstadt 41–2
  fires (1736 and 1737) 43–4

C's ceremonial re-entry into 127–8
great flood 257–8
St Petersburg (Dutch vessel) 57
St Petersburg News 57, 69, 77, 78
St Petersburg Public Library 330
St Sophia Cathedral, Tsarskoye Selo
250
Saint-Germain, Treaty of (1679) 25
Saldern, Caspar von 189, 219, 230
Saltykov, Count Nikolay 295, 303, 307
Saltykov, Field Marshal Peter 14, 160,
204, 206, 208, 212, 213
Saltykov, Sergey 87, 92, 178, 190, 197,
328
Saltykov family 14
Salzdahlum, Lower Saxony 29
Samoiedes 174
Sanches, António 49
Santi, Count 56–7, 58, 59, 60
Saratov 227, 236
Sarti, Giuseppe: *Te Deum* 294
Saxe-Gotha, Duke of 223
Saxe-Gotha, Princess Louise of 220
Saxe-Gotha, Prince William of 34
Schaden, Professor Johann: 'On the
Spirit of the Laws' 160
Schilling, Dr 113
Schleswig 120
Schlüsselburg fortress, near St
Petersburg 12, 124, 308
Schönbrunn, Vienna 191
Schönhausen palace, Berlin 37
Schroeder, Paul 301
Schumacher, Andreas 124–5
Schütze, Johann Christoph 33, 34
Schwedt an der Oder 37
Sechënov, Archbishop Dimitry 14, 19,
123, 151, 160, 166, 171, 176, 178

Secret Chancellery 90
Ségur, Count 272, 274, 283, 287
Seleucco (Pasquini) 79
Seltsa estate 220
Semënovsky Guards 44, 54, 123, 208,
255
Senate, the 9, 14, 95, 121, 133, 175, 190,
230, 271, 324
Senate Building, St Petersburg 97
Senate Palace, Moscow 16
Sennoye 251
Senyavin, Admiral 208
Serafim of Sarov, St 8
Serbia 248
serfdom 129, 154, 163, 172–3, 175, 271,
272, 277, 290, 292, 310, 320
Sevastopol 287, 289
Seven Years' War (1756–63) 14, 103,
105, 106, 119, 128, 157, 159, 184, 186,
187, 194, 195
Sèvres 262
Shafirov family 111
Shakespeare, William 93
Julius Caesar 310
Shakhovskoy, Yakov 116, 133
Shcherbatov, Prince Mikhail 95–6,
118–19, 143, 333
Shcherbatova, Princess Darya 190,
290
Shcherbatsky, Metropolitan Timofey
7, 14
Shepelëv, Ober-hofmeister 92
Sheremetev, Count Nikolay 288
Sheremetev, Count Peter 5, 60, 117,
127, 139
Sheremetev Palace, St Petersburg 140
Sheremeteva, Countess Anna 177, 178
Sheridan, Richard Brinsley 298

Sheshkovsky, prosecutor 308
Shirley, Henry 173–4
Shishkova, Alexandra 323
Shklov 251
Shubin, Fëdor 305, 312
Shuvalov, General Alexander 90, 92
Shuvalov, Count Andrey 162, 176,
    182, 195, 311
Shuvalov, Ivan 91, 94, 95, 97, 109, 113,
    115, 168, 193, 307, 314, 315
Shuvalov, Peter 62, 96, 110, 113, 115,
    157
Shuvalov family 102, 105, 106, 114, 119
Siberia 256, 292
Siegen, Prince Nassau 293
Sievers, Count Karl 21, 135, 146–7,
    220, 234
Sievers, Yakov 93, 140, 229, 240, 273
Silistria 229, 235
Simbirsk 169
Simferopol 287
Simonetti, Giovanni 33
Skavronska, Countess Catherine (née
    Engelhardt) 255
Skavronsky, Count 255
Skavronsky, Counts 143
Skavronsky family 70
Slavonic-Greek-Latin Academy,
    Moscow 7
Slizov, Konstantin 3–4, 239
smallpox 23–4
    inoculation 188–90, 247–8, 262, 284
Smolensk 240, 278, 281–2
Smolny Cathedral, St Petersburg 79
Smolny Convent 99, 205
Smolny Institute 130, 178, 303
Society for the Education of Young
    Noblewomen 130

Society for the Translation of Foreign
    Books 199, 261
Sofia, near Tsarskoye Selo 250, 265,
    278, 314
Sollogub, Countess Natalia 284
Solms, Count 126, 195, 207, 216
Solzhenitsyn, Alexander 171–2
Somov, Konstantin 331
Sophia, Tsarevna 12, 13
Sophia Dorothea of Württemberg see
    Maria Fëdorovna, Grand Duchess
Sorbonne, Paris 188, 190
Soubise, Cardinal de 142
Spanish Succession, War of the (1701–
    14) 25
Sparrow, Charles 210
Spectator, The 198
Speransky, Mikhail 325
Spiridov, Admiral 202
Sreznevsky, Ivan 322
Stable Chancellery, Moscow 59
Stählin, Jacob 64, 77, 111, 115, 117, 128,
    136
Stalin, Joseph 171–2
Stanisław August Poniatowski, King
    of Poland see Poniatowski
Starov, Ivan 246–7, 275, 294, 305
State Duma 331
Stedingk, Baron 294–9
Steele, Richard 198
Steen, Jan: Revellers 193
Stephen the Little 196
Sterne, Laurence: Sentimental Journey
    292
Stettin (now Szczecin, Poland) 23, 24,
    25, 28, 32, 333
Stockholm, Court of 92
Stockholm, Peace of (1720) 25

Stone Island 140
Stowe, Buckinghamshire 94
Stroganov, Alexander 140, 141–2, 160,
 171, 172, 178, 193, 250, 251, 256, 261,
 302, 321
Stroganov, Baron Sergey 95
Stroganov Palace 115, 141
Stroganova, Countess 143, 177
Sudermania, duke of 314
Sukhodolsky, Vasily: *Astronomy* 110
Sumarokov, Alexander 22, 51, 122, 327
 Ode to Potëmkin 237
 'On the First Day of 1763' 17
 Sinav and Truvor 110, 146
Sumarokov, Peter 14, 322
Summer Annenhof, Moscow 51
Summer Garden, St Petersburg 36,
 128, 256, 258
Summer House, St Petersburg 81–2,
 83
Summer Palace, Moscow (1730) 47
Summer Palace, St Petersburg (1741–
 4) 55, 57, 61, 68, 78, 83, 113, 128, 145,
 149, 180, 236, 258, 295, 320
Sutherland, Richard 307–8
Suvorov, Field Marshal 235, 291, 296,
 299, 300, 303, 309, 311, 322, 333
Svenskund 293
Svinin, Pavel 328
Sweden
 Great Northern War 9, 288
 as the dominant Baltic power in the
  seventeenth century 24
 spoils of the Thirty Years' War 24
 Russia celebrates peace with (1744)
  65
 suspension of the 1720 constitution
  217

restoration of the monarchy's
  absolute powers 217
 and Nevsky 246
Swedish fleet 290, 293
Swift, Jonathan: *Gulliver's Travels* 199
Synodal Palace, Moscow 9

T

Tacitus: *Annals* 101
Taininskoye 151, 160
Talyzin, Admiral Ivan 14, 124
Tamerlane 237
Tames, John 9
Tatars 17, 167, 168, 174, 246
Tatishchevo 233
Tauride Palace, St Petersburg 46,
 299–300, 304, 305–6, 311
 Gobelins Room 299
 Winter Garden 300, 305
 converted into stables 320
Tauride province 263–4, 280
Teplov, Grigory 9, 125, 130, 132, 212
 supervision of Kiriil Razumovsky's
  education 131
 translates Araja libretti 131
 drafts C's early edicts 131
 Commission on Church Lands 131
 Imperial Assembly secretary 133
'theatres of piety' 54
Theodore I, king of Corsica 93
Thirty Years' War (1618–48) 24
Three Bishops (ship) 202
'thunder-rock' 204–5
Times, The 166, 289
Titian: *Danaë* 193
Todorsky, Archimandrite Simon 51, 60
Tooke, William 123, 299–300
Torre, M. de la 257

Torzhok 272, 273
  monastery of Boris and Gleb 273–4
Transfiguration, Cathedral of the, St
  Petersburg 45
Treasury (British) 98
Treasury (Russian) 308
Trezzini, Domenico 42, 151
Trinity Cathedral, St Petersburg
  246–7, 294, 315
Trinity Lavra 79, 170
Trinity St Sergius monastery 49, 51,
  67, 85, 124, 150–51, 239
'Triumphant Minerva' (street pageant)
  22
Tronchin, François 193
Troppau, capture of (1758) 114
Troshchinsky, Dimitry 311
Trubetskaya, Princess Yevdokiya 190,
  230
Trubetskoy, Prince Nikita 116, 121
  C's wedding 62
  and C's coronation 7, 8, 9, 13, 21
Trubetskoy family 14
Tsar Boris's Ponds 127, 170
Tsaritsyn 236
Tsaritsyno 276, 326
Tsarskoye Selo, near St Petersburg
  15, 46, 55, 69, 72, 76, 79, 82, 95, 100,
  108, 109, 126, 137, 177, 178, 189, 192,
  193, 197, 205, 209, 210, 215, 216, 219,
  220, 223, 229, 230, 233–4, 243, 249,
  250, 258, 261, 264, 266, 267, 268,
  274, 278, 281, 289, 293, 304, 305, 312,
  314, 322, 323
  Picture Gallery 220
  redesign of (Charles Cameron)
    258–9
  Lyon room 259
  Chinese room 259
  Arabesque room 259, 294
  C's study 259
  bronze doors for C's bedroom
    262–3
  Cameron Gallery 299
  C's library 306
Tula 288
Turchaninov, Peter 312
Turgenev, Alexander 325, 328
Turgenev, Nikolay 325
Turin: royal library 142
Turkish navy 202–3
Tuscany 254
Tver 158, 159, 160, 162, 166, 273, 322
Tver (C's galley) 161, 162, 164
Tver province 240, 275

U
Ufa 230
Uglich 161
Ukhtomsky, F.F. 150
Ukraine *see* Little Russia
Ulrich, Duke Anton 29
Ural mountains 228, 233, 235
urban government 271
Utkin, Nikolay: *Lady with a dog* 323

V
Valeriani, Giuseppe 76, 141
Vallin de la Mothe, Jean Baptiste
  136–7, 138, 191
Vanbrugh, Sir John 138–9
Varel, Oldenbourg 34
Varennes 301
Vasilchikov, Alexander 230
  C's new favourite 216, 217
  no substitute for Grigory Orlov 218

C's boredom with him 225, 232
supplanted by Grigory Potëmkin
229, 232
Vasilevsky Island, St Petersburg 44,
211
Vechelde, palace of, near Brunswick
29
Veilly, Jean-Louis de 15, 21
Veldten, Georg 137, 138, 191, 258
Velë 265, 278
Venice 254
Venturi, Franco 196
Verdi, Giuseppe: *Un ballo in maschera*
308
Verela 294
Vernet, Pastor Jacob 141
Versailles 29–33, 57, 76, 94, 147, 193,
288
Vicenza 279
Vienna 207, 254, 262, 270
Imperial Court 33
Virgil: *Aeneid* 294
Virgin of Kazan 60
Vladimir, Prince 54
Vladimir, St 285
Vladimir Aleksandrovich, Grand
Duke 332
Vladislavova, Praskovya 13, 99
Voice, The (newspaper) 331
Volga River 155, 158–61, 163, 166, 168
Volkonsky, Prince 213
Volkov, Dimitry 99, 118–19, 134, 162,
171
Volkov, Fëdor 22
Voltaire 67, 68, 93, 109, 152, 222, 224,
239, 295, 310
correspondence with C *see under*
Catherine II the Great

Huber's cycle of portraits 193
bust commissioned by C 261
death 261
Anecdotes on Peter the Great 77
Candide 191
Vorobëvo 80
Voronezh 278
Vorontsov, Count Alexander 89, 96,
107, 134, 268, 270, 282, 287, 290, 292
Vorontsov, Chancellor Count Mikhail
62, 73, 94, 96, 97, 106–7, 111, 114,
133, 142
Vorontsov, Count Roman Larionovich
119
Vorontsov, Count Semën 134, 182, 235,
270, 298
Vorontsov family 105, 106, 113, 114,
134, 281
Vorontsov Palace, St Petersburg 95, 295
Vorontsova, Countess Anna Katlovna
15, 18, 21, 74, 109–13, 118
Vorontsova, Countess Anna
Mikhailovka 74, 109–13, 142–3
Vorontsova, Elizabeth 16, 92, 104, 110,
115, 124
Votiaks 168
Voulgaris, Eugenios 294, 304
Vyazemsky, Prince Alexander 134,
233, 237, 274, 285, 306, 308, 333
Vyazemsky, Prince Peter 327
Vyborg 293
Vyshny Volochëk 272, 275

W

Wagner, Pastor Friedrich 26–7, 28
Wailly, Charles de 288
Wallachia 203, 229
Walpole, George, 3rd earl 261

Walpole, Horace 241, 261, 308–9
Walpole, Sir Robert 261
War of American Independence
(1775–83) 263
Warsaw 219, 301, 309, 311
Washington, George 275
Watteau, Antoine 193, 304
Wedgwood, Josiah 261
Weimar Republic 33
Weitbrecht, Johann 310
Westminster Abbey, London 16
Whately, Thomas: *Observations on
Modern Gardening* 210
Whitworth, Charles 323
Wilkes, John 261
Wilmot, Catherine 321, 323
Wilmot, Martha 321, 322, 323
Winter Annenhof (later Golovin
Palace), Moscow 47
Winter Palace, St Petersburg 45, 55–6,
58, 60, 66, 79, 278
Winter Palace, St Petersburg (stone)
95, 119–20, 121, 123, 130, 135, 136–9,
181, 189, 200, 221, 225, 265, 269, 280,
299, 302, 315
  Amber Room 83, 231
  Chevalier Gardes' Room 132, 137,
  318
  Portrait Room 137
  Diamond Room 138, 232, 315
  Mirror Room 138
  library 138
  massive proportions 138
  audience chamber 141
  Orlov's rooms above C's 145
  theatre 146
  extravagant masquerade (1770) 205
  Potëmkin's apartments 233

  and Sophia's reception in Russia 245
  great flood of 1777 258
  Constantine's apartments 313
  St George's Hall 315
  and C's death 316, 317–19
  Grand Gallery 318
  requiem service for Peter III 319
  loss of interiors in great fire of 1837
  138
Winter Palace, St Petersburg
  (temporary wooden structure) 95,
  112, 113, 115, 147
Wolff, Jacob 97–8
'World of Art' group 331
Wörlitz 32
Wortman, Richard 332
Wouvermans, Philip 193
Wraxall, Nathaniel 214, 235
Württemberg, Eberhard Ludwig,
  Duke of 31
Württemberg, Frederick, Prince of
  281
Württemberg, Zelmira, Princess of
  (Princess Auguste of Brunswick)
  281

Y
Yaik Cossack host 228
Yakovlev, Savva 127, 163
Yakubovsky, Ivan 316
Yaroslavl 163–4, 165
Yauza River 10
Yekaterinburg, Siberia 209
Yekaterinburg fortress 84, 94
Yekaterinhof suburban palace 68, 82,
  83, 234
Yekaterinoslav (now Dnipropetrovsk,
  Ukraine) 280, 304, 311

Yekaterintal Palace, Reval 204
Yelagin, Ivan 130, 135, 165, 171, 178,
    195, 234, 235, 333
    a lifelong servant of C's 131
    arrested with Bestuzhev 132
    connection with English Masonic
        lodges 132
    and the Imperial theatres 148
Yenikale 239
Yermolov, Lieutenant Alexander 272,
    274
    relationship with C 270–71
    the 'white negro' 270
    rapid downfall 270
    inveigled into an intrigue against
        Potëmkin 270
    dismissed and sent abroad 270
    extended 'retirement' 270
Yeropkin, Senator Peter 44, 206–7,
    208
Yevreinov, Timofey 66, 99
Yorke, Charles 93
Young Court 65, 66, 69–70, 79, 90,
    105, 133, 140, 141, 143, 178, 219, 222,
    303
Yusupov, Nikolay 321

Z
Zagryazhskaya, Natalia 328
Zaporozhian Cossacks 9, 238
Zatrapezny, Ivan 163
Zavadovsky, Peter 270, 278, 281,
    282–3, 290, 324

relationship with C 28, 241, 242–3
promoted to major general 242
temporary retirement to Lyalichi
    243
long career at Court 243
Commission of National Schools
    248
and the Russo-Swedish War 293
and the second Russo-Turkish War
    294
and Poland's third partition 309–10
Zemtsov, Mikhail 44, 60
Zerbst, family seat at 24, 28, 33–6, 66,
    106
Zherebstova, Olga 322–3
Zhurzha (now Giurgiu, Romania) 208
Zimmerman, Dr Johann 277, 280, 283,
    321
    Solitude considered with respect to its
        influence on the mind and the heart
        271
Zips (Spisz) 207
Znamenskoye 127
Zorich, Semën 243, 251–2
Zorin, Andrey 297
Zorndorf, battle of (1758) 112
Zosima, Abbot 165
Zubov, Count Nikolay 315
Zubov, Platon 291, 294, 295, 300, 301,
    306, 307, 308, 310, 311, 314, 316, 322
Zubov, Valerian 296
Zwinger complex, Dresden 33